THE RUSSO-TURKISH WAR, 1768–1774

THE RUSSO-TURKISH WAR, 1768–1774

CATHERINE II AND THE OTTOMAN EMPIRE

Brian L. Davies

Bloomsbury Academic
An imprint of Bloomsbury Publishing Plc

B L O O M S B U R Y
LONDON · OXFORD · NEW YORK · NEW DELHI · SYDNEY

Bloomsbury Academic
An imprint of Bloomsbury Publishing Plc

50 Bedford Square	1385 Broadway
London	New York
WC1B 3DP	NY 10018
UK	USA

www.bloomsbury.com

BLOOMSBURY and the Diana logo are trademarks of Bloomsbury Publishing Plc

First published 2016

British Library Cataloguing-in-Publication Data
A catalog record for this book is available from the British Library.

ISBN: HB: 978-1-4725-1293-2
PB: 978-1-4725-0801-0
ePDF: 978-1-4725-1279-6
ePub: 978-1-4725-1415-8

Library of Congress Cataloging-in-Publication Data
Names: Davies, Brian L., 1953-
Title: The Russo-Turkish War, 1768-1774 : Catherine II and the
Ottoman Empire / Brian L. Davies.
Description: London : Bloomsbury Academic, an imprint of Bloomsbury
Publishing Plc, 2015. | Includes bibliographical references and index.
Identifiers: LCCN 2015023204 | ISBN 9781472512932 (hardback) |
ISBN 9781472508010 (paperback) | ISBN 9781472512796 (ePDF) | ISBN 9781472514158 (ePub)
Subjects: LCSH: Russo-Turkish War, 1768-1774. | Catherine II, Empress of
Russia, 1729-1796. | Russo-Turkish War, 1768-1774–Influence. | Russo-Turkish War,
1768-1774–Diplomatic history. | Russia–Territorial expansion–History–18th century. |
Turkey–History–Ottoman Empire, 1288-1918. | Borderlands–Russia–History–18th century. |
Borderlands–Turkey–History–18th century.
Classification: LCC DR553 .D38 2015 | DDC 947/.063–dc23 LC record
available at http://lccn.loc.gov/2015023204

Typeset by Integra Software Services Pvt. Ltd
Printed and bound in Great Britain

CONTENTS

Contents

PREFACE

Many years ago when I was still a graduate student my imagination was captivated by William S. McNeill's magisterial *Europe's Steppe Frontier, 1500–1800* (University of Chicago Press, 1964), which surveyed the development of Pontic Europe—the steppe frontier zone of southeastern Europe—over the early modern period and its gradual incorporation into three great competing agricultural Empires, Ottoman, Russian, and Habsburg. In addition to the breadth of knowledge McNeill's book displayed, I was impressed at how skillfully it interwove the geopolitical and military narrative with the history of colonization, economic development, social policy, and statecraft within the three expanding empires and the frontier polities they absorbed. I was inspired to devote my own research to examining the imperial competition for Pontic Europe in closer detail, making use of Russian-language sources.

So far this project has resulted in four studies. My *State Power and Community in Early Modern Russia: The Case of Kozlov, 1635–1648* (Palgrave MacMillan, 2004) relied on archival sources to reconstruct Muscovite frontier colonization policy and the ways in which it structured state–society relations in the southern Russian forest-steppe zone in the early seventeenth century. My next book, *Warfare, State, and Society on the Black Sea Steppe, 1500–1700* (Routledge, 2007), was intended for a broader audience and dealt with Russian steppe colonization and military development in the larger context of Russia's intensifying competition with Poland-Lithuania and the Crimean Khanate for mastery of Pontic Europe. A third book, *Empire and Military Revolution in Eastern Europe: Russia's Turkish Wars in the Eighteenth Century* (Continuum, 2011), continued the narrative of this competition over the course of the eighteenth century as it became more focused on Russian struggle with the Ottoman Empire. Now, in *The Russo-Turkish War (1768–1774): Catherine the Great and the Ottoman Empire*, I offer a more detailed study of the most decisive and transformative of the eighteenth-century Russian-Ottoman wars.

The Russo-Turkish War of 1768–1774 had enormous repercussions for Eastern Europe. It resulted in the defeat and ultimately the annexation to Russia of the Crimean Khanate. It led to the partitions of the Polish–Lithuanian Commonwealth. It completed the incorporation of Ukraine into the Russian Empire and the dissolution of the Zaporozhian and Don Cossack Hosts. It reduced Ottoman power in the Black Sea, along the Danube, and even in the eastern Mediterranean and emboldened Europeans to begin treating the Ottoman Empire as the "Sick Man of Europe." The war also stabilized the political fortunes of Empress Catherine II and enabled her to promulgate reforms further centralizing provincial government, accelerating the colonization of the southern steppe, and establishing broader foundations for state finances.

The military and diplomatic narrative of Catherine the Great's first Turkish War will be largely unfamiliar to most English-language readers, but those especially interested in military history should find useful its comparison of Russian and Ottoman military organization and its identification of certain Russian technical and tactical innovations that could be argued represented a European "Military Revolution." In explaining the circumstances by which Ukraine and Crimea joined New Russia in the Russian Empire, the book illuminates some issues that have recently become flashpoints in Russian relations with Europe and the United States. We do not, however, take any position on what territories rightly "belong" to what modern states, for we see speculations about organic national "identity" and "historical right" as useless and even counterproductive to writing serious and objective history.

The military narrative here relies by default largely on Russian-language sources. I would have liked to compare them with Ottoman accounts of the war but as I do not read Turkish some important Ottoman primary sources, such as the court histories compiled by Sadullah Enveri and Ahmed Vasif Efendi, were not available to me. The one notable exception was Ahmed Resmi Efendi's *Hülasat al-itibar* (1781), which was recently translated into English. I have tried to balance my account of the war with a sympathetic understanding of Ottoman capabilities and security interests, and I hope to learn from whatever dialog with Ottomanists my book might engender.

With the exception of places most familiar to readers in traditional English transliteration (Moscow, Warsaw, Istanbul, Kiev, Bucharest, Zaporozhia, etc.) I have tried to render toponyms according to modern atlas usage (thus: Dnepr, Dnestr, Chernihiv, Iași, Focșani). The names of towns and fortresses under Ottoman control are presented in the fashion most likely to be recognized by Ottomanists (Akkirman, Bender, Ibrail, Rusçuk, etc.). In a few instances I have chosen to transliterate from Russian because during the period under examination these places figured largest in Russian discourse (thus Khotin rather than Chocym or Hotyn).

Unless otherwise indicated all dates are given in the Old Style, that is, in accordance with the use in Russia (until 1918) of the Julian Calendar. In the eighteenth century Julian dates were eleven days "behind" Gregorian dates.

I wish to thank the following people for their patience and encouragement: Jeremy Black, Carol Belkin Stevens, Gregg Michel, Kolleen Guy and her children, my wife Paula, and my editor at Bloomsbury, Claire Lipscomb.

MAP

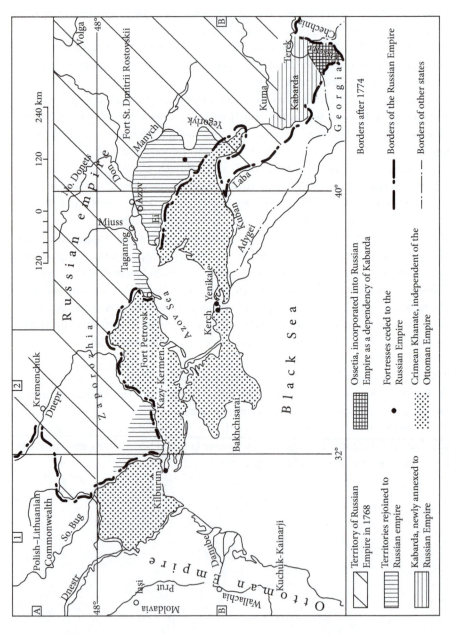

Territorial readjustments from the Kuchuk-Kainarji Treaty, 1774.

CHAPTER 1
THE RUSSIAN EMPIRE AT A STRATEGIC CROSSROADS, 1762–1768

Empress Catherine II felt both exhilaration and nervous uncertainty in the months following the June 28, 1762, coup that deposed her husband Emperor Peter III and confirmed her as sole ruler of the Russian Empire.[1]

On the one hand, she had been delivered from persecution at the hands of her detestable husband and given tremendous power over a vast and powerful empire. On the other hand, she was aware that she was widely and rightly viewed as a usurper and would be given little time to prove herself worthy of respect and obedience. She wrote to her former lover Stanisław Poniatowski, "It behooves me to be very cautious, as the least important man of the Guards can, on seeing me, say to himself: 'This is my doing.'" To the French ambassador Louis Auguste de Breteuil, she compared her plight to that of a hare pursued by hounds. When Chancellor Bestuzhev-Riumin proposed that she begin her reign boldly by assuming the title of *Mother of the Fatherland*, she responded that she did not dare as it would be met with ridicule. She confided to her advisors and intimates that she gave herself just five years in which to consolidate her power and win acceptance from the Russian nobility and international opinion.[2]

Peter III had issued 220 decrees in his 186 days on the throne. Many of them were on matters of great consequence, and Europe was waiting to see whether Empress Catherine II would reject or confirm them. A decree emancipating the Russian nobility from compulsory service had been issued by Peter III on February 18, 1762, much to the surprise of Russian nobles;[3] would she confirm it, and how would she adjust finances and the army manpower accordingly to accommodate the end of the service requirement? Peter III had limited the powers of the Senate and disbanded the Conference, Empress Elizabeth Petrovna's war cabinet; how would Catherine placate the Senatorial magnates and the army's high command? Peter III had alienated the Russian Orthodox Church by taking steps toward secularizing its estates and by measures rehabilitating the dissident Old Believers; could Catherine II afford politically to endorse such a campaign against the interests of the Church?

Most urgent of all was to resolve the question of what kind of grand strategy the Empire was now to follow. How should relations with Denmark and Prussia be managed? Should she abandon her late husband's plan of war against Denmark? Should she sustain the armistice with Prussia and perhaps even follow it up with further political rapprochement? Did the Ottoman Empire and the Crimean Khanate pose threats serious enough to require her heightened vigilance?

Under Empress Anna Ioannovna (r. 1730–1740) and Empress Elizabeth Petrovna (r. 1741–1761) Austria had been considered Russia's natural ally, a vitally necessary counterweight to France, Prussia, and the Ottoman Porte. Austria had allied with Russia against the Turks in 1735–1739, and although there had been disappointment in St. Petersburg as to Austria's lack of resolve in that war, Russia continued to align with Austria during the War of the Austrian Succession and most of the Seven Years' War. Aleksei Petrovich Bestuzhev-Riumin (Vice-Chancellor 1741–1744 and Chancellor 1744–1759) had been the chief spokesman for maintaining strategic partnership with Austria and expanding that partnership to include Britain. But he had spoken out against bringing Russia to war against Prussia in 1756, and he was removed from office after his political client General Stepan Apraksin was dismissed on charges of cowardice. His successor as chancellor, Mikhail Illarionovich Vorontsov, was also a firm Austrophile but was suspected of taking bribes from the French and did not protest Peter III's sudden *volte-face* in favor of Prussia. Bestuzhev-Riumin had been an early confidante of Catherine Alekseevna against Peter III, and Catherine II now returned him to court and gave him the rank of Field Marshal. Vorontsov had been late in supporting her coup in 1762, but she left him in place as chancellor.[4]

The alternative to continued partnership with Austria would be presented by Nikita Ivanovich Panin (1718–1783), ambassador to Sweden in 1747–1760 and from 1760 *oberhofmeister*, tutor and governor to the Imperial heir Grand Duke Paul. Panin had been adroit in maintaining good relations with both Bestuzhev-Riumin and Vorontsov and had advanced with the help of their patronage despite the very apparent differences in their diplomatic agenda by 1762. Catherine II owed her throne to him—he had played a crucial role in the coup deposing Peter III—and he and his faction offered greater governing experience than the Orlovs could, so she was now inclined to give Panin's counsel preference. She made him acting President of the College of Foreign Affairs even while keeping Vorontsov on as chancellor.[5]

Panin favored restoring the Senate's powers to protect against the kind of autocratic despotism Peter III had embodied. A rehabilitated Senate would restore to the Empire its natural leadership, the great families of the high nobility traditionally dominating the Senate; it would also reaffirm long loyal service in the state bureaucracy "rather than imperial favoritism as the main upward route to political power."[6]

Panin sought peace and the opportunity to rebuild the Empire's finances, so he considered the late Peter III's project for a war upon Denmark as potentially catastrophic. However, he believed that Peter III's unexpected armistice with Prussia presented the opportunity to avoid war with Denmark and enter a new age of peace based upon further rapprochement with Prussia. It had to be recognized that the recent Seven Years' War had simplified the balance of power in Europe by sorting the leading powers into two great bipolar blocs: one dominated by Bourbon France and Habsburg Austria, and the other led by Britain and Prussia. Peace between these two blocs could be maintained by treaties, by recognizing spheres of interest, and by enlisting new allies to restore the balance of power. Thus Britain could counter French power on the continent by maintaining her domination of the sea lanes and overseas colonies; and Britain might welcome Russia as a useful ally to counter French influence in the Ottoman Levant and the Black Sea region, rewarding Russia by making her a commercial and political partner in the Baltic. Because Austria was now aligned with France, it was no longer possible to share Bestuzhev-Riumin's and Vorontsov's confidence in Austria as Russia's "natural" ally. On the contrary, it was in France's interest now to rely on Austria to block Russian power in southeastern Europe and to encourage the Ottoman Empire, Poland, and Sweden in active opposition to Russia. It followed that Russia had no alternative but to pursue a "Northern Accord" with Denmark, Prussia, and Britain.[7]

By 1763, Panin had prevailed in this policy debate; Catherine II endorsed the construction of a Northern Accord. It avoided the risk of war with Denmark and renewed tensions with Prussia; it also offered opportunity to expand Russia's role in the Baltic trade. Panin had read court politics more shrewdly than his opponents. There had been greater animosity between Vorontsov and Bestuzhev-Riumin than between Vorontsov and Panin, so Vorontsov agreed to cede the field to Panin. The empress offered Vorontsov two years' leave to travel abroad for his health; he did not actually leave, but his continuance as chancellor was in name only.

Catherine II and the Polish project

The construction of the Northern Accord assigned an especially important role to Poland-Lithuania. The Commonwealth could not be allowed to become a pawn of France and Austria; it needed to be secured as an ally, a partner in the Northern Accord. But her partnership had to be a junior one, with Russia increasing, rather than relaxing, her hegemony over the Commonwealth. On the other hand, the Polish–Lithuanian Commonwealth had to be strong enough to be a useful ally. Panin therefore expected the empress to support measures strengthening the Polish monarchy, increasing its fiscal and military power and giving it a stronger hand over the fractious magnates in the Diet (*Sejm*).

Vorontsov, by contrast, had been skeptical that Poland-Lithuania could be turned into a reliable ally in a Northern Accord. In 1761, he had written to Empress Elizabeth Petrovna, "Poland, being plunged into internal discord and disorder, will always be beset by them as long as she preserves her constitution, and so she does not deserve to be considered among the European powers."[8] A 1762 memorandum to Empress Catherine II, unsigned but probably authored by Vorontsov, was more explicit: "The weakness and disorder of Poland's governance is so great that this monarchy can be neither useful nor threatening to anyone, which is why all neighbouring nations have an interest in not allowing anyone to put its government into better order."[9]

Panin's project of taming the Commonwealth while strengthening it could be undone by any one of the three political elements in the Commonwealth: magnates and lesser nobles who were angry that Russian interference had humiliated the Commonwealth, destroyed their Golden Liberty, and undermined the hegemony of the Catholic faith; the new king Catherine II would select for Poland, if he should become nervous about the tenability of his own position, obliged to placate St. Petersburg while confronting the magnate opposition; or reform-minded Commonwealth magnates who sought to strengthen the Polish monarchy beyond the point acceptable to the Russian empress. In fact, the empress' Polish project would be complicated by all these three elements.

The Polish–Lithuanian Commonwealth presented Russia with another potential problem: the more obvious became Russian political dictate to the Polish monarchy, the more that would alarm the Ottoman government. It had been under Russian auspices that August II had regained the Polish throne in 1709, the army of Peter I having defeated the Swedes at Poltava and ended the rule of Charles XII's ally Stanisław Leszczynski; however, it was also the case that August II had needed the friendship of the Porte to reconsolidate his rule. Hence, he had renegotiated the Karlowitz treaty and obtained the Porte's recognition of his right to the throne, as well as recognition of the Commonwealth's sovereignty over Right Bank Ukraine. In return the sultan had exacted from him a promise that Russian troops would be removed from Commonwealth soil. But they were not; August II lacked the power to force them out; and in fact, the Russians soon became more indispensable to him as mediators of his conflicts with the confederations of Polish and Lithuanian magnates opposing his perceived inclination toward "Saxon absolutism." Russian troops were present in Warsaw in early 1717 when the Diet ratified an agreement dissolving the confederations and permanently capping the Crown army at 18,000 Polish and 6,000 Lithuanian troops supported from 5.3 million złotys a year. This left the Commonwealth with one of Europe's smallest armies in proportion to population, thereby guaranteeing that the Commonwealth would remain militarily dependent on Russia.[10]

The final years of King August III (r. 1734–1763) were ones of political paralysis in the Commonwealth. Norman Davies compared the king's temperament to that of "a pudding—soft, sweet, and inert."[11] August III had been more preoccupied with his duties as Elector of Saxony than with governing Poland-Lithuania, so he spent most of his reign residing in Saxony, leaving executive authority in the Commonwealth in the hands of Count Heinrich Bruhl. Bruhl recognized that both of them held their power only on the good will of the Russians, so Bruhl in turn let the Russian ambassador and the Russian Army free to do what they willed. The Diet was incapable of reaching any political consensus—it was sharply polarized between a pro-French faction led by the Potockis and the *Familja*, a pro-Russian faction headed by the Czartoryskis—and so most of its business had to be passed down to the provincial dietines. This left central government and the Crown Army moribund. Political and military power devolved upon a few provincial magnates and their private armies.[12]

When Catherine II took the Russian throne, it was already apparent that August III was dying and a succession would have to be arranged. She was resolved that a native Pole, a Piast, should be elected to the Polish throne—not a prince of a foreign dynasty. But that Polish successor would have to be someone congenial to Russian interests. She expected that any Russian candidate for the Polish throne would be opposed by France,

Austria, Saxony, the Porte, and perhaps Sweden; also, she knew that to have her hands free to pursue this project, she would first have to settle relations with Denmark, Saxony, and Prussia.

Peter III had suddenly withdrawn Russia from the coalition against Frederick II to prepare for war against Denmark to reunify Schleswig and Holstein. Catherine sent Baron I. A. Korf to Copenhagen to reassure Frederik V that she intended to keep the peace with Denmark and was ready to renounce claims to Holstein in exchange for the lesser duchies of Oldenbourg and Delmenhorst. In August 1762 Frederik V accepted these overtures providing that she acknowledged him as guardian of Grand Duke Paul (a Holsteiner, as the ostensible son of the late Peter III).[13]

Her next step was to reaffirm Peter III's May 5, 1762 peace treaty with Prussia on terms more advantageous to Russia. In December 1762 she wrote to Frederick II urging him to conclude peace with Austria and reminding him, "I have sacrificed substantial gains of war to my love of peace. Let us hope that others will follow this example … But if my best intentions do not bear fruit … I shall be forced to resort to steps contrary to my wishes, my inclinations, and my feelings of friendship."[14] More explicit threats proved unnecessary; Prussia, Austria, and Saxony were too exhausted to continue the war and they signed a peace treaty at St. Hubertusberg on February 15, 1763. By the summer of 1763 Catherine was ready to go even farther and propose an alliance with Prussia to further her Polish project and the construction of Panin's Northern Accord. Bestuzhev-Riumin, who had been fiercely pro-Austrian and anti-Prussian, was ordered to undertake talks with the Prussian ambassador Count Friedrich von Solms. In August 1763 Vorontsov was encouraged to travel to Europe to attend to his health. From this point, Panin became unofficial supreme authority on diplomatic affairs and was given free hand to set foreign policy. Meanwhile, Frederick II had reached the conclusion that France and Austria would not risk further war by contesting Catherine's plan to put a puppet Piast on the Polish throne.

Catherine also exploited the declining powers of August III to reduce Polish and Saxon influence in the eastern Baltic to the benefit of Russo-Prussian rapprochement. Karl of Saxony had been placed on the ducal throne of Courland by his father August III in 1759, with the consent of Empress Elizabeth Petrovna. But Catherine II considered him a burden; he was a Roman Catholic, and aloof and politically inattentive, and she thought it unlikely that he would be able to control the largely Lutheran nobility of Courland. So she credited reports that Karl was conspiring with the courts of Saxony and Austria to throw off Russian dependency, and she pressed the ailing August III to get him to renounce the throne in 1763. Catherine II then pressured the Courland barons to elect as his successor Ernst Johann von Biron, recently returned from Siberian exile. Biron earned his rehabilitation by conducting himself circumspectly in Courland.[15] With Courland once more under close Russian control, Catherine would have greater leverage to press August III and Bruhl to cede part of the Commonwealth's Baltic coast to Prussia, allowing Frederick II to win a land bridge connecting western and eastern Prussia.[16] It would now be easier for Russian forces to get transit rights through Courland and access to the port at Riga.

King August III died on September 24 (OS)/October 5, 1763. Catherine had already decided in August that her candidate to succeed him was Stanisław Antoni Poniatowski (1732–1798). On October 6 she decided with her Cabinet that the succession would be "assisted" by dispatching N. V. Repnin, Panin's nephew by marriage, to Warsaw as ambassador and by stationing Russian forces on the Commonwealth's frontier.

The Poniatowskis were an old magnate family. Stanisław's father had been grand treasurer of the Lithuanian Army and his mother was Konstancja Czartoryska, making him a member of the *Familja*, the Czartoryski faction. He had been a deputy in the Diet, had travelled widely in Europe, and had resided at the Russian court in 1755–1756—at which time he had been Catherine's lover. Frederick II snidely remarked that Catherine had selected as her candidate a man "who has long been known to the Empress of Russia, and whose person is agreeable to her."[17]

It was now Frederick II's turn to make himself indispensable to Catherine's Polish project to negotiate a Russo-Prussian alliance on favorable turns. In November 1763 the Ottoman diplomat Ahmed Resmi Efendi made an unprecedented visit to the Prussian court; Frederick greeted him with an equally unprecedented pomp and publicity to convey the impression he was contemplating signing a formal alliance with the Porte. That was not actually his intent, as it would have stuck him with the obligation to defend the Porte in the event it went to war against Russian. But by making a show of rapprochement with the sultan, Frederick could keep Austria on edge and signal to Catherine II that she needed to secure alliance with Prussia.[18]

An alliance of mutual defense between Russia and Prussia was signed in St. Petersburg on March 31, 1764. Each nation would contribute 10,000 foot and 2,000 horse to the defense of the other, or a subsidy of 400,000 rubles a year; this mutual defense pact would last for eight years. Secret articles on the Polish question obliged Russia and Prussia to maintain peace and security in the Commonwealth, act in concert to get a Piast elected king, and defend the Commonwealth militarily if necessary. Neither nation was to make changes in the Commonwealth's constitution. However, both Prussia and Russia had the responsibility to sponsor toleration for religious dissidents (Orthodox, Protestants) in the Commonwealth, including holding the new king of Poland to the policy of religious toleration.

This marked a true diplomatic revolution and the first steps taken toward Panin's Northern Accord. But Panin recognized that Poland-Lithuania also had a potentially important role in protecting Russian interests in the south, as an ally of Russia in the event of a war with the Ottomans. This is why he planned to use Stanisław Poniatowski's royal authority to enlarge the Polish–Lithuanian army to 50,000 men and to allow the Russians to base armies between the Dnepr and the Dnestr.[19]

Bestuzhev-Riumin and Vorontsov were skeptical of this alliance with Prussia and a strengthened Commonwealth, but they were no longer in any position to argue for an alternative policy. Of greater importance for the future was the opposition to Panin's Polish plans from two rising figures in the army, War College Vice-President Zakhar Chernyshov and General-*anshef* Grigorii Orlov—especially as Orlov was the empress' current favorite and lover and the father of two of her illegitimate children. Chernyshov and Orlov wanted to see the Commonwealth further weakened politically, so that it could be partitioned. A few months before, Chernyshov had submitted a secret plan to annex Kreuzburg, Dinaburg, Lifland, Polotsk, Vitebsk, and part of Mstislav palatinates upon the death of August III. He considered that this annexation could easily be carried out by the Russian army when it was sent into Poland to supervise the election of the next king.[20]

Saxony was not able, at this time, to raise major obstacles to the election of Stanisław Poniatowski, for it was in political disarray after the recent deaths of August III, Bruhl, and ducal heir Friedrich Christian I. France, of course, tried to rouse the Polish magnates against Stanisław's candidacy, but its efforts were uncoordinated. France had "as many as three envoys at Warsaw, two of whom were in the king's confidence, which made five cabals. They stirred the whole world into confusion, and destroyed all parties; they only succeeded in throwing the minds of men into all disorder, and in destroying the small amount of respect which France still commanded."[21] Once Stanisław was elected he would expel all these French agents. France could still hope to incite the Turks against Russian machinations in Poland, but for the time being, the government of Sultan Mustafa III could not be roused to protest. The sultan's envoy to France declared, "Who shall be the next king of Poland is a matter of little interest to us; his name means nothing; what interests us only are the conditions under which he will rule."[22] Some Polish nobles sought to pre-empt Catherine II by advancing their own Piast candidate, Crown Hetman Jan Branicki, but Branicki was elderly and ailing, and his faction could raise no more than three thousand troops to demonstrate against the 14,000 Russian soldiers entering the Commonwealth in March 1764. Meanwhile, ambassador Repnin was distributing large sums—perhaps 1.5 million rubles in all— to bribe leading members of the Diet.[23] The funds spent over the next three years to maintain the Diet's compliance with Repnin and King Stanisław would amount to some 7–8 percent of the Russian Empire's state budget.[24]

Catherine's Polish project got further assistance from the *Familja*. Stanisław's election was supported by a confederation organized by his uncle Michał Czartoryski. This confederation had other political objectives of its own, ones more radical than Catherine and Panin had anticipated: to abolish the *liberum veto*, a practice that had paralyzed past Diets; to limit the power of the upper house of the Diet, the Senate, by forming a Supreme Executive Council; to form within the Diet special commissions to initiate military and fiscal reform; to ban vendetta wars among the magnates and abolish their private armies; and to increase taxes and establish a customs service enforcing protective tariffs. For the time being Catherine and Panin made no quarrel with this program, for the Czartoryskis were crucial in winning the Diet's election of Stanisław and supporting the goal of enlarging the Crown army, and they recognized that the *liberum veto* had been a source of chaos and political weakness.[25] On September 7, 1764, the Diet elected Stanisław Poniatowski King of Poland (Stanisław August, r. 1764–1798).[26]

But resistance among the Polish–Lithuanian *magnaterja* and *szlachta* began to build when Repnin and the Prussian ambassador to Warsaw put the king and Diet on notice that the Commonwealth would have to sign a formal alliance with Russia before the Polish Crown army could be expanded. Many Polish nobles feared that such an alliance would provide some pretext for the Russians to alter the Commonwealth's political constitution. This fear was not without foundation; Russian ruling circles had long been on record as declaring the Commonwealth's republican government a prescription for anarchy and an obstacle to Russo-Polish cooperation.[27] A second new Russian demand was that the *liberum veto* be retained after all, so that the Czartoryskis might be checked from entirely dominating the state. A third Russian demand proved even more inflammatory. Inspired by grievances submitted by Mohylew's Orthodox bishop Iurii Konisskii, Repnin announced for the empress that alliance required King Stanisław and the Diet to now guarantee religious toleration for the Commonwealth's Orthodox and Protestant subjects. A bill of Toleration would allow Dissidents to be elected to the courts, the provincial dietines, and perhaps a third of the seats in the Diet. This was, of course, completely unacceptable to most Catholic nobles and to the hierarchs of the Catholic Church. The possibility must be considered that Catherine II realized this would provoke the Catholic nobles to form confederations in revolt, and that she counted on this happening to provide a pretext for Russian military intervention on an even larger scale.[28] Repnin subsequently threatened that 40,000 Russian troops under General Saltykov would enter the Commonwealth if the Diet did not comply and pass a Toleration bill.

This greatly alarmed King Stanisław, who feared that it would provoke his overthrow. He wrote to Catherine, "You cannot have meant, in elevating my person, to raise a target for your arms ... But I entreat you to take note of the fact that if all that Prince Repnin has threatened is carried out, there can be no middle course for me. I must expose myself to your blows, or I would betray my nation and my duty."[29]

Repnin's ultimatum also enraged the Czartoryskis, who took it to mean that Repnin and the empress were now abandoning the *Familja* and placing all their bets on the Orthodox and Protestant nobles and the Russian army. The Czartoryskis rejected Toleration and so they now had greater cause to drift over to the camp of the Catholic nobility and join the resistance to Repnin's dictatorship. The mounting opposition to the empress's plans made it necessary for Repnin to bring more Russian troops onto Commonwealth soil and distribute more subsidies to Orthodox and Protestant nobles to support the formation of Dissident political confederations for the next Diet. A confederation of Orthodox nobles emerged at Slutsk and a confederation of Protestant nobles formed at Torun with Prussian assistance. Polish and Lithuanian nobles opposed to the reforms of the Czartoryskis formed a large confederation under the magnate Karol Radziwiłł, who agreed to commit it to Toleration and a Polish–Russian alliance in return for Russian assistance in repaying his debts and recovering his estates.

The Diet reconvened in summer 1767. It was, of course, fiercely polarized even though 1,200 Russian troops were in Warsaw. Kajetan Sołtyk, the Bishop of Cracow, emerged as the spokesman of a "Republican" bloc of Catholic nobles resisting any Toleration bill, protesting the Russian military occupation, and opposing King Stanisław. The other leaders of this bloc were Hetman Wacław Rzewuski, the *wojewóda* of Cracow; Adam Krasiński, the Bishop of Kamianets; Michał Krasiński; Joachim Potocki, Lithuanian Grand Cup-bearer and Lt. General in the Crown Army; and Josef Pułaski, a prominent jurist once adhering to the *Familja* and now close to Bishop Sołtyk. Bishop Sołtyk was the most vocal representative of this bloc in the Diet, whereas the Krasińskis were the most active behind the scenes in trying to enlist foreign powers, especially the Porte, in the cause of delivering *ultimata* for expelling the Russian troops and defeating the Dissidents.[30] While the election of Stanisław had not much bothered Sultan Mustafa III, the build-up of Russian forces in Poland did; after all, the presence of Russian troops in Poland had been a *casus belli* for the Russo-Turkish Wars of 1711–1713 and 1735–1739. In 1764 two Russian divisions had been on Commonwealth soil—Volkonskii's, near Warsaw, and Dashkov's, near Grodno; in late 1767, Repnin had brought in more troops, to hold Torun, Slutsk, and Warsaw and to intimidate the Diet, raising the number of Russian troops in the Commonwealth to about 40,000; and by early 1769, fighting with the Confederates would require an additional 26,000 Russian reinforcements.[31]

After Repnin ordered the arrest of Sołtyk and Rzewuski on October 13, the Krasińskis and Josef Pułaski stepped up their efforts to enlist Ottoman and French support. Bishop Krasiński left Warsaw and returned to Kamianets, just across the border from Moldavia, and he sent agents to Istanbul to negotiate for Ottoman backing of a Polish resistance; he also sent an agent to Vienna to try to secure a pledge of neutrality from Austria in the event of a new Russo-Turkish war. Pułaski asked the sultan for 100,000 ducats to help organize resistance.[32]

Sultan Mustafa III also came under greater pressure from France now that the Duc de Choiseul had returned as French foreign minister.[33] Sorel contends that Choiseul's "dominating idea was to avenge the Seven Years' War upon England. For this it was necessary to secure the neutrality of the Continent—that is to say, Prussia and Russia. He counted on Austria to hold Prussia in check; but he had to seek everywhere for enemies for Russia: in Poland, where he sent money and officers to the Confederation of Bar; in Sweden, where took the part of the king; and finally in Turkey, where he strained every nerve to rouse the Turks."[34] Vergennes, the French ambassador to Istanbul, was sent three million *livres* to distribute as bribes to turn the sultan's government against Russia. Choiseul explained to him that it did not matter whether the Turks had the military capacity to prevail against the Russians. "In good truth, the rottenness of the Turks in every department might make this trial of strength fatal to them; that matters little to us, provided the object of an immediate explosion be attained."[35]

The temporary silencing of the Republican bloc in the Diet allowed Repnin to ram through a vote on February 13 (OS), 1768, to form a commission to write a military alliance between the Commonwealth and Russia.[36] By its terms Russia would defend the Commonwealth against her enemies and preserve her laws, her elective monarchy, and even her *liberum veto* for particular matters of state (for it might prove useful in the event that a future Polish king was less friendly to Russian interests). In return Commonwealth law would have to acknowledge religious equality and open offices to non-Catholics and ban vendetta war among the nobles.[37]

Catherine II had intended to withdraw Russian forces from the Commonwealth once her project had been achieved. But on February 29, 1768, the Krasińskis and Pułaskis assembled 300 prominent Republicans at Bar, in Podolia near the Moldavian frontier, and announced the formation of a military confederation to annul the alliance and drive out the Russians. Michał Krasiński was acclaimed as the Bar Confederation's provisional marshal and Josef Pułaski as marshal of its armed forces. With funds provided from the Carmelite Monastery at Berdichev the Bar Confederation began assembling an army, and by summer, it had enrolled about 8,000 men: men from the magnates' private bands, soldiers from some Crown garrisons, and even some Tatar volunteers. The Bar Confederation was initially able to field 13 banners of *husarz* heavy cavalry, 6 banners of *pancer* light cavalry, and 2,000 lance comrades. After the fall of its base at Berdichev in July (and the temporary imprisonment of its commandant, Colonel Kazimierz Pułaski)[38] military command of the Confederation was transferred to Joachim Potocki.

The Confederation's Manifesto of October 12, 1768, called on the nation to revolt in defense of the Catholic Church and the integrity of the Commonwealth's councils, tribunals, dietines, and Diet; to liberate senators and bishops held prisoner by the Russians; and to defeat the *haidamak* rebels they believed had been unleashed by Repnin's efforts to empower the Dissidents.[39] Adam Zamoyski characterizes the Bar Confederation as consisting of "poorly trained bands, with no supplies, no bases, no strategy, and no leadership." Yet the Bar Confederation survived for the next three years, skirmishing with the Russians all across the Commonwealth and continuing to draw thousands of men to its banner. It endured as long as it did because patriotism, anti-Russian feeling, hatred of the king, and religious zeal and the crusading impulse combined with "conservatism, the bitterness of the magnates, and the grievances of the poor *szlachta*."[40]

King Stanisław was caught in a dilemma. He was reluctant to commit Crown troops against the Confederates lest this plunged the Commonwealth into civil war; but Repnin informed him that if he did not honor his debt to Russia by ordering in the Crown army, the Russians would deal with the Confederates on their own—and would take no prisoners. Stanisław reluctantly ordered Hetman Branicki to take the Crown army into the field against the rebels but to avoid battle with them and to use the army to try to separate the Confederates from the Russians and the haidamak insurgents.[41]

Haidamak revolt

For several decades the Kiev, Bratslav, and Podolia regions in Right Bank Ukraine had experienced raiding by bandit gangs called *haidamak*s attacking the estates of Polish nobles and terrorizing the Jews. Most of these bandits were economically marginalized and estranged elements of the Zaporozhian Sich, although some of their captains had defected from the private forces of Polish magnates. During the 1735–1739 Russo-Turkish War haidamak bands had swept across Kiev, Bratslav, Volhynia, and Podolia and Russian forces had taken advantage of them to seize Brody, Zbarazh, and other towns from the Confederates loyal to Stanisław Lesczynski. Haidamak raids were a regular annual occurrence in Kiev and Bratslav in 1741–1763 and the Commonwealth usually had to field four or five thousand Crown, county, and manorial troops against them.[42]

A new wave of haidamak revolt broke out in Right Bank Ukraine in spring 1768. Polish Catholic and Ukrainian Uniate nobles blamed it in part on Russian encouragement of the Dissidents, while the haidamaks saw themselves as responding to the threat presented by the mobilization of Catholic nobles in the Bar Confederation.

In May 1768 Maksim Zalizniak, a retired colonel of the Zaporozhian Host residing as a lay brother at the Motronyn Monastery, led a band of seventy Cossacks across the Dnepr south of Kiev to raise a new haidamak rebellion against the Bar Confederates and against the Catholic Polish *szlachta*, the Jews who collected their rents and ran their liquor monopolies, and the Catholic and Uniate clergy. Zalizniak appears to have been inspired by the religious nationalist propaganda of the Motronyn archimandrite Melchizedek Znachko-Iavors'kyi, and he took advantage of the fact that Znachko-Iavors'kyi had found official refuge on Russian soil to assure his followers that the Russians would assist their revolt. He even forged a "Golden Charter" from Catherine II calling on Orthodox Ukrainians to rise up and slaughter the Catholics, Uniates, and Jews.[43]

Within weeks Zalizniak had assembled a haidamak army of several thousand Ukrainian peasants, Zaporozhians, and Cossacks defecting from the private bands of the Polish magnates. Their revolt spread as far to the northwest as Zhytomyr and as far south as Podolia and the edge of the Zaporozhian Sich; the towns of Fastiv, Cherkasy, Korsun, Bohuslav, and Lysianka fell to them; in June 1768 they demanded the capitulation of Uman, a town belonging to the estate of Kiev *wojewóda* Potocki. By this time several thousand Poles, clergymen, and Jews had taken refuge at Uman and in camps outside its walls. Ivan Gonta, the commander of a Cossack militia assisting Polish forces in garrisoning Uman, defected to Zalizniak and the two of them conducted a massacre. Haidamak artillery blasted the barricaded synagogues in which Leib Shargorodski and Moses Menaker were leading the Uman Jews' defense. Estimates of the number of people slaughtered at Uman range from 2,000 to 20,000. Other haidamak bands conducted pogroms at Balta, Tulchin, Rashov, Fastiv, and other towns.[44] Zalizniak's revolt became known as the *Koliivschyna* (Ukr. *kola*, "pike").

By late June most of Kiev and Bratslav palatinates and parts of Podolia and Volhynia were under haidamak control and Russian authorities began to worry that the southward spread of disorder could carry into Left Bank Ukraine or provoke a border incident with the Ottomans. Catherine II therefore ordered Russian troops under Brigadier Mikhail Nikitich Krechetnikov to aid Polish Crown forces against Zalizniak's bandits. In April 1769, one of the last operating haidamak bands, Guba's 700 men raiding in Bratslav and Kiev palatinates, was destroyed by a force of 2,000 Don Cossacks and 60 jaegers under Major Vuich. By summer 1769 the *Koliivshchyna* had been suppressed. Zalizniak and other ringleaders were exiled to Siberia; Polish authorities had Ivan Gonta flayed and quartered. From his headquarters at Kodynka, the Polish commander Jozef Stępkowski conducted trials and executions that reportedly took 7,000 Ukrainian lives. This ended what Orest Subtelny considers "the last great uprising of the Ukrainian peasantry against its Polish lords."[45]

The Balta incident

In the first months after the formation of the Bar Confederation the sultan had still balked at providing substantial support for the Confederates. His position was that the Porte "does not intend to intervene in the Confederates' affairs, as all her actions are inclined only to the protection of her honor and security."[46] "A vagabond named Potocki came into the Sublime State's protection with three to five hundred soldiers," Ahmed Resmi Efendi wrote. "Those who escape the hands of an aggressive tyrant and seek refuge with another state bring ruin and misfortune because of their misdeeds, while those involved in this kind or patronage, inviting the enemy into their own territory, suffer distress and hardship."[47] But threats to the Porte's frontier and the security of her Moldavian and Crimean vassals were another matter. The haidamak raids violating the Ottoman Empire's borders would finally spur Sultan Mustafa III to declare war on Russia.

In March 1768 Jozef Pułaski had again asked the grand vizier to assist the Bar Confederates against Russia by pointing out that Russian forces were within ten miles of the Porte's northern border, a violation of the 1700 Constantinople Treaty and 1739 Belgrade Treaty.[48] A. M. Obreskov, the Russian ambassador to Istanbul, had tried to explain that Russia was increasing its military presence in Poland only temporarily, to protect the Dissidents, and he issued another 70,000 rubles in gifts to placate the grand vizier and other ministers. However, they continued to harangue him about reported Russian intrigues fomenting unrest in Montenegro and Greece.[49]

In mid-June 1768, soon after the massacre at Uman, a detachment of Zalizniak's haidamaks was pursuing some Confederates through Podolia toward the Kodyma River and entered the town of Balta on the Moldavian side of the border. Something happened in Balta that resulted in the massacre of about a thousand inhabitants and combat between the haidamaks and the janissary garrison.[50] An attack on Balta involving Cossacks who had come from the Zaporozhian Host—in other words, Russian subjects—could be viewed in Istanbul as a very serious provocation. Balta was an important market town—the Nogais often brought their horses and cattle here for sale, and many Turkish, Tatar, Greek, Armenian, and Jewish merchants regularly traded there. Balta was also of considerable strategic value to the Porte because it stood at the junction of the Bug, Dnestr, and Prut rivers and from it ran the roads east across Bucak to Crimea and northwest to Kishinev, Iaşi, and Khotin in Moldavia.

After the Balta incident the sultan's ministers were no longer satisfied by Obreskov's reassurances that Russian troops had not been involved and that Russian forces in Poland would be drawn down once the Confederate and haidamak revolts were controlled.

The sultan's diwan was also enraged that the Russians seemed to be exploiting instability in Moldavia, Montenegro, Kabarda, and Georgia and were building new fortresses in New Serbia and near Bender. Branicki, head of the Bar Confederation, was urging the sultan to give the Russians an ultimatum, and the sultan was also being pressed toward war by his physician, Ghobis. On July 26 the Prussian resident in Istanbul reported to Berlin, "Matters here are at a critical stage. If Russia does not give the satisfaction which the Porte demands, and does not withdraw her troops from Podolia, war between Russia and the Porte is almost inevitable."[51] At the end of August, Grand Vizier Muhsinzade Mehmed Pasha was removed and replaced by Silahdar Hamza Pasha (who lasted just a month), and then by Mehmed Hindi Emin Pasha, who was of a more militant disposition.[52] According to the Ottoman court historian Ahmed Vasif, Obreskov was forced to acknowledge that there were, by this time, 27,000 Russian troops in Poland, not 7,000, and that Russian troops had been involved in the Balta incident.[53] A *fetva* from the Grand Mufti ruled that war was justified because innocent Muslim blood had been shed. On October 6, 1768, Obreskov was arrested and confined to the dungeon of the Seven Towers. War was now at hand.[54]

CHAPTER 2
THE OTTOMAN EMPIRE AND ITS FRONTIER
IN PONTIC EUROPE

The construction of a Northern Accord had been quick work. By late 1764 Denmark and Prussia had been enlisted in alliance, and a king loyal to Empress Catherine had been placed on the Polish throne. But in summer 1767—the beginning of the sixth year of Catherine's reign—her government's decisions to arrest leading Polish Republicans and force the Diet to enact a Toleration bill had provoked armed resistance in Poland. The Confederation of Bar revolted against the king and the occupying Russian army, and in the course of the struggle between Catholic Confederates and Orthodox haidamaks, the Ottoman border had been violated at Balta. The Porte now declared war on Russia.

Panin had expected the Northern Accord to lead to peace. He had not anticipated that the Russian power project in Poland, key to achieving a Northern Accord of Baltic powers, would lead indirectly but so quickly to another war on Russia's Black Sea frontier.

Vorontsov had been skeptical of the value of a Northern Accord, preferring that Russia preserved its strategic partnership with Austria. He had also warned that the Turks had found, and would continue to find, reasons to interfere in Russia's business with Poland. In his 1761 memorandum to Empress Elizabeth Petrovna, Vorontsov identified the leading causes of tension between the Ottoman and Russian Empires, although he was still confident that these tensions could be managed through diplomacy and deterrence.

"When the town of Azov, at the mouth of the Don, was in the possession of the Ottoman Porte, the Porte's border had directly adjoined that of Russia's southern provinces, and the Porte had therefore been considered an extremely dangerous neighbor." But the demilitarization of Azov has reduced this danger, so that the immediate threat to southern Russia now came only from the Crimean Khanate.

"However, at the present moment the Ottoman Porte can harm Russia in respect to several considerations: 1) in Polish affairs, in which the Porte takes part and on some of which it has observable influence; 2) in negotiations about Persia, if the Porte should seek to recoup its losses there, especially along the Caspian; 3) and through the Crimean khans, who make attacks on Russia."[1]

The Turks for their part feared Russia when Russia had control of Azov and the Don mouth, and maintained naval forces there; "now Russia cannot harm the Turks—except through its religious unity with various peoples who are subjects of the Turks, comprise the largest and most significant part of the Turkish domains in Europe, and conduct themselves enthusiastically towards Russia. Russia could, in event of need, be of secret or open aid to them. This prospect disturbs the Turkish court and causes it anxiety."[2]

Vorontsov urged vigilance over the longer term to prevent the Turks from intervening in Polish affairs or seeking *revanche* against Persia, thereby interfering with Russian trade; and Russia must also look for the opportunity "to obtain Crimea and the Don mouth as places to maintain a Russian fleet in the Black Sea." But for now "as long as the Azov region remains in its current state neither empire need have much to do with or much to fear from the other."[3]

Vorontsov considered Russia's alliance with Austria crucial in maintaining peace with the Porte. "Russia and Austria, seeing in the Porte a common enemy, formed a close alliance and in separate secret articles concluded in 1746 agreed that in the event of a war with the Turks each would assist the other, declaring war even if that side was not already at war, excluding from military operations only the Asiatic domains of the Russian Empire and the Italian domains of the Austrian Empire." In 1753 a special act made this article eternal and independent of all other treaty obligations. Vorontsov considered this Austro-Russian mutual defense treaty sufficient for "establishing a balance of power against the Turkish forces."[4]

Certain points of dispute with the Ottoman government remained unresolved. The main specific grievances from the Porte were that the new Russian fortresses of St. Dmitrii and St. Elizabeth violated the border and that Russia had broken certain treaty terms by taking some Nogai hordes under protection in 1742. Russia's main concerns were about possible Ottoman interference in the Caucasus and in Polish politics, or Ottoman aggression against Austria.

As to the likelihood of these disputes provoking war, Vorontsov speculated, "It is to be noted further that Turkish power is approaching exhaustion and decline (*iznemnozhenie i upadok*) through the generally effeminate and luxuriant life now installed in it, and from internal disorders. But it must be considered that a wise sovereign could use his autocratic power and the abundant resources in that empire to correct all these disorders in a short period, without difficulty—which would have to be reckoned extremely dangerous for our neighbors and for all Christianity." He characterized the Porte as a military despotism dependent upon military adventures and victories to "strengthen the body politic and nourish its nerves. From protracted peace it would experience not only exhaustion but ultimate destruction. It follows from this that the Ottoman Porte by the very nature of its government is necessarily forced to break peace with its neighbors." For fifteen years, sultans Mahmud I and Osman III had kept their empire at peace—but it was because they were weak, despised by their subjects, and feared bringing together in mobilization their janissaries and the regular army. "But the now reigning Sultan Mustafa is inclined to war, and is held back from it only by his Grand Vizier."[5]

Vorontsov saw it as a fundamental law of politics that war was most likely to be actively sought when a long peace had begun to erode a nation's military spirit; when population growth had increased the number of "spongers" and exploiters and provoked internal discord and banditry; or when campaigns to suppress rebels and purge the realm of evildoers presented the opportunity to embark upon new conquests. But if the Turks returned to war, Vorontsov thought, it would be more likely against neighboring Austria, tempted by the rich military resources so near at hand in Hungary and Transylvania.[6]

"Exhaustion and decline"

The defeat of the Ottoman army at Vienna in 1683; the capture of Azov in 1696; the Karlowitz and Constantinople treaties imposing on the Porte and Khanate fixed frontiers enforced under international law; and Prince Eugene's victories over the Turks in 1716–1718 had dramatically altered European perceptions of Ottoman military power. Ottoman armies were now viewed as undisciplined fanatical masses and the Ottoman government seen as less able to manage military resources because of corruption and incompetence. The Terrible Turk of seventeenth-century sermons and broadsides had become the Comical Turk parodied in the comic operas of Haydn and Mozart. Nicholas I was not the originator of the meme of the Ottoman Empire as "the sick man of Europe": this idea was already being promulgated by European philosophers in the mid-eighteenth century. Montesquieu wrote in *The Persian Letters* (1721) of the Ottoman Empire, "whose sick body was not supported by a mild and regular diet, but by a powerful treatment, which continually exhausted it."[7]

The idea that the Ottoman Empire was in decline and increasingly dysfunctional fed Europe's confidence that, with the right military leadership and resolve, Austria and Russia could finish off the Porte as a great power. Voltaire wrote a poem in 1716 celebrating the victories of Prince Eugene:

Chase the Moslems
Break soon the barrier
Make the impertinent circumcised bite the dust
And full of a warrior passion,
Trampling their turbans,
Finish with this mission
In the palace of the Ottomans.[8]

Early in the Russo-Turkish War of 1735–1739, Marshal Münnich had predicted that Russia would retake Azov in 1736, conquer Crimea, the Kuban, and Kabarda in 1737, occupy Bucak, Moldavia, and Wallachia in 1738, and "in 1739 the flags and standards of Her Highness will be hoisted … where? In Constantinople."[9]

Part of the reason for this confidence in Europe was relief that the Köprülü viziers' program of renewed conquest in Europe had been defeated. The War of the Holy League had been won and the Turks pushed out of Podolia, Transylvania, and Hungary. After 1739 the Porte tried to avoid military conflict, to the extent that it stood aside from the War of the Austrian Succession and the Seven Years' War. This could be interpreted in Europe as the Porte's acknowledgment of its weakened military capacity. Part of the new European strategic confidence was also derived from the fact that the only available information for assessing Ottoman intentions and capabilities came from ambassadors at Istanbul and Edirne reporting what they observed at court: the rapid ministerial leapfrog of grand viziers, janissary mutinies, intrigues among *diwan* secretaries, and acceptance of the bribe money proffered by these same European ambassadors. The ambassadors' knowledge of administration and politicking in the outlying provinces was much more limited. In other words, the ambassadors were positioned to witness the dysfunction of central institutions but were not able to observe whether power was being efficiently decentralized in compensation.

Thus Veshniakov, Russian ambassador to the Porte during the 1735–1739 war, wrote, "I must bluntly if honestly report that in Turkey now there are no political leaders, no military commanders, no sound financial administrators: everything is in terrible disorder and with the slightest misfortune would be pushed to the edge of the abyss. The Turks' terror derives from one conviction: that the Turks are completely different from before. Previously they were inspired by glory and ferocity, now they are faint-hearted and fearful, all apparently sensing the end of their lawless power … There is no concern for the general welfare in Turkey, they are entirely preoccupied by private profit; the distinguished and talented people have all been ruined and destroyed, with only the mediocre surviving … The Tatars know this, as everyone here can attest, and are now wavering in heir loyalty to the Porte. As regards the Christian subjects, the Turks fear they will all revolt as soon as the Russian army approaches the frontier."[10] Some of the same observations were being made by Ottoman courtiers in their "advice literature" warning the sultans of the paralysis of central government and the breakdown of order and erosion of virtue.

Historians studying Ottoman administration in the seventeenth and eighteenth centuries have observed the breakdown of certain fiscal and military institutions that had traditionally been essential to the "autocracy" of the sultans and the efficiency of their army. Institutional breakdown resembled the fall of a chain of dominoes, with the failure of particular institutions forcing substitutions or adaptations that created more new problems in turn.

Thus rural overpopulation led to the shrinking of peasant farms within *timar* grants and the resulting decline in *timar* revenue yields led, in turn, to the reduction in the timariot *sipahi* cavalry formation and the compensating expansion of the janissary and militia infantry formations. But the janissaries and militias, unlike timariots, had to be paid out of the treasury, forcing the government into heavier deficit spending.[11] The combat-effectiveness of the janissary corps eroded as a result of the decision under Sultan Murad IV to end *devshirme* recruitment, to open up janissary service to Muslims, to allow sons to follow their fathers in janissary service, and to allow janissaries to augment their quarterly pay by engaging in shop trade. To combat mounting pay arrears and budget deficits, the government raised tax rates, made formerly extraordinary taxes permanent annual levies, debased the currency, and converted *timar* and *zeamet* grants into *iltizam* tax-farms. From 1695 it became possible to pay fees to have tax-farms turned into *malikane*, life-term leaseholds. Military elites scrambled to obtain *malikane* as compensation for their declining *timar* and salary income. Since merchants with significant accumulated capital had the advantage in bidding for tax-farms and coming up with the payments to convert them to life leaseholds, the expansion of *malikane* accompanied the emergence of a new landlord class of merchant origin that wielded additional social power as tax collectors and creditors to the government. These new landlords may have been social upstarts in relation to the traditional social hierarchy, but they quickly consolidated their power as "new notables" (*ayan*) at the local and regional levels by cementing patron–client relations with officials, janissary officers, and *ulema*. They purchased additional offices or won offices from the district and provincial governors by assisting with taxes and requisitions for the army and by offering loans, so that those especially successful in acquiring offices were able to leave the ranks of the *reaya* commoners altogether and get reclassified as *askeri* of the ruling institution. They also accomplished this by purchasing at auction janissary salary tickets (*esame*), with the result that many on the janissary salary rolls performed no actual military service. Some took advantage of their private capital and their access to tax revenue to form their own military households (*has*) out of dispossessed *sipahi*s, mercenaries, and peasant *sekban* troops.

Some historians therefore see the introduction of *malikane* tenure in the 1690s as beginning what they call the Age of the *Ayan*, marking a fundamental change in the character of the Ottoman state.[12] They emphasize the debilitating effect of the change: it weakened Ottoman military effectiveness and led to the rollback of Ottoman power from southeastern Europe. Shaw characterized the seventeenth century as a period of "decomposition" followed in the eighteenth century by "internal anarchy...combined with the loss of integral parts of the empire."[13]

But others (Virginia Aksan, Karen Barkey) have more recently argued that the shift in power from the sultan's court to the provincial *ayan* had an economic and military logic, the Ottoman regime was experiencing some of the same problems besetting other eighteenth-century European powers, and Ottoman institutions were responding through *reconfiguration* rather than collapse.

Most of the grand viziers of the period recognized the need to reform finances and reduce the size of the army, particularly the overprivileged janissary corps, and these things might have been accomplished if factionalism had not denied these reforming viziers longer tenure in office.[14] The tax-bearing population did indeed suffer as taxes multiplied and tax rates rose—but this was happening across much of Europe. The relative weight of the *timar*-based *sipahi* cavalry in the army did decline sharply, but the *sipahi* were tactically obsolete anyway and the expansion of the infantry was an unavoidable expense if the army was to remain effective on the battlefield. Some of the new notables did respond to the commercialization of the rural economy by dispossessing the peasantry and enclosing lands and pastures to establish large plantation farms (*çiftliks*). However, these plantations were not that numerous, were usually devoted to livestock ranching rather than cereal cultivation, and were ordinarily established on waste land and did not alienate that many direct producers—so that it would be a distortion to compare the spread of *çiftlik* tenure in the Ottoman Empire to Eastern Europe's Second Serfdom.[15] *Multezim* and *malikane* tax-farmings were logical responses to the commercialization of the economy and the need for military modernization. The *mukataa* revenue source held as a tax farm was a more flexible budgetary unit than the old *timar* revenue grant, and the initial conversion fees and smaller annual renewal fees tax farmers paid to hold *malikane* actually made it easier for the government to budget for both pressing financial needs and routine annual expenses. Karen Barkey notes that the readiness of military elites to accept *malikane* contracts "further legitimated the state at a moment of fiscal crisis because they thereby signaled their continuing support of the state and their willingness to extend credit to this central institution." Over the course of the eighteenth century, the total income from *malikane* tax farming increased by about 1,400 percent. It was not impossible to achieve a balanced budget providing that the state developed and maintained a more ramified and task-specialized fiscal administration, and resorted to a carefully considered complex mix of revenue sources: "a variety of cash taxes, including the annualized 'household' levies, increased poll taxes, excise duties on tobacco, coffee, and wine, in addition to income from new tariff stations and short-term revenue farms."[16] The initial *malikane* conversion down payments alone provided about 10 percent of all state revenue. By 1698–1699 the state deficit was reduced to 63.5 million *akces*; by 1701–1702 the treasury had a surplus of 111.8 million *akces*.[17]

Political reconfiguration affected not only fiscal and military administration but also the distribution of power across the ruling class. Under the old system, power had been concentrated in a single household (*kapi*), that of the sultan and his *kapikulu* officials and officers, many of whom were of slave and *devshirme* origin. Over the course of the seventeenth century, the grand viziers and pasha military governors developed their own *kapi* households modeled upon the sultan's. This occurred as much from the expanding size, increasing complexity, and functional differentiation of the state apparatus as from the weakening of the sultans' power. The Köprülü viziers had taken the lead between the 1660s and 1680s in building from kinship and clientage ties their own households to maintain their hold on power and distribute subordinate offices; these households "provided an alternative route of recruitment into politics, different from the palace and the military that had been until then controlled solely by the sultan's household." Gradually, multiple household political machines emerged, some attached to high figures in the palace administration, others to pashas serving as military governors and army commanders, and these machines allowed some pashas to jump to palace administration and become grand viziers. "Vizier and pasha households became strong patronage networks of men, members of an extended family, friends and clients who were offered training and education for government positions in return for loyalty and service. Members of the pasha's household could become part of a pasha's retinue for war or follow him in the palace administration. The pasha households in effect reproduced the model of the household of the sultan, where the most effective and developed patronage system was prevalent." But they were increasingly effective in exercising their own patronage power, enabling men trained in or still attached to *kapi* households to obtain about half of all key posts in central and provincial administration.[18]

This had the effect of endowing high officials with greater patronage power over a larger range of subordinate offices—while also intensifying factional contestation of appointments, since those appointed were considered to owe patronage to fellow members of their household and were seen as blocking patronage opportunities for members of other households.[19]

Thus, political power had been decentralized—shifted from the sultan and his court to the households of the provincial governors, the pashas and *sancakbey*s and the new notables. These provincial households came to play a more important role in frontier defense and in the campaigning field army. Those pashas most inclined to independent action were those governing districts closest to the military frontier guarded by large garrisons: Ismail, Ibrail, Silistra, Giurgiu, Rusçuk, Vidin, and Belgrade. Those pashas most servile to the sultan and the central government were those governing territories closer to Istanbul, such as Shumla and Edirne.[20]

Decentralization and army organization

The Ottoman field armies campaigning on the lower Don and in Ukraine in the seventeenth century had sometimes exceeded 100,000 men, counting Tatar and Moldavian and Wallachian auxiliaries. The expeditionary army led by Hussein Deli, Pasha of Silistra, to recover Azov from the Don Cossacks in 1641 comprised 20,000 janissaries, 20,000 *sipahi*s, 10,000 Circassians, "a greater number" of Moldavians and Wallachians, and 50,000 Tatars.[21] Grand Vizier Kara Mustafa reportedly marched on Chyhyryn in 1678 with at least 105,000 troops and sappers: 15,000 janissaries, 15,000 *sekban* infantry, 15,000 "pioneers," 30,000 (sic—probably 3,000) court *sipahi*s, 15,000 "other guards," 2,000 gunners, 800 engineers, 10,000 Moldavians and Wallachians, 80,000 (sic—probably 30,000–50,000) Crimean Tatars, 59 great siege guns, 130 field guns, 15 mortars, 8,000 ammunition wagons, 10,000 proviant wagons, 5,000 camels, and 8,000 shepherds.[22]

Grand Vizier Baltaci Mehmed's army defeating Peter I's army on the Prut in 1711 numbered 119,000–121,000: 19,000–21,000 *sipahi*s, 36,000–38,000 *cebelü* retainers; 23,400 janissaries, 10,000–12,000 *cebeci* armorers, 20,000 Bosnians and Albanians, 7,000 gunners, and 1,400–1,500 sappers.[23]

However, there are two important things to be observed about the composition of Ottoman field armies over this period: the number of *timar*-supported provincial *sipahi* cavalrymen declined, while the proportionate weight of salaried standing *kapikulu* troops no longer exceeded about 70,000. In 1670, the standing *kapikulu* component topped out at 70,926: 48,212 janissaries (39,470 janissaries and 8,742 janissary cadets); 14,070 in the six standing cavalry regiments (*sipahi* guards, *silahdar*s, *ulufeci*s of right and left, *gureba* of right and left); and 8,014 artillerymen (*cebeci* armorers, *topçu* gunners, *arabaci* wagoneers).[24]

In estimating the total strength of the Ottoman armed forces at the start of the 1735–1739 war, the Russian military historian A. K. Baiov relied upon calculations by Luigi Marsigli.[25] The standing core of the field army, equipped and salaried from the sultan's treasury, consisted of the *kapikulu* troops (Slaves of the Porte). On paper, the *kapikulu* numbered 54,222 janissary infantrymen, 15,284 *sipahi* cavalry Guards of the Six Regiments, several thousand artillery gunners (*topçu*), bombardiers (*humbaraci*), mining engineers (*mimari*), and about a thousand support troops (water-boys and *cebeci* armorers to clean and repair guns). Excluding the un-enumerated artillerymen and support troops, this gives a potential strength of 74,148 men. But only 29,956 were actually called up into the field army. Of the janissaries, 21,426 were in garrison service; 430 guarded the three imperial residences; 3,020 were janissaries' sons, not in service but living from shares of their fathers' salaries; and about 10,000 were men holding janissary salary tickets but not performing actual janissary duty. The elite *sipahi* cavalry guards of the Six Regiments appeared in full strength only when the sultan in person was with the army on campaign; otherwise, only about two-thirds of them appeared in the field army. On some occasions, the treasury hired *levendat* mercenaries for short-term service to make up the shortfall of salaried standing troops.

The field army also contained *Serhat Kulu*, "provincial troops," some in standing units, and others formed on occasion of campaign. They were equipped, provisioned, and paid from the *has* courts and client lists of the more powerful provincial pashas. The *Serhat Kulu* included some 20,000–26,000 *azab* light infantrymen and *sekban* (Hound-Keeper) infantrymen. The *azab* infantrymen were either recruited locally or were mountaineers brought in from Albania or Bosnia; they served just three to four months each year and were organized by day shifts rather than by *orta* companies. *Sekban* militiamen were raised from the local peasantry for temporary duty, upon military need; they did receive firearms, but older ones of lower quality, and they had virtually no training. The *Serhat Kulu* cavalry were more useful. They included the *betli* light cavalry, standing troops raised and paid from the provinces, officered by local men, and assigned the duty of raiding and attacking. As select standing troops were trained by officers from their own milieu, the *betli* tended to show more *esprit de corps* than other elements of the Ottoman cavalry. The *deli* (Daredevils) were not a standing force but did have some prestige as the personal cavalry guards of the pashas. There was also a standing cavalry formation, locally raised, called the *dzhiundzhuli* (in Baiov's transliteration), but they were for garrison duty, not for the field army. The *Serhat Kulu* had an artillery force, nonstanding, performing defense duty in frontier towns; and as support services, it had *lağimci* engineers accompanying the field army as miners and sappers, and *musselimi* sent ahead of the army to build bridges and repair roads.

Traditionally, the largest part of the army had consisted of *toprakli*, provincial *sipahi* cavalry, and their *cebelü* retainers remunerated and outfitted through *timar* village revenue grants. Timariot *sipahis*, *zeamat*-grant *sipahis*, *beyler* officers, *beylerbey* commanders, and pasha governors were expected to provide one cavalryman or retainer from every 3,000 aspers of *timar* revenue they held. The *toprakli* cavalry were organized in regiments and equipped like the elite *kapikulu* cavalry, and their maximum paper strength was 126,292. But there were seldom more than 64,000 *toprakli* in a field army; at any time, a sixth of them were exempt from campaign duty, and it took so long to mobilize the rest that typically less than half of them had appeared in the field army by the second or third year of war. As they were not standing troops their training and combat effectiveness tended to be deficient.

It had also been traditional for the Ottoman field army to rely upon auxiliary troops, mostly cavalry, contributed by the Moldavian and Wallachian hospodars and the Crimean khans: usually 4,000 men from each of the hospodars and 12,000 or more

Nogais and Crimean Tatars. The hospodars were required to provide these troops at their own expense, in addition to helping with the provisioning of the field army, as part of their obligations as tributary vassals. Although the Crimean khans paid tribute to the Porte, they were reimbursed for the warriors they brought on campaign with the field army.

Baiov concluded that the maximum strength of the Ottoman armed forces in the 1730s was about 220,000 men, but that 109,000–115,000 was the maximum actual strength of the field army. In extreme circumstances another 30,000 might be added to the field army by stripping manpower from the provincial garrisons. He considered it a potential problem that such a small part of the army consisted of standing salaried *kapikulu* troops under the control of the central government, not only because they would have been better trained but because they were presumably more politically reliable than provincial troops.[26]

The reconfiguration of power relations since the 1690s had indeed affected the size and structure of the field army and the combat-readiness of its troops. Trained janissaries were a smaller proportion of the infantry now; the bulk of the infantry now consisted of seasonal *azab* militiamen or *sekban* mercenaries hired by the pashas or the central treasury. The smaller number of provincial *sipahis* participating on campaign did reflect the reduction of *timar* revenue for *toprakli* and also the failure of some provincial officials to find funds to subsidize *Serhat Kulu* cavalry. In 1744, twenty-three *sancaks* in three *pashaliks* were ordered to mobilize 120,000 provincial *sipahi* cavalrymen for war against Nadir Shah; because of poor management and shortage of funds, just 12,000 men appeared for service. *Sancakbey* Suleiman of Janina had been ordered to provide 400 Asian and 250 Rumelian *sipahis* as his retinue; he was able to come up with just six or seven men.[27]

Comparing Ottoman military performance in the sixteenth and eighteenth centuries therefore becomes more complicated: it is not enough for the historian to focus on decision-making in the central government and the turnout of standing *kapikulu* troops; for the eighteenth century it becomes necessary to examine the performance of the pashas and other provincial authorities as mobilizers, provisioners, and *seraskir* commanders of provincial troops.

Decentralization and military finance

From the fifteenth century the Ottoman political economy had been ostensibly patrimonial, with the sultan claiming ownership of three-fifths of the land and the rights to requisition what he needed for war and distribute revenue grants in exchange for military service. Now it was becoming a more obviously capitalist economy in which private property in land, military manpower hire, and market purchase of military provisions counted for more. The rise of *ayan* power in the provinces, although it came at the expense of the central power of the sultan's autocracy, had the effect of "unleashing" market relations. The shift toward *malikane* tax-farming soon covered the deficits run in the late seventeenth century and provided revenue growth through the first sixty years of the eighteenth century. The expansion of commercial economy and the curtailment of government deficit spending were further promoted by the central government's steady commitment to peace between the 1740s and 1760s and its reluctance to raise tax rates.[28]

There were several points of vulnerability within the Ottoman fiscal system—obsolete cadastral records led to unrealistic tax quotas, and much potential revenue was lost to the continued practice of donating real estate to tax-exempt *vakif* trusts. However, the European ambassadors tended to overstate the Empire's fiscal problems because what was most visible to them was the reduced revenue reaching the central treasury. Baron de Tott blamed this on the rapaciousness of "the Pachas, who were at once the farmers of the revenue, and the governors of the provinces," their greed forcing the central government to keep a suspicious eye over them and look for every opportunity to confiscate their "corrupt gains" so as to compensate the treasury for lost revenue. Tott saw a kind of "war" over revenue being waged between the center and the provinces, with Sultan Mustafa III assiduous in uncovering and confiscating illegal gains from his tax-farmers. "The system of the Turkish finances consists in placing on the surface a great number of sponges, which swelling with the dew, afford the Sovereign the means of acquiring all, by squeezing them into a reservoir, of which only he keeps the key."[29] Tott estimated the actual annual tax revenue of Sultan Mustafa's treasury, not counting confiscations, at about 3.2 million livres, with the bulk of treasury revenue (400 million livres) coming from the regalia from royal domains, much of which had to be kept in reserve for emergencies; he therefore considered Mustafa to have begun to "exhaust his wealth," and by the time of the sultan's death in 1774, his janissaries were owed twenty seven months' pay.[30]

Under the old patrimonial system of the sixteenth century, the aim of military finance had been the expansion of trained standing forces, which required that the state maintained its central monopoly over revenue and its power to impose requisitions. Under the new *ayan* regime, the test of effective military resource mobilization became the pashas' ability to work with contractors and military enterprisers to raise and support militias and mercenary troops. That had not been clearly tested during the peaceful decades of the 1740s to the early 1760s; it would now be tested in the 1768–1774 Russo-Turkish War.

In the Age of the *Ayans*, the Empire was more commercially developed and more wealth available for taxing for the army, at least potentially. But political decentralization had made budgeting and provisioning less predictable and more contentious.

Under the old patrimonial regime, it had been easier for the sultan's central treasury to plan initial disbursements over the winter months to assemble and equip a campaign force and then issue additional funds over the spring to cover the expenses of launching the campaign and marching the army to the front. It had also been easier to keep up the network of imperial granaries and supply stations (*menzil-hane*) along the main march routes. It had been the usual practice to levy provisioning taxes and support services on registered tax-exempt service groups, while the army was within the core of the Empire—and then turn to contracting for supplies and support services on a cash-and-carry basis, ideally at prevailing market rates, once the army left the core and moved into border regions. In the event costs exceeded original projections supplemental taxes for provisioning, including emergency taxes (*avariz*), could be levied on border taxpayers. But the state had tried to keep emergency taxes and forced contributions to a modest and occasional role in provisioning, and up until the end of the seventeenth century, "an orderly relationship between suppliers (provincial residents) and requisitioners of supplies (the state as represented by its armed forces) was maintained."[31] One of the reasons they could be kept in balance was the practice of entrusting most recordkeeping in local government to *kadi* judges appointed from the local *ulema*. Because the *kadi*s served for two-year terms, they were less intimidated or tempted to enter the patronage networks of local notables, and because the *kadi* offices archived the tax records and cadasters and produced a great deal of paper documentation of local administration, they made available to the Empire a standardized accounting system for military procurements.

Rhoads Murphey considers the seventeenth century *menzil-hane* network and military commissariat organization not only up to the task of supporting large field armies but "leagues ahead of their European contemporaries." Only in the eighteenth century would the European powers develop magazine networks and commissarial corps surpassing the old Ottoman model in effectiveness at centralized resource extraction and allocation for war.[32]

But one of the consequences of the decentralization of power during the Age of the Ayans was the shift of military accounting out of the *kadi* offices into committees comprised of *malikane* tax-farmers and representatives of the local notables. These committees were less formally connected than the *kadi*s to the *sancakbey*s mobilizing the *toprakli* troops and the commandants of the frontier garrisons, and they could not be monitored as closely by the central government. Questions about tax and service obligations and contracting prices were more likely to become contentious the more they impinged upon the patronage interests of the local notables. Mounting tax arrears in the 1710s convinced Istanbul of the urgency of updating and correcting *cahiers* and tax records. In some cases, the provincial committees of notable did a creditable job of this reallocation work; in other instances they produced inaccurate records, and in still other instances they abused the reallocation process to enrich themselves and their cronies by exempting certain estates from taxation or attaching indebted peasants to tax-farming creditors. Central treasury accounting was less able to step in and correct the local committees because it was already overburdened dealing with the consequences of the booming popularity of *esame* salary tickets, which artificially inflated the muster rolls and made it harder to calculate salary costs for standing troops.[33]

Ottoman military "obsolescence"

The ordinances of the major European armies had developed complex instructions for handling arms, extending and doubling lines, forming columns, firing by platoon or volley, and so on. By comparison, Ottoman infantry and cavalry appeared to follow no systematic tactical doctrine at all and so their tactics struck Europeans as formless and primitive. P. A. Tol'stoi, the Russian ambassador to the Porte in 1703, wrote that even the standing janissary *ortas* conducted themselves in battle as if ignorant of military art. "All their military cunning and power derives from their numbers ... If the enemy beats them and forces them to withdraw, they cannot maintain any order but flee and perish, because they are not used to battle order, and if the enemy pursues them, they throw off their officers and leave them behind and run off, not to be recalled."[34] Baron de Tott maintained that the janissary infantry had only their ferocity and fanaticism to rely upon: "An Ottoman army once attacked, is broken to pieces without being beaten; but the first shock of the Turks, when they are determined to make the first attack, is always dangerous and difficult to sustain. At the affair of Grotska, to get possession of a redoubt, they heaped the ditches with their dead; and fanaticism carried some of them so far in the last war against the Russians, as to make them brave the fire of the artillery by rushing, like madmen, to hack with their sabres the mouths of the enemy's cannon."[35]

Whereas the prevailing tactical model for European armies was to deploy infantry in two or three lines a few ranks deep to maximize firepower across a broad front, Ottoman tactics for attack placed greater reliance on cold steel than infantry or artillery fire. Ottoman forces infantry and cavalry typically attacked in what Petr Panin called "heaps" (*kuchi*), which made repeated attempts to penetrate the enemy line as wedges. If a heap was successful in breaking through, it would then spread out like a fan, lashing out with its yataghans and sabers to widen the gap and disrupt the rest of the enemy's front line; with enough ferocity in individual combat, adroit horsemanship, and the willingness to make repeated attacks against European musket and cannon fire, this could give them victory. This was why Austrian and Russian armies fighting the Turks learned that they could not afford to deploy battalions along their lines at intervals, as had been customary when fighting other European armies; when facing the Turks, those intervals would have to be closed up or blocked by regimental guns and cavalry squadrons.

The Ottomans made greater use of their infantry and artillery firepower when they were on the defensive, and their preference from the late seventeenth century was toward defending from trench lines and other field fortifications. This was especially the case in the first two years of the 1768–1774 Russo-Turkish War. But Russian commanders had devised new methods of attack by divisional squares that rolled over Ottoman field fortifications, and after their defeats at Larga and Kagul, the Turks were forced to avoid large-scale open battle and adhere to a purely defensive strategy of maintaining large fortress garrisons along the Danube to deter the Russians from crossing the frontier.[36]

The janissary infantry companies seem to have lost much of their combat effectiveness since the end of *devshirme* and the opening of their companies to Muslims, sons of janissaries, and parasites who held salary tickets but never performed janissary duty. It was also the case that fewer *toprakli sipahi* cavalrymen came out on campaign and that their discipline and resolve had eroded.

This raises the question of why the Ottoman government seemed incapable of reforming its army and replacing such "obsolete" formations with new model infantry and cavalry of European type.

European observers tended to invoke Ottoman cultural backwardness and "superstition" to explain the state's reluctance to modernize its forces. Baron de Tott gave as an example the resistance his efforts to Europeanize the Ottoman artillery had engendered at court and among the clerics. When the baron demonstrated the ability of his new *süratçi* gunners to match Russian artillerymen in rapid firing, the grand treasurer (*defterdar*) objected to the fact that Tott's gunners were using rammers with brushes made of hog's bristles. The baron responded by producing an artisan who testified that hog-bristle brushes were used to whitewash and paint the walls of Istanbul's mosques and that some bristles were invariably left stuck to the mosque walls after painting. "You see, then," Tott told the grand treasurer, "that as the hogs' bristles do not defile your Mosques, there can be no harm in making use of them against your enemies."[37] Tott's low estimate of Ottoman gun-casters, engineers, and gunners became conventional wisdom throughout Europe. But it was without much foundation in fact, based upon cursory observations by a man whose arrogance exceeded his own limited expertise. Tott admitted that he had never seen a foundry before, and his complaint about superstition blocking military reform overlooks the fact that Sultan Mustafa III had initiated the program to improve gunnery and continued to invest in it until his death.[38] The French ambassador de Peysonnel wrote a devastating critique of Tott's memoirs, charging him with unfairly dismissing Ottoman military technology.

It was true that many Ottoman court historians subscribed to "Ottoman exceptionalism," the idea that the Ottoman Empire was divinely favored, just in its waging of *jihad*, and destined to endure forever. Ottoman defeat could therefore be explained only as *istidrâc*, divine punishment: God giving unbelievers victory to test the Muslim faithful while making the unbelievers prideful and setting them up for defeat and damnation. But it was also the case that some Ottoman intellectuals—Ibrahim Muteferrika (1674–1745), Ahmed Resmi Efendi (1700–1781), and Ahmed Vasif Efendi (c. 1730–1806)—were devising a new philosophy of history that distinguished between "universal events," which were divinely preordained, and "particular events," which could be shaped by human agency. They argued that God had empowered man to take initiative and act upon particular events as a moral duty. Thus Ahmed Resmi Efendi in his *Summary of Admonitions* characterized Russian victory in 1774 as an *istidrâc*, but he also harshly condemned those conservative officials who had plunged the Porte into that avoidable war out of stubborn confidence that the religious piety of the Turks would assure them victory. Ahmed Vasif Efendi (an associate of Ahmed Resmi's, a veteran of Kartal, and a participant in the peace talks at Bucharest) had gone even farther in his 1804 chronicle of the 1768–1774 war, acknowledging that the Russians had prevailed not just because of the will of God but because they had tended to preparations for particular events: their troops "were trained in the newly developed principles of war and combat; they were obedient to their officers; they were assiduously drilled in all the means of artillery; they were prevented from luxury and kept from rest."[39] This new philosophy of history acknowledging greater role for free would help embolden Sultan Selim III to undertake military reform.

The greater resistance to modernizing the army probably derived less from religious fatalism and general neophobia than from political anxieties about the social disruption attending military reform. It should be remembered that the janissary corps, the gunners' Hearth, and the elite *sipahi* guards regiments had been in existence for centuries, that they dated back to the beginning of the Ottoman gunpowder revolution, and that for those fortunate enough to be enrolled in them they had taken on important social welfare and status-marking functions. Their members were defined as tax-exempt *askeri* rather than taxable commoner *reaya*. This is why Muslim subjects had clamored for opening up the janissary corps to non-*devshirme*, so they could enroll their sons and make janissary status inheritable; it was why so many paid at auction to acquire *esame* tickets. Members of these standing formations were entitled to treasury salaries, bonuses, and to particular privileges with regard to artisanal enterprise and trading; they were officially marked as *kapikulu*, Slaves of the Porte, and thus honorific kin in the sultan's household, sons under the solicitude of the sultan as father. This patriarchal culture was replicated within the *orta*s, where commanding colonels were called *çorbaci* ("soup-ladlers") and all the subordinate ranks had titles pertaining to the kitchen and commensal nurture. "The crescent formation order of the military forces which the Ottomans employed in major open field confrontations, even as the new technical and strategic developments dictated otherwise, was driven by the idea that the military apparatus of the state was just that: an expression of the order and proximity to the privileges granted by the sultan, or his substitute, the grand vizier. This is to say, the deployment of Ottoman assembled forces on the battlefield was representative of the political hierarchy of the Ottoman state."[40]

In other words, some minds may have recognized the need to liquidate the janissary corps and replace it with European-style New Formation Troops (*Nizam-i-jedid*) after the Empire's defeat in 1774, but the project met with strong resistance and took decades to carry out because it conflicted with the Ottoman exceptionalist tradition, shook up the social hierarchy, and threatened status and livelihood.

Border defenses

In the eighteenth century the Ottoman field army still had one very significant advantage: the front along which it engaged Habsburg and Russian forces was clearly defined in both political and strategic terms—fixed in international law after 1700 (with temporary exceptions with regard to the status of Azov) and marked off by a horizontal chain of strong fortresses along the Danube and along the northern coast of the Black Sea. The principal march routes leading from Istanbul and Edirne to the fortress-defended border were short and led through territory that was mostly densely populated and economically developed. This meant that field armies could be assembled north of Edirne or in Dobruja, which is already close to the frontier, and could make a quick march to intercept the enemy at or beyond the fortress line. Waging a war of posts to protect the Empire from enemy invasion was therefore a fairly straightforward proposition, relying on established procedures and a permanent *menzil-hane* network of supply posts. Undertaking invasions penetrating deep into southern Poland, Ukraine, or southern Russia was a more difficult matter, but in the event it became necessary there was also a chain of large fortresses (Akkirman, Bender, Sorocha, Khotin) running south–north along the Dnestr—perpendicular to the primary fortress line—which could support field armies coming up from the south.

An example of successful exploitation of this advantage was the 1711 campaign into Moldavia undertaken to block the Russian army's march down the Prut to the Danube and into Wallachia. Grand Vizier Baltaci Mehmed Pasha was ordered to assemble the standing *kapikulu* core of the field army above Edirne, march it north through Dobruja—attaching provincial troops and Tatar auxiliaries en route—and cross the Danube at Isaccea before the Russians and their Moldavian renegade allies could reach Isaccea and turn into Wallachia to join with the rebel hospodar Brancoveanu. Baltaci Mehmed's secondary mission, if time proved on his side, was to push north past Isaccea and join with the Tatars (and if necessary, troops from the Dnestr garrison of Bender) to defeat Peter I's Russian army on the Prut River before it could "liberate" the southern half of Moldavia.

The core elements of Baltaci Mehmed's army marched from Edirne between May 1 and May 14. Their progress toward Isaccea was facilitated by the fact that the infrastructure of supply depots and rest camps along their march route was already in place (much of it for generations). Between Edirne and Isaccea, for example, there were five bridges and twenty way-stations, ports at Burgaz and Varna, as well as four sea-reinforced supply depots near the mouth of the Danube. Beyond Isaccea as far as Falçiu Geçidi, where Baltaci Mehmed's army halted the Russians, there were more bridges, seven way-stations along the eastern bank of the Prut, four supply depots on the Prut, and another three depots just to the east along the Dnestr below Bender. Tsar Peter's army moved much more slowly because it had to rely on long supply lines into Poland and found it difficult to get water, grain, or fresh mounts in Moldavia. By June 28, while the Russians were still in the vicinity of Iaşi, Baltaci Mehmed's army had already left Isaccea far behind and was advancing up the Prut to intercept.[41] Ottoman naval power in the Black Sea and eastern Mediterranean also made it possible to deliver to Baltaci Mehmed janissaries from Egypt and arnauts from the western Balkans and Anatolia, so that by the time he encircled the Russians at Stanileşti, he had about 120,000 troops.[42]

After 1700 the Ottoman Empire avoided aggression in southeastern Europe (in contrast to the Caucasus) in order to maintain peace and gain a breathing spell in which to manage the transition to a more decentralized regime and repair its finances. It was less important now to build forces to pursue a war of annihilation to be won through overwhelming superiority; it was enough to maintain the ability to win a war of posts to defend the Empire's border in Europe and deter further European aggression. The lesson of Baltaci Mehmed's decisive victory on the Prut seemed to be that a war of posts could be won without a costly modernization of Ottoman forces, providing that the army made good use of its long experience in logistics.

But what if the political reliability of border elites could no longer be counted upon in a crisis and border logistics should be disrupted? What if the Russians or the Austrians should take advantage of the decentralization of the Ottoman state, or religious conflicts, or taxpayer unrest in the border provinces and frontier client polities of the Porte, and turn them against the army and the Empire?

Moldavia and Wallachia under phanariot rule

Before Tsar Peter's Moldavian campaign in 1711, the hospodars of Moldavia and Wallachia had been most useful to the Porte as Christian vassal lords contributing troops to border defense and the sultan's campaigns. But the fact that the hospodars of both Moldavia and Wallachia had wavered in loyalty and welcomed the Russian army to the Prut forced the sultan's government to curb their military power and reorient them to the primary task of tax-farming for the sultan's treasury. In 1714 the Turks dethroned and beheaded Wallachian Hospodar Brancoveanu for treason and took the opportunity to transform the administration of vassal Moldavia and Wallachia. Henceforth, the boyars of Moldavia and Wallachia were deprived of the right to elect their own hospodars; the sultan would instead entrust the governance of vassal Moldavia and Wallachia to *phanariots*, Greek or Hellenized political clients of the sultan's government—usually dragoman interpreters residing in Phanar, the Greek quarter of Istanbul—on the basis of the bids they offered to hold the hospodarate thrones for three-year terms and collect *kharaj* tribute for the treasury of the Porte. A phanariot seeking appointment as hospodar was required to make a bid for the investiture kaftan; he could retain the throne beyond the initial three-year term by offering an additional bid similar to the French *paulette*. The traditional council of boyars advising the hospodar was replaced by a *diwan* packed with clients of the phanariot and other office-seekers from Phanar. The phanariot hospodar was allowed to invest his share of the *kharaj* in trade, and because of his political connections, his enterprises became monopsonic within the principality's economy. He gradually increased his authority over the Orthodox Church, so that his consent was required to invest elected bishops (now more often Greeks). The traditional national levy was scaled back and the army transformed into a guard for the hospodar.[43] The defense of the principality henceforth relied primarily upon the Turkish fortress garrisons—for Moldavia the garrison at Khotin, in particular.

There were just a handful of Phanar families with the wealth and connections to win appointment (the Mavrocordatos family, the Ghica family), so the title of hospodar tended to be rotated among two or three of them.[44] The Porte was thereby reassured that it was working with vassal rulers whom it knew intimately; this also checked the multiplication of boyar factions. Because the phanariot system placed first emphasis on revenue-farming, it tended to be fiscally rapacious. This was especially true in the first half of the century. In Moldavia, for example, the total tax and tribute burden rose three-fold between 1714 and 1750.[45] Heavy taxes in turn provoked peasants to curtail cultivation or flee and pressed the boyar landlords to compensate by raising feudal rents. Some peasant tenants fled across the Danube into Ottoman territory, or into Austrian Banat and Transylvania; census data suggest that Wallachia lost half its peasant population to flight just in the years 1741–1745.[46] Others peasants turned to *hajduk* banditry.

Baron de Tott, traveling through Wallachia and Moldavia in 1767, considered the rapaciousness of the phanariot hospodars to have "laid waste the two finest provinces of the Ottoman empire." Candidates for investiture as hospodar borrowed enormous sums at 25 percent interest to purchase appointment and to defeat the intrigues of rival candidates; then, they had to raise taxes to recover this investment and obtain a profit, "as if the Despot, solely bent on destruction, thought himself entitled to increase his exactions in proportion to the diminution of his people, and the loss of the fertility of their lands. I was myself witness, in passing through Moldavia, to the levying of the eleventh poll-tax in that year, though we were then only in the month of October."[47] Tott considered the boyars cruel oppressors as well. "It is rarely that they live on good terms with their Prince, and their intrigues are generally pointed against him; Constantinople is the center of their maneuvers. It is there that both parties carry their complaints, and their money, and the Sultan Seroskier, of Bas-Arabia, offers a constant refuge to such boyards as the Porte is disposed to sacrifice in its tranquility … These different outgoings, for which the boyards reimburse themselves by partial persecutions, joined to the taxes imposed by the Prince to complete his annual tribute … oppress Moldavia to such a degree, that the richness of the soil is scarcely adequate to the purpose."[48]

This heavy exploitation may explain why many Moldavians welcomed the Russian army into Iaşi in September 1739 (Hospodar Gheorge II Ghica had already fled to Falçiu). But Marshal Münnich soon forfeited their support when he imposed a Protective Act holding the Moldavian people liable for heavy taxes, troop quartering, and labor services. Within days, Münnich received word that the Austrians had signed a separate peace with the Porte at Belgrade. The Russian government reluctantly signed the Belgrade treaty on September 19, and five days later, Münnich was ordered to evacuate the Russian army from Moldavia.[49]

Oltenian Wallachia had been in Austrian hands from 1718 to 1739, and Vienna had carried out some reforms regulating landlord–peasant relations and the taxation there. As a consequence of the Treaty of Belgrade, Oltenia was restored to the principality of Wallachia, and Wallachia's new hospodar Constantin Mavrocordatos took some inspiration from the Oltenian reforms to address the problem of peasant unrest and thereby reinforce his power. In 1744 he limited peasant tenant labor rent to just twelve days a year, and a few years later, he limited serfdom by offering state bounties for peasants to buy their freedom. In moving to reduce rents, he intended to turn the rural population into state peasants able to pay more taxes to the state; hence, he awarded state lands and free pasture rights to land-poor peasants and introduced a new quarterly land tax. He put the counties under pairs of appointed officials, the *ispravnici*, and his reforms culminated in the reorganization of the Wallachian boyars as a service nobility of three ranks receiving state salaries from taxpayer revenue. He reproduced these reforms in Moldavia in 1748–1749.[50] But some Moldavian boyars were outraged at his limitation of their manorial rights and they succeeded in getting him deposed and exiled to Lemnos in 1749. Over the next several years his reforms were watered down or left to lapse. Ottoman pressure for more revenue raised quotas again so that the land tax was now collected twenty times a year rather than four, while the boyars won the right to increase labor rents. In 1759 Iași was wracked by mob violence provoked by heavy taxes and incited by some boyars opposed to Hospodar Ioan Teodor Callimachi.[51]

Whatever anxieties the Ottoman government may have entertained about the political stability of the phanariot regimes in Moldavia and Wallachia were apparently offset by satisfaction with the tribute and trade revenue they were yielding, and by confidence that Poland and Austria still offered sufficient political bulwarks against Russian expansion into the Danubian principalities. After 1739, the prospect of Austrian expansion into Wallachia declined. Moldavia remained a possible target of Russian expansion, but the district of the greatest fortress garrison in Moldavia—Khotin, in the far north on the Podolian border—was under direct Ottoman control as a *pashalik*, while Moldavia's eastern frontier was thought to be protected by the Tatar hordes in Bucak (Bessarabia) and the Ottoman fortress of Bender.[52] But Khotin was not invincible—the Russians had taken it in 1739, opening their road to Iași—and the Bucak region was left less secure in the 1750s when the Yedichkul Horde began migrating eastward and the Bucak hordes started negotiating for Russian protection.

The Ottoman Balkans, Bucak, and Ochakov

The Belgrade Treaty of 1739 restored Oltenia to the principality of Wallachia and returned to the Porte northern Bosnia and northern Serbia (the territory above Nis' as far north as Pozarevac, including the city of Belgrade). This meant that the entire length of the Danube was re-established as the northern border of the Balkan provinces of the Ottoman Empire. In the northwest the border ran along the Danube just below the vassal principalities of Wallachia and Moldavia, and extended nearly to the Sava River in Habsburg Croatia–Slavonia and to Venetian Dalmatia. The Ottoman *pashalik* of Belgrade lay across the Danube from Habsburg-ruled Banat. In the northeast, just across the Danube from Wallachia and Moldavia, stood Dobruja (from Silistra in northern Bulgaria to Babadagh and the delta of the Danube); and just to the north of Dobruja, between Moldavia and the Black Sea as far east as the Bug River, lay an expanse of steppe called Bucak ("The Corner"). Bucak abutted Ukrainian Podolia and the Zaporozhian Sich and so was heavily militarized; sovereignty here was shared between the pashas commanding the Ottoman garrisons of Ismail, Bender, Akkirman, Kilburun (Kinburn), and Ochakov and the allied Bucak, Yedichkul, and Yedisan Nogai Hordes.[53]

The Serbs probably numbered about one million in the late eighteenth century. About 650,000–680,000 of them were Habsburg subjects residing in Croatia–Slavonia (where they manned the *Grenze* defense line) and in southern Hungary (Voivodina). The Serb subjects of the Porte resided mainly in Belgrade and Leskovac *pashalik*s and as elements of the populations of Bosnia, Montenegro, and the Vidin *pashalik*. Serbian emigration across the Danube into the Habsburg domains had occurred in two great waves, in connection with the wars of Austro-Turkish wars of the 1690s and 1730s, and the settlement privileges the Habsburgs extended to them had by mid-century left them more culturally independent and prosperous than their counterparts within the vast Ottoman *pashalik* of Belgrade, where grain production took a distant second place to animal husbandry, especially pork production for export to the Habsburg Empire.

Much of the arable in Belgrade *pashalik* was on *çiftliks* (larger service-conditional revenue "farms") held by a few hundred families of *sipahi* cavalrymen, absentee landlords receiving in revenue a tenth of the Serbian peasant tenants' grain harvests, some limited labor services, and various small dues and fees. Garrison janissaries often became the resident stewards of these *sipahi* landlords. The *çiftlik* system caused "not so much intolerable taxation as intolerable insecurity"[54] as a succession of janissary stewards tried to amass wealth and power as revenue collectors and feudal "protectors" of *çiftlik* tenants. On the whole, the rent and tax burden imposed by the Ottoman ruling class was not particularly onerous, except in wartime when extraordinary levies and requisitions were added, and the Serbian peasantry was partly shielded from Ottoman authority by *millet* religious autonomy, the right to police itself and collect rents and taxes through their own elected village headmen, and the continued practice of combining families in large extended *zadruga* households. There was infrequent contact between Serbian villagers and Ottoman officials, and so little friction.

In contrast to the situation in Greece or in Habsburg Serbia, the Orthodox Church in Ottoman Serbia had not yet come into cultural dialog with the Enlightenment and lacked the organizational power to rouse Ottoman Serbs against their Turkish overlords, for the Patriarchate at Pec and the Metropolitanate at Karlowitz had been declining in authority for decades and the former would be abolished by the sultan in 1766.[55]

During 1709–1711, Moldavian Hospodar Cantemir and Wallachian Hospodar Brancoveanu had encouraged Peter I to bring the Russian army in to liberate their principalities by holding out to him the prospect that his intervention would rouse 30,000 Serbs to revolt against the Porte. Far fewer Serbs actually took up arms when the Russians finally marched into Moldavia in 1711.[56]

The Serb majority in Montenegro (*Chernogoria*) was small in number—probably about 15,000 adult males—but was more restless. Montenegro had been granted some limited autonomy by the sultans; they recognized the Metropolitan of Cetinje as the head of its administration in return for turning over tribute payments to the pasha of Shkoder in Albania. The Montenegrin economy was even less commercialized than in Belgrade *pashalik* and there was more clan and tribal conflict among the Montenegrin Serbs. *Hajduk* banditry was endemic here. Because of Montenegro's location, the Metropolitan of Cetinje found it easier to appeal to foreign powers for intervention—to the Austrians and Venetians, and also to the Russians as fellow Orthodox.

Even before 1700 Peter I had noted the Montenegrin mountaineers' resistance to Ottoman domination and had contemplated the possibility that Russian alliance with an independent Montenegro might someday give Russia access to the Adriatic. Hence he invited the refugee Matija Zmajevic to help organize the Russian Baltic fleet, and in 1710 the tsar prepared for his invasion of Moldavia by issuing propaganda promising the liberation of Montenegro. Some Montenegrin tribes did rise up against the Turks but were brutally suppressed by Ottoman forces from Shkoder and Bosnia after the tsar was defeated on the Prut.[57] But Metropolitan Danilo resumed diplomacy with the Russians, Austrians, and Venetians the following year, and Metropolitan Sava made even more concerted diplomatic efforts during the Russo-Turkish War of 1735–1739. Sava and his successor Metropolitan Vasilije travelled to St. Petersburg in 1742 and 1752–1754 to try to negotiate alliance, and the Montenegrin tribes rose up against the Turks again in 1756. Finally, in 1760, Empress Elizabeth Petrovna sent Colonel Puchkov to Montenegro to assess the situation. But Puchkov's report persuaded her not to get Russia involved: "The people are wild; they live in disorder; heads roll for the least offence; the clergy are grasping; the churches are deserted; Russian assistance is distributed among the Bishop's cousins."[58] Metropolitan Vasilije traveled again to Russia in 1766 to make an appeal to Empress Catherine II but was refused an audience and died in St. Petersburg. Catherine's condolence decree urged the Montenegrin chiefs "to live together with their neighbours in peace, tranquility and unity and as far as possible to eliminate all cause for discord, hate, or warfare."[59]

One of the stranger episodes in Montenegrin history was the short rule of Stepan the Small (r. 1767–1773), a purveyor of herbal medicines who managed to convince Metropolitan Vasilje's opponents to acclaim him as Russia's Emperor Peter III, miraculously delivered by God to deliver the Orthodox in Montenegro from the Ottoman yoke. The Venetian Republic, the Porte, and Russia all denounced him as an impostor. Venetian agents tried but failed to poison him; Catherine II sent Vladimir Dolgorukov into Montenegro in 1769 to try to get the tribal chiefs to repudiate him; and Sultan Mustafa III twice sent armies against him. But Stepan survived and even managed to lay some foundations for orderly government. He was finally murdered in his bed in 1773 by a servant bribed by Ottoman officials in Albania.[60]

The strategic and economic heart of the Ottoman Empire in Europe were the five *sancaks* in Bulgaria, south of Dobruja. The Porte's long peace between 1739 and 1768 had brought Bulgaria enough security and stability to promote agriculture, artisanal craft, and trade. Market towns and seasonal fairs grew and multiplied. Istanbul, of course, remained the primary market for Bulgarian commodities, but trade across the Danube with Voivodina and other Habsburg domains also increased, and there was trade out of the Black Sea port of Varna with the French. As in Ottoman Serbia, the growth of commercialized agriculture promoted the multiplication of larger *çiftlik* farms, which dispossessed Bulgarian villagers of their commons and then turned them into contract laborers or sharecropper tenants. Landless peasants unable to find *çiftlik* employment turned to banditry and guerrilla raiding, especially in the Rodope Mountains. On the other hand, the commercialization of the economy also turned some Bulgarian peasants into peddlers, contract provisioners, tax-farmers, and money-lenders.[61]

There had been three great revolts against Ottoman rule in western Bulgaria in the late 1680s—the Tarnovo, Chiprovtsi, and Karposh revolts—but they had broken out in response to the Habsburg victories at Vienna and Belgrade and had been confined to the mountainous northwest of Bulgaria and to central Bulgaria around Sofia. Eastern

Bulgaria had been more quiescent, perhaps because Muslim Turks comprised a larger part of its population and because this region was more easily monitored from nearby Edirne and Istanbul. The emergence of a national resistance spirit may also have been retarded by Bulgarians' resentment that their largely Greek clergy filled benefices by auction or nepotism and marginalized Slavonic liturgy. There was, however, one circumstance that could destabilize eastern Bulgaria: if it was repeatedly trampled by Ottoman field armies imposing ruinous requisitions.[62]

The sociopolitical situation in Ottoman Greece was especially complicated. On the one hand, the Porte provided privileges and power to the phanariot elite, which used its political connections with the Ottoman court to promote their clients into the administration of the Orthodox Patriarchate, as well as the upper ranks of the sultan's bureaucracy. The expansion of Ottoman trade during the Long Peace was also an enormous boon to Greek merchants and sea captains, who were able to take advantage of the frequent wars between Britain and France, and fill the vacuum created by the disruption of British and French trade in the Mediterranean. "The Greeks seized the opportunity to transport to Central Europe Balkan raw materials such as cereals, wool, cotton, and leather. In return they brought back manufactured articles that hitherto had been imported directly by the Western merchants in the port cities. Before the end of the eighteenth century, prosperous Greek trading communities had grown up in Vienna, Buda, Bucharest, Trieste, Venice, and other foreign cities."[63]

On the other hand, Greek peasants held less of the land, there were more çiftliks supporting Ottoman soldiers and officials, and these çiftliks tended to be smaller, more oriented toward rent collection than toward cereal or cash-crop production for the market—so "Greek villagers typically sharecropped and surrendered one-third to two-thirds of their product to Turkish landlords, depending upon the quality of the land and the portion of the stock of equipment which they latter supplied. They also had to contribute to the increasingly regular additional taxes (imdat, taksit) which supported the local administration."[64]

The most restless part of Greece was probably the mountainous Mani (Gr. mania, "wild") peninsula in the Morea, a region in southern Peloponnesus that had been given loose autonomy in return for tribute. The Turks had reconquered this region from Venice in 1715. Here many Greek peasants supplemented their farming with smuggling and piracy, and policing was entrusted to special militias of local mountaineers called armatolikia. These militias were based in hilltop forts and elected a bey confirmed by the Ottoman government; but they were distinguishable only by their patents of police authority from other armed bands of fugitive peasants turned brigands (klephts, from Gr, klephtein, "to steal"), and in times of political crisis, armatole militias could renounce their allegiance to the sultan and unite with klepht bands in revolt. In the second half of the century, about 14,000 Maniots belonged to armatole or klepht bands.[65]

In 1766 a Thessalian Greek named Papazoli serving as a captain in the Russian artillery received leave from General-anshef Grigorii Orlov to take three years' leave in Greece to establish an intelligence service, recruiting Greek and Serbian agents from

Venice, Ragusa, and Trieste. Papazoli was also tasked with identifying Greek sea captains who might later be recruited into Russian naval service, and he helped subsidize Stepan the Small in Montenegro. Meanwhile, another intelligence network was established on Malta by six Russian naval officers who had been sent to study Mediterranean shipbuilding. These networks would late prove useful for the Russian naval campaign in the Aegean and Sea of Marmara.[66]

The Porte's northeastern frontier with the Danubian principalities, Russian Ukraine, and the Crimean Khanate comprised the regions of Dobruja and Bucak—sparsely settled but strategically important and heavily militarized zones.

Dobruja today comprises part of the Black Sea coast of Romania and Bulgaria. It ran from the Danube delta, Tulcea Hills, and Măcin Mountains as far west as Galați, narrowed along the Medgidian Plateau, and widened in the south to include the districts of Constanta, Silistra, and Dobrich. This made it the shield of Ottoman Thrace and the roads to the Ottoman capitals of Edirne and Istanbul, and for this reason it was the traditional corridor used by Ottoman armies marching on Wallachia, Moldavia, and Podolia. The main assembly point of the Ottoman field army in the eastern Danubian theater was Babadagh, just behind the Tulcea hills. The coast of Dobruja also supported Ottoman naval operations on the Black Sea into the Danube delta and up to the Crimean peninsula. Dobruja's population was not of dubious loyalty, as it was a mix of Turks, Nekrasovite Cossacks turned renegade from the Zaporozhian Host, and Moldavian peasants seeking an escape from boyar manorialism. But the northern border of Dobruja was weak in that the main garrisons holding the Danubian crossings at Tulcea, Isaccea, and Măcin were small and in need of repair, and it was possible that a Russian army could circumvent them by crossing the Danube at Hârșova or Chernovody to pin down the Ottoman field army at Babadagh.[67]

Dobruja therefore relied heavily on the protection offered by Bucak on its northern border. Bucak was bounded by the Tigheci Hills in the north, the Dnestr River in the east, the Black Sea in the southeast, the Danube in the south, and the Prut River in the west. In the Middle Ages, the Genoese had built fortresses at Montecastro, Tighina, and Kiliia to protect their trade operations on the Black Sea coast and in Crimea. The Wallachian princes and, after them, the Moldavian princes became the masters of Bucak in the fourteenth century and fifteenth centuries. The Ottomans conquered Bucak over the period 1484–1538 and took over and enlarged the old Genoese fortresses, renaming Montecastro as Akkirman and Tighina as Bender.[68] They built a new fortress at Ismail that gradually superseded Kiliia, and in 1492 the Tatars transferred to the Turks the facing fortresses at Ochakov and Kilburun guarding the Dnepr estuary. By the seventeenth century, Ochakov had become the capital of an Ottoman *eyalet* comprising eleven *sancaks*.

Sultan Bayezid II had granted the Bucak steppe to Crimean Khan Mengli Girei as reward for his aid in capturing Kiliia and Montecastro, but in 1501 elements of the Great Nogai Horde migrated across the Dnepr into the Bucak steppe. These Nogais were Mangit Mongols, ethnically and culturally different from the Crimean Tatars, and their arrival initially complicated Ottoman attempts to secure the Bucak fortresses as well as

Crimean Tatar efforts to enforce their own claims to the Bucak steppe. But within a few years the Nogai nobles vassalized themselves to the Crimean Khan and so were left in place. The khans monitored them through *agas* stationed at the village of Khankyshla. By 1650 there were probably about 45,000 of these Nogais. In summers, the Nogai clans nomadized on the steppe with their cattle and in winters, they retired to small *aul* villages in southern Bucak. The soil was fertile enough for wheat cultivation, but there were few rivers and summers were hot and arid; for lack of wood, the villagers fueled their fires with dung. Sources usually refer to them collectively as the Bucak Nogai Horde, or sometimes the Bilhorod Horde, because they guarded Akkirman. At mid-century, the Bucak Nogai Horde numbered under 40,000 warriors.[69]

Other Nogai tribes roamed the steppes just beyond Bucak. The Yedisan Horde nomadized to the northeast, between the Dnestr and Southern Bug, above the fortress of Ochakov. The Jamboiluk Horde roamed the lands between the Southern Bug and the Dnepr. The Yedichkul Nogais resided on the steppe north of Perekop, directly under the sovereignty of the Crimean khans. The Kuban Tatars were to be found to their northeast, above Azov and as far east as the Kuban River.[70] These tribes kept to separate valleys and resided in tent encampments ranged along lines about thirty leagues in length.[71]

But managing these hordes presented three challenges to the Ottomans and Crimean Tatars. Sometimes the Nogai hordes undertook their own unauthorized raids into Poland and Ukraine, which risked embroiling the Porte and Khanate in war. The hordes sometimes migrated far to the east of their assigned grazing lands, to the lower Volga or to the Kuban, and after colliding with the Kalmyks and the Russians fled back home and requested special resettlement protection from the Crimean khans. They also complained of oppression by the Crimean khans in disputes over transit, grazing rights, military requisitions, or shares of raid plunder, and so petitioned to transfer their fealty directly to the sultans. The years 1701–1706 had seen Sultan Mustafa II and the Crimean khan in a tug-of-war over which of them was to receive the direct fealty of the Bucak Horde. In the course of this struggle the sultan had to send troops into Bucak to pacify the Horde, the khan tried to incite the Bucak Nogais into attacking the Ottoman fortresses at Kiliia and Akkirman, and even the Yedichkul Horde began protesting Crimean Tatar domination.[72] Tott's Turkish military escort through Bucak was forced to travel on alert because of reports of unrest among the Yedisan Nogais angered by heavy grain taxes.[73]

By the 1760s these tensions had escalated to the point that Russian diplomats considered that the time was ripe to detach the hordes from Ottoman or Crimean Tatar suzerainty and place them under Russian protection. Fifty Yedisan Horde Nogais defected to Poland in 1759; another 150 went to Mohylew and asked for letters of transit so that they could enter the service of Frederick II. That year 250 Bucak Nogais (including a hundred nobles) went to the Ukrainian border near Kiev and asked to be taken into Russian service and given refuge in the Volga–Kuban steppe against the oppressor Khan Kirim Girei. Russians traveling through Bucak in 1768 reported that the Bucak Nogais "secretly despise the Turks."[74]

The Crimean Khanate

Vorontsov's 1762 memorandum to Catherine II maintained that the Crimean Khanate remained a significant danger to Russia. The Khanate "is wholly inclined to plunder and villainy, skillful in fast and unexpected military undertakings, and before the last Turkish War Russia suffered perceptible harm and offense connected with their frequent raids, their taking prisoner of many thousand of many inhabitants, their rustling of cattle and their plunder of estates ... from which many were devastated and impoverished to the final extremity. This comprises the chief industry and profit of these wild steppe peoples."[75]

The Khanate had been founded in the 1440s by Haji Girei, a Chingisid prince in revolt against the disintegrating Great Horde. After the fall of Constantinople in 1453 the Ottomans turned to conquering the old Genoese and Moldavian fortresses along the northern coast of the Black Sea. Their campaign accelerated with Tatar military aid after Khan Mengli I Girei pledged vassalage to Sultan Bayezid II in 1475. By 1500 the Ottomans garrisoned Akkirman, Kiliia, Kafa, Gozlev, Arabat, and Yenikale and controlled most of the Crimean coast and hills between Inkerman and Kafa, linking this stretch of coast to the Ottoman domains of Bucak and Dobruja. The Turks also established a large garrison at Azov (old Tana), near the Don's mouth on the Sea of Azov, thereby bounding the Khanate on the east. The Azov garrison policed the lower Don steppe and the Kuban steppe, deterring Cossack raids and Muscovite attacks and reinforcing the khans' claims of sovereignty over the Kuban Horde. The Turks' control over most of Crimea's coasts and ports had the effect of turning the Black Sea into "the Ottoman Lake," and Istanbul, the Ottoman Balkans, and the Anatolian coast became dependent upon the Khanate's exports of slaves, lumber, grain, wax, silk, butter salt, fish, cattle, and sheep.[76]

In principle, the khans' vassalage to the sultans was not unlike the vassalage of the Moldavian and Wallachian hospodars before 1713: the khan was under obligation to the sultan to be "the enemy of thy enemy, the friend of thy friend," to contribute troops when the sultan called for them, and to pay tribute gifts to the sultan; otherwise, he was permitted enough sovereignty over his own domains to mint his own coins and collect his own tribute from the Nogai hordes, the Poles, and the Russians. The khan frequently received subsidies from the sultan—in 1769, about three million piasters—and a command of janissaries was stationed at Bakhchisarai as his personal guard. After the 1620s, the khans were essentially appointed by the sultan rather than elected by the *kurultai* assembly—another indication that the Porte was attempting to tighten its control over them.[77]

The first khans had sometimes found it necessary to negotiate temporary alliances with the Polish kings or Muscovite grand princes, but by the early 1500s the Crimean Tatars had become essential to what Ottoman writers called the Stratagem of Selim:[78] the sultan now exercised closer control over the Khanate's foreign policy and directed the Tatars to attack either Muscovy or Poland-Lithuania, whichever power seemed to be ascendant at the moment, while the sultan disavowed any responsibility for their attack. Because Tatar cavalry was effective at reconnaissance, foraging, raiding, and envelopment, it became frequent practice from the 1590s for Crimean Tatar and Nogai cavalry—sometimes as many as 20,000 warriors—to accompany the sultan's field armies on campaign. They served on the Danubian front in the Long War and on Sultan Mehmed IV's 1683 Vienna campaign; in the Caucasus, down to the 1760s; and in Ukraine during the 1678–1681 Russo-Turkish War. Renegade Ukrainian hetmans also relied heavily on the Tatars as their allies against the Poles or Russians (1648–1650, 1659–1660, 1671–1676, 1709–1713).

But the Khanate also remained dangerous because its economy and its value to the Porte depended so heavily on the slave raiding it conducted in Poland, Lithuania, Ukraine, and Muscovy. Slave raiding occurred in the course of the great punitive invasions led by the khans and sanctioned by the sultan, but it had been a chronic problem, sometimes occurring several times a year, when conducted on smaller incursions led by particular Tatar princes and chiefs seeking plunder. The harvest in slaves taken during the great invasions could sometimes be enormous. Khan Devlet I Girei led 40,000 Tatars deep into central Muscovy in 1571, burning Moscow and allegedly killing 80,000 and carrying off 150,000 as slaves.[79] Polish sources report that in 1575, Khan Devlet Girei invaded Podolia and Ukraine with 100,000 warriors and withdrew with 100,000 captives, including 35,340 Polish nobles.[80] By the Soviet historian Novosel'skii's calculation, the cumulative toll of captives taken from Muscovy in great invasions and chronic raiding over the period 1600–1650 was somewhere between 150,000 and 200,000.[81] Slave harvesting was of enormous economic value to the Khanate. A fifth of the human booty had to be turned over to the sultan as tribute, and a share was distributed among the khan, the many princes of the Girei house, and the beys of the great Tatar clans. Some prisoners were put to labor in Crimea or in the *auls* of the Nogais. But a large number were sold at the slave markets at Kafa, Bakhchisarai, and Karasubazar, with the price of one healthy male averaging about fifty rubles and the khan collecting a duty of 10 percent.[82]

Tatar raids on southern Russia, Sloboda Ukraine, and against the Don Cossack Host continued to occur almost annually in the early eighteenth century. A grievance sent to the Ottoman grand vizier from Vice-Chancellor Ostermann in 1736 listed attacks every year between 1713 and 1722. The Tatar raids into Voronezh Governorate and the Kharkov regimental territory in 1713 killed over two thousand and took 14,300 prisoners; the 1717 attack on Tsaritsyn and the lower Volga districts took 30,000 prisoners.[83]

But after the 1650s the military initiative and effectiveness of the Crimean Khanate declined. The khans were more likely to hold back from assisting Ottoman field armies in open battle or undertaking diversionary attacks on the Russians, Poles, or Austrians, and they were more likely to undertake their own diplomatic rapprochements in defiance of the sultan. For such insubordination, the Turks found it necessary to depose Aadil Girei in 1671, Selim I Girei in 1678, Murat Girei in 1681, and Saadet Girei II in 1691. Khans who did undertake high-risk campaigns provoked intrigues among the Crimean nobles or mutiny by the Nogais; Safa I Girei was overthrown in 1692 when the army he had ordered into Wallachia mutinied against him.[84] Tatar raids and invasions into Ukraine, southern Poland, and Russia were less common, briefer, penetrated not as far, and yielded smaller captive harvests.

There were a number of reasons for this. Over the course of the seventeenth century, Kalmyk attacks on the Kuban Horde had blocked the expansion of Crimean power in the east. Zaporozhian and Don Cossack naval and land raids had depopulated Tatar and Ottoman towns and villages on the Crimean coast, and the resulting reduction in head tax revenue from these settlements' Greek, Armenian, Jewish, and Circassian millets forced the Ottoman government to shift more defense responsibility to the khans to spare on Porte revenues. As for the khan's own revenue, Tott estimated it to be just 600,000 *livres* a year, most of which went to the upkeep of the court and for subsidies to particular favored mirzas. The army required no revenue as it was raised from service lands and remunerated only with plunder,[85] but the number of Nogai warriors able to heed the call to campaign appears to have been reduced in the late seventeenth century by plague and anthrax epidemics killing off their herds.

It could be argued that tactical innovations in the Habsburg, Commonwealth, and Muscovite armies (improved artillery and infantry firepower, fast-moving strikes by light cavalry *corps volantes*, moving armies across the steppe in *wagenburg* trains, the use of dragoons and grenadiers to attack Ottoman fortifications) inflicted heavier casualties on the Tatars and raised the risks of direct engagement.[86]

Through ambitious programs of military colonization and fortress construction, the Russian tsars had been able to establish successive advancing defense perimeters that had been especially effective in throwing the Khanate and the Nogai hordes on the defensive. The Belgorod Line, which ran for 800 kilometers from Tambov to Akhtyrka in Ukraine, was built between 1636 and 1653; two years later, additional segments had extended the defense line to Simbirsk on the Volga. The Iziuma Line, built in 1679–1680 to link the eastern end of the Belgorod Line to Tsarev-Borisov and Kolomak, extended the Russian fortified frontier another 160 kilometers southward and brought it within 150 kilometers of the Black Sea coast. Between 1731 and 1740 the Belgorod and Iziuma lines were augmented by a Ukrainian Line 285 kilometers long, shielding the Poltava and Khar'kov territories from the Tatars. Several thousand men were resettled in Land Militia regiments along the Ukrainian Line.[87] By the end of the seventeenth century, Kazykermen and Azov, the Ottoman fortresses protecting the northwestern and northeastern borders of the Khanate, had fallen to the Russians, and as long as the Russians held them, the khans were cut off from the Bucak and Kuban hordes.

The Karlowitz and Constantinople treaties in 1699–1700 turned the northern edge of the Khanate into a belt of no man's land forbidden to settlement or garrisoning. This demilitarized zone ran from the Siniukh River, a tributary of the Bug, through a point just above the Ottoman fortress of Ochakov, along the Bol'shaia Verda River to the mouth of the Miuss River on the Sea of Azov, and from the Miuss to the Don. Because Azov was in Russian hands until 1712, the Russians had claimed the Ei River as their border with the Khanate in the Kuban region. Since the Karlowitz and Constantinople Treaties had the unprecedented consequence of setting a fixed frontier in Europe for the Porte and Khanate, the maintenance of this frontier required that the Porte exercise much closer political control over Tatar and Nogai raiding operations; raiders crossing the frontier had to be treated as violators of the border and threats to peace. This reduced raiding opportunities in Russia and Ukraine that the Tatar slave-raiding economy survived only by stepping up predation upon the Kabardans and Circassians in compensation. Khan Devlet II Girei found the sultan's ban on raiding so constraining that he led a revolt against it in 1701–1702.[88]

The Russo-Turkish War of 1736–1739 revealed that the khans could no longer defend their own core territory. Three times (1736, 1737, 1738) Russian expeditionary armies managed to break through or circumvent the Or-Kapi Line and push deep into Crimea, driving the Tatar nobility into the hills (and on one occasion forcing Khan Fet'ih Girei to take refuge at sea). The Russians burned Gozlev, Karasubazar, and the khan's palace at Bakhchisarai and took control again of the Ottoman fortress at Azov. The sultan had khans Kaplan Girei and Fet'ih Girei deposed for their incompetence. The Kuban Horde was overwhelmed by the Kalmyks and for a while vassalized to the Kalmyk *taishis*.[89] Just one major Tatar raid into Russia occurred during the war, in October 1736, when Tatar forces passed through an undermanned section of the Ukrainian Line and fanned out on a raiding front of about twenty kilometers; but only 6,000 Tatars were involved and they did not manage to carry off many prisoners. The Russian responded by stationing two *corps de reserve* behind the Ukrainian Line to plug such gaps in the future.[90]

The 1739 Belgrade Treaty required the Russians to evacuate Crimea and destroy again their fortifications at Azov, but the treaty left them in control of steppe extending Russia's border about twenty miles closer to the Khanate.[91]

Khans Selamet II Girei (r. 1740–1743), Selim II Girei (r. 1743–1748), and Arslan Girei (r. 1748–1756) pursued a very cautious foreign policy so as not to give the Russians any provocation. Sultan Mahmud I kept them on a tight leash so that he could maintain peace with Christian Europe and focus on the struggle in the Caucasus with Nadir Shah, and these khans anyhow had their hands full rebuilding Bakhchisarai, reviving the Crimean economy, and bringing the Kuban Horde back under their sovereignty. There were some border incidents with the Zaporozhian Cossacks, but the khans sought to resolve them through diplomacy rather than war.[92]

Meanwhile, the Russians had been expanding their defense lines and militarized zones in the south. The Ukrainian Line had eighteen fortresses, 140 redoubts, and twenty-two military colonies by 1740, and in 1752 and 1754 Empress Elizabeth Petrovna permitted several thousand Serbian emigres from the Habsburg Empire to settle as hussar and *pandur* infantry colonists in "New Serbia" and "Slavonic Serbia" on the western and eastern edges of the Zaporozhian Sich.[93] Lest the ratification of an Ottoman–Persian peace treaty (1746) encourage the Turks and Crimean Tatars to resume aggression in Europe, Empress Elizabeth Petrovna signed a twenty-year renewal of Russia's alliance treaty with Austria, committing both powers to support each other in the event of an Ottoman attack, and she took efforts to make the news of this treaty appreciated in Istanbul and Bakhchisarai. This treaty was renewed in 1753. Vorontsov considered it successful in establishing "a balance of forces" against the Turks.[94]

Vorontsov's 1762 memorandum identified three remaining threats from the Khanate. The khans had settled about 10,000 Yedichkul Nogais on the lower Dnepr near the Zaporozhian Host and the Ukrainian Line, increasing the danger of Tatar attacks on the Zaporozhian Sich or New Serbia; Khan Kirim Girei supported the sultan in opposing the construction of Fort St. Dmitrii; and Kirim Girei could mobilize up to 70,000 warriors if he chose to invade Ukraine, either with or without the sultan's permission.[95]

But Vorontsov considered the Khanate's military power to be declining and an opportunity emerging to detach the Khanate from the Porte—a project worth pursuing given the Khanate's strategic location as "the key to the Russian and Turkish domains." "As long as the Khanate remains subject to the Turks," he wrote, "it will always be a terror to Russia; but when it is placed under Russian rule, or no longer be dependent of anyone, then not only Russia's security would be reliably and firmly confirmed, but Azov and the Black Sea would be under her [Russia's] power, and the nearer eastern and southern lands would be under her guard, which would inevitably draw their commerce to us."[96]

Such a project could be built upon some foundations already laid over the past twenty years. One of the foundations was the policy of encouraging certain Nogai seraskirs and chieftains to throw off Ottoman and Crimean suzerainty and place their *ulusy* under Russian protection. In this regard, an important preparation for war was made in 1768 when P. I. Panin, commander of the Second Army in Ukraine, began channeling gifts and money through the Zaporozhians to the leaders of the Yedisan and Bucak hordes.[97]

Another foundation was the establishment of a Russian consulate at Bakhchisarai. In 1740 Kiev governor M. I. Leont'ev, who had succeeded in invading and occupying Crimea in 1736–1739, proposed establishing a Russian officer in Crimea to mediate trade disputes between the Tatars and the Cossacks. Ambassador Obreskov had repeated this proposal to Sultan Mahmud I in 1752, adding that if a second such consul were posted in the Sich, there could be much better mediation of Cossack–Tatar conflicts. Crimean Khan Kirim Girei finally accepted this proposal in 1763, partly under pressure from the sultan and partly out of recognition of the benefits of conflict mediation. Catherine II subsequently appointed a consul, Aleksandr Nikiforov, and he established residence at Bakhchisarai in 1764.[98] Her instructions authorized Nikiforov to do more than mediate disputes; he had to use his residence to collect useful intelligence "on the state, political, social, military and economic structure of the Crimean Khanate, reports on topographic and strategic conditions of the peninsula, on civil laws and judicial methods, on military organization, size of the population, income of the khan, and on the customs of the Tatar peoples."[99] However, Selim III Girei expelled Nikiforov in 1765 for failing to offer satisfactory response to complaints that Cossacks were raiding Crimean territory.[100]

The third foundation was the liberation of Kabarda. "There needs to be a free people in Kabarda serving as a barrier between both powers [the Porte and the Russian Empire]," Vorontsov wrote. That principle had been established in the 1739 Belgrade treaty. But the taming of Kabarda had not been completed, it had not yet come under a "strong hand" that would allow Russia "to intervene for her own interests."[101]

Some way would also have to be found to tame the Zaporozhian Sich and Don Cossack Host. Vorontsov considered the "Zaporozhian Cossacks and other frontier commands uniformly inclined towards willfulness (*samovol'stvie*), so there occur frequent disputes and disorders among them, which cause the present Russian court many unpleasantries and troubles, sometimes even to the brink with the Ottoman Porte."[102]

The Kuban steppe and the Caucasus

To secure their eastern front against the Don Cossack Host, the Kalmyks, and the Russians, the Crimean khans had to devote great attention to maintaining their control over the Kuban Horde—the Nogai tribes nomadizing the steppe above Azov over to the lower Volga and as a far south as the Kuban River, the edge of the northern Caucasus. This task was complicated when the fortress of Azov was in Russian hands (1696–1711 and again in 1736–1739), but that setback had been partly countered by the erection of a new Ottoman fortress below the Sea of Azov, at Akchu.[103] But a further complication for them was the growing reluctance of the Nogai Horde to subordinate their own campaigns of self-aggrandizement in the North Caucasus to their assigned role as the Khanate's buffer zone in the northeast. Signs of Kuban Nogai insubordination were already clear by 1706. In 1742 and 1746 some Kuban Nogai mirzas offered to recognize Russian suzerainty in return for permission to resettle across the Terek under Russian protection against the Kalmyks.[104]

The largest ethnic group in the northern Caucasus were the Circassians (*Cherkessy*), speakers of the Adygei language. They resided in two regions: below the Kuban River in the western part of the Caucasus, and to the southeast near the Kuma and Terek rivers, above Ingushetia. The former population, remaining under tighter Crimean Tatar control, came to be known as the Beslenei; the latter were called the Kabardans and had undergone greater social differentiation to the point of generating a feudal nobility. Both the Beslenei and the Kabardans had accepted the suzerainty of the Crimean khan in 1519, although this did not exempt them from being occasionally raided for slaves and livestock by the Crimean Tatars and Kuban Nogais. They were also targets of religious proselytization, the Crimean Tatars trying to convert them from paganism to Islam.

Having observed with interest Russian expansion down the Volga to the north coast of the Caspian in the 1550s, some Kabardan nobles sent envoys to Moscow to negotiate alliance with Tsar Ivan IV. In 1557 the son of nobleman Temriuk Indarko was left at Moscow as honor hostage; he converted to Orthodoxy, took the name Mikhail Temriukovich Cherkasskii, and received the rank of boyar. Three years later, Temriuk's daughter, Gwashchenei was awarded to Ivan IV in marriage and ruled as Tsarina Mariia Temriukovna (1561–1569).

The alliance with the Kabardans quickly took on great importance for the Russians; it provided a counterweight to Crimean–Nogai power in the northeast Caucasus, helped shield the new Russian colony at Astrakhan, offered access to the Dar'ial Pass (the "Iron

Gates," the pass leading into Georgia), and checked the northward expansion of the Muslim Shamkhal Kingdom in what is today Daghestan.[105]

In 1570 Crimean Khan Devlet I Girei crushed the Beslenei and the Kabardans. Tsar Ivan IV countered by establishing a Muscovite fortress on the Sundzha River in eastern Kabarda (Lesser Kabarda). This was followed by the formation of a Cossack host to hold the Sundzha–Terek river frontier and the founding of a second fort, Tersk gorodok. Henceforth, the Terek Cossack Host would shield Lesser Kabarda on its north and Cossack settlement would expand into central Caucasus.

After Peter I evacuated Azov (January 12, 1712) Sultan Ahmed III and Khan Saadet IV Girei decided to launch operations from Kerch, Yenikale, and Akchu to restore their control over Kabarda. An army of 40,000 Tatars invaded Kabarda in 1720 and re-imposed tribute on two of the four great clans. The overthrow of Persia's Safavid Dynasty by Mahmud Ghilzai in 1722 created a power vacuum in Shamkhal and the other Muslim domains in southeastern Caucasus, drove Armenia and the Georgian kingdom of Kartli to revolt against Ottoman domination, and forced the Safavid prince Tahmasp II to ally himself with the Russians to regain his throne. This provided Peter I with the opportunity to invade the Caucasus in 1722 with an army of 100,000 men to establish a Russian protectorate over Kabarda—five more Russian garrisons were established along the Terek River—forge alliance with Christian Armenia and Kartli, and secure the Dar'ial and Derbent passes into the southern Caucasus. By August 1723, the invading Russians had taken the Shamkhal capital, Tarku, seized Derbent, and occupied Baku, Gilan, and Mazandaran. A treaty signed with Tahmasp II on September 12, 1723, ceded to Russia all this territory—the western coast of the Caspian as far as Shirvan. But the treaty remained unenforceable until 1729, and by 1732 Tahmasp had been overthrown by Nadir Shah. Maintaining an occupying army in the southern Caspian provinces of Persia had overstrained Russian finances and logistics, so in 1732 Empress Anna Ioannovna signed the Treaty of Resht restoring them to Nadir Shah. This meant that Russian forces in the Caucasus had to be drawn back to the Terek.[106]

Sultan Mahmud I considered his own 1732 Treaty with Persia permission to resume the subjugation of Kabarda, and when 20,000 Crimean Tatars invaded Kabarda in 1735, war broke out between the Ottoman and Russian Empires. Part of this war was fought in the North Caucasus, pitting the Crimean Tatars and Kuban Nogais against the Russians, Terek Cossacks, Kalmyks, and some Kabardan nobles. In the course of the 1735–1739 Russo-Turkish War, the Russians built a major fortress at Kizliar at the delta of the Terek (in Daghestan) and more Cossack garrisons in the northeast. Kizliar now superseded Terek as the major Russian garrison in the North Caucasus. It reduced the power of the Kuban Horde by hemming in part of their grazing territory. In 1763, Kizliar and the other new Cossack stations would be linked up along a fortified line running 250 kilometers west to the new fortress of Mozdok in what is today Northern Ossetia.[107]

The Treaty of Belgrade (1739) made the following stipulations about Greater and Lesser Kabarda: "As for the two Kabardas, Greater and Lesser, and the nations that inhabit therein, the two parties agree that the two Kabardas shall remain free, and will submit to neither of the two empires, but will be considered as a boundary between the two; and on the part of the Sublime Porte, neither the Turks nor the Tatars shall interfere in [the internal affairs of] of these [two] countries, and, according to old custom, the Russians shall continue to have the right to levy hostages from the two Kabardas, the Sublime Porte being also free to levy the same for the same purpose; and in case the above mentioned peoples of the Kabardas give ground for complaint by either of the two powers, both are permitted to punish them."[108] The actual consequence of this was to embroil the Kabardas in further Ottoman–Russian–Persian competition, with the Crimean Tatars raiding Kabarda in the 1740s and the Russian Empress Elizabeth Petrovna sending troops to intervene in conflicts between pro-Russian and pro-Ottoman nobles. In 1742 and 1745 Russian forces at Astrakhan and Kizliar were expanded to deter Nadir Shah and Sultan Mahmud I from renewing their efforts to conquer the Kabardans, Shamkhal Kumyks, and Chechens. In 1746 the Porte and Persia reached stalemate and signed a treaty restoring their borders in the Caucasus to the 1639 status quo.[109]

These conflicts also weakened Crimean Tatar hegemony over the Kuban steppe. The Crimean *kalga* Shirin Girei led 5,000 Tatars into the Kuban steppe in spring 1754 with the aim of forcing the Kuban Horde to assist in pacifying the Beslenei and Abazins. But the *kalga* was soundly defeated by the Beslenei on the Karasu River and was forced to retreat from the Kuban. He ordered twenty of his officers beheaded as punishment.[110] The Kuban Nogais subsequently drove out some of their Crimean Tatar princes and began negotiating alliance with the Beslenei and Abazins.

After Kizliar was linked to Mozdok the Kabardans were pushed about sixty kilometers farther south. Those remaining in the north near the Russian defense line came under greater pressure to convert to Orthodoxy. The Russian government also stepped up efforts to convert and resettle the Ossetians, Ingushetians, and Vainakhs (Chechens).[111]

Vorontsov's 1762 note to Catherine II suggested that the Kabardans be distrained from "resistance" (*protivnost'*) by holding some of their nobles as honor hostages to answer for their conduct. He estimated that there were about 6,000 warriors in Greater Kabarda and 3,000 in Lesser Kabarda, and that they trained from childhood in the use of musket and saber, kept nimble mounts, and "no other irregular force could compare with them."[112]

At the southern end of the Caucasus were the Georgian kingdoms of Imereti, Kakheti, and Kartli—Imereti in the center west, running to Anaklia and Poti on the Black Sea coast, with Kutaisi as its capital; Kartli to its east, with Tiflis (Tbilisi) at its core, extending from the Kura River in the south to the Terek in the north; and east of Kartli, the kingdom of Kahketi, bordered on its east by Leketi (Daghestan) and Shirvan on the Caspian coast. These three kingdoms had been vassal polities of the Safavid shahs, who intermittently extended tolerance to their growing Christian populations in return for tribute payments and military service against the Turks. Mahmud Ghilzai's invasion of Persia in 1719 had placed Imereti under Ottoman domination while pushing Kakheti and Kartli toward rapprochement with the Russians.[113]

When Peter I's army captured Derbend (August 1722), the king of Kartli, Vakhtang VI, had decided to throw in his lot with the Russians and pledged joint operations with them—while reassuring Shah Tahmasp II he would continue to command the forces defending northwestern Persia. Kakheti troops and Lesghians attacked Tbilisi in May 1723, forcing Vakhtang to take refuge on Russian territory at Astrakhan.[114] Tsar Peter's death in 1725 restrained the Russians from further involvement in Kartlian affairs. This gave the Turks a few years to try to free to tighten their control over all three Georgian kingdoms, but that control quickly dissolved when Nadir Shah came to power in Persia (1732) and invaded Shirvan and the Georgian kingdoms (1734). From that year until Nadir Shah's death in 1747, the Georgian kingdoms were wracked by his heavy taxes, Lesghian raids, and war between pro-Ottoman and pro-Persian Georgian princes.

Under King Irakli II (ruler of Kakheti 1747–1762, ruler of Kartli and Kakheti 1762–1798), the east Georgian kingdoms underwent significant state-building and some cultural Europeanization. The numerous petty Muslim warlords were unable to receive assistance from Persia and were played off against each other and brought under fealty to Irakli; a long campaign to pacify the Lesghians was undertaken; Greek and Armenian advisors were brought in; tax exemptions were offered to refugee peasants to repopulate abandoned estates and crown lands; border block-houses were built; and foundations were laid for a regular army augmented by seasonal conscript militias and Kabardan, Kalmyk, Nogai, and Ossetian mercenaries. St. Petersburg took notice of Irakli's success in expanding Kartli–Kakheti territory southward into Karabagh and Ganj, and signed a mutual assistance pact with King Solomon of Imereti (1758).[115] The foundations for a unified Georgian kingdom were being laid.

In 1760 King Teimuraz II of Kartli traveled to St. Petersburg to sound out Empress Elizabeth Petrovna on the possibility of Russian assistance in defending Kartli against Karabakh and Kubin, the two remaining Muslim khanates strong enough to pose a threat to eastern Georgia. Teimuraz died in St. Petersburg in 1762 without accomplishing this project.[116] A second invitation to Russia to help liberate the Georgian kingdoms from the Turks originated in Imereti in 1764 when King Solomon faced dethronement by the sultan for trying to suppress the slave trade. Irekli II would later agree to bring Kartli–Kakheti into the war against the Turks, providing that the Russians were forthcoming with real military assistance.[117]

The decision for war

Ahmed Resmi Efendi considered Sultan Mustafa III's decision in October 1768 to declare war on Russia a mistake, a choice neither inevitable nor advisable. The Ottoman government had remained at peace and aloof from European great power conflicts for nearly thirty years and had some economic recovery to show for it. Vorontsov had identified points of dispute between the Russian and Ottoman Empires but had remained confident that they could be resolved by diplomacy; war would occur only if the sultan was desperate to have it, in order to restore the Empire's discipline and military prowess.

Russian historians, especially those writing for popular audiences, have tended to attribute the hostility between the Ottoman and Russian Empires to French machinations—French diplomats were agitating and passing bribes to incite the Porte against Russia, in order to advance French power projects in Central Europe and the Middle East. In evidence, they cited the correspondence of Vergennes, de Bruel, and Bretieul stating that it was the purpose of French diplomacy to "excite the Porte against Austria and Russia" and deprive Russia of "the possibility of playing any kind of role in Europe…One must make it fall into an entirely lethargic dream, and if it is to be awakened from this dream, let it be by means of a convulsion, for example, through internal revolt."[118] Certainly this was French strategy—which is why Catherine II would investigate whether French money and French propaganda had any role in provoking Pugachev's Revolt. But attributing Ottoman conduct entirely to French *diktat* treats the Ottoman government as if it were incapable of articulating its own strategic interests and ignores the many important junctures (e.g., the outbreak of the Seven Years' War in 1756) at which the Porte ignored French blandishments and bribes and refused to act in concert with France.

While one could speak of a long-term strategic antagonism between the Russian and Ottoman Empires, it did not express itself in continual warfare. Russia and the Porte did not come to outright war until fairly late in the seventeenth century—whereas Russia and the Crimean Khanate had been in nearly constant conflict since the early sixteenth century. Even Muscovite campaigns in support of the Holy League's war against the Porte—Golitsyn's 1685 and 1689 expeditions against Crimea, Peter I's 1695–1696 Azov campaigns—focused on fighting the Crimean Tatars and avoiding major collisions with Ottoman field armies.

After the Constantinople peace, the basis of Ottoman–Russian adversity changed. Tension now derived from the threats the Porte perceived in the stationing of Russian troops in Poland, Russian interference in Moldavia and Wallachia, and Russian adventurism in the Caucasus. The first two of these threats were deemed provocative precisely because Sultan Ahmed III (r. 1703–1730) and Sultan Mahmud I (r. 1730–1754) saw themselves as adhering to a largely defensive strategy in southeastern Europe, protecting the borders established in the Karlowitz and Constantinople treaties; the third threat was considered serious because the Russian military presence in the Caucasus could thwart the one remaining opportunity for Ottoman imperial expansion and Crimean Tatar slave-raiding.[119] The longest and most destructive war between the Russians and Ottomans thus far had been the war of 1735–1739, which was sparked by Russian and Crimean Tatar military competition in Kabarda and then deliberately escalated by Chancellor Ostermann and Field Marshal Münnich in an attempt to recover Azov and, with Austrian assistance, to liberate the Balkans from the Turks. This war was a major blow to Ottoman strategic confidence because it put Crimea, Moldavia, and some of the key Ottoman border fortresses under temporary Russian occupation. But after 1739 the Ottoman government sought peace and resisted invitations to enter the War of the Austrian Succession and the Seven Years' War.

The best explanation for why the government of Sultan Mustafa III saw cause for war in 1768 was its perception that recent actions had thrown the security of most of its northern frontier in doubt. The balance of power in the northern Caucasus had tilted away from the Crimean Tatars; the Nogai hordes were beginning to defect to the Russian Empire; the Russian army was more solidly entrenched in Ukraine than ever before, poised again to attack Crimea and Bucak; Wallachia and especially Moldavia were restless again; large numbers of Russian troops were again stationed in Poland and were likely to remain for years; and the Russians had begun subverting even the Morean Greeks and Montenegrins.

CHAPTER 3
THE RUSSIAN EMPIRE AND ITS BLACK SEA STEPPE FRONTIER

Catherine II issued a manifesto on July 6, 1762, pledging to the nation that she would dedicate her rule to preserving "the unity of the Empire and Our autocratic power, which has through misfortune been somewhat undermined," while also guaranteeing that her government would "carry on its activity within its power and proper bounds, so that in the future every state office would possess its limits and laws for the observance of good order in everything."[1] This was an attempt to avoid the mistake of Empress Elizabeth Petrovna, who had allowed the conduct of the Seven Years' War and the administration of the Empire to be weakened by factionalism within the court nobility and undue influence exercised by her favorites. On the other hand it also repudiated the example of Peter III, who had acted despotically toward the nobility and ruled arbitrarily, even to the point of pulling Russia out of the coalition against Frederick II at the moment it stood at the edge of victory. Catherine II had set herself the difficult task of reestablishing independent, strong, and consistent monarchical power while honoring the state law precedents and natural laws that checked arbitrary despotism. This middle course was considered to adhere to the model of governance prescribed by Peter the Great: the "regulated state" (*reguliarnoe gosudarstvo*).

Catherine saw the breakdown of regulation as the most immediate challenge to the stability and power of the Empire. The revenue demands of the Seven Years' War had led to massive deficit spending and the exhaustion of the government's credit: the state deficit in 1762 stood at seven million rubles and the army had not been paid for the last eight months. The civil service was no longer able to subsist on its salaries and had returned to soliciting bribes and "feedings." Dangerous monopolies had been allowed to form in key branches of manufacture and commerce. Excessive reliance on tax farming was costing the treasury potential revenue; for example, farming of customs duty collection was bringing in just 2 million rubles. Her government did not even have complete and accurate accounts of its revenue and expenditure in 1762: in that year the Senate had recorded receipts of 16 million rubles, but a special audit conducted two years later revealed that receipts had actually been closer to 28 million rubles.[2] She was considering re-dividing the Empire into general-governorships which are subdivided into districts of more uniform population size (10,000–30,000 revision souls), but the Senate did not even have maps of all the regions or lists of all the Empire's towns.[3] Before the staffing reform of 1763 there were only about 12,000 officials in central and provincial administration to govern a population of about 22 million spread over a territory of about 14 million square kilometers.[4]

Catherine also found some hard policy choices that could make it more difficult to secure the political support of the Empire's elites. She hoped to win Russia a breathing spell from war, beginning with the conclusion of a stable peace with Prussia and Denmark. "Peace is necessary to this vast empire," she wrote, "We need population, not devastation; we need to populate our great spaces as much as possible."[5] But her closest advisors fell into different camps as to the wisdom of continuing strategic partnership with Austria or taking up construction of Panin's Northern Accord. She had not yet won political acceptance by the Russian nobility. Peter III's February 18, 1762, decree "emancipating" the nobility from compulsory state service confronted her with an unprecedented situation: the emergence of a provincial nobility "privileged yet separated from state service, whose way of life was in conflict with the laws and institutions established by Peter the Great."[6] The great noble families and the petty provincial nobles alike were waiting to see whether she would confirm this decree and how she intended to redefine the nobility's privileges; but it was as yet unclear to her how to accommodate nobles' requests for retirement or exemption while finding some way to improve staffing of the middle and lower levels of the provincial bureaucracy.

For the past several years, Vorontsov, Münnich, and then Panin had bemoaned the distortion of central decision-making by "caprice" (*proizvol*): Empress Elizabeth Petrovna's competing favorites had pulled policy back and forth, while Peter III had ignored all his councilors and conducted himself as an unchecked despot. Within a month of Catherine's accession Panin proposed establishing an Imperial Council to guide her, restore order to decision-making, and contain caprice. The membership of this Imperial Council should be comprehensive enough to represent both of the main competing court "parties"—the Bestuzhev–Orlov bloc, and Panin's own bloc—thereby offering the empress the opportunity to keep factions in balance. It could also combat the influence of favorites by limiting the exercise of authority that did not derive from official position; thus the six to eight members of the Imperial Council as envisioned by Panin would each have portfolios and sit as "state secretaries" responsible for different functions (War, Marine, Foreign Affairs, Internal Affairs, etc.). The Senate's work supervising the central colleges would be improved by dividing the Senate into six departments, each supervised by the appropriate state secretary. All business requiring the empress' decision would have to be reported up from the Senate to the Imperial Council for discussion and could only become law with the signature of the empress and the counter signature of the relevant state secretary.[7]

The Bestuzhev–Orlov faction was suspicious of this proposal and tried to convince Catherine that an Imperial Council would grant too much power to these state secretaries and reinforce the magnate oligarchy already entrenched in the Senate. The Orlovs argued that the empress' survival depended on her maintaining political flexibility, which required that she preserve the authority to advance her favorites and entrust political tasks to them.

On December 15, 1763, Catherine II decided to compromise. She went ahead with Panin's recommendation to divide the Senate into specialized departments, but instead of subordinating the Senate departments to state secretaries in an Imperial Council, she strengthened her own personal control over the Senate by appointing as General Procurator of the Senate A. A. Viazemskii, a trusted figure unaffiliated with either of the two court parties.[8] In a special instruction to Viazemskii the empress wrote, "You will find two parties, but a reasoned policy on my part requires that neither be respected in the least; deal with them firmly and they will disappear more quickly. I have watched them with an unsleeping eye and employed those people according to their ability for one or another matter. Both parties will now attempt to win you to their side. In the one you will find honest men, although without great foresight; in the other, I think, their views extend much farther but it is not clear that they are always for the best purposes."[9] As for Panin's proposed Imperial Council, she put the project on hold from October 1763 and kept the two parties preoccupied by assigning her circle of advisors to a special conference on the Polish succession and to a Commission on Noble Freedom examining how to respond to Peter III's 1762 decree ending compulsory state service. In this manner she managed to balance court factions without surrendering any of her power to an Imperial Council. During her first Turkish War, the military would indeed be directed by a council of her advisors, but it would be a new Council of State attached to the Imperial Court, specifically created for supervising the war effort.

Recruit levies and the soul tax

The two main mechanisms for mobilizing resources for war had been bequeathed by Peter the Great: the recruit levies (*rekrutnye sbory*) raising troops for the army, introduced in 1705, and the soul tax (*podushnaia podat'*), decreed in 1718. Both had fallen on the Empire's tax-bearing population with heavy brutality in Peter's lifetime, but Peter's successors had found ways to put the recruit and soul tax burdens in a bearable balance with population growth and the burden of other services, taxes, and rents.[10]

The norms for the recruit levy of course rose sharply in wartime, especially during the longer Turkish War of 1736–1739 and the Seven Years' War.[11] Wartime levy rates could disrupt the agricultural and commercial economies of peasants and townsmen by stripping households of males of peak labor age. But at the war's end the recruit rate usually dropped off so that the cumulative rate over the century averaged 1–1.5 men per 100 souls, which could be considered a natural equilibrium in relation to the rate of population growth. Population growth in the decades after the death of Peter the Great was sufficient to allow the military establishment to expand to 331,422 by 1756 and cover the army's high mortality and desertion rates without forcing Russia to place a larger proportion of its subjects under arms than Prussia or France.

The recruit levies were undoubtedly a brutal experience for those snatched up in them as the term of service for commoners was for life,[12] so a young man taken up in a recruit levy would probably never see his family and village again. Formal leave was permitted only for noblemen who had to tend to their estates and to cavalrymen on the southern frontier who lived nearby along the Ukrainian Line; common recruits could only gain leave unofficially and illegally, by bribing their regimental commanders. But from the government's point-of-view the recruit system was effective because the levies were able to "mobilize manpower early and at low cost, and to convert raw recruits into reliable soldiers under the command of an effective officer corps."[13]

From 1762 to 1766 Catherine II took no recruit levies in the name of fiscal austerity and allowed the size of the military establishment to fall to 303,529 by 1765.[14] In 1767 she resumed recruit levies, taking one man from every 300 male souls (projected yield: 20,778 men; actual yield: 22,373). In 1768, during preparations for her Turkish War, she ordered two recruit levies to expand the army and Land Militia, again at the rate of one recruit per 300 souls (actual yield, 50,747 men). The manpower demands of the following year required the rate to be raised to one recruit from 150 souls (actual yield 46,583), and in 1770 to one recruit from 100 souls (actual yield 49,583).[15]

Through Catherine's reign it was the policy to make the recruiting burden fall mainly upon the peasant population of Great Russia. The Baltic provinces, the population of partitioned Poland and Lithuania, and New Russia were privileged with lower levy rates. After 1762 taxpayers subject to the soul tax were allowed to purchase substitutes. Factory owners, merchants, and landowners could substitute cash payments depending on their rank and the number of serfs they held. The age limits for recruits were also changed over the decades: in the 1730s the age range for taking recruits had been set at 15–30 years, but this was raised to 20–35 in 1754; the need for manpower in Catherine II's Turkish Wars compelled her to lower the age for recruiting eligibility to 17. The height requirement was initially set at 5 feet 3 inches but lowered in wartime, although shorter men were supposed to be sent into the navy or into garrison units. The new General Establishment on Recruit Levies (1767) also recognized the right of recruits to form eight-man *artel'* collectives pooling part of their pay for mutual aid under the supervision of their corporals.[16]

During the Seven Years' War expenditure on the army and fleet had ranged from 7 to 10 million rubles per year. In the war's final year (1762), it had reached 10.4 million rubles, or 63.1 percent of all state spending, with expenditures exceeding state revenues by 1.2 million rubles (and by 2.0 million rubles in 1763). The *Oberkrigskomissariat* had already fallen into debt to military contractors by 1759, and by the following year the debt to contractors had reached 5 million rubles.[17]

The Empire's main direct tax was the soul tax, which was earmarked for the support of the army and fleet. It was collected by the War College (*VK, Voennaia kollegiia,* founded in 1718) from all adult males entered on the census registers as tax-bearing subjects: that is, nobles were exempt from it on the grounds they were rendering military or administrative service, as were soldiers and parish clergy. When first devised in 1718 the base rate of the soul tax had been set at 74 kopeks from each registered taxpayer with the expectation that this would produce revenue of 4 million rubles a year, enough to support 73 regiments. By the time the collection actually began in 1724, the base rate had undergone additional adjustment so that taxpayers not subject to the rent demands of noble landowners would pay somewhat more (state and court peasants now paid an additional 40 kopeks, and taxpayers in town *posad* communes paid an additional 50 kopeks).

Scholars have disputed whether the rate for Peter I's soul tax was as ruinously heavy as some anecdotal evidence has suggested, or whether the protests and taxpayer flight the soul tax provoked derived from the fact that it was collected in a brutal manner, by the army itself, in connection with billeting, and because introduction of the soul tax increased the monetary proportion of the peasant tax burden at a time of currency devaluation and volatility in grain prices.[18] In any case, after the death of Peter I the Supreme Privy Council took alarm at rising soul tax arrears and signs of civil unrest and decided to reform collection technique and lower the rate of the soul tax by a few kopeks. This was expected to be welcomed by the nobility, as it would leave more peasant surplus product available for rents to landlords. Newly expanded or added military formations—a larger artillery corps, the Ukrainian Land Milita, etc.—would instead be paid from the *obrok* rent levied on state peasants and *odnodvortsy*.

This would remain the preferred fiscal strategy through the rest of the century. Whereas revenue from the soul tax increased from 4 to 10.4 million rubles over 1726–1796, revenue from *obrok* on state peasants increased from 700,000 rubles to 14 million rubles.[19]

In 1763 Catherine reined in spending, reducing reduced army and fleet expenditures to 9.12 million rubles out of total state expenditures of 17.23 million rubles. By 1768 spending on salaries to officials, on the army and fleet, and on collection costs had raised total expenditures to 23.63 million rubles. To pay down the state debt over these years Peter III and Catherine II raised the total yield of the soul tax without raising soul tax rates—that is, by placing Left Bank Ukraine under *guberniia* administration in 1765 and extending liability for the one-ruble soul tax to Ukraine's male taxpayers. Peter III's 1762 decree on secularizing the estates of the Orthodox Church also made it possible for Catherine to raise more revenue in the form of state *obrok*, as the Church owned about a seventh of the entire rural population: *obrok* levied on Church peasants reclassified as state peasants yielded 1.37 million rubles a year, of which only 463,000 rubles had to be paid back to churchmen in the form of salaries. In 1764 the empress raised the *obrok* rate on former Church peasants to 1.5 rubles per soul and the rate on *odnodvortsy* to 1 ruble. *Obrok* in 1765 brought in 2.4 million rubles while the soul tax on private serfs yielded 3 million rubles. Thus the yield of direct taxation was grown 1.6-fold by 1765 without much new inconvenience to noble serf-owners, as the increase came at the expense of state peasants. In that year, the government's direct and indirect revenues reached 23 million rubles. By the eve of the war in 1768 the empress had managed to build up a reserve of 5 million rubles.[20]

Catherine II also took steps to grow the national economy by lifting duties on Russian grain exports. Over 1751–1760 the annual average of wheat and rye exports had been 71,565 quarters (*chetverti*); this rose to 370,038 quarters over 1761–1770. In the 1760s grain exports still counted for just 200,000 quarters out of total commercial grain consumption of 6.3 million quarters, but grain exports would be more than double by the 1770s and would increase 47-fold by the end of the century providing significant stimulus to the commercialization of Russian agriculture.[21]

In Elizabeth Petrovna's reign, the main supplement to the soul tax for supporting the army and fleet had been the crown's salt and liquor monopolies, which accounted for 8 percent and 25 percent of state revenues respectively. Senator Count Petr Shuvalov, Empress Elizabeth Petrovna's principal economic advisor, had urged raising salt and liquor revenues so as to cover reductions in the soul tax and placate the nobility. Revenue from the liquor monopoly had nearly doubled between 1749 and 1758, and revenue from the salt tax had risen 2.7-fold. Most of the liquor monopoly had been turned over to tax-farmers—mostly nobles, and in certain districts, to merchants. Catherine II viewed monopolies and tax farming as corrupting and socially dangerous, and she had moved already in 1763 to dismantle the worst of them, beginning with the potash and tar monopolies and the tax farming of customs collections; she did not abolish tax farming of liquor sales, but from 1767 she did regulate it more closely. The liquor monopoly would continue to supplement revenues for her Turkish War, and liquor revenues would increase 1.6-fold over 1764–1771.[22]

Although these measures had accumulated a healthy treasury reserve by 1768 they would not be enough to pay for the enormously expensive Turkish War, and Catherine would soon be pressed to resort to additional steps (the introduction of paper *assignats*, the negotiation of loans from Dutch bankers and a subsidy from Prussia).

Provincial administration and staffing

Peter I had recognized that running the recruit levies and collecting revenue for the army could not be managed completely from the *prikazy*, the traditional offices of central government, and that the burden on the *prikazy* could be significantly reduced if much of the management of military resource mobilization was passed down to regional authorities held accountable to the center. In 1708 he had therefore divided the realm into nine super provinces called governorates (s. *guberniia*; pl. *gubernii*), each under a governor (*gubernator*) with his own chancery staff (*kantseliariia*): the Moscow, Petersburg, Arkhangel'sk, Ingermanland, Smolensk, Kazan', Kiev, Azov, and Siberian governorates. Before this military, policing, administrative authority had been concentrated in the hands of "town governors" (*gorodovye voevody*) appointed by the Military Chancellery to govern small districts (*uezdy*) not much larger than a town and its hinterland. There had been about 300 such districts toward at the end of the seventeenth century, and their secretarial/clerical staffs had been small (on average six personnel total); they were now subordinated to the governor and his chancery and their *gorodovye voevody* were refashioned as commandants (*komandanty*).[23]

The new governorates were expected to prove their superiority in several ways: by serving as administrative arteries connecting the central bureaucratic heart to the district capillaries; by providing greater regional coordination of military resource mobilization and other functions;[24] by improving information processing about local needs and conditions; and by placing regional administration in trusted hands, that is, the hands of Peter's nine closest comrade deputies, members of the inner ruling circle such as

A. D. Menshikov, F. M. Apraksin, and D. M. Golitsyn. The historian Anisimov compared them to "satraps of a distinctive sort."[25] Yet it was also expected that the governors would gradually expand their chanceries and create new subordinate offices—*komissar*s to supervise recruit levies, *fiskal*s to monitor abuses of authority—that could be held by appointed local nobles and merchants, giving local elites more of a stake in in office-holding and review and control of the governors and their chanceries.

A second stage of reform began in 1711. While off on his Moldavian campaign, Peter I had established a Senate to supervise the realm in his stead. The central *prikazy*, including the War Chancery (*Voennaia kantseliariia*) and the War Provisioning Commissariat (*Krigskommisariat*) were subordinated to the Senate, as were the governors and their chanceries. This allowed more functional specialization in the central administration so that the War Chancery could tighten its focus on central coordination of the recruit levies while the War Provisioning Commissariat could focus on provisioning and logistics. The Senate took charge of staffing the governors' chanceries, appointing noblemen as land councilors (*landraty*) to perform secretarial duty in the chanceries and sit as boards to check governors and commandants from abusing their authority. In 1715, these land councilors were converted into officials in charge of the fiscal administration in the 147 new tax-lot units (*dol'ia*, standardized at 5,536 tax-paying households) that had replaced the old *uezd* districts. Each tax-lot was assigned to the support of one regiment. Over 1712–1715 measures were taken to improve governorate supervision of military manpower by placing the commandants of smaller outlying town garrisons under the command of the governor's *ober-komandant*; this turned the smaller outlying garrison locale into an *oberkomandantskaia provintsiia*, a military-administrative unit above the *dol'ia* but under the governorate capital.[26]

The third phase in Tsar Peter's reforms of provincial administration was in 1719–1725. This phase was more explicitly cameralist and aimed at enhancing administrative specialization, regulation, and unification. Having recognized that many locales had too few nobles to sit as land councilors checking abuses of authority by commandants and governors, Peter I decided to exercise tighter control over provincial officials from above by reforming central administration and then following its organizational principles in restructuring the governors' chanceries. Therefore in 1717–1720 Peter established at St. Petersburg nine Swedish-style Colleges (for Foreign Affairs, War, Navy, Revenue, Treasury, Auditing, Commerce, Mining, Manufactures), each with a ten-man board under a President, deciding business collegiately. It was hoped this would produce a simpler and clearer division of labor in central government that could be followed in turn in reorganizing the governors' chanceries to better prepare the governorates for the new task of collecting the soul tax. At this time a number of new specialized policing, judicial, and fiscal offices (*kamerir* accountants, *rentmeister* bursars, *zemskii* commissars, and magistrates) were established below the governor's chancery as new capillaries carrying power out from the governorate artery. These new officials were appointed by the Senate and the Colleges. The crucial link between them and the governor were the secretaries in the governor's chancery, who had to be in the higher ranks in the Table of Ranks and who were therefore supposed to be hereditary nobles; their appointments had to be approved by the Senate and Heraldmaster's office.[27] But in practice so few of these nobles were available locally that Peter was forced to transfer nobles out of St. Petersburg or Moscow to fill secretarial posts. Most growth in the number of provincial officials was confined to the lower clerical and servant posts, which could be held by those who had not acquired the ranks bestowing hereditary nobility. In compensation Peter now devoted greater attention to issuing ordinances standardizing office procedures and regulating remuneration and rewards (amplifying upon the 1714 law on salary remuneration and the 1722 Table of Ranks). This third phase did not produce entirely satisfactory results: there remained a staffing shortage, especially at the higher clerical and secretarial levels; it was becoming difficult to honor the 1714 salary law and pay salaries to all in full and on time; and there was still inadequate coordination between the Senate and the Colleges.

After Peter's death the government of Catherine I decided to economize by shutting down the offices of the magistrates, *kamerirs*, *prokurors*, and *rentmeisters*; to compensate for the elimination of these lower-level offices the district (*uezd*) was reestablished. Thus by 1728 the Empire was now divided into fourteen governorates under *gubernatory*, subdivided into forty-seven provinces (*provintsii*) under *provintsial'nye voevody*, and further subdivided into 250 districts (*uezdy*) under *uezdnye voevody*. This also represented a partial rehabilitation of the pre-Petrine practice of concentrating administrative, financial, and judicial authority in the hands of an executive—*gubernator* or *voevoda*—thereby making "caprice" and abuse of power more likely. Meanwhile the economies Catherine I and her Supreme Privy Council had taken had left officials at all three levels less able to perform their duties. For example, salaries were now paid only to secretaries and to those lower officials who had been in salaried posts before 1700. That left most of lower officialdom unsalaried and more tempted to resort to bribe-taking and embezzlement in order to survive. It also made it more difficult to find qualified men to fill posts. In 1755 the Senate set a staffing norm of thirty officials and servants in governorate chanceries, fifteen in province chanceries, and ten in district chanceries, but these norms were rarely met.[28]

When Catherine II came to the throne she therefore faced four problems: 1) expanding the governorate system to accommodate territorial expansion and better integrate newly acquired lands into the Empire; 2) improving Senate supervision of the colleges and the governors' chanceries; 3) improving the staffing of provincial administration, especially at the higher clerical/secretarial levels; and 4) finding a way to achieve Peter I's goal of a universally salaried officialdom.

By restructuring administration in Siberia and northwestern Russia and by taking advantage of colonization in eastern Ukraine Catherine's government created seven new governorates in 1764–1767: Little Russia, New Russia, Sloboda Ukraine, Azov, Irkutsk, Pskov, and Mogilev. This brought the total number of governorates to 23.[29] It also had the effect of bringing the apparatus for the soul tax and recruit levies into Ukraine, the staging ground for army operations in the approaching Turkish War.

On April 21, 1764, the empress promulgated a Precept to Governors (*Nastavlenie gubernatoram*) enumerating their full range of duties in tax collection, recruit levies, supervising customs and the post, policing, supervising magistrates, maintaining roads and bridges, and supervising the management of hospitals, schools, and bridges. The Precept was a fairly comprehensive summary of her views on the responsibilities of cameralist statecraft. It placed special emphasis on the governor's duty to provide the Senate with detailed information about changing conditions of population, agriculture, and commerce.[30]

A 1763 commission headed by Prince Iakov Shakhovskoi, former Procurator of the Senate, proposed increasing to seven the number of governorates with enhanced military authority as *general-gubernii* (St. Petersburg, Moscow, Belgorod, Orenburg, Smolensk, Kazan', and Siberia). To prevent such centralization from promoting greater caprice by *general-gubernators* Shakhovskoi proposed attaching to them special associates (*tovarishchi*), some of them elected from the local nobility and merchantry. At the governorate level the governor would have a board of four associates, one of them elected from the local nobility; at the province level there would be elected noble associates and also elected noble commissars to adjust army provisioning quotas to the condition of the tax-bearing population. Shakhovskoi also endorsed Panin's proposal to divide the Senate into six departments, centralizing in one department control over the seven colleges and *kontora* offices dealing with commerce, industry, revenue and expenditure. Only this last recommendation was implemented by the Senate at this time, the Senate balking at the magnitude of the task involved in restructuring the *guberniias*.[31] But the suggestion that elected representatives from the nobility be given a larger role in provincial administration would shape the empress' approach when she resumed reform after the Turkish War.

The Shakhovskoi Commission had greater success in addressing the problem of salary remuneration. In 1714 Peter I had envisioned an officialdom entirely remunerated by salary, no longer dependent on income from their estates and paid well enough to resist the temptation to solicit bribes and tips. But this had soon proven unrealistic. By 1760 the majority of officials in central and provincial government, especially in the middle and lower ranks, were unable to live off their salaries and had to supplement their income with "feeding" exactions and bribes. In 1760 expenditure on the bureaucracy had been 198,400 rubles: 125,100 rubles (63 percent) to officials in central administration and 73,300 rubles (37 percent) to officials in the governorates. Through economies and the exploitation of new revenue sources Catherine II found it possible to increase expenditure on the bureaucracy 5.5-fold by 1763.[32] The larger expenditure allowed paying better salaries to higher officials and also made it possible to begin offering pensions (at half salary rate) for those who had served more than 35 years. After 1765 officials with noble rank in the Table of Ranks could take four months' leave without salary on permission of the Senate. By increasing the number of procurators it was possible to prosecute corruption more aggressively; there were major prosecutions in Smolensk, Belgorod, and Voronezh in this period. But the scale of corruption appears to have declined in this period; the universalization of salary remuneration, together with lower prices, does seem to have made it easier for officials to subsist on their salaries.[33]

The biggest remaining problem was the shortage of administrative personnel. It had been possible to reestablish salary remuneration for officials because there were in all just 16,500 officials in central and provincial administration in 1763.[34] The shortage was especially acute at the middle level—the level of the clerical staff, where offices were not *chinovnik*, that is, were below the eighth rank in the Table of Ranks, too low to confer hereditary noble status. The clericate usually recruited from non-taxpayers who were sons of clerks, merchants' sons, clergymen's sons, or sons of impoverished service nobles who had not risen enough in rank to get confirmation of hereditary nobility.

Peter III's Manifesto of February 18, 1762, "emancipating" the Russian nobility from compulsory state service,[35] had raised the possibility that noblemen taking advantage of the new opportunity to retire from active military duty and return to the countryside to tend their estates might be brought into provincial officialdom, either as salaried officials or elected representatives of the local noble estate (hence Shakhovskoi's proposal for elected noble "associates" and commissars). After all, the Manifesto still expected nobles to educate their sons for service and to perform service from patriotic duty and from respect for the good opinion of their peers, if no longer out of compulsion.[36] The Manifesto may have been partly motivated by calculations of winning that popularity among the nobility that had so eluded Peter III, or by cameralist considerations that the economy could be grown by closer noble stewardship of the land. But its main motive had been to economize on salary expenditures, especially on officers' pay: now that Peter III intended to take Russia out of the war against Prussia, he envisioned a smaller, leaner military establishment and a bureaucracy staffed by motivated volunteers. He would not allow a sudden mass exodus from state service, however; it would have to be timed and controlled.[37] The Manifesto was therefore in harmony with the post-Petrine practice of allowing exit from state service on a limited basis, in peacetime, when it was in the interest of reducing salary expenditures.[38]

The number of nobles retiring from military service in 1762–1771 was 6,590. Enough of them were interested in taking up salaried posts in the civil bureaucracy that they were required to apply for the Heraldmaster's Office for reassignment to civil posts. But the Heraldmaster's office could find vacant posts only for 1,330 of these men, especially as the majority of them had expected posts in the upper ranks of the provincial civil service. The typical retired officer in this period was aged 39 and had twenty years' military service, but he owned few or no serfs and was middling to poor in literacy and arithmetical ability. By social pretension he expected to serve in the upper bureaucratic ranks, yet his skills ill-equipped him for clerical duty, where the personnel shortage was most acutely felt. Thus the 1762 Manifesto had not yet fulfilled the expectation that educated noblemen would turn to service in provincial government. In 1767 Governor-General Sievers wrote to Catherine II, "Since the nobility was free from all compulsory service, the provincial government has had great difficulty finding people for the endless number of positions that it must constantly fill."[39]

Thus the tendency in state administration in the Russian Empire was the opposite of Ottoman administration. Whereas the Ottoman political trajectory over the eighteenth century was toward decentralization and the transfer of military authority into the hands of provincial *ayan* households, Catherine II sought ways to tighten central government control over military service and military resource mobilization in the provinces—to the extent that some previously free social elements were converted into state peasants liable for the soul tax, and territories that had been previously treated as politically autonomous were absorbed into the Empire as governorates.

Security, colonization, and economic development in Russia's Black Soil south

South of Moscow and the Oka River a great arc runs from Orel through Tula, Riazan', Simbirsk, and ends at Ufa near the Urals. This arc was the northern edge of the Russian part of the vast belt of black soil (*chernozem*) that extended as far south as the Black Sea coast and the Kuban steppe.[40]

The Black Soil south held tremendous potential for the agricultural development of Russia and Ukraine, for this soil was humus-rich, considerably more fertile than the leached gray soil (*podzol*) of central and northern Russia, and the growing season here was longer. For this reason yields of rye (the principal cereal crop) reached 11:1 in the eighteenth century, one-and-half times greater than in the northern gray soil region.[41]

But Muscovite colonization and agricultural exploitation were long delayed by risks of attack by the Nogais and Crimean Tatars. Khan Mengli I Girei insisted that the districts of Briansk, Starodub, Novgorod-Severskii, Ryl'sk and Putivl, and Karachev were part of his *yurt*, and he raided them in 1514 to extort their arrears in tribute. Tatar invasions and raids in the first half of the sixteenth century often reached the Ugra and Oka rivers and sometimes crossed them, exposing Moscow and its environs to attack in 1521 and 1571.[42]

Tsar Ivan IV and his successors responded to this threat by investing enormous resources in successive waves of fortified line construction and military colonization in order to gradually expand Muscovy's defense perimeter and enclose more of the Black Soil forest-steppe and steppe. An Abatis Line running from the Volga to the Zhizdra River was built over the second half of the sixteenth century. After Tatar raids in 1632–1633 that broke through the Abatis Line, about 800 kilometers of its length were substantially repaired and a new fortified defense line farther south was begun from the newly founded garrison town of Kozlov. Eighteen new garrison towns were founded along this Belgorod Line, which ran for over 800 kilometers from the Kozlov satellite garrison of Chelnavsk to Akhtryka on the border of Ukraine. By 1655 more defense line segments were added in the east, extending the line from Chelnavsk through Shatsk, through Simbirsk on the Volga, and as far east as Menselinsk on the Ik River.[43]

During this second wave of defense line construction it had become apparent that the norms for service land grants and retinues accompanying servicemen to mobilization were no longer supportable, especially on the sparsely populated southern frontier where servicemen would find it difficult to hold peasant tenants. The Military Chancellery therefore decided to concentrate on enrolling in Belgorod Line defense duty *odnodvortsy* ("single-household-men"), yeomen with smaller cash bounties, smaller service land entitlement rates, smaller service land grants, and few or no peasant tenants. These smallholders would be cheaper to support, and it was not supposed to matter that they had no peasant tenants because they were expected to perform only local duty defending the nearest segment of the Belgorod Line; it was not intended that they be called up with retainers for campaign duty in the field army. Since they were to be settled on a nucleated pattern in villages along the defense line, it became the practice to assign them rotating shares in a village bloc of service land rather than separate individual service land tracts; this meant the *odnodvorets* village would periodically repartition and redistribute plowlands among its members somewhat in the fashion of the peasant village commune.

The decision to pursue *odnodvorets* military colonization had enormous consequences for the Black Soil region. It enabled the region to significantly reduce the threat of Tatar raiding already by the 1680s. But it also delayed the emergence of manorial agriculture in the south and muffled the sociopolitical voice of its population in Imperial security and trade policy. This can be illustrated by looking at the example of Kozlov district in Voronezh Governorate.[44]

Kozlov servicemen ended up doing more than patrolling and defending the nearest segment of the Belgorod Line; after 1650 Moscow departed from its original intent and started taking more and more of them into the field army defending the western end of the Line and campaigning in Ukraine and the lower Don. Kozlov and its satellite garrisons at Dobryi and Sokol'sk provided about half of the 8,000 troops in the four new formation infantry regiments founded at Iablonov in 1652; another 3,385 men were taken from Kozlov, Dobryi, and Sokol'sk for the Belgorod Army Group; and by the 1670s troop levies here were sometimes violating the rule that two men per household be left in local service or labor support for every man taken into the regiments. Kozlov district provided troops for the 1677–1678 campaign to defend Chyhyryn against the Turks, for the 1685 and 1687 expeditionary armies marching on Crimea, and for Peter I's campaigns against Azov in 1695–1696. In 1700 Peter I began taking males younger than fifteen years and as short as 1.53 meters, leading to the complaint from Kozlov yeomen that "no one was left on the plowland, they enroll everyone who meets the measuring stick."[45] From the 1660s those Kozlov yeomen left in local defense service, exempted from duty in the regiments, had to pay a grain tax called *chetverikovyi khleb* to support the regiments; by 1674 its rate had increased nine-fold. Meanwhile reductions in service land entitlement rates, service land grant rates, and population growth forcing the subdivision of service lands had reduced the standard actual service land grant from 50 quarters per field in 1637–1639 to 6.6 to 40 quarters per field in 1675.[46]

The need for revenue during the Great Northern War and the lower frequency of Crimean Tatar and Nogai raids on the Belgorod Line districts brought about a radical change in the juridical status of most Kozlov *odnodvortsy*. Beginning in 1699 southern frontier *odnodvortsy* registered in town service rather than field army duty were subject to a special cash tax assessed on individuals rather than their land resources—in other words, a precursor to Peter I's soul tax. This collapsed most of the legal distinction between *odnodvortsy* and state peasants paying *obrok* rent from state lands. Then in 1710 census-takers redefined "*odnodvortsy*" to mean "men of the old services" who now bore taxes. By 1728 24,000 of Kozlov's 27,000 former servicemen were registered as tax-bearing *odnodvortsy* paying the new soul tax.[47]

There were some 510,000 *odnodvortsy* in the Empire in 1762. They were liable for the soul tax at the higher rate borne by state peasants; they provided recruits for the army at the rate of one man from every 25 or 50 households; they were liable for fifteen years' service in the Land Militia along the Ukrainian Line; they supplied the army with fodder and food, and they performed *corvee* on fortifications and magazines. The only privileges they had retained from their original condition as state servicemen were that they were allowed by law to acquire their own serfs (in principle, in the very rare instances in which they could afford it); they were permitted to sell or rent land, although their lands still officially belonged to the state; they could not be transferred by the state to private landowners; and unlike state peasants they remained unbound by communal collective surety.[48]

Under Peter I and again under Empress Anna some new fortress foreposts were built south of Kozlov and Tambov: Borisoglebsk (1696), Pavlovsk (1709), Tranzhament (1711, renamed St. Anna in 1730), and Novokhopersk (1716). They were of value in securing a Russian presence on the lower Don after Azov was turned back over to the Turks, and they encouraged families from Kozlov and Tambov to begin colonizing the steppe to their south along the rivers Matyra, Bitiug, Khoper, Surena, and Tokai.[49] There were 107 settlements in Kozlov district in 1722; the number rose to 134 by 1744.

Tranzhament/St. Anna soon became the western terminus of a new defense line running from the Don to the Volga, the Tsaritsyn Line (built 1718–1720), and the eastern terminus of the Ukrainian Line (built 1731–1740). The latter defense line would play an important role in supporting the Russian attacks on Azov, Perekop, and Ochakov in the 1735–1739 Russo-Turkish War. To man the Ukrainian Line it was decided to expand the Ukrainian Land Militia, and two of the new Land Militia regiments resettled along the Ukrainian Line were from Kozlov and Tambov—*odnodvortsy* taken back into military service as military colonists holding plowlands within thirty kilometers of the Ukrainian Line.[50] There was a political rationale to this as well, for by transplanting Russian *odnodvortsy* in Land Militia service along the Ukrainian Line the role of the cossack regiments of Ukraine and Sloboda Ukraine in the defense of their own frontier was reduced. This resettlement of the *odnodvortsy* still capable of military service was affordable because by the 1730s the forest-steppe and steppe between the Don and the Volga had been sufficiently secured against the Tatars.

A few Belgorod Line towns had found viable economic specializations and had grown: Voronezh, for example, as a major grain and cattle market, a locus for some cloth factories, a wharf and shipyard for the Don River flotillas, and a *guberniia* capital; Ostrogozhsk, as a grain market, distilling center, and fairground; and Tambov, as a grain and livestock market with links to the Volga, the Don, and the old Tatar road moving up the Tsna toward Moscow.[51] But many of the old towns of the Belgorod Line now lost their significance as garrisons and administrative centers and lost population, shrinking to the size of large villages. Kozlov was surpassed by Tambov, which became the province capital, though Kozlov's urban population did increase slightly, from 2,861 in 1685 to about 5,300 (males and females) in 1762. But Kozlov's urban population remained *odnodvorets*—79.5 percent in 1719, still 43 percent at the end of the eighteenth century.[52]

Kozlov's rural population in 1762 was still two-thirds *odnodvorets* and one-third serf, the serfs tenanting fairly small estates. Large-scale manorialism by wealthy metropolitan nobles had never taken hold in the Kozlov–Tambov region, with one exception: the estate Prince Aleksandr Menshikov acquired near Ranenburg at the beginning of the century. It had comprised twelve villages in Kozlov district and nine villages in Tambov district and had reached a peak population of about 5,000 male and female serfs in 1714. But Nekrasovite Cossacks raided it, and when Menshikov was disgraced and exiled to Siberia in 1727 the Ranenburg estate was confiscated by the government and its serfs converted into state peasants. With the greater frontier security provided by the Tsaritsyn Line the lands of the Kozlov–Tambov region in the 1740s finally began drawing investment by some metropolitan nobles (General A. G. Zagriazhskii, Prince G. S. Meshcherskii, Prince N. A. Shekhovskoi), but the estates they founded here contained no more than 100–500 souls.[53]

Although noble manorialism was still underdeveloped in the Kozlov–Tambov region conflicts between *odnodvortsy* and nobles did arise there, as in Tambov district in 1775, when the nobleman Shpikulov seized the lands and livestock and burned out the homesteads of some neighboring *odnodvortsy* and tried to impose on others cartage *corvee* and other services. Such conflicts were more common farther north in the Black Soil region, closer to Moscow. *Odnodvortsy* from Efremov district attending the empress' 1767 Legislative Assembly petitioned, "The nobles cause us no little poverty and ruin, and coming to the homesteads, they commit theft and robbery, and take the hay from the fields, and take … the hayfields themselves, and hunt in our woods, take horses and other animals, and hunt our cattle in the fields, and their cattle take our grain."[54]

Odnodvortsy lacked the political influence to affect state frontier policy; they did not even feel empowered to regulate their own condition. At the 1767 Legislative Assembly the Empire's *odnodvortsy* were represented by forty-two deputies (compared to 205 deputies representing nobles, 167 deputies representing merchants, and forty-four deputies from Cossacks), and their *cahiers* and speeches mostly complained "of the burden of military service, of the additional services demanded of them … of delays in promotion to commissioned rank … [and] of their inability to secure justice from the local administration …. They were almost unanimous in demanding self-government as a separate social 'estate.'"[55]

Odnodvortsy generally lacked the resources to expand their acreage deeper in the steppe, and in the period 1725–1763 the area of cultivated plowland increased only from 25,000 *desiatiny* to 29,000 *desiatiny*, and then mostly at the expense of forest.[56] Kozlov's economy remained localized. Its primary products—rye, meat, leather, fish, honey, some cloth—were mostly traded across the other Belgorod Line districts; occasionally merchants came down from Moscow, Tula, Kursk, and Iaroslavl' to make purchases; the merchants permanently based at Kozlov were mostly local men (*odnodvortsy*, clerks' sons, churchmen, house serfs, court peasants) dealing in small lots with sale and purchase values under thirty rubles, and they had unstable capital and were only sporadically involved in the market.[57]

Thus enormous treasury investments over a period of two hundred years had settled the forest-steppe south of the Oka River and the steppe between the Volga and the Don and gradually made these settlements safe against Tatar raiding. But the region's *odnodvorets* population had made enormous sacrifices in the process. From 1650 they had made major manpower contributions to the field armies defending the Belgorod Line and campaigning in Ukraine, and from the 1720s the *odnodvorets* population had assumed the obligation to support the army as payers of the soul tax as well as suppliers of recruits levied for the regiments.

This region could be expected to continue providing grain, revenue, and recruits for the army in the event of another war with the Ottoman Empire and Crimean Khanate. But it was unlikely to push for such a war to further its economic interests, for its population remained predominantly *odnodvorets*, without a prosperous nobility committed to commercialized agriculture for export. "The security situation made stable agriculture impossible for 100 years after its [Tambov's] founding [in 1636], and a plantation-type economy unfeasible for another hundred years after this."[58] The districts on and below the Belgorod Line lay at too great a distance from the major markets at Moscow and St. Petersburg, and at the time the prospects for trading down the Don and across the Black Sea seemed bleak.

By contrast the nobility of central and northern Russia opposed the Turkish War as wasteful and postponing the launching of Panin's Northern Accord, which held out to them the promise of expanding exports of flax, hemp, timber, tar, and grain from their estates across the Baltic to English and Dutch markets. The great nobles oriented their production and their political expectations toward the Baltic, to the extent that they had already "lost interest in the southern steppes .... Although the land between the Oka Basin and the Black Sea was very fertile and much of it lay unclaimed, the landowners of the eighteenth century were far less interested in occupying it than their sixteenth- and seventeenth-century predecessors had been. Once St. Petersburg began to exert its influence on commodity prices, fertile land became less important to landowners than access to markets, and the lands south of the Oka Basin had no water transport to the markets of the north. Because the rivers that traversed the fertile southern steppes flowed southward to the Black Sea, estates in that region were productive but unprofitable, growing crops that could not be sold."[59] What finally disposed the nobility to accept the empress' Turkish War was more likely the opportunity it provided for the partitioning of Poland.

The Don Cossack Host

In the sixteenth and seventeenth centuries the inhabitants of southern Russia's Black Soil region had a social pressure safety valve: those facing exploitation as serf tenants or *odnodvortsy* could move farther south, beyond the Belgorod Line, and take up residence in the encampments and small forts of the Don Cossack Host on the lower Don River near Azov and the Kuban steppe. Here they might find service in the Host or attach themselves to Host Cossacks as support workers or working lodgers.

By the 1620s the barracks settlements and winter camps on the lower Don held about 5,000 active duty Cossacks. They made their living by hunting, fishing, bee-keeping, and especially by raiding, ransoming captives, and hiring out as mercenaries. Field agriculture and animal husbandry were not much developed among them until the end of the century. They considered themselves "free cossacks" with the right to elect their own ataman and captains and conduct raids and wars on their own initiative, in their own interest, and for this reason they long resisted attempts by the tsar's officials to take census of their numbers. The Don Cossacks might sometimes serve the Moscow tsars by gathering intelligence and intercepting Tatar raiders threatening the southern Russian towns or by making their own raids upon the Crimean Tatars and Nogais with the tsar's encouragement—reward for which the tsars began shipping down the Don as an annual subsidy in the form of cash, grain, gunpowder, and liquor distributed among their *starshina*. But they continued to view themselves as standing outside the Muscovite state: they were neither the Sovereign's servicemen nor his men of tax draft and reserved for themselves the right to choose their own masters. Moscow recognized this by placing the handling of Don Cossack affairs in the Ambassadors' Chancellery, thereby treating with them as with a foreign power.

In the course of the Belgorod Line's construction fugitive peasants and servicemen defecting from garrison duty began to settle south of the defense line along the Voronezh and northern Don (the "Upper Reaches") and tried to imitate the Don Cossack condition, insisting on their freedom to move about the steppe unregulated, trade duty-free with the Russian border towns, and occasionally attend the general Cossack assemblies at Razdory electing the Host atamans and their officials. But these self-styled cossack villages of the Upper Reaches were less stable in population precisely because they operated as way-stations for migration between the Belgorod Line towns and the Host settlements on the lower Don. The cossacks of the Upper Reaches lived too far north to participate very often or deeply in Host affairs—they did not live under permanent company (*stanitsa*) discipline—and in the late seventeenth century Moscow would begin dealing with them very differently than with the Host companies residing on the lower Don.[60]

The Host ataman's headquarters at Monastyrskii gorodok was just 60 kilometers from the Ottoman fortress at Azov and just across the Miuss River from the Crimean Khanate. The Don Cossacks were also strategically situated vis-à-vis the Nogais on the Kuban steppe. Their endurance as a vassal military population was therefore of great value for the security of the Russian garrison towns on the Lower Volga as well as the

Don. The Host also asserted itself in naval warfare by undertaking frequent longboat raids along the Black Sea coast, making attacks upon Trebizond, Sinope, and even Istanbul itself. But at particular junctures these land and sea raids on Ottoman and Tatar territory risked embroiling Muscovy in war with the Porte (as in 1637–1642, when the Don Cossacks captured and occupied Azov, provoking Sultan Ibrahim to send a large army to expel them).[61] This gave Moscow reason for regretting it exercised so little control over the Host, and so from 1644 the Muscovite government began two practices aiming at constraining the Host's behavior: making adjustments to the size of the annual subsidy shipment, to tie subsidy generosity to Cossack *starshina* cooperation; and sending troops from the Belgorod Line for seasonal deployment on the lower Don, ostensibly to support Don Cossack operations but also to keep watch over Host Cossacks and restrain them from unauthorized raiding.[62] These deployments of Muscovite regiments to the lower Don would lay the logistic foundations for Peter I's expeditions against Azov in 1695–1696.

The growing Muscovite military presence on the lower Don—along with the construction of new Ottoman fortresses at the mouth of the Don to defend Azov and the Khanate—may have made it harder now for the Don Cossacks to initiate their own naval raids on the Black Sea. Certainly the tsars preferred to see the Don Cossack Host serving as auxiliaries to the field army than operating as independent raiders. A more critical problem for the Host was population pressure. The greater military security from the Belgorod Line encouraged more migration farther south into the cossack villages of the Upper Reaches and the company settlements of the lower Don. But cossack settlements could not provide sound livelihood to all these new migrants. This was true even in the more agriculturally and commercially developed Upper Reaches, which now drew the attention of the colonels of Sloboda Ukraine, who obtained grants and leases to plowlands, the salt works at Bakhmut, and the more productive fishing banks. This left the less economically diversified Host settlements of the Lower Don all the more dependent upon the tsar's Don shipment subsidy, which the *starshina* tried to monopolize for itself; and that in turn heightened tensions between a *starshina* elite more dependent on Muscovite subsidy and a "rabble" (*chern*) more desperate than ever to find new opportunities to raid for plunder.

In 1670–1671 the Host ataman's ban on raiding on the Volga and Caspian sparked a bloody revolt led by Stepan Razin. Among his 3,000–10,000 followers were many impoverished Cossacks of the Upper Reaches.[63] After overwhelming the Muscovite garrisons at the Volga towns of Tsaritsyn and Astrakhan, Razin announced his plan to march up the Volga into central Muscovy to punish the boyars for starving the cossacks and "barring the way to the sea." His forces were defeated at Simbirsk, Kazan', and Korotoiak, so Razin returned to the lower Don and attempted to seize Cherkassk and assassinate Ataman Iakovlev but failed. Razin was delivered in chains to Moscow and executed in Red Square on June 6, 1671. Among the measures taken to pacify the Don Cossack Host after the defeat of Razin were the imposition of an oath of eternal loyalty to the tsar; levies to provide Cossack *corvee* on new border fortifications; the establishing of roadblocks to check the flow of refugees to the lower Don and regulate Don Cossack travel to the Muscovite border towns; and the stationing of more Muscovite troops on the lower Don to surveil the Don Cossacks as well as the Ottoman fortresses.

The 1699 Karlowitz and Constantinople Treaties establishing a thirty-year armistice ending the War of the Holy League had enormous consequences for the Don Cossack Host. Muscovy was confirmed in possession of Azov and allowed to build new a naval base at Taganrog and a fortress at Miussk, but to keep the peace with the Porte and Crimean Khanate a fixed frontier was now drawn—a demilitarized strip of land running from the Miuss River to Perekop, with the Kuban steppe north of the Kuban River as a second demilitarized zone. Don Cossack settlements within these demilitarized zones had to be evacuated. The Don Cossack Host also had to abjure raiding and burn their longboats; their military activity had to be confined to patrolling their side of the frontier for the tsar. One would assume the ban on raiding economy would have caused great consternation among the Don Cossacks, given that it had been the original purpose of their military organization, but they took it largely in stride—at least in comparison with the Crimean Tatars—in part because they expected to find some compensation in the service with the tsar's field army and the opportunity to trade with the Khanate and the Muscovite garrisons at Azov, Taganrog, and Miussk.[64]

However, the transition to fixed frontiers was much harder on the population of the Upper Reaches.[65] Peter I decided the Don Cossack population should be concentrated on the lower Don, to defend and provision Azov and Taganrog. The scattered cossack settlements in the Upper Reaches overburdened the policing resources of the towns of the Belgorod Line; their men could not be taken into garrison service along the Belgorod Line, for there were not enough vacancies to accommodate them; the state could not permit them to turn to agriculture, as they might then begin to draw fugitive peasants as tenants; and the Don shipments could not support them, as this subsidy was intended first of all for the *starshina* on the Lower Don. Therefore Peter ordered over 1,500 cossack households on the Bitiug steppe burned and their inhabitants resettled at Azov. He planned to resettle the Bitiug basin with court peasants transferred from central Muscovy. In 1703 he initiated a census across most of the Upper Reaches with the aim of deporting to their districts of previous residence all those who had settled in cossack villages before 1695. Two years later he authorized the evacuation and destruction of all Upper Reaches cossack villages settled after 1695. Their inhabitants were to be deported to the left bank of the Northern Donets River.[66]

Thus Peter I shrank and "encapsulated" the Don Cossack Host, even if it was not his intention to abolish all Host privileges. Brian Boeck characterizes Russian policy over 1671–1708 as recognizing the host as a separate community, only now *within* the borders of the Russian Empire.[67]

The southward spread of Old Belief dissent from the official Orthodox Church stiffened resistance among the Upper Reaches cossacks facing the destruction of their homes. In the Bakhmut region, the bridge between the Upper Reaches and Sloboda Ukraine, Kondratii Bulavin raised a force of a few thousand rebel cossacks and ambushed and killed Colonel Iurii Dolgorukii, the commander Tsar Peter had charged with the task of purging the Upper Reaches (1707). Bulavin subsequently expanded his army to 15,000–25,000 men by welcoming under his banner fugitive peasants, army deserters, runaway laborers from the Voronezh shipyards, refugee Old Believers, and some Zaporozhian Cossacks. He seized Cherkassk in April 1708 and beheaded Host Ataman Maksimov, but then he overreached by trying to campaign against the Russian garrisons at Azov and on the lower Volga. By July 1708 Bulavin had been killed and punitive detachments from the Russian army had restored order at Cherkassk. The commander of the punitive expedition, Vasilii Dolgorukii, avenging brother of the late Iurii Dolgorukii, had orders from the tsar to complete the purge of the Upper Reaches: Tsar Peter may have feared that the Bulavin insurgency might spread west through Bakhmut and link up with the rebellions of Hordienko's Zaporozhians and Mazepa's Ukrainian Cossacks. By Vasilii Dolgorukii's own count his suppression of the Bulavin Revolt claimed 23,500 rebel cossack lives. It is possible that 90–95 of the cossacks of the Upper Reaches were killed or dispersed.[68]

After the Upper Reaches had been emptied and the lower Don restored to order, St. Petersburg kept the Host busy defending its eastern border on the Kuban steppe, which was vulnerable to raids by the Kuban Horde and the Nekrasovite Cossacks.[69] In 1711 the Russian army's defeat by the Turks on the Prut River in Moldavia forced Peter I to accept an armistice that restored Azov to the Porte. A new survey was conducted to redefine the border between the Don and the Dnepr and the Don Cossacks were ordered to respect this border and live in peace with the Crimean Tatars and Azov Turks. They largely did so; Don Cossack raids for slaves ceased, and the Don Cossacks remained active in raiding economy only peripherally, as mediators and ransom brokers for prisoners the Azov Turks, Nogais, and Kalmyks had taken from each other. This peace was broken only for a brief interval, during the revolt of Crimean prince Bakhty Girei (1715–1718), who attempted to establish his own new horde on the Kuban steppe.

But there were no official restraints on the Don Cossacks involving themselves in the military struggle in the North Caucasus. They provided volunteers to assist the Terek Cossacks against the Chechens and other mountain peoples of the Caucasus; they contributed a few thousand men for Peter I's 1722 expedition into northern Persia; and in the later 1720s and 1730s some 3,000–4,000 Don Cossacks—about a quarter of the Host's total strength—performed annual garrison duty in Russian-occupied northern Persia.[70]

In the course of the Russo-Turkish War of 1735–1739 Empress Anna ordered the mobilization of all adult males in the Host, making the Don Host "the first region in the Russian Empire, and most likely the first in modern Europe, to experience universal military mobilization."[71] So many men were sent off to serve with the Russian field army that the Don region was left undefended and the Nekrasovites raided in 1737 inflicting heavy losses in people and livestock. This forced the Don Cossacks to join with the Kalmyks in retaliatory attacks on the Nekrasovites and Kuban Horde, and in 1740 the Nekrasovites had to request the sultan to find them new refuges in other parts of the Ottoman Empire.[72]

The Belgrade Treaty (1739) once again handed back Azov to the Porte and reestablished the borders of 1700. The Russian government now sought to exercise tighter control over the Host to prevent the occurrence of anything like another Bulavin revolt while at the same time keeping the Don Cossacks ready for future service with the Russian field army. To achieve this it relied upon four control devices.

The first of these involved redefining the authority of the Ataman of the Host so that he exercised greater authority over the Cossack rank-and-file but answered directly to St. Petersburg. Most of the traditional liberties of the Host would still be recognized, but starting in 1738 the Cossack general assembly would lose its right to elect its ataman. Danilo Efremov (r. 1738–1753) would instead be appointed ataman by Empress Anna; his son Stepan Efremov (r. 1753–1774) would likewise succeed him by Imperial appointment. It had already become established practice for St. Petersburg to confirm loyal atamans "in perpetuity" and encourage them to build enough patronage power to tame the *starshina* and dictate to the general assembly. The Efremovs were so successful in their practice of patronage politics they were able to amass considerable fortunes in cash, land, livestock, and slaves; Ataman Stepan Efremov owned over five hundred serfs.[73]

Second, the central government's administration of Don Cossack Affairs was reorganized. In the seventeenth century the Don Host had been under the jurisdiction of the Ambassadors' Chancellery (*Posol'skii prikaz*), acknowledging the Host's status as an independent vassal polity whose inhabitants were not direct subjects of the tsar. Then Peter I's *guberniia* reform of 1708–1709 had classified the Host as a special autonomous region within Azov Governorate, with the Azov governor exercising higher command authority over the Host in military affairs. In 1720, the Host was placed under the jurisdiction of the War College (VK), reflecting the new view that the Don Cossacks were first and foremost a formation of irregulars within the Russian field army deriving their special privileges from that military function.[74]

The third control device was the juridical redefinition of the Cossack condition. In connection with Tsar Peter's First Revision for the soul tax a census was taken of all males in the Don Host. The census was then used to compile an official register of "legal" hereditary Don Cossacks—those in active service and descendant from men who had settled on Host territory before 1696. Those males who did not meet these tests were classified as "resident *burlaki*" permitted to reside in the region but without the rights to enroll in Cossack service or receive shares of the cash subsidy the tsar issued to the officially registered Cossacks. This allowed St. Petersburg to permit in-migration while preventing it from overloading and "diluting" the Cossack register.[75] The Host *starshina* were reclassified as holders of officer rank in Imperial service by appointment by the VK, with the right to pass on their rank to their sons; in other words, the *starshina* now became government-accredited hereditary nobles.[76]

The final control device was the enforcement of universal military service obligations through collective security bonds upon Cossack villages, which carried fines of ten rubles for every settlement failing to meet the Russian field army's mobilization quota. This burden was offset, however, by relaxing the traditional stricture against Cossack agriculture. Now that the Cossack register had been fixed but in-migrant *burlaki* permitted to remain in residence, it made sense to allow Cossacks to use *burlak* labor to cultivate the land so that the Host frontier could be conquered agriculturally as well as militarily. It also made sense to remove the ban on in-migration by Ukrainians (1763). There would be no repeat of the purge of the Upper Reaches as had occurred in the 1690s, when Peter I had ordered the burning of cossack agricultural settlements on the upper Don.

However, the diversification of Don Cossack economy would intensify social differentiation and feed resentment of the privileged *starshina* by the *chern'* they were attaching as their tenants.[77] Riots against Ataman Stepan Efremov in 1772 would force Catherine II to depose Efremov and investigate for possible linkages of this unrest with the new rebellion among the Iaik Cossacks led by Emel'ian Pugachev, a deserter from the Don Host.[78]

Frontier populations and the Black Sea trade

The government of Empress Elizabeth Petrovna had recognized the potential value of a Black Sea trade but had seen little opportunity to begin building it. The 1739 Belgrade Treaty had required that the Russians evacuate Azov and that any Russian wares exported across the Black Sea be carried on Turkish ships. Enough Russian interest in trade with the Ottoman Empire remained that Russian customs houses were set up along the border, at Kremenchug, Perevolok, Cherkassk, and at Temerikov at the confluence of the Don and Temerik rivers (1749), near the site of Fort St. Dmitrii, where the Don Cossacks could do some trading with Greek, Armenian, and Turkish merchants from the Ottoman lands.[79] But these stations received less traffic than Nezhin, to the west in Ukraine; Turkish ships visiting Cherkassk, for example, often departed unladen.[80]

In 1745, Prince Boris Grigor'evich Iusupov, President of the Commerce College, had written to the Russian resident in Istanbul asking him to sound out Italian, Greek, Armenian, and Turkish merchants in Istanbul as to the prospects of developing Russian trade across the Black Sea on Turkish carriers or, ideally, on Russian ships. Iusupov dreamed of the day the Black Sea might be as commercially exploited as the Baltic and the Caspian, and he thought English and Dutch trading interests might welcome the Black Sea trade as a safer alternative to the Levantine and trans-Caucasian trades with Persia.[81]

The reply from resident Nepliuev was not encouraging. The sultan's government remained firmly opposed to allowing Russian vessels on the Black Sea; any Russian commodities coming across the Black Sea would have to be carried on Turkish ships. In 1738 the sultan had not even allowed French ships to transport Ottoman troops to Crimea. Nepliuev emphasized the French would continue to press the sultan to block Russian maritime power on the Black Sea in order to protect their commercial interests in the Levant. The only significant Russian–Ottoman trade at this time was overland, to Nezhin, and confined to regional circulation. Nepliuev observed that European merchants in Istanbul never saw any Russian wares and had no apparent interest in them—not even the Venetians. Although the Russians still had a base at Taganrog, it was inadequate as a trade and shipping *entrepot*; it was militarily insecure, poorly provisioned, and unvisited by foreign merchants.[82] The lower Don customs house at Temerikov had observed some increase in Urals iron purchases by visiting Ottoman merchants, and in 1757 a Russian trading company was established at Temerikov with the intent of lobbying the Porte to permit Russian vessels on the Black Sea. But despite the bribe money it circulated among Ottoman officials the sultan's government held firm on its ban.[83]

The Commerce College therefore had to turn its attention westward to Ukraine in search of profitable trade routes. In 1759–1761 court councillor Dmitrii Lodygin investigated for the Senate the trade opportunities at Nezhin, the Zaporozhian Sich's trade with the Turks, and the possibility of getting the Porte to acknowledge as protected a trade route from southern Poland through Bender to Ochakov, with a branch linking Ochakov with New Serbia and the Zaporozhian Sich. But ambassador Obreskov cautioned that the Ochakov-New Serbia branch was vulnerable on the Bucak steppe and that it would be costly to ship Russian commodities all the way through southern Poland. In anticipation that such routes might become more feasible in the future, however, the Russian government invested in the agricultural and commercial development of New Serbia and Slavonic Serbia. In 1760, their inhabitants were given privileges for a duty-free horse trade, liquor sales, and grain sales at the new customs house at Orlik and at Balta. To connect this trade with the lower Dnepr Lodygin proposed in 1762 that wharves be built at Nikitin Urochische and Russian and Hetmanate military convoys be organized.[84]

Thus by Catherine II's reign projects for exploiting the Black Sea trade had been raised, but they could not be put into action as long as the Porte stood by its ban on Russian maritime traffic in the Black Sea.

Left Bank Ukraine: the fate of the Hetmanate

The incorporation into the Russian Empire of the Hetmanate (Left Bank Ukraine, that is, Ukraine east of the Dnepr, with Kiev) occurred very gradually. Some would argue that it was already foreshadowed in the terms of the Russian protectorate Bohdan Khmelnyts'kyi had negotiated with Tsar Aleksei's envoy at Pereiaslav in 1654. But the incremental reduction of the sovereignty of the hetmans in fact took several decades and at each stage was apparently driven by Russian military needs rather than any Russian repudiation of Hetmanate sovereignty in principle. The Hetmanate administration was suspended more than once when particular hetmans demonstrated their political unreliability, but it was not finally abolished until 1765.[85]

An important early instance of Russian military exigencies invoked to reduce hetman authority occurred during the Great Northern War. In 1707 Peter I saw the need to intensify military resource mobilization in Ukraine and integrate the defense of Left Bank Ukraine with that of Sloboda Ukraine. Therefore he created a Russian imperial Governorate of Kiev. This turned the commandant of the Russian garrison at Kiev, Dm. M. Golitsyn, into a *gubernator* with direct administrative authority over some of the larger or more strategically situated eastern Ukrainian towns (Kiev, Pereiaslav, Chernihiv, Nezhin, Kamennyi Zaton). There were now two uneasily coexisting military administrations in Left Bank Ukraine: that of the Hetmanate, based at Baturyn, and that of the Kiev Governorate.

This reduction of the territory and military power of the Hetmanate alarmed Hetman Ivan Mazepa, but it was not the main reason he turned renegade and joined with the Swedes in 1708. Mazepa went over to Charles XII because he saw that Charles XII was turning his army south toward Ukraine; that Ukraine was about to become the main theater of war and suffer horrific devastation; and that the Russians stood to be defeated. But Mazepa tragically miscalculated. The Russians destroyed the Swedish army at Poltava and Perevolok in summer 1709; Peter I had Mazepa anathematized as a traitor and dethroned; and Mazepa died soon after at the Ottoman fortress of Bender. His secretary Pylyp Orlyk tried from Bender to assemble an alliance with the remnants of Charles XII's army, the Turks, Crimean Tatars, and the Polish adherents of Stanisław Leszczynski, but by 1713 he had failed. The Russians replaced Mazepa with Hetman Ivan Skoropad'skyi (r. 1708–1722), who retained Tsar Peter's trust and was able to convince the tsar to reaffirm most of the hetman's powers as defined in the 1687 Kolomak Articles.

Skoropad'skyi was succeeded by unconfirmed acting Hetman Ivan Polubotok (r. 1722–1724). Polubotok was arrested and executed in 1724 because he had tried to sabotage the work of the new Little Russian College attached to his court for "bringing an end to the disorder that has arisen in the Ukrainian courts and army."[86]

The Little Russian College represented a more serious Russian limitation of the powers of the hetman. It was a board of six Russian officers from the dragoon regiments garrisoning Ukraine; it reported directly to the Imperial Senate at St. Petersburg; it received cash and grain collections from Ukrainian taxpayers and supervised their distribution as pay to the officers of the Ukrainian Cossack regiments; it oversaw the billeting of Russian troops in Ukraine; and it came to expect that every order from the hetman's administration be submitted to it for countersigning.

The Hetmanate was suspended from 1724 to 1727 while St. Petersburg looked for a new hetman "completely faithful and reputable." Danilo Apostol' appeared to fit this requirement and the Hetmanate was restored for him in 1727; Russian supervision of Ukrainian administration was removed from the Senate and restored to the College of Foreign Affairs. But when Apostol' died in 1734 Empress Anna's government left the office of hetman unfilled and placed Ukraine under a new Governing Council of the Hetman's Office, a board of three Russians and three Ukrainians overseen by a Russian general. This was probably not intended as a definitive solution of the question of Ukrainian autonomy, but it did allow St. Petersburg to tighten its control over Ukrainian manpower and revenue in order to build the Ukrainian Line and strengthen the Russian army deployed on Ukraine's southern frontier. During the 1735–1739 Russo-Turkish War the population of Left Bank Ukraine was required to support the stationing of 50–75 Russian regiments at an annual cost of 1.5 million rubles. About 35,000 Ukrainians perished in this war.[87]

While touring Ukraine in 1744, Empress Elizabeth Petrovna was petitioned by some *starshyna* officers to dismantle the Governing Council of the Hetman's Office and allow the election of a new hetman. She finally agreed to this in 1747. Part of the reason was that she had at hand a candidate of obvious political reliability, Kyrilo Rozumovsky, already at age 22 a field marshal and major landowner in Ukraine and the younger brother of the empress' morganatic consort Count Oleksii Rozumovsky. Another likely reason was that Count Shuvalov's project of eliminating the customs barrier between Ukraine and Russia provided the opportunity to reform the finances and administration of the Hetmanate.[88] In 1750, Rozumovsky was elected by the *starshyna* at Hluhiv and confirmed by St. Petersburg. He could resume the tradition of governing through his General Military Court and General Military Chancellery, and the traditional territorial administrative structure of Cossack regiments, companies, and barracks (*polki, sotny, kurenia*) was reaffirmed; but the *rada* councils would be held less frequently now and would represent only officers. Most importantly a Russian state councilor was attached to Rozumovsky to exercise control over finances. All revenues and expenditures would have to be reported to St. Petersburg. Nor could the hetman appoint his own missions to foreign courts or refuse to contribute Ukrainian troops to Russian campaigns.[89]

Under Hetman Rozumovsky the *starshyna* was able to amass estates with large numbers of peasant tenants, in imitation of the Russian higher nobility. Andrei Polubotok held 1,269 households, for example; the Kochubeis had 1,193 households; Galaganov and Lizogubov had three or four hundred each.[90]

From the outset of Empress Catherine II's reign Rozumovsky worked hard to ingratiate himself with her, and generally succeeded. He also allied with Nikita Panin. But he could not get himself accepted by Catherine's favorite Grigorii Orlov or the faction of Bestuzhev-Riumin. In 1763 Rozumovsky overreached by holding a special *rada* with his *starshyna* and putting his name to their petition calling on the empress to confirm their traditional rights by permitting them to recreate the judicial system authorized by the Lithuanian Statute and establish a parliament modeled on the Polish Diet; for his own part Rozumovsky expressed the hope the empress would confirm the Rozumovsky family's hereditary rights to the title of Hetman.[91] The empress' secretary, Grigorii Teplov, who had served several years as Rozumovsky's financial controller, sent her a secret memorandum painting a bleak picture of Ukraine's administration. Teplov portrayed Rozumovsky as the puppet of the *starshyna* colonels, who were able to use their power to rig the elections of their captains, purchase exemptions from military duty, and buy up the lands of impoverished Cossacks. Teplov believed that there was too much peasant tenant mobility, that landlords were able to draw new tenants with promises of temporary rent exemption but unable to keep their tenants once the period of exemption had passed; to raise agricultural productivity and tax receipts it would thus be necessary to introduce full serfdom as practiced in Russia. Teplov warned her that the *starshyna* were content with enjoying their traditional rights and privileges but bent on expanding them at Russia's expense; they needed to be reminded that Ukraine was Little Russia (*Malorossiia*), always a part of Russia, not a realm separate.[92]

On December 10, 1763, Catherine issued a decree confirming that peasant tenants in Ukraine still had the right of departure, provided their landlords gave permission; but her decree echoed Teplov's argument that peasants ought to be induced to settle permanently in one place so that agriculture and taxes did not suffer. There were rumors that Grigorii Orlov was pressing the empress to remove Rozumovsky so that Orlov could receive appointment as field marshal of Ukrainian Cossack forces. Finally, in February or March 1764 she held a private interview with Rozumovsky and convinced him to relinquish the title of Hetman in return for a pension of 50,000 rubles. Soon after the College of Foreign Affairs recommended abolishing the Hetmanate and restoring the Little Russian College under a Russian President and Governor General. This Little Russian College was established at Hluhiv on November 10, 1764, with four Russian members (Brandt, Meshcherskii, Khvostov, and Natal'in) and four men from the Ukrainian *starshyna* (Kochubei, Tumansky, Zhuravki, and Apostol'). As its President and as Governor General of Malorossiia the empress appointed Petr Aleksandrovich Rumiantsev, who had spent part of his childhood in Ukraine and had distinguished himself in the Seven Years' War.[93]

Catherine II acquainted Rumiantsev with Teplov's diagnosis of Ukraine's ills and instructed him to integrate Ukraine into the Empire by following the manner in which Lifland and Finland had been managed: by finding reasonable men within the native elite, arranging their election to offices, and bestowing privileges on them so that Ukrainians would cease to "look upon us as a wolf in the forest." Rewards would have to be liberally distributed, as "the last Hetman loved to be depicted for his generosity of bounty and hospitality."[94]

In his term as Governor General and President of the Little Russian College (1765–1769) Rumiantsev made an inspection tour of the Ukrainian Line, placed Russian officials on the judicial board of the General Court, extended Russian military law over the Cossacks, and found new revenue sources for the Russian treasury by introducing stamped paper and turning the hunting lands of the hetmans into state lands and taxing their inhabitants. He took the first measures toward introducing serfdom into Ukraine: In 1766, the Ukrainian *starshyna* was allowed to purchase villages as allodial property; in 1767 the *starshyna* was given the privileges of the Russian nobility (*dvorianstvo*), including the right to send representatives to Catherine's Legislative Commission and place their sons in the Noble Corps of Cadets.[95]

But his most important act was introducing a variant of the soul tax for the support of the Russian army on Ukrainian soil (September 9, 1765). Ukraine was divided into twenty military districts, each district electing a propertied man as commissar to supervise quarterly collection of a new "ruble tax" from every male taxpayer. This new cash tax would replace the old provender and forage taxes collected in kind. The projected annual yield from this new ruble tax was about 250,000 rubles—more than twice what Ukrainians had paid for maintaining the Russian regiments in the 1740s.

The Russian military presence in Ukraine could now be tripled in number over the Russians stationed there in Ukraine in 1731, for the commissars could manage their billeting as well as provisioning. Rumiantsev announced in 1768 the stationing of a Ukrainian Division of seven dragoon, carabinier, and hussar regiments and eight infantry regiments—19,981 troops in all. These regiments were of Russian recruits, many of them from central and northern Russia, and the regiments were posted to most of the major towns in Ukraine: Starodub, Myrhorod, Poltava, Chernihiv, Kiev, Priluki, Khar'kov, Akhtyrka, Valuiki, Lubny, Belgrade, Kremenchug, Hadiach, Perevoloch'nia, and Izium. Since the commissars found just 30,000 households in which to billet these 20,000 troops, a billeting rate of two Russian soldiers in every three households became the norm.[96] Many of the Ukrainian *cahiers* presented at the empress' Legislative Commission in 1767 were devoted to complaints about billeting.

Rumiantsev also notified the Senate that it was necessary to reform the Ukrainian Cossack territorial regiments (*polki*) in order to prepare them for the approaching war. The *polki* varied greatly in strength: some had one to three thousand Cossacks, others just a few hundred. Rumiantsev proposed there be 20,000 Cossacks and officers, in regiments of one standard strength.[97]

Otherwise Rumiantsev worked very shrewdly, co-opting the friendlier elements in the *starshyna* by offering them posts and lands while simultaneously presenting his reforms to the peasantry and Cossack rank-and-file as efforts to combat the socioeconomic differentiation that had been servilizing them to their own *staryshyna*. Since the late seventeenth-century antagonism between the *starshyna* and the Ukrainian peasantry and townsmen had been fed by the colonels' increasing power to engross land and labor. By recognizing the *starshyna* as privileged members of the Imperial noble estate Rumiantsev's reforms guaranteed there would be no major outcry from the *starshyna* over the abolition of the Hetmanate. And for the time being the spirit of social revolt among the Ukrainian and Zaporozhian lower classes was deflected outwards as support for *haidamak* religious warfare in Right Bank Ukraine. But it was also the case that the new ruble tax soon fell into arrears and the heavier tax burden provoked further peasant tenant flight.[98]

From Sloboda Ukraine to the Khar'kov and New Russian governorates

One of the last parts of the Pontic steppe to undergo Russian and Ukrainian colonization was the region running along the Northern Donets, above the territory of the Zaporozhian Cossacks, between eastern Ukraine and southern Muscovy. This region had been freely nomadized by the Nogais in the sixteenth and early seventeenth centuries. Two developments finally opened it up to Russian and Ukrainian colonization in the mid-seventeenth century: the construction of the Belgorod Line, bringing Muscovite military colonization to its eastern edge; and the Ukrainian Cossack revolts against the Polish Crown, which drove the colonels and captains of some eastern Ukrainian Cossack regiments to emigrate and request service and protection under the Moscow tsars. In 1638 a party of Ukrainian Cossacks under Iakiv Ostrianyn received permission from Tsar Mikhail to settle at Chuguev and perform border defense service for Muscovy. The intensified cossack unrest in Ukraine over the next several years led another 10,000 Ukrainian emigres to resettle in this region; the Muscovite government came to call them *Cherkasy*, but the Ukrainian colonists referred to themselves as *Slobozhane* because they settled in small "free settlements" (*slobody*) exempt from taxation. In 1652 Colonel Dzinkovs'kyi settled a large number of Ukrainian Cossack on the Tikhaia Sosna River. Moscow agreed to allow the construction here of a fortress, Ostrogozhsk, and stationed sixty volunteer musketeers and gunners at Ostrogozhsk to assist in its defense.

This established a precedent for the next few decades of colonization in what would be called Sloboda Ukraine. The region was claimed as Muscovite territory but its service population was to be mixed, with some Russian service colonists under the jurisdiction of the Belgorod Army Group and the Military Chancellery, while the majority of military colonists were Ukrainian Cossacks salaried from the tsar's treasury, exempt from Muscovite taxes, privileged with the rights to distill liquor and exploit hunting and fishing appurtenances duty-free, and enjoying the right to elect their own captains and atamans. Because Ukrainian Cossacks predominated in the region Sloboda Ukraine came to be subdivided into four Cossack-style regimental territorial administrations: the Ostrogozhsk Regiment, the Khar'kov Regiment, the Sumy Regiment, and the Akhtyrka Regiment. The largest of these regiments was the Ostrogozhsk Regiment, with 1,000 registered Cossacks; the other three regiments had strengths of 600–800 men each. In order to coordinate the defense of these territories with the Muscovite garrison forces and the districts of the Belgorod Line the Cossack regiments were placed under the military command authority of the Belgorod Army Group.[99] The completion of the Izium Line in the late 1680s provided a stronger southern shield for Sloboda Ukraine and made it possible to spin off from the Ostrogozhsk Regiment a fifth Sloboda regiment, the Izium Regiment.

By the end of the century the population of Sloboda Ukraine approached 120,000, most of them ethnic Ukrainians. Sloboda Cossack communities underwent social differentiation in order to support life military service by the able-bodied. The colonels and captains came to be recognized as a privileged *starshyna* with the right to own peasants. The rank-and-file Cossacks held service lands in repartitionable collective blocs, like the *odnodvortsy* of the southern frontier, and supplemented their cash salaries with income from duty-free enterprise. Those not selected for service in the Cossack regiments were categorized as either "supporters" (*podpomoshchniki*), assigned to provide provender and forage to Cossack households and to raise funds for the purchase of mounts and equipment, or as "working lodgers" (*podsosedki*), free but economically dependent support laborers residing in the homes of active-duty Cossacks and helping to till their lands.[100]

Originally the Sloboda Cossacks were supposed to be tax-exempt, privileged with exemption from excise and appurtenance duties, and used entirely for border defense. But Moscow soon broke these promises very much in the manner it had redefined the *odnodvorets* condition in southern Muscovy. From 1666 Sloboda Cossacks had to pay a few thousand rubles annually in state rent on bridges, mills, stud farms, and customs houses to the Belgorod Army Group. From 1687 they began serving on long-distance campaigns with the tsar's army: in 1687, on Golitsyn's expedition against the Crimean Khanate; in 1691, on the lower Don; in 1697, on the Azov campaign of Peter I; in 1700 far off to the north, on the Pskov front, against the Swedes; in 1705, against the mutineers at Astrakhan; and in 1725–1727 a thousand Sloboda Cossacks were stationed in Russian-occupied northern Persia. Having burdened the Sloboda regiments with distant campaign duty, Peter had to take measures to tighten Russian control over Sloboda Ukraine and insulate it against the unrest spreading from the Zaporozhian and Don Cossack Hosts. During the Bulavin Revolt (1707–1708) the tsar ordered the new Russian fortress of Pavlovsk built at the confluence of the Osereda and Don rivers to prevent Bulavin's rebels from bringing their insurgency into Bakhmut and Sloboda Ukraine. Peter's decree of December 18, 1708, dividing the Empire into eight governorates to facilitate military resource mobilization also affected Sloboda Ukraine: it was directly incorporated into the Empire, divided between the Kiev and Azov governorates along the Orel, Mozha, Donets, and Vol'cha rivers. After the defeat of Charles XII at Poltava part of the Russian army was quartered in Sloboda Ukraine and all supreme military and civil authority in Sloboda Ukraine was concentrated in the hands of the commander-in-chief of the quartered Russian division; this included the authority to order Sloboda Cossacks relocated to new settlements. Sloboda *podpomoshchniki* were required to provide the billeted Russian regiments with flour, groats, hay, salt, and oil. This condition lasted down to 1734.

Peter I had tried to impose a ruble head tax on every male support worker in 1697 but Cossack petitions had forced him to back down. But starting in 1722 the soul tax was levied on all male support workers and working lodgers in Sloboda Ukraine, and in 1729 all the Sloboda regiments save the Ostrogozhsk Regiment lost their traditional Cossack structure and were given the same organization as Russian line regiments.[101]

The soul tax and the *corvee* obligations of southern Russian *odnodvortsy*, Sloboda inhabitants, and Ukrainian taxpayers were applied to the construction in 1731–1740 of an imposing new defense line, the Ukrainian Line, which ran from the Orel River south of Perevolochnia to the Northern Donets south of Izium (a distance of 285 kilometers) in order to augment the old Belgorod and Izium Lines. By 1740 the Ukrainian Line had eighteen fortresses and 140 redoubts and military colonists at twenty-two *sloboda* colonies. In this case, however, the military colonists were Land Militia foot and mounted regiments mobilized from southern Russia (Tambov, Kozlov, Riazhsk, etc.) rather than colonists from Sloboda Ukraine or Left Bank Ukraine. In other words Russian military colonization was being extended westward to separate Sloboda Ukraine and Left Bank Ukraine from the territory of the Zaporozhian Host.[102] The military administration of the Ukrainian Line and its colonists was headquartered in the Land Militia Chancery at Fort Belev (until the dissolution of the Land Militia regiments in 1765); civil administration of the territory of the Ukrainian Line was divided in 1740 between the province of Belgorod in Belgorod Governorate and, for Line territory from Bakhmut eastward, the chancery of Bakhmut Province in Voronezh Governorate.[103]

Not surprisingly the Ukrainian Line reduced the significance of the Sloboda regiments for frontier defense. Sloboda Cossacks continued to serve with the army on campaigns abroad—in Poland in 1733–1735, and in Crimea in 1736–1739—but their role in defending the steppe east of Poltava and west of Izium had shifted to the Land Militia regiments of the Ukrainian Line. The opinion that the Sloboda Cossacks were militarily obsolescent was expressed by Adjutant General Shakhovskoi, who conducted a general census of Sloboda Ukraine in 1732 and headed a special chancery in 1733–1737 examining tax and provisioning matters and reviewing deeds and property titles. Shakhovskoi proposed permanently capping the Akhtyrka Regiment at 1,000 Cossacks and the other four regiments at 800 Cossacks each; all five regiments were to be under a brigade commander who would in turn answer to the commander-in-chief of the army's Ukrainian Division; the officers of the Cossack regiments were to be deprived of their duty-free appurtenances and the right to rent land and required to live off their cash pay from the Treasury; all support workers and working lodgers—indeed all non-noble and non-clerical inhabitants not in regimental service—were to be ascribed to Cossack households as peasant tenants; and those Cossacks most fit for service were be transferred into a new dragoon regiment. The Shakhovskoi System proved so unpopular with Sloboda Ukrainians that Empress Elizabeth ordered it nullified in 1743. She also expanded the Cossack register to 7,500, but in order to transfer the best Cossacks into a Sloboda Hussar Regiment.[104]

Hussar units had become the new preoccupation of the War College and the raising of them now dictated new colonization campaigns and administrative reorganization across eastern Ukraine. During 1733–1741 Field Marshal Münnich had experimented with the formation of hussar companies raised from immigrant Serbian, Moldavian, Hungarian, and Georgian volunteers. They had performed creditably on Münnich's Turkish campaigns and Russian cavalry commanders had come to see them as tactically superior to both dragoons and cuirassiers. It was also seen as an advantage that they came into Russian service with their own gear and mounts, making them cheaper troops; the College of Foreign Affairs calculated that it cost forty guldens to ready one Serbian hussar for war, but 200 guldens to prepare one Russian recruit.[105] The cooling of relations between the Habsburg and Romanov empires in the 1740s delayed for a decade Russian efforts to recruit more Serbian hussar volunteers, but by 1751 Elizabeth Petrovna's government was prepared to resume it, in part because Vorontsov, Bestuzhev-Riumin, and Shuvalov were advising her to step up Russian agitation on the behalf of the Orthodox Slavs of the Balkans. In the summer of 1751 the Austrian *Hofkriegsrat* granted the request of Colonel Ivan Horvat and some other Serbian officers to transfer into Russian service. In October 1751 Horvat and 281 Serb officers, subalterns, and their families arrived in Kiev. The following March Bestuzhev-Riumin asked the Austrians for permission to recruit another 1,200 Serbs for Russian service.[106]

In spring 1752 Empress Elizabeth Petrovna invited the Serbian volunteers to settle on two territories on the western and eastern edges of Zaporozhia. Ivan Samuilovic Horvat was authorized to form 432 Serbs, Macedonians, Bulgarians, and Wallachians into the nuclei of a regiment of hussars and a regiment of *pandur* infantry on steppe territory east of the Dnepr, from Kavarly River to Kamenka and Omel'ianka. This territory was to be called New Serbia (*Novaia Serbiia*), although Moldavians were actually about two-thirds of Horvat's group. Horvat's colonists would be organized in 20 redoubt colonies under their officers, much in the old manner of the *polk* Cossacks of Sloboda Ukraine; their commander would answer to Major-General Ivan Glebov, commandant of the Ukrainian Line fortress of St. Elizabeth, and to the War College. The territory assigned to New Serbia included lands formerly part of the Ukrainian Poltava and Myrhorod Cossack *polki*, but Ukrainian settlers in New Serbia would have to leave: only the invited Serbian immigrants were allowed to settle here. Hetman Rozumovsky protested this but was ignored. By 1758 there were about 10,000 settlers in New Serbia. In 1759 the Senate formed a New Serbia Chancellery to oversee their administration. Over the course of the 1750s St. Petersburg spent about 50,000 rubles a year maintaining New Serbia.[107]

A second group of volunteers under Sevic and Drepreradovic was given permission to settle in sixteen redoubt colonies south of Sloboda Ukraine in the triangle above the Bakhmut and Lugan rivers. This territory was called Slavonic Serbia (*Slavianoserbiia*). Settlement here began only in 1754 and proceeded more slowly than in New Serbia, and it proved harder here to forbid colonization by Ukrainians moving down from Sloboda Ukraine.

Thus the western and eastern edges of Zaporozhia had been detached from the control of the Zaporozhian Cossack Host and turned over to foreign colonists, who assumed much of the steppe patrol and field army duty previously performed by the Zaporozhians.

Meanwhile General Glebov, commandant of St. Elizabeth on the Ukrainian Line, began transforming the service population of the Line. Previously the Line garrisons had been Russian *odnodvortsy* from the northeast. Glebov began colonizing the Line with Ukrainian immigrants from Left Bank and even Right Bank Ukraine, enrolling them in a New Sloboda Cossack Regiment (*Novoslobodskii kazach'i polk*) directly under the War College.[108] Many of those enrolling in the New Sloboda Cossack Regiment were Ukrainian settlers who been driven out of New Serbia.

This was a kind of replication of old Sloboda Ukraine, only deeper in the steppe and closer to the Crimean frontier. Old Sloboda Ukraine was now treated as a mere rear reserve because its Cossack regiments were no longer viewed as useful for either frontier defense or field army service.

The next steps in the political reorganization of the eastern Ukrainian frontier were taken at the outset of Catherine II's reign. Her decree of June 11, 1763, opened New Serbia to free colonists from Poland, Left Bank Ukraine, Sloboda Ukraine, and Russia. Many of these were fugitive serfs or Old Believers, but the empress allowed some of them to enroll in the hussar and *pandura* regiments and the rest to till the land under six years' initial immunity from taxes. Russian landlords whose fugitive peasants had already found refuge in New Serbia were paid compensation by the Imperial Treasury. This demilitarization of New Serbia was followed by a decree of June 11, 1764, removing the special autonomy of New Serbia, Slavonic Serbia, the Ukrainian Line, and the New Sloboda Cossack Regiment and incorporating them directly into the Imperial administrative system as the constituent parts of a new governorate called New Russia (*Novorossiiskaia guberniia*).[109] By 1767, Elizavetgrad Province, the most densely settled core of New Russia Governorate, had about 73,000 inhabitants. After the 1768–1774 Turkish war a government-organized settlement program would produce dramatic demographic expansion in New Russia.

In 1765 old Sloboda Ukraine was dissolved. Catherine II decided that the Sloboda Cossack regiments were obsolete and should be replaced with hussar regiments; Sloboda Ukraine, previously divided between Kiev and Belgorod governorates, should be reunified as its own new governorate. In decrees of December 16, 1764, and March 3, 1765, the empress established a new Khar'kov Governorate capitalled at Khar'kov and comprising the provinces of Akhtyrka, Sumy, Ostrogozhsk, and Izium. Major Shcherbinin of the Izmailovskii Guards was charged with the task of abolishing the old Cossack regiments and forming their best men into five new hussar regiments. Traditional Cossack administration was thereby abolished; military administration now followed the ordinances of the Russian army and civil administration the laws of the Empire. Each province was to elect six commissars to oversee the legal and fiscal transformation. The support workers and working lodgers were reclassified as "military treasury inhabitants" subject to the soul tax (although at the slightly reduced rate of 85 kopeks per soul from men not holding stills and 95 kopeks from men having vodka distilling privileges). Peasant tenants on hussar or noble estates were recognized as landlords' serfs. However, the provender, forage and equipping money Sloboda inhabitants delivered to the hussar regiments would be paid for by the Imperial Treasury, which earmarked another 100,000 rubles for salarying and equipping the new hussar regiments.[110]

Thus the population of Sloboda Ukraine had been relegated to the same fate as the *odnodvortsy* of southern Russia: a minority was kept in service but the vast majority was turned into state peasants liable for the soul tax. There was one important difference, however: after the 1768–1774 Russo-Turkish War eliminated the threat from the Crimean Khanate larger-scale manorial economy would develop on a larger scale in Khar'kov region, with the result that by the end of the century about half of its population had been turned into private serfs, most of them working estates held by their former *starshyna*, who had been granted hereditary noble status on the basis of officer rank.[111]

The Zaporozhian Cossack Host

The Zaporozhian Cossack Host headquartered at the *Sich* ("clearing") near the lower Dnepr rapids had launched Bohdan Khmel'nytskyi's cossack revolution establishing the Hetmanate in Left Bank Ukraine. But it had striven thereafter to preserve its independence from the Hetmanate in order to pursue a raiding economy unrestrained by any other power. It conducted land and naval raids upon the Commonwealth, Muscovy, the Crimean Khanate, Bucak, and sometimes Anatolia and Istanbul itself. It often rebelled against Left Bank hetmans it considered too servile toward the Muscovites or toward the Ukrainian *starshyna* elite. At the peak of the Zaporozhian Host's power from the 1660s to the 1680s it controlled territory covering about 80,000 square kilometers, directly abutting the Crimean Khanate in the south, the Hetmanate in the west, the Don Cossack Host in the east, and Sloboda Ukraine to the north.[112]

The 1686 Eternal Peace between the Commonwealth and Muscovy had confirmed Zaporozhia as a protectorate under the tsar, but a protectorate separate from the Hetmanate. Tsar Peter I and Hetman Mazepa both tried to tame Zaporozhian raiding by resettling border populations, building border fortresses, and controlling provisioning and trade, but neither was entirely successful. Locust invasion, famine, and plague in 1690 exacerbated social antagonisms within the Zaporozhian Host and divided it into two factions, one looking for opportunity to raid the Crimean Khanate, the other willing to ally with the Crimean Tatars to destroy the Russian fortresses, overthrow Mazepa, and restore true independence to the Host. For the next ten years Mazepa had to wage war against the latter faction, led by Host Secretrary Petryk. Petryk's insurgents were unable to rouse Left Bank Ukraine to their cause but they found a more enthusiastic welcome in Right Bank Ukraine. The decade of cossack warfare in western Ukraine did much to defeat the efforts of the Polish nobility to recolonize the Right Bank. The treaties of Karlowitz and Constantinople (1699–1700) dashed Petryk's hopes that the Crimean Tatars and Turks would come to his aid, and by the terms of these treaties the Zaporozhian Host was required to curtail its raiding in order to keep the peace.

For some of them the ban on raiding was no easier to accept than it was for the Crimean Tatars, and the Zaporozhians provided some support for Kondratii Bulavin's Don Cossack revolt against Russian authority in 1707–1708.[113] Dissatisfaction with inadequate cash and powder subsidies from the Russians and disputes with Russian authorities at the border fortress of Kamennyi Zaton convinced Host *Koshevyi Otaman* Kost' Hordienko to join with the Crimean Tatars and support Mazepa and the Swedes against the Russians in 1708.[114] In response Peter I had the Zaporozhian Sich burned and most of its inhabitants massacred on May 19, 1709.[115]

Hordienko's Cossacks were given refuge by Crimean Khan Devlet II Girei and established a new Sich at Oleshki on the lower Dnepr. They did not thrive. Although the khan paid them a subsidy for defending the Khanate's northwestern border, they were denied fishing rights and the land around Oleshki proved unsuitable for keeping cattle. They lacked the numbers to reestablish a military organization based on federated barracks settlements. When the Ukrainian Hetmanate was restored under Apostol' in 1727 the Oleshki Sich began petitioning St. Petersburg for amnesty and resettlement at the old Chortomlyk site. Empress Anna finally met this request in 1734, finding it wisest to detach the Zaporozhians from the Khanate and the Porte in view of the approaching war with the Ottomans; General Weissbach had also advised her that the Zaporozhians could provide material support and reserves for the defense of the new Ukrainian Line. *Koshevyi Otaman* Malashevich was therefore permitted to return the Zaporozhians to a new Sich near Chortomlyk and bring them back into allegiance to Russia.[116] In 1751 Ukrainian Hetman Rozumovsky was given authority over Zaporozhia.

The completion of the Ukrainian Line emboldened a flood of Ukrainians, some from as far off as the Right Bank, to resettle on the empty lands of western Zaporozhia. Most of these new settlers were peasants fleeing the consolidation of serfdom in Ukraine, or former Cossacks dropped from the Ukrainian Register; in Zaporozhia they took up farming and stockbreeding but showed no interest in joining Cossack military service. Eastern Zaporozhia also experienced an influx of Russian *odnodvorts*y from Kursk and Voronezh governorates. Most of these immigrants gravitated to the south, resettling behind the Ukrainian Line in what became in 1764 New Russia Governorate.[117]

Thus Zaporozhia was no longer the exclusive preserve of the Zaporozhian Cossack Host. One compensation for having to share it, however, was that the Zaporozhian *starsyhna* was able to attract some peasant tenants and turn toward agriculture and animal husbandry, taking advantage of the fact that most of Zaporozhia's southern frontier (except for the small segment facing the Ottoman fortress of Ochakov) had become safer from Ottoman or Tatar attack. With the take-off of Zaporozhian agriculture the Host also become less dependent on food imports from Left Bank Ukraine. Zaporozhian grain, horses, and cattle were sold to the Nogais, and Ukrainian tobacco and linen and some Russian manufactures were carried through Zaporozhia to Crimea or to Ottoman and European merchants at Nezhin. Crimean salt, Turkish textiles, and dried fruit and wine from the Aegean and Anatolia were imported into Zaporozhia. Most Zaporozhian agriculture and animal husbandry was undertaken by Cossack *starshyna* officers, exploiting the labor of tenants who were rank-and-file Cossacks fallen into poverty or recent immigrants. Poorer Cossacks no longer had opportunity to practice raiding economy except in connection with haidamak banditry in Polish Ukraine. Over 1760–1770 the population of Zaporozhia increased 63 percent, to 30,600 male souls, most of whom were not Sich Cossacks. [118]

The Ukrainian Line and the garrisoning of Left Bank Ukraine and Sloboda Ukraine by the Russian army had greatly reduced Russia's need to rely on the Zaporozhian Host to guard the southern frontier; and anyway the Host's reliability as an ally continued to be suspected given that after renewing their fealty to Russia in 1734 many Zaporozhian Cossacks remained in friendly contact with those elements of the Host still enjoying the protection of the sultan. In the 1750s and 1760s land and appurtenance disputes between Zaporozhian Cossacks and the immigrants settling in New Serbia, the New Sloboda Regiment, and Slavonic Serbia had often turned violent, escalating into what St. Petersburg called Cossack "brigandage." The Zaporozhian Host also angered the Russian government and the Russian and Ukrainian nobility by offering haven to refugees fleeing the serfdom spreading through Left Bank Ukraine and Sloboda Ukraine.[119] After the lands on Zaporozhia's southern frontier were transformed into New Russia Zaporozhia was entirely encapsulated and any reason for preserving Zaporozhia as an autonomous Cossack enclave inside the Russian Empire vanished. In the course of Catherine's Turkish War the Russians would established four new fortresses in Zaporozhia to enhance political surveillance, and at war's end the Sich would be destroyed and the Zaporozhian Host liquidated.

Between 1707 and 1765 Russian imperial policy toward the Ukrainian lands had succeeded in tightening Russian administrative control in order to extract more revenue for war while shifting the primary role in frontier defense from Ukrainian, Sloboda, and Zaporozhian Cossack forces to the regiments of the Russian field army. This made it possible to eliminate the political autonomy of such "anachronistic" polities as the Hetmanate, Sloboda regiments, and Zaporozhian Host and incorporate them directly into the Russian Empire.

Cameralist management of subject nationalities and frontier populations

Because of its vast size and the historical circumstances of its territorial expansion the Russian Empire of the mid-eighteenth century still preserved some features of a composite state. In regions where manorialism and serfdom were underdeveloped different conceptions of property right and different obligations of landholders toward state service prevailed (among the state peasant population of the north along the White Sea coast, for example, and among the yeomen *odnodvortsy* of the southern Black Soil steppe). The Kazan' region along the Middle Volga had many Muslim Tatar and pagan Finnic inhabitants, and through most of the seventeenth century they had been spared pressure to convert to Russian Orthodoxy and their Muslim elite had been granted *pomest'e* service lands and integrated into the state service nobility. The elites in territories on the western frontier that underwent gradual and treaty-defined integration into the Empire (Ukraine, the Baltic states, and eventually Poland-Lithuania) were granted special legal privileges and some administrative autonomy to reconcile them to incorporation, and those non-Russian elites with the educational and cultural accomplishments desirable for enriching the Russian Enlightenment and rationalizing Russian administrative and military service (the Baltic German nobles in particular) were given rapid promotion up the Table of Ranks and entrée into the court and army high command.

Making some exceptions from heartland administrative, social, and cultural practice for certain regions and minority populations therefore made both political and economic sense because it allowed the state to adapt its service and fiscal demands to what was realistic within particular environments and to offer concessions to woo the allegiance of recently subjugated elites.[120]

But it was also the case that the urge to centralize power by promoting institutional uniformity across the Empire was reinforced in the eighteenth century by the popularity of cameralist thinking among Russian rulers and high officials. Catherine II in particular strongly believed that the policy of the state should be to intervene in all facets of public life in order to increase the productive capacity and resources of the nation. Making policy exceptions observing the composite origins of the Empire was sometimes necessary, but striving for the uniformity of institutions and administrative practices was to be preferred whenever possible because uniformity was associated with *systematic* governance, and system was equated with good order and efficiency, in keeping with Peter I's vision of a "regulated state." Government guided by cameralist principles should be able to shape policy in accordance with what could be identified as uniform in human nature and what was environmentally and historically particular in human culture. It was therefore cameralist policy to assist and raise up subject cultures at lower levels of development, encouraging them to abandon nomadism and turn to settled agriculture, for example; to use state power to accelerate the colonization of economically or strategically valuable frontier regions; and to promote "European style estate structures for the Russian population, in particular to foster the middle class of merchants, tradesmen, and small manufacturers that was still lacking in spite of the efforts of Peter I."[121]

Thus policy initially acknowledged and accommodated differences but treated these differences as temporary, eventually to be surmounted in order to achieve uniformity and integration. Despite the vast expanse of the Russian Empire it did attain "a basic uniformity which is striking when compared with contemporary France and Prussia, not to speak of the Habsburg monarchy."[122]

Since Peter I's reign cameralist thinking had a very great impact on Russian frontier policy in particular. It had been invoked to justify inviting in Serbian, Hungarian, and German immigrants with desirable *grenzer* and farming skills and resettling them with special privileges along the Zaporozhian frontier and the Volga. It had weighed the military service capacity of the yeoman smallholder servitors (*odnodvortsy*) of southern Russia against their potential value as taxpayers and turned most of them into a kind of special category of state peasants liable for the soul tax. Once it was recognized that permitting the continued independence of vassal polities like the Ukrainian Hetmanate and the Zaporozhian and Don Cossack Hosts was no longer worth their strategic value and policing costs, it placed them under the *guberniia* system of provincial government, issued privileges bringing their *starshyna* elites into general legal equality with Russian noblemen, and imposed the imperial soul tax and Russian customs system.

On the eve of her Turkish War Catherine II had devoted special attention to encouraging frontier colonization by foreigners with useful skills. In 1762, she issued a decree inviting all foreigners except Jews to resettle in Russia, and in 1763, she created a Chancellery for the Guardianship of Foreigners to compile a register of lands free for distribution and to arrange subsidies for settlers (now including Jews). Special recruitment agents were empowered to offer land grants, tax exemptions, and other financial incentives to free settlers.[123] The state spent about 200,000 rubles per year on colonization programs over 1764–1774.[124] Such programs would be used to accelerate the colonization of New Russia and the Tauride in the 1780s and 1790s.

Thus the Russian Empire and Ottoman Empire stood on the edge of war in 1768 with considerably different approaches to the mobilization of resources for war. In the Russian Empire the centralization of state power had intensified in order to engage in such cameralist re-engineering of frontier society "from above," whereas in the Ottoman Empire the sultan's government had permitted significant decentralization in order to leave the management of frontier life up to local elites and market forces. The war would test the respective strengths and weaknesses of both approaches.

CHAPTER 4
THE RUSSIAN ARMY AT MIDCENTURY

The Russian army in the Seven Years' War

At Peter I's death in 1725 the Russian armed forces numbered about 289,000 men.[1] Under his successor Catherine I, there was anxiety in the Supreme Privy Council that the soul tax could not continue to maintain such a large military establishment without overburdening peasant taxpayers and provoking rural unrest, and it had even been proposed to demobilize two-thirds of the army. But in the 1730s, in the reign of Anna Ioannovna, the Land Army Commission (*Voinskaia sukhoputnaia kommissiia*) headed by Burkhard Christoph von Münnich found ways to avoid this while lowering the soul tax rate: Münnich enlarged those formations (the Land Militia, the artillery) that were supported from state peasant *obrok* rather than the soul tax, and most of the field army regiments he disbanded were in the Lower Corps stationed in the Caucasus, in connection with the withdrawal of forces required by the Treaty of Resht.[2] In 1732 Münnich became President of the War College (VK); he also served as commander-in-chief of Russian forces in the War of the Polish Succession and the Russo-Turkish War of 1735–1739.

Münnich was toppled and sent into Siberian exile by the 1741 coup that overthrew the infant Emperor Ivan VI Antonovich and his Brunswick regents and placed Elizabeth Petrovna on the throne. But his military reforms remained largely intact through the 1740s, because the campaigns of the Russian army in this decade—the 1741–1743 war against Sweden and the 1748 demonstration in Franconia on behalf of Austria—were limited in scale and did not seriously test Russia's military capabilities.[3] The only significant changes in the 1740s were the reintroduction of grenadier companies in the infantry regiments (Elizabeth Petrovna especially favored the grenadiers) and the formation of the Orenburg Cossack Host. Field Marshal Lacy did form a special commission, the War Staff (*Voinskii shtat*), under the Senate to examine matters of staffing and logistics. It reviewed existing infantry ordinances but did not issue any new ones. It found enough need for reform that Count Petr Shuvalov formed a new commission within the VK in 1754. The work of the Shuvalov Commission focused on improving service from the Cossacks and other irregular light forces, reorganizing the hussar regiments and the Land Militia, working up new manpower norms for infantry regiments, preparing new ordinances for infantry and cavalry training and tactics, establishing more magazines and foreposts, and organizing engineering and artillery schools within the Corps of Cadets.[4]

By the start of the Seven Years' War, the land forces of the Russian Empire had grown to 331,422 men: 172,440 field army troops, 74,458 garrison troops, 27,758 Land Militia troops (mostly dragoons), 12,937 troops in the Artillery and Engineering corps, and 43,739 irregulars (Cossacks, hussars, and Kalmyks). The Russian army was thus the largest in Europe.[5] The maximum manpower mobilizable for campaign against the Prussians was about 220,000, including irregulars.

The Shuvalov Commission's staffing norms (*shtaty*) for the infantry set the structure of a line infantry regiment at three battalions, each of four companies, with two of the twelve companies consisting of grenadiers.[6] But the grenadier companies were larger (200 men) than the musketeer companies (144 soldiers and six under-officers), so the total paper strength of an infantry regiment was 2,541, of whom 11 percent on average were ineffective support personnel (*nestroevye*). This was more than twice the size of an infantry regiment in Münnich's time (1,049 men, 10 percent of whom were *nestroevye*). Actual strength often fell below this standard by a few hundred soldiers. This larger size may have reduced the effectiveness of mobilizations and administration. The train of a regular infantry regiment was supposed to be capped at 102 vehicles and 219 transport horses, but in practice, it was usually much larger because there was no limit on the number of baggage vehicles officers could take on the march.

There were also four regiments entirely of grenadiers stationed in the eastern Baltic provinces, formed in 1756 by taking men from the grenadier companies of the musketeer regiments; from 1756 to 1760 there was an Observation Corps with regiments of four-battalion structure.

Forty-six infantry regiments and three elite Guards regiments were liable for field army duty, but a decree of March 30, 1756, assigned fourteen of these infantry regiments and the three Guards regiments to "internal" duty. Also performing internal duty were the forty-nine infantry regiments and seven dragoon regiments in garrison service. Most garrison forts had just one infantry regiment. Garrison troops were expected to assist in convoying and training recruits for the field army, perform fortifications and road *corvée*, and stand as a reserve for replacing losses in the field army, but their salary rates were lower than those for field army troops, and their combat-readiness was so low commanders in the field army dreaded receiving them as replacement transfers.[7]

As had been the case under Münnich, the defects of the Russian cavalry were of special concern. Not counting irregulars and garrison dragoons, the cavalry in 1756 numbered 39,546 troopers and officers in twenty-nine dragoon regiments, three cuirassier regiments, and one Life Guards regiment. Most regiments were under-staffed and the Shuvalov Commission was dissatisfied with their combat-readiness, especially that of the dragoons, who had too few mounts and too often had to be let out for foraging and haymaking, because they received forage money only for the colder months.[8] The organization of cavalry units was also a problem: the standard-size squadron was clumsy, too large to be easily turned, whereas the standard company was too small to deliver much shock in a cold steel charge. The Commission therefore recommended that forage money rates be doubled and dry forage issued year-round. The squadron should be reduced to forty-six troopers, and dragoons should be equipped with the *palash*, a heavy-slashing sword, rather than the lighter *shpaga* rapier (cuirassiers retained the latter). To contain expenditures, the Commission proposed reducing the regular cavalry by 7,000 men, to be achieved by lowering regiment *shtaty* and by eliminating two dragoon regiments. But it intended to double the number of heavy cuirassiers, from three regiments to six, and to establish five new regiments of mounted grenadiers organized out of reformed dragoons. More dragoon regiments were to be shifted from field army duty to internal and garrison duty. The regular cavalry to be prepared for campaign against the Prussians would comprise five cuirassier regiments, five mounted grenadier regiments, and four dragoon regiments. Most features of this reform had not yet been implemented when the war broke out (the Commission had estimated that making all these changes would take four years), and it was all the less likely that the cuirassiers would perform as hoped given that the Commission had instructed that they buy all their mounts inside Russia in order to save on costs.[9] Mounts produced in Russia tended to be undersized and weaker, so Elizabeth Petrovna's cuirassiers were unlikely to carry home a charge as effectively as Frederick II's cuirassiers, who were expected to cover the first 4,000 yards at a trot, the next 1,800 yards at a gallop, and the final 300–400 yards at full rush.[10]

The Ukrainian Land Militia in 1756 consisted of twenty regiments of dragoons, six of which performed service along the Ukrainian Line and eleven of which were stationed as forepost troops along the western front between Smolensk and Kiev. The Trans-Kama Land Militia also continued to exist; it comprised three regiments of dragoons and one regiment of infantry.

Münnich's reforms in the 1730s had doubled the number of regimental guns to improve the artillery's ability to sustain fire. Shuvalov's 1755 *shtaty* required each infantry regiment to have two three-pounder regimental guns (range 500 paces) and four six-pounder mortars; dragoon regiments should have one three-pounder gun and two six-pounder mortars. But the Seven Years' War saw significant improvements in the Russian artillery beyond this. Part of the reason for this was the more imposing industrial foundations of the Russian military machine by the 1750s, especially in the form of mining and metallurgy in Urals and arms manufacture at Tula; part of the reason was the enterprising spirit of *General-fel'dtseikhmeistr* Petr Shuvalov. His "unicorn," introduced in 1757, was a conical-barreled gun that was half the weight of the standard regimental gun, able to fire eight different charges, including bombs, grenades, *brandskugel* naval incendiary shells, and canister, and at ranges nearly up to a kilometer. His slot-bored "secret howitzer" could spread canister across a wider front, and he introduced *blizniat* mortars for higher altitude short-range bombardment. By reducing the weight of field guns, he was able to double the mobility of field gun batteries while increasing their ranges; he made more explosive rounds and canister rounds available; and he assigned officers from the Field Artillery Regiment to the infantry regiments to train gunners for the regimental guns.[11] By 1760 Russia had a larger artillery park than any other European nation: 8,272 field, siege, regimental, and garrison guns; 391 howitzers; 282 unicorns; and 756 mortars.[12]

Less successful was Shuvalov's 30,000-man combined-arms "superdivision" called the Observation Corps (*Observatsionnyi korpus*). Its tasks were to cover the movement of other corps and the Field Artillery Regiment, and to support sieges and blockades: for this reason, its infantry regiments were of double size—four battalions—a quarter of its infantry companies were grenadiers, and it had more field guns. The Observation Corps was supposed to be formed by transferring the 420 most experienced troops from every garrison regiment, but this proved unable to provide more than 12,000 men, forcing Shuvalov to supplement these transfers with raw recruits and Land Militia and garrison dragoon horsemen. The Observation Corps performed poorly at Zorndorf and Kunersdorf, taking heavy losses in both battles. It was dissolved in 1760, and its infantry taken into regular musketeer regiments.[13]

On the urging of Grand Chancellor A. P. Bestuzhev-Riumin, a Conference attached to the Imperial Court (*Konferentsiia pri vysocheiskom dvore*) was founded on March 25, 1756, for the purpose of presenting the empress with regular reports and discussion about important foreign affairs. Beyond this, its mission was to produce "a general and systematic plan to reduce the powers of the King of Prussia and to make him no longer dangerous to the Russian Empire."[14] The project to manage the Prussian threat was to be accomplished militarily as well as diplomatically, so when Russia entered the war against Prussia in December 1756, the Conference took on broad responsibility for managing the war effort, including operational planning, and this usually came at the expense of the initiative of the VK (which was left so much out of the loop it had to get its information about Russian losses at Gross Jägersdorf from foreign newspapers). The Conference included M. P. Bestuzhev-Riumin, Vice Chancellor M. I. Vorontsov, Procurator General Prince N. Iu. Trubetskoi, Senator Field Marshal A. B. Buturlin, Senator M. M. Golitsyn (President of the Admiralty College), General Field Marshal S. F. Apraksin (President of the VK), Field Marshal A. I. Shuvalov, and his brother *General-fel'dtseikhmeistr* P. I. Shuvalov. Empress Elizabeth Petrovna was too often ill to enforce a productive symphony of voices in the Conference, so it was usually dominated by Grand Chancellor Bestuzhev-Riumin.

The Grand Chancellor envisioned the Conference as functioning like the Austrian *Hofkriegsrat* and supervising nearly all matters affecting the army and fleet, including provisioning and appointments and promotions. But by refusing to divide authority with the VK, his Conference soon got swamped in petty details. It had two other serious flaws: unlike Catherine II's Council of State, the Conference tried to impose operational plans on commanders, denying them any initiative; because the Grand Chancellor desired the closest possible coordination of Russian operations with Austrian operations, his Conference often subordinated Russian military objectives to those of Austria at unfortunate critical junctures. In the first months of the war, the Conference denied Field Marshal Stepan Apraksin of the power to issue any orders or instructions that were not countersigned by the Conference, and it kept him uncertain as to whether he was to prepare his army to invade East Prussia or to swing across Poland into Silesia. Apraksin withdrew the army to Tilsit in September, but the Conference ordered him to prepare for an immediate counteroffensive; he refused and was removed and court-martialed for treason. Apraksin died of a stroke soon after.[15] In 1759 the Russian field army's commander-in-chief was the far more capable Count Petr Semenovich Saltykov, but the Conference issued him contradictory orders and several times kept him from following up his victories and exploiting new opportunities (such as the drive upon Berlin after Kunersdorf) to placate the Austrian commander Leopold Von Daun. The Russian generals considered Daun too slow and cautious and too ready to let the Russians bear the brunt of the campaign. This eventually engendered such distrust of the Austrians among the Russian generals that they held back from committing to major battles in 1760 and 1761—thereby sparing Frederick II from complete defeat.[16]

In 1756 the Conference had estimated the war would cost just six million rubles, affordable given that the year's revenues were over eleven million rubles; by the end of 1760 the accumulated cost of the war exceeded forty million rubles. *General-fel'dtseikhmeistr* Petr Shuvalov became *de facto* chief of war finances and eventually had some success in meeting war costs by raising the *obrok* rent on state peasants, devaluating the currency, establishing a public Artillery Bank, and increasing sales for the state vodka and salt monopolies.[17]

One of the army's greatest deficiencies in the war was its dysfunctional provisioning system. The foundations for a capable quartermastery had been laid by *General-fel'dtseikhmeistr* James William Bruce in 1704 and further improved by *General-kvartirmeistr* William Fermor in 1736, but the theater of the Seven Years' War presented its own special challenges given its distance from the Russian frontier. Pomerania and the Oder basin may have been more densely settled than the Black Sea steppe, but their road transport was just as poor and they did not have food stocks sufficient to feed the Russian army beyond early autumn, at which point commanders had no choice but to take the army into winter quarters.

At campaign's start troops marched from their base magazines with ten day's rations in their backpacks and a mobile regimental magazine with another twenty days' rations. When these supplies ran out, the regimental quartermasters were expected to draw from the rear magazines in Lithuania and Livonia or to use the funds they had been issued to purchase additional provender from sutlers or from local inhabitants. But most of the rear magazines were small and hastily organized—some captured from the Prussians; the few sutlers who did appear tended to charge more than the soldiers' *arteli* could afford; purchasing stores from the local population, supposed to be done at market price with prompt payment, often degenerated into forced requisition. Resorting to coercion was especially common in the first year of the war when Apraksin was in command. On Polish territory coerced requisition was excused on the grounds that the Russian army was campaigning in defense of the king of Poland; in East Prussia it was carried out as punitive requisition or as outright looting. This sparked peasant flight and partisan resistance. By 1761 St. Petersburg had acknowledged that requisitions in East Prussia had to be regulated if the conquered province was to be held, so East Prussia's new governor, V. I. Suvorov, who was also *General-fel'd-intendant*, introduced a schedule of requisitions (for grain and fodder, horses and wagons) worth about 400,000 rubles. When Fermor succeeded Apraksin, he tried to organize supply at the front by creating a Field Proviant Chancery under a *General-proviantmeistr-leitenant*, but it was unable to achieve good coordination between field officers and the supply officers of the Main Proviant Chancery within the VK.[18]

The new infantry ordinance produced by Zakhar Chernyshov in 1755 has been judged by several Russian military historians as inferior to Peter's 1716 War Ordinance (*Voinskii ustav*), and considered fundamentally conservative and blindly conforming to German military doctrine. Certainly, the ordinance was preoccupied with maximizing firepower at the expense of mobility and shock; it still prescribed the unrolled line formation (*razvernutyi stroi*) of four ranks, the first and second ranks at knee, all ranks with fixed bayonets, in battalions flanked by grenadiers.[19] It gave preference to firing by half-divisions during attack and firing by platoon during withdrawal, but permitted firing by ranks, files, volley, and on the oblique. It reintroduced the counter-march, which Peter I had abandoned. The goal of getting up a rapid rate of fire was undermined by an overly complicated manual of arms that required about twenty steps (*ruzheinye priemy*) for loading, aiming, and firing; too much emphasis at drill on rushing through these steps tended to reduce the accuracy of fire. At a marksmanship exercise by the Kiev fusilier regiment, for example, only 691 of the 2,709 bullets fired hit any part of the target.[20]

One feature of the 1755 infantry ordinance is seen as "progressive," however. Although it said little about using the bayonet on attack, it did reflect awareness of recent French doctrine on the value of attacking in company or battalion columns, presumably with bayonet, to break the front of the enemy.[21] By the end of the Seven Years' War, Rumiantsev would be training his troops to attack in massed columns of two or even four regiments. By freeing commanders to make marches by grand division columns, the ordinance was able to double the average daily march rate from five miles to ten miles. Catherine II's army was able to make even better time, in part through improved training and by more often marching unencumbered by large trains.[22]

The cuirassier and dragoon exercises of 1753–1755[23] have also been criticized for reinforcing the turn Münnich had made in the 1730s away from "proper" Petrine doctrine: they prescribed cavalry attack in deep formation rather than closed-up, at trot rather than gallop, and required training in firing pistols and carbines from horseback. Peter I had discontinued firing from horseback in 1706. Little such training in mounted firing had been held before the outbreak of the war, which may have been part of the reason that Apraksin's fourteen regiments of regular cavalry in 1756 were found ill-prepared for combat and had to be reformed. The Russian cavalry was still useful in reconnaissance, allowing Fermor and Saltykov to locate the enemy and choose the ground of battle, but it played little role in combat until later in the war, at Palzig, Zorndorf, and Kunersdorf, where it charged with cold steel.[24]

There was no new comprehensive artillery ordinance in the 1750s; the artillery still used the ordinance of 1730, supplemented by some new precepts Petr Shuvalov developed over 1757–1758 and published in 1760. The new rules prescribed an order of battle in which three-quarters of the field guns were stationed along the front infantry line and one-quarter in front of the second battle line, on higher ground so that they could fire over the heads of the first battle line. The larger caliber guns along the front line were to open fire on the enemy at a distance of 1,500 meters, first aiming at the enemy's artillery and caissons; when the enemy infantry or cavalry came within 500 meters the field guns switched to canister fire. The smaller caliber field guns and the regimental guns first opened fire at a range of 800 meters, switching to canister at a range of 140 meters. The reserve field guns, usually a single battery, were placed at some spot between the two battle lines but were ready to be moved to whatever part of the front line was in more danger from the enemy, or to be pulled back to support the second battle line. Canister fire had to be halted when the Russia line went on the attack, but when the infantry was withdrawing, covering fire from the field guns had to be kept up.[25]

Shuvalov's reformed artillery won recognition for its effectiveness. An Austrian military attaché observed that some batteries could fire at an unprecedented rate of eighteen rounds per minute.[26] Over the course of the war greater reliance was placed on battery mobility and on canister fire. It was also an advantage that the Russian army usually had numerical preponderance in artillery over the Prussians; at Zorndorf, there were six Russian guns for every 1,000 troops—twice the rate as for the Prussians. The Prussian defeat at Kunersdorf a year later owed much to the Russian and Austrian batteries on the Kleiner-Spitzberg heights. Rumiantsev and William Fermor used unicorns very effectively to bombard Schwedt and Cüstrin in 1758.[27]

If the infantry and cavalry ordinances of 1753–1755 were anachronistic, it may not have mattered so much that the army had so little time to train under them before the war broke out. Mastery of complicated exercises may have been less crucial than other forms of training. At the battle of Zorndorf (August 25, 1758), Fermor's infantry regiments, deployed on unfavorable ground facing uphill and into the sun, held firm for hours against repeated attacks and withering enemy fire. They took 16,000 casualties yet finally withdrew in good order and spirit, leaving Frederick II—who had lost 12,800 of his own men, a third of his army—instilled with lasting fear of the ferocity of the Russians. One of the Prussian survivors wrote, "The terror the enemy inspired in our troops is indescribable."[28] At Kunersdorf (August 12, 1759), Frederick II lost another 18,500 men against Saltykov and Gideon Laudon, causing Frederick to write to Finckelstein, "I will not survive this … I have no more resources, and speaking frankly, I consider everything lost. I shall not outlive the downfall of my country. Farewell for ever!"[29]

The Prussian Field Marshal Keith judged the Russians as "still novices maneuvering; they do not know how to move, but they hold firm."[30] Walter Pintner has speculated that something in the training or composition of the Russian army imbued the Russian soldier with "a spirit, or at least a willingness to be killed, that exceeded that of his contemporaries in the armies of Western Europe." Perhaps, the *rekrut* composition of the Russian army made its soldiers less likely to break or desert than the soldiers of the Prussian army, who were a mix of mercenaries, volunteers, and impressed men.[31]

By B. Ts. Urlanis' estimate, total Russian fatalities in the Seven Years' War were about 120,000 men (18,000 killed in action, 5,000 dead of wounds, and 97,000 dead of disease).[32]

The Russian experience in the Seven Years' War demonstrated the shortcomings of conservative training ordinances, mismanagement of provisioning, and overcentralization of decision-making in the Conference at St. Petersburg. This was partly compensated by the consolidation of the spirit of technicalism in military policy over the first half of the eighteenth century.[33] Peter I could be seen as a forerunner of Russian military technicalism in that he gave priority to mobilizing specialized technical expertise to build and maintain a "regular" army, even though his personal experience with technical matters had been limited to gunnery and shipbuilding. Bruce, an accomplished mathematician and engineer, had organized Russia's first Artillery School, put Russian gunnery on a scientific footing, and laid the foundations for a Quartermastery Service. Although a mediocre field commander, Münnich had further strengthened the artillery; devoted greater attention to supervising logistical support from Ukraine to his army on the march; improved the medical service in response to the enormous losses caused by cholera and dysentery; founded a Dnepr flotilla for landing and resupplying troops; based promotions on aptitude reports inspired by Fenelon's "natural psychology"; and introduced more technical training in the Noble Corps of Cadets to reshape it along the lines of the Prussian and Danish *ritterakademien*. The Shuvalov brothers further refined these practices and achieved a closer, more coherent connection between military development and industrial and fiscal policy.

Furthermore, during the Seven Years' War there had still been periodic opportunities for the more independent-minded commanders—Rumiantsev, Saltykov, Petr Panin—to make their own choices about concentrating their forces, selecting objectives, and making effective use of their reserves. Rumiantsev's bombardment and blockade of Kolberg (June–December 1761), a joint operation with the Baltic Fleet, were well executed, demonstrated the value of attack columns and harassing fire by jaegers, and nearly won the war for Russia, leaving Frederick II convinced his only salvation now was from some miracle, perhaps the Ottoman Empire's entry into the war.[34]

Military reform on the eve of Catherine II's Turkish War

In Catherine II's first few months on the throne, efforts at military reform concentrated on eliminating the more unpopular innovations of Peter III to reassure the military establishment it was being restored to its condition under Elizabeth Petrovna (although at peacetime strength, with reduced manpower owing to the suspension of the recruit levies).[35]

In December 1762, however, a more ambitious reform program was launched through a special Military Commission chaired by *Fel'dmarshal* P. S. Saltykov, hero of the Seven Years' War.[36] It was guided by a thirty-three-point instruction presented by the empress. The commission's first task was to work out new *shtaty* for the infantry, cavalry, and artillery—not to expand the number of troops in absolute terms, since the recruit levies were in abeyance for a while, but to determine optimal battalion, regiment, and company sizes and structures so as to make best use of existing supply and training and command-and-control measures. The *shtaty* the Military Commission published in 1763 set the standard that an infantry regiment must comprise two battalions, five musketeer companies, and one grenadier company per battalion, with two of the musketeer companies in quarters in reserve for training new recruits. That would leave the fighting strength of each battalion at 800 men. Counting officers and *nestroevye*, standard regimental strength was 2,092 men. In all the infantry arm was to comprise three guards regiments, four grenadier regiments, and forty-six musketeer regiments, with a total strength of 104,654 men (26,146 fewer than under Elizabeth Petrovna).[37]

By 1765 the Military Commission had expanded the infantry arm to sixty-three regiments by folding most of the Ukrainian and Trans-Kama Land Militia Regiments into the regular army as eleven new infantry regiments. Under Elizabeth Petrovna and Peter III, the twenty infantry regiments of the Ukrainian Land Militia (22,700 men) and the single infantry regiment of the Trans-Kama Land Militia (1,286 men) had been a "settled" auxiliary force, mixed but predominantly infantry, with the special function of defending certain sections of the steppe frontier. The Military Commission's decision to reform them as infantry regiments in the regular field army meant they could be deployed beyond those regions, although this increased the service burden upon the *odnodvortsy* serving in the Land Militia. By 1779 they would be issued the same uniforms, equipment, and salaries as regular line regiments and thereby ceased to exist as an identifiable separate formation. For a few years beyond the 1765 reform, 11,000 men remained in Land Militia cavalry service, in fourteen mounted regiments.[38]

The Military Commission also committed to expanding the role of jaeger riflemen in the infantry. Rumiantsev had organized a small command of volunteer jaegers for his 1761 Kolberg campaign, and they had shown themselves useful as sharpshooters and skirmishers. They could be dispersed ahead of the infantry lines for skirmishing or formed into lines or squares to cover the flanks of division squares. In 1763, Petr Panin had formed a command of 300 jaegers within his Finland Division, assigning five jaegers to each of his infantry companies. In 1765, the Military Commission placed sixty-man jaeger commands in twenty-five infantry regiments along the northwestern front. By 1767 there were 3,540 jaegers in the army, and by 1769 there would be jaeger commands in all infantry regiments. Eventually, their numbers would be greatly enlarged and they would be organized separately into ten four-battalion jaeger corps.[39]

From the experience of the Seven Years' War the Military Commission had concluded that the army should maintain a two-to-one ratio of infantry to cavalry. Not counting the new Land Militia infantry regiments, this would call for twenty-five regiments of heavy cavalry, each of five squadrons, at two companies per squadron. Peter III had sought to establish eleven regiments of cuirassiers; the Military Commission limited this to six regiments. His six regiments of mounted grenadiers were abandoned and their troopers combined with those from thirteen of the twenty dragoon regiments to form nineteen regiments of carabiniers.[40] Whereas the cavalry of Peter the Great had consisted mostly of dragoons, the Military Commission was following European preference for heavier cavalry, for greater shock; during the Seven Years' War the Russian army had nearly 40,000 dragoons, but only 7,000 of them had seen action in major battles. The lighter dragoons were now mostly removed from the field army and assigned to garrison duty except for seven settled regiments (8,000 troopers) stationed near Poltava and Smolensk and along the Orenburg Line.[41] Light cavalry still had important functions to perform: reconnaissance, flank defense, and pursuit of the defeated enemy. But these functions could still be performed by hussars, *pikinier* lancers, and Cossacks. Five regiments of "field hussars" were created out of Cossacks not in active service, and one regiment of Sloboda Hussars formed during the Seven Years' War. The number of Serb, Hungarian, Moldavian, and Georgian immigrants who had settled in New Serbia and Slavonic Serbia as volunteer hussars in the 1730s and 1740s had declined during the Seven Years' War; three field regiments of them remained by 1767, while some of their number were reformed as three *pikinier* regiments. No more foreign volunteers were taken into hussar service. A hussar or *pikinier* regiment comprised six rather than five squadrons. By 1765 the cavalry arm numbered 44,634 troopers in forty-five regiments: 23,550 in the heavy cavalry, 12,812 in the dragoons and mounted Land Militia, and 8,272 in the field hussars. As for Cossack cavalry, at mid-century, there had been eleven regiments and thirteen smaller commands of Cossacks in the field army, excluding the Ukrainian Cossack regiments; the largest complement contributed to the field army came from the Don Host, which could mobilize up to 9,000 men. The other Cossack hosts were the Volga, Iaik, Greben', and Azov hosts.[42]

The Shuvalov reforms during the Seven Years' War had left the artillery in largely good state, and Catherine's first *General-fel'dtseikhmeistr* A. N. de Villebois was a competent manager of ordnance.[43] He founded an Artillery Academy and Engineering Academy within the Second Corps of Cadets, retained the lighter unicorns and secret howitzer, further standardized calibers, and strove to increase the number of regimental guns. The norm had been two three-pounder guns for each infantry, dragoon, and carabinier regiment; Villebois sought to increase this to four three-pounders for an infantry regiment, each with a crew of eight men and six horses, and three three-pounder guns for every cavalry regiment.[44] Shuvalov's combined-arms Observation Corps had already been abolished in 1760 after its failure at Zorndorf; its two regiments of field guns were returned to the Field Artillery, which Catherine II organized into five regiments (one Bombardier, two Cannoneer, and two Fusilier regiments); by the end of the Turkish War, the field artillery would comprise 350 guns.[45] The infantry of the Observation Corps were reassigned to the Fusilier Regiment of the field artillery. The other change the Military Commission made to the artillery eliminated the Bombardier Battalion Peter III had created within the Life Guards, which was reformed into Bombardier companies in the Preobrazhenskii Guards Regiment and smaller artillery commands in the Semenovskii and Izmailovskii Guards.[46] The siege artillery was gradually reduced to a *shtat* of 164 cannons, unicorns, and mortars.

The engineering service was left substantially unchanged, organized as a Pioneer Regiment of two pioneer, two miner, and two master companies. In 1771 it was expanded to a Pioneer Battalion and in 1775 to an Engineering Corps.

During the Turkish War manpower for the field army was of course prioritized, yet the social disorders of those years also called for the expansion of the garrison forces, from 64,905 troops in 1764 to 89,619. This was accomplished by relegating to garrison duty "obsolete" formations like the Land Militia and dragoons, some of the newer recruits, and invalids. In this period, there were fifty-five garrison regiments (forty-eight infantry regiments, seven dragoon regiments) and a number of smaller "commands." Most garrison regiments comprised just two battalions. For administrative purposes, the VK distinguished between Interior garrisons and Ostsee garrisons defending the Baltic frontier. Continued skepticism about the quality of service performed in the garrison regiments discouraged the VK from treating them as a ready Reserve for the field army.

One of the concerns of the Military Commission was to make mobilization, supply, and reserve functions easier to coordinate by more closely aligning the administrative organization of the army—its peacetime basing and billeting—with the tactical organization of the army on campaign. During the Seven Years' War, the advantage of the division and corps principles of tactical organization had been acknowledged. The Military Commission now decided it made sense to make this permanent and to assign quartering regions to eight divisions and three corps (by 1775, eleven divisions and three corps).[47] It did not intend thereby to divide the army for territorial defense but to enable territorially quartered forces to mobilize quickly into concentrated forces for operations in one or more strategic sectors such as the Baltic Front or Black Sea Front. Each new territorial "division" command consisted of several regiments of infantry and cavalry grouped in brigades under the command of a full general and his staff of Major-Generals. Each regiment had its permanent quarters in a particular town or village. "The deployment of each division was designed to carry out the task assigned to each sector within the strategic plan of the entire field army while retaining the possibility of shifting forces to another sector as circumstances required."[48]

In regard to the southern frontier, the territorial division reform could also be seen as assisting political centralization, a new stage in the consolidation of the Empire: first had come decades of military colonization having the effect of encapsulating the territories of the Hetmanate and Don and Zaporozhian hosts; then the transfer of southern Russian Land Militia regiments and foreign volunteer hussar regiments to the Ukrainian Line; extension of the governorate system to Ukraine and Sloboda Ukraine, establishing the Little Russian and New Russian Governorates; the inclusion of the Ukraine and Sevsk Divisions in the new territorial division scheme; and finally, soon after the Turkish War, the liquidation of the final remnants of autonomy of the Zaporozhian and Don hosts.

Although the territorial division system bore some resemblance to the strategy of legion deployment in the early Roman Empire under the Flavian and Severan emperors,[49] it may be a coincidence that the Military Commission next turned its attention to experimenting with smaller territorial combined-arms units called Legions and Cohorts. In response to the outbreak of the Bar Confederation revolt in Poland-Lithuania, the Military Commission formed a Petersburg Legion and a Moscow Legion out of recruits from those territories augmented by transfers from dragoon and hussar regiments outside those territories. Each legion was supposed to number 5,577 troops in four battalions of infantry, four squadrons of carabiniers, two squadrons of hussars, a Cossack command, and regimental guns. The semi-improvised complection of these legions and inexperience with combined-arms operations at this low a unit level eventually convinced the VK to do away with the legions after the Turkish War. Experimentation with smaller two-company "commands" of mixed infantry and cavalry was somewhat more successful as long as it was limited to territorial defense in the rear—against Pugachev's rebels, for example—and not expected to perform a reserve function for the field army.[50]

The officer corps at the beginning of Catherine II's reign probably numbered about 9,000.[51] The rank hierarchy went from *Fel'dmarshal* down through General-*anshef* (full General), Lieutenant-General, Major-General, Brigadier, Colonel, First Major, and Second Major (Colonel and Major were "staff officer" ranks), and then below them to the junior officer ranks of Captain, Captain-Lieutenant, Lieutenant, and Sub-Lieutenant.

As before, nearly all officers were from the nobility (*dvorianstvo*) and had come out of the Guards regiments, the Corps of Cadets, or more slowly out the lower ranks of the regular line regiments. The Guards regiments continued to be the path towards officer commission most preferred by young men from the more exalted metropolitan noble families—promotion from Guards Sergeant major to commissioned officer in a line regiment was pretty automatic—but the Guards sometimes produced "plungers" more interested in shining in society than in military duty. Catherine II appears to have preferred that candidates come out of the Corps of Cadets, and to encourage this, she nearly doubled the Corps to six hundred cadets in 1762. She entrusted the broadening of the Corps' curriculum to Count Betskoi, an admirer of Fenelon and Rousseau, who was convinced that an officer's education should awaken love of work as well as technical qualification. Betskoi started taking sons as young as five or six into the Corps to protect them from the corrupting influences of home life and intensify their commitment to the elite boarding-school values of the Corps.[52]

A nobleman pursuing an army career in a line regiment entered service while still a minor. After one to three years' service, he could get from his regimental colonel promotion to *kaptenarmius* or *fur'er* and then to sergeant and sergeant major. But to get a commission to officer rank, he would have to be recommended by his corps or divisional commander, pass an examination, and win a ballot among the officers of his regiment. His subsequent promotions were supposed to be determined by his seniority and by confirmation from the VK of his meritorious service. In the 1760s it was typical for a junior officer to take three or four years to rise to captain and to spend the next seven or eight years at captain's rank. Commission as a staff officer, colonel, or general was issued by the empress upon recommendation of the VK. Kinship and clientage ties had considerable bearing on promotions up to captain, given how interconnected the *Generalitet* was, and promotions by the VK to majors and above could be affected by VK President Chernyshov's factional alliances with the Rumiantsev and Kurakin clans or by "fees" paid to the staff of the VK. Because promotions above captain required the intercession of the VK and the empress, there tended to be a vast gulf in status and privilege separating staff officers from captains. A further problem with the promotion system was that promotion within one's original regiment was not always guaranteed;

promotion often involved transfer to another regiment or even to a different branch of service, and this limited the opportunity of officers to get to know their troops and establish trust with them.[53]

Under Peter the Great, officers no longer fit for field service were transferred to garrison duty or to provincial reserve regiments training recruits. Peter III's 1762 Manifesto emancipating the nobility from state service allowed such men to take voluntary retirement, and most of them who chose retirement did so after making the rank of major.[54]

Although Russians represented an increasingly large part of the officer corps as a whole, it remained the case early in Catherine's reign that foreigners and Baltic German-speakers (Imperial subjects, but privileged) were numerous in the higher ranks, in part because the lifting of the compulsory service obligation from the nobility in 1762 for a while caused a shortage of officers and required that more officers be recruited from abroad. Of Catherine's 402 officers of staff rank or higher, non-Russians made up 41.3 percent. Russians were 56.2 percent of the Generals-*anshef*, 36.3 percent of the Lieutenants-General, 47.9 percent of the Majors-General, 64.2 percent of the Staff, and 63 percent of the Colonels.[55] During the 1768–1774 Turkish War, many of the more important general officers in the field armies of Golitsyn, Rumiantsev, and Panin were foreigners or Baltic Germans (the Stoffelns, Bauer, Weissman, Berg, Elmpt, Essen). There were occasional expressions of resentment about the number of non-Russians, some of this prompted by memories of the *Bironovshchina* in Anna's reign, some of it prompted by Elizabeth Petrovna's frequent claims that she was defending Russian honor by guarding against the revival of German clique power. But in the campaigns of 1769–1774, conflicts between Russians and non-Russians in the *Generalitet* were no more common than conflicts over competing claims of seniority.

In connection with the preparation of new training ordinances, the Military Chancellery found it advisable in 1764 to issue two "Instructions to Colonels": one for managing cavalry regiments and the other for managing infantry regiments. These instructions dealt in greater detail than previously with the responsibilities of company captains and regimental colonels for the five-month initial training of their recruits.[56] The VK preferred to give the greater role in troop training to staff officers under the assumption that lower officers were still lacking in experience.

Saltykov's Military Commission had concluded that the army's operations in the Seven Years' War had been hindered by the lack of a General Staff to collect and analyze information concerning quartering, provisioning, reconnaissance, and cartography. Up to this point, those functions had been performed by the Quartermaster Section, which consisted of officers on temporary postings to divisions and regiments and which lacked a formal central organization. It was the Military Commission's recommendation that the Quartermaster Section be converted into a General Staff. In response, Zakhar Chernyshov formed a General Staff of forty officers, ten sitting in the VK and thirty detailed to the field army (1763). The next year they were given their own distinct uniforms. Their early work demonstrated need for further improvement, so in 1769 Major-General Friedrich Wilhelm Bauer, General Quartermaster of Frederick II, came to Russia and reorganized the General Staff, increasing the number of its senior officers so that more could be spared for detail to the field army. Rumiantsev enthused about the value of Bauer's organizational talents and mastery of military science.[57]

The plans, maps, and other materials prepared by the General Staff were maintained in the archive of the VK, to whose Vice-President the General Staff reported. Meanwhile, some 1763 reforms of Catherine II's Military Commission had the effect of reducing the VK's dependence upon the War Department of the Senate and increasing the VK's direct accountability to the empress, to whom the VK now had to report each week.

The approach of war with the Ottoman Empire pushed the empress to establish in 1768 a council of war, the Council of State (*Gosudarstvennyi sovet*, sometimes called the Council of War, *Voennyi Sovet*). Whereas Panin's proposed that Imperial Council had been intended first of all to balance the court factions intent on advising and influencing the Sovereign, the Council of State also gave the empress the opportunity every Monday and Thursday morning to receive written and oral reports from the most senior figures in the diplomatic and military establishments: Count Nikita Ivanovich Panin, Acting Chancellor and Acting President of the College of Foreign Affairs; his brother Count Petr Ivanovich Panin, veteran of Gross Jägersdorf and Zorndorf and General-*anshef* since 1762; Count Grigorii Grigor'evich Orlov, Catherine's favorite and Chief of Artillery; Prince Mikhail Nikitich Volkonskii, former General-*anshef*, nephew of former Grand Chancellor Bestuzhev-Riumin; Prince Aleksandr Mikhailovich Golitsyn, former minister to London, General-Adjutant, now Vice-Chancellor; Prince Aleksandr Alekseevich Viazemskii, Procurator General, the Council's liaison with the Senate (he was related by intermarriage to the Saltykovs and Trubetskois and was a close ally of General Rumiantsev); Count Kyrilo Rozumovsky, last Hetman of Ukraine, now General-*Fel'dmarshal* of the Petersburg military region; and Count Zakhar Grigorevich Chernyshov, President of the War College from 1763, brother of Admiralty College President Ivan Chernyshov, and related by marriage to the Panins. Major-General and Privy Councillor S. F. Strekalov served as its Secretary. In 1768 the Council was still *ad hoc* and met just ten times, but on January 13, 1769, the Senate decreed it a regular state institution with authority to discuss all military and political matters relating to war.[58]

The Council of State proved more sophisticated, more diligent, and less distracted by petty details than Elizabeth Petrovna's Conference. For example, in planning for the coming war with the Porte, the Council of State made a close examination of the records on Münnich's campaigns against the Turks, and it drafted an operational plan for three years, with multiple variants adapted to the different courses of action the enemy might be anticipated to take. The Council "thrashed out the issues, recommended options, and set the limits of the possible before an assertive ruler whose dynamic mixture of idealism and cynicism needed at times to be guided and restrained."[59] Over the next few years, there would be occasional disputes between the Council of State and field commanders, Rumiantsev in particular, but Rumiantsev ultimately accepted its authority because the Council was less frustrating than an Austrian-style *Hofkriegsrat* directed by men of little military experience.[60]

The training ordinances of 1763

One of the most important changes by the Military Commission was the publication on March 12, 1763, of a new Infantry Ordinance, the *Pekhotnyi stroevyi ustav*.[61] It had been found necessary because of the training and tactical deficiencies the recent war had exposed in the 1755 Ordinance. While reaffirming preference for line formation, the 1763 Ordinance gave commanders freedom to select from a wider range of formations, including columns and squares, and it simplified firing procedures.

The 1755 Ordinance had prescribed unrolled formation (*razvernutyi stroi*) in a front line four ranks deep; the 1763 Ordinance gave preference for an unrolled formation in a battalion front line three ranks deep, with the front line divided into four divisions and platoons (*vzvody*) at eight to twelve ranks per platoon. Grenadier companies were on the flanks of the battalion line. The distance between ranks was set at three paces, the distance between battalions along the line at eight paces. The number of steps in loading, presenting, and firing (*ruzheinye priemy*) was reduced to get up a faster rate of fire. The first two ranks fired from knee, the third rank standing at ready; it was now expected that all three ranks have their bayonets attached while firing, although the ordinance had nothing to say about training for a bayonet attack; the front was forbidden to advance immediately after firing without having loaded another round. There were several different firing systems permitted, the most common of which were: firing by platoons; by platoons *vystupnye* (just before firing each platoon stepped forward so that its third rank came even with the first rank of the rest of the battalion); by platoons *otstupnye* (stepping back from front line, when battalion is withdrawing); by divisions (all three ranks firing, the firing shifting by division in the order of 1, 3, 2, and 4); by half-divisions; by firing on the oblique;[62] by files; by ranks (in order of 3, 2, 1); and by general volley (*zalp*) of all three ranks. Most European armies were finding platoon firing most effective, however, for it provided more continuity of fire: immediately after he fired, each soldier could stand up and reload without having to change position or wait until other ranks behind him had finished firing.

Under the inspiration of French military thought and experiments during the Seven Years' War by such Russian commanders as Saltykov and Rumiantsev, the 1763 *Pekhotnyi stroevoi ustav* gave greater attention to circumstances in which unrolled formation was unaffordable and folding into columns or squares advisable. When crossing uneven ground or passing through a defile, for example, the battalion or half-battalion should form into a column one platoon, one-third of a rank, or one half-rank wide; the grenadier files on the right end of the line would usually march first, and when this first division had advanced a distance twice the width of the column to be formed, the next division of the battalion would start to march behind it. Upon reaching firing position, the column would make *deployade* back into unrolled formation, with the first division already firing (though this first time not from knee) as soon as the third division had come into line alongside the second division, their soldiers taking a half-step to the side so as to space the line. Forming unrolled line from column had to be carefully executed so as to make the line straight and files properly spaced; conversely, folding from line into column took some time, so it was not advisable to do it without withdrawing from the firing line.

The 1763 infantry ordinance aimed at providing more training for movement in columns but did not yet follow French doctrine from the 1750s on attack by column (*le ordre de profound*). French ordinances recognized that columns could be used to attack sections of the enemy line or fortified points using cold steel. They prescribed massed attack by two parallel columns, each with a front of two platoons and a depth of sixth platoons, advancing at ordinary pace and then closing in on the enemy line section at double the time with their bayoneted muskets raised. They had also worked out procedures for forming a column of retreat back to the front of the line and for doubling, tripling, and quadrupling the width of a column in movement.[63]

It had long been the Russian practice to take field armies across the steppe in great *wagenburg* squares or oblongs to protect against Tatar cavalry attacks. During Empress Anna's Turkish War, Marshal Münnich had employed a single square or column of regimental squares for the march and experimented with battalion, division, and half-division squares for combat. The 1763 infantry ordinance recommended that when facing cavalry attack, a regiment in unrolled line formation should form into a square with musketeers on the front and rear faces, grenadiers on the sides, and field guns and regimental guns at the corners. It retained Münnich's predilection for further protecting the front of the square with chained swine feathers (for which a regiment was expected to transport 3,500 swine-feathers). Sometimes the regiment might form an oblong square with alternate sections along the flanks stepped-out for firing.[64] One of Rumiantsev's contributions to Russian infantry tactics during Catherine II's first Turkish War was to form an order of battle consisting of four or five great *corps* squares, formed from attack columns, dispersed enough to be able to "attack the enemy from different directions, while being close enough to lend mutual support."[65] Smaller battalion squares of jaegers and two-rank lines of cavalry were positioned between these corps squares. Catherine II's first Turkish War subsequently saw corps operating in regimental squares (Foçsani, 1770), and Suvorov deploying battalion and company squares against the Turks (Turtukai, 1773).

In 1763 the Military Commission issued a new ordinance for cavalry, the *Ustav voinskii o konnoi ekzertsitsii*.[66] It reflected the doctrine that the primary function of the cavalry was to break a section of the enemy's front by mounted attack from the flank to prepare it for attack by the Russian infantry. This meant cavalry shock rather than firepower was to be emphasized. For that reason, the heavy cavalry had been enlarged through the creation of the nineteen new mounted carabinier regiments. The carabiniers augmented the more expensive armored cuirassier regiments in that their sturdy mounts and *palash* swords (long, heavy swords with straight and wide blades) gave them more shock value than dragoons, while their carbines allowed them to perform the same dismounted firing function as the old dragoons.[67] Much of the 1763 cavalry ordinance repeated the prescriptions from 1755—the basic formation for the march as well as for combat was the unrolled line, in three ranks. One change was that attack by company columns was still permitted, but forming cavalry battalion squares was now discontinued as useless. Another departure was the more explicit instruction concerning firing carbines. Carbines were not to be loaded or fired from horseback, except when facing a lightly armed enemy, when surrounded, or when further advance was blocked; instead carbine firing was to be made dismounted, and in two rather than three ranks, as experience had shown that in three-rank firing the middle rank, encumbered by their swords, had not the space to comfortably go to knee. Pistol firing was still to be conducted mounted, on the trot, one rank at a time, but the new ordinance said little about training for this (nor about mastering riding).[68] Within a few years, Rumiantsev, Suvorov, and Potemkin would all de-emphasize pistol fire and place their reliance on the cavalry attack with cold steel.

For the first several years of Catherine's reign, Shuvalov's 1756 and 1759 artillery ordinances were left largely unchanged. They had prescribed that guns be deployed in batteries, at sixteen to twenty-four guns per battery, grouped in four to six gun divisions positioned in extended line. This line deployment was intended not just for firing but for advancing onto the battlefield and moving to new firing positions. Guns were always to be moved by horse team, not by men. Gun "squares" firing in all four directions were permitted in theory but were never actually used. The maximum range for a twelve-pounder field gun elevated to five degrees was about 1,200 meters, but it was preferable to fire within 500–800 meters, and canister was to be used at the range of 200 meters or closer.[69] A new general ordinance for artillery had to wait until 1788. During the empress' first Turkish war, however, Rumiantsev issued his own *Precepts to Battery Commanders*, which placed importance on having pioneers assist the artillery train on the march, with separate columns for different calibers of guns and their caissons. Rumiantsev recommended that firing at longer ranges be kept to a minimum.[70]

Doctrine and innovation

While some scholars see in its ordinances the Military Commission's failure to break out of its "hypnosis by the Frederician system,"[71] this is overstated. The 1763 infantry ordinance was open to other influences, notably French doctrine about columns, and we should note that such French military thinkers as Puysegur, Maizeroy, de Broglie, and Guibert were turning at this time to experimentation with divisions, columns, and skirmishing precisely because they did not think that French soldiers could accept the level of rigid mechanical drilling required to achieve the rapid firing and complex maneuvering potential of the Frederician line formation.[72] During the Seven Years' War, some Russian commanders came to the same conclusion about their own troops and doubled down on training their men to stand firm under a faster rate of Prussian fire. Furthermore, Rumiantsev had not been the first to recognize that "Prussian exercises" would not suit for warfare against the Turks, who did not practice linear tactics and rapid platoon fire.[73] Finally, it should be kept in mind that ordinances designed for training on the parade ground might be abandoned early on as useless by commanders gaining combat experience. This had already happened on some occasions during the Seven Years' War, and as early in the Turkish War as May 1769 Rumiantsev began issuing his own training ordinances for his Second Army.[74]

In other words, technicalism might naturally strive to codify military doctrine as fully and authoritatively as possible, but the soundest doctrine was that empirically tested and revised through combat experience. Conservative training ordinances aiming at imposing standards from conventional wisdom might not be mastered in actual troop training, or commanders might alter or abandon them in light of what they learned in battle and the other military writers they were reading. The Frederician model was not the only available one, even if it was still preferred in the Russian ordinances. For example, both Shuvalov and Rumiantsev were fascinated by the *Essai sur l'art de la guerre* (1754) of Comte Lancelot Turpin de Crisse.[75]

Several historians of eighteenth-century Russian military development consider the Russo-Turkish War of 1768–1774 as a crucible of new Russian military doctrine. They see this new military doctrine as pioneered by Rumiantsev, Suvorov, Potemkin, and for some, by Panin. They argue that the new Russian military thinking represented a coherent and superior alternative to the Frederician model and anticipated some of the ideas and practices later refined in France's Revolutionary and Napoleonic wars.[76] Others, especially Soviet historians writing in the postwar Stalin era, go further and view its progressive and "superior" character as due to its rejection of all foreign models, which was somehow uniquely Russian, a revival and refinement of the original Russian "national" mode of warfare created by Peter the Great.[77]

The following innovations in strategy and tactics appearing over the course of 1768–1774 have been cited as examples of the new emerging Russian military doctrine.[78]

Rumiantsev disliked getting mired in a protracted war of posts, maneuvering, and occasionally giving battle to seize territory (ground, hard points) and deny them to the enemy. He sought to take and maintain the offensive, carry the fighting to the enemy's territory, and find the opportunity to deal a decisive blow destroying the enemy's army in the field. This has been contrasted to Frederick II's strategy in the second half of the Seven Years' War, when the loss of territory and reduced manpower forced Frederick to maneuver his army to avoid risky general battle against unfavorable odds and to wear down the logistic capabilities of Prussia's enemies.

Rumiantsev rejected the Austrian-preferred *cordon strategy* of dispersing troops evenly along a frontier for defense and for basing of offensives, on grounds it spread forces too thin, reduced resources available as reserves, and slowed concentration against enemy attacks. Cordon tactics might serve Austrian commanders well-enough along narrow fronts in the Low Countries or Northern Italy, but they were ill-suited for the vast open plains of Ukraine and Moldavia. One might be tempted to adopt cordon tactics to defend the fortress chain along the Danube—as the Turks themselves did after 1770—but this forfeited the chance to defeat the enemy decisively in open battle.[79] Rumiantsev instead embraced the VK's new commitment to divisions and corps as tactical as well as administrative units in order to station his field army across the theater of war by divisions or corps, in three to five areas of concentration, staggered for stationing in greater depth. Enhancing force mobility would then enable divisions and corps to march to each other's defense and to combine or divide to conduct simultaneous offensives over different sections of the front.

Perhaps under the inspiration of Turpin de Crisse, Rumiantsev took to devising his plan of campaign on the basis of a series of staged objectives, each achieved objective establishing a new "parallel" from which the division would proceed to the next.

This in turn enabled Rumiantsev to devise a more sophisticated logistics network of tertiary, secondary, and primary magazines in parallel lines with connecting interval bases, observing standard procedures for more regular transfer of provender and materiel from rearward to forward magazines closer to the army's front lines. This bore some resemblance to Henry Humphrey Evans Lloyd's ideas immediately after the Seven Years' War on the "line of operations," which should be as short and straight as possible in connecting an army with its convoys and magazines. Later in the century, Adam Dietrich von Bülow would produce a "geometry of operational lines," which prescribed an angle of 90° as the optimal angle of attack upon an objective.[80]

More careful planning of operational lines connecting divisions with their magazines made it possible to undertake offensive operations with smaller forces, moving faster because of reduced supply trains. In the last three years of the war, many of the more effective offensive operations undertaken by parts of Rumiantsev's First Army were undertaken as flying raids (poiski) by small forces of a few infantry battalions and cavalry squadrons. These small forces frequently defeated Ottoman forces much greater in size.

Rumiantsev anticipated that his greatest technical challenge would be taking troops quickly across the Danube. Therefore, he began training his troops for landing operations (including night desants) and building a flotilla of small gunboats permanently stationed at bases along the eastern end of the Danube.

Münnich had trained his army to cross hostile steppe territory in one great army column. Rumiantsev achieved a faster rate of progress by marching in less-dense multiple division or corps columns moving in parallel by pairs. He assigned separate night bivouacs for each column, so they could resume column formation more quickly for the next day's march. Rumiantsev and Suvorov also gave their troops more training for rapid forced marches and night marches.[81]

The column now served not only for the march but for the order of battle. Kagul (1770) established the precedent of advancing in four or five corps or division columns which then assumed battle order as squares, supported in their intervals by cavalry, jaegers, and artillery.[82] One or two squares were assigned the task pinning down the enemy's front, while the others rolled over the enemy's rear or flanks. Prussian and Austrian military doctrine had given reference to line formation because it took time to form squares on the battlefield, but in combat against the Turks, the Russians discovered that they were more likely to come into contact with large enemy cavalry forces earlier in the battle, and so the battalions in line would have to meet the cavalry by forming squares, by shortening their lines, and shifting more troops to defend their flanks.[83]

This new Russian preference for the division square is considered by some foreshadowing of the transition during the Napoleonic War from line tactics to "impulse tactics," in which divisions and brigades "formed separate grand tactical 'impulses' that were often separated from their neighbor by sizable distances."[84]

The primary role in attacking by square was given to the infantry, but it now required combining firepower with mobility, the column offering maneuverability which the unrolled line could not provide. The third element of effective force, shock, could be supplied by the bayonet charge. To maximize infantry maneuverability, protective swine feathers were gradually discontinued, a process completed in the Russian army by the 1780s. In contrast to Rumiantsev, Suvorov disapproved of the *demonstratsiia*, the feint attack designed to reconnoiter and distract the enemy; he considered it a waste of manpower and an operation preferred by more timid commanders unready to go all out for victory.

In combat (unlike in reconnaissance or foraging), the cavalry played a reduced role, in part because of deficiencies in Russian cavalry training and in part because it could nearly always be assumed the Turks would have numerical superiority in cavalry. In battle, the cuirassier and carabinier cavalry moved through the intervals of the squares to cut down separated "heaps" of enemy troops and protect the infantry squares from being outflanked. It was usually Cossack and hussar light cavalry that was sent in pursuit of the routed enemy.

Artillery now played a more active role in the attack, because batteries were no longer kept massed at the rear or flanks of the order of battle but were "castled," shifted forward, and moved about from point to point over the course of the battle, to reconcentrate artillery fire and establish crossfire with the infantry to support the main blow or protect units coming under threat of counterattack. The precedent for such castling of guns had been established at Kunersdorf.

One of Rumiantsev's most successful innovations was in the way he used jaegers. In the last year of the Seven Years' War, he had experimented with jaeger companies in his infantry regiments; during the Turkish War, he made it a practice to defend the flanks of his infantry squares with jaeger battalions. At Larga, he even combined the jaeger battalions from Bauer's and Repnin's corps into their own separate square to maneuver with aimed fire against Turkish cavalry trying to attack Bauer's and Repnin's squares.[85]

Rumiantsev maintained that a well-founded division should not only combine arms but also contain the range of functionally specialized formations within each branch of arms. Hence, a musketeer regiment should have grenadier and jaeger companies, and different kinds of cavalry missions should be tasked to heavy, medium, and light cavalry units. Tactical specialization would allow simplified and streamlined training while preparing the regiment for combat against very different enemies (Prussians, Austrians, Turks) under very different theater conditions.

Rumiantsev and especially Suvorov issued their own ordinances for infantry and training to step up the pace of platoon firing. They even introduced aimed firing, which was now expected not only from jaegers with rifled guns but also from musketeers in loose order, firing by squads following direction by platoon corporals. However, training in marksmanship still took up just a few days for month; the emphasis remained upon rapid and uninterrupted rather than accurate firing.[86]

Suvorov laid even greater stress than Rumiantsev on intensive training to raise morale and unit cohesion as well as proficiency; he sought to produce soldiers who possessed fighting spirit, self-confidence, and initiative as well as mechanical mastery of ordinance exercises. The initial five-week training given to new recruits should be reinforced by holding training camps on a regular seasonal basis, and training should proceed from individual instruction (ten days a month) through platoon and company training (two to three days a month), culminating in regimental exercises and maneuvers (three to four days a month), so that basic concepts could be mastered by repetition at higher unit levels and the regiment prepared for the introduction of more complicated exercises. "Train hard—fight easy" was one of Suvorov's dicta. Physical discipline should reinforce training—the rod still had its place—but soldiers should be punished for insubordination, not for making mistakes, and officers ought to cultivate a firm but patient paternal authority rather than act as brutal short-tempered martinets. Officers ought to be able to explain their expectations in simple language peasant recruits could understand. Above all, officers should tend to their own training so as to develop the skills required for keeping the army on the offensive: speed, quick assessment (*coup d'oeil*), and striking power. Suvorov's training doctrine would evolve over the next decades and culminate in his 1795 pamphlet *The Art of Victory*, written in simple reiterative language for his own troops, whose text is often cited by those historians arguing for the special "moral" strength of the Russian national military idea.[87]

For the most part, Catherine II's Council of State did not restrict Rumiantsev from implementing these tactical and strategic innovations, which made it possible for him to keep his armies on the offensive through most of the 1768–1774 war and avoid (except in 1771) the Austrian error of getting bogged down in a war of posts. These innovations frequently brought the Russians decisive victories over larger Ottoman forces, and with far fewer casualties on the Russian side. Rumiantsev's *Obriad sluzhby* ordinances crafted for his First Army in 1770 would be adopted by the rest of the army in 1776; after the war, Suvorov would elaborate upon these ideas to achieve his own successes in the next war against the Turks and the war upon revolutionary France. The new military thinking represented by Rumiantsev and Suvorov did not entirely replace the older doctrine of line tactics; however, their tactical prescriptions were reserved for certain types of warfare, especially for warfare against the Turks. Hence, Suvorov recommended in 1778, "Against regular forces—line tactics, as in the Prussian War; against irregular forces, as in the last Turkish War."[88]

CHAPTER 5
THE KHOTIN CAMPAIGN, 1769

Catherine II had resisted committing to Panin's proposal for an Imperial Council, and she had recognized that Elizabeth's Conference had over-centralized military planning during the Seven Years' War and stifled commanders' initiative. But now that Sultan Mustafa III had declared war she found it politically necessary to bind the factions into a central war council to reach consensus for a general war plan. This new Council of State (*Gosudarstvennyi Sovet*) had its first meeting on November 4, 1768.[1]

After listening to reports from Chernyshov and Nikita Panin reviewing the events leading to the sultan's declaration of war, the lessons of Empress Anna's war with the Turks, the state of the army, and the political situation in Europe, the Council voted unanimously to prepare for an aggressive war rather than awaiting the enemy's first move. Orlov was especially vocal about the need to identify war aims, specific advantages that could realistically be won. The empress would offer her own answer to this question at the next session, on the sixth: the war should recover the fortress ports of Azov and Taganrog from the Turks and acknowledge Russia's right of free sailing on the Black Sea; it should also establish permanent inviolable borders for Poland-Lithuania and secure Poland-Lithuania's peace.[2] Over the next few days, the Council approved more ambitious objectives: rousing Dalmatia and Morea to revolt by implementing Orlov's proposal to send a fleet into the Mediterranean, and liberating the Kabardans and the Georgians in the Caucasus.[3]

The Russian war plan

The two most likely threats to Russia, the Council decided, were an attack on New Russia by combined Tatar and Ottoman forces and an Ottoman strike up the Dnestr against Kamianets to link up with the Bar Confederates. It was also acknowledged that the Turks, Kuban Tatars, and mountain peoples of the Caucasus could pose a threat to Russian forces on the lower Volga and lower Don and prevent the recovery of Azov. On their own the Bar rebels were too scattered and uncoordinated to pose as much danger, so a smaller Russian reserve force could be left in Poland.

It was therefore decided that the Russian armed forces should be divided into three parts: a First Army of 80,000 men, to assemble at Kiev and move into southwestern Poland and to defend Kamianets and wage offensive war against the Ottoman garrison of Khotin and other Ottoman fortresses farther down the Dnestr River; a Second Army of 40,000 troops (not including Cossack and Kalmyk auxiliaries), to assemble at Ust' Samara near Elizavetgrad and at Bakhmut to defend Ukraine as far as the Bug and southern Russia as far as the Northern Donets; and an Observation Corps of 10,000–15,000 troops stationed at Warsaw and Vilnius to defend Poland-Lithuania against the Bar rebels (if necessary, it could march west to join with the First Army near Staro-Konstantinov). Two regiments would also be sent from Orenburg to Astrakhan to help defend the lower Volga, leaving Orenburg to be guarded by three dragoon regiments and one infantry regiment. On Grigorii Orlov's suggestion, a squadron out of the Baltic Fleet, commanded by Aleksei Orlov, would be sent into the Mediterranean if British permission could be secured.[4]

The command of the First Army was given to General-*anshef* Prince Aleksandr Mikhailovich Golitsyn.[5] The Second Army was entrusted to General-*anshef* Count Petr Aleksandrovich Rumiantsev.[6] The Russian forces currently in Poland under the control of ambassador Repnin were to be reorganized as the Observation Corps under General-*anshef* P. I. Olits (soon transferred to the First Army and succeeded by Lt. General I. I. von Weimarn). Golitsyn's and Rumiantsev's appointments were a disappointment to the Panin party, which had hoped to secure the First or Second Army for Petr Ivanovich Panin.[7]

If the Turks managed to mobilize early and advance quickly up the Dnestr, crossing near Kamianets and joining up with the Confederates, Golitsyn was to wage a war of posts, avoiding general battle and using the First Army to deny the enemy food and forage and block them from pushing farther into the interior of Poland. If the Turks were delayed in coming up toward Kamianets in great force, the First Army should secure Kamianets, establish magazines on the Polish side of the Dnestr, and cross the river and seize the Ottoman fortress at Khotin. But if it became apparent the Turks were directing their main blow against Rumiantsev's Second Army in Ukraine, Golitsyn should be ready to send Rumiantsev's assistance while reinforcing his own positions.

The primary tasks of Rumiantsev's Second Army were to defend Ukraine and to maneuver to protect the rear of the First Army. Beyond this the Second Army was to support an operation by the Black Sea Flotilla and the Don Cossacks to seize Azov, an expedition under Major-General Medem into Kabarda, and an expedition into Transcaucasia under Count Todtleben.

As for Count Aleksei Orlov's naval expedition into the Mediterranean, it would have to be undertaken by elements of the Baltic Fleet sailing from Kronstadt across the North Sea, past Portsmouth, and through Gibraltar. Admiral G. A. Spiridov would have command of the First Squadron: thirteen ships of the line, five of them mounting eighty guns each, six with seventy guns, and two with three guns; three galiots, two transports, five big sloops, thirty-nine small sloops, and four galleys; accompanying the thirteen ships of the line would be five big sloops, thirty-nine small sloops, and four galleys with 8,910 sailors and 1,600 soldiers. The Second Squadron would be commanded by Counter-Admiral John Elphinstone: four ships of the line with sixty guns, two with fifty-four guns, three with thirty-two guns; five galiots, two galleys, two pinks, three half-galleys, three large sloops, and twenty-four small sloops; 3,960 sailors, 860 soldiers. Once in the Mediterranean Count Orlov would exploit his political contacts in Dalmatia and Greece and harass the Turks on land as well as sea,[8]

The Empire's previous two recruit levies had each yielded about 31,000 men. On November 14, the Senate decreed that the revised levy for 1768 would aim at delivering 50,747 recruits at the rate of one man from every three hundred male souls.[9] The Council also reluctantly decided to reinstitute one of the decrees of the late Peter III: introducing paper assignats to help cover the costs of the war. By decree of December 29 all private parties receiving payments from the treasury had to accept 25 of every 500 rubles in paper bills, which could be exchanged in the state banks at Moscow and St. Petersburg.[10]

The Turks might be having difficulty raising provisions in Moldavia, but that did not mean Golitsyn could count on getting supplies out of the Moldavians once the First Army crossed the Dnestr; whatever the Ottoman commissars had not gathered up in Moldavia would probably be concealed. The First Army would therefore have to rely on provisions from garrisons in Poland and delivered by Russian convoys. Originally, it had been proposed to establish regimental depots, each with twelve days' provisions for one regiment, supplemented by a mobile magazine supply system of 4,667 wagons, each wagon pulled by four oxen and carrying ten quarters (*chetverti*) of grain and oats, the wagons arriving once a month. But it was soon recalculated that a month's supply for an army of 80,000 men would actually require 5,165 wagons. In this one respect, it was fortunate that Golitsyn gave up on trying to mobilize 80,000 men and set off for Khotin with an army half that strength, supported by just 3,367 wagons, and planning not to live off the wagon supplies alone. It would become necessary for the First Army to contract for deliveries from Polish estate owners at current market price, paying in cash or issuing promissories. In last resort Golitsyn was allowed to demand "contributions" in kind or cash, but this was to be avoided lest it drive Poles into the arms of the Confederates. It was subsequently decided that the First Army would also have to draw provisions from Ukraine, delivered monthly by wagons from Kiev.

Twice over the course of the 1769 campaign, Golitsyn would have to halt operations against Khotin and withdraw back into Poland because of provisioning problems. He had sufficient stores in his magazines in Poland but he had not established magazines closer at hand on the Moldavian side of the Dnestr.

Rumiantsev's slightly smaller Second Army did not require as many monthly supply wagons—just 1,300 wagons—as it had more stationary magazines nearby at Kiev, Bakhmut, and Fort St. Dmitrii. These magazines were being filled in advance of the spring campaign, *General-proviantmeister* Khomutov having sent out commissioners to Orel, Mtsensk, and Kursk, the largest grain markets, to purchase groats and flour at prevailing prices (1.80 rubles for a 147-kilo lot of rye, 70–80 kopeks for the same in oats). At the time the war plan was under discussion, there were about 73,000 quarters of flour, 4,600 quarters of groats, and 13,000 quarters of oats in all the magazines in Ukraine, but another 75,000 quarters would have to be amassed by May 1 in order to fill the main campaign magazines at Kiev and Fort St. Dmitrii. Handmills would also have to be distributed to the companies of the Second Army, so they could grind flour from grain they obtained along their march route.[11]

The Ottoman war plan

Ahmed Resmi Efendi considered the only real threat to the Porte posed by Russian forces in Poland the possible Russian military occupation of Podolia, which had been an Ottoman *eyalet* up to 1699 and bordered on Moldavia and Bucak. He had considered the dispatch of 30,000–40,000 reinforcements to the Ottoman border fortresses sufficient to deter such a move by the Russians. He remained skeptical of the capabilities of the Bar Confederates and opposed to Ottoman forces intervening in Poland on their behalf.[12]

But Grand Vizier Silahdar Hamza Pasha was thought to have endorsed a more ambitious aggressive war plan that required mobilizing a much larger army at much greater expense. Ottoman forces were to attack on three fronts. The grand vizier would lead the main field army (over 100,000 men, perhaps as many as 400,000) up the Dnestr in spring to reinforce Khotin, cross the Dnestr, and seize Kamianets—thought to be an easy matter, as the Bar Confederates were reassuring the Turks that the Polish commandant of Kamianets was ready to surrender to them. Then, Potocki and Krasiński would bring over 80,000 Confederate troops and the grand vizier's army would push deeper into Poland, enter Warsaw, and overthrow King Stanisław. After driving Russian forces from Poland it might even be possible to take the Ottoman army further east in two great columns, against Kiev and Smolensk. A second army of 60,000 Crimean Tatars reinforced by some Ottoman units would be led by Khan Kirim Girei on a raid into New Russia to tie down Russian forces in Ukraine.[13] A third army would secure Azov and the lower Don, link up with Kuban Tatars and Lesghian mountaineers, and make a diversionary threat against Astrakhan.[14]

How much of this plan actually existed is impossible to know. It may only have corresponded to what St. Petersburg could have expected from the Turks in a "worst instance" scenario, and that was quickly rendered moot by several things—logistical problems that held up the grand vizier's army on the Ottoman side of the Danube until June; the refusal of the French and the Austrians to proffer any assistance; the weakness of the Confederate forces; and the premature exit of Kirim Girei's Tatars from New Russia in January 1769. The Turks took no measures to reinforce Azov, which the Russians were able to occupy without a fight on March 6, 1769. When Yağlıkçızade Mehmed Emin Pasha replaced Silahdar Hamza Pasha as grand vizier and finally took the army across the Danube on June 2, he evidently had no idea how to proceed and had to ask his officers for recommendations.

Over the winter and spring, the Turks did have time to reinforce their border fortresses in the west, especially by raising *levendat* militias: 17,650 men for Khotin, 14,200 for Ochakov, 31,000 for Bender, 6,000 under Dukakin Karaman Pasha for the interior of Moldavia, 2,000 for Khan Kirim Girei's guard, and 24,000 for Kafa and other garrison in Crimea. Bender also received 15,500 elite *sipahis*. In addition to these 81,670 garrison reinforcements, the field army the grand vizier was assembling at Hantepesi grew quickly; to its core of 60,000 janissaries were added large numbers of militiamen and volunteers from the Balkans and Anatolia and even as far off as Daghestan, Kabarda, Arabia, and Egypt, so that it soon far exceeded 100,000 men. But about 70 percent of them were raw recruits, even in the *Serhat Kulu* units, and there were another 20,000–30,000 camp followers ("tent pitchmen, servants, beggars and hucksters, parasites, perhaps Jews and infidels, and the riff-raff of Istanbul" in the opinion of Ahmed Resmi Efendi), who put a greater strain on rations while they remained with the army and spread disorder when they later deserted. The militiamen were also prone to desert: a provincial pasha would deliver "enough men for a battalion, within three days they were all gone."[15]

As in the past, the plan for provisioning and transport aimed at filling magazines at the frontier fortresses and the *menzil-hane* depots along the traditional march route for the field army. Army commissars were to arrange with *ayan* councils across the realm to obtain 2.5 million kilos of wheat, barley, flour, and biscuit by forced purchases at fixed prices and ship it to the fortresses and depots from the central distribution centers at Istanbul, Gallipoli, and Isaccea. Some of the flour came from as far away as Egypt, Cyprus, Sinop, Kafa, and Thessalonika. Moldavia and Wallachia would not be able to supply as much as in the past, however; this was partly for political reasons—concern that heavy requisitions would provoke pro-Russian sentiment there—and partly because unusually dry weather in 1769 had led to harvest shortfalls. Procurements would also turn out to be hampered by inflation and hoarding, which were further exacerbated when the government minted a flood of new coins. It is also possible that some provincial *ayan* were less diligent or more corrupt in arranging procurements, as the central government had recently let lapse a rule that *ayan* appointments no longer required confirmation by the sultan.[16] Logistical problems would prove serious enough to undermine both the Khotin and Bender garrisons and the grand vizier's field army in 1769; thousands would desert when it was discovered the biscuit stored at Isaccea had been adulterated with dirt and the flour stored at Bender became useless because ovens had not been built.

The Tatar invasion of New Russia

The first operation of the war was undertaken by Khan Kirim Girei, instructed by the sultan to invade Russian Ukraine and southern Russia "for devastation and for taking captives."[17] Kirim Girei was then aged sixty, and Baron de Tott, who accompanied him on this campaign, quite admired him, describing him as able to assume at pleasure "the appearance of a gentle affability, or of a commanding severity."[18] It was Tott's mission to coordinate the khan's campaign with operations by the Bar Confederates, who at the time were in their largest concentrations near Kamianets (2,500 men under Count Gaddick at the forts of Zhvanets and Okop) and Dankovtsy (Count Potocki, with 2,000 men).[19]

Kirim Girei assembled his army at Tombachar in Bucak. He called up three horsemen from every eight households from the Nogai hordes. Some mirzas did not obey his call to arms and had to be jailed, and Tott probably exaggerates when he claims 100,000 men were mobilized for the khan's main army, 40,000 for the *kalga's* army, and 60,000 for the *nuraddin's* army. Petrov estimates the mobilization yielded half that number: Kirim Girei's army comprised 40,000 Nogais from the Bucak and Edisan hordes augmented by 3,030 Ottoman arnauts, 3,000 Nekrasovite Cossacks, 7,000 Ottoman *sipahis*, and 20,000 janissaries, while the *nuraddin* had 30,000 warriors and the *kalga* 20,000.[20] In either case, this was the last great mobilization by a Crimean khan.

Kirim Girei planned to march to Balta, rendezvous with the Ottoman troops, receive some field guns from the Confederates, and then cross the southern Bug River to raid in Bratslav palatinate in southern Poland and the Elizavetgrad province of New Russia. Then he would detach 8,000 warriors and send them to Ladyzhin to join with Potocki's Confederates in raids on the Uman region. The *nuraddin* and *kalga* would campaign east of the Dnepr—the *nuraddin* taking his warriors against Bakhmut, where the eastern wing of Rumiantsev's Second Army was stationed, whereas the *kalga* raided the Zaporozhian winter encampments near the Dnepr.

The army of Kirim Girei marched from Bucak on January 7, 1769, fording the Dnestr and sending their supplies across on eight rafts. It halted at Balta for eight days to gather victuals and receive the Ottoman troops. A few Confederates appeared, but without artillery. To Tott Balta appeared "the most frightful picture of devastation." Most of the inhabitants had fled, as the *sipahi* cavalry awaiting the khan's arrival had already plundered and burned most settlements in the vicinity. Food and forage were unavailable and it was bitter cold. Tott was unimpressed by the quality of the Turkish *sipahis*: "This body of cavalry, accustomed to the comforts and inactivity of a long peace, no way formed to fatigue, uninured to the cold, and so ill-clothed withal, as not to be able to withstand it, could be of no effectual service whatever. Their bravery was not less suspected by the Kam of the Tartars, than are in general their principles of religion."[21]

On January 15 Kirim Girei's army left Balta and crossed the Bug near Orel, entering Russian territory. "Without any fixed order, the army had thrown itself naturally into twenty files deep, and in lines tolerably well formed," Tott wrote. "Each Sultan Serasker, with his little court, formed an advance group before his division. The centre of the line, occupied by the Sovereign, formed of itself a pretty considerable advanced corps, the arrangement of which formed a picture no less military than agreeable. Forty companies, each composed of forty horsemen, four abreast, led the van, in two columns, and formed an avenue, lined on each side with twenty pair of colours. The Grand Equerry, followed by twelve led hordes, and a covered sledge, marched immediately after, and preceded the body of horse which surrounded the Kam. The standard of the Prophet, borne by an emir, as well as the two pair of green colours which accompany it, came next, and were seen blended with the standard of the Cross, belonging to the troop of Inat Cossacks [Nekrasovites], attached to the Prince's bodyguard, which closed the march."[22] At this point the *nuraddin* and the *kalga* separated from Kirim Girei and took their divisions toward Zaporozhia and Bakhmut.

Reports of these movements moved Golitsyn to send a force under A. A. Prozorovskii from Liakhovitsy to Konstantinov to threaten Kirim Girei's army from the rear. He was actually too far off and too short of cavalry to catch up with Kirim Girei, but there were also a few Russian battalions and regiments at Gorynets, Liakhovitsy, Zaslavl', and on approach to Balta, providing enough support so that Prozorovskii could either strike against the 8,000 Tatars raiding near Uman or turn to engage the Confederate forces near Kamianets.[23]

At this time Rumiantsev was in Kiev discussing operational plans with Golitsyn, and his cavalry were busy pursuing haidamak bands. His Second Army was stationed north of Fort Elizavetgrad, between Poltava and Bakhmut.[24]

Kirim Girei encamped his army upon reaching the Ingul River, just on the border of former New Serbia. Emissaries from the Zaporozhian Sich arrived, promising that the Zaporozhians would observe neutrality if spared the *kalga*'s attack. This convinced Kirim Girei to detach one-third of his force, "composed of volunteers, under the orders of a Sultan [Seraskir] and several Mirzas. It should pass the river at midnight, divide itself into several columns, and successively sub-dividing, should overrun New Servia, burn all the villages and crops which were gathered in, carry off all the inhabitants, and drive off their cattle."[25] The *sipahis* were invited to join this strike force but most declined; the exception were the *Serdengeçti* (Forlorn Hope troops), "volunteers determined to conquer or die; but neither the one nor the other ever happens to them."[26] The remaining two-thirds of the khan's force would cross the Ingul and march northwest against Fort Elizavetgrad to protect the Tatar forces raiding across New Serbia.

By January 19, forward elements of the khan's army had come within five *versts* of Fort Elizavetgrad, the rest of his troops were about twenty *versts* behind, near Kalinovka on the Adzhamka River. The cold rainy weather suddenly turned to a frost so severe "that it was with difficulty the tents could be folded up. Small hail, violently drifted by the wind, cut our faces, and made the blood come out of the pores of the nose, and the breath freezing to the whiskers, formed icicles so heavy, as to be very painful. A great part of the Sipahis, maimed in the preceding marches, perished on that day; the Tatars themselves suffered very severely, but nobody dared to complain." Tott estimated that 3,000 men and 30,000 mounts died from the frost that day. Kirim Girei took ill and could no longer ride; he had to take to a covered sledge.[27]

Fort Elizavetgrad was garrisoned by 1,800 infantry, 2,000 light cavalry, and 2,000 Ukrainian Cossacks. Its commander, Major-General A. S. Isakov, had already requested reinforcements, but the nearest Russian forces were at Kremenchug and Tsybul'ev. For the time being, his fortress was surrounded, and he would later explain he lacked the means to make an effective sortie: his infantry would be too slow, and his Ukrainian Cossacks were mostly unfit for mounted service and had been assigned to man the fortress walls.[28] Yet Kirim Girei was reluctant to send his army to attack the fortress; in fact, he feared his army "was in so sad a state, that it had everything to fear from a sally" by the Russians. Nor did his warriors have the energy to make a quick circumvention of the fortress. He decided to give his warriors shelter at the Adzhamka village and wait for the return of his raiding parties. In the meanwhile, he sent a party of three hundred volunteers "to go at sunset to insult St. Elizabeth, to keep the garrison on the defensive."[29] By the twenty-fifth, his raiders had returned and he had burned Adzhamka and begun to withdraw toward Savran, moving in seven columns in slow stages. Major-General Isakov sent his 2,000 cavalry under Prince Bagration to follow, whereas Isakov led his infantry regiments toward Myrhorod and Uman to try to intercept some of the Tatar raiding parties; but they were not fast enough to prevent the raiding of several Polish towns.

Tott describes the Nogai raiders escorting their captives on the khan's return march to Savran.[30] "Five or six slaves, of different ages, sixty sheep, and twenty oxen, the prize of a single man, do not embarrass him. The children, with their heads peeping out of a sack, hanging by the pommel of the saddle; a young girl sitting before, leaning on her left hand; the mother behind on the crupper, the father on a led horse, the son upon another, sheep and oxen before them, everything in a march, and nothing goes astray from under the vigilant eye of the shepherd of this flock." According to Russian reports, the Tatars had seized in Elizavetgrad Province alone 1,183 captives, 13,567 head of cattle, 17,100 sheep and goats, and 1,557 horses. They had killed 126 people and burned four churches, six mills, 1,190 homes, a distillery, 6,377 quarters of grain, and 920 hayricks.

On January 27 the *nuraddin*'s force raiding near Bakhmut had been defeated by a detachment from Rumiantsev's Second Army under Major-General Romanius and had retreated to Crimea after abducting just 794 and killing four. The *kalga*'s detachment operating near Vol'chye Vody against the Don Cossacks had also been put to flight.[31] The human toll and property damage from Tatar raiding around Uman and in Bratslav palatinate is undocumented. Tott judged that Kirim Girei's division had burned 150 villages and had harvested 20,000 prisoners and "innumerable" livestock. The khan's own share was 2,000 captives; he sent the sultan a gift of 600 women. From Savran, the Nogais were sent home with their booty while Kirim Girei himself proceeded to Bender. His illness had worsened, and he died at Bender under the treatment of a Greek physician to the Wallachian hospodar (Tott suspected him of poisoning the khan). Ahmed Resmi Efendi believed that "had there been favorable fortune, had Kirim Giray invaded Poland at that time, in truth he was certain to have wrought utter havoc on the Russians and fearlessly impeded their attack on Hotin."[32]

General-*anshef* Rumiantsev sent a harsh letter to Isakov rebuking him for failing to sortie against the Tatars upon their first approach. He ordered Dolgorukov's corps to take up new positions along the Dnepr, deploying infantry at Omel'nik, Kremenchug, Potok, and Perevolochnia and the cavalry at Vlasovka, Goltva, and Kishenka.[33] The Turks replaced Kirim Girei with Devlet IV Girei, whom Ahmed Resmi Efendi considered a "wretch" released from the Rumelian appanage, where the sultan warehoused his spare Gireis.[34]

The First Army, April–May 1769

The instructions issued in the late 1768 had expected Golitsyn to mobilize the First Army numbering 71,530 troops (47,280 infantry, 14,250 regular cavalry, and 10,000 Cossacks). During the months of its assembly at Kiev (November 1768–February 1769) and its first stationing at Polish territory between Staro-Konstantinov and Polonnoe (March 1769), it had not been possible to bring these regiments to full strength, with the result that the First Army's actual strength was at 44,531 men—5,683 of them *nestroevye*, noncombat effectives—by the time it crossed the Dnestr on April 11: two cuirassier regiments, fourteen carabinier regiments, five hussar regiments, three grenadier regiments, some jaegers from the Finland Division, twenty-six regular line infantry regiments, 100 field guns, ten small unicorns, 100 pontoons, 6,000 Don Cossacks, and 3,000 Ukrainian Cossacks.[35]

But with the Confederates now driven from their trenches around Kamianets, it was possible for Golitsyn to begin his march to Kamianets and Khotin. On March 25 the First Army crossed the Bug River and set up a new main base at Medzhibozh for the artillery train and mobile magazine, with the reserves at Derazhna and Prozorovskii's vanguard of Cossacks at Bar for reconnaissance along the Dnestr. From these three points the army would assemble in full force in six days when it came time to cross the Dnestr at Kalius and approach Khotin.[36] But protracted operations on the other side of the Dnestr would overstrain the supplies at Medzhibozh, and the other larger magazines were far off in the rear at Berdichev, Polonnoe, and Olyk.

At this time about 20,000 Ottoman garrison troops and recently arrived reinforcements were at Khotin under the command of Yegen Hussein Pasha, along with a recently arrived detachment of 10,000 cavalry under Dukakin Karaman Pasha. Khotin had 120 big guns. There were another 13,000 Ottoman troops farther downriver at Sorocha and 30,000 at Bender. Khan Devlet IV Girei and 80,000 Tatars were at Căuşeni, near Bender. But the grand vizier's field army was far off; it had begun its march from Edirne only on March 31, and by mid-April it was still immobilized at Isaccea, where its bridge across the Danube, begun in November, was still under construction—it would not be able to cross the Danube into Moldavia until June 2. This meant that the largest force that Golitsyn was likely to encounter at Khotin was Hussein Pasha's garrison. There were other small enemy forces at points along the Dnestr—a few thousand arnaut volunteers, Potocki's 6,000 followers, and Pulaski's 3,000 Confederates—poised to raid into Ukraine and Poland near Bar and Balta, and it was possible that Confederate forces based near Cracow might take advantage of the First Army's movement to the east and attack L'viv, but these were smaller threats Prozorovskii's flying column and Weimarn's Observation Corps could deal with. There was encouraging intelligence from Bishop Dosifei about the depth of anti-Ottoman feeling within Moldavia, and despite the expenditure of 350 million piasters, Ottoman quartermasters were far from filling their magazines on the Dnestr, Pruth, or even the eastern Danube. Some Ottoman magazines in Moldavia had even been attacked and burned by local inhabitants.[37]

On April 15 the First Army crossed the Dnestr at Kalius in an order of battle of two echelons (each of several infantry brigades, with cavalry) commanded by P. I. Olits and Golitsyn and followed by a reserve (eight battalions grenadiers, six carabinier regiments, and several thousand Cossacks) under C. von Stoffeln.[38] Twenty of the larger field and siege guns were left behind, and Golitsyn ordered his troops to carry just eight days' rations and five days' fodder so as not to slow their march to Khotin. Golitsyn was counting on taking Khotin quickly, by storm rather than protracted siege.

Officers of the Khotin garrison urged Yegen Hussein Pasha to order a sortie against the Russians before they could reach the fortress. He refused and put them to digging a big entrenchment along the face of Khotin's south wall. They mutinied and assassinated him and acclaimed Dukakin Karaman Pasha as his replacement.[39] Dukakin Karaman Pasha's 10,000 cavalry sortied on April 18, but were beaten by Prozorovskii's reserve corps near Novoselitsa. That allowed Golitsyn to bring his army out of the woods and take up position opposite Khotin's southern and eastern walls. As it was already dark, it was decided to put off the attack until the next morning.

On the morning of the nineteenth, the first echelon under Olits advanced to within musket range of the south wall and from a battery atop a hill just to their north began a bombardment of the Turkish troops in Khotin's suburb and in the new trenches along the south wall. Olits' left and right flanks were protected by squares of light and heavy cavalry; the commanders of sections of the first echelon were C. von Stoffeln, J. Bruce, I. P. Saltykov, V. V. Dolgorukov, A. A. Stupishin, Gorchakov, Glebov, Izmailov, Prozorovskii, Aleksei Golitsyn, Kamenskii, and Colonel of Artillery Melissino. Golitsyn had charge of the second echelon, which was positioned behind the first at cannon-range.[40] After three hours of bombardment, the Turks fled their trenches into the fortress or south into the interior of Moldavia. Infantry under Izmailov, Dolgorukov, and Stoffeln advanced to occupy the trenches, but the Turks had managed to set ablaze the Khotin residential suburb. It now became obvious that Khotin was not about to fall to an immediate storm attack and Golitsyn would have to withdraw back over the Dnestr, returning when he had more guns and stores for a longer siege. The Russians had lost just five dead and thirty-six wounded in this action, but among the casualties was Major-General Dolgorukov, whose wound proved fatal.

In the course of withdrawing in two columns on April 21, the army had to throw back an attack upon its front wagons by 5,000 of Abaza Mehmed Pasha's *levendat* cavalry. Prozorovskii and Stoffeln pursued the enemy cavalry as they retreated back to the Prut.[41]

The empress sent a letter congratulating all the commanders on their bravery but singling out Melissino for special praise. She did not rebuke Golitsyn for withdrawing so early—her Council of State had approved his operation plans and had shared his expectation that Moldavians would rise up *en masse*—but she did strongly recommend that next time he should establish his magazines much closer to Khotin.[42]

The First Army withdrew to Derazhna and remained there for most of May and June. To be fair, Golitsyn was not the only one who considered it impossible to make an immediate return to attack Khotin. At a council of war held on April 19, all Golitsyn's generals save Prozorovskii acknowledged it was impossible: the army was too far from its magazines, its mounts were running low on hay, and larger enemy forces in the south might be advancing (Olits thought the grand vizier's field army might reach Khotin within the next two weeks). But not all of them had favored taking the army back to Derazhna. Stoffeln thought it would be better to set a fortified camp closer to Khotin, near Kalius, Mohylew, or Iampol, so that the First Army could station itself closer to Rumiantsev's Second Army while still guarding its supply line back to Medzhibozh. Essen, Bruce, Stupishin and Izmailov proposed encamping the army on the Moldavian side of the Dnestr, between that river and the Prut, to engage the grand vizier's field army before it could link up with the forces at Khotin. Prozorovskii argued for making a final storm assault on Khotin—a surprise attack at dawn—while sending a flying column through Moldavia to threaten the bridge and storehouses at Isaccea; if these measures failed and the grand vizier approached Khotin, the First Army could fall back to Stanislavov to strike the grand vizier's army in the rear, or to the woods of Marianpol to hit them in the rear if they marched against Rumiantsev's Second Army.[43] Another option not seriously discussed was marching against Iaşi, the Moldavian capital—which lay just eight days away and was defended by only 25,000 Turks—then waiting for the Second Army to come through Dubossary and join forces for a battle against the grand vizier's army.

With Golitsyn's First Army sitting inactive at Derazhna, Rumiantsev was placed at a disadvantage: his Second Army had to defend the broad Ukrainian front while simultaneously keeping itself ready to march west if it proved necessary to come to the relief of the First Army.[44] In May, Rumiantsev therefore took the Second Army across the Dnepr and camped on its eastern bank near Kriukov Shanets. He sent a detachment of light cavalry under Major-General Zorich toward Elizavetgrad and then toward Bender for reconnaissance. The only corps of the Second Army now left on the eastern side of the Dnepr was G. G. Berg's, near Bakhmut, which was charged with the tasks of guarding against Tatar attack and covering operations at Azov and Taganrog. Rumiantsev took these measures reluctantly, worried that he was spreading out his forces too far in violation of his preference for force concentration.[45]

Rumiantsev was greatly dissatisfied with the war plan imposed on him. He had not received its details until January 5, 1769. Those details had set the strength of the Second Army at 43,728 troops: five regiments of regular cavalry, seven hussar regiments, four pikinier regiments, 9,000 Cossacks, fourteen regiments of infantry, and forty guns.[46] He was uneasy that St. Petersburg expected him to defend such a vast Ukrainian front and assist the First Army with so few troops. With those numbers he could patrol the Ukrainian front but might have difficulty holding it against Tatar and Ottoman armies. The Second Army was deficient in regular cavalry and too many of his regiments had come from the Baltic front and were inexperienced in steppe warfare. The Ukrainian Division, which he had created while Governor-General of Little Russia, had been transferred to Golitsyn's First Army. He had been promised five regiments of regular cavalry and fourteen infantry regiments from the Moscow Division but had been given just two regiments of carabiniers and four regiments of infantry from that division. His pikiniers were less effective Land Militia military colonists and anyhow remained under the authority of F. M. Voeikov, the new Governor-General of Little Russia.

Rumiantsev's experience in the Seven Years' War had convinced him of the uselessness of the "cordon strategy" the Austrian commanders had employed, and he had written to the VK back in September 1768 arguing that only garrison forces should be assigned the function of cordon defense in Ukraine; his Second Army should be given the task of mobile defense and for this purpose should be stationed in three large concentrations, one on the Dnepr and the others on the eastern and western flanks, with maximum coordination among them. He repeated this proposal in a late December letter to Nikita Panin.[47] He could now cite Kirim Girei's recent defeat in New Russia in support of a mobile force strategy: Isakov's Elizavetgrad garrison had been less useful in defeating the Tatars than Romanius' regiments.

He had also argued in December that Golitsyn's proposed campaign against Khotin would prove of less value to the Russian war effort than his own proposal, an attack by the Second Army on Ochakov and Perekop. Even if Golitsyn managed to take Khotin on the first attempt, he had written, it would not much affect the operational capacity of the grand vizier's field army sitting idle farther down the Dnepr, and it was unlikely that Ottoman forces would link up with the Confederates and drive into Poland. But if Perekop were taken, Tatar forces would be bottled up in Crimea and unable to reinforce the Ottomans on the Danubian–Dnestr front, and if Ochakov fell to the Russians, the Turks would lose one of their most important naval bases on the northern coast of the Black Sea and would find it harder to provision their forces at Bender and Khotin; the grand vizier's army would likely have to put aside plans to march on Khotin and concentrate instead of defending Bender.[48]

The recovery of Azov and Taganrog

Although Golitsyn's first attempt to take Khotin had failed, at least Khan Devlet IV Girei and his 80,000 Crimean Tatars had not yet moved from Căuşeni in Bessarabia, where they had been stationed since Kirim Girei's death. This left the Crimean peninsula poorly defended and provided the opportunity for the Second and Third divisions of Rumiantsev's Second Army to undertake two important operations that had been part of their original mission: recovering Azov and Taganrog and making a diversionary raid into Crimea.

Lt. General F. P. Vernes had been appointed to command a flotilla to sail down the Don and occupy the half-destroyed fortress of Azov, which had been assigned to the demilitarized zone by the 1739 Treaty. By spring, Vernes had assembled at Fort St. Dmitrii a flotilla of seventy-five vessels, mostly prams and double-sloops, with 1,035 guns and 12,400 crewmen and troops. This force arrived at Azov on March 6 and garrisoned it. While Azov's crumbling defense works were being renovated and expanded, a detachment of 500 Cossacks under Brigadier Zhederas reconnoitered Taganrog, twenty *versts* west from the mouth of the Don, and found it abandoned. Zhederas returned on April 2 with more Cossacks and a thousand laborers and took control of Taganrog. Patrols sent out as far as the mouth of the Kal'miuss turned up no sign of the enemy.

Thus Azov and Taganrog had been restored to the Russian Empire. But to retain control of the Sea of Azov would require a larger and more sea-worthy fleet. In June, the first vessels of this new fleet, two 44-gun prams, arrived at Azov from the shipyards on the upper Don, and A. N. Seniavin, now promoted to Vice-Admiral, was able to begin building a great harbor at Taganrog. The water here was conveniently deeper here than at the mouth of the Don, although there was not much potable river or well water in the vicinity.[49] Here would be laid the foundations for a new Black Sea Flotilla, a true sea-going fleet that could not only defend the Don delta but also support the invasion of Crimea and challenge the Ottoman navy for mastery of the Black Sea.[50]

While construction and settlement were underway at Azov and Taganrog, the Third Division of the Second Army under Lt. General Berg provided cover by pushing south from Bakhmut to threaten the Khanate.[51] On June 1, they reached Vol'chye Vody; on the seventh, they entered Crimea through Zheleznaia Balka and camped at the Torets River. On June 10, near the heights of the Kal'miuss River, Berg divided his division in half: Berg accompanied a column under Major-General Karl von Stoffeln heading toward the Berestovaia River, while a column under Major-General Romanius marched on Mokrye Ialy, rendezvoused there with 11,000 Kalmyks, and then crossed the Vol'chye Vody and proceeded along the Verda River.[52]

Stoffeln's column made rapid progress and reached Kal'chik on June 22. It joined here with 50,000 Kalmyks and with the Tambov infantry regiment of the Ukrainian Line, guarding the approaches to Azov. After building a food magazine at Kal'chik to receive shipments from Bakhmut and Izium, Berg and Stoffeln took their column along the Verda River, reuniting with Romanius' column on June 27. Patrols were sent ahead toward the Tokman' River. On the twenty-ninth, the Russians and Kalmyks advanced toward Verda Creek in three columns, with Berg's troops in the center column and Kalmyks on the right and left. Berg encountered a Tatar reconnaissance force of 500 warriors near Balka on July 4 and skirmished successfully with it. The next day his column reached Molochnye Vody.[53]

From here the only passages into the Crimean peninsula were through the heavily fortified line at Perekop or across the Sivash Shallows, the lagoons and marshes of the Rotten Sea. Berg chose the latter route, which Field Marshal Peter Lacy had followed in 1737. He managed to get across the Sivash at Shamgur but had to halt at Genici. The Tatars had not appeared in force to block his advance, but they had burned all the grass and the water for miles around was foul, presenting real hardship for his cavalry. Anyway, his force was too small to safely move deeper into the interior.[54] So he withdrew to the Kal'miuss and deployed for defense. But his march on Crimea had provided enough of a diversion to give Russian forces time to consolidate their control of Azov and Taganrog.

Golitsyn's second attempt on Khotin, July–August 1

Grand Vizier Yağlikçizade Mehmed Emin Pasha finally took his army across the Danube at Isaccea on June 2, 1769.[55] His planned itinerary was to Kartal, then to the main supply depot at Hantepesi, to Bender, to the magazine at Riabaia Mogila, and finally to Khotin. But his logistical preparations had not been completed. His advance would be slowed by the necessity of taking along thousands of wagons from Hantepesi to under-supplied Bender, and at Bender five or six thousand of his troops deserted after finding no ovens for baking their bread.[56]

The grand vizier had been a *diwan* secretary without military command experience, and he was seriously ill. At the council of war he held at Hantepesi, he showed his dismayed commanders just how little thought he had given to this campaign. He admitted that he had no idea as to what Russian movements to expect or what steps to take next and asked his commanders for recommendations. According to Ahmed Resmi Efendi, the grand vizier doubted that the Russians would make another attack on Khotin after failing there in April, and he thought they would have moved against Bender already if that had been their intention. His preference was for beginning the campaign with raids into New Russia. The council decided to appoint Gülpaşazade Ali Pasha *Seraskir* of Khotin; Moldovanci Ali Pasha was put in charge of the garrison at Iaşi, mostly because the grand vizier disliked him and wanted him away from his camp.[57] Eventually, it was decided to take the army up the Prut River to the camp and magazine at Riabaia Mogila, roughly equidistant from Bender and Khotin, and wait there to see where the Russians would move next. By mid-June, about 100,000 of the grand vizier's troops were concentrated at Riabaia Mogila—its magazine was not sufficient to feed more—and the rest were distributed between the Sărat River and the Dnestr.[58]

The sultan demanded an invasion of Poland and so ordered the grand vizier to march his army to Khotin, cross the Dnestr, and attack Kamianets by June 26. But the grand vizier's staff was reluctant to comply: there were not enough provisions around Khotin to support an invasion of Poland, and Potocki, upon whose intelligence they replied, dreaded the prospect of a large Ottoman field army devastating Poland. Potocki was continuing to argue for a strike into New Russia instead—40,000 Tatars had already moved to Dubossary to prepare for this—and he had convinced the grand vizier that Khotin and Bender could be held against the Russians with two divisions from the field army as reinforcements while the rest of the field army maintained its present position so as to tighten control over provisions collections from Moldavia.[59] Therefore Potocki and Mehmed Pasha arrived at Khotin on June 9 with fresh stores and reinforcements for the Khotin garrison and Abaza Mehmed's cavalry corps: 8,000 janissaries, 15,000 cavalry, a few hundred *sipahi*s, and twelve guns. This brought the Ottoman forces at Khotin up to 35,000, and another 40,000 Tatars were reportedly advancing toward Khotin from Balta. Mehmed Pasha received appointment as *Seraskir Rumeli-Valasi* on June 12. But on their arrival at Khotin his troops were reportedly filled with foreboding by sight of a sandstorm and blood-red moon.[60]

Reports that new forward fortifications and a bridge across the Dnestr at Braga were under construction pressed Golitsyn to hold a council of war on June 5 to discuss returning to Khotin. As there was also intelligence that the Turks were planning to raid New Russia, it was decided to deploy some forces from the First Army farther south along the Dnestr to block further enemy reinforcement of Khotin, and Rumiantsev was asked to move the Second Army to Ermolintsev. A second council of war in late June resolved that the First Army should cross over the Dnestr at Simoshin, a few kilometers above Khotin.

This crossing was undertaken by pontoon on June 24. The Turks were not aware of it until it was already underway; at that point, Potocki journalled, he had tried to convince

Ali Pasha to send cavalry to hit the Russians in the rear and a detachment of infantry, cavalry, and guns to block their further advance. But Ali Pasha had decided to wait until he could concentrate all his forces and then encircle and destroy the Russians.

The first elements of the First Army to cross at Simoshin were Prozorovskii's light vanguard and Stoffeln's reserve corps. They entered Bukovin Forest, through which Golitsyn had planned to march the rest of the army, moving in front and rear columns in preparation for a battle order of two echelons. Golitsyn had artillery and *chevaux-de-frise* with him, but to shorten his train he had ordered his mobile magazine left behind at Simoshin under guard by a small force of infantry and cavalry. This meant that his troops were carrying just four days' rations. Colonel Shirkov was sent with a small detachment to Stanislavov to establish a second magazine to receive stores brought up from Medzhibozh. Johann Rennenkampf's division remained on the Polish side of the river to protect the line of communications to Kamianets.

On reaching the defile through Bukovin Forest, Golitsyn decided against entering it—his columns were too long—and so the First Army circumvented the forest on their left and camped at the village of Rogoza, a few miles from Khotin, on June 28.[61] On July 2 the First Army took up a new position just beyond the village of Pashkvitsy, about six kilometers southeast of Khotin fortress.

By this time the Ottoman, Confederate, and Tatar forces assembled at Khotin and its outlying forts under the command of Hussein Pasha and the *Seraskir Rumeli-Valasi* Mehmed Pasha approached 85,000; Khotin's outworks had been repaired and the number of guns brought up to over 400, although there were not yet enough gunners to man them. A few thousand more Confederates under Marozowiecki were expected to arrive within days, and once the grand vizier received report of Golitsyn's approach on Khotin, he was thought likely to send Moldovanci Ali Pasha from Iaşi and more of the khan's Tatars in reinforcement.[62]

Before dawn on July 2, Golitsyn received report of a large enemy force to his north. He formed his army into a vast square, with light cavalry on his left and Stoffeln's reserve on his right. Along the front of his camp was a small creek, easy to cross but rising on the Russians' side to a high bank covered in dense vegetation; he sent part of Stoffeln's reserve corps—five of his grenadier battalions—to occupy this bank. They were followed by two regiments of Izmailov's carabiniers and some Cossacks and hussars, who took position on the right of Stoffeln's grenadiers. Around 5:00 a.m., thousands of Ottoman cavalry crossed the creek and charged the bank, breaking and scattering the Cossacks and hussars and then falling upon Stoffeln's grenadiers from the right and from the front. The grenadiers were quickly overrun despite their *chevaux-de-frise*. Fortunately, two more battalions of Stoffeln's grenadiers came up through a ravine from the reserve at this moment and helped the others reform their line and push back the Turks under support from Golitsyn's batteries. A second attack by the Turkish cavalry failed, and Golitsyn brought the rest of his square up to the bank, followed by his train in a *wagenburg*. He again covered his right flank with light cavalry brought up from the army's original position at Pashkvitsy. This action had succeeded in part because Golitysn had reacted quickly and ordered the grenadier battalions sent forward from his reserve, and because the artillery had inflicted heavy losses on the attacking enemy, who had attacked with cavalry alone and with no supporting fire from their own field guns.[63]

Golitsyn's square resumed its advance toward Khotin fortress, but it had not proceeded more than a kilometer beyond the creek when it suddenly came under attack from all sides by a huge force of Mehmed Pasha's cavalry. Mehmed Pasha made several attempts to break the Russian square but was thrown back each time by heavy infantry and artillery fire; finally, he changed his strategy and attacked the weaker right flank of Cossacks and light cavalry. The Russian right flank would have collapsed if not for its reinforcement by the Apsheron Infantry Regiment and two battalions of grenadiers and fire from a battery shifted to high ground on the right. By 11:00 a.m. Mehmed Pasha's cavalry had retreated, and not entirely in good order; while some fell back to Khotin and others fled toward the Prut River. Golitsyn's square continued its advance that afternoon, reaching Kaplivka, about three kilometers south of Khotin, by 5:00 p.m.[64]

From his unfortunate experience in April, Golitsyn had learned Khotin could not be taken simply by storm; it would first have to be subjected to protracted bombardment. He began bombardment on July 3, from batteries along both sides of the Dnestr. As Rennenkampf's division occupied good ground on the opposite bank for batteries, he sent Rennenkampf reinforcements, built two bridges across the Dnestr near Okop, and founded a new magazine at Okop with stores transferred from Medzhibozh and Stanislavov. He also blocked the roads between Khotin and Kamianets, Iași, and Bender with the intent of keeping the Turks bottled up and hungry inside Khotin fortress.[65]

Large relief forces from Iași under Moldovanci Ali Pasha and from Căușeni under Khan Devlet IV Girei were en route to Khotin, and the grand vizier himself started marching the rest of his field army from Bender back toward Riabaia Mogila. But Golitsyn had placed a blocking force under Prozorovskii athwart the Iași road to provide warning of their approach, and the grand vizier's advance was significantly slowed by desertions provoked by a provisioning crisis of his own making.[66]

A Tatar vanguard was repulsed by the artillery of Bruce's corps on July 19 near Lipkany, about thirty kilometers south of Khotin. Prozorovskii had begun to pursue the Tatars southward, but he and Bruce were called back once it was decided that this Tatar detachment must be a diversion assisting Moldovanci Ali's advance from Iași.[67]

The vanguard of the First Army had its own fortified camp north of Rukshan village woods, whereas the main camp was along a narrow rise to its north, protected by a creek running through Rukshan to the Dnestr, two other creeks to the rear, five small redoubts facing Rukshan, and another four redoubts on the camp's right flank facing open field. Prozorovskii's new position was a little to the southeast, on the road to Bender, protected by a trench line and two more redoubts. Seven more redoubts facing the field and running from the main camp to Prozorovskii's position were still under construction.

Around noon on July 22 a large enemy force—probably Tatar cavalry—attacked Prozorovskii's trench line. Repulsed several times by artillery fire, the enemy then drew out into line on the left with the intention of expanding its assault to include Golitsyn's main camp on the right flank. For a moment, the enemy even succeeded in breaking through and cutting Prozorovskii off from Golitsyn, but Saltykov took his heavy cavalry out and struck the enemy in the rear; this and canister fire from the main camp finally put to flight the enemy forces attacking Prozorovskii. But the Tatars continued their attack upon the redoubts on the right, and Turkish cavalry and infantry from Khotin fortress began a simultaneous sortie. A counterattack by eight battalions of Stoffeln's grenadiers threw the Tatar cavalry back, while four infantry regiments and some cavalry defeated the Khotin sortie detachment. By evening the enemy had withdrawn on all sides, falling back to the fortress and fleeing south. This engagement may have worsened morale among Khotin's defenders by revealing the weakness of their infantry, their inability to lift the Russian blockade, and the need to keep to defensive operations while awaiting rescue from without.[68]

Another attack came on July 26, this time by 50,000 troops in a vast half-moon formation, the horns attacking Prozorovskii's division and Rennenkampf's position at the Okop bridges and the center throwing itself against the redoubts along Golitsyn's right flank. This attack was repulsed as well, apparently with heavy losses, and Prozorovskii's cavalry pursued them some distance.[69]

The next morning, Turks from the Khotin garrison began work on new fortifications while their cavalry pitched camps along the river above and below the fortress. According to Potocki's journal, he had convinced Khotin's commandants that they had enough troops to withstand a long Russian siege provided they use part of their forces to weaken Golitsyn's lines of supply and communication. He had recommended that they dig approach trenches toward Golitsyn's camp and await the arrival of Moldovanci Ali and the grand vizier while several thousand other troops were sent to seize the Okop bridges and magazine and march toward Chernovitsy to block Golitsyn from receiving supplies from the Moldavian interior or withdrawing through Pokutia.[70]

But Potocki's plan could not be implemented. On August 1 Golitsyn's bombardment and siege of Khotin entered its twenty-seventh day. Four days before the Ottoman, garrison at Khotin had exhausted its flour and biscuit, and although forward elements of Moldovanci Ali's army had probed Golitsyn's defenses, Moldovanci Ali had chosen to hold to position to receive an attack rather than advance closer to give one. But Golitsyn doubted the strength of his own position. Weeks of blockade and bombardment had not forced Khotin's capitulation, and Golitsyn lacked the heavy siege guns to bring it to a quicker close; his First Army was low on provisions and fodder, too; and enemy forces in the theater greatly outnumbered the First Army, especially if the nearby army of Moldovanci Ali really numbered 70,000 men. Therefore Golitsyn convened a council of war to discuss withdrawing across the Dnestr.

Several of his generals spoke in favor of continuing the blockade and even preparing to attack Moldovanci Ali, but the council finally decided to begin an immediate evacuation. The First Army crossed back over the Dnestr at Okop on August 1–2 and headed for Kniagino.[71]

His previous dispatches to the Council of State had painted a picture of mounting successes, so report of Golitsyn's second withdrawal from Khotin caused consternation in St. Petersburg. It also moved Frederick II to offer another quip, "Catherine's generals were ignorant of fortification and tactics; those of the Sultan had even less knowledge, so that to form a clear idea of this war, one must imagine one-eyed men who have given blind men a thorough beating and gained a complete ascendancy over them."[72]

Rumiantsev also stepped up his criticism of Golitsyn's conduct on the Khotin front. For the past few months, Rumiantsev had been complaining to St. Petersburg that Golitsyn had failed to share intelligence with him while repeatedly demanding he take the Second Army west from the Dnepr to other stations even while Golitsyn was taking the First Army farther out of his range. He had also criticized Golitsyn's plan to take Khotin by blockade as naive.[73] In mid-July, Rumiantsev had rejected Golitsyn's request to bring the Second Army toward the Bug; he had instead left most of it concentrated near Elizavetgrad while sending Berg's division against Crimea and reconnaissance detachments into Poland and toward Bender and Ochakov. He viewed this as sufficient assistance to Golitsyn, as these movements had confused the grand vizier as to the Second Army's actual position and strength and had caused the grand vizier to reverse the march he had begun toward Khotin.[74] For Rumiantsev, the dispatch of troops toward Bender and Ochakov had the added advantage of demonstrating again the necessity of adhering to a mobile force strategy.

On August 13 the empress decreed that Golitsyn was to relinquish command of the First Army and return to St. Petersburg for consultations. Rumiantsev was appointed to replace him as commander-in-chief of the First Army. Petr Ivanovich Panin would take over the Second Army. The VK issued their new orders the following day.[75] The Panin clan was disappointed by this, preferring to see command of the First Army go to Petr Panin, whom they argued was more likely to inspire the army than the bookish and methodical Rumiantsev. They insinuated that Rumiantsev owed his new appointment to a cabal of powerful court women headed by his mother and his sister Countess Bruce.[76]

But the empress' rescript appointing Rumiantsev to take over the First Army was clear in communicating her expectations. The fact that lack of forage had forced Golitsyn to cross back over the Dnestr "has undoubtedly given the enemy encouragement, even if without cause. But I hope that your skill and agility will not allow the enemy to long entertain such empty vainglory when you take under your command an army that has already in the last five months put to flight six times the innumerable disorderly mob of the enemy, and that you will endeavor not only to recover the abandoned advantage but to win us new advantages."[77]

The stalemate at Khotin also had repercussions for Ottoman command. When news came that "the Russians had been crushed anew at Hotin and retreated across the Dniester … the realm rejoiced," wrote Ahmed Resmi Efendi. "Yet what was the use? The Muscovites were not the type to change their ways, to relent when routed, nor to withdraw, saying 'Winter has come.' They prepared to continue on until the job was done. They crossed the Dniester, putting their affairs in order in Poland, and awaited our army's fatigue and dispersal."[78] Scapegoats were needed. Grand Vizier Yağlıkçizade Mehmed Emin blamed garrison commandant Dukakin Karaman and had him summoned to his pavilion at Hantepesi to hear pronouncement of his death sentence. Dukakin Karaman did not take this stoically; he drew his pistol on the grand vizier and had to be subdued.

On August 2, the grand vizier himself received orders to relinquish his command and go into exile at Dimetoka. On September 11, he was executed on order of the sultan. Moldovanci Ali Pasha was appointed the new grand vizier.[79]

The fall of Khotin, August 29–September 10

On August 14, the day Golitsyn's replacement with Rumiantsev was announced, the First Army was encamped on the Polish side of the Dnestr near Kniagino, close to Kamianets. A few days before, Golitsyn had sent some light cavalry under Prozorovskii to conduct reconnaissance between the Dnestr and the Prut; Major-General Potemkin had also taken two carabinier regiments and one infantry regiment south along the Dnestr to respond to raids by Tatars arriving to reinforce Khotin. The First Army camped at Kniagino was therefore left with the following commanders and units: second in command was General-*anshef* Petr Ivanovich Olits; Lt.-Generals Christopher von Stoffeln, Petr Plemiannikov, Christopher von Essen, Count James Bruce, Count Ivan Saltykov, Johann Rennenkampf, Nikolai Saltykov, Baron Ivan von Elmpt (Quartermaster General), and Prince Nikolai Repnin; Major-Generals Gavrila Cherepov, Karl von Tranze, Aleksei Stupishin, Prince Ivan Gorchakov, Fedor Glebov, Aleksandr Kheraskov, Ivan Podgorichani, Ivan Izmailov, Prince Aleksandr Prozorovskii, Semen Chernoevich, Aleksandr Zamiatnin, Mikhail Kamenskoi, and Prince Aleksei Golitsyn; two cuirassier regiments, twelve carabinier regiments, five hussar regiments, three grenadier regiments, twenty-seven line infantry regiments, 6,000 Don Cossacks, 3,000 Ukrainian Cossacks, an unspecified number of Moldavian *arnaut* volunteers, 100 field guns, ten small unicorns, thirty-two supplemental regimental guns, a field artillery command of 2,705, and 4,405 staff, auditors, priests, surgeons, clerks, farriers, and clerks.[80] This was roughly the same strength as in April—under 39,000 men.

At noon on August 14 Ottoman troops began erecting a pontoon bridge across the Dnestr under the cover of Khotin's fortress guns; Ottoman cavalry and infantry also began fording the river at its shallows. These troops were from a large army of 70,000–80,000 men the new Grand Vizier, Moldovanci Ali Pasha, had brought up from Hantepesi.

On receiving this news Golitsyn ordered the First Army out of its Kniagino camp and closer to the river. By the end of the day the army's right flank had reached Gavrilovtsy, about three *versts* from the river. Detachments of Cossacks and hussars sent ahead to attack the first enemy elements across the river were thrown back and the enemy was able to claim the heights above Braga and open fire on redoubts held by the company of Azov Grenadiers. A battalion of F. I. Fabritsian's jaegers also came under attack. About 10,000 Turks had by this point made it across the river. Three hussar regiments under Brigadier P. A. Tekelli and some infantry battalions under Major Bonenberg and Colonel Gudovich came to reinforce Fabritsian and they slowed the Turkish advance, killing about a thousand of the enemy. But enemy forces continued to cross the Dnestr by pontoon, boat, or fording all the next day. The total strength of enemy forces near Khotin now approached 100,000 (including Tatars and Confederates), and the enemy had twenty large field guns and 240 small "mule guns."[81] A captured Confederate officer related that Moldovanci Ali was expecting an additional 20,000 foot and 3,000 horses from Riabaia Mogila, where the janissary *aga* had taken temporary command following the deposition of Grand Vizier Yağlikçizade Mehmed Emin.[82]

On August 16 Golitsyn moved the First Army from Gavrilovtsy to a new camp closer to the river. Major-General Demolin fortified this new camp with five lunette earthworks on its corners, seven surrounding redoubts, two larger forward redoubts with fleches and wolf-traps, and lines of abatis (*zaseka*) in the forest along the left flank.[83] The redoubts provided a triple line of fire on the flanks and in front and a double line of fire in the rear. The right flank faced the Dnestr; Rachev Forest ran along the front as far as the village of Babshino, where the enemy was likely to send foraging parties, there being no other site on this side of the river offering good fodder for horses.

The Turks completed their bridge across the Dnestr on August 20, crossed in force on the 22nd, and secured their bridgehead with an entrenchment on the 23rd. Golitsyn sent 4,000 troops under colonels Weissman, Igel'strom, Sukhotin, and Krechetnikov to destroy the bridgehead. They were able to capture the entrenchment but were unable to burn the bridge, which was of green wood.[84] Golitsyn's next move was to occupy Babshino and station there infantry that could attack the Turks in the rear; for this purpose, he sent into the woods near Babshino a detachment of cavalry under Lt. General Saltykov, twenty companies of grenadiers under Major-General Kamenskii and Colonels Rzhevskii and Kashkin, and six grenadier regiments under Major-Generals Glebov and Potemkin. At sunset on August 28 Saltykov's, Glebov's, and Potemkin's cavalry and grenadiers took up position in the woods behind Babshino while the twenty grenadier companies followed the road from the camp along the edge of the woods and entered the forward part of the woods already occupied by Russian advance posts.

The deployment near Babshino had been intended to ambush Turkish foragers and position Saltykov's forces for a strike against the enemy's rear. But from his point within the Babshino woods Saltykov was unaware that the enemy forces advancing from the bridge at dawn on August 29 were Moldovanci Ali's main army, 20,000 cavalry in the vanguard, heading for the right flank of Golitsyn's camp. At 7:00 a.m., the Turkish guns along the Khotin side of the bridge opened fire on the Russian camp and Turkish infantry began digging trenches facing the abatis lines along the left flank of the camp.

A cavalry attack on the camp's right flank was repulsed by heavy fire from Melissino's battery and crossfire from the redoubts, and the Turkish infantry behind them froze when deprived of their cavalry screen.[85]

The enemy's remaining momentum was therefore brought mostly to bear on the three abatis lines defended by Bruce and Aleksei Golitsyn. Along most of the abatis lines, the Russians were thinly spread in just two ranks and, along some stretches, just one, supported by a handful of regimental guns, with a hundred men stationed at an additional gun off their first line of jaegers, to the right, separated from the jaegers by a path through the woods. At 8:00 a.m. 6,000 Ottoman infantry made a column attack through a ravine against the center of the middle abatis, while another 4,000 Ottoman infantry struck the middle abatis on its right flank and Ottoman cavalry separated the St.

Petersburg and Fourth Grenadier regiments from the rest of Bruce's men, forcing them to fall back to the rear abatis.

But by positioning to attack the abatis lines, the Turks had moved past Saltykov's post in the woods, and Saltykov now realized that they comprised the enemy's main attack, not a forage party. He divided his force in three: Kamenskii leading eight grenadier companies to strike at the Turks attacking the middle abatis, Rzhevskii with four grenadier companies and some jaegers heading toward the right flank of that abatis, and Saltykov himself leading the eight remaining grenadier companies against the rear of the enemy attacking the center section of the middle abatis. Saltykov arrived in time to save the Fourth Grenadier Regiment, which had found itself completely surrounded; the Fourth was then able to make a bayonet attack and drive the Turks back. Saltykov, Rzhevskii, and Kamenskii were then free to go to the relief of the rest of Bruce's command, which had been pushed back to the rear abatis. The Turks were beaten back from the third abatis, then from the second abatis, and then pushed back into the woods beyond. A flank attack on their right by four companies of Bruce's grenadiers combined by an attack on their front by Saltykov succeeded in driving the Turks back to their bridgehead by 3:00 p.m.[86]

Around noon, 20,000 Ottoman cavalry had entered the meadows separating the two halves of Rachev Forest and made three attacks on Glebov's forces in the rear of Babshino, forcing Glebov to turn his front toward the left to expose his attackers to artillery fire from Golitsyn's camp. But Golitsyn did not spare cavalry from his camp to reinforce Glebov, and this seems to have convinced Moldovanci Ali that victory was at hand; he tried to use his cavalry to attack the main camp from three sides, defying the intense fire from the Russian batteries. Glebov maneuvered again to try to hit the attacking Turkish cavalry in their rear, but before he could strike, the Ottoman cavalry attack broke up on its own after incurring heavy losses from the Russian guns. An attack by a separate Ottoman cavalry force against Golitsyn's train near Kamianets also failed. Golitsyn's cavalry finally sortied from their camp and pursued the Turkish cavalry back to the Dnestr. By 7:00 p.m. the battle was over.[87]

Figures on Turkish and Tatar casualties in this battle are not available, although the Russians estimated about 3,000 enemy dead had been left on the battlefield. The losses in the First Army were two staff officers, three over-officers, and 177 soldiers killed, and fourteen over-officers and 323 soldiers wounded.[88]

Moldovanci Ali sent Orai Uglu and a force of 5,000 infantry and 7,000 cavalry back over the Dnestr bridge on September 6, but they were thrown back by Russian grenadiers and suffered heavy losses (the Russians lost eighty-nine killed and 500 wounded). Then heavy rains and flooding caused the collapse of the Turks' pontoon bridge. On the night of September 7/8, Major-General Demolin opened fire on Khotin fortress from a new battery set up near Braga. The Khotin garrison had already suffered privations and low morale, and Moldovanci Ali's army was short on food and fodder; so Moldovanci Ali decided on September 8 or 9 to withdraw his army to Hantepesi. The Khotin garrison was evacuated as well. "The troops were extremely weakened and reduced by hunger, enemy fire, and the cold, so no one wanted to stay. The pasas who were appointed [as commandants] went in one door of the fortress and went out the other," Ahmed Resmi Efendi wrote. The evacuation was not orderly; many parties of deserters were captured by the Russians or drowned trying to cross the Dnestr. At Iaşi, mutineers tried to assassinate Moldovanci Ali and he was forced to flee with a guard of forty men to Riabaia Mogila.[89] Moldovanci Ali was dismissed and replaced as grand vizier by Ivaz Pashazade Halil Pasha. This did not prevent the sultan's government from celebrating the battle of August 29 as a great victory and bestowing the title of *Ghazi* on Sultan Mustafa III.

When the First Army entered Khotin on September 9, they found only twenty men of its garrison remaining. Golitsyn left Brigadier Weissman and four infantry regiments to garrison Khotin from a camp outside the fortress (its inside had not yet been emptied of corpses). Lt. General Elmpt was ordered to take a small corps south to follow the retreating Turks; Golitsyn took the rest of the First Army back across the Dnestr on September 13. En route to the army's base at Medzhibozh, it stopped at Chercha for a few days to await its new commander, Rumiantsev.[90]

Rumiantsev arrived and took command on September 18. He decided that most of the First Army ought to enter winter quarters at Letichev near the Bug River; in the meantime, Elmpt's operations in Moldavia were to be strengthened by sending a detachment of light forces under Prozorovskii along the western bank of the Dnestr for reconnaissance and support. Prozorovskii was instructed to head in the direction of Bender to rendezvous with Wittgenstein's detachment out of the Second Army. Once Stoffeln had pacified Iaşi and northern Moldavia, his corps was likewise to rendezvous with Prozorovskii and Wittgenstein near Bender. This would finally resolve the old problem of the 400-kilometer gap between the First and the Second armies and facilitate coordination between both armies for the next task, a campaign against Galaţi and Ibrail. Rumiantsev intended to remain on the offensive, this time with the Danube as his objective.[91]

The First Army in Moldavia, September–December

On September 10 Golitsyn had ordered a small corps of grenadiers, carabiniers, and Cossack cavalry under Lt. General von Elmpt to move south to pursue the fleeing Turks, seize Iaşi, and rouse the Moldavians to revolt. After Moldovanci Ali Pasha had fled to Riabaia Mogila, just 300 Turks and Confederates were left to defend Iaşi. Elmpt reached the outskirts of Iaşi on the twelfth. He sent a detachment of light cavalry under Prozorovskii around northeastern Moldavia calling on the inhabitants to come to Botoşani and swear allegiance to Russia. On September 26 an advance party of hussars under Colonel Khorvat took possession of Iaşi for Elmpt. The nearest large Ottoman forces were off at Riabaia Mogila and Bender, so the Russians met with no significant opposition when their cavalry pushed on toward Cecora and toward the Danube crossing at Isaccea; in fact, their movements convinced Grand Vizier Ivaz Pashazade Halil Pasha to hasten the Ottoman army back over the Danube, leaving behind guns, supply wagons, and stragglers. Ekaterina Bibikova, future wife of Mikhail Kutuzov, wrote that she saw 20,000 Turkish horses dead along the road from Iaşi to Bucharest.[92] One is left to speculate what would have happened if Golitsyn had sent the rest of his army following Elmpt toward the Danube instead of returning to Medzhibozh.

The appearance of Russian forces in Iaşi emboldened a "liberation movement" in Moldavia. Clerics appeared at Botoşani and Iaşi pledging allegiance to Empress Catherine II and support with provisioning; peasants and townsmen enlisted in volunteer detachments that raided Ottoman magazines.[93] There was also pro-Russian agitation in Wallachia, where a faction of boyars and clerics grouped around the Cantacuzene brothers had been gathering intelligence for the Russians since May.

In early October Elmpt left a detachment under Major-General Prozorovskii to garrison Iaşi and took the rest of his corps back through Khotin to the First Army's winter camp near Tinna. Prozorovskii was instructed to form a provisional government for liberated Moldavia. Major-General Chernoevich was appointed president of the Moldavian *Diwan*; Major-General Zamiatnin was made president of the Wallachian *Diwan*. Rumiantsev, who wanted to demonstrate early on he would use the First Army more aggressively than had Golitsyn, criticized Elmpt's decision to rejoin the First Army leaving Moldavia more vulnerable to an Ottoman counter-offensive. To rectify the situation, Rumiantsev reinforced Prozorovskii by sending five infantry regiments under Christopher von Stoffeln to secure the interior of Moldavia and maintain communications among Bucharest, Iaşi, and the Russian reserve at Focşani, so that Stoffeln could then try to capture the fortresses at Ibrail and Galaţi to drive a wedge between Ottoman forces and the Crimean Tatars. He also issued a manifesto on October 31 calling on all Moldavians and Wallachians to rise up against the Turks and support the Russian army.[94]

Moldavian and Wallachian volunteer forces did provide some useful support, especially around Focşani, Bucharest, and Galaţi. By the end of the year there would be over 6,000 Moldavian volunteers under arms, Moldavian hospodar Konstantin Mavrocordatos would be dead of wounds received resisting arrest, and Wallachian hospodar Grighore III Ghica would be in Russian custody.[95] The Russians and the Moldavians and Wallachians accompanied their operations with considerable religious rhetoric about freeing the Orthodox faithful of the Danubian principalities from "Hagarite slavery" and "the abyss of impiety." The Cantacuzenes reassured St. Petersburg that Sultan Mustafa III was on the verge of being overthrown and replaced by his brother Bayezid.[96]

Ottoman forces finally responded in mid-November. On November 11, Fabritsian, with just 1,600 troops, defeated six or seven thousand Turks near Botoşani, north of Iaşi; some 1,200 Turks were killed, including Abaza Pasha, and Hospodar Mavrocordatos was captured. Fabritisian then seized Galaţi, losing just twelve killed and forty-six wounded. Stoffeln sent two grenadier battalions to reinforce Fabritsian and three jaeger battalions under Major-General Anrep toward Bucharest. Anrep captured Hospodar Ghica and entered Bucharest on November 21. The next objective of these divisions was Ibrail, garrisoned by 10,000 Turks. There were reports that a large Ottoman army was marching from Isaccea to the relief of Ibrail, while other Ottoman forces were assembling in Silistra to occupy Focşani and besiege Anrep at Bucharest. Rumiantsev therefore decided that he would send Stoffeln three more battalions of grenadiers to reinforce the Russian garrisons at Bucharest, Galați, and Focșani while he took the rest of the First Army to Iași (December 13). On November 28–29, Fabritsian was forced to march from Galați to Berești to relieve one of his advance posts, under attack by 1,000 janissaries and 5,000 Ottoman cavalrymen; they fled when he approached, but in Fabritsian's absence from Galați, a detachment of enemy troops from Ibrail garrison attacked and burned Galați.[97]

Stoffeln's corps was diverted from Ibrail by an attack of six thousand Turks out of Giurgiu; Ottoman forces from Ibrail under Abdi Pasha also threatened Anrep at Bucharest and Zamiatnin at Focșani. Stoffeln reinforced the latter, while Anrep sent 300 jaegers under Karazin from Bucharest on December 10 to block Suleiman Aga's Turks coming from Giurgiu.

Outnumbered, Karazin's jaegers were forced to take refuge within Koman Monastery. Anrep led troops to his relief on December 13. Several hours' battle at Koman gave inconclusive results; Suleiman Aga could not take the monastery, but Anrep was forced to withdraw and in the course of leading his troops out along a narrow defile, he and 153 jaegers were killed in ambush.[98] Suleiman Aga then joined forces with Abdi Pasha and reinforced Ibrail. Rumiantsev had ordered Stoffeln to try to seize either Ibrail or Giurgiu, but Stoffeln thought this impossible at this time—Rumiantsev had taken the rest of the First Army back across the Dnestr—and so he withdrew his troops to winter quarters around Bucharest and Focșani. With the exception of the Turks reinforcing Ibrail and Giurgiu, most of the Ottoman army had crossed back over the Danube to winter at Babadagh.[99]

Operations against the Bar Confederates

In early 1769 the biggest challenge the Bar Confederation had presented to Golitsyn and Rumiantsev was Potocki's force of 6,000 rebels near Khotin supporting Ottoman operations against the First Army and trying to incite action out of Bender and Căușeni against the Second Army. Krasiński was at Iași, appealing for French, Saxon, or Austrian intervention; there were bands of Confederates active around Balta and near Plotsk, and Golitsyn's planned campaign against Khotin was complicated by the presence of small Confederate garrisons at Okop and Zhvanets, just outside Kamianets, as well as the suspected Confederate sympathies of General De Witt, the Polish commandant of Kamianets. The rest of Poland-Lithuania seemed quiet, so Major-General Weimarn, charged with the task of policing the Commonwealth against Confederates and haidamaks, could be expected to keep his Observation Corps, stationed at Vilnius and Warsaw, free enough to protect the rear of Golitsyn's First Army while it campaigned across the Dnestr.[100]

On February 26 Major-General Izmailov drove the 400 Confederates from Zhvanets and the 320 Confederates from Okop.[101] This was an important precondition for the First Army's crossing of the Dnestr. The surviving Confederates in the Kamianets region followed the Pułaski brothers east toward Cracow to link up with the detachments of

Lubomirski and Kosiński; over the next few months, they would make repeated attempts to capture L'viv but would be defeated by light forces under Prozorovskii sent from the First Army and forces under Drevich sent from Weimarn's Observation Corps. Small Confederate bands also made several cavalry raids on Russian magazines. In Lithuania, Michał Pac and Josef Sapieha formed a Lithuanian Confederacy, but it did not cooperate with Bar Confederation forces in Lithuania. The Pułaskis were also increasingly reluctant to coordinate plans with Joachim Potocki.[102]

The possibility that the Confederates might invite intervention by other powers remained a concern to the Russians, however. Spies sent to Białystok reported that Crown Hetman Branicki was plotting to betray King Stanisław and was communicating with French, Austrian, and Saxon agents. Reports that an army of 40,000 Saxon troops was preparing to enter Poland were unfounded, but it was true that Kamianets Bishop Krasiński was negotiating with the French and Austrians and receiving subsidies from them.[103]

In mid-August 1769 the young brigadier Aleksandr Suvorov[104] arrived at Warsaw to take command of the Suzdal', Smolensk, and Nizhegorod infantry regiments. Weimarn put him to work chasing the Confederate cavalry detachment of Kazimierz and Francisek Pułaski reportedly moving toward Kobrin in Lithuania pursued by detachments under colonels Renne and Drevich. The Pułaskis had about 2,000 men and two guns. To speed his march, Suvorov left most of his brigade and marched against Pułaski with just two battalions of grenadiers, a squadron of dragoons, fifty Cossacks, and two guns; Renne and Drevich likewise left behind the larger part of their commands. On September 2, they caught sight of the Confederates near the village of Orzechowo. Suvorov, Renne, and Drevich were separated from each other by marsh, while the rebel guns controlled the only bridge, so they had to attack across the marsh, firing and then pressing in with bayonet. Suvorov's infantry had used their grenades to set fire to the village, through which the Poles might otherwise have counterattacked. The Confederate forces lost about a hundred men and fled, pursued by Russian cavalry. The next day, some of Renne's carabiniers caught and killed Francisek Pułaski.[105]

Suvorov had made enough of an impression to get himself called to Lublin, where M. N. Volkonskii, Repnin's successor as Russian ambassador to Warsaw, put him in charge of a plan to organize a more formal defense network of eleven block-posts to police assigned territories and keep open Warsaw's lines of communication with Lublin, the First and Second Armies, and Nummers' division in Lithuania. Suvorov would operate from the central node of this network at Lublin with an enlarged mixed brigade of infantry, cuirassiers, dragoons, carabiniers, Cossacks, and artillery and a number of watch-posts distributed within 50–80 kilometers of Lublin. Weimarn would remain in Warsaw, using Drevich's mobile corps as a reserve to assist any of the garrisons of the network. On January 1, 1770, Suvorov was promoted to Major-General.[106]

Suvorov began developing a new tactical doctrine for fighting the small Confederate guerrilla bands popping up over Poland and Lithuania. It envisioned using Lublin as a central hub from which small *corps volantes* would make quick marches against the enemy, and it emphasized the principles of *coup d'oeil*, speed, and staying on the attack.

In support of this new tactical doctrine, he began developing his own training manual for his Suzdal' Infantry Regiment, the *Polkovoe uchrezhdenie*, which prescribed a training sequence: training the individual in the manual of arms and the basics of forming lines, squares, and columns; next, platoon training, with the assistance of veteran corporals; then company training; and finally training of the regiment. The *Polkovoe uchrezhdenie* prescribed firm discipline to snuff out insubordination but also urged officers to know their recruits and their personal skills and capacities, explain to recruits what officers expected of them, and refrain from beating them simply for making mistakes. Over the next three decades, Suvorov would refine these instructions and achieve remarkable results in troop proficiency and *esprit de corps*.

In response to Suvorov's operations from Lublin, the Confederates strove for unified command. Krasiński was elected marshal of Confederate forces in October and began reconcentrating them near Cracow.

The Caucasus in 1769–1770

There were two reasons for Major-General I. F. Medem's campaign in the North Caucasus in 1769: St. Petersburg saw it as a way of further diverting Ottoman military resources by opening a fourth front in the war; and the outbreak of a Russo-Turkish War was expected to engender conflict here anyway, given the "neutrality" and political divisions of the Kabardans left from the 1739 Treaty. Since then Russian military colonization had exacerbated these tensions among the Kabardan nobles. The new Russian fortress of Mozdok had been built on the traditional pasturelands and woodlands exploited by the Kabardan nobles, so they considered the territory theirs and were especially angry when Mozdok became a refuge for their runaway slaves. In 1765–1769 there had been repeated Kabardan attacks on the Russian forts of Mozdok and Kizliar.[107] To defend Mozdok and strengthen the Terek Line, Catherine II ordered part of the Volga Cossack Host transferred to new settlements along the Terek between Mozdok and the Greben' forts. This new Mozdok Regiment was charged with keeping peace among the Kabardans, the Chechens to the southeast, and Kalmyk herders on the south bank of the Terek.[108] In the week before Sultan Mustafa III declared war on Russia, the Kuban Tatars responded by appealing to Muslim Kabardans to acknowledge the sovereignty of the Crimean khan and join the Tatars in an attack on Mozdok to punish the "Moscow kaffirs."[109]

Therefore Medem was recalled from the Orenburg Corps and transferred to Mozdok in April 1769 to command a force consisting of one regiment of Astrakhan' garrison infantry, two squadrons of dragoons, two squadrons of Georgian hussars, four guns, 1,000 Don Cossacks, 497 Volga Cossacks, and 150 Greben' and Terek Cossacks. But his instructions did not stop at defending Mozdok and Kizliar; he was also expected to "raise the tribes of the Caucasus against the Turks."[110] Three thousand Russian regulars and Cossacks were obviously not sufficient for this task, so Medem began organizing a force of Daghestani, Ingushetian, and Chechen volunteers under the command of Hamza

Alishev, Arslan-bek Aidemirov, and Kudenet Bamatov.[111] The brunt of the fighting would be done by 20,000 Kalmyk auxiliaries under Khan Ubashi, "Viceroy of the Kalmyks." Twenty thousand of Ubashi's Kalmyks rendezvoused with Medem on the Kalaus River on April 28; Medem attached a small command of dragoons and Cossacks under Lt. Col. Kishenskii to Ubashi's army for liaison and support.[112]

On April 29 Khan Ubashi and Kishenskii encountered a force of 6,000 Kuban Tatars under the command of two princes of the Girei house, Arslan and Maksiut. The Tatars withdrew into a gulley and suffered heavy losses when Kishenskii's two guns joined the Kalmyks in firing down on them from above. The number of Tatars killed or captured was not recorded, but over 5,000 horses were seized from them.[113]

Medem's and Ubashi's columns then entered the Beshtava Mountains (near present-day Piatigorsk), where the Kabardan nobility was especially polarized between pro-Ottoman and pro-Russian factions. The pro-Russian *pshis* quickly presented themselves to swear allegiance to Empress Catherine and turned over their sons as honor hostages. To flush out and subjugate the four remaining pro-Ottoman clan leaders and their followers, Medem sent Major Ratiev with a squadron of hussars, 800 Cossacks, 3,000 Kalmyks, and two guns. Ratiev's force killed about fifty Kabardans and took 300 prisoners, and by June 7 most of the remaining Kabardan leaders had submitted and sworn allegiance.[114] Soon after, envoys from the Tapanta and Mysylbai clans of the Abazas came down from the highlands along the upper Kuban to submit to the empress.

Medem and Ubashi finally reached the Kuban River on June 21, but it was in flood from the mountain thaw and Medem had to defeat another force of Kuban Tatars on July 1–2 before his army could occupy the one bridge across the river. Enemy losses in this battle were again apparently significant, for about 30,000 head of livestock were captured, twelve Cossacks and Kalmyks were killed, and thirty-three were wounded. Reports that Chechens were raiding Kizliar forced Medem to return to Mozdok. Khan Ubashi took his Kalmyks to attack the Kuban Tatar capital at Kopyl', which had been rebuilt on an island in the Kuban River. But the Kalmyks discovered that the new Kopyl' was heavily fortified and be able to withstand long siege because their guns could not be brought across the river to bombard it.[115]

By February 1770 most of Lesser Kabarda was peaceful and the Kuban Tatars were no longer able to incite Chechen attacks on Kizliar. Delegations from Ingushetia and eastern Ossetia were appearing at Kizliar and proffering oaths of allegiance to the empress. Major Dmitrii Toganov was posted to Kabarda to lay the foundations for the Russian administration of Kabarda and its integration into the Terek Line.[116]

But Medem was increasingly critical of Khan Ubashi for continuing his fruitless campaign against Kopyl', and Ubashi had his own reasons for estrangement from the Russians: St. Petersburg was trying to interfere with his own *zargo* council and was granting steppe land south of the Tsaritsyn Line to German colonists. So, after taking his Kalmyks back to their winter grazing lands in the late 1769, Ubashi threw off Russian service. In spring 1770 three quarters of the Kalmyk population—about 150,000 people—crossed over to the eastern bank of the Volga and began the long trek back to their homeland in Dzhungaria. Only one-third of them would survive the journey.[117]

With the Chechens and other peoples of the North Caucasus now drawn into the Russian sphere of influence, it was time for Todtleben's Transcaucasian Corps to link up with Irakli II and Solomon, the Christian kings of western Georgia.[118] The list of questions Catherine II had sent her College of Foreign Affairs in November 1768 suggests just how belated St. Petersburg had been in recognizing Russian strategic opportunities in Transcaucasia and how quickly the empress now wanted to make up for lost time in exploiting them. She wanted accurate maps showing where the Georgian kingdoms lay, whether they had ports on the Caspian or Black Sea, where Tiflis was located (her existing maps varied on this), and whether the Georgian kings were Orthodox or Catholic.[119]

Todtleben's corps of 3,767 marched from the Terek Line and in summer 1769 accomplished the difficult task of crossing the Caucasus range through the Dar'ial Pass. At Kobi, it was met by Irakli II, King of Kartli and Kakheti, who sought alliance with the Russians to defeat the Lesghians, recover Samstkhe, and keep the Persians at bay. Outside the Turkish fortress of Atskveri, they were joined by Solomon, King of Imereti (Irakli's ally since 1758, at war with the Turks for the past ten years). Todtleben's corps assisted Solomon in liberating Kutaisi in summer 1770, but then the allies had a falling-out. It became apparent that Todtleben was more interested in extracting Georgian nobles' allegiances to Russia than in helping Irakli and Solomon form a united independent Georgia; he abandoned Solomon on the battlefield at Akhaltsikhe, and he had got bogged down in an unsuccessful siege of Poti to win that Black Sea port for the Russian navy. When Solomon protested this, Todtleben tried to incite the nobles of Mingrelia and Guria to rebel against him. His own officers denounced him to St. Petersburg and Catherine II had to recall him in disgrace in the late 1770. The siege of Poti continued under his successor Sukhotin, but after Sukhotin lost half his army to disease St. Petersburg began to lose interest in operations in Transcaucasia. Russian forces were withdrawn to the Mozdok Line in 1772, first in anticipation of the Focşani peace talks and then to avoid antagonizing the Persian shah and protect against the spread of the Pugachev Rebellion. Irakli and Solomon were left to fight the Turks without Russian assistance. Irakli begged the empress for help, offering up his own sons as hostages and substantial revenue to support Russian garrisons, but the terms of the 1774 Kuchuk–Kainarji Treaty denied the Georgian kings protectorate status and gave the Turks a free hand south of the Rioni River.[120]

CHAPTER 6
THE YEAR OF VICTORIES, 1770

The winter war in Moldavia and Wallachia

While the First Army remained in winter quarters intense fighting continued in Wallachia and Moldavia. For the time being Grand Vizier Ivaz Pashazade Halil Pasha lacked the logistics to move large forces back to Riabaia Mogila, and the recapture of Khotin was entirely out of the question.[1] But the Turks could take advantage of the distance separating Stoffeln's Moldavian Corps from the winter quarters of the rest of Rumiantsev's First Army, so smaller forces of 20,000–25,000 Turks and Tatars under Suleiman Aga, Abdi Pasha, Mehmed Pasha, and Ismail Pasha could be sent up from Bucak to try to retake Bucharest and Focşani or at least reduce the Russian threat to the Ottoman fortresses at Ibrail, Giurgiu, and Galaţi.[2] On January 3 Abdi Pasha and a force of 2,000 cavalry, 800 infantry, and eleven guns reached the Rimna River and opened fire on Russian pickets about six kilometers from Focşani. Major-General Podgorichani managed to halt the enemy at the Rimna River even though he had with him just half his command—about 600 hussars and 300 Cossacks and Moldavian volunteers. The next day Abdi Pasha was reinforced by 2,000 cavalry and 6,000 infantry under *Seraskir* of Wallachia Suleiman Aga, while Major-General Grigorii Potemkin came to Podgorichani's aid with 1,500 infantry and 900 cavalry. Potemkin departed from established practice by dispensing with swine-feathers and forming his infantry into three squares—a central battalion square of 800–900 men, with flank squares of 300–400 troops each, the squares within about 500 meters firing range of each other. This allowed Potemkin's infantry to maneuver while withstanding five attacks over thirteen hours, and even after janissaries penetrated the central square, his troops were able to drive them out by bayonet. Potemkin's infantry and Podgorichani's cavalry then joined in a devastating counterattack. They lost just twenty-six killed and fourteen wounded; the Turks suffered far heavier losses and Suleiman Aga himself was wounded.[3] This was the earliest known instance of deployment of Russian troops in three squares rather than one large square, facing Ottoman cavalry without swine-feathers.

With Hospodar Grighore III Ghica now a prisoner of the Russians, the task of organizing Wallachian resistance to the Russians fell to Monolaki, the *Ban* of Craiova, who assembled a force of Albanians and Turkish reinforcements from Vidin and skirmished several times with Russian forces between Bucharest and Oltenia. The sultan was sufficiently impressed to appoint Monolaki Hospodar and send him more reinforcements, raising his army's strength to 20,000 with the hope that he could retake

Bucharest. But Major-General Zamiatnin was easily able to repulse Monolaki's attack on Bucharest on January 14, and after this the initiative passed to the Russians. The Turkish detachments in Wallachia fell back to reinforce Ibrail.

As Ibrail's garrison now numbered 15,000 troops, it remained the most immediate threat to the Russian army in Wallachia and Moldavia. Podgorichani and Potemkin marched on Ibrail, followed by Stoffeln's division from Focşani. Their drive south was hampered by frost and harsh wind and the absence of forage opportunities—there were no villages for over forty-five kilometers, until Tunsha. At Kurbeşti, twelve kilometers from Ibrail, Stoffeln skirmished with 2,000 Turkish cavalry.

The next day, January 18, Stoffeln, Potemkin, and Podgorichani reached the edge of Ibrail. It was not difficult for them to drive the enemy infantry from their trenches back into the fortress, enabling Rzhevskii and Potemkin to enter the town; but then their troops found their movement constricted by Ibrail's narrow streets and they came under heavy fire from the eighty large-caliber guns of Ibrail's citadel. Fires began to spread through the neighborhoods they occupied, and the next morning Stoffeln's inspection convinced him that he would be unable to take the citadel without siege guns. Therefore he withdrew from Ibrail on January 21 after burning the residential section to the ground. Detachments from his division fanned out along that part of the Danube, burning 260 villages and driving their Christian inhabitants into the Wallachian interior. Upon reports that Monolaki was concentrating his forces at Giurgiu for a second attempt on Bucharest, Stoffeln divided his forces to reinforce Zamiatnin at Bucharest and hold Focşani and the Rimna River.[4]

On the morning of February 4, in a dense fog limiting visibility to twenty paces, Stoffeln, Potemkin, and Zamiatnin attacked Giurgiu in three squares: two infantry squares in the first line, each of two grenadier battalions and an under-strength musketeer regiment, and a third square of cavalry in the second line.[5] Giurgiu was defended by 16,000 Turks under Çelibei Pasha of Rusçuk, and the town had a well-fortified stone citadel with twenty big guns. As at Ibrail the Russians were quickly able to clear the enemy trenches before the town, but once inside the town they found themselves under heavy fire from the citadel guns and from barricades along the narrow streets. It became necessary to send Potemkin with three battalions of grenadiers and Major-General Tekelli with the hussars and light cavalry to block a Turkish cavalry force arriving from the Danube, while Zamiatnin's troops were sent to storm the citadel. But the citadel was protected by a bend in the river and Zamiatnin could find no boats to land troops at its foot. The attack on Giurgiu had taken about 3,000 Turkish lives. It cost the Russians seventy seven dead and 294 wounded (including Zamiatnin), and their stores were running low. Stoffeln decided to abandon the siege on February 7. But before leaving he had most of the town burned to the ground, destroying about five thousand homes, and as at Ibrail he dispatched parties to burn 143 Turkish villages along the eastern Danube as far as the Prut—a distance of about 250 kilometers. The loss to the Porte was estimated as equivalent to 3 million assignat rubles.[6] Some Christian villages were of course among those destroyed, and the empress declared Stoffeln's tactics barbaric. Rumiantsev agreed that they were counterproductive but suggested that Orlov explain to her that in waging war against the Turks, one could not observe the rules of warfare against fellow Europeans.[7]

Reports in March and early April that the grand vizier was completing his Danube bridge at Isaccea and 30,000 Tatars were massing at Iagorlik for an attack on Iași spurred Rumiantsev to order Stoffeln to prepare for the resumption of military operations—with the proviso that Stoffeln refrain from laying waste the countryside. But by this time the usefulness of the Moldavia Corps was limited by a new crisis: the spread of bubonic plague. It had first appeared at Iași in October 1769, reportedly transmitted by Turkish prisoners of war in the military hospital.[8] Rumiantsev had urged Stoffeln to take quarantine measures by moving his troops out of Iași into camps outside town. But Stoffeln disobeyed, and apparently from fear of incurring the empress' wrath for failing to protect the health of his troops, he got local doctors to certify that the disease was merely a malignant fever. Therefore the plague had spread to Focșani by April 1770, and by May 3 it had reached Khotin. The death toll at Iași just over April 25–28 had been forty-six civilians and seventeen soldiers; over April 29 to May 1 another twenty-three soldiers and forty-seven civilians died of plague. Rumiantsev demanded further quarantine measures and the establishment of roadblocks to try to keep the epidemic from spreading across the Dnestr into Ukraine and Poland and infecting the rest of the First Army. He sent Dr. Gustav Orraeus, a leading specialist of the day, to Khotin to ascertain whether the epidemic was actually bubonic plague. Stoffeln finally began confining the infected in a separate hospital, but he refused to evacuate the garrison from Iași, and by the end of May he was himself dead of plague. Of the 1,500 patients received into the Iași plague hospital between May 18 and August 18, 1770, only 300 survived.[9]

The plague did subsequently spread into Ukraine, reaching Briansk by August 1770, and by December 1770 cases were being reported in hospital in Moscow. Moscow began experiencing about a thousand plague deaths per day and the Governor-General and the *ober-politsmeitser* fled the city. By the time it had finally burned itself out in 1773, the plague had cost Moscow nearly 100,000 lives—about half the population.[10]

The First Army in winter quarters

The empress' War Council had expected Rumiantsev's First Army to take up winter quarters along a broad front from the eastern bank of the Dnestr so as to provide a cordon defense extending far enough east to offer closer support for Panin's Second Army. But Rumiantsev kept to his preference and concentrated most of his regiments between the Dnestr and the Bug in territory about 80 kilometers long and 40 kilometers deep, from Staro-Konstantinov and Chmelnik in the north to the line Satanova-Grudek-Savitsy-Bar in the south, with his infantry and artillery in the southern part, his cavalry in the north, and his reserves at Derazhna and Letichev. He believed that this would allow him to quickly move forces in any of three directions: into Polish Pokutia across the upper Dnestr; toward Khotin and northern Moldavia; or toward

Mohylew and Bratslav. He expected the First Army's primary mission in 1770 to move south through Moldavia against the Turkish fortresses in Bucak.[11] He needed the next months to bring the First Army backup to strength, organize its logistics for the spring offensive, and update its training.

In a memorandum from late 1769 he expressed the conviction that the Turks would make redoubled efforts in the spring despite their defeats in 1769. They would replenish and likely expand their infantry, so the infantry of the First Army must spend the winter resting and rebuilding, and fresh replacements should be sent to the garrison at Khotin. The First Army's cavalry should be enlarged, especially its light cavalry. Although the Ukrainian Cossacks had performed poorly in 1769, they should be handled gingerly and not antagonized, so their maintenance over winter should be equalized with that of the Don Cossacks; the elite Ukrainian Cossacks could be used in the spring to man advance posts and guard magazines along the Polish border. Forces of Bar Confederates would undoubtedly try to threaten the rear of the First Army; to protect the army's lines of communication through Poland Rumiantsev intended to station units of jaegers at Sandomir, L'viv, Lublin, and Stanislavov.[12]

Rumiantsev anticipated that the first major objective in 1770 would be the Ottoman fortress at Bender, south of present-day Kishinev. He preferred the task of taking Bender fall to Panin's Second Army, with his own First Army helping to accelerate the fall of Bender by marching to the Black Sea coast and seizing the Ottoman fortresses on the lower Danube.[13] Taking Bender would require Panin to march with at least 20,000–25,000 infantry, as many cavalry as he could amass, and more artillery transferred from Kiev. The Zaporozhian Cossacks could be used as auxiliaries defending against the Crimean Tatars and patrolling the lower Dnepr.

The First Army would concentrate on tightening Russian control over Moldavia and over Wallachia as far west as Oltenia and as far east as the mouth of the Danube. Operations by the First Army should be confined to the territory between the Dnestr and the Prut or between the Prut and Sărat, with the primary objective of holding Moldavia and deterring the Turks from crossing the Danube. Stoffeln's Moldavian Corps would have to be strengthened and more magazines established: a primary depot at Iaşi, and subsidiary fortified magazines at Taburev and Sărat along the Prut, Sorocha on the Dnestr, at Botoşani between the Prut and Sărat, at Suçeava on the Sărat, and in the rear at Chernovtsy. Supply should be entrusted to contractors at double the going rate and to transfers from distant magazines to nearer ones. The army should not expect to obtain adequate supplies from the Moldavian population, but at least the Turks would encounter the same problem once they crossed the Danube. As the First Army neared the Danube, it should be on guard not only against the Ottoman fortresses at Ibrail and Kiliia but also against diversionary attacks from the southwest, from Giurgiu, Craiova, Orsova, and Vidin.[14]

The process of equipping Moldavian volunteer units and preparing them for joint operations with the First Army had begun after Rumiantsev's October 1769 Manifesto to the Moldavian people. By January 1770 about 6,300 Moldavian volunteers had been enlisted. They would participate in several of the larger battles of 1770. Negotiations were also underway with Pirvu Cantacuzene and other Wallachian boyars to raise Wallachian volunteer units.[15]

Over the winter Rumiantsev refined his plans for the spring offensive. He decided that the First Army would push south toward the Danube by moving along the eastern bank of the Prut River, thereby avoiding the plague in Moldavia. He selected Riabaia Mogila as the place to assemble the First Army's forward elements and main body. To initiate such concentration, he ordered Repnin's corps to pull out of Wallachia into Moldavia, to north of the line Byrlad-Vaslui, and sent Zorich's cavalry toward Riabaia Mogila for reconnaissance and livestock raiding. The main force of the First Army would march out of winter quarters once Riabaia Mogila had been scouted. Stoffeln's Moldavian Corps would have the task of defending against Tatar forces moving up the Prut from Bender and Căuşeni, which required him to retain control over Moldavia and Wallachia as far as Cecora. In the event Rumiantsev had to link up with Stoffeln, he could use the bridge across the Prut at Cecora. But it was preferable for Rumiantsev to stay on the eastern side of the Prut, to keep the First Army closer to Panin's Second Army and present a greater threat to the Turks. There was one disadvantage to this plan, however; the First Army would have to drag a larger supply train. If he had chosen to advance down the western side of Moldavia he could have gathered more provisions en route. But that of course would have run greater risk of infection from the plague.[16]

The recruit levy rate for 1770 remained at one man from every 150 households. Eventually, this yielded 49,583 recruits, about 3,000 more than the levy of 1769. They started arriving at the First Army in January 1770, but at a trickle, so it took some months for Rumiantsev to bring his regiments up to full strength. He resorted to several devices to try to accelerate this. To simplify regiment assignments he set standard regiment size at five to six companies for infantry regiments, five squadrons for cuirassier regiments, and eight squadrons for carabinier regiments. He increased the proportion of combat-effectives to *nestroevye* support personnel by relegating some of the latter to garrison service and replacing combat-effectives with hired Ukrainian transport personnel. Prior to this, new recruits had been sent from Kiev to Berdichev and Medzhibozh for preliminary training, then to Khotin for further training and assignment to their regiments; Rumiantsev now arranged for the recruit parties to be sent directly from Kiev to the winter quarters of their regiments. Responsibility for training new recruits was thereby shifted from special battalions at regional headquarters to the regimental and company officers where new recruits were assigned to serve.[17] This had the additional advantage of enabling Rumiantsev to oversee their training directly and implement new training ordinances of his own devising.

Rumiantsev's new training ordinances

These new ordinances incorporated the lessons Rumiantsev had drawn from his service in the Seven Years' War—especially from his successful Kolberg campaign—combined with judgments he had reached as to the advisable tactics for fighting the Turks and

Tatars on the steppe frontier. They were also intended to correct what Rumiantsev saw as deficiencies in the infantry, cavalry, and general field service ordinances of 1763–1766. On March 8, 1770, Rumiantsev issued his *Rite of Service* (*Obriad sluzhby*) as a new general ordinance for his First Army.[18] It prescribed new rules concerning march order; setting and protecting camps, pickets, and watches and making rounds; lazarettes and field hospitals; supervising sutlers and rations distributions; foraging; and infantry and cavalry exercises and firing schemes.

Several important departures from past practice can be noted in it.

Regimental and company officers, sergeants, and under-officers assisted by veteran soldiers were now required to devote more attention to training and monitoring new recruits, since training now began in the regiment of duty assignment rather than at the regional headquarters of special training battalions. This meant that in turn officers had to show greater diligence in their own study and practice of exercises and tactics. A progression of training levels (individual training, company, battalion, regiment, and army training) was to be followed.

Previous ordinances had prescribed unrolled line deployment in three ranks per line as the best way to maximize infantry firepower. The Rite of Service prescribed a two-rank line and introduced a new manual of arms to increase the rate of fire. The rate of quick march was increased.

The cavalry line was also reduced to two ranks in depth. Attack was now to be made at full gallop, with saber raised to eye level and the line maintained "without fail." To increase attack speed the cuirassiers gave up their cuirasses. Firing from horseback was allowed, but only when necessary to drive back a numerically superior attacking enemy.

One of the most striking changes was in the order of battle. For fighting the Turks and Tatars Rumiantsev preferred the infantry square to extended line deployment. In Münnich's time the army had sometimes marched and fought in one great army square, flanked by cavalry and wagons, with the faces of the square protected by chains of swine-feathers. Rumiantsev viewed the army square as limiting maneuverability and speed. He prescribed instead attack by multiple divisional squares of infantry, with the cavalry interspersed between the squares as well as on the flanks and jaeger skirmishers and grenadiers along the front and on the flanks. The wagons were consigned to the rear and no longer used for shielding the flanks. The commanders of the infantry squares had discretion to change direction to counter sudden enemy movements and try to divide the enemy and catch elements of the enemy force in square crossfire. Swine-feathers were to be abandoned because they hindered infantry mobility. "They are a shield for cowards, but an obstacle for brave men," Rumiantsev wrote.[19]

The new ordinances also placed much greater emphasis than before on the combat roles of jaegers and grenadiers. Besides a fifth company of grenadiers in certain regiments, Rumiantsev established separate four-company grenadier and jaeger battalions which were used to lead the advance across uneven terrain, conduct reconnaissance, break the enemy's lines of communication, divide enemy forces and overpower their smaller fragments, and sometimes to deliver the first attack blow. They were trained to attack either in unrolled line deployment or in column.[20]

Riabaia Mogila

In late April the divisions of Rumiantsev's First Army began assembling at Khotin for the march down the Dnestr-Prut corridor. Heavy rains and complications in crossing the Dnestr made it impossible to begin the march out of Khotin until May 25. That day the First Army's reported strength was 31,125 combat effectives, 5,203 *nestroevye*, and 2,122 men on the sick list.[21] But the army marching from Khotin would actually number only about 25,000 combat-effectives because 4,000 troops had to be left to garrison Khotin and another 7,000 left in Poland under Essen to guard lines of communication.

When the First Army left Khotin on May 25, it marched southeast in three divisional squares: Rumiantsev and Olits in the center, with eight regiments of musketeers, one battalion grenadiers, one battalion of jaegers; Plemiannikov on the right flank with five regiments musketeers and four battalions grenadiers; and Bruce on the left with four regiments musketeers and four battalions of grenadiers. Saltykov's cavalry was on the right flank and between the right and center infantry squares; Glebov's cavalry was on the left flank and between the left and center squares. The artillery was along the front and in reserve in the rear. To make better time, the infantry squares moved in seven columns, their grenadier battalions at the front, and all the light baggage in a separate parallel column.[22] Their progress was slowed by the weather—hot days, chilly nights, and heavy rains—and bad road conditions, as well as the need to circumvent plague-infested settlements. Rumiantsev hoped the Turks were under the misapprehension that his army was larger than it really was. On May 27 and June 3 several thousand Ottoman and Tatar cavalry crossed the Prut at Podolian and Falçiu but were beaten back by Russian vanguard forces before they could catch sight of the rest of the First Army.[23]

But on June 6 the First Army had to detour on a forced march from Agiria to reach Cecora Bridge in time to rescue Repnin, whose Moldavian Corps vanguard on the other side of the Prut near Riabaia Mogila was endangered by 20,000 Tatars and 15,000 Turks under Khan Kaplan II Girei and Abaza Pasha of Ruşçuk. On June 8 Rumiantsev realized that he was not going to arrive in time, so he sent to reinforce Repnin a detachment under General-Quartermaster Friedrich Wilhelm Bauer.[24]

On June 9 Repnin managed on his own to defeat the Turks attacking him near Riabaia Mogila, but the next morning Bauer's relief force was blocked by 20,000 Tatars near the Podolian crossing on the Prut. Although greatly outnumbered, Bauer attacked first, sending his cavalry around their flanks and leading his jaegers through the woods against their front. The Tatars retreated, pursued by Bauer's cavalry for about twenty kilometers to a fortified camp at Riabaia Mogila. Repnin crossed over the Prut to rendezvous with Bauer on June 11. By June 12 the rest of the First Army had pitched camp at Orland, just six kilometers from Bauer and Repnin.[25]

By this point the enemy forces defeated at Cecora and Podolian had reassembled to reinforce other elements holding a fortified camp at Riabaia Mogila. Abaza Pasha and the khan therefore had about 20,000 Turks and 50,000 Tatars dug in atop a high hill overlooking the marshes of the Prut. The northern side of their camp was protected by Călmăţiu Creek and several long trenches and forty-four guns; the marshes along the

Prut guarded its western side, to a depth of about a kilometer; and a deep ravine (Dolina Chora) protected its southern flank.[26]

The First Army attacked the enemy camp at Riabaia Mogila on the morning of June 17. It began forming in three attack columns after 2:00 a.m., keeping its bivouac fires burning so as to deceive the enemy; Bauer's corps, at the head of Rumiantsev's main column, quietly moved south down the banks of Nyrnova Creek toward the northern face of the enemy camp, while Repnin's corps, fronted by Plemiannikov's cavalry, advanced on the right to strike the enemy in the rear, where the Dolina Chora ravine neared the Călmățiu. Potemkin's light cavalry and jaegers, with Fabritsian in the vanguard, pushed down the opposite bank of the Prut with the task of crossing by pontoon and attacking the enemy's positions from the hilltops above the Dolina Chora ravine.

At dawn rockets signaled the Russian attack. Under cover of heavy artillery fire, Bauer's column formed in square and attacked the center of the trench line on the north side of the camp, seized the hillside above the trenches, and brought up their batteries to fire down upon the Turkish infantry. Rumiantsev's regiments then came up and attacked the section of trenches just to the right. This sufficiently preoccupied the khan and Abaza Pasha that they were caught by surprise on their right flank, where Repnin was now advancing in two infantry squares with Saltykov's cavalry in between. When this was finally discovered, Turkish and Tatar cavalry were sent to attack them, but they were quickly driven back, allowing Repnin and Saltykov to push farther down the enemy's right and join Fabritsian and Potemkin in a strike on the rear of the enemy camp. The Russian squares held firm, and they were distributed across such a broad space and moved in such coordination that the Turks may have thought they were under attack by a much larger army; so the Turks and Tatars broke and fled southward from their camp, pursued for several kilometers by the Russian cavalry. By Podgorichani's count about four hundred dead enemies were left behind, including the khan's son Kerim Deli Sultan. The Russians lost just seventeen killed and thirty-seven wounded.[27]

Larga

It was still considered possible that the Turks might come up in force through Moldavia along the left bank of the Prut to cut Rumiantsev's lines of communication with Khotin. There was also the danger that Tatar and Turkish forces could come up from the Danube and cut the First Army off from Panin's Second Army, which had just crossed the Bug and was still a long march from the Dnestr. Therefore, Rumiantsev decided that the First Army must continue in haste down the Prut to deter the grand vizier from taking his army across the Danube at Isaccea. Repnin's and Bauer's corps would take the vanguard; Potemkin would take his jaegers and light cavalry back across the Prut near Falçiu to reconnoiter and to prevent Turkish forces out of Ibrail from attacking Rumiantsev's supply train.

This was fruitful, as Moldavian *Seraskir* Abdi Pasha was indeed marching from Ibrail with 20,000 troops, and Potemkin spotted them several kilometers from Falçiu on June 21. Intelligence from Repnin's patrols subsequently revealed that Abdi Pasha's army had camped on a high plateau above the bend of the Larga River, north of Lake Babikul, just across the Prut in Moldavia; that Ismail Pasha's army and the remnants of Abaza Pasha's and the khan's armies were reassembling near the Larga; and that these 80,000 Turks and Tatars were awaiting the arrival of the grand vizier's field army. It was necessary to destroy this enemy concentration at Larga before the grand vizier could reinforce it, so Rumiantsev called Potemkin's corps back over to the eastern side of the Prut. Leaving a small detachment under Colonel Kakovinskii to guard the bridge over the Prut, Rumiantsev took the rest of the First Army across the Tsyganka River to approach the enemy camp from the hills along the right bank of the Larga. Bauer and Repnin reached the Larga River on July 1; the rest of the Russian army came up on the fourth. Rumiantsev's Cossacks, grenadiers, and Moldavian volunteers skirmished with Tatar forces for two days and on July 5 Rumiantsev convened a council of war to plan at attack.[28]

The enemy camp was situated near the confluence of the Prut and Larga, on steep slopes between the gullies of the Larga and Babikul rivers, protected by the marshes of the Larga on the north and the swamps of the Prut on the west. Its eastern approaches were guarded by earthworks and fortifications, and the positions of the 30,000 Ottoman infantry within this pocket were separated by ravines and fortifications. The council of war decided there was no choice but to direct the main attack from the northeast, between the Larga and Babikul rivers, on the enemy's right flank; this would be attempted by Rumiantsev's, Bauer's, and Repnin's corps—about 31,000 men. Plemiannikov would lead another 6,000 troops in a diversionary attack across the Larga against the center of the enemy trench lines.[29]

On the night of July 6 Bauer's troops erected a bridge across the Larga and dug in on the heights across the river; Repnin's and Rumiantsev's regiments followed across by midnight. At around 2:00 a.m. Plemiannikov's cavalry and two squares of infantry fell upon the Turkish pickets along the Larga to begin their diversion. Two hours after dawn, the main attack began: Bauer's infantry in a square on the left, Repnin's and Potemkin's in two squares on the right, cavalry in between, and the Cossacks and Moldavian volunteers infiltrating along the gulley of the Babikul. Rumiantsev's regiments stood in square in reserve. Melissino's seventeen field guns began bombarding the enemy positions from hilltop batteries between Repnin's and Potemkin's squares. This pinned the Turks down in their tranches and gave Bauer's, Repnin's, and Potemkin's jaegers and grenadiers time to approach the Turkish trenches. The khan threw most of his Tatar and Turkish cavalry along the Babikul gulley to stop their advance, but Rumiantsev countered by sending a brigade of Major-General Rimskii-Korsakov's grenadiers and one battery of field guns to fire into the gulley. They were soon reinforced by Cossacks, Moldavian arnauts, and more of Melissino's field guns that turned the enemy cavalry to flight, and Saltykov's cavalry gave pursuit.

By this time Plemiannikov's force had crossed the Larga and fallen upon the front trench lines. Turkish cavalry attempted a counterattack but were thrown back when Plemiannikov was reinforced by two infantry regiments from Rumiantsev's reserve.

Janissary infantry from the largest of the left flank ravines also offered fierce resistance but were ultimately put to retreat by heavy musket and artillery fire and bayonet attacks. On the right Repnin's troops took one Turkish infantry position after another, and then Bauer's jaegers rushed ahead and set up a firing line 200 paces beyond on the highest ground in the camp. Field guns brought up to this firing line loosed canister fire on the nearest part of the enemy rear. After eight hours of fighting, the Turks and Tatars began to abandon their positions in panic. It was just a little past noon.[30] Plemiannikov's cavalry did chase some of the fleeing Turks and Tatars, but the Russian infantry was too exhausted and low on rations to join in the pursuit. About a thousand Turks had been killed, and some others may have perished in the marshes while retreating; twenty-three of the enemies were taken prisoner. The First Army lost twenty-nine dead and sixty-two wounded.[31]

Larga has attracted attention from several military historians as a vindication of Rumiantsev's new doctrine of independent divisional squares, the use of light mobile jaeger battalions supported by their own field guns, night maneuver to achieve surprise, and yet another demonstration of the effectiveness of the castling of field guns. It should be noted that the battle was won largely through the efforts of the three forward squares under Bauer, Repnin, and Potemkin, without Rumiantsev having to commit his main force.[32] Larga also had an important immediate strategic consequence: it brought to an end for some while joint operations between the Tatars and the Turks. From Larga the Tatars fled across the Sal'cha River to Ismail and Kiliia, while the surviving Turks withdrew to their magazine at Reni.

Kagul and Kartal

On July 8, reconnaissance by Bauer's vanguard revealed that the Turks defeated at Larga had encamped near the Kagul River about twenty kilometers to the south of the First Army and eighty kilometers from the Danube. On July 14, Grand Vizier Ivaz Pashazade Halil Pasha finally took his army across the Danube at Isaccea, using 300 boats rather than waiting any further for the bridge to be completed. Although Bender was under siege by Panin, the grand vizier had decided not to go to the relief of Bender but to march toward the Kagul River to attack Rumiantsev, and to that end he had ordered the Crimean Tatars to head back across the Sal'cha and position themselves to attack the First Army from its rear. Over July 16–20, the grand vizier's army arrived at the Kagul camp. By July 17 the Rumiantsev's First Army was camped at Grecheni—a vulnerable spot, given that it could be struck between the Kagul and Ialpukh rivers and had high hills to the rear limiting the Russians' maneuverability. Despite the overwhelming superiority of the enemy—perhaps 150,000 Turks and 80,000 Tatars—Rumiantsev decided that he had no choice but to attack the Turkish camp at Kagul.[33] To guard his rear, he put his train in *wagenburg* under 8,000 troops and Colonel Volkonskii. With his remaining 25,000 troops and 118 guns, he began the march toward Kagul.[34]

The grand vizier's camp faced the Kagul River on the west and south and an old earthern dyke called "Trajan's Wall" on the north.[35] Parallel to the river were four high mounds running north to south. On the camp's eastern side, an open glade ran southeast from the dyke to within a kilometer or two of the river. The Turkish camp was toward the bottom of this pocket protected by three parallel lines of tranches fronted by a deep ditch. The disadvantage of this position was that it was tightly hemmed in on the south, with room to maneuver only along the glade on the northeast side. The Ottoman cavalry were under the command of Abdi Pasha, Kaipkaran Aga Pasha commanded the janissaries, and Abaza Mehmed Pasha had the rest of the infantry. Also present were several double-horsetail pashas, Reis Avni Efendi Pasha, the diplomat Ahmed Resmi Efendi, and most of the Ottoman court elite; only the *kaimakam*s and lesser courtiers had remained at home with the sultan.[36]

The grand vizier may have planned to attack the Russians from his trenches on the morning of July 21. But Rumiantsev used the night of July 20–21 to position his forces to attack first. Once again, his order of battle made use of columns—five of them—compressible into divisional squares. The vanguard consisted of Bauer's division of 4,000 troops on the right flank, which had the task of moving down the high ground past the village of Vulcaneşti to attack the enemy's left, and Repnin's 5,000 men on the far left flank, which was to march across three crests and attack the Turks from the glade on their east. The three middle squares comprised Bruce's division (3,000 men), Plemiannikov's division (4,500 men), and the main division of 7,500 troops with Olits and Rumiantsev; they were to cross the earth dyke and hit the Turkish trench lines in the center. Saltykov's cavalry, Dolgorukov's carabiniers, and the Akhtyrka and Serbian hussars were placed in the intervals. Melissino's field artillery was positioned on the sides and corners of the infantry squares to provide fire support and to facilitate castling on new firing lines. About two-thirds of the guns were with Olits and Bauer, to support the main blow upon the enemy's left flank.

At about 1:00 a.m., the columns began to advance. At 5:00 a.m., Repnin, Bruce, and Olits had reached Trajan's Wall, at which point their squares came under attack by Turkish cavalry. Bruce and Repnin had to peel off some of their grenadiers and musketeers to form two new squares to prevent enemy encirclement. After three hours, the Turkish cavalry retreated in the face of canister fire from Melissino's guns and the arrival of infantry regiments from Rumiantsev's reserve; the Turkish cavalry never rejoined the battle. At 8:00 a.m., Bauer's and Plemiannikov's squares had nearly reached the first line of enemy trenches when 10,000 janissaries erupted from a gulley on the left flank and attacked with cold steel. They managed to break into Plemiannikov's square on its right face and push apart his four regiments, forcing some of the Russians to flee to Olits' square.[37] According to Rumiantsev's report to the empress, he prevented a rout by coming up and calling on the troops to hold their ground and then bringing up Ozerov's brigade of grenadiers and some field guns. The janissaries fell back and Plemiannikov's square reformed and resumed its advance with the cry of "*Vivat* Ekaterina!"[38] Saltykov's and Dolgorukov's cavalry then put the janissaries to flight.

This action in the center apparently diverted the grand vizier's attention from what was happening on his left flank. A battalion of grenadiers, followed by the rest of Bauer's division, reached the Turkish trenches and subjected them to heavy musket and field gun fire. At this same time, the Turkish right came under attack by Bruce's division, and Repnin's division completed its movement down the eastern glade and reached the enemy rear. By about 9:00 a.m. the Turks concluded that they were about to be encircled and overrun. They started to abandon their camp and their guns and flee—most of them on foot—southward to the Danube.[39] Rumiantsev estimated that about twenty thousand enemies had been killed, and he mentioned prisoner testimonies that guessed the toll could have been twice that number.[40] The Russians had lost 353 killed, 550 wounded, and eleven missing.[41]

At 4:00 p.m. Bauer's resupplied division was sent on forced march in pursuit of the retreating enemy. Part of the grand vizier's defeated army had managed to get across the Danube at Isaccea by boat—the bridge was still unfinished—but several thousand Turks were still at the landing on the opposite bank, at Kartal. Bauer devised two infantry squares and attacked them on their right flank. The grand vizier tried to come to their aid by sending transports across the river supported by three frigates, but fire from Bauer's guns sank some of the vessels and prevented most of the transports from reaching shore. Ahmed Resmi Efendi was there and described the debacle. "Those remaining at Kartal awaited the boats as if it were Judgment Day. The next day the boats came to the fords, but they could not land; they could not be boarded…. If they approached the shore, three hundred men collected and sank the boat. If they stayed back, they could not be boarded. Well, with a thousand difficulties, the janissaries were resettled. After that, those with the strength threw themselves into the water and drowned. The majority had crossed over by that evening."[42] But about a thousand were taken prisoner by the Russians.

Those Turks who had fled in the direction of Ismail were pursued by Igel'strom's brigade, which caught up with them and destroyed their rear guard near Ialpukh on July 22. That emboldened Rumiantsev to send Repnin's division to attack Ismail.

The Second Army and the siege of Bender

As of December 1769 General-*anshef* Panin's Second Army in its winter quarters in Ukraine comprised eleven cavalry regiments, fourteen infantry regiments (including jaegers and grenadiers), 3,000 Don Cossacks, 4,000 Ukrainians, 5,000 Kalmyks, and ninety-seven field guns and unicorns. Its corps and regiments were commanded by General-*anshef* V. M. Dolgorukov, Lt. Generals Berg, Dalke, Rennenkampf, and Vernes, and Major-Generals Lebel, Wittgenstein, Karl von Stoffeln, Romanius, Shcherbatov, Zorich, Musin-Pushkin, Olsuf'ev, and St. Mark.[43] In April, Panin was ordered to detach some troops to Ladyzhin, to guard the Dnestr and the road into Poland; in exchange eighteen companies of infantry and the newly formed Moldavian Hussar Regiment were transferred to the Second Army.

Panin's mission in 1770 was to leave the left wing of the Second Army to guard Elizavetgrad Province and march with the rest to besiege and take Bender, one of the most powerful Ottoman fortresses, located on the Dnestr south of Kishinev.[44] Căuşeni, just a few kilometers south of Bender, was the encampment of most of the Crimean Tatar army supporting Turkish army operations on the Dnestr and the Prut; so the capture of Bender could be expected to push the Turks and Tatars back to the Black Sea coast, to Akkirman and Ochakov, and to clear Bucak as far as the Danube.

The Second Army left winter quarters on March 20–25, nearly a month before Rumiantsev's First Army, but its progress east was slowed by a shortage of pontoons and fodder and by heavy rains turning the roads to mire. It took until May 12 for it to cross the Dnepr at Kremenchug and it reached Iagorlik on the Dnestr on May 22. At Iagorlik, the Second Army was rejoined by the units earlier shifted to Ladyzhin. This brought the strength of the Second Army to 45,750 men with 174 guns.[45]

The long march down the Dnestr to Bender took another three weeks. Fortunately, the Second Army met no major challenge out of Bender and Căuşeni, perhaps because the khan was under the impression that Panin was headed against Ochakov and the Crimean steppe, while movement from Bender was being deterred by Prozorovskii's light cavalry and Don Cossacks, sent down the Dnestr from the First Army. Meanwhile, Berg's corps had begun marching from Bakhmut toward Perekop to keep the rest of the Tatar forces bottled up in Crimea.[46]

On July 5–7 the Second Army's vanguard skirmished with enemy forces north of Bender. The rest of the Second Army reached the outskirts of Bender on July 15. By this point the number of combat-ready troops not in hospital or detailed to guarding lines of communication was 32,904.[47] Petrov notes that July 15 was a week after Rumiantsev's great victory at Larga and that if Panin had reached and taken Bender a week earlier, the Second Army could then have proceeded east and linked up with the First Army at Grecheni in time to help Rumiantsev achieve an even more decisive victory at Kagul.[48] But Panin's siege of Bender could not have brought such rapid results, for Bender would prove very difficult to take.

The excavation of trenches and parallels began on July 19 and bombardment began three days later. Panin appears to have planned his approaches well, except that it took longer than expected to shore them up because the material for gabions and fascines had to be shipped in from Chernovtsy and Kalius on the northern Dnestr. Over the rest of the summer, Panin's engineers slowly brought their zigzag trenches and parallels closer to Bender's walls, their progress frequently slowed by enemy bombardment, countermining, and sorties. By mid-August, the guns of the Bender citadel were firing on average 200–300 rounds every 24 hours, while the Russian guns were responding with 500–750 rounds per day against the citadel. On August 3 the Russians fired 1,439 shells against the citadel and enemy sorties. The Turks made two strong sorties against the besieging Russians, on August 29 (killing sixty-seven Russians and wounding 138) and September 3 (killing ninety-nine Russians and wounding 265).[49]

On September 15 Panin learned that detachments under Igel'strom and Rzhevskii were coming from the First Army to reinforce him at Bender. This brought matters to a head: if he were to receive exclusive credit for victory at Bender that victory had to be achieved now. Panin therefore ordered a storm assault for the night of September 15–16. Eleven thousand troops were to attack the ditch and walls, in three columns: jaegers leading, grenadiers comprising the larger part of the assault force, and two battalions of musketeers in support, with covering fire from twenty-six siege guns, thirty field guns, and seven mortars. The signal for the assault was the explosion at around 10:00 p.m. of an enormous mine, a *globa de kompresion* packed with 6,400 kilos of gunpowder. The first soldier to breach the wall was promised a reward of 100 rubles.

The assault lasted for ten hours and encountered fierce resistance, both along the wall and in the narrow streets of the town, where the Turks had put up guns and snipers behind retirades. During the Russian assault, a force of 1,000 Turkish cavalry and 500 Turkish infantry sortied from the main gates and headed along the high banks of the river on the Russians' left flank, apparently with the intent of circling around and seizing the Russian baggage train and camp, protected by Lt. General Rennenkamp's regiment. Several units supporting the storm assault were turned on their commanders' own initiative to come to the defense of the camp: first During's squadrons of Moldavian volunteers, then Fel'dkerzam's jaegers, and then units under Elmpt, Taliazin, Ilovaiskii, Vernes, and Zorich. The enemy sortie force was nearly wiped out, and the sight of this (along with fires spreading through the town) may have caused the resolve of Bender's remaining garrison to waver, for at 8:00 a.m. a deputation came out to surrender.[50]

The Turks had lost about 5,000 dead, the larger part during the Russian storm assault; 11,794 Turkish soldiers and civilians surrendered, including more than 5,000 janissaries and *sipahi*s. But the fire had left little for the Russians to hold and garrison, and the Second Army had taken 6,236 casualties, of whom 2,561 had been killed or wounded in the course of the storm assault. A fifth of Panin's army had been lost. This dismayed the empress, who wrote, "To lose so many and to gain so little, it would have been better not to have taken Bender."[51] Panin did receive the order of St. George in "appreciation," but only a third of the officers he named for commendation went rewarded. With supplies low and winter approaching he began to take the Second Army back into winter quarters. On November 7 Panin was released from military service "as a mark of the Sovereign's kind consideration."[52]

Ismail, Kiliia, Akkirman, and Ibrail

With the fall of Bender, the army of Grand Vizier Ivaz Pashazade Halil Pasha also halted operations and withdrew behind the Danube to winter quarters at Isaccea. The recent Russian victories at Kagul and Bender made it less likely that large Ottoman forces would be sent across the Danube before spring, and that left vulnerable several of the hard points along the Ottoman fortress chain along the Danube. Rumiantsev decided to keep the bulk of the First Army encamped near Lake Ialpukh but send detachments south to try to seize the fortresses of Ismail, Kiliia, Akkirman, and Ibrail.

In the first few days after the battle of Kagul reconnaissance by Brigadier Igel'strom and Major-General Podgorichani showed that the retreating enemy had divided, some following the grand vizier to Kartal with Bauer's corps in pursuit, and another twenty thousand or so fleeing around Lake Ialpukh toward Ismail. Rumiantsev decided to exploit the division of enemy forces by sending Prince Repnin's corps past the lake toward Ismail—ideally to obtain its surrender without a lengthy or destructive siege.

Repnin's corps reached Ismail on July 26 and deployed in four squares, with Potemkin on the right (four battalions of grenadiers and four field guns), Rzhevskii on the left (two battalions of grenadiers and two guns), and Fabritsian (two battalions of jaegers) and Igel'strom (one battalion of infantry, a regiment of carabiniers, and four guns) in the two middle squares; three regiments of heavy and light cavalry were distributed in the intervals of the squares. It was expected that they could take Ismail without a long siege, for its northern face had an outer earth wall but no redoubts, and most of the Turkish cavalry and infantry—20,000 men—had been wasted on a failed attack on the advancing Russians and put to flight toward Kiliia. As soon as Potemkin's square advanced right up to Ismail's walls, the rest of the Turkish garrison surrendered. Repnin had lost eleven killed and ten wounded, but he had forced the withdrawal of about 20,000 Turks and killed 1,000 and taken 972 prisoner. He left three battalions of infantry to garrison Ismail and continued on toward Kiliia. Rumiantsev sent down the engineer Major-General Golenishchev-Kutuzov to oversee refortification and prepare Ismail to serve as the base for a Danubian Flotilla.[53]

En route Repnin received a deputation from Kiliia's citizens. They informed him that most of Kiliia's Turkish garrison had already evacuated, leaving just a hundred soldiers behind, and the Christian inhabitants had taken up arms and were waiting to welcome the arrival of their Russian liberators. But when Repnin reached Kiliia on August 10 he found 4,000 Turks still holding Kiliia and no sign of armed Christian volunteers. About 400 Turks sortied and set the outer works ablaze. Repnin was forced to settle in for a siege. On August 18 he brought up a breach-battery to within eighty paces of the walls, but his bombardment met with steady return fire from the enemy guns and the Turks made effective sorties. By the time Kiliia's commandant Mufti Efendi agreed to capitulate (August 19), Russian losses at Kiliia reached forty-two killed and 158 wounded. Vnukov, one of the heroes of Larga and Kagul, had been killed and Fabritsian had been wounded. Mufti Efendi and his troops were allowed to give parole and depart unharassed for Tulcea. Repnin finally took possession of Kiliia on August 21.[54]

Akkirman was not much easier. Once again Repnin was mistaken as to how many Turks remained in its garrison—there were actually over 1,100, not 400—and the detachment he sent against Akkirman was inadequate: Brigadier Igel'strom with four battalions of grenadiers, a squadron of hussars, 250 Cossacks, and no siege guns. Akkirman was perhaps the most solidly built of all the Ottoman fortresses on the eastern Danube, with stone inner and outer walls with large bastions, a stone escarpment and counter-escarpment, and an outer ditch fourteen meters deep. Igel'strom soon found it necessary to detach two companies of infantry, seventy Cossacks, and two unicorns to establish a small fort at the mouth of the Dnestr to protect against Tatar attacks and cut Akkirman's lines of communication with Ochakov.[55] Igel'strom's entrenching work, bombardment, and mining lasted from August 15 to September 25, when he received substantial reinforcements from Panin's Second Army.[56] Mufti Efendi surrendered Akkirman that day.[57]

Ibrail was next, attacked by Major-General Glebov, just arrived from Focşani. Ibrail had a garrison of 6,000 Turks and seventy four guns, so it withstood Russian bombardment from September 27 to October 24. Glebov attempted to take it by storm, attacking the fortress before dawn on the twenty-fourth with just 1,700 troops, no reserve, and without the support of heavy siege guns. Although night attacks had recently worked well for the First Army, on this occasion Glebov's three assault columns got tangled in the darkness and missed their assigned attack points. Heavy canister and musket fire killed five Russian officers and 484 soldiers and wounded fifty-three officers and 1,284 soldiers in just two hours. Report that enemy reinforcements from Bucharest were a few miles away gave Glebov further reason to lift the siege and withdraw his survivors to Maksimen.[58] But soon after this, the commandant of Ibrail decided that he would be unable to withstand a second siege—stores were low, and he feared that 12,000 Russians had concentrated at Maksimen for a second attack—and so he ordered its garrison to evacuate. Colonel Leont'ev took control of Ibrail on November 10.[59]

Four days later, Brigadier Gudovich and Kakovinskii reoccupied Bucharest.[60] Craiova, a Turkish fortress to the west of Bucharest and the temporary seat of the Ottomans' Wallachian hospodar, capitulated soon after. Rumiantsev left Major-General Weissman in command of the captured territory between the Prut, the Danube, and Bender, including the Russia units garrisoning Bender.[61] From Iaşi on November 29, 1770, Rumiantsev issued a manifesto to the Wallachians announcing the surrenders of the Ottoman fortresses at Akkirman, Kiliia, Ismail, and Ibrail and the liberation of Wallachia from the Turks. To the largely Turkish Muslim population of Craiova he promised protection and fair treatment. The First Army was now positioned to resume operations against the two remaining eastern Danubian fortresses, Giurgiu and Tulcea, come spring.[62]

In November the sultan replaced Khan Kaplan II Girei with Selim III Girei, perhaps due to suspicions the former was negotiating with Panin for a separate peace. At the end of the year Grand Vizier Ivaz Pashazade Khalil Pasha was sent into exile and replaced by Silahdar Mehmed Pasha.[63]

Orlov's Aegean expedition

On November 4, 1768, the empress and her new Council of State, responding to report of the imprisonment of Ambassador Obreskov and the immanence of an Ottoman declaration of war, had voted to undertake an offensive war against the Porte. At that time Nikita Panin had expressed the hope that the scale and duration of such a war would be limited. But Grigorii Orlov, Vice President of the VK and the empress' favorite and lover, had argued that Russia ought to be prepared for a protracted war on a larger geographic scale if she were to reap valuable territorial gains. Given that it was Panin's Polish project which had now provoked a war with the Turks and Orlov had not yet proposed how far to extend the Russian war effort, the Council was not inclined to dismiss Orlov's recommendations out of hand; and on November 12, at the Council's third session, it agreed to Orlov's proposal that the war effort include a naval expedition into the Aegean as a diversionary action.

Orlov did not yet speak to what squadrons would undertake this expedition—would they have to come out of the Baltic Fleet, given that the Turks still controlled the Dardanelles?—or whether the squadrons were to pursue the additional mission of supporting anti-Ottoman revolts in Greece and Montenegro. But Catherine was intrigued by the possibilities that Russian naval power might be used to incite revolts in the Balkans and perhaps even obtain for Russia an island or land port in the Mediterranean. In a December 20 letter to I. G. Chernyshov, her envoy to London, she wrote that her tendency "to build Spanish castles" had been awakened.[64]

From the beginning of her reign Catherine II had expressed interest in developing Russian maritime trade and naval capability in the Eastern Mediterranean as well as the Black Sea. In 1763 she had endorsed the project of some Tula merchants to form a Mediterranean Company and the next year, a special armed merchantman frigate specifically decided for Mediterranean sailing, the *Nadezhda Blagopoluchiia*, had been launched and sent on a test voyage to Livorno. D. M. Golitsyn, Russia's ambassador to Vienna, began negotiations with the Kingdom of Naples and Duchy of Tuscany to secure their support for the Mediterranean Company. The empress also took measures to strengthen the Baltic Fleet by arranging for Russian midshipmen and shipbuilders to obtain training and experience at Port Mahon on Malta and for several British naval officers, most notably John Elphinstone and Samuel Greig, to be loaned to Russian service. There were some limits to cooperation with Britain—while it became possible to resolve disputes about export dues and navigation rights and ratify a Russo-British trade agreement in 1765, Britain still resisted signing any alliance treaty.[65] But it became easier for the empress to win British support for a Russian Aegean expedition from 1768 now that Ivan Chernyshov, a member of the Russian Admiralty College, was in London as her extraordinary envoy and Charles Cathcart was posted to St. Petersburg as Britain's envoy. When the crucial time came, Britain would rebuff French demands and allow the Russian Baltic Fleet through the Gibraltar straits.

Grigorii and his brothers Aleksei and Fedor Orlov had in fact been working since 1762 to prepare for a Russian naval expedition in the eastern Mediterranean, and some of their undertakings had been cleared with the empress. The Orlovs took advantage of the contacts they had made while traveling in Italy to recruit Georgios Papazoli, a Thessalian Greek in the Russian artillery; Manuel Saro, a Greek ship captain and smuggler; and Ivan Palatino, a Cretan with connections to the Patriarchate at Constantinople. These three men would run an intelligence service out of Venice to identify and recruit insurgent leaders in the southern Peloponnesus, southern Albania, and Montenegro. Papazoli, who had been handling the Mediterranean Company's correspondence with the *Nadezhda Blagopoluchiia*, was entrusted with the additional task of spreading universals from the empress, in Greek, declaring that she offered herself as protector of the Greek Rite. By 1767 they had recruited into Russian service Marquis Piano Marucci, a Venetian banker of Greek Epirote extraction, to liaise with the Venetian government and convince the Corsican rebel leader Pascual Paoli to secure access to Corsican ports for Russian ships. Marquis George Andre de Cavacalbo agreed to make Malta available to the Russian fleet.[66]

In 1768 Aleksei Grigor'evich Orlov, the oldest and most diplomatically adroit of the brothers, was given leave to travel to Italy to attend to his health. He may actually have been ill for a while, but the medical leave was also a ruse to allow him to organize the Orlovs' intelligence and logistics network in the Mediterranean without alarming Nikita Panin, who remained opposed to the Aegean project. Aleksei Orlov was accompanied by a large suite of officers and en route he stopped in Vienna to discuss Balkan intelligence with D. M. Golitsyn. He sent two of his officers into Montenegro to try to convince Stepan the Small to drop his imposture of Peter III and lead his people in revolt against the Turks. Orlov also sent agents into the Khimara region of southern Albania, where for some years the kings of Naples had recruited a special Macedonian mercenary regiment. In December 1768 Orlov wrote home to the empress, "I have found here many like-minded men who wish to be under our command and serve in the present circumstances against the Turks."[67]

On January 29, 1769, Catherine II appointed Aleksei Orlov supreme commander of the Aegean Expedition and provided him with 500,000 rubles. Orlov had no naval experience (and would sometimes infuriate his squadron admirals, Spiridov and Elphinstone), but he was politically essential to the mission in that he had negotiated its logistics in the Mediterranean and apparently recruited the elements for an anti-Ottoman insurgency across much of the Balkans. However, the empress' instructions were not explicit as to how large a role supporting Greek and Slavic insurgents was to play in the Expedition's mission. She instructed Orlov that he had to make an effective diversion forcing the Turks to transfer troops and ships from the Danubian-Pontic front; that diversion could involve support for Balkan revolts, but she said nothing about one of his tasks being the "liberation" of the Balkans. Catherine did issue on the same day a Manifesto to the Greeks and southern Slavs stating that the arrival of the Russian fleet would provide them with the opportunity to struggle for their freedom, but the fleet was coming for "the easing of their lot"—Panin had crossed out "liberation" (*osvobozhdenie*) and substituted this phrase.[68] Nor did Catherine make it official that it would be squadrons of the Baltic Fleet sent into the Mediterranean; Nikita Panin would have protested. Preparations of the Baltic Fleet would be kept secret until May 1769.

In spring 1769 John Dick, the English consul at Livorno, and Teodor Aleksiona, a Greek at Port Mahon, assisted Orlov in amassing food stores and munitions at Livorno, on Minorca, and on Sardinia and helped recruit Greek captains and corsairs. Agents in Trieste put Orlov in contact with Giorgios Mavromichalis, the most powerful warlord of the Maniots. But Major-General Iurii Vl. Dolgorukov, secretly sent into Montenegro to prepare it as an insurgent *place d'armes*, failed to convince Stepan the Small to cooperate, and on Corsica the French crushed Paoli's revolt before it could secure Corsican ports for the Russians. Orlov's preparations were not that much of a secret in European capitals, and the Turks knew much about what the Orlovs had been undertaking since at least 1767.[69] They had countered by arresting suspected conspirators and simultaneously instructing their pashas to avoid provoking their subjects.

In March 1769 Admiral G. A. Spiridov[70] was given command of the First Squadron of the Aegean Expedition fleet: the line ships *Sviatoslav, Tri Ierarkha, Sv. Ianuarii, Evropa, Tri Sviatitel'ia, Severnyi Orel, Sv. Evstafii Plakida*; the frigate *Nadezhda Blagopoluchiia*; the bombardier *Grom*; the pinks *Solombala, Lapomink, Saturn*, and *Venera*; and the packetboats *Pochtal'on* and *Letuchii*—640 guns and 5,582 crew in all. The heaviest ship of the squadron was the *Sviatoslav*, with eighty guns and a crew of 830, commanded by Brigadier Captain I. Ia. Barsh; the next largest was the *Tri Ierarkha* (sixty six guns, 576 crew) under Brigadier Captain Samuel K. Greig.[71] The *Nadezhda Blagopoluchiia* had made the test run to Livorno a few years before. The line ships of the First Squadron were sheathed with an additional layer of planking caulked with sheep's wool to protect against damage from sea worms. This increased their weight, however, and slowed their speed.[72]

Spiridov had outfitted and crewed the squadron, but he was not confident that it would succeed in its mission and pleaded illness so as not to have to take command of it. He reluctantly accepted after the empress and Admiralty College insisted and promoted him to full Admiral on June 4. An indication that Catherine II still did not have a clear idea as to the possible repercussions of the expedition can be seen in her June 15 instructions to Spiridov, which set his primary mission as blockading the Dardanelles with the assistance of Elphinstone's Second Squadron: supporting Orlov's efforts on land to rouse the Greeks to revolt was of secondary importance, and nothing was said about engaging the Turkish fleet in battle.[73]

In fact the First Squadron lacked experience in sailing beyond Denmark. Both Paris and London were dubious that their expedition to the Aegean would succeed, while the Panin party protested that detaching ships from Baltic duty might reduce the ability to respond to any new Swedish naval challenge. The route from Kronstadt to the Mani coast of the Peloponnesus was over 8,300 kilometers, and although Britain had arranged for access to Portsmouth, Gibraltar, and Port Mahon for repairs and the hire of additional crew, the First Squadron made difficult progress.

The First Squadron left Kronstadt on July 19, 1769. It took it a month just to reach Copenhagen (it had taken Captain I. D. Mishukov just seven days in 1758). In August, leaks and a broken foremast forced the *Sv. Estafii Plakida* and *Sviatoslav* to return to Revel' for repairs.[74] The VK and Admiralty grew suspicious that Spiridov's reports were undercounting the sick, so when the squadron reached Hull, the Russian ambassador Chernyshov made an inspection. He found that 700 men were on the sick list. He also found that half of the squadron's crewmen were peasants from central Russia with no prior maritime experience. By the time the First Squadron arrived at Port Mahon on Minorca in late December, 332 men had died and 313 men were still sick.[75]

On October 9, 1769, the Second Squadron set sail from Kronstadt under Counter-Admiral John Elphinstone.[76] Elphinstone's mission was defined more narrowly: he was to assist in the blockade of Istanbul, and he was to serve under the authority of General-*anshef* Orlov but independently of Spiridov. The Second Squadron consisted of the four line ships *Ne tron' menia, Saratov, Tver'*, and the repaired *Sviatoslav*, with the frigates *Afrika* and *Nadezhda* and two small support ships. Leaks and storm damage slowed the squadron's progress and forced it to spend late December and most of January in Portsmouth for repairs.[77] Claude-Carloman de Rulhiere expressed the skepticism common in England as well as France toward the Aegean expedition: "One can hardly describe the amusement with which the English viewed these ships of pinewood, their enormous heaviness in maneuvering, their poops loaded with relics, the unhandiness of the sailors, the incredible dirtiness of their equipments, which was the veritable cause of a contagion that consumed them. Sometimes five or six English sailors would amuse themselves by working, in a moment and with extreme quickness, a ship of the same size as the Russian ship, which was hardly got under way by two or three hundred sailors of their nation."[78]

The Morean revolt

Spiridov's First Squadron arrived at Malta on February 4, 1770, and made final preparations for landing Russian troops and guns on the Mani peninsula of the Peloponnesus. On February 17 the squadron reached the Mani coast and entered the harbor of Vitullo (Oitylo). Its prefabricated half-galleys were assembled ashore and used to convey two detachments of Russian infantry and a battery to the wharf. Contact with Maniot rebels was soon made, and captains Barkov and Saro were sent to Passavo to recruit rebels for an "Eastern Legion" to attack Ottoman garrisons in the interior. By February 21 this Eastern Legion had over 1,200 volunteers—but only twelve Russian soldiers. Most of its Maniots were followers of the Grigorakis clan, which was burning to avenge itself on the Turks. Papazoli and Palatino were insisting that 40,000 rebels could be raised in Mani and another 100,000 across the rest of the Peloponnesus and that the revolt could carry as far as the Corinthian isthmus.

The Eastern Legion made its first contact with the enemy on February 26 when it attacked a fortified camp of 3,000 Turkish soldiers outside Misitra. The Turks withdrew to Misitra after taking about a hundred casualties; the Eastern Legion lost thirty dead and eleven wounded. After besieging Misitra for nine days, Barkov accepted the surrender of its garrison on parole, and by March 8 another 3,500 Ottoman soldiers and armed civilians had come in to Misitra from neighboring districts to lay down their arms. However, this did not satisfy some of the Legion's Maniots, who massacred about four hundred of the disarmed Turks, and Barkov was able to stop further atrocities only by locking the rest of the Turks up in local homes under guard. When Maniots began firing on the Russian guards, Barkov decided to divert their attention by allowing them to plunder Misitra.[79]

At Vitullo a Western Legion had also been formed from twelve Russian soldiers under Prince Petr Dolgorukov and about 500 Maniots under Giorgios Mavromichalis.

The Western Legion pushed farther into the interior of the Peloponnesus and seized Kalamata, Leontari, and Arkhadia, while other Russian landing forces from the squadron laid siege to the coastal fortresses of Koroni and Methodi. For a while Aleksei Orlov thought that the Russian occupation of the Isthmus of Corinth was nigh. But the ferocity the volunteer legions displayed toward the Turks began to stiffen the resistance of Ottoman garrison commanders, and 15,000 Albanian reinforcements now entered Morea. When Barkov's Eastern Legion (now exceeding 8,000 men, with forty-four Russian sailors and soldiers) placed the Turkish garrison at Tripolis under siege on March 29, the Turks sortied and surrounded and slaughtered them. Barkov and Saro barely escaped by fleeing down a narrow defile. Saro returned to Misitra to try to organize its defense; Barkov returned to Spiridov's squadron. The Eastern Legion was finished, and the Western Legion had to abandon Arkhadia and head toward the coast at Navarino.[80]

Efforts by the squadron to seize the port of Koroni by bombardment and storm were also having no success. Aleksei Orlov wrote the empress that these defeats "dispelled hope of success on land," and he blamed them on the Maniots' "inclination toward servility and their frivolity."[81] He decided to end land operations in Morea and concentrate the squadron's resources on taking the fortified port of Navarino (Pylos), which offered a better harbor and wharf than Vitullo.

The assault on Navarino had begun on March 24 when Spiridov took the *Sv. Ianuarii*, *Tri Sviatitel'ia*, and *Sv. Nikolai* into Navarino Bay and anchored out of range of its fortress guns. On April 3, Captain Borisov landed 300 troops and I. A. Gannibal, commander of the squadron's artillery, set up ten heavy guns and two unicorns in two batteries on the heights east of Navarino. For the next six days Gannibal's batteries and the guns of Spiridov's ships bombarded Navarino. When its walls were finally breached, Navarino's commandant decided to surrender rather than face a Russian storm assault. On April 14, Aleksei Orlov reached Koroni on the *Tri Ierarkha*; learning that Navarino was in Spiridov's hands, he ordered the fruitless siege of Koroni lifted and hastened to join the squadron at Navarino.[82]

The Maniot rebels were now left to their own devices. It was true that their Russian officers had found them difficult to control, but it was also the case that the squadron had given them very little assistance, while Russian propaganda, repeated by the Greek clergy, had left them with the mistaken impression that the Russians were fighting to liberate them from the Turks, not just to divert Turkish forces from the Danubian front. Pandasi Paleolog pleaded for more Russian help, at least in the form of money, arms, and small ships, claiming that there were still 20,000 Maniots ready to resume operations against the Turks in Morea and central Peloponnese.[83]

Chios and Çeşme

Elphinstone's Second Squadron arrived in the Aegean on May 9. On May 11 it landed some troops and guns at Rupino in the Gulf of Kolokythia. Here Elphinstone received reports that a large Ottoman fleet under *Kapudan* Ibraim Hassan Bey Pasha had entered the Gulf of Nafplion to the east. Elphinstone's squadron consisted of just four line ships, two frigates, and four pinks, while Ibraim Hassan had ten line ships, two frigates, and seven smaller vessels. But Elphinstone decided to sail against this Turkish squadron before Spiridov could arrive in reinforcement from Navarino with four line ships and two frigates.[84]

On May 16 the squadrons of Ibraim Hassan and Elphinstone engaged in a brief battle in Nafplion Gulf. Ibraim Hassan overestimated the size of Elphinstone's squadron, misidentifying his frigates and pinks as line ships, and withdrew up the gulf to the harbor of Nafplion (Napoli di Romania). Elphinstone followed. At dawn on the next day Elphinstone attacked the Turkish squadron while it was at anchor in Nafplion harbor under the protection of shore batteries. He was closing in on them in wake column when the wind suddenly died and his ships had to drop anchor. Ibraim Hassan now gauged the real size of the Russian squadron and counter-attacked. After about three hours of firing, the Russian ships were forced to retreat down the bay, the Turkish vessels in pursuit—but they finally left off the chase when they learned that Spiridov's First Squadron was approaching. Elphinstone had got off lightly with just six men killed and three wounded, most of them on the *Sviatoslav*. The Turkish captains had been slow to attack, their rate of fire had been low, and their gunners had aimed at the Russian's topmasts instead of trying to hole their sides.[85]

Elphinstone's and Spiridov's squadrons rendezvoused off the island of Cerigo (Cythera) and then turned northeast to reengage Ibraim Hassan's fleet. They caught up with it near the island of Spetses on May 24. Spiridov's squadron fell behind by forming its *corps de battaille* prematurely and losing speed; so only the two forward ships of Elphinstone's squadron were able to exchange fire with the enemy. When the wind fell the Turkish squadron slipped away in the darkness under tow by their sloops and galleys. Spiridov and Ephinstone had repeatedly quarreled over seniority, so some semblance of unity of command was restored at Spetses when Aleksei Orlov, aboard the *Tri Ierarkha* and accompanied by the bombardier *Grom*, joined the Russian squadrons. He had been forced to evacuate Navarino and blow up its defenses. The fall of Navarino marked the end of Russian operations in Morea. The squadrons' mission was now to find and destroy the Turkish fleet.[86]

The combined Russian squadrons now comprised nine line ships, three frigates, one bombardier, one packetboat, three pinks, and thirteen smaller vessels. On June 11 they headed from Milos across the Aegean toward Paros in the Cyclades in search of the enemy fleet, Orlov having received report that enemy ships had passed Paros three days before. Brigadier Captain Lupandin was sent with the *Rostislav* and two support ships to scout the waters to the northeast of Paros. At around five o'clock in the afternoon of June 23, Greig signaled that he had spotted the enemy fleet in the strait between Chios Island and the Anatolian mainland.

This was a larger enemy flotilla than the one encountered at Nafplion: sixteen line ships, six frigates, and fifty brigantines and xebecs. Greig reported that three of these line ships had eighty to ninety guns and crews of 800–900 men; seven of them had seventy guns, and six had sixty guns; the total strength of the Turkish fleet at Chios exceeded 14,000 men and 1,430 guns. Ibraim Hassan had only nominal command over it; the real command authority was vested in Hassan Bey Jezairli, an Algerian, a far more experienced and braver admiral. Orlov later acknowledged that the sight of so many ships and guns initially unnerved his crews.[87]

The remaining Russian ships joined with Greig and took up attack formation on the morning of the June 24: Spiridov on *Sv. Evstafii Plakida*, followed by a *corps de battaille* of four ships under Orlov on the *Tri Ierarkha*, and behind them a line-ahead column of three ships under Elphinstone, who was on the *Sviatoslav*. They came into the strait at a near right angle to the Turkish ships, which were standing at anchor in two lines in a half-moon formation, the heavier ships of line in the front and the smaller vessels in the second line spaced to fire through the intervals of the first line at targets of their choosing. Hassan Bey Jezairli left the attack to the Russians, confident that his half-moon deployment was a strong position and that another Ottoman squadron would soon be arriving in reinforcement. But by forfeiting the chance to maneuver he let the initial course of the battle be determined by the Russians, who had the wind on their side.[88]

The Turkish ships opened fire when Spiridov's vanguard came within three cable lengths. Spiridov's ships continued to hold their fire and close in further, as yet not much damaged because the Turkish gunners were aiming too high. But their battle formation broke when the captain of the *Evropa* veered off to avoid a reef, exposing Spiridov's *Sv. Evstafii Plakidka* to fire from five enemy ships when she came up to within fifty meters of Hassan Bey's flagship, the 84-gun *Real-Mustafa*. The *Sv. Evstafii Plakida* could not turn away from the *Real-Mustafa* because much of her rigging had been cut. Carcasses (explosive fused spherical ordinance) fired from the *Sv. Evstafii Plakida* set the *Real-Mustafa* ablaze under her quarterdeck and Spiridov's crew boarded her. But they had to withdraw when the fire spread to her sails and across the rest of the *Real-Mustafa*. The crew of the *Real-Mustafa* began jumping overboard and trying to swim to shore. The flames soon spread to the *Sv. Evstafii Plakida*. She did not burn as fast because of the direction of the wind, so Spiridov and Fedor Orlov and some sixty of crew had just enough time to abandon ship and take to the admiral's cutter and longboats before the blazing mainmast of the *Real-Mustafa* fell across the bow of the *Sv. Evstafii Plakida* and the latter blew up. The *Real-Mustafa* burned for another quarter of an hour and then she too exploded.[89]

The *Tri Sviatitel'ia* had maneuvered around the burning *Sv. Evstafii Plakida* and plunged into the middle of the Turkish first line, followed by the *Sv. Ianuarii* and the *Tri Ierarkha*. Greig and Aleksei Orlov brought the *Tri Ierarkha* alongside the second Turkish flagship, the *Kapudan-Pasha*. When the anchor cable of the *Kapudan-Pasha* was destroyed, her prow turned toward the *Tri Ierarkha* and she remained caught in this position for a quarter of an hour, unable to use most of her guns while the guns of the *Tri Ierarkha* raked her repeatedly. *Rostislav* followed in and the second line of Turkish ships now came under heavier fire.

The rest of the Turkish fleet feared that the wind would carry the fire from the *Real-Mustafa* to their own ships, so they began cutting their cables and putting on sail or arranging for tow to withdraw into nearby Çeşme Bay. They retreated in such haste that some of their vessels lost their bowsprits. The *Tri Ierarkha* led the Russian squadrons in pursuit for two hours but halted outside Çeşme Bay at about 2:00 p.m.[90]

For some time, Aleksei Orlov feared that his brother Fedor had been lost on the *Sv. Evstafii Plakida*. Then he learned that Fedor and Spiridov had managed to reach safety on the packetboat *Pochtal'ion*. Sloops and longboats had headed in to try to rescue other survivors from the *Sv. Evstafii Plakida*, but they found only her captain, Aleksandr Kruz, one cuirassier, and an artillery officer clinging to spars and other pieces of wreckage. The destruction of *Sv. Evstafii Plakida* had taken the lives of 628 men, including thirty officers. But the rest of the squadron's losses were just nine killed, thirty-five wounded, all on the other line ships.[91]

Spiridov's tactics at Chios—making a line ahead ("wake column") attack nearly at the perpendicular, holding fire until just a cable length away from the enemy—were not those preferred in the Russian Naval Ordinance, but neither were they a complete novelty: the English had occasionally made effective use of them since the Seven Years' War, and Nelson would later use them with great success at Aboukir Bay and Trafalgar. Kruz had probably studied line-ahead tactics during his eight years' training in England. Ships attacking in wake column are initially under disadvantage in that those behind the lead ship cannot use their guns until they close in and turn, and for much of their approach they are vulnerable to fire from across the front enemy line. But if they keep up a speed of two to three knots, the enemy's field of fire is greatly reduced by the time the attackers come within two cable-lengths.[92] Line-ahead tactics were also suitable for concentrating a blow against an enemy flagship, which might confuse and paralyze the rest of the enemy squadron—it certainly did in this instance—and one might speculate that Kruz and Spiridov chose a line-ahead attack at Chios because most of their squadron was inexperienced and it was simpler to instruct them to just follow the lead of the captains in front of them.

Although the Turkish fleet had fled, it had not been destroyed, and until that was accomplished, the Russian squadrons would not be able to freely operate in the Aegean. The surviving seventy to eighty Turkish vessels had taken shelter in a small, congested harbor without much room to maneuver, but they had positioned their eight heaviest ships in a line guarding the entrance to the bay and there were shore batteries protecting both of their flanks. Spiridov had brought the bombardier *Grom* up to the mouth of the bay to keep them immobilized under unicorn and mortar bombardment, while the Russian flagmen and captains held a council of war to determine how to proceed. It was decided to attack at night on June 25–26 rather than to blockade or withdraw; Greig would lead the line ships *Evropa*, *Rostislav*, *Ne Tron' Menia*, and *Saratov*, the frigate *Afrika*, and the *Grom* to within one or two cable-lengths of the first Turkish line and pound them with their guns, while the frigate *Nadezhda Blagopoluchiia* concentrated its fire against the northern shore battery; then four Greek ships converted into branders would exploit the smoke and confusion and slip through the enemy line to spread fires through the second, third, and fourth lines of the Turkish fleet.

At Chios much of the Russians' action had been improvised; at Çeşme everything unfolded according to plan. Greig's *corps de bataille* approached the outer enemy line after midnight and opened fire; the first to close in was the *Evropa*, followed within the half-hour by the other four line ships and the frigate *Afrika*. Within an hour and fifteen minutes, fire from the *Grom* had set ablaze the topsails of at least two enemy ships. The fire from the enemy line began to weaken at this point, so Greig sent in the branders against the as yet undamaged part of the Turkish fleet. Two of the branders were unable to get through, and the third, captained by Gagarin, was blocked by an enemy ship already ablaze. But Lt. D. S. Il'in managed to bring the fourth brander alongside a large line ship of eighty-four guns and set it afire.[93] By 2:00 a.m. the conflagration had spread across much of the Turkish fleet, and when a powder magazine blew at around 3:00 a.m. the Turks stopped firing and began abandoning their ships. Gunners at the shore batteries and the fortress at Çeşme also abandoned their posts, some fleeing as far as Izmir.[94]

Greig's combined artillery-brander night attack on an enemy in harbor was an historical first. It resulted in the destruction or abandonment of every enemy vessel in the harbor: fourteen line ships, six frigates, and fifty smaller vessels burned, while one line ship and five galleys were captured. Only about 4,000 Turkish crewmen made it ashore; the other 11,000 perished. Russian losses were negligible; eleven men were killed, most of them on *Evropa*; the only Russian vessels sunk were the four branders, and their crews had managed to get away by sloop. As had happened at Nafplion, the Turkish gunners had aimed too high to inflict many casualties on the Russians.[95]

The empress expressed her satisfaction in a letter to Rumiantsev declaring the Çeşme victory the most illustrious yet and thanking God for the miracle. She awarded Aleksei Orlov the Order of St. George, First Degree and the title *Orlov-Chesmenskii*; Captain Greig won the Order of St. George, Second Degree, and Admiral Spiridov received the Order of St. Andrew.[96]

On June 28 Orlov wrote to the empress, "Now there remains for me no other task than closing the trade to Constantinople and thereby trying to compensate the State for the expenditures on this expedition."[97] The Turks still had three large ships docked at Istanbul and a few at Rhodes and Mytilene, but these were not enough to break a Russian blockade of the Dardanelles. Orlov therefore set Elphinstone with three line ships and two frigates to block the Dardanelles and cut Istanbul's grain provisioning from Egypt. Elphinstone's squadron met with no resistance when it took up position at the mouth of the straits on July 15; it ventured into the straits a few times but generally contented itself with patrolling the mouth. The rest of the Russian Aegean expeditionary fleet was divided between Orlov and Spiridov and headed for Lemnos, about seventy kilometers from the Dardanelles, where Orlov wanted to establish a base for the Dardanelles patrols. On July 19 Orlov's and Spiridov's squadrons concentrated near Lemnos and began a long siege of the fortress of Pelari. In September Elphinstone detached the *Sviatoslav* to assist in the siege of Pelari, but it foundered on a reef. Orlov had to give up the siege of Pelari, and blamed Elphinstone for it. But in December a new base for the squadrons was obtained at Port Auza on the island of Paros, and on December 25 the Third Squadron under Admiral I. N. Arf arrived at Port Auza. Arf's squadron comprised the line ships *Sv. Georgii Pobedonosets* (sixty-six guns), *Vsevolod* (sixty-six guns), *Aziia* (fifty-four guns), the frigate *Severnyi Orel* (forty guns), and fifteen chartered English transports. This increased the landing forces of the Aegean fleet to 2,167 infantry. Arf's arrival also delivered stores badly needed for repairs and made the patrolling of the Dardanelles less sporadic. But some historians have speculated whether a more intense blockade might have had great effect, given the panic then prevailing in Istanbul.[98]

Austria alarmed, 1770

Until 1769, Emperor and Co-Regent Joseph II and Count Kaunitz had considered the highest priority of Austrian foreign policy the diplomatic containment of Prussian power. They had disapproved of the Russo-Prussian alliance in 1764 and Catherine II's Polish project—preferring to see a Saxon Wettin on the Polish throne—but they had remained neutral in Russia's war against the Porte, initially welcoming the war in the expectation that it would weaken both powers.

In May 1769 Dmitrii Golitsyn, the Russian ambassador at Vienna, asked Count Kaunitz if the emperor still considered Austria obliged to observe the terms of the 1753 Russo-Austrian Treaty. Kaunitz responded that the 1753 treaty had been nullified when Russia had signed alliance treaty with Prussia, and he informed Golitsyn that Austria and the Porte had reached agreement on a treaty of perpetual peace, which Austria intended to honor as long as the sultan did likewise. But Kaunitz reassured Golitsyn that Austria would remain neutral with regard to the Russo-Turkish War and would not interfere in Polish affairs.[99]

But the events of late 1769–1770—the fall of Khotin, followed by Rumiantsev's victories at Larga and Kagul and the destruction of the Ottoman fleet at Çeşme—filled the Austrians with alarm. The Porte appeared on the edge of military collapse and might accept peace upon Russian terms inimical to Austrian interests. The prospects of Russian armies indefinitely occupying Moldavia and Wallachia and a Crimea wrenched from the Porte and vassalized to Russia were very troubling to the emperor and Kaunitz. At summits held at Neisse in October 1769 and Neustadt in October 1770, Joseph II and Frederick II traded complaints about the dangers of Russian hegemony in Poland and Rumiantsev's advance upon the Danube. Joseph II stressed the need to press Russia to end its war with the Porte as soon as possible and on terms minimizing damage to the balance of power; Frederick II suggested in turn that Austria now had more to fear from the growth of Russian power on the Danube than from the Turks themselves. He did his utmost to beguile Joseph II with his proposal of a new Condominium of "German patriotism" that would render Prussia less reliant on alliance with Russia while enabling Prussia and Austria to better resist being dragged into war between England and France. Neither of them was yet prepared to threaten a coalition war upon Russia, however; Joseph II's program of military reform—introducing Prussian-style cantonal conscription—was just beginning and had not yet borne much fruit,[100] and Frederick II had found it safer to renew his treaty with Russia in October 1769, ahead of schedule.

The second summit at Neustadt brought both sovereigns to agreement that Catherine II must be pressed to recognize Austria and Prussia as mediators to reach a quick and stabilizing peace.[101] The vague threat of a possible combination of Austria and Prussia against Russia might be necessary to convince her, as she undoubtedly recalled the lesson of French "mediation" in the 1739 Belgrade peace talks with the Porte, and the military situation by late 1770 would have suggested to her that the sultan was ready to settle for peace on whatever terms she offered.

In September 1770 the sultan asked the governments of Prussia and Austria to mediate and arrange peace talks. But Catherine II held firm and insisted that if the Turks wanted to negotiate, it should be through Rumiantsev and any mediation by other European powers should include Britain. The terms for peace she communicated to Frederick II on December 9, 1770, included Russian retention of Azov and Taganrog; Russian navigation rights on the Black Sea; the cession to Russia of Greater and Lesser Kabarda; the return to Imereti and Kartli of the Georgian territories the Turks had seized in 1770; and the sultan's pledge that the Christian millet in Ottoman lands would be protected from oppression. In early 1771 she attached additional terms: recognition of the Crimean Khanate's independence from the Porte, and the demand that the Ottoman government pay Russia an indemnity of 25 million rubles, which could be secured through continued Russian occupation of Moldavia and Wallachia for the next twenty-five years.[102] Frederick called these terms "exorbitant and intolerable."[103] Vienna rejected them in early summer 1771, declaring that the Turks would never accept such terms. Meanwhile, the Austrian army began building new magazines on the Transylvanian frontier as an intimidating gesture.[104]

In the interval, Kaunitz sought to gain advantage for Austria by conducting a separate secret diplomacy with the Turks. Franz Thugut, the Emperor's envoy to Constantinople, drafted a secret treaty of alliance with the Porte in June 1771: Austria would restore the *status quo ante bellum* providing that the Turks pay 11 million gulden and cede to Austria Oltenia, Vidin, and Belgrade. The 11 million gulden was to compensate Austria for the cost of withdrawing troops from Italy and the Netherlands for redeployment along the Moldavian and Wallachian frontiers as a deterrent to the Russians.

It was unprecedented that the Habsburgs would sign a treaty with their hereditary enemies, the Ottomans, but the treaty Thugut was proposing was really for a concert, not a true alliance, as it did not promise any joint military operations. Austria would not declare war on Russia but would restore prewar borders simply through diplomatic mediation and by deploying troops on her Hungarian, Transylvanian, and Polish frontiers to "deter" Russia from sending forces across the Danube. But the sultan was desperate for Austria's timely intervention in the peace process, and Thugut had given him the impression that Austria might take some military action in Poland to replace King Stanisław and undermine Russian army logistics. Thugut's treaty was signed in Istanbul on July 6–7 but not yet ratified in Vienna, and it was supposed to be kept a secret for the time being; Catherine would finally learn of it in October.[105]

To apply additional pressure on Catherine II, Frederick II had sent his brother Prince Henry to St. Petersburg in October 1770. Prince Henry aimed at convincing her that there was a real danger Austria might declare war on Russia if she continued to reject Austrian mediation in peace talks with the Turks; Russia was already in some danger in the Baltic, as the French were intriguing to conduct a coup in Copenhagen and pull Denmark out of her alliance with Russia; if the empress insisted on renewing her war with the Turks and sent her armies across the Danube, the Austrians could be pushed to ally with France and Prussia might have to halt its subsidies to Russia and retreat into neutrality.

By January 1771, in his final days at the Russian Court, Prince Henry was floating an intriguing proposal: by offering territorial concessions in Poland-Lithuania, Russia could restore friendly relations with Austria and secure continued Prussian support. Such an idea had already been presented to the Russian government in February 1769 by the Prussian ambassador Count Solms, who represented it as a proposal made years before by the Danish diplomat Count Rochus zu Lynar.[106] At that time Catherine II had expressed no interest in it, as she felt no pressure then to placate the Austrians and doubted Joseph II and Frederick II were anywhere close to resolving their disputing claims to Silesia. But when she became aware of Thugut's treaty with the Ottomans in October 1771, she decided she could not afford to reject out of hand Prince Henry's proposal.

Frederick II correctly calculated that Vienna would embrace his proposal for a tripartite partition of Polish-Lithuanian territory—first because it allowed Austria to avoid the collision course with Russia Thugut's treaty with the Turks might have set; second, because Kaunitz had already drafted some partition proposals of his own; and third, because it legitimated actions the Austrians were already taking on their Carpathian frontier. For years the Habsburgs had sought the opportunity to reclaim Zips, a copper-mining region on the Hungarian border that had been pawned to the kingdom of Poland in the fifteenth century. When Zips became a haven for Bar Confederates in 1769, Vienna had responded by establishing a protective military cordon here, and the next year this cordon was extended another twenty miles to cover some Polish Crown domains in Nowy Targ and Nowy Sącz. For the time being the Austrians had to reassure King Stanisław August that the cordon was a temporary defensive measure and a permanent border would be renegotiated once order was restored in the kingdom of Poland. The Prussians had also taken steps toward a partition in 1770 when Prussian troops established a cordon through Polish Prussia west of the Vistula to protect against the plague sweeping across Poland. Bar Confederates in this territory were impressed into the Prussian army and the city of Danzig, which had given refuge to army deserters, was forced to pay reparations.[107]

For Prussia the proposal offered the opportunity to avoid conflict with either Austria or Russia, and it also delivered territories Frederick II had coveted for some time. In his 1768 *Testament Politique*, Frederick had set as one of the duties of his successor the acquisition of Polish territories along the Vistula—Danzig, Torun, Elbing—as a land bridge connecting Pomerania and East Prussia.[108] He had also begun to establish his own *cordon sanitaire* through part of Polish Prussia in 1770, ostensibly to protect against the plague and to impress Bar Confederates into the Prussian army.[109]

News of Thugut's treaty with the Porte reached St. Petersburg in October 1771. Panin was outraged by it and by Austria's occupation of Polish territory, but he acknowledged that this made it necessary to commit Russia to the partition proposal to salvage the empress' terms for peace with the Turks. Let Kaunitz know that "Russia has taken steps in consequence; she has reinforced her troops in Poland, and extended her alliance with Prussia to meet all possible cases of rupture … The Czarina, in agreement with the King of Prussia, has resolved to bring upon the heads of the Poles the consequences of their ingratitude, and to make certain convenient acquisitions at their expense, to the advantage of the frontiers of the Empire and those of her ally, the King of Prussia, following in this the example of the Court of Vienna. It is at the present time indispensible that Prince Kaunitz be brought to realize that we have settled everything already, and that it would therefore better repay the Court of Vienna also to make acquisitions, and rather than expose itself to the uncertainties of a war, to enlarge its territory at the expense of Poland without further delay, a course to which no opposition will be offered either by the King of Prussia or by ourselves."[110]

At a secret convention in St. Petersburg on February 17, 1772, Russia, Prussia, and Austria agreed to proceed with the partition of the Polish-Lithuanian Commonwealth. On February 28 the Austrians gave Frederick II reassurance that they had abandoned their claims to Silesia and would accept Polish territory in compensation. On March 8 the Austrians gave Catherine II reassurance that they would press the Turks to enter peace talks at Foçsani, to be mediated by Thugut.

CHAPTER 7
STALEMATE AND BREAK-OUT

A war of posts

By the end of 1770 the First Army had driven most Ottoman forces in Bucak, Moldavia, and Wallachia back across the Danube. The only significant exceptions were the large Ottoman fortresses at Giurgiu and Turnu, and the threat they posed was to Russian-held Bucharest and Oltenia more than to Russian forces on the lower Dnestr. But Rumiantsev was unable to campaign in 1771 the way he had in 1770; he could not concentrate the divisions of the First Army and push farther south to try to crush the grand vizier's army in the open field, as he had done at Larga and Kagul. The new Grand Vizier, Silahdar Mehmed Pasha, formerly the Pasha of Bosnia, differed from his predecessor in having chosen to remain on the defensive and not invade Moldavia or Wallachia in great force. So Silahdar Mehmed concentrated fewer troops in the Isaccea-Babadagh invasion staging area and devoted more of his resources to strengthening the remaining Ottoman fortress garrisons along the Danube: Turnu and Giurgiu on the northern bank, and Vidin, Nikopol', Sistovo, Rusçuk, Turtukai, Silistra, Hârşova, Măcin, Tulcea, and Isaccea on the opposite bank. He also attempted to replace irregulars with more combat-effective regular troops and to increase the number of French-trained gunners in the field army. By early summer the Turks had 15,000 troops and 250 guns at Ochakov; 15,000 troops and 50 guns at Isaccea; 5,000 troops at Măcin; 4,000 troops at Hârşova; 11,000 troops and 6,000 arnauts at Nikopol' and Turnu; 15,000 troops at Rusçuk; 10,000 troops at Tulcea; and 20,000 troops at Vidin. The field army at Babadagh and Diyarbekir numbered about 45,000 troops with 200 guns. Meanwhile Khan Selim Girei had brought 7,000 Tatars to the field army at Babadagh, and Moldovanci Ali Pasha had been assigned 40,000 troops and 1,000 guns to defend the Dardanelles against the Russian fleet.[1]

This forced Rumiantsev to resort to a war of posts to hold the zone of Russian occupation along the Danube from its mouth as far west as Oltenia. The river fortresses remaining in Ottoman hands enabled smaller enemy forces at the eastern end of the Danube to cross the river and attack Russian-held Akkirman, Kiliia, and Bender or for larger enemy forces to cross over to Turnu and Giurgiu and threaten Bucharest from those points or from Vidin. The *Voennaia Kollegiia*'s war plan for 1771 expected the First Army to stay largely on the defensive, making occasional small raids and diversionary moves across the Danube when possible, with the offensive role to be assigned instead to Dolgorukov's Second Army, which was assigned the task of invading Crimea and detaching it from its alliance with the Porte.[2]

The First Army was at lower strength than in the previous year, and Rumiantsev had to spread it across a broad front; so in assigning winter quarters he had separated its three main divisions at considerable distances. Rumiantsev and the First Division (about 23,000 troops under Major-Generals Stupishin, Khrapovitskii, Tekelli, and Brigadier Engelgart) would winter in Moldavia, at Iaşi and Maksimen, ready to shift across the Prut or to move across the Sărat River bridge southwest into Wallachia, if necessary. General-*anshef* Olits and the Second Division, the "Wallachian Corps" (about 17,000 troops under Major-Generals Glebov, Podgorichani, Kheraskov, Grotenhelm, Iurii Trubetskoi, and Krechetnikov), would guard the right flank and Bucharest by standing in southern Wallachia between the Sărat and Olt rivers. Major-General Weissman and the Third Division (about 13,000 troops, with Major-General Ozerov) would hold the left flank east of the Prut by camping on the heights of Ialpukh River and in Bucak.[3]

Conducting a war of posts from these points required a more sophisticated logistics than had the campaigns of 1769 and 1770. It was no longer enough to operate from a few big magazines in Poland; Wallachia, Moldavia, and Bucak had to be integrated into the magazine system so that the Polish magazines could be relegated to the role of a tertiary network; a secondary network could be established at Focşani, Falçiu, and Bucharest, and a primary network composed of magazines at Iaşi, Roman, and Bender could issue the six-month ration "portions" to the three main divisions of the First Army.[4] Collection into magazines and transfers out of fuller tertiary magazines down to secondary and primary magazines was supervised by the First Army's *ober-proviantmeister* stationed at Ianov, who had charge of 2,173 officers stationed across the magazine networks. Some collection of provisions was entrusted to private contractors like Baron Hartenberg, who made purchases of food and fodder in Poland. Certain districts in Moldavia, Wallachia, and Poland were required to turn over to officials all surplus above a certain amount for personal consumption, to be paid out of the Polish, Moldavia, and Wallachian treasuries at fixed prices (concealed surpluses were to be confiscated without compensation). In Bucak Weissman bought provisions on the local market at free market prices, with payment made in cash upon delivery to his regiments or payment upon presentation of receipts to the Moldavian *Diwan*. This proved more successful than Rumiantsev's and Olits' efforts, which relied mainly on requisitioning surpluses at fixed prices. War and plague had driven many Moldavians and Wallachians from their plowlands, and control over the district *ispravnici* supervised by the Moldavian *Diwan* had deteriorated after Stoffeln had been replaced by Chernoevich and then by Rzhevskii.[5]

The six-month rations and fodder portions to the First Army in 1771 were delivered by its mobile magazine, which consisted that year of 3,890 wagons, 15,408 oxen, and 3,890 drivers. Some of the wagons, oxen, and drivers were requisitioned by the *ober-proviantmeister*'s officers at fixed rate; some were obtained in Poland by contractor Hartenberg. Petrov considers Rumiantsev's provisioning system to have worked reasonably well in 1771, except for Potemkin's Oltenian battalions, which were too far away from the magazines. The total cost of First Army provisioning in 1771 was 3,291,376 rubles, which at the time seemed affordable enough given that the payments were being made mostly in paper assignats.[6] However, by November 1773, grain collections from the Polish peasantry had apparently taken so much many peasants were fleeing westward into the new districts annexed by Austria.[7]

Conducting operations along and across the Danube presented a special challenge. Rumiantsev had to monitor actions along 600 kilometers of the river's length, from its mouth on the Black Sea as far west as Vidin. The width of the Danube varied from 170 meters to three kilometers—at Isaccea, the crossing point of preference for the grand viziers, it was about 640 meters—and the average depth of the river was about 20 meters. Crossing from the Russian to the Turkish side was complicated by the fact that the southern banks were lower and densely covered with reeds, making approaching Russian forces more visible to Turkish troops so the Turks could fire on them from batteries concealed among the reeds on the islands and banks they controlled. Rumiantsev complained to the VK that he did not even possess maps of the course of the Danube. This is part of the reason the First Army was not prepared to make larger offensives across the river until 1773–1774.[8]

The Turks were better able to use the Danube to their advantage, for their fortresses along the river were more frequently serviced by military transports as well as merchant ships, and they had two centuries of experience building bridges to bring armies across the river. Rumiantsev therefore recognized the need for the Russians to create their own Danubian Flotilla to land troops across the Danube for raiding in 1771 and for invasion later in the war.

The first elements of this Danubian Flotilla were Cossack *chaika* longboats, a few captured enemy vessels, some hired river craft, and small flat-bottomed boats built at Ismail, Ibrail, and Galați. The construction of new vessels went slowly because masts and some planking and rigging had to be brought in from Ukraine and Russia, so Rumiantsev assigned to Captain Nogatkin the task of building ships at the old wharf Peter I had established near Voronezh and sailing these craft along the western coast of the Black Sea and up the Danube. Weissman's raid on Tulcea brought in some more captured ships and guns, so that by the end of November 1771 the new Danubian Flotilla assembled at Ismail numbered 67 small vessels (galiots, rowing brigantines, Turkish *konchebasy*, and *dubbel-shliupki*) mounting a total of 174 guns and falconets, manned by 421 sailors, and capable of landing 2,553 troops with stores for two to three months' campaigning. When the VK began planning for the Danubian Flotilla to undertake raids on Istanbul, Admiral Charles Knowles would be brought into Russian service and given command of the flotilla in early 1772.[9]

In January and February Rumiantsev's biggest concerns were the enemy build-up at Vidin and Turnu, which foreboded a drive across the Danube into Oltenia against Craiova, and the concentration of enemy forces at Giurgiu, which posed a major threat to Olits' Wallachian Corps defending Bucharest. Rumiantsev ordered Krechetnikov to make a diversion across the Olt and Danube against Vidin and instructed Olits to march on Giurgiu; he thought the time was ripe to capture Giurgiu, now that the Turks were preoccupied with Russian raids to its west and east.

Olits' expedition to Giurgiu was with 3,130 regular infantry, 347 cavalry, and some Cossacks and Wallachian arnauts. But he lacked siege guns, and he was deathly ill, and this delayed his march and gave the Turks time to reinforce Giurgiu. When Olits' troops finally reached Giurgiu on February 17 they faced an enemy who were three times their number. Olits was able to drive back an attack by enemy cavalry on the eighteenth and sent Brigadier Saltykov's grenadiers and jaegers to seize the outer trench line, but when night fell Saltykov's battalions holding position in Giurgiu's suburb came under a sortie attack. The Turks encircled and nearly overwhelmed his battalions until beaten off with heavy casualties.

Olits was finally stormed Giurgiu on the night of February 20–21. Four Russian columns assaulted Giurgiu, two from the suburb and two from the right flank. Their progress was hampered by a shortage of fascines and ladders, but after three hours' combat the Ottoman troops defending the outer wall fell back to their citadel. The castle's 84 guns and mortars and Olits' three batteries along the river bank and opposite the citadel bridge continued to exchange fire for the next three days. After the citadel's powder vault exploded, its garrison finally surrendered on February 24. Two thousand Turks were allowed to evacuate on parole, as well as a hundred of Potocki's Polish Confederates. Four thousand Turks were reportedly killed in the siege, and another two thousand had fled farther up the Danube. But Olits' corps had paid a heavy price for taking Giurgiu: it had lost 173 killed and 794 wounded, with Major-Generals Demolino and Grotenhelm among the wounded. Olits returned to Bucharest on March 1, leaving Second-Major Genzel and just 600 troops to garrison Giurgiu.[10] On April 2, command of the Wallachian Corps was transferred to Major-General Gudovich. Five days later Olits died at Bucharest.

The fall of Giurgiu left Turnu's 6,000 troops as the remaining Ottoman garrison on the north bank of the Danube. To discourage the enemy from reinforcing Turnu Major-General Potemkin was conducting raids out of Craiova against Vidin, whereas in the east Major-General Weissman was raiding Tulcea and Isaccea from Ismail. Prince Repnin, who had recently assumed command of the Wallachian Corps from Gudovich, marched on Turnu but decided after reconnaissance that it could not be taken without a lengthy siege that might leave Bucharest vulnerable to attack out of Nikopol' or some other point along the Danube.[11]

In fact the greatest point of vulnerability along the Russians' Danubian front remained Giurgiu, which Olits had left inadequately garrisoned. Muhsinzade Mehmed Pasha amassed large forces at the fortress of Rusçuk on the opposite bank just a few kilometers away, and on May 25–26 they made landings on an island opposite Giurgiu and at Slobozia village about three kilometers upriver. On the twenty-sixth they moved a small battery up to the outer walls of Giurgiu and opened fire. Instead of using his many fortress guns to suppress the Turkish battery, Genzel decided to undertake a sortie by volunteers. They failed and had to retreat back into the fortress, allowing enemy cavalry and infantry to push all the way up to the other end of the citadel bridge. Repnin began marching from Bucharest to Genzel's relief, calculating that Genzel ought to be able to hold Giurgiu for about two weeks. But by May 29 Genzel's garrison had taken so many casualties that he had only 379 men remaining under arms, and Turkish artillery fire had severed the chains controlling the citadel drawbridge, so that the only thing holding the Turks at bay was Russian canister fire across the lowered drawbridge. Genzel therefore surrendered on May 29 in exchange for the promise of safe evacuation on parole. Repnin reached the outskirts of Giurgiu just hours later. Finding it occupied by 14,000 Turks, he turned back to Bucharest.

Rumiantsev learned of Giurgiu's surrender on June 2. He was furious and had Genzel and officers Koliubakin and Ushakov court-martialled at Khotin. They were sentenced to be shot, but this was later commuted to deprivation of rank and confiscation of their estates.[12]

After retaking Giurgiu Ottoman forces were emboldened to undertake strikes across the Danube at several points: from Hârşova against Russian outposts at the mouth of the Ialomiţa; from Măcin against Cossack pickets; against Negoeşti; and a major strike by *Seraskir* Ahmed Pasha and 10,000 Turks from Giurgiu in the direction of Bucharest. This last operation ended in a major battle against 10,000 of Repnin's and Potemkin's troops on the Sambor River on June 10, resulting in 500 Turks killed and Russian casualties of 41 dead and 109 wounded.[13] Rumiantsev was forced to move the First Division up to Feleşti. He decided it was essential to retake Giurgiu from the Turks. This time the task fell to Repnin. But Repnin, too, had fallen ill, and his corps had just 17,450 troops to hold the entire Wallachian front, with rations for just two weeks' campaign. Provisioning his Wallachian Corps had been complicated by factional disputes among the boyars on the *Diwan* at Bucharest alarmed by rumors that peace talks were close at hand and might result in the restoration of Wallachia to the Porte.

On June 25 Repnin went on leave and turned command of the Wallachian Corps over to Lt. General von Essen. Essen proved far more daring. Despite the presence of 20,000–25,000 Turks around Giurgiu, Essen rejected Rumiantsev's suggestion that he tried to draw their forces out to defeat them in the field. Instead he marched all the way to Giurgiu with 6,000 troops with the intention of seizing it by siege or storm.

Essen tried to storm Giurgiu at night on August 7. He did not make enough use of his artillery or give his troops enough ladders, so none of his three assault columns was able to get over the top of the enemy breastworks; his troops were felled by enfilading fire or Ottoman pikemen pushed them off their ladders into the moat. The commanders of all three assault columns, Majors-General Czartoryski, Olsuf'ev, and Gudovich, were wounded—Czartoryski fatally. Essen lost about a third of his command.[14] He was forced to retreat; fortunately the Giurgiu Turks did not pursue him.

In late August and September the grand vizier reinforced Giurgiu and Turnu to 40,000 men. Testimonies by prisoners taken in a raid on Hârşova suggested that the grand vizier was planning for September a three-pronged offensive across the Danube, with 50,000 troops from Isaccea, Babadagh, and Măcin striking against Ibrail; Mehmed Pasha leading 40,000 troops from Giurgiu and Turnu against Bucharest, and Muhsinzade Mehmed Pasha taking another 30,000 troops from Vidin into Craiova and hitting Bucharest from the west. To Rumiantsev, September seemed too late in the year for an Ottoman offensive, but he took the threat seriously enough to strengthen patrols along the main roads and ordered Essen and Bauer to take up new positions closer to Bucharest.[15]

Muhsinzade Mehmed fell ill and could not make his march from Vidin, but Ahmed Pasha did advance on Bucharest in mid-October with 7,000–8,000 infantry and 30,000–40,000 cavalry. On the 20th, his army clashed with Essen's division of 13,000 troops at Văcărești Monastery about four kilometers from Bucharest. Essen followed the Rumiantsevan model of deploying his infantry into three squares (under Essen and Major-Generals Igel'strom and Dolgorukov) with cavalry in the intervals and stationing a smaller reserve square under Gudovich in the rear protecting the road to Bucharest. During the night Major-General Tekelli's light battalion had made a forced march to circle around the enemy, so that in the first hour of the battle Tekelli's battalion struck the Ottoman infantry from the rear while Essen's square collided with their front. Unable to make use of his disorganized infantry, Ahmed Pasha ordered his cavalry into action— not to rescue his infantry, but to cross over the Dîmbovița River and seize the road to Bucharest. But they were blocked by Dolgorukov, who sent Kantemir's cavalry and some of Gudovich's infantry and artillery to the Dîmbovița; canister fire from Gudovich's guns broke up the Turkish cavalry. Ahmed Pasha's infantry and cavalry fled south, pursued by Dolgorukov and Igelstrom, with Essen right behind. About two thousand Turks had been killed and 350 taken prisoner. Russian losses were 55 killed and 199 wounded.[16]

The pursuit of Ahmed Pasha amassed sufficient momentum to take Essen's division all the way to Giurgiu. On October 24 Lt. Colonel Kantemir's detachment approached Giurgiu's outer works and discovered most of its garrison had fled, leaving a remnant encamped outside the citadel. Kantemir seized the bridge and broke into the citadel; lacking artillery of his own, he had his Cossacks and hussars turn the citadel's guns upon the enemy camp below while he attacked it with his pikiniers and Cossack cavalry. The Turkish camp was quickly overwhelmed. Its defenders fled to small islands on the Danube or drowned trying to cross the river. Giurgiu was finally back in Russian hands, and with it an enemy mobile magazine of a thousand ox-teams.[17]

By the end of 1770 the resistance at Craiova led by Ban Monolaki had been broken and most of the Ottoman troops west of the Olt River had been driven back across the Danube. But the battalions of Krechetnikov and Potemkin had been expected to stand guard against Turkish forces reinfiltrating into Oltenia from the fortresses at Turnu and Vidin, which the grand vizier reinforced in January 1771. Soon after this Krechetnikov had to request medical leave and transfer command of his troops to Potemkin. Potemkin had been given a difficult mission: securing the territory west of the Olt with just a few thousand men, mostly light troops and some Greek arnauts, undertaking raids across the Danube to keep the enemy forces at Vidin and Turnu on the defensive, yet avoiding any provocation to Austrian forces.[18] Although Potemkin's troops were short on rations and equipment, they performed some remarkable feats in May and June. On May 5, they raided across the Danube at Hârșova. The next day Potemkin led a flying detachment of 600 grenadiers and 200 jaegers against Zimbri, burning its magazines, capturing a hundred Turkish vessels, and ferrying 2,620 Christian inhabitants back to the Russian side of the Danube. His detachment suffered just one fatality. Four thousand Turks retaliated on May 17 by crossing over the Danube and marching up the Olt River, but Potemkin defeated them; the Turks lost 300 dead, Potemkin 39 dead and 32 wounded.[19]

Ten days later he defeated another attack by 10,000 Turks from Turnu and rendezvoused with Repnin at Copaceni to march to the relief of the besieged Russian garrison at Giurgiu.

There were also successful raids across the river by General-Quartermaster Bauer and some Zaporozhian Cossacks against Hârşova, resulting in the destruction of Hârşova's powder magazine and the burning of a hundred Turkish vessels (August 23–24); by Miloradovich, against the enemy camp near the fortress at Măcin (December 20–21); and the most effective of them all, raids undertaken out of Ismail by Major-General Weissman against Tulcea (March 23), Isaccea (April 16 and October 19–24), and Babadagh (October 20 and November 17). These three points comprised the main *place d'armes* of the grand vizier's field army, each was defended by 3,000–9,000 Turks, and the enemy troops stationed across this eastern Danubian front totaled 40,000, whereas Weissman was raiding with much smaller forces.[20] Yet upon their approach, the Turks usually fled from their fortresses and camps—Tulcea's garrison evacuated after mistaking Weissman's force for the entire First Army, and when he advanced on Babadagh, most of the Turks fled to Bazarjik, so that "It was not possible to muster 2,000 men to stand against the Russians; the townsmen loaded their wives and children onto wagons and had them evacuated .... The grand vizier ... seized the sacred banner and disembarked with the sipahi and silahdar agas and present statesmen."[21]

Weissman's raids denied Grand Vizier Silahdar Mehmed Pasha the magazines, boats, and bridges necessary to cross the Danube into Bucak. The grand vizier may not have been able to mount a more effective resistance, because he was already preoccupied with a Mamluk revolt in Egypt. In November, he was replaced with Muhsinzade Mehmed Pasha and Ahmed Resmi Efendi was named second in command of the army. Muhsinzade tightened military discipline and began rebuilding the field army at Shumla.[22]

By the end of October it was safe for the First Army to retire to winter quarters. Rumiantsev's division was stationed between the Sărat and Prut, with headquarters at Iaşi; Essen's division camped near Bucharest; and Weissman's division stood at Ismail and between the Dnepr and the Bug. The Danubian flotilla established bases at Ismail, Ibrail, and Giurgiu, whereas Dolgorukov's corps protected the army's magazines in Poland. The empress notified Rumiantsev of her discussions with Nikita Panin and their agreement that it was now time to propose peace talks to the sultan.[23]

All through 1771 Rumiantsev's division had remained in Moldavia and had not risked pitched battle against the grand vizier's field army. Russian operations had been limited to smaller forces out of the eastern and western divisions conducting sieges and raids against enemy fortresses; while most of these operations were successful enough to keep the enemy on his side of the Danube, some writers have wondered why Rumiantsev was so reluctant to take the massed First Army across the Danube for a decisive battle to annihilate the enemy's field army. A. B. Shirokorad sees Rumiantsev as trying the patience of the empress and VK by offering a thousand excuses not to invade across the Danube, and he finds the argument that Rumiantsev feared heavy casualties unconvincing, given that the First Army was already suffering great losses from disease by keeping to its quarters in plague-infested Moldavia.[24] A. N. Petrov argues that the

Danubian flotilla was still too small to take the First Army across the Danube quick enough so that it would not be struck on the flanks or in the rear by the enemy forces based at Rusçuk, Turtukai, Sistova, Silistra, Nikopol', Hârşova, Măcin, and Vidin. Under such circumstances the preferred strategy would be to use small elements of the army to deny the enemy the means to invade across the Danube.[25] It should also be kept in mind that the general points of First Army's war plan for 1771 had been formulated by the VK in St. Petersburg, and the VK had the responsibility of anticipating diplomatic events reshaping military objectives—such as the new pressure from Austria and Prussia to negotiate a speedy peace with the Porte, a peace that might require the empress to soften her terms or offer some territorial concessions.

Conquest of Crimea

Rumiantsev's victories at Larga and Kagul and Panin's capture of Bender had given the Nogai hordes even more reason to think the Crimean Khanate would not be able to sustain another Russian invasion. Some mirzas of the Yedichkul and Jamboiluk hordes, approached through Zaporozhian Cossack envoys, had already entered into negotiations with General-*anshef* Panin to establish terms for throwing off the suzerainty of the Ottoman Sultan and accepting Russian protection; Panin was encouraging them to bring into the talks representatives of the Yedisan and Bucak hordes as well. There was a reason to think this could be achieved, as the Yedisan and Bucak hordes had refused to support Khan Kirim Girei's 1768 raid into New Russia, and on July 6, 1770, five Yedisan mirzas under Jan-Mambet Bey signed a treaty of friendship and alliance with Russia.

At this stage, Panin's intention was to bring the four Nogai hordes under Russian protection and guarantee them independence under their own laws in a homeland in Kuban; they would have to be evacuated from the steppe west of the Dnepr, as it was expected this territory would be annexed directly to Russia. As yet Panin's negotiations did not touch upon the subject of the Tatars within Crimea. But the empress now saw the opportunity to use the defection of the Nogai hordes to pressure the Crimean Tatars to repudiate the Porte and thereby "deprive Turkey of its right hand."[26]

In November 1770 the Russian negotiating strategy therefore shifted to focus upon the Crimean Tatars, offering them independence under Russian protection and restoration of the Crimean khans' authority over the Nogai hordes.[27] Panin was dismissed from the negotiations, partly because of his illness and partly because command of the Second Army was transferred to General-*anshef* Vasilii Mikhailovich Dolgorukov—an appointment generally believed to be a political victory for Zakhar Chernyshov.[28]

Dolgorukov would handle negotiations with the Crimeans; the continuing negotiations with the Nogais would be handled by Major-General E. A. Shcherbinin, the governor of Sloboda Governorate, and by P. P. Veselitskii, Shcherbinin's Tatar Commissioner, formerly attached to the Secret Expedition of Consul Nikiforov in Crimea.[29] A Russian translator, Mavroev, was sent to Crimea with Jan-Mambet's brother

Melisa Mirza to try to start negotiations among the Crimean Tatar mirzas, while Khan Selim III Girei was still off on the Danube.[30]

Although the Nogais could be induced to ally with Russia, it was recognized that the Crimean Tatars would require the stick as well as the carrot, so on May 10, 1771, Catherine II wrote Dolgorukov instructing him to prepare the Second Army for an invasion of Crimea and to borrow funds from Shcherbinin's Tatar Commission to suborn the Crimean mirzas.[31] A Russian military occupation of Crimea could be expected to set favorable terms for the Khanate's new relationship with Russia besides presenting the Nogai hordes with the *fait accompli* of their restored vassalage to the Crimean Khan.

In 1736 Marshal Münnich, leading an army of 80,000 men, had demonstrated that it was possible to break through the Perekop Line and seize Gozlev and Bakhchisarai—although the summer heat, lack of fresh water, and spread of dysentery had forced him to withdraw from Crimea after two months. Marshal Peter Lacy had greater success invading Crimea in 1737 and 1738 by improving his army's medical service, arranging for greater support from the Azov Flotilla, and by avoiding a direct assault on the Perekop Line and instead crossing the Genici Strait by pontoon bridge and entering Crimea on the Arabat Spit. The massing of Ottoman and Tatar forces near Karasubazar and shortages of fodder and water had forced Lacy, too, to withdraw, but it was noted that actual armed resistance to his troops inside Crimea had been minimal.[32] This augured well for Dolgorukov's new attempt, provided he made careful logistic preparations and most of the Crimean Tatar army remained off on the Danube.

In fact, Dolgorukov's Crimean expedition was better planned and financed than Münnich's or Lacy's and more attentive to the special conditions of campaigning on the Perekop steppe and the arid interior of the Crimean peninsula. Whereas Münnich and Lacy had aimed at destroying the Crimean army, the diplomatic groundwork already laid by Panin left Dolgorukov with a simpler and more easily attainable military objective: seizing the Kerch Straits and the harbors along the Crimean coast, driving their inhabitants into the interior to deny the Khan Ottoman reinforcements, and forcing the Crimean nobility to repudiate their vassalage to the Porte.[33]

When Khan Selim learned that Mavroev and Melisa Mirza had arrived at Bakhchisarai, he sent orders for their arrest and execution. But they were saved by the intervention of Shahin Girei, Seraskir of the Nogai Hordes and son of former khan Mehmed Girei.[34] Shahin Girei argued that taking the life of Mavroev would do nothing to deter the Russians from invading Crimea, which was defenseless at this time given that the Khan was far off at Babadagh with most of the army and the Ottomans were unlikely to come to their aid. On April 8, 1771, Shcherbinin informed St. Petersburg that he had received a letter from *kadiasker* Abdul Kirim Efendi that the leading mirzas had met in Bakhchisarai and resolved to depose Selim III Girei and elect Sahip Girei in his place. Shahin Girei was sent to St. Petersburg to get the Russian government's acknowledgment.[35]

In April, Dolgorukov assembled the Second Army near Poltava and Bakhmut. Its total strength was about 53,000 men. The plan of campaign, worked out by Zakhar Chernyshov in the VK, called for the Second Army to operate in three separate corps. The main corps of 23,950 troops, under Dolgorukov, was given the task of marching from the new Dnepr Line to break through the Khanate's Perekop Line and drive south against Kafa.[36] A "Sivash Corps" of 3,395 troops under Major-General Shcherbatov would cross the Sivash marshes with the aid of Admiral A. N. Seniavin's Azov Flotilla (17 warships and 57 smaller landing vessels) and capture the Turkish fort on the Arabat Spit, then push on to occupy Kerch and Yenikale and seize control of the straits separating the Sea of Azov from the Black Sea. A third corps of 2,500 troops commanded by Major-General Braun would separate from Dolgorukov's main corps and seize Gozlev. The Azov Flotilla was to land Shcherbatov's Corps near Genici at Sivash and anchor at the mouth of the Verda River to shuttle stores from Taganrog to Shcherbatov; in the event an Ottoman fleet approached Genici, the Azov Flotilla would reposition itself off Fedotova Kosa to block it. Lt. General Osterman would have charge of another 21,000 troops from the Second Army performing cordon defense along the Ukrainian Line, whereas the Don Cossacks would patrol the steppe between the Dnepr and Azov and a force under Major-General Wasserman would stand at the mouth of the Chartaly River to defend the Dnestr-Bug steppe against any enemy attacks out of Ochakov and to provide a link between the second and first armies.[37]

Spring of 1771 offered a good window of opportunity for Dolgorukov's expedition. Khan Selim III Girei and much of the Tatar army were off at Babadagh with the grand vizier; the Ottoman garrisons in Crimea, under the command of Ibraim Pasha, were undermanned; most of the Turkish fleet was preoccupied with operations in the Aegean.[38]

On April 20, 1771, Dolgorukov's division began its 290-kilometer march toward Perekop, keeping within a few kilometers of the Dnepr and making good time; the weather was warm, and there was already abundant spring grass for grazing the army's mounts and transport animals. The division crossed the Samara River during May 7–13, using a newly built bridge and proceeded toward Konskie Vody in four columns. At Konskie Vody on May 25, Dolgorukov's division was reinforced by some of Lt. General Berg's regiments, come down from Bakhmut; two days later, Shcherbatov's Sivash Division separated for its landing upon the Arabat Spit. Near Kazykirmen, where the Dnepr road and the road to Perekop split, Dolgorukov founded a magazine guarded by a redoubt manned by two companies of infantry, 600 Cossacks, and a few squadrons of carabiniers; wagons from this magazine would supply Dolgorukov's division for its march to Perekop, about 70 kilometers to the east. On May 17 Vice-Admiral Seniavin launched the Azov Flotilla on the Sea of Azov, which had been closed to Russian ships for the last seventeen years.

Dolgorukov set up camp about four kilometers from Perekop on June 12. Here his division made their first contact with the enemy—a small reconnaissance detachment, which was easily put to flight.

The Perekop Isthmus connecting the Crimean peninsula with the mainland and separating the Black Sea from the Sivash Sea is only about five to seven kilometers wide, and most of its width was protected by a fortified line manned by Ottoman and Tatar troops from the fortress of Or-Kapi, which guarded the road into Crimea. There were five batteries along its span; its wall was 8.5 meters high, and there was a ditch or moat 6.4 meters deep along its face. The Perekop Line had withstood Vasilii Golitsyn's huge armies in 1687 and 1689, but Münnich and Lacy had been able to penetrate it during Empress Anna's Turkish War, and since then, its defenses had undergone further dilapidation. The Crimean Tatars' strength along the Perekop Line and at Or-Kapi in June 1771 was estimated at 55,000 by the VK; the Turks defending these positions numbered about 7,000.[39] But Dolgorukov decided to assault the Perekop Line at night (June 13–14) by sending Prozorovskii with some light cavalry and infantry on a diversionary attack on the eastern end of the Line, near the Sivash Sea, whereas the larger part of Dolgorukov's division would move out from their *wagenburg* in three squares of grenadiers and jaegers under the command of V. P. Musin-Pushkin to attack the western end of the Line, crossing its ditch and scaling its wall by siege ladder.

Prozorovskii's troops were counterattacked by enemy cavalry as they neared the Line, but he drove them back and took possession of that end of the wall; Musin-Pushkin's infantry soon after captured the other end of the wall. The Line's surviving defenders fell back to Or-Kapi fortress, which surrendered the following day (June 15). Dolgorukov allowed the defeated Turks to evacuate to Gozlev on parole, but to escort them to Gozlev, he sent Major-General Braun with 2,500 infantry and Cossacks and instructions to occupy Gozlev. The rest of Dolgorukov's division marched on Kafa.[40]

Shcherbatov's Sivash Division had embarked on vessels of the Azov Flotilla on June 12 at Fedotova Spit. Despite strong winds and rough seas, Shcherbatov's troops were landed on Arabat Spit the next day. On the fifteenth, Seniavin took part of his flotilla—a squadron of eight warships and double-sloops—toward the Kerch Straits upon report that an Ottoman squadron was approaching to land 10,000 troops to reinforce Kerch and Yenikale. Seniavin's ships encountered fourteen Turkish xebecs and half-galleys off Arabat Fortress point on June 19, but two days of squalls prevented him from engaging them in battle; by the time he took up battle order on the twenty-first to try to block them from entering the Sea of Azov, the entire Turkish squadron had retreated beyond the Kerch Straits back into the Black Sea.[41] In late June, some vessels' crews met with enemy fire while replenishing their water ashore near Kerch, and Seniavin had to land a few battalions to put the Turks to flight, but only two marines were killed in this operation and it marked the last Ottoman attempt to challenge Seniavin's mastery of the Sea of Azov.

Shcherbatov's division reached the fortress of Arabat on June 17 and stormed it on the night of June 18 with three battalions of infantry and 100 jaegers, and with fire support from ships of the Azov Flotilla. Of Arabat's garrison of 500 Turks, 70 were taken prisoner and the rest were killed or fled, pursued by Shcherbatov's cavalry. The Russian casualties at Arabat were 12 killed and 39 wounded. Shcherbatov established batteries near Arabat Fortress and on the opposite shore, across the Rotten Sea, to prevent the Turks from landing again on Arabat Spit. The appearance of Seniavin's flotilla off Kerch drove Abaza Mehmed Pasha's squadron back out to the sea, so there was no landing of Turkish troops to hinder Shcherbatov from advancing farther down the Spit to the stone fortress of Kerch. Most of the Turks garrisoning Kerch had already fled, so it surrendered after little resistance on June 21. By July 11 Shcherbatov's division had captured Taman' Island and the Ottoman fortress at Yenikale, on the other side of the Kerch Straits.

Russia had thereby achieved one of the principal objectives of the war: control of the Kerch Straits separating the Sea of Azov from the Black Sea. Russian naval forces could now freely enter the Black Sea.

Abaza Mehmed Pasha made no further attempt to land Ottoman troops on Arabat Spit and took his fleet back to Sinope.[42] Ibraim Pasha, commander of the 10,000 Ottoman troops remaining in Crimea, turned back to Kafa instead of continuing to Karasubazar. Khan Selim III Girei had returned to Crimea upon word of Dolgorukov's breakthrough at Perekop, but he now took refuge at Bakhchsarai with a few members of his court rather than take the field against the Russians.[43] Dolgorukov decided to send a cavalry detachment to Bakhchisarai to capture the khan, but the khan fled by sea to Istanbul.

Dolgorukov was therefore able to cross the Salgir River and reach the outskirts of Kafa by June 29. A force of Tatar cavalry attacked but were driven all the way back to Kafa's outer works by the Russian hussars and carabiniers. Dolgorukov's infantry advanced upon Kafa in three battle lines, the cavalry on their flanks, the guns concentrated in forward batteries. The artillery played an especially important role in Dolgorukov's attack: besides bombarding and quickly clearing Kafa's forward trenches, they fired on anchored Turkish warships and forced them out to sea. As Dolgorukov's infantry seized the forward trenches, the light cavalry on his left flank drove along the shore to prevent Turkish troops from attempting any sortie out of Kafa fortress. Dolgorukov then moved his batteries in closer and began bombarding the fortress itself. It quickly capitulated. Ibraim Pasha and 700 Ottoman troops were taken prisoner. About 3,500 Turks had been killed, but Dolgorukov's casualties were limited to 54 wounded.[44]

Braun had already seized Gozlev without a fight on June 22. On June 29 his division rejoined Dolgorukov's at Kafa after repulsing several attacks by much larger Tatar forces. Tatar resistance now collapsed; the Tatar army melted away into the hills. Although the Tatars in the highlands may have numbered as a many as 60,000, they had broken up into small uncoordinated groups unable to pose much threat to the Russians along the coast, so Dolgorukov had no need to carry the war into the hills. He had sundered the Khanate's lines of communication with the Turks and had occupied Bakhchisarai, Sudak, Yalta, Balaklava and Akhtiar with little resistance, giving his Second Army control of most of the eastern and southern coasts of the Crimean peninsula. This remarkable achievement was due in part to faster movement, better intelligence, and better provisioning and medical services than attended Münnich's 1736 Crimean expedition, on which 30,000 Russian troops had died of thirst and dysentery.[45]

The ease and rapidity with which Dolgorukov had conquered Crimea had convinced even the Shirin clan to join the other Crimean nobles in abandoning the Porte and accepting alliance with Russia. Shirin Mirza Ismail and Azamet Aga had presented themselves at Dolgorukov's camp on June 22 as "representatives of all of Crimean society" and had requested that the empress take Crimea under her protection. On July 8 Dolgorukov received a letter from Shahin Girei announcing that the Crimean nobles had repudiated Khan Selim and were in the course of choosing a new Khan. This forced Khan Selim himself to acknowledge Russian suzerainty on July 13 in exchange for

Russian recognition that he retained his throne—though after a few days he abdicated and fled to Sinope, perhaps fearing Ottoman retaliation.[46] On July 27, 1771, the Shirins, lesser notables, and clerics assembled at Karasubazar and elected Sahip Girei as the new Khan, his brother Shahin Girei as *kalga*, and their nephew Batyr Girei as *nuraddin*. The Karasubazar assembly swore an oath of allegiance to Russia and requested protectorate status, assuring Dolgorukov this was also the wish of the twelve Tatar clans in the Kuban. This encouraged the empress in August to authorize Shcherbinin's Tatar Commission to press the beys of the Nogai hordes to submit to the authority of Khan Sahip Girei.[47] In November, Shahin Girei arrived in St. Petersburg to formalize a treaty of alliance and protectorate and get Russian confirmation of Sahip Girei's sovereignty over Crimea and the Nogai hordes.

Dolgorukov turned over command of the Second Army in Crimea to Major General Prozorovskii on September 25, 1772. Prozorovskii still found it necessary on occasion to use armed force against groups of Tatar rebels, and in the intervals between peace talks it was also necessary to guard against further enemy efforts to land troops. On intelligence about enemy plans to land janissaries at Taman' in March 1773, the Azov Flotilla was expanded to 56 vessels[48] and organized into three squadrons for cruiser patrolling: two squadrons under captains Sukhotin and Kingsbergen patrolling the Crimean coast out of Balaklava and Kafa, and a squadron under Seniavin patrolling the Kerch Straits and convoying Russian transports to Crimea.

On May 29, 1773, Sukhotin's squadron encountered an enemy flotilla of about thirty merchant ships converted into troop transports in the gulf of Sucuk-Kale (future Novorossiisk) on the Abkhazian coast. The Turks were reported to be preparing to land troops at both Taman' and Ochakov. Sukhotin attacked at night and burned six enemy transports, and captured two more the next day. On June 23, Kingsbergen with the shallow-draught frigates *Taganrog* and *Koron* engaged two enemy ships and two enemy xebecs off Balaklava in a six-hour battle in which four Russians were killed and 26 wounded; the enemy withdrew, having suffered heavier damage. On August 23, 1773, Kingsbergen, with *Azov, Giurgiu, Modon*, frigate *Vtoroi*, a brander, and a sailboat, engaged off Sucuk-Kale a Turkish squadron of three ships-of-the-line, four frigates, three xebecs, and seven or eight transports. The enemy squadron fled to the harbor of Sucuk-Kale, where they took protection under its fortress batteries.[49]

The last Black Sea naval engagements of the war occurred in June 1774. An Ottoman flotilla of 5 line ships, 9 frigates, 17 galleys and xebecs, 1 bombardier, and 3 transports anchored in the fog between Kerch and Taman' on June 23. This may have been Grand Vizier Muhsinzade Mehmed's final gamble of the war: a landing at Kerch timed to coincide with a Crimean Tatar attack on Prozorovskii's camp on the Salgir River. But the attack on Prozorovskii was crushed, and the Turkish ships off Kerch were driven off by the squadron of Counter-Admiral B. Ia. Chichagov (*Koron* and *Azov, Pervyi, Vtoroi, Chetvertyi*). This Ottoman flotilla returned to the Kerch Straits on June 28 but was again driven away, this time by Seniavin, who was with the *Azov, Giurgiu, Khotin, Pervyi, Vtoroi, Chetvertyi*, and two bombardiers. Twelve days later, the Kuchuk-Kainarji Peace was signed.[50]

The Russo-Turkish War, 1768–1774

Russian naval power in the eastern Mediterranean

After the victory at Çeşme, the Aegean Expeditionary Fleet was in search of a mission. The Morean revolts had been largely crushed, so there was no opportunity for further amphibious operations in support of the rebels. The Turkish fleet had withdrawn beyond the Dardanelles, leaving another general naval battle unlikely. This left the task of blockading the Dardanelles to keep Istanbul hungry and on the defensive. This would have been easier if Orlov and Spiridov had been able to hold the fortress of Pelari on the island of Lemnos, just 50 kilometers away, but the Turks took advantage of the temporary easing of Elphinstone's blockade after the foundering of the *Sviatoslav* to make a raid on Mudros Bay and land 3,500 troops on Lemnos, forcing the Russians to evacuate Lemnos in late October. They found themselves a new base for the fleet on the island of Paros, at Port Auza, and it was easily captured. But it was much farther from the Dardanelles.

The Third Squadron, under Counter-Admiral I. N. Arf, arrived at Port Auza on December 25, 1770. Arf brought into the fleet the new line ships *Vsevolod* and *Sv. Georgii Pobedonosets* (both 66 guns), the *Aziia* (54 guns), the frigate *Severnyi Orel* (40 guns), and 15 English transports. He also delivered materiel badly needed for repairs and additional troops bringing the size of the fleet's landing force to 2,167 men.[51] This made it possible for Spiridov's squadron to resume the Dardanelles blockade in June and July and for Spiridov and Greig to extend the blockade down the Anatolian coast as far as the Chios Strait in August, burning storehouses and seizing grain transports from Egypt.

Over the next three years, the Aegean Fleet at Port Auza was reinforced by the Fourth Squadron under Counter-Admiral Chichagov (arriving August 1772) and the Fifth Squadron under Greig (launched from Kronstadt in October 1773 arriving September 1774 after the war had ended). This added more big line ships, such as *Chesme* (88 guns), *Sv. Velikomuchenik Isidor* (74 guns), and *Graf Orlov* (66 guns). New vessels were also built at Port Auza and ten captured Turkish frigates were rechristened and reoutfitted, so that by late 1771, the Aegean Expeditionary Fleet had ten ships of the line, two bombardiers, twenty frigates, four transports, one packetboat, and eleven xebecs.[52] Losses due to combat and to poor maintenance facilities were therefore covered, although at great expense.

The Aegean Expeditionary Fleet conducted only one more significant engagement with Turkish squadrons at sea—on October 26–29, 1772, when a Turkish squadron of nine frigates and sixteen xebecs was defeated off Patras by a squadron of two line ships, two frigates, two poliaks, and one xebec under Captain M. T. Koniaev.[53] But there was no attempt to force the Dardanelles. Baron de Tott considered Istanbul to be in such a state of panic after Çeşme that Orlov had made a great blunder in not immediately forcing the Straits before Tott had made his "improvements" to their defenses (the value of which Tott may well have been overstated).[54] A more likely explanation was that Catherine II's naval strategy had shifted—to using her Aegean fleet for cruiser patrolling across the eastern Mediterranean, making occasional landing raids along the coasts of Anatolia, the Levant, and northern Egypt, and founding a "Republic of the Archipelago" to demonstrate to Europe as well as to the Porte that Russia was now an established great power in the eastern Mediterranean.

Thus we see her fleet making raids on the island of Mytilene to destroy a Turkish wharf (November 1–5, 1771) and on the Egyptian coast to destroy some enemy frigates in Damietta harbor (October 21, 1772).[55] Blockading the Dardanelles ultimately required cruiser patrolling across much of the eastern Mediterranean to seize cargoes deemed bound for Istanbul and impound vessels that could be considered enemy combatants. Cruiser patrolling was onerous; however, it had to be kept up constantly, and it required caution so that the ships of the French, English, and other neutrals were not harassed. As the squadrons based at Port Auza were not large enough to patrol all of the eastern Mediterranean, the Aegean Expeditionary Fleet issued patents of patrol to some Greek and Slavic captains and ship owners under the direction of Count Major Ivan Voinovich, but this made Russia responsible for their actions. Cruiser patrolling also made the Aegean Expeditionary Fleet responsible for catching Albanian corsairs taking advantage of the rollback of Ottoman naval power. In early 1772 Albanian pirates seized two Russian ships and began using them for piracy, forcing Spiridov and Orlov to warn Turkish as well as neutral vessels against them.[56]

During the Morean campaign of 1770, Catherine II and Aleksei Orlov had begun thinking about the desirability of using the Russian squadrons to secure a permanent harbor or island base. At that time, this goal was secondary to supporting amphibious operations in Greece, but after the collapse of the Morean revolt it became more important not only to support blockading and cruiser actions but also for its potential value as an additional source of geopolitical pressure on the Porte. Nikita Panin also became interested in this project, especially if it could be made to take the form of a federation of several Aegean islands under Russian protection—the fall of Lemnos having demonstrated the vulnerability of basing the Russian naval presence on just a single island. Aleksei Orlov took the first steps toward this goal in October 1770, when he issued an appeal to the inhabitants of all the islands of the Aegean archipelago to place themselves under Russian protection. In February 1771 the clergy and local officials of fourteen islands accepted this offer, partly because they hoped for an end to disruption of the archipelago's grain trade.[57]

Fleet Lieutenant Anton Psar, a native of Mykonos, was appointed to assemble elected deputies from the fourteen islands and devise a protectorate federation. Spiridov then began defining its shape: the islands would preserve their self-government, but to preserve their freedom, they would enter into a military union supporting the Aegean Expeditionary Fleet; they would pay a tithe for the upkeep of the fleet, and contract for its provisioning; unlike the subjects of other Russian protectorates, their federal government would take the form of a Republic, perhaps on the model of the Venetian Republic, with an elected Senate and with a Republic chancery office on each island; islands would organize their own militias to police themselves and to assist the Russian fleet in common defense; until the departure of the fleet, the formation supervision of this Republican regime would be supervised by Orlov and Spiridov.[58]

The war would end and the fleet would be withdrawn to the Baltic before the constitutional details of this arrangement were fully worked out to define what "protectorate" and "subjects" would actually mean. But what is historically significant about the Archipelagan Republic proposal was that it partly encouraged the empress' later "Greek Project," and for the time being—until the end of her first war with the Ottomans in 1774—it stengthened her claim that Russia had by conquest established herself as a sovereign Great Power in the Mediterranean.

This can be seen in the expansion and sophistication of Russian diplomacy and trade with Venice, Genoa, Tuscany, Algiers, Tunis, and Mamluk Egypt, and most vividly, in the Russian occupation of Beirut.

At the beginning of the war the sultan had instructed Ali Bey, the Mamluk governor of Egypt, to contribute troops to the Ottoman army. Ali Bey had been born in Abkhazia, the son of a Georgian priest, and his treasurer and oracle, Rizk Abdullah, a Coptic Christian, had prophesied the fall of the Ottoman Empire. Ali Bey decided to revolt against the Porte and to send an army into Syria, either to pressure the Sultan Mustafa III to recognize his full sovereignty in Egypt or to revive the project of a Mamluk Empire independent of the Ottoman Empire. In alliance with the Sidon Pasha Dahir al-Umar, his forces occupied Damascus and Sidon in June 1771. In December 1771 Ali Bey and Rizk Abdullah sent letters to Paros arranging an alliance with the Russian fleet. Although Ali Bey had been driven out of Egypt by March 1772, it was in observation of their alliance that Orlov and Spiridov sent on patent Greek ships and Greek and Albanian mercenaries to Damietta and then to Beirut, the last port the Ottomans still controlled in embattled Greater Syria. On June 18, 1772, they sank the Turkish ships in Beirut's harbor, bombarded the town, and sacked its bazaar. A second flotilla from the Aegean Fleet landed artillery, Albanian mercenaries, and some Russian officers at Jaffa to support Ali Bey and Dahir.[59]

A third expedition by a Russian squadron of five frigates, six xebecs, and seven smaller vessels under Captain Mikhail Kozhukov and Major Voinovich placed Beirut under blockade and bombardment from July 23 to September 5, 1773. Kozhukov and Voinovich extorted 300,000 piastres from Emir Yusuf as terms for lifting the bombardment, and on September 18, they landed troops in Beirut. Russian troops assisted Dahir in driving back an Ottoman force approaching from the Bekaa Valley. Russian forces occupied Beirut until January 2, 1774, and left behind a garrison of 300 Albanian mercenaries until Yusuf paid the remainder of his tribute. Thus, Beirut remained under Russian control until February 1774.[60]

After the signing of the Kuchuk-Kainarji peace treaty, Port Auza was evacuated and the ships of the Aegean Expeditionary Fleet were gradually returned to the Baltic. Most were in poor condition, in part because of inadequate maintenance on Patros. "In all the Russians had sent 20 battleships, five frigates, and eight lesser vessels to the Aegean and bought 11 frigates and two bombs. Of these 13 battleships and all the frigates returned to Russia. Of the 12,200 men sent to the Aegean, 4,516 did not return."[61] These losses could be considered acceptable given what the fleet had accomplished in naval action and diplomacy, especially as "Catherine II had risked the better part of her naval resources as well as the credibility of Russia as an emerging Great Power in a naval and amphibious deployment at a distance from its home bases that beggared description at the time. She did so with an untried assembly of ships and men faced with problems and challenges at all levels."[62]

The defeat of the Bar Confederation

After his defeat at Orzechowo, Kazimierz Pułaski had withdrawn to the Tatra Mountains on the Hungarian border to rebuild his forces. In September 1770 he returned to southern Poland and occupied the fortress of Czéstochowa Monastery, successfully withstanding siege by Drevich's regiments in December and January 1771.[63] Winter 1770–1771 also saw failed attempts by Confederate commander Jozef Miączynski to capture Sandomierz and Cracow. Suvorov marched from Lublin to give battle at Meliec, and Miączynski's 1,700 cavalry and 300 infantry fled back toward Cracow, some of them taking refuge in the castle of Lanckorona. Suvorov attacked Lanckorona with 800 men and four guns, but the artillery of Lanckorona cost him several of his best officers, including his nephew, Lt. Nikolai Suvorov. Recognizing that he lacked the artillery to take Lanckorona Castle by siege, Suvorov withdrew his troops to Sandomierz.[64]

The French foreign minister Choiseul had long hoped that the Bar Confederates, if properly supported, could provide enough of a diversion in southern Poland to force Rumiantsev to withdraw Russian troops from the Danubian front. In 1769 the Chevalier de Chateaufort had reported to Choiseul that he found the Bar Confederates unpromising allies: "They have no defined aim, no policy, no unity among themselves, no means, no resources."[65] But Choiseul had not given up; in 1770 he sent the Chevalier de Taules into Poland with funds to identify and subsidize the most effective of the Confederate bands. De Taules returned to Paris with his funds unspent, so Choiseul next turned to General Charles Francois du Perier Dumouriez, who was sent into Hungary to negotiate with Krasiński and the other Confederate leaders sheltering there.[66]

Dumouriez found that Kazimierz Pułaski, Potocki, Zaremba, Savva, and Miączynski could probably field more than 16,000 rebel troops—provided some way could be found to get these fierce rivals to work together. Dumouriez began assembling a more imposing Confederate army than had existed before, spending money to raise a militia of 25,000 peasants in the Cracow and Sandomierz regions, hiring 2,000 deserters from the Austrian and Prussian armies, and shipping the Bar rebels muskets and artillery from Silesia and Hungary. A Polish Crown regiment of dragoons went over to his banner, and Prince Karl of Saxony, who had been deposed in Courland by Biron and the Russians, sent several thousand Saxon infantry and cavalry. Dumouriez developed a plan by which the leading Confederate commanders would cooperate in spreading guerrilla war across most of southern Poland, occupying so many small castles and fortresses that the Russian forces policing Poland could not recover them all and it would become necessary for Rumiantsev to shift regiments from the Danubian front into Poland. Cracow and Sandomierz would be Dumouriez's immediate objectives; then Pułaski would raid the

Russian magazines in Podolia with 8,000 men; Jozef Zaremba and Jan Zalinski would march from Poznań against Warsaw with another 10,000; and Lithuanian Grand Hetman Michał Kazmierz Ogiński would join the revolt and lead 8,000 Lithuanian troops against Smolensk. Dumouriez, counting on having 20,000 infantry and 8,000 horse under his command, intended to follow up the capture of Cracow and Sandomierz by marching either upon Warsaw or Podolia, wherever greater opportunity presented itself.

He doubted that Russian forces in Poland could suppress the fast-moving cavalry guerrilla warfare sweeping through so many districts. There were only about 12,000 Russian troops in Poland, and a third of them were Cossack irregulars. Lt. General Essen had about 4,000 troops in Kiev and other parts of Ukraine, as a Reserve for Rumiantsev's First Army; Major-General Weimarn and Colonel Drevich were covering Warsaw with another 4,000 men, and Major-General Suvorov had 4,000 men based at Lublin.[67]

But the chances of Dumouriez's plan succeeding declined over the winter of 1770–1771. He could not get the other Confederation commanders to coordinate action with him; even Pułaski, the best of the lot, insisted on acting independently. On December 24, 1770, King Louis XV dismissed Choiseul for scheming to bring France into an Anglo-Spanish war over the Falkland Islands. Choiseul's replacement as foreign minister was Emmanuel Armand de Richelieu, Duc de Aiguillion, whose "zeal for the Poles was more ostentatious than effective."[68] Suvorov was about to mount serious resistance to Bar operations in southern Poland; he had already established Cossack pickets at key points in the Cracow region as far as the Silesian border, and he had trained his regiments to make forced marches out of their Lublin hub at short notice.[69]

In early spring Dumouriez did manage to divert Suvorov's attention from the region of Cracow by using his peasant militias to light ominous night bonfires across several districts. This gave Dumouriez the opportunity to seize Bobrek, the major crossing on the Vistula, and the castles of Tyniec and Lanckorona near Cracow. A night attack on Cracow on April 19 gave Dumouriez temporary control of the city. Weimarn sent Suvorov to liberate Cracow; he started with just 1,600 men (two battalions infantry, five squadrons of cavalry, and eight guns), but Drevich reinforced him with another 2,000 troops en route. On May 9 Suvorov's force reached Tyniec Castle, guarding the outskirts of Cracow. But Walewski's Confederates were well dug in there, and Suvorov's first attack on the castle was repulsed, costing him 30 casualties to the Confederates' 100. So Suvorov left off and marched toward Lanckorona, where Dumouriez was standing with 4,000 troops.

Dumouriez's army had taken up strong positions along a high ridge above two pine forests with the castle of Lanckorona on his left flank. About 600 troops and 30 fortress guns were in Lanckorona Castle; twenty guns were on his right flank; and 200 French jaegers and two field guns were hidden in the woods below the ridge.

Suvorov's attack on these positions on May 10, 1771, began with a move that was so tactically unorthodox it took Dumouriez by surprise: a cavalry attack uphill against fortified positions. About 150 mounted Cossacks circumvented the woods in scattered formation and then rejoined and began ascending the hill, heading for the center of the French-Polish line, followed by an echelon of mounted carabiniers. When Suvorov's cavalry reached the top, Dumouriez ordered Antoni Orzheszka to attack them with his Lithuanian troops. But Orzheszka's counterattack failed and he began to retreat in such hurried desperation that he killed Kajetan Michał Sapieha when the latter tried to restrain him. Schutz's hussars fired just one volley against the Russians and then they too began to retreat. Miączynski tried to attack the Russians but was taken prisoner. Suvorov's two infantry regiments used their grenadiers to clear the woods of snipers and proceeded to follow his cavalry up the hill. By this point the French-Polish center had collapsed completely. Dumouriez joined his jaegers in exfiltrating through the woods, while other survivors fled to Lanckorona Castle. The fighting was all over in just a half-hour. The Confederates had suffered 300–500 killed and 200 taken prisoner. Suvorov's losses were four or five missing.[70] Dumouriez fled to Hungary; he would not return to Poland.

Pułaski remained a threat, however; he had refused to join Dumouriez at Lanckorona and had instead marched from Dunajec to Zamość, which opened its gates to him. As long as he controlled Zamość, he endangered Suvorov's lines of communication with Lublin. Therefore, Suvorov decided not to besiege Lanckorona Castle—he lacked the artillery for this, anyway—and instead hastened toward Zamość, which his regiments retook on May 22. Pułaski managed to slip away, heading for Lithuania and then reversing course to take refuge back at Lanckorona.

In August, Lithuanian Crown hetman Ogiński joined the Confederates with his personal army of 3,000 men. At Rzeczyca, he forced the surrender of a Russian detachment of 300 men after their commanding officer, Colonel Albychev, was killed. Ogiński then marched to Nesvizh, in accordance with Dumouriez's plan to carry the war over the Lithuanian border into Russia. Drevich was ordered to move from Minsk and Suvorov from Lublin to stop him. At Biała, Suvorov divided his forces so he could lead a flying column of 902 men and five guns to intercept Ogiński. At dawn on September 12, 1771, he attacked Ogiński's army while they were asleep in camp at Stolowicze, near Minsk. The Lithuanians took heavy losses and Ogiński himself was forced to take to a borrowed horse without his boots and flee to Prussian Köningsberg.[71]

In place of Dumouriez, Paris sent to Poland General Viosmenil with fifty French officers.[72] It was unclear what they could accomplish campaigning with the Confederates, however, and Count Kaunitz had just informed Paris that the Confederate cause would no longer enjoy as much open support from Vienna as in the past; there would be no more Austrian assistance with troops or with money.[73] Puławski and the other surviving Confederate commanders in desperation began concocting a plan to kidnap King Stanisław August and use him to negotiate for the withdrawal of Russian forces. They had repudiated his sovereignty already in 1770, when the Confederation had issued manifestos denouncing him as a traitor and declaring the Polish throne to have been vacant from 1763.[74]

On the night of November 24, 1771, the king was returning to his palace in Warsaw from a visit to Chancellor Michał Czartoryski when his carriage, travelling without its usual lancer escort, was stopped by a party of thirty armed horsemen led by Colonel Stanisław Strawiński.[75] They assaulted his postilion and aides, wounded the king lightly, and placed him on a horse and rode off with him. But once outside the city limits, the band split up and his remaining captors got lost in the darkness, leaving the king alone with just one nervous guard, Kuzma Koziński. Stanislaw August managed to convince Koziński to stop and wait with him at a nearby mill until a rescue party from the palace arrived. The next morning King Stanisław August was returned to safety in his palace, slightly battered and shaken.

The episode had backfired badly on the Confederates. To Frederick II, it demonstrated that "pathetic Stanisław" could not be trusted to control the Polish nation, which was "just as it had been at creation, brutish, stupid, and without instruction." Catherine II saw it as proof that additional measures were needed to contain the "anarchy" in Poland. The attempted kidnapping of Stanisław August thereby provided Austria, Prussia, and Russia with additional cause to proceed with plans for the partition of Poland. On February 19, 1772, Joseph II and Maria Theresa, Frederick II, and Catherine II signed the St. Petersburg Convention authorizing the tripartite partition of the Polish–Lithuanian Commonwealth.[76]

The final operation of the Rebellion of the Bar Confederation was attempted in January 1772 and was initiated by Viosmenil and the French officers rather than by any of the Polish or Lithuanian Confederate commanders.

Wawel Castle in Cracow had great symbolic importance as the royal palace of Poland's Jagiellonian kings; it also had an arsenal and a dungeon holding some Confederate prisoners. It was an imposing stronghold with high and thick walls, but there were only about thirty Russian soldiers guarding it, and their commanding officer, Colonel Stalkenberg, was devoting less attention to his night watches than to his dalliance with a local lady. On the night of January 21–22, Brigadier Claude Gabriel de Choisy sailed a command of 600 cavalry and jaegers down the Vistula from Tyniec to the foot of Wawel Castle. Sixty of his men managed to infiltrate the castle through a drainage pipe and underground passages, overcome Stalkenberg's guards in a short firefight, and open the gates to their comrades. Suvorov had been preparing to march into Lithuania when he got word that morning that the enemy had captured Wawel; he immediately set out for Cracow with his regiments, accompanied by Crown Hetman Branicki with five regiments of Polish uhlans. Between them they had 3,500 troops, enough to invest and blockade the castle, but they did not have the big siege guns necessary to bombard it, so they had to settle for firing with musket and smaller regimental guns from the upper storys of the houses adjoining the castle. Choisy defended Wawel fiercely, making several sorties that Suvorov had to beat back by musket fire and bayonet, and an attempted Russian storm assault on the night of February 18 failed, costing Suvorov and Branicki a hundred wounded and fifty killed, including Colonel Geisman. But Choisy was unable to lift the blockade, and an attempt by Szymon Kossakowski to break through and reinforce him was defeated. At the beginning of April, Russian siege guns arrived at Cracow and Suvorov began mining galleries under Wawel's walls, but he remained reluctant to risk his troops on another storm assault because Puławski was reportedly nearby. By mid-April, Choisy's command was near starvation and he was being forced to shoot attempted deserters, so he finally surrendered his 43 officers and 739 soldiers on

April 15. Suvorov sent the French officers to L'viv and Biała but had the ordinary soldiers convoyed to Smolensk.[77]

On April 19 the Confederates learned of the immanent partition of Poland. The entry of Austrian and Prussian troops to occupy northern and southern Poland and western Ukraine forced the Confederates to abandon their remaining refuges at Tyniec, Lanckorona, and Czéstochowa. Pułaski, facing prosecution for the attempted kidnapping of the king, was forced to flee Czéstochowa for Dresden. The Russians sent their 14,000 Polish and Lithuanian prisoners to Omsk and Tobol'sk in Siberia; nonofficers had to make this march on foot and many of them did not survive. Other prisoners were impressed into the Russian army.[78]

The First Partition of Poland

After the fall of Cracow, the Bar Confederation was essentially finished. In the course of its rebellion, about 100,000 adult male Poles and Lithuanians had been killed or taken prisoner and many others had been forced into exile in Silesia, Moravia, and Hungary. The secret convention of Partition signed in St. Petersburg in February 1772 would not be announced to King Stanisław August until March 1771, and he did not initially believe it. But the convention pact had already provided the pretext for Russia to increase its military presence in the Commonwealth to 30,000; 10,000 Prussian troops had entered northwestern Poland between the Warta and Vistula Rivers; and 20,000 Austrian troops had advanced beyond the Zips cordon into Cracow and part of Sandomierz palatinates.[79] They met with almost no organized resistance, as most of the Bar commanders had already fled abroad; the Confederation's final manifesto of protest, throwing full blame upon the king, was issued at Lindau in Bavaria on November 23, 1772.[80]

The formal treaty of Partition was signed on July 25/August 5, 1772. It cost the Polish–Lithuanian Commonwealth 211,000 square miles of territory and 4.53 million inhabitants—28.7 percent of the Commonwealth's total territory and about a third of its subjects. The treaty's preamble offered as justification "the spirit of faction, the troubles and intestine war which had shaken the Kingdom of Poland for so many years … which give just apprehension for expecting the total decomposition of the state."[81]

Austria added to her recent acquisitions in Zips and Nowy Sącz, the southern part of Małopolska with the towns of Belz and Szeszów, and part of western Ukraine as far as the Zbruch River, with the towns of L'viv, Galich, Tarnopol', and Peremyshl'. These territories together formed the new Province of Galicia-Lodomeria. Austria thereby acquired 83,000 square kilometers and 2.13 million inhabitants.

Prussia acquired the districts of West Pomerelia, Netze, and Ermeland, that is, the West Prussian land bridge connecting Pomerania with East Prussia. This included the towns of Elbing, Marienburg, Graudenz, Dzikowa, Culm, and Bromberg, but excluded Torun and Danzig—the latter upon Panin's insistence that the loss of Danzig would cripple Poland's trade with Russia. Prussia's gains from the First Partition totaled about 36,000 square kilometers and 580,000 inhabitants.

To Russia went southern Livonia with Marienhaus and Dinaburg and the Lithuanian Belarus' districts on the eastern bank of the Dvina River: Polotsk, Vitebsk, Mstislavl', Mogilev, and Gomel. These were annexed to Russia as the Governorates of Polotsk and Mogilev under Governor-General Zakhar Chernyshov. Russia thereby gained about 92,000 square kilometers and 1.3 million inhabitants.

While Austria gained considerably in territory and new subjects, Galicia-Lodomeria was economically underdeveloped and it would require decades of resettlement by German nobles and peasants to dispossess the Polish landlords. Frederick II had done very well for himself, though: his new West Prussian districts were commercially prosperous and had finally made Prussia a contiguous united state. He would move quickly to resettle 57,000 Prussian families in the region and impose his own customs duties on Danzig.[82]

The new Russian ambassador to Warsaw, Otto Magnus von Stackelberg, informed King Stanisław August in September 1772 that the empress expected him to convene a Diet to ratify the treaty of Partition. If he did not comply he was likely to be dethroned and "lose everything down to his last spoon" and Poland would cease to exist. The king tried to stall for time, hoping for some kind of French intervention, but he had few loyal supporters: Catherine II had forsaken him, the Czartoryskis were less powerful now, and Stackelberg had set about creating new political puppets in the Senate, Adam Poniński and Michał Radziwiłł. Most magnates were sufficiently intimidated that when the Senate was convened in October only twenty-eight Senators dared attend, and when the Diet opened in April 1773, just half of the deputies showed up. Stackelberg had to spend 120,000 rubles "hiring" replacement deputies. He reminded the king that if the Diet did not produce the required results, the Austrian, Prussian, and Russian troops garrisoning Warsaw might loot the capital.[83] The Diet finally ratified treaties with Austria, Poland, and Russia over the course of August 21–September 18, 1773, and King Stanisław August signed on October 8.

The peace talks at Giurgiu and Bucharest

The agreement by Austria, Prussia, and Austria to partition Poland meant that the sultan could no longer rely upon Thugut's alliance proposal to deter the Russians and would have to begin negotiating peace. Kaunitz wrote to Thugut on April 8, 1772, instructing him to explain to the sultan that Austria had promised to protect the Turks against Russia, but not against Prussia as well. Prussia's alliance with Russian to execute the partition of Poland nullified the pact Thugut had proposed, and the sultan himself had nullified it by ceasing to pay Vienna the subsidies promised. The Thugut Pact would therefore not be ratified. The sultan should choose the prudent course and enter peace talks with the Russians; Kaunitz and Thugut would still use their good offices to assist the Turks in such talks.[84]

But Nikita Panin had already made it clear that the empress expected the Austrians to support Russia's terms for peace and leave the Turks to their own devices in the event they rejected those terms.[85]

So in early March 1772 Grand Vizier Muhsinzade Mehmed Pasha accepted Rumiantsev's proposal to begin peace talks.[86] A ceasefire to be observed until June 1 led to the first round of talks being conducted near Giurgiu between State Councilor I. M. Simolin and Pasha Abdul Kerim. Support from the Austrian and Prussian envoys to Istanbul helped produce a convention on armistice which Rumiantsev signed on May 30.

The next stage was to negotiate a treaty of peace. These negotiations began at Focşani in early August. The Porte was represented by Yenişehirli Osman Efendi and Sheikh Yasincizade Efendi. The garrulous bore Osman Efendi would do his best to drag out negotiations, whereas Yasincizade Efendi, speaking on behalf of the *ulema*, would throw up many objections from shar'ia to some of the Russian peace terms. Catherine sent to Focşani Grigorii Orlov and Aleksei Obreskov, "my two angels of peace, who are now face to face with the vile bearded Turks." For this, the sultan had been forced to release Obreskov from the prison in which he had been confined since October 1768. The personal trust Orlov enjoyed as Catherine's personal had begun to wane, but she may have appointed him as a counterweight to Obreskov, who was seen as an ally of Nikita Panin. This time active support from Thugut and the Prussian envoy Zegelin was no longer welcome; they were not allowed to attend the early sessions.[87]

The empress' instructions to Orlov (dated April 21) were to adhere to those peace terms most guaranteed to reduce the Porte's ability to attack Russia in the future and to obtain maximum compensation for the losses Russia had endured in the war. This compensation had to include Ottoman formal recognition of: Russian rights of free trade and navigation on the Black Sea; Russian rights to "protect" the Christians of the Caucasus and the Georgian kingdoms; Russian sovereignty over Greater and Lesser Kabarda, and the extension of the border from Kabarda across the Kuban steppe to Azov; Russian retention of Azov; and above all, Russian protectorate over the Crimean and Nogai Tatars, guaranteeing they would henceforth remain "independent" of the Porte. Orlov was instructed to show some flexibility on the future status of the Moldavian and Wallachian principalities and the amount of monetary indemnities the Turks were to pay, the empress recognizing that some appearance of reasonable concession would be necessary to get the Turks to agree to the biggest sticking-point, the independence of the Crimean Khanate and Nogai hordes.[88]

The first sessions at Focşani produced an extension of the truce to September 21 but bogged down on the issue of the Khanate's independence from the Porte, Yasincizade Efendi protesting that the sultan could not agree to such an abrogation of shar'ia law. In mid-August, the talks broke down and the Ottoman envoys prepared to return home. Two events had convinced them that the Russians would not be able to prevail: in Poland, King Stanisław August was still refusing to convene the Diet to ratify the Treaty of Polish Partition, and in Sweden, King Gustavus III had arrested his Diet and suspended the constitution, perceiving that a recent coup in Denmark, the Partition of Poland, and the Russo-Turkish peace talks would reinforce Russian hegemony in the Baltic. Panin's Northern Accord was collapsing. For the moment, there was a chance Russia would have to go to war against Sweden, and under those circumstances, Frederick II might renounce his alliance with Russia. Grigorii Orlov now had a personal reason for quitting the conference, too; Lieutenant A. S. Vasil'chikov had just replaced him as the empress' favorite. He delivered a final ultimatum to the Turks and then returned to St. Petersburg. Obreskov and Nikita Panin blamed the collapse of the Focşani talks on Orlov's intransigence, that he had no real desire for peace and expected further advantages for himself and his brothers if the war resumed. Joseph II opined, "The Congress has been broken up, solely by Orlof's fault. His credit is diminishing, and as his duties demanded residence, he is almost certain that another has taken them up in the interim."[89]

However, Obreskov and Panin both wanted to salvage the peace process and the grand vizier despaired of any quick reversal of the strategic situation on the Danubian front. The grand vizier therefore wrote to Rumiantsev on September 7 proposing another six months' armistice and the resumption of peace talks, this time at Bucharest. Rumiantsev welcomed this because he considered the First Army too exhausted by combat and epidemic to resume operations at this time. The empress agreed to resume talks, but she expressed to the Council of State her judgment that a peace treaty "would not be worth a penny, would be more shameful than the Prut or Belgrade treaties" if it did not obtain the terms she had laid out in her April instructions to Orlov.[90]

The talks at Bucharest began on October 29. By this time, the Crimean nobles had elected Sahip Girei as Khan and it was clear he was on the verge of signing a formal treaty of Crimean independence at Karasubazar. This presented the Ottoman plenipotentiary to Bucharest, Abdurezzak Reis Effendi, with a *fait accompli*; he would have to concentrate his objections now on Obreskov's demands that the Russians be guaranteed free navigation rights on the Black Sea and permanent control of Kilburun, Kerch, and Yenikale. When this was communicated to Istanbul, Osman Efendi and some other conservatives denounced Russians for "trick and guile." Obreskov's terms were rejected by the sultan's *diwan* and the Bucharest talks ended two months before the armistice expired on March 21, 1773.[91]

The strains of war

Despite Russian successes in 1771–1772, Rumiantsev welcomed peace negotiations, because he was concerned about the manpower shortage hampering his ability to conduct a major offensive across the Danube. It had been difficult to cover the First Army's losses, especially those due to the spread of the plague. Rumiantsev wrote, "The armistice has not lasted long enough for us to stock enough supplies of war materiel. No conscripts and little of the ammunition needed have been brought forward. Thus, if a campaign begins in March, we will hardly have the forces here to defend the territory we now occupy … much less mount significant operations of our own."[92]

The VK hoped to increase the strength of the First Army to 116,000 to encourage Rumiantsev to take it across the Danube, and the recruit levy for 1773 had therefore been raised to one recruit from every 100 souls (the rate for 1772 had been one per 150). This yielded 74,739 recruits for the armies, garrisons, and fleets. But the manner of convoying recruits to the front had always been brutal and wasteful, and now that the plague had expanded into central Russia Rumiantsev was alarmed at how many recruits were perishing even before reaching his regiments. To make matters worse, the threat of war with Sweden led the VK to order him to send eight infantry regiments off to Pskov on the Baltic front. He considered this unwise, because it weakened the First Army at the very point it was necessary to intimidate the Turks into accepting Russian terms at the Bucharest conference. The 1773 levy had also aimed at building a larger trained reserve, so it was stipulated that replacements for the First Army be taken out of garrison service, with some of the new recruits replacing in the garrisons for training those transferred to the Danubian front. Although the soul tax (at half rate) had just been extended to the territories just annexed from Poland–Lithuania, St. Petersburg did not yet dare to impose the recruit levies on those territories.[93]

Over 1768–1771 state expenditures had totaled 118 million rubles. A little under half of this expenditure had gone to the conduct of the war with the Porte:

Year	Expenditures on the army	Expenditures on the fleet
1768	10.013 million rubles	1.3 million rubles
1769	10 million rubles	1.4 million rubles
1770	9.904 million rubles	1.445 million rubles
1771	10.232 million rubles	2.578 million rubles

The government accomplished the remarkable feat of keeping military spending stable over the next two years as well:[94]

Year	Expenditures on the army	Expenditures on the fleet
1772	10.508 million rubles	1.378 million rubles
1773	10.812 million rubles	1.433 million rubles

The primary revenue source for military expenditure remained the soul tax and the *obrok* on state peasants, which had risen from 9.712 million rubles in 1768 to 12.238 million rubles, much of this due to territorial and population expansion. But soul tax and *obrok* revenue decline slightly thereafter, to 12.219 million rubles in 1772 and 12.18 million rubles in 1773. The mounting arrears in the soul tax (3.9 million over 1769–1772, and 4.17 million rubles by 1773) gave cause for concern, but it could be partly offset through the traditional remedy of increasing the *obrok* on the state peasantry. The Russian Empire was fortunate that it now had a broader range of revenue sources to cover total state expenditures: for 1768–1771, these revenue sources were 99.3 million rubles in total direct and indirect taxes, a residue of 8.4 million rubles from previous years, special military levies totaling 2 million rubles, 1.2 million rubles in subsidies from Prussia, foreign loans of 3.6 million rubles, and 10.67 million rubles in assignats.[95]

The decision to issue assignats—paper certificates serving as bonds to cover the state debt—had been made by the Council of State in November 1768. In 1769, 2.629

million rubles in assignats had been issued; this rose to 3.758 million in 1770 and 4.291 million in 1771. By 1774 about 20 million rubles in assignats were in circulation and it was becoming common to treat them as currency. This led to high inflation from 1772. Especially worrisome was the inflation of bread prices, which caused suffering among the lower classes in Moscow and St. Petersburg in particular and encouraged landlords to raise *barshchina* and *obrok* rents on their peasant tenants.[96]

Rising bread prices, harvest shortfalls, and epidemics combined to provoke serious social unrest. The first signs of the plague's arrival in Moscow came in November 1770; in the following summer, the city was in panic. Between March and September 1771, 20,049 people died of plague in Moscow and about three-quarters of the population fled the city, including Governor P. S. Saltykov. On September 15 many of the remaining inhabitants rioted over quarantine measures. The riots lasted for three days and even took the life of Archbishop Amvrosii, who was lynched for trying to forbid a "purifying" ikon procession. Order was finally restored when Grigorii Orlov and Dr. Orreus arrived.[97]

There was unrest in the Don Cossack Host in 1772. Its ataman, Stepan Efremov, was openly disobeying the VK's orders to transfer "volunteers" to garrison duty on the Mozdok Line and at Azov and Taganrog; he had failed to bring Don Cossack units to the Second Army; there were charges that he was in unauthorized dealings with the Kuban Tatars; and there had been complaints that he had taken large bribes to enroll clients in the *starshina*. He resisted calls to come to St. Petersburg and explain himself, so he was finally arrested and tried. He was sentenced to hang, although the empress commuted it to exile to Livonia.[98]

The most serious disturbances, however, were those beginning in far-off Orenburg Governorate in the autumn of 1773. They would spark a Cossack rebellion that in its later stages pushed westward into the Volga region and inspired peasant jacqueries terrifying the landowning nobility. This upheaval was called the Pugachev Rebellion (*Pugachevshchina*), and to suppress it, the VK would have to devote considerable resources and recall commanders from the First and Second armies.

The Pugachev Rebellion is one of the most studied subjects in Russian and Soviet historiography and the literature on it is vaster than on the subject of Catherine II's Turkish wars,[99] so rather than reconstructing its course in detail, we will confine ourselves here to four observations.

First, the rebellion was provoked by the techniques for military colonization and management of frontier populations that had been preparing the Russian Empire for its war with the Porte. The settlement of Orenburg Governorate had begun in 1734, by means of military colonization along a new defense line, the Orenburg Line, to control the nomadic Bashkirs and Kazakhs and protect eastern Astrakhan and the Land Militia settlements along the Trans-Kama line to the northwest. But this had encroached upon the grazing lands of the Bashkirs and driven them to bloody revolts in 1735–1741 and 1755, and there were signs of renewed unrest among the Bashkirs by 1772. At this time, there were just 6,719 regular infantry and dragoons garrisoning Orenburg and the larger forts along the 1,800-kilometer Orenburg Line.[100] Defense of the region therefore had to rely heavily upon the smaller hard points manned by the Iaik Cossack Host (4,800 men in active duty). But there were mounting tensions between the rank-and-file Iaik Cossacks and their *starshina*, whom they accused of embezzling their salaries, and for the last thirty years the VK had further alienated the Iaik Cossacks by depriving them of the right to elect their own ataman and officers, placing them under the jurisdiction of the Governor-General of Orenburg, and selecting Iaik Cossacks for compulsory service in distant theaters. In 1769 the Iaik Host was ordered to contribute several hundred Cossacks for duty in a new Special Legion under Brigadier General Kar, for service against the Turks. Those facing selection for the Special Legion considered it a punishment not only because it was so far from their homes but also because once taken into a regular army unit they would be required to shave their beards (many of them were Old Believers).[101] In January 1772 they rioted at Iaitsk Gorodok and killed Commandant von Traubenberg, sent to investigate their complaints against their *starshina*. In response, St. Petersburg sent a punitive expedition of 1,500 dragoons and jaegers under General Freyman to crush their mutiny and impose an enormous fine of 36,000 rubles.

Therefore there was considerable fresh bitterness among the Iaik Cossacks when Emel'ian Ivanovich Pugachev, a Don Cossack deserter from Panin's Second Army, arrived on the Iaik in November 1772 and revealed himself to be Emperor Peter III, miraculously delivered from murder plotted by the wicked nobles supporting the usurper Catherine. He joined up with some dissident Iaik Cossacks who had managed to escape punishment and issued manifestos promising to restore the Host's independence, protect the Old Belief and the Islam of the Bashkir nomads, and fight to reclaim his throne from the usurper. His closest followers probably did not actually believe he was Peter III, but his arrival was timely and it was politically convenient to use him as a Pretender so as to challenge the Imperial government without repudiating the Emperor's sovereign legitimacy. By late summer 1773 Pugachev had amassed a following of perhaps over 12,000 men—Iaik Cossacks, Bashkirs, mutinous factory serfs, and other elements— and had begun besieging Orenburg.

Second, the eventual spread of the Pugachev Rebellion westward along the Volga between June 1774 and spring 1775 may have been connected with the fact that rising grain prices and the 1762 Manifesto permitting nobles to leave state service to concentrate on their estates had accelerated manorial colonization and intensified *barshchina* exploitation in this region. In its Volgan phase, the rebellion would also find support from some *odnodvortsy* unable to defend their lands against encroachment by politically connected nobles acquiring lands and resettling their serfs. Among the magnates who had recently acquired large estates along the Volga were Petr Panin and the Orlovs.[102]

Third, the strain of coping with the Pugachev Rebellion while simultaneously continuing the war against the Ottoman Empire naturally suggested to Catherine II and her inner circle the notion that the two conflicts might be causally connected, Pugachev's rebels possibly being supported by French or Ottoman gold. One of Aleksei Orlov's letters to Potemkin wondered if the Pugachev Rebellion was not "a joke by the French."

The empress had received an intercepted letter to the grand vizier from the Pretender "Princess Tarakanova" at Livorno urging the Turks to support Pugachev with money and arms to save Poland and rebuff Catherine's peace terms.[103] There were some grounds for fearing the involvement of Polish Confederates in the Pugachev Rebellion, as there were about a thousand exiled Confederates in Orenburg Governorate and another 7,000 in Kazan' Governorate. Interrogations of Pugachev's lieutenants subsequently confirmed there had been some exiled Confederates riding with the rebels, but they had not officered rebel bands or served on Pugachev's staff.[104]

Fourth, before the signing of the Kuchuk-Kainardji Treating ending the war with the Turks in July 1774, there were few regiments available to send east to suppress the rebellion. For example, when rebel detachments began turning west toward the Volga in October 1773, the entire governorate of Kazan' had just three battalions of garrison troops for its defense and had to be augmented by calling up retired soldiers. In October 1773 the VK sent Major-General Kar to oversee operations against the rebels in Kazan' and Orenburg governorates, but he was given just 3,468 troops and eight field guns. He failed to relieve Orenburg and was replaced in November by General-*anshef* A. I. Bibikov, a political client of Nikita Panin's and a veteran of the campaign against the Bar Confederates. Bibikov was promised over 6,000 troops but most of them did not arrive until spring 1774, when the revolt was entering its final phase, so he was compelled to appeal to the nobles of the Volgan districts to raise at their own expense squadrons of uhlan militia at the rate of one man from every 200 peasant souls.[105] Only after the end of the war with the Porte had been signed could the Pugachev Rebellion be crushed by fielding against the rebels large numbers of regular troops under experienced commanders transferred from the Polish and Turkish fronts (Major-General P. M. Golitsyn; Lt. Colonel I. I. Mikhelson, a veteran of Zorndorf and Kunersdorf as well as Kagul; General-*anshef* Petr Panin, the conqueror of Bender; and even Suvorov).[106]

Given all these challenges, it is remarkable that Catherine II did not lose her nerve in late 1773, especially as she was already in some personal danger from the fragmentation of the inner circle that had placed her in power. The year before several young officers of the Preobrazhenskii Guards Regiment had been arrested for conspiring to confine her in a convent and bring her son, Grand Duke Paul, to the throne. She had to refuse to see Grigorii Orlov upon his return from Focşani, because his many infidelities had finally been brought to her attention. But without a trusted favorite it might become much harder for her to steer about the shoals of court factionalism, and a new rivalry was emerging between VK President Chernyshov and Peter Panin, who was insisting upon his rehabilitation and reappointment to command. Nikita Panin no longer possessed as much influence as at the beginning of the war; the partition of Poland and the coup in Sweden had damaged his Northern Accord and estranged Prussia, and Catherine was suspicious that Panin, *oberhofmeistr* and tutor to Grand Duke Paul, might have endorsed the Guards putsch on Paul's behalf. Catherine would be out of danger only after spring 1774, after the Kuchuk-Kainarji Treaty, the crushing of the Pugachev Rebellion, and her alliance with her new favorite, Grigorii Potemkin.[107]

The Danube Front in 1773

The peace talks at Bucharest broke down in January 1773 and the cease-fire they had established was scheduled to lapse in March. The VK was increasingly concerned about the need to shift forces to the Baltic to deter a possible threat from Sweden. In the event of a Baltic war, it might even become necessary for the First Army to evacuate the fortresses and territory it had seized from the enemy on the southern side of the Danube. Therefore Catherine II wrote to Rumiantsev on February 28 that he should prepare to "seize by force of arms that which you have been unable to secure up to now by negotiations, by dispatching the army or part of it across the Danube and attacking the vizier's main army," which was concentrated at Shumla. But Rumiantsev was very reluctant to take the First Army across the Danube, not only because of lack of manpower and materiel but because Rumiantsev himself was quite ill—"attacks of illness have so sapped my strength that I can last barely a short time if there is a winter campaign." He would be hit repeatedly by bouts of fever and fatigue over the course of 1773. His reluctance to force the Danube was shared by his division commanders Weissman, Saltykov, and Potemkin, whose misgivings about crossing the Danube he communicated to the empress.[108]

They supported Rumiantsev's opinion that a massed attack on Shumla facing an Ottoman field army that might exceed 100,000 troops would require shifting too many regiments from the territories on the left and right wings, making it difficult to defend Wallachia against attacks out of the other enemy fortresses along the Danube. Saltykov stated that he would need another 2,000 infantry just to seize the enemy fortress at Rusçuk, which surely would have to be taken first before Shumla could be attacked; he was certain Potemkin would also have to take Silistra first before he could rendezvous with Saltykov and march against Shumla. Potemkin was not confident that he had enough troops, particularly infantry, to capture Silistra. Weissman judged that he would have to secure Karasu before moving against Shumla and that would require his corps be reinforced to over 17,500 men with rations and fodder for two months.[109] Rumiantsev instead suggested to the empress that Obreskov find some way to extend the armistice until May, by that time the First Army would have more supplies and replacement recruits, but even then he intended to limit First Army operations to sending smaller forces on raids across the river to keep the enemy on the defensive, as had been done so effectively in 1771, rather than driving *en masse* deep into the Balkans. Without a First Army push against Shumla, the Turks would still feel pressure to capitulate from the Russian occupations of Crimea and Bender and the blockade of the Turkish Straits by the Russian fleet in the eastern Aegean.[110] But the empress reiterated her demand for an attack on Shumla.

In April, enemy forces out of Rusçuk and Silistra struck across the Danube against Saltykov's corps, thereby endangering Giurgiu and Bucharest. This finally pressed Rumiantsev to prepare the First Army for forcing the Danube, although he still insisted Silistra would have to be taken first before Shumla could be attacked. Rumiantsev and Ungern would attack Shumla from Silistra, while Weissman's corps and Saltykov's division struck Shumla's eastern and western flanks.[111]

The arrival of spring meant there was now enough fresh fodder to allow the army to come out of winter quarters, so Rumiantsev began preparing the magazines and bridges for a Danubian crossing and instructing Weissman and Saltykov to prepare for diversionary raids on the enemy's right and left flanks.[112] At this point, Rumiantsev's plan entailed crossing the Danube at Hârşova and attacking the enemy fortress at Silistra. He sent Potemkin ahead to reconnoiter the crossing at Hârşova and Weissman to surveille the roads from Hârşova to Silistra. The enemy was likely to respond to these movements by attacking Saltykov's division in the west, so as an additional diversion, Rumiantsev ordered Lt. General Suvorov, newly transferred to the First Army upon his own request, to take charge of a detachment from Saltykov's division at Negoeşti and make an attack on enemy camps near Turtukai.

Potemkin seized Hârşova by the end of April. To help consolidate this foothold and support Saltykov's planned attack on Rusçuk, Suvorov arrived at Negoeşti on May 5 and began preparing a force of 1,950 men (760 infantry, 370 carabiniers, 480 Cossacks, 7 guns, and 17 boats) for an amphibious attack on Turtukai on May 9–10. Another 500 men were to guard the embarkation point near Negoeşti. Suvorov planned to make the landing from the mouth of the Argeş River in three waves, his infantry in the first two and his cavalry in the third.

A Turkish reconnaissance command of 1,000 horse, bearing for the Olt River and unaware of Suvorov's preparations, stumbled across and attacked his camp at Negoeşti toward dawn on May 9. They had the advantage of surprise for Suvorov's Cossack pickets were inebriated from a holiday celebration, and there was such fierce fighting it looked for a moment that the Russians might be overwhelmed and Suvorov killed or captured. But finally, the Turkish cavalry were routed and 85 of them were killed and their *bimbashi* commander taken prisoner. The prisoners confirmed there were about 4,000 Turks in three camps on the outskirts of the village of Turtukai. Suvorov decided to proceed with his landing the night of May 10.

The crossing no longer had the element of surprise and had to be executed under heavy fire from the enemy's forward batteries opposite the Argeş. Fortunately, their fire was ineffective and all three waves were able to get across without casualties. The Turkish batteries were quickly seized and Suvorov drew up his force in three small columns— infantry in the front columns, cavalry in reserve—to ascend the ridge between the enemy camps. Once in position for attack, the columns then unfolded into squares. Colonel Baturyn's square cleared the smaller enemy camp, while Colonel Maurinov's square cleared the next; Maurinov's square was then reassigned reserve duty while Colonel Rebok's square, up to that moment the reserve, was sent against the largest enemy camp, the one on the Rusçuk side of Turtukai. Rebok drove the Turks from that third camp and then attacked and burned the town of Turtukai. All of this took just four hours. The Turks lost perhaps 1,500 killed; the survivors fled toward Rusçuk and Shumla. Suvorov captured 80 ships and 16 enemy guns and had 187 families of Christian Bulgarians transported across the Danube to Wallachia. The Russians had lost two dead and seven killed in the *bimbashi*'s attack on their camp, and they suffered another twenty-four killed and thiry-five wounded in their attack on Turtukai.[113]

This was Suvorov's first battle against Turks, and it was tactically remarkable in a number of ways: it was a model of a forced amphibious landing; he had successfully attacked 4,000 enemy with just 700 troops (most of his cavalry and all his guns had been left at the landing site); he had trained his men to rapidly and smoothly reform from squares to columns and back to squares, and shift from attack role to reserve role at a moment's notice; and Suvorov had moved his jaegers far to the flank and ahead, which D. F. Maslovskii considered the kind of "perpendicular tactic" that would become more common in the wars of the French Revolution. The strategic value of the first battle of Turtukai was limited, however; while it succeeded in its mission of helping Potemkin dig in at Hârşova, Rumiantsev soon after decided that Hârşova was unsuited as the crossing-point for the First Army.[114]

It had been hoped that reconnaissance would find at Hârşova sites for troop transport docks along both banks of the river, terrain protecting the landing site from flank attacks, and good roads leading toward Silistra. None of these advantages were found, so Rumiantsev decided on June 3 the First Army would cross instead at Gurobaly, one march-stage closer to Silistra. There were just 6,000 Turks defending Gurobaly, and here the Danube was just a kilometer wide, with some small islands that could conceal Cossack longboats. But Gurobaly also presented some risk: there was a line of enemy batteries on its east, and the land on its western side had not been reconnoitered. To secure the crossing, Weissman would have to be in the heights around Lake Goltino as well as Kuchuk-Kainarji, a village in the rear. Silistra was just thirty kilometers to its west, and its garrison had 15,000 troops. Five kilometers below Silistra a 35,000-man field army under Osman Pasha was encamped; Shumla had besides its own garrison the grand vizier's reserve corps of 10,000.[115] Rumiantsev's main corps would therefore have to make the crossing at Gurobaly with the assistance of diversionary attacks by Saltykov on Hârşova and Weissman on Karasu and Basarjik, and the landing site would first have to be secured by Potemkin's corps. The Danubian flotilla was assigned the task of blocking the mouth of the Danube to Ottoman troop transports, while the Zaporozhian Cossacks were to make diversionary boat raids above Silistra. Suvorov was also expected to make a second diversionary attack on Turtukai.[116]

This operation was set for June 7. Rumiantsev's main corps would approach the Danube from the Ialomiţa River, with Lt. General Stupishin commanding the regiments on its right flank and Potemkin the regiments on its left; the total strength of these divisions was about 21,380 regulars and 74 field guns.[117] Infantry far outnumbered cavalry.

On the night of June 6–7, Weissman circled around the northern edge of Lake Goltino and attacked the eastern flank of the enemy camps at Gurobaly; then Potemkin joined the attack, landing part of his command in front of the enemy camps and sending another part of his infantry, with some guns, to rendezvous with Weissman's column on the eastern flank. The enemy did not put up lengthy resistance; 300 of them were killed and 61 taken prisoner, and the survivors fled toward Osman Pasha's camp five kilometers from Silistra, pursued part of the way by the Russians. That evening Rumiantsev and Stupishin began floating their regiments across the river. It took them until June 11 to bring them all across. By that time the Turks had begun to regroup behind the Galitsei River. But an attack by Stupishin and Potemkin drove them out the next day.[118]

Potemkin's and Weissman's corps approached Silistra on June 15–16. Cherkes Pasha, whom Weissman had defeated at Karasu on May 27, attempted to attack them from the rear but was defeated and forced to withdraw to Bazarjik. However, when Potemkin and Weissman seized one of the hill redoubts overlooking Silistra they saw that they lacked the men and guns to capture the fortress by storm or to safely blockade it. The fortress was on broken, heavily wooded ground and Silistra's garrison probably now exceeded 30,000 troops, reinforced by soldiers fleeing from Gurobaly, Galați, and Cherkes Pasha's force. There was intelligence that Numan Pasha was marching from Shumla with 20,000 Turks to strike them in the rear, and counting the grand vizier's field army at Shumla and the enemy garrisons at Rusçuk and Nikopol' there may have been as many as 70,000 Turks in the Silistra sector. Potemkin and Weissman were low on supplies, and their lines of communication with Rumiantsev had been stretched too far. Therefore, Rumiantsev held a council of war on June 20. It decided that the army should fall back and concentrate near the Galați River for a return crossing of the Danube and that Weissman should cover the eastern flank of this withdrawal by taking up a position near Kuchuk-Kainarji, fifteen kilometers away.

Numan Pasha tried to attack near Kuchuk-Kainarji on June 22. Weissman, with just six battalions of infantry and some cavalry, counterattacked and routed Numan Pasha's army, killing 4,000–5,000 of them and driving them back to Bazarjik. This secured Rumiantsev's withdrawal toward the Gurobaly crossing, but at a dear price, for Weissman was shot through the heart leading his charge.[119]

The first attempt at breakout had failed. Rumiantsev had managed something unprecedented—bringing the Russian army across the Danube. But he had landed insufficient forces to achieve his next objectives, attacks on Silistra and Shumla. If some positive results were now to be retrieved from the situation, it would have to be in the form of smaller strikes at least initimidating the grand vizier's army from venturing out from Shumla. Weissman's victory at Kuchuk-Kainarji could be seen as partly fulfilling this objective; what was also necessary now was decisive action from Saltykov, who had been ordered to make new attacks on Turnu and Turtukai.

Up to this point, Saltykov had been inactive. On June 12 Rumiantsev had ordered Colonel A. S. Meshcherskii to take troops from Saltykov's division on a second raid against Turtukai, which had been reoccupied by about 4,000 Turks under Sari Mehmed Pasha. Upon Suvorov's return to Negoești from Bucharest, this mission was reassigned to him. Saltykov had finally reinforced the Negoești detachment, although Suvorov still considered it undermanned, in particular in regard to infantry. But Suvorov proceeded to make another night raid across the river from the mouth of the Argeș on June 16–17 with 2,565 troops—1,300 infantry and jaegers, 700 regular cavalry, some Cossacks and arnauts, and fifteen regimental and siege guns, including some unicorns and Coehoorn mortars. On this occasion he had the element of surprise and just the camps of Turks to clear.[120] He conducted his attack much in the manner of his first raid against Turtukai, sending his attack columns along the ridgeline and then unfolding them into squares for the descent upon the enemy camps. Both camps were cleared in short order, but there was now the danger that enemy forces a few miles away would counterattack through the woods, as his Cossacks and carabiniers had been observed while crossing the river before dawn. Those of Suvorov's troops still atop the ridgeline were vulnerable to enemy fire, as the parapet was low. Just as a force of Turks began rushing up the hill, some of Suvorov's cavalry struck them in the rear at the moment the rest of Suvorov's troops began pushing downhill. The enemy was forced to flee in the direction of Rusçuk after losing 800 killed, including Sari Mehmed. Suvorov's losses were six killed and 107 wounded, but his men had captured fourteen guns and thirty-five river craft. St. Petersburg awarded Suvorov the Order of St. George Second Class, and instead of sending him against Rusçuk transferred him to his own independent command at Hârşova.[121]

Except for the forces at Hârşova, the rest of the First Army was led back over the Danube over June 20–24. Rumiantsev explained to the empress and the VK that he had no choice but to withdraw from the Gurobaly/Silistra sector: he had too few infantry, the roads from Gurobaly were poor, fodder hard to find, and his men had been exhausted by the campaign thus far. The disposition of enemy forces had placed the First Army in danger of destruction. "If we plan to continue military actions there, we must not only double but triple the army. An unassailable stance requires this many troops, for without them it is impossible to defend our position on account of the breadth of the river behind us and the difficult fords, during which we could be cut asunder from all sides. We would have to post special corps so as not to tie the hands of those participating in the offensive, who will have to blaze a route through forest and mountains." He may also have been referring to the increasing squabbling among his commanders—Dolgorukov's criticisms of Suvorov, for example—when he described his distress "that my intercession on behalf of numerous people serving under me has not benefited them. Without this, devotion declines among subordinates, whom I have no other way to encourage." [122]

News of the failure of the Silistra campaign caused great dismay in the Council of State, which feared it could encourage Ottoman diplomats to even greater obduracy and prolong the war. It was wondered how a commander as talented as Rumiantsev could have embarked on the Silistra campaign without having accurately assessed in advance the resources necessary. He was complaining he did not have enough infantry to accomplish his mission—yet look what he had achieved at Larga and Kagul with just 17,000 effectives! Zakhar Chernyshov did indicate he was prepared to satisfy part of Rumiantsev's manpower demands by transferring to the First Army Bibikov and some regiments from Poland. Catherine II took some offense at Rumiantsev's insinuation that unnamed political "enemies" (presumably Orlov and Chernyshov) had eroded her confidence in him; she replied, "I do not know who these enemies are ... and I have not heard about them except from you. Indeed, it was impossible for me to hear about them, since I close my ears to all private quarrels." But she also tempered her obvious disappointment with expressions of sympathy for Rumiantsev's predicament; she understood how difficult operations on the other side of the Danube must have been, "but having known your skill and tested your assiduous zeal, I do not doubt that you will know how to extricate yourself with honor from any difficulties in which you find yourself."[123]

Although Ottoman forces still tended to suffer defeat and heavy losses in battles with smaller Russian forces, there had been less opportunity in 1773 for Rumiantsev to achieve victories on the scale of Larga and Kagul. Muhsinzade Mehmed Pasha was less likely than Silahdar Mehmed Pasha or his other predecessors to risk his field army in a general battle. On the other hand, the pashas commanding smaller forces raiding out from the Danubian garrisons showed greater persistence than in 1770–1772. They were able to recuperate from heavy losses and resume operations more quickly. This perhaps demonstrated one of the advantages of the decentralization of military authority: these commanders were provincial *ayan*s, "defending home territory with their own troops."[124]

In August the VK granted Rumiantsev's request for additional troops. He could have up to 116,000 men for the 1774 campaign. But Catherine II pointed out that this was the sixth recruit levy since 1767, that thus far 300,000 recruits had been raised, and that she was signing the newest levy authorization "with a heavy heart ... seeing that the levies have yet to bring an end to the war despite our wreaking considerable damage on the enemy and ourselves suffering terrible losses of our men."[125] She asked Rumiantsev to reassure her he had a sound plan of campaign for the next year that would not waste more recruits.

After the withdrawal across the Danube Rumiantsev's and Stupishin's division stood near Slobozia, guarding the front from the Ialomiţa to the mouth of the Prut; Lt. General Ungern had taken over Weissman's corps, stationed near Ismail; Saltykov again held the western sector, from the Olt to the Argeş; Potemkin's reserve was at Negoeşti, covering the territory from the Argeş to the Ialomiţa; and there was a separate detachment under General Kamenskii holding Giurgiu. Their priority now was defense. Rumiantsev hoped to see greater coordination of effort among these commanders to rebuild the Russian defense network along the Danube and allow the First Army to find secure winter quarters as close to northeastern Bulgaria as possible. It was anticipated that the grand vizier, emboldened by the Russian withdrawal across the Danube, might make his own strike across the river, probably from Rusçuk in the direction of Bucharest. There were also reports that 20,000 Turks were massing at Karasu for an attack on Hârşova. In late July, Rumiantsev decided to reinforce Kamenskii at Giurgiu while preparing for diversionary attacks on the western and eastern flanks: Saltykov's corps was to make a demonstration march against Turnu and a raid upon Orsova, while Ungern was to take 6,000 men on a raid against Babadagh and then Karasu.[126] Eventually Karasu could be attacked from east as well as west, by Ungern and Dolgorukov, and once Karasu was seized, there might be an opportunity to cross the Danube again and place Silistra under bombardment and siege.

On August 6 Ungern camped near Babadagh and sent patrols toward Karasu. His intelligence suggested that Ahmed Pasha was planning to march from Turnu with 20,000 troops to attack Giurgiu from the rear, while the grand vizier's forces from Shumla struck Giurgiu from the front. Fortunately, Ahmed Pasha mistook Saltykov's division near Giurgiu for a Russian army of 40,000 and he halted his advance. Giurgiu did come under attack on August 12, but only by a detachment from Rusçuk, which was handily defeated. The grand vizier then altered his plans and prepared to attack Hârşova, one of the most strategically important hard points the Russians held on the southern bank of the Danube.

It was Suvorov's task to hold Hârşova. He had only 4,000 troops under his command, with just four regiments of infantry, and Hârşova's fortifications were in disrepair. He had hoped that he could coordinate the defense of Hârşova with Ungern and had proposed that if the Turks attacked Hârşova Ungern would strike in their rear; in reciprocation, he would march to the defense of Ungern if the latter were attacked by enemy forces from Karasu or Babadagh. But Rumiantsev considered this too risky. He ordered Suvorov to stay at Hârşova and Ungern to remain at Babadagh.[127]

When 7,000–10,000 Turks from Ahmed Pasha's vanguard appeared south of Hârşova in the morning of September 3, Suvorov had a trap awaiting them. He had placed his two weakest regiments in two masked redoubts under instructions to lay low and hold their fire. The enemy passed by both positions, assuming they were empty. Suddenly they came under canister fire from a third, northern redoubt that had become visible only when the enemy had passed some low hills. Suvorov had the strongest of his regiments in this third redoubt. Their artillery fire was followed by a bayonet attack and then a sortie by some squadrons of hussars. The enemy was routed, and as they fled south, they came under attack from the other two redoubts. The Turks lost about a thousand killed; Suvorov lost ten killed and 167 wounded.[128]

Suvorov's victory at Hârşova convinced Rumiantsev to approve Suvorov's proposal of joining with Ungern to attack Karasu; as neither had more than 3,000 troops available, Rumiantsev instructed them to rendezvous with Dolgorukov, thereby giving them an additional three regiments of infantry and a regiment of cavalry. On October 15 Dolgorukov, Ungern, and Suvorov joined forces at Karamurat, and two days later they captured Karasu, killed 1,500 Turks, and took prisoner 775. Most of Karasu's 15,000 defenders had fled at first sight of the approaching Russians. Momentum carried them on to Bazarjik, defended by just 3,000 Turks under Cherkes Pasha, who surrendered to them on October 23 without firing a shot.[129]

Rumiantsev intended the Karasu/Bazarjik operation to support drives against two more important objectives. He wanted Saltykov to set up island batteries to place Rusçuk under bombardment, and he expected Potemkin to cross at Gurobaly again and place Silistra under bombardment. Even if neither fortress fell, this would keep up enough pressure on the enemy until it came time to take the First Army into winter quarters; it would perhaps satisfy the empress and the VK that elements of the First Army, if not its main corps, had returned to operations across the Danube; if it produced favorable conditions, he could send Suvorov, Ungern, and Dolgorukov to attack the grand vizier's reserves at Shumla.

But while he was still capable of planning such ambitious aggressive operations, Rumiantsev was not in the condition to execute them himself; everything had to be entrusted to his division commanders. Rumiantsev had fallen so ill—probably with malaria—he had to transfer command of the main corps to Glebov and retire to Focşani for treatment. On September 14 N. V. Repnin reported from Focşani, "I found the Field Marshal still extremely weak and unable to get out of bed, although he is now out of danger. He looks pitiful, as does everyone else here. The whole town has been turned into a hospital. Igel'strom was quite ill, but is already up and about. Zavadovskii is on his back, Asch, Velda, Prince Andrei Nikolaich also—in short, practically everyone is sick with high and low-grade fevers. Of all the Field Marshal's staff, only his huntsman is healthy. All others are either in bed or barely dragging themselves about."[130]

The success of 1773's final operations therefore devolved upon the division commanders, and the mixed results appear to have been due to bad weather and their failure to coordinate action.

Saltykov established two batteries on an island opposite Rusçuk and began bombarding the fortress on October 24. On November 3 he sent regiments across the Danube and captured an enemy camp at Martineşti, ten kilometers from Rusçuk. Potemkin, reinforced by 4,500 of Glebov's troops, forced the Danube on October 30 and placed Silistra under siege bombardment. But both sieges bogged down, and Saltykov and Potemkin were unable to shift forces from these sites to support the strike against Shumla; Glebov had to march from Ibrail to reinforce Potemkin at Silistra. Meanwhile, Ungern and Dolgorukov, charged with the mission of joining some of Glebov's troops in a march from Bazarjik toward Shumla, quarreled with each other and went off in different directions, Dolgorukov toward Shumla and Ungern against Varna on the Black Sea coast. Ungern's reconnaissance of Varna was sloppy and so his storm assault on October 30 was defeated; 211 of his officers and soldiers were killed and a larger number wounded. On word of Ungern's failure at Varna, Dolgorukov left off his march on Shumla. This brought the campaign of 1773 to an end. Ungern and Saltykov reported that further operations were impossible due to heavy rains and snow, the flooding of bridges and roads, the shortage of fodder, and illness among their troops. In Saltykov's division on just one night (November 6), fifteen men died and 447 were seriously ill. Most Russian forces now entered winter quarters, except for Potemkin's, which continued to bombard Silistra from the island of Kegai.[131]

The break-out

With the First Army in winter quarters and Rumiantsev recovered sufficiently to resume his correspondence, he wrote to the empress with his views on the past year's campaign and what plans he considered feasible for 1774. On both of their sides, this correspondence was respectful but noticeably curt and testy. He asked not to be straitjacketed in a "Cabinet plan" he was not free to alter, but to be given complete freedom of initiative and the authority to alter plans in the face of new exigencies. Catherine insisted that he present some concrete plan for an offensive, at one point suggesting simultaneous strikes on Silistra and Varna. Rumiantsev rejected this on the grounds that these targets were 200 kilometers apart and capturing them would require forces so large as to leave the rest of the Danubian frontier unguarded. He asked that the Azov Flotilla and part of Dolgorukov's Second Army be shifted from Crimea and sent to besiege Ochakov and Kilburun and close the mouth of the Danube to Ottoman warships and transports. The empress responded that the Second Army would keep Ochakov under observation but would be expanding its campaign into the Kuban; the Azov flotilla would be strengthened by spring and a new squadron of four line ships and two frigates would be arriving to reinforce the Russian fleet in the Aegean and maintain blockade pressure on Istanbul. Meanwhile, what she expected from Rumiantsev was a commitment to gaining a firm foothold in northern Bulgaria, for only that would force the sultan back to the peace table.[132]

It was finally decided that the spring campaign would take the form of an offensive blockading the Ottoman fortresses of Rusçuk and Silistra while concentrating the main blow against the grand vizier's army at Shumla. This would avoid dispersing Russian forces across too broad a front, as all these targets were in a pocket of northern Bulgaria just 100 kilometers across, allowing divisions to march to reinforce each other.

Some of the promised new recruits came in over the winter, so by March the First Army had a total strength of about 77,000 men. But that was on paper; excluding troops in hospital or running logistical missions in Poland, its actual strength was about 55,000. The First Army was stationed in the following manner:

Near Ibrail, Rumiantsev's *corps d'armes* (First Division) of nine regiments infantry, eight regiments cavalry, two regiments of Cossacks, and thirty-eight siege guns; on the Right Flank at Slobozia, Suvorov's Second Division of six regiments infantry, five regiments cavalry, one regiment Cossacks, and twenty field guns; on the Left Flank, at Ismail, Lt. General Kamenskii's Third Division of five regiments of infantry, two battalions of grenadiers, one battalion of jaegers, one regiment of hussars, six regiments of Cossacks, and twenty-three guns; at Orasha, Suvorov's *corps de reserve* of three regiments of musketeers, two battalions of grenadiers, one battalion of jaegers, two regiments of regular cavalry, one regiment of Don Cossacks, 2,000 Zaporozhians, and eight guns; and the Wallachian-Banat Corps under Saltykov, comprising ten regiments of infantry, six regiments of cavalry, two jaeger battalions, five Don Cossack Regiments, and thirty-three guns guarding Giurgiu and Oltenia in the west. The magazines in Poland were guarded by Major-General Shirkov with twenty-two infantry and grenadier companies, one cuirassier regiment, and 1,500 Ukrainian Cossacks; and there were seven regiments and five battalions garrisoning Bender, Akkirman, Kiliia, Ibrail, Bucharest, Khotin, and Iaşi.[133]

The winter had also seen two important political developments offering greater optimism for bringing the war to a close. In December, Sultan Mustafa III had a heart attack and died after a few weeks; he had wanted to take the field himself to reinvigorate his army's efforts, but his advisors had forbidden it on grounds of his poor health. He had intended his son Selim to succeed him, but the throne instead went to his brother Abdul Hamid I, a gentle soul who had spent the last 43 years confined in the *Kafes*, the Gilded Cage. This presented an opportunity for the grand vizier and Ahmed Resmi Efendi, who had opposed the war from the beginning, to press for a return to peace talks.

The second development was foreshadowed in a letter from the empress sent to Potemkin while he was conducting the bombardment of Silistra in December. "Since on my part I am most anxious to preserve fervent, brave, clever, and talented individuals, I beg you to keep out of danger. When you read this letter, you may well ask yourself why I have written it. To this, I reply: I've written this letter so that you should have confirmation of my way of thinking about you, because I have always been your most benevolent, *Catherine*."[134] They had met several times before this; their encounters had left them both charmed with each other, and they had been conducting correspondence for some time, although she had complained he had kept himself too busy to answer all his letters. Potemkin knew her well enough to recognize that she had chosen him to succeed Vasil'chikov as her favorite.

Potemkin was able to offer Catherine far more as lover, confidante, and political advisor than Vasil'chikov, and his rapid political rise reflected her urgent need for his political services. He offered her a way to advance her own agendum, steering between the Orlov and Panin parties, neither of which could object to his influence compared to the nonentity Vasil'chikov's. For a few months, Petr Panin even welcomed his new influence. On Potemkin's return to St. Petersburg on February 4, he was immediately ushered into Catherine's private apartments; they soon became inseparable. In April, he took new rooms directly below hers in the Winter Palace; from late May, they began referring to themselves in their letters as husband and wife. On May 30, 1774, Potemkin was promoted to General-*anshef*; by June, he was Vice-President of the VK.[135] The empress had found a way to transcend the policy squabbles of the Orlovs, Panins, and Chernyshov—just in time to see the Turkish War to satisfactory conclusion and to turn to suppressing the Pugachev Rebellion.

The First Army's 1774 campaign began in early April when Kamenskii crossed the Danube at Isaccea with 10,850 troops and 23 guns. He circumvented Tulcea on his left flank and advanced through Babadagh, Karamurat, and Karasu toward Bazarjik, where he was supposed to rendezvous with Suvorov for an attack on the grand vizier's 50,000-man army at Shumla. Suvorov crossed the Danube at Hârşova in May, with 14,000 men and field guns. On May 16 Suvorov reached Chernovody, from where he began marching in close parallel with Kamenskii's division. Given past experience, it did not seem unlikely that 25,000 troops could defeat the grand vizier's 50,000, and anyhow 25,000 was as many as Rumiantsev could spare, for he needed to use the rest of the First Army to blockade Rusçuk and Silistra, to secure Kamenskii's and Suvorov's rear.

Therefore, Saltykov's division of 10,000 men began moving down the Argeş on May 21 and crossed the Danube on June 2. On June 6 Saltykov reached Turtukai and dispersed a camp of 3,000 Turks; on the ninth, he was attacked by 15,000 Turks but defeated them, killing or capturing about 2,500; and on June 16, Saltykov arrived at Rusçuk and placed it under siege.

Rumiantsev and Glebov crossed at Gurobaly on June 10. Two days later they divided their force, sending part southeast to reinforce Suvorov and taking the rest toward Silistra. On June 19 Rumiantsev camped on the shores of Lake Galați, about 6 kilometers from Silistra, hoping this would draw out the Silistra garrison from open battle making a siege unnecessary. Although Silistra was only about 30 kilometers from Gurobaly, it took until June 22 for some of his infantry and artillery to catch up with him, as heavy rains had made the roads a morass.[136]

But by this time, Suvorov and Kamenskii had already effectively ended the war, even without completely effective coordination between them.

On June 2 Kamenskii captured Bazarjik, defeating 5,000 Ottoman cavalrymen, who retreated toward Kozluji. At that moment, Suvorov's division was at Karacha, a little to the southwest. On June 9 their forces met up near the village of Iushenla and began marching on Kozluji, with Suvorov's Cossacks in the vanguard. The next day, while Suvorov's vanguard was proceeding along the road through the dense Deliorman Forest, at a point about 12 kilometers outside Kozluji, they were attacked by surprise and nearly surrounded by a force of about 15,000 Turkish cavalry. Behind the enemy cavalry were about 25,000 infantry: Reis Efendi Abdurrezak had marched from Shumla with the greater part of the grand vizier's army, leaving only about a thousand troops behind at the Shumla camp. In a fierce battle lasting most of the afternoon and early evening, three enemy attacks were beaten back by Suvorov's bayonet countercharges and artillery fire. The rain may have helped Suvorov by suppressing the janissaries' firepower. Abdurrezzak's force was routed, leaving between 500 and 1,000 dead. Russian losses were seventy-five dead and 134 wounded.

Their dispatches are at odds as to whether this victory was achieved by Suvorov alone, or whether Kamenskii's column had joined in the fighting—there was considerable animosity between the two commanders. Kamenskii claimed credit for the victory at Kozluji. But the road to Shumla, just two march stages ahead, now lay open. Suvorov had taken ill again and had to turn over his command to Miloradovich, but according to Suvorov's reports, he had called on Kamenskii to continue pursuing the enemy to Shumla. But Kamenskii instead rested his division for four days, giving the enemy time to regroup at Shumla. When he finally resumed the march, Kamenskii had to first defeat a vanguard of 5,000 Turks at Yenibazar, and another enemy force had assembled near Achibaba. When Kamenskii arrived at Shumla on June 17, he therefore decided not to risk being taken on his flanks while concentrating on storming Shumla; he decided instead to place Shumla under blockade. This would make it easier for him to spare troops to patrol the roads to Razgrad and Varna and protect against attacks on his flanks.[137]

Over June 21–29, the Shumla garrison made three attempts to sortie against the besiegers, but they were unable to break out. The blockade continued; Kamenskii even became confident enough to move his division back to expand his blockade ring. As provisions ran low at Shumla its garrison began to desert. Kamenskii sent Brigadier Zaborovskii with a command of 2,500 men forty kilometers beyond Shumla, and at Chaplyk-Kovak, Zaborovskii routed a force of 4,000 Turks under Iusef Pasha heading for the relief of Shumla. Meanwhile, Saltykov had won a victory at Turtukai and brought the rest of his division over the river to besiege Rusçuk, and Rumiantsev had Silistra under blockade and could link up with Kamenskii along the Silistra road.[138]

With his army at Shumla disintegrating and Russian forces pushing deeper into northeastern Bulgaria, Grand Vizier Muhsinzade Mehmed Pasha was ready to call an end to hostilities. On June 20 he had asked Rumiantsev for a ceasefire; Rumiantsev had rejected this, insisting on no less than a commitment to negotiations for a final peace. On June 28 the grand vizier accepted the proposal for peace talks, suggesting they could be held on an island off Rusçuk or Giurgiu. Rumiantsev wrote back that any such talks should proceed upon the conditions and demands already laid down by Russia at the Focşani conference. On July 5, 1774, Ahmed Resmi Efendi and Reis Efendi Ibrahim Munib arrived at Rumiantsev's headquarters at the village of Kuchuk-Kainarji to begin peace talks with the Russian envoy N. V. Repnin.[139]

CHAPTER 8
PEACE, REFORMS, AND PROVOCATIONS

According to A. S. Musin-Pushkin's reports from Istanbul, Sultan Abdul Hamid I and Grand Vizier Muhsinzade Mehmed Pasha were already inclined to peace talks by spring of 1774. The subsequent Russian blockades of Silistra and Rusçuk and the approach of Rumiantsev's First Army toward Shumla exerted further pressure on them. The moment was also diplomatically favourable for Russia, as Prussia and Austria were satisfied for the while with their gains from the partition of Poland and Britain was well disposed toward Russia. The French envoy to Istanbul, the Comte de Saint-Priest, was still urging the sultan to continue the war, but France could not exert as much influence now, for Choiseul had been sent into retirement and the new king, Louis XVI, was not focused on relations with the Ottomans.

Until late spring 1774 there had been some dispute within the empress' Council of State as to what terms to demand for peace. Nikita Panin, nervous about the spread of the Pugachev Rebellion, had urged that Russia soften any demands that might complicate and delay a peace agreement, and for that reason he suggested Russian demands for the cession of Kerch and Yenikale be dropped; Russia could be satisfied with Kilburun or Ochakov in their stead. This idea was strongly opposed by Grigorii Orlov, however, who argued that Russian possession of Kerch and Yenikale was crucial to guarantee the Crimean Khanate's independence from the Ottoman Empire.[1] In March, however, Rumiantsev took the initiative and began consulting with Obreskov, recently released from Ottoman captivity, and on June 17 Rumiantsev took his army to within five kilometers of Shumla. When the grand vizier wrote Rumiantsev on June 20 proposing an armistice conference, Rumiantsev responded, "Concerning a Congress, much less an armistice, I cannot and will not listen. Your Radiance knows our final will in this: if you desire to make peace, send envoys to conclude peace, but not to discuss the main articles, which have already been long discussed and explained. Until these main articles are ratified our military action will not cease."[2]

The Treaty of Kuchuk-Kainarji

On July 5, 1774, the grand vizier's envoys Ahmed Resmi Efendi and Reis Ibraim Munib Efendi were escorted to the site of the peace talks, in Rumiantsev's camp at Kuchuk-Kainarji (Turkish, Küçük Kaynara). The negotiations began that same morning. Obreskov's arrival had been held up by a flood on the Danube, so Rumiantsev appointed to his place Lt. General N. V. Repnin, former ambassador to Warsaw and commander of the Wallachian Corps. To expedite matters Rumiantsev hinted that he might march upon the grand vizier's army at Shumla if the talks did not produce results within five days.[3] He also insisted that the usual rituals demanded by diplomatic protocol should be omitted. In fact, most points of controversy were resolved already on the second day of the talks, and a courier was sent to notify the grand vizier on the 7th. The grand vizier sent his response on the 10th, and the Treaty of Kuchuk-Kainarji was signed that day.[4]

The speed with which the terms were accepted reflected the extremity of the grand vizier's military and political situation and gave rise to the legend that the treaty had been signed on a drumhead inside Rumiantsev's tent.[5] But obligations left unclarified and consequences unforeseen would later spark conflicts drawing the Russian and Ottoman Empires back into war in 1787.

The Treaty of Kuchuk-Kainarji provided for a perpetual peace with mutual amnesty for past hostile acts. The Russian army would withdraw from Bulgaria back to the left bank of the Danube, upon which Hârşova would be returned to the Porte, followed by the evacuation of Russian troops from Wallachia and Bessarabia and the return of the fortresses of Giurgiu, Ibrail, Kiliia, Ismail, and Akkirman, this evacuation to be accomplished within two months' time. The Russian army would leave Moldavian territory and cross over the Dnestr, turning over to the Turks the fortresses of Khotin and Bender, within five months. The Russian fleet and land forces would also leave the islands of the Archipelago "as soon as possible." The fortress of Kilburun and the angle of the uninhabited lands enclosed by the Bug and Dnestr were to be retained by Russia in perpetuity, however, and Azov would also remain the "perpetual and incontestable property of the Russian Empire."[6]

"All the Tatar nations of Crimea, Bucak, Kuban, Yedisan, Jamboiluk, Yedichkul', with no exception whatsoever, shall respectively be recognized by the Two Empires as free and independent of all foreign power and as being in the immediate power of their own Khan, descendant of Genghis Khan, elected and established with the unanimous consent of the Tatar peoples, and who shall govern them according to their laws and ancient customs, without being accountable to any foreign power." Neither Russia nor the Porte may interfere "in any manner with the election of the said Khan, nor in domestic affairs, political or civil," except that the Tatar people, as Muslims, may regard the sultan as the ruling Caliph safeguarding Muslim law. Russia will cede back to the Khanate "all the cities, fortresses, habitations, lands, and ports conquered in Crimea and in Kuban by Russian forces, the districts between the Berda, Kuskaia Voda, and Dnepr rivers, as well as the land extending to the Polish border between the Bug and Dnestr," except for the fortress of Ochakov, which shall be retained by the Porte, and the fortresses and ports of Kerch and Yenikale, which shall be retained by the Russians, thereby guaranteeing for Russia control of the Kerch Straits and entry into the Sea of Azov. The Porte may not introduce any troops or commissioners into Crimean territory but must "permit to all the Tatars the enjoyment of their freedom and independence, as the Russian Empire does."[7]

The Treaty established "a free and unmolested navigation for all vessels and merchant craft belonging to the two Contracting Powers on all the seas that bathe their shores, and the Sublime Porte permits Russian vessels and merchant craft free passage in her ports and in all places, in exactly the manner as the other Powers possess it, in the commerce they carry on from the Black Sea to the White Sea [Mediterranean] and similarly from the White Sea to the Black Sea." In other words, Russian merchant ships would have rights of free navigation on the Black Sea and in the eastern Mediterranean, but this right did not extend to Russian merchant ships trying to pass through the Bosporus and Dardanelles (likewise closed to European merchant ships).[8] It should be noted that the Treaty was not explicit as to the navigation rights of Russian warships, guaranteeing that this matter would be the subject of contention in the future. Greek merchants acquired the right to sail under the Russian flag. For purposes of paying customs duties and protecting the rights of merchants, Russia may establish Consuls and Vice-Consuls "in all places where the Russian Empire shall judge expedient, and they shall be considered and esteemed as the Consuls of other friendly powers."[9]

In resuming his suzerainty over Bessarabia, Wallachia, and Moldavia, the sultan promised them amnesty for their acts of rebellion; protection of the free exercise of the Christian religion; restoration to their monasteries and to individuals of lands "unjustly seized;" and the right of emigration, provided emigration be made within one year from the signing of the Treaty, so that families may put their affairs in order. In light of the great hardships the inhabitants of these territories incurred during the war, the Ottoman government may make no demand for payment of debts or contributions within the next two years, and thereafter it must "employ all kindness and generosity in the imposition of all monetary tributes and to receive them by means of Commissioners sent every five years." The people of Moldavia, Wallachia, and Bessarabia are to be "permitted the same advantages they enjoyed in the fortuitous reign of Mehmet IV." The sovereign hospodars of Moldavia and Wallachia shall have the right again to send to the sultan "Christian ministers in charge of Christian and Greek religious affairs … and these same Ministers shall protect the interests of the said Principalities." In addition, the Ministers of the Imperial Court of Russia "may speak in their favor, and the Sublime Porte promises to have respect for these representations in conformance with all friendly consideration and the respect that Powers have for one another."[10]

The Russian army would evacuate the kingdoms of Georgia and Mingrelia and return the Ottoman fortresses captured by Russian forces (Kutaisi, Shirvan, and Bagdati) "to those who possessed them in former times, a long time before they were owned by the Sublime Porte." Russian recognized the peoples of Georgia and Mingrelia as subjects of the Porte and would no longer interfere with their affairs, while the Porte pledged that it would offer them full amnesty and would renounce "ever again to demand a tribute of young children, be they girls or boys, nor any other form of tribute."[11]

As for Greater and Lesser Kabarda, "being on account of their closeness to the Tatar lands in greater contact with the Khan of Crimea, it is left to the said Khan to consent, with his council and the elders of the Tatar nation, to letting these lands become the property of the Imperial Court of Russia."[12]

Articles VII and XIV would subsequently come under controversy in pledging the Ottoman government to the "lasting protection of the Christian religion and of the

Churches of that religion," and permitting the Imperial Russian government to represent on every occasion the cause of "the Church constructed at Constantinople."[13] Several historians (Ulianitskii, Zhigarev, Miliukov, and Hammer-Purgstall) have interpreted this to mean that Russia claimed the right to protect Orthodox subjects in all Ottoman lands, and it was this right that Tsar Nicholas I invoked in declaring war against the Ottoman Empire in 1853. The right of Christian Europe to interfere in Ottoman affairs to protect the Christian millet from oppression was thought to date from this point, and Albert Sorel took on authority the judgment of the Austrian diplomat Thugut—who had not yet actually examined the text of the Treaty—that "by the dexterous combination of the articles of this treaty, the Ottoman Empire becomes from today a sort of Russian province."[14]

But literally interpreted, Article XIV of the Kuchuk-Kainarji Treaty indicates that the right of the Russian Government to protect Orthodox Christians extended only to the clergy and caretakers of a new church, to be built in the outskirts of Galata, a Russian Orthodox Church of Greek Rite that was subject to the Patriarch of Moscow rather than to the Greek Orthodox Patriarch of Istanbul. The Treaty does speak of the right of the Russian Government to make representations in defense or protection (*zashchita*) of the Orthodox faith, but the Turkish version of the treaty uses *siyanet* (preservation) in place of "defense" and commits the Porte only to "receiving with attention" the representations made by the Russian government; in that sense the protectorate is exercised by the Ottoman government, not the Russian government.[15] However, it would not take long for the Russian government to begin asserting its own protectorate, at least symbolically and for Russian public opinion, for on March 17, 1775, Catherine II issued a manifesto declaring "Our Orthodoxy is henceforth under Our Imperial guardianship in the places of its upspringing, protected from all oppression and violence."[16]

The final article of the Treaty stipulated that the Porte must pay the Russian Empire an indemnity of 7.5 million piasters (4.5 million rubles) for the expenses of the war, in three payments over 1775–1777.[17]

One can therefore discern in the Treaty four points of dispute upon which Russo–Ottoman relations could someday founder: 1) the "independence" of the Crimean Khanate, which required the stability of its administration and its safety from dynastic or factional division; 2) the freedom of navigation allowed the Russian Black Sea war fleet, as guaranteed by Russian control of the Kerch Straits; 3) the ability of the Crimean Khan to guarantee the Kabardas remained pacified under Russian sovereignty; and 4) the limits of the authority of the ministers and consuls of the Russian government to make "representations" protecting Orthodox subjects in Moldavia, Wallachia, and possibly even in Greece.

The reform of provincial government

In September 1774, following report of Pugachev's capture, Petr Panin sent Suvorov east to pacify the Bashkir tribes while Panin focused on restoring order to the Volga region.

On one hand, Panin's reports to St. Petersburg detailing the administrative malfeasance and corruption that had fed the rebellion did prove useful to the empress in crafting her 1775 reform of provincial government, and Panin authorized the purchase of 90,000 quarters of grain to distribute as famine relief.[18] On the other hand, he sent out his regiments on punitive expeditions to restore order through terror and cruel reprisals. He announced that those who had murdered officials, gentry landowners, and priests were to be quartered and beheaded, their remains posted on blocks along the roads and streets; if the murderers could not be found, the villages where the crimes had occurred "shall be compelled to hand over the guilty by drawing lots among them, every third man to be hanged; and if by this means they still do not give them up, then every hundredth man by lot shall actually be hanged by the rib, and all the remaining adults be flogged."[19] Panin reported that between August 3 and October 10 his punitive detachments crushed sixty-three rebel bands, killed 10,000 rebels, and took 9,000 prisoners.[20] Pavel Potemkin's commission at Kazan' was more selective in its repressive measures; it released many of the 10,000 prisoners it had in custody and prosecuted and punished only the more important ringleaders. But there were also prisoners held by the Secret Commission and Orenburg Commission and in the custody of local officials and garrison commanders, so in all, probably about 20,000 people beyond those arrested by Panin's troops were held under investigation.[21]

On May 17, 1775, Catherine II issued a manifesto commemorating the glorious peace obtained in the Turkish War and demonstrating her maternal love for her subjects by bestowing forty-seven favors upon the nation. These favors included the abolition of certain extraordinary, superfluous, or unnecessarily burdensome taxes; a pardon for all fugitive serfs if they returned to their owners by the end of 1776; a pardon for deserters; the end of corporal punishment without trial for the lower ranks of the army; and her reaffirmation of the 1754 decree prohibiting capital punishment.[22]

In reviewing the course of the Pugachev Rebellion the empress had reached agreement with General-*anshef* Panin that "the weak conduct of the civil and military authorities in various places … [had been] just as harmful to the common good as Pugachev and his riffraff." This was also the view of Governor-General of Moscow M. N. Volkonskii and the new Governor-General of Kazan' M. S. Meshcherskii, who both argued that the larger governorates had too few officials to ensure police order and efficient collection of taxes. They urged immediate reform to restore order and regain the trust of the gentry. Over the next few months the empress drafted a reform with the aid of Novgorod Governor Yakov Sievers, an Anglophile who shared her interest in Blackstone's *Commentaries on the Laws of England*.[23]

The Statute for the Administration of the Governorates of the Russian Empire was promulgated by the Senate on November 7, 1775.[24] Its purpose was to "strengthen and secure the general tranquility and safety" of the realm by addressing the problem of territorially vast governorates with inadequate chancery staffs, which had limited the division of administrative labor—between revue and disbursement, for example, and between criminal and civil justice. This lack of division of labor had promoted "sluggishness, neglect, and procrastination … arbitrariness and chicanery."[25]

The Statute replaced the previous twenty-one governorates and seventy-one provinces with forty-one new governorates (by the end of Catherine's reign there would be 50). The new governorates were formed upon the principle of population: each comprised between 300,000 and 400,000 taxpaying souls and was divided into *uezd* districts of 20,000–30,000 souls. They had more ramified and more uniform administrative structure with clearer separation of administrative, judicial, and fiscal functions. The old post of provincial *voevoda* was abolished. The *gubernator* reported directly to the empress and had a seat on the Senate when he was in St. Petersburg; he was now assisted by a deputy governor in charge of finances and a board of appointed councilors that collegially refined decrees and instructions to lower organs and supervised the civil and criminal courts. There were two subsidiary boards for tax collection and expenditure and for the management of hospitals and schools. At the district (*uezd*) level there were separate courts for the nobility, townsmen, and peasants, a lower land court consisting of a land commissar and two assessors elected by the district nobility, and a *kapitan-ispravnik* for policing. This more ramified apparatus employing more officials permitted some administrative decentralization, so that some functions previously concentrated in the central colleges could be passed down to the governorates.[26] It became possible to shut down all but two of the central colleges dealing with internal administration. General central control was maintained, however, through the Procurator-General of the Senate, whose supervisory powers were strengthened through the procurators of the new governorates.

There was one feature of the reform that placed political convenience over bureaucratic rationality. The Statute had left intact the Petrine principle of entrusting certain governorates to trusted intimates with magnified powers; thus certain pairs of governates were combined into viceroyalties (*namestnichestva*) under governors-general. The governors-general were unwilling to allow their procurators to regulate their power from below or allow the Procurator-General to regulate them from above, they retained their Senatorial rank, and they treated their postings to the viceroyalties as interruptions of their military careers, so "they were an element of instability, and their relationships with the central government and the governors were really never defined."[27] In the case of Governor-General Potemkin this freedom from regulation was all to his benefit: he obtained enormous power to settle and develop New Russia according to his own vision and counted on his intimacy with the empress and his cooperation with the Panins to define his relations with the center. On the whole, however, the governors-general represented a contradiction within the 1775 reform. "While Catherine granted a watered-down measure of gentry self-government with one hand, with the other she set up a counter-balance so powerful as to negate the substance of decentralization. The government of the Russian Empire remained in the hands of the autocrat and a small coterie of courtiers."[28]

Nearly all the new governors and governors-general appointed after 1775 were military commanders, many of them recommended by Potemkin or Rumiantsev, men not yet retired but for whom new military commands had not yet been found, so that "seldom was the invasion of the countryside by Major Generals so sudden and so extensive as in the late 1770s. The result was to raise the status of the central government's representative in all the guberniia capitals by one or two ranks over that of his predecessors." The creation of viceroyalties for governors-general had an added political effect: the elite nobles who had consolidated their power at the capital and in the army now "fanned out into the provinces as well ... to dispense their patronage and coopt new members." John Le Donne therefore characterizes the political content of the reform as "a redistribution of authority within the ruling class."[29]

For the time being the legal rights and degree of autonomy in provincial government permitted the gentry as an estate were left unclear; the Statute of 1775 had allowed for the creation of local assemblies of the nobility and their right to elect a marshal, but their role in taxation and other matters had not been spelled out and the empress had not even officially acknowledged the 1762 Manifesto emancipating the nobility from compulsory state service. These matters still had to be addressed if the 1775 Statute was to expand the scale of elective office-holding within provincial administration.

On April 21, 1785, in celebration of her birthday, Catherine issued a Charter to the Nobility and a Charter to the Towns. The Charter to the Towns, partly inspired by Swedish and Prussian law, divided the urban "middle estate" (*meshchane*) into six categories based on property, wealth, and education. Those with a minimum income of fifty rubles were entitled to participate in municipal-elected self-government. They could elect a town assembly every three years; it could discuss matters and make representations to the governor, although its main function was to select a six-man board to police the town, maintain public buildings, run hospitals and other urban services, and adjudicate disputes between guilds—under the supervision of the governor, of course. The Charter of the Nobility confirmed and expanded the legal rights and privileges of the nobility: freedom from compulsory service, the right to own serfs; freedom from personal taxation and billeting; the right to travel and to enter service abroad; and freedom from corporal punishment and from deprivation of property or rank without trial by peers. Those noblemen who had annual incomes of 100 rubles (equivalent to ownership of twenty-five serfs) and had reached through service the rank of commissioned officer could be elected from their district to the governorate's noble assembly (convened by the governor every three years), elect a marshal of nobility, and make representations to the governor, the Senate, and the empress. Those who had not reached the rank of commissioned officer, or who had not served at all, could sit in the noble assembly but without the rights of elected deputies, that is, the right to vote or to hold elective post. It should be noted that the Charter of the Nobility sorted out nobles into six status categories, awarding higher precedence status to men of lineage of at least a hundred years and to those who had rise to noble rank through military service; and it did not provide voting rights in the noble assembly to nobles who had no estates or owned fewer than twenty serfs—who comprised over half of the nobility.[30]

Liquidation of the Don and Zaporozhian Hosts

Although Potemkin still recognized the value of Cossack light cavalry as a supplement to the slower cuirassier cavalry, especially on the southern frontier,[31] the Efremov affair and the Pugachev Revolt convinced him that dangerous Cossack revolts could reoccur as long as Hosts preserved their autonomy under elected atamans. Removing the Don Host's Ataman Stepan Efremov for corruption had been difficult; the *starshina* of the Don Host would have made a stand for him—they were ready to kill Major-General Cherepov, sent to Cherkassk to arrest Efremov—and it was only with luck that Captain Rzhevskii and three squadrons of hussars had been able to spirit Efremov away.[32] For the past several years the Zaporozhian Host's *Koshevyi otaman* Petro Kalnyshevs'kyi had threatened to place the Sich under the sultan's protection if St. Petersburg did not address the Zaporozhians' grievances.[33] Potemkin believed that it was time to place the territories of the Cossack Hosts under the same administrative system as the rest of the Empire—the *guberniia* system.

Once the Pugachev Rebellion had been suppressed the Russian government moved to resolve the problem of the Don and Zaporozhian Cossack hosts.

Efremov had been replaced in 1773 by Don *Nakaznoi ataman* Semen Sulin, who had contributed forces to the campaign against Pugachev. But Sulin was left in command only for a year; in February 1774 another veteran of the campaign against Pugachev, General Aleksei Ivanovich Ilovaiskii, was appointed by Potemkin and the VK as the new *Nakaznoi ataman* of the Don Cossack Host. He would remain in this post until 1797. Under Ilovaiskii the old military system of *stanitsa* settlement assemblies and general assembly electing the Host's *starshina* and managing military affairs was preserved, but the Don Cossacks were placed in 500-man regiments under staff officers and colonels holding patents from the VK. Ilovaiskii, now promoted to Major-General, retained his Campaign Chancery (*Pokhodnaia kantseliariia*) supervising Don Cossack military affairs but also now presided over a new Host Civil Administration created by Potemkin and comprising six *starshina* officers, four elected annually and two permanently appointed by Governor-General Potemkin. The Host Civil Administration was treated as the equivalent of a *guberniia* chancery within the Azov province of the new Azov Governorate. One of its major tasks was to administer the Cossack land fund and regulate the flood of new immigrants into the Host, who were no longer distributed among the *stanitsa* settlements but were either assigned to the Cossack regiments of the Russian field army or attached to *starshina* officers as dependent laborers. As Governor-General of New Russia and the Don Potemkin had ultimate authority over the military and civil administrations of the Don Host. In the judgment of General Aleksandr Rigelman, Ilovaiskii and the dual administration of the Don Host had fully pacified the Don Host by 1778.[34]

The Zaporozhian Host met with a harsher fate. Its *Koshevyi otaman* had chosen to provoke St. Petersburg on precisely the issue that had already convinced Catherine's government that the Host was an unnecessary anachronism. The territory of the Zaporozhian Host—about 8 million *desiatiny*—had already been encapsulated within the Empire in the 1750s, confined in the south by New Serbia, Slavonic Serbia, and the Sloboda Cossack regiment; in 1764 all three of these had been folded into the newly created Governorate of New Russia; and by 1774 the neutralization of the Crimean Khanate had completed the process of rendering the Zaporozhian Host's southern frontier defense role obsolete. Yet since 1765 *Koshevyi otaman* Kalnyshevs'kyi had been bent on the Host's territorial expansion, demanding that Russia cede to the Host lands on its southern as well as northern boundaries.[35] Zaporozhian raids on the Nogais had complicated the negotiations for the neutralization of the Crimean Khanate, and elements of the Zaporozhian Host had participated in the raid on Balta provoking the war with the Ottoman Empire. Kalnyshevs'kyi was not restraining his Cossacks from making raids into New Russia and enticing or herding into Zaporozhia some 8,000 inhabitants of the Moldavian Hussar Regiment. Landlords in Left Bank Ukraine were complaining to St. Petersburg that the Zaporozhians were luring or abducting thousands of their peasant tenants. "Surrounded on all sides by Russian possessions, Zaporizhzhya not only was no longer useful; rather, it proved to be an obstacle to Russian colonization and trade in the south. Zaporozhian diplomats were unable to grasp this change."[36]

The Council of State therefore decided on May 7, 1775, to liquidate the Zaporozhian Host altogether, disperse its Cossacks, and open its territory to Russian colonization. "The camp of these Cossacks, as the source of their unruliness, must be destroyed. When order is restored among them, authority will be established over them. Fugitive families from New Russia, who have settled among them, shall be returned to their abodes."[37] On June 4, 1775, some regiments from St. Elizavetgrad under the command of Lt. General P. A. Tekelli placed the Sich at Oleshki under blockade and demanded the arrest of Kalnyshevs'kyi and three other *starshyna* officers. They were handed over without a fight and the three thousand Cossacks at Oleshki were dispersed by June 16. The Zaporozhian Host was thereby dissolved. Its territory was divided between the New Russia and Azov governorates.

The empress' manifesto justifying the liquidation of the Host, issued on August 3, was written by Potemkin (ironically, an honorary Zaporozhian Cossack).[38] It explained that the Host had to be dissolved because it had become a "political monstrosity": having outlived its usefulness for guarding the frontier against the Tatars and Turks, it had tried to reconstitute itself as an independent but wild and lawless state within the Empire through territorial aggrandizement and abduction of labor from Russian provinces.

The Zaporozhian Host had numbered about 30,000 male souls. *Starshyna* officers who swore allegiance to the empress were made officers in the dragoon and hussar regiments of the Russian army. Many of the rank-and-file Zaporozhians were resettled at Astrakhan and in the Kuban, where they would be reformed in 1787 as a Black Sea Host (Kuban Host). Some others were left on their lands outside the Sich, although with insecure title and in danger of being enserfed, for colonization by Russian magnate landowners now began in earnest. Some Zaporozhian Cossacks followed the example of the Nekrasovites and fled into the Ottoman Empire, resettling along the Danube.[39]

Ukraine

The elimination of the military threat from the Crimean Khanate "terminated the historical justification of the Ukraine as a borderland." Malorossiia, with its population of just over a million male souls, had become encapsulated, "an internal province of the Empire for which the maintenance of a separate status was no longer justified."[40]

Two factors militated against a more assertive and organized Ukrainian resistance to the further administrative integration of Malorossiia into the Russian Empire. One was the scale of the Russian military presence garrisoned and billeted in Malorossiia, which St. Petersburg intended to maintain beyond 1774 as a deterrent to the Turks and Crimean separatists. The other was the political isolation of the Ukrainian *szlachta*. The *szlachta* had been enlarged by the laws of 1767 and 1768 recognizing the cossack *starshyna* as possessing the privileges and allodial landowning rights of Imperial Russian nobles. It retained some nostalgic loyalty to the idea of the Hetmanate and the Kiev Metropolitanate as symbols of Ukrainian special autonomy; and for the time being it expressed opposition to the introduction of full serfdom in order to preserve existing administrative and judicial institutions. At the empress' Legislative Assembly, Hryhorii Poletyka had called for a fully empowered *szlachta* to restore the Hetmanate and Ukrainian autonomy. But at the same time the *szlachta* was politically co-opted through its interest in winning appointments to the Russian imperial bureaucracy, and the absence of any Diet or estate-representative assembly made it all the more difficult for the *szlachta* to represent itself as a Patriot party speaking for rank-and-file Cossacks, the townsmen, peasantry, and clergy as well as for themselves.[41]

Catherine II intended her 1775 Statute for the Administration of the Governorates to be applied across the entire Empire to standardize administrative organization and practice and better serve the enlightenment of the realm. The haidamak rebellions, the recent lawlessness of the Zaporozhian Host, and the Pugachev Rebellion might have argued for bringing the administration of Malorossiia in line with the new system of the Statute as quickly as possible. Governor-General Rumiantsev had moved the capital of the Malorossiia Governorate from Hlukhiv, the old capital of the Hetmanate, to Kiev in 1775. However, the empress waited until 1779 to order Rumiantsev to implement the other new administrative structures prescribed by the Statute, and Rumiantsev cautioned her that the process must be gradual and permit some compromises to deal with some of the special privileges and attachments to "autonomy" rooted in the old Hetmanate. As Rumiantsev still had considerable military responsibilities—administering all cavalry forces in Malorossiia, guarding the Polish border, and monitoring political conflicts in Crimea—the empress appointed General Andrii Myloradovich as subordinate Governor and passed to him much of the work reorganizing the administration of the Governorate. This was politically shrewd, as Myloradovich was not only a respected veteran of the recent Turkish War and one of Rumiantsev's staff generals, but also a well-connected member of the Ukrainian *szlachta*.[42]

Myloradovich conducted a new census over 1779–1781, and on its basis Malorossiia Governorate was subdivided on the basis of population into three provinces with capitals at Kiev, Novhorod-Sivers'k, and Chernihiv. Each province comprised eleven districts. The Treasury and the Accounting Commission of Malorossiia were closed and their functions transferred to Treasury Boards in the three new provinces. Closing down the Little Russian College took until 1786, as it first had to resolve a backlog of court cases within its General Military Court. The devolution of fiscal and judicial authority to the chanceries of the three provinces' governors was counterbalanced by enhancing the power of Governor-General Rumiantsev as Supreme Viceroy, the empress' direct representative, accountable directly to the empress alone (bypassing even the Imperial Senate), with the authority to countermand the orders of the provincial governors and all government institutions of Malorossiia.[43] To further enlarge his authority Rumiantsev's tenure as Governor-General was confirmed for life. "Together with his position as commander-in-chief of all troops ... this made the territory of the former Hetmanate his virtual satrapy."[44] The provincial governors also served long terms. Myloradovich, for example, served as Governor of Chernihiv province for fifteen years.[45]

The last of the nonmilitary Cossack administrative offices of the old Hetmanate were abolished and their functions transferred to the judicial, fiscal, and police organs of the three provinces. However, there was a political compensation offered here in that the new provincial governors (Myloradovich, Zhurmna, and Zavadovs'kyi) were all of Ukrainian *szlachta* background, the new elective and appointive offices of their districts were staffed by the former company commanders of the Cossack regiments, and the chanceries of the provinces provided positions for the regimental colonels and employment to many "former regimental and company clerks, young graduates of the Kievan Academy, and even literate rank-and-file Cossacks. Due to the presence of this officialdom, the provincial capitals—Kiev and Novhorod-Sivers'k in particular—became the social and intellectual centers for the Ukrainian elite." By accepting without protest the Statute of the Administration of the Governorates and embracing service in its institutions, however, "the Ukrainian gentry lost their autonomous position, based on historical rights and privileges, and assumed the role of mere servitors for the imperial bureaucracy. This was the crucial transformation in the demise of Ukrainian autonomy."[46]

The dissolution of Cossack territorial *polk* civil administration cleared the way for Rumiantsev to abolish the Cossack *polk* regiments themselves. Cossack military ranks were redefined as equivalent Russian regular army ranks and Cossack officers and rank-and-file were transferred into ten new regiments of carabiniers in 1783. The ten new carabinier regiments took 73,576 men from 14,320 households of elite and registered Cossacks. Only Cossacks were recruited, their officers were from the Cossack *starshyna*, and for a while these ten carabinier regiments retained the names of ten of the eleven traditional territorial *polki*, recruiting from the cantons of the same original territories— in these regards the reform of 1783 paid respect to the Cossack military legacy. But the carabinier regiments were smaller (828 men) and therefore excluded some Cossacks; service in them was for just five years, so that complete turnover in composition was achieved every five years; and each year forty-eight of the best troopers were transferred into elite regiments of the Russian army. In 1786 the principle that the Malorossiian military establishment was supposed to be of Cossack origin was broken; in that year a dragoon regiment of 3,974 men was created, and it combined one thousand Cossacks transferred from the carabiniers with peasants levied from recently secularized monastery lands. This had the effect of collapsing the distinction between the free Cossack soldier and the peasant *rekrut*.[47]

The further socioeconomic integration of Ukraine into the Empire was promoted by the introduction of serfdom. Rumiantsev had already introduced the soul tax in Malorossiia in 1765, and a decree of 1770 had authorized the return of runaway peasant tenants to their landlords so that payment of taxes would not be avoided. With the completion of the census by Myloradovich, it was expected that St. Petersburg could now move to protect its fiscal interests by legislating *de facto* serfdom in Malorossiia. The decree accomplishing this, dated May 3, 1783, did not actually use the word "serfdom," but it did readjust Rumiantsev's "ruble duty" to correspond to Russian social estate gradations of the soul tax, and it announced that taxpayers were henceforth bound to the places and status in which they had been registered in Myloradovich's census.[48] The Ukrainian peasantry responded to this with tenant flight on a large scale. Over 1783–1795, 23,700 male souls fled from Kiev province, most of them to the lower Don and the Black Sea coast of New Russia.[49]

From the viewpoint of St. Petersburg, the liquidation of Cossack administration and the imposition of the Statute on Provinces represented a political compromise: "On the one hand, abandonment of the old regimental organization and acceptance of the partitioning into three *gubernii* fitting within the norms of the Organic Law;[50] on the other, absorption, in a territory where Cossacks were becoming a minority, of the Cossack sociopolitical order into the new administrative structure of the *uezd*. Police and justice were administered and taxes were collected by the former company commanders, while the former colonels staffed the *guberniia* agencies and continued to uphold, through a network of personal and family relationships, the unity of Little Russia."[51]

New Russia

One of Potemkin's most impressive achievements after the war was the colonization and economic development of New Russia (*Novorossiiskaia guberniia*), which experienced a population increase in 86.4 percent over the 1780s and 1790s, years in which Left Bank Ukraine experienced an increase of just 1.3 percent.[52] Much of the increase in New Russia came at the expense of Left Bank Ukraine, in the form of peasant flight from serfdom. This constituted a geopolitical shift as dramatic as that of the partition of Poland: Ukraine was no longer central to Russian control and exploitation of the Pontic steppe.

The greater frontier security provided by the Ukrainian Line had made it possible by summer 1764 to form New Serbia, Slavonic Serbia, the New Sloboda Cossack Regiment, the Ukrainian Line east of the Dnepr, Bakhmut district, and parts of the Hetmanate territorial regiments of Myrhorod and Poltava into the Governorate of New Russia. Its area at that time had been about three million *desiatiny*, and its first governor at Elizavetgrad (from 1765, at Kremenchug) had been Lt. General Aleksei Mel'gunov. Because of New Russia's militarized administration Mel'gunov and his successors through to 1774 were called commanders-in-chief (*glavnye komandiry*) rather than governors and their military resources depended partly on those shared by the Governor-General of Malorossiia at Kiev. The commandant of Ft. Elizavetgrad garrison had his own chancery and played an important role in governorate administration, which took on even more military responsibilities once Azov and Taganrog were reoccupied by Russian forces and annexed to New Russia in 1769.[53] Most of the settled regiments for regional defense—three hussar regiments, a pikinier regiment, and a Bug Cossack regiment formed from Moldavians and Bulgarians—were concentrated in Elizavetgrad province, Bakhmut, and the lower Bug. During the war New Russia received some further protection when work began on the new Dnepr Line along its border with Zaporozhia. However, Khan Kirim Girei's 1769 invasion of Elizavetgrad province had inflicted losses on its colonists; therefore, in 1773, the governorate's total population was only 162,930 males and females.[54]

New Russia's history entered a new phase in 1774–1775. In 1774 Potemkin became Governor of New Russia; General Ilovaiskii ended the autonomy of the Don Cossack Host, bringing their lands and Bakhmut district into Azov Governorate; and the Treaty of Kuchuk-Kainarji annexed to New Russia Kilburun and the Bessarabian corner of land between the Dnepr and the Bug. In 1775 the Zaporozhian Sich was abolished, its territory brought into New Russia; the empress issued her Statute for the Administration of the Governorates, reorganizing the administration of New Russia and introducing viceroyalties under governors-general; and Potemkin became Viceroy Governor-General over New Russia and Azov Governorate.

With Zaporozhian lawlessness curbed and Crimea no longer vassalized to the Porte, the Pontic coast and steppe were now much safer for Russian colonization, and it could proceed according to the plan already worked out by the empress, Mel'gunov, and Petr Panin a decade earlier: the "Plan for the Colonization of New Russia Governorate," approved by the Senate on April 2, 1764.[55] Its guiding principles were physiocratic: the state should organize and promote accelerated colonization by volunteers accorded the full rights of Russian subjects and endowed with state land held as hereditary private property possessed in perpetuity. The right to settle on state land as colonists applied to foreigners as well as Russians, to group colonies as well as to individuals, and to all social estates except for *odnodvortsy* and private serfs, who lacked the right of mobility to resettle. State peasants could resettle with treasury land allotments provided they got permission from the government. Volunteers would receive settlement subsidies and loans from the state and enjoy a period of immunity from taxes and military service; for an initial period they could also trade duty-free; the treasury lands allotted to them would be standardized in size to facilitate the eventual assessment of land taxes and military service obligations. The state would offer interest-free loans at 6 percent interest and ten years' exemption from customs duties to encourage the settlement of entrepreneurs willing to establish workshops and factories to diversify the economy and provide material support to the army.

More specifically, the Plan called for New Russia to be divided into seventy districts, fifty-two of which were reserved for volunteers ready to take up military service, the rest designated for settling rural farmers and urban *meshchane*. In these seventy districts the arable was divided into 700 land parcels averaging twenty-six *desiatiny* of forested land or thirty *desiatiny* of unforested land, corresponding to what was considered necessary to support a single household. Those volunteers who settled within three years and promised to remain as farmer settlers or soldiers were entitled to hold their parcels for the next six, eight, or sixteen years exempt from land taxes, depending on the productivity of their lands and the hardship of their resettlement circumstances; thereafter they paid *obrok* in the manner of state peasants, as a land tax, but they were not assessed the soul tax. If they took up military service they remained exempt from *obrok* for as long as they were in active service. Those colonists entering military service in New Russia had to have at least two supporting laborers in their households (or four if they were serving in the mounted pikiniers). If they had no male heirs able to take over military service, the land parcel would be turned over to another household that did have such an heir.

Recruitment of volunteers from other parts of Russia and Europe was entrusted to special agents incentivized by rank promotion. Agents who recruited 300 or more settlers into military service (or recruited 600 as farmers) won the rank of major; those who recruited more than 150 into military service won the rank of captain.

Potemkin and the empress were especially interested in resettling foreigners with useful skills, so foreign colonists were invited to settle either in the villages or in the towns, as individual settlers or in group colonies, and were provided with transit funds, interest-free construction loans, up to thirty *desiatiny* of land per household, thirty years' exemption from duties and taxes, and permanent exemption from military or civil service. They were also guaranteed freedom of worship and even freedom to proselytize.[56] The earliest foreign colonists to arrive were Greeks, Moldavians, Wallachians, Bulgarians, and Albanians, many of whom settled in the cavalry regiments. From 1776 Polish Jews were invited to settle, to promote the crafts and trade. In 1778 Suvorov transported to New Russia and Azov 32,000 Greeks and Armenians from Crimea, who resettled in the new towns of Mariupol' and Nakhichevan, and in 1785 Catherine II would extend the resettlement invitation to Danzig merchants and manufacturers unhappy with the oppressive Prussian tariff system.

The Plan also made allowance for the higher social estates to obtain blocs of up to forty-eight land parcels per applicant, for a maximum of 1,440 *desiatiny*. The blocs of land obtained thereby were called *pomest'ia*, and after the lapse of the period of tax immunity their owners paid land tax at half the rate paid by the lower estates. Eventually, it became necessary politically to allow noblemen and wealthy industrialists to obtain more than 1,440 *desiatiny*, and this was done by tacitly permitting them to establish multiple *pomest'ia* at different sites (although Potemkin tried to require them to reside on one of them). The liquidation of the Zaporozhian Sich brought much more land into New Russia, making it possible to enlarge settler land parcels to sixty *desiatiny* per household and *pomeshchik* estates from 1,440 *desiatiny* to 12,000 *desiatiny*.[57] By the 1780s some nobles of high rank had established estates out of treasury land in New Russia, mostly around Elizavetgrad: Bezborodko, Prozorovskii, Viazemskii, and Rumiantsev. Staff officers and higher officials also obtained lands on such scale to make New Russia an "El Dorado … for all those Second-Majors, Registrars, and Archivists."[58]

To foster industry and enlightenment the Plan provided for some revenue sources to found and manage schools, including girls' schools and group homes for orphans.

Potemkin was also committed to using revenue to build roads, canals, and wharfs. But the land tax paid by settlers was dedicated especially to the hussar and pikinier regiments, which were expanded in 1776 from four hussar regiments to nine, and from four pikinier regiments to six (total 10,404 troopers) by enrolling military colonists and former Zaporozhian Cossacks.[59]

Over the years 1774–1784 the New Russia and Azov governorates distributed to settlers and *pomeshchiki* over 4.47 million *desiatiny* of treasury land, endowing 53,511 males at an average of eighty-three *desiatiny* per man.[60] Some of those recipients lived as tenants on *pomest'ia*, but it is interesting that in this period it remained illegal to enserf them; they preserved their freedom to move, and the government offered freedom to fugitive serfs willing to resettle in New Russia and Azov. A decree of May 5, 1779, invited fugitive peasants from Zaporozhia and Ukraine to return within two years and receive parcels of treasury land, personal freedom, and temporary exemption from taxes. In these years estate owners were unable to obtain remands of fugitive serfs resettling in New Russia under the Plan. A decree of April 17, 1780, extended the period of resettlement to such fugitives. As had been the case on the southern Russian frontier between 1635 and 1654, the state's policy of satisfying the nobility's interest in consolidating and perpetuating serfdom was temporarily suspended to favor the state's interest in rapidly settling and securing the frontier. The population of the New Russia and Azov governorates had increased from 162,920 males and females in 1773 to over 530,000 by 1782. About 200,000 of them were treasury peasants on small allotments; but only 4,514 of them were held as private serfs.[61]

The early waves of resettlement occurred primarily in the northern part of New Russia, on forest-steppe above the line running from Voznesensk to the mouth of the Northern Donets, but subsequent waves would begin to exploit the more fertile soil of the steppe south of this line, and they would work it more efficiently using heavy moldboard plows drawn by ox-teams rather than the traditional horse-drawn or man-drawn light *sokha*, which was unable to turn as deep as a slice of topsoil. The southern half of the region produced higher yields and was better suited for growing winter rye, oats, barley, fruit, and vegetables and for livestock grazing. However, before the annexation of Crimea, markets and fairs remained more numerous in the northern part of New Russia.

By 1782 there were ten towns in the New Russia and Azov governorates. Some fortresses along the Ukrainian Line—Belev'sk, for example, which became the *uezd* capital Konstantinograd—had grown into towns with *posad* settlements; Taganrog surpassed old Azov in population, and Forts Aleksandrovsk and Petrovsk had grown into towns. Potemkin had founded entirely new towns to support the Black Sea Fleet and link Black Sea commerce to the New Russian hinterland: Kherson (1778), Pavlograd (1780), and early Ekaterinoslav (1776).[62] Greeks transferred from Crimea founded Mariupol', and Armenians from Crimea settled at Nakhichevan on the lower Don. New towns also arose at Nikopol', on the Dnepr south of the old Zaporozhian Sich, and at Pavlograd on the Vol'chie River.[63] The Greek names given several of these towns reflect Potemkin's intoxication with his Greek Project.

The Black Sea Fleet

With the Russian occupation of the Kerch Straits, the Azov Flotilla along with the Danube Flotilla became part of the Black Sea Fleet.[64] Although it was confined to the Black Sea and could not enter the Dardanelles, it still had an important mission in deterring the Turks from landing forces in Crimea to reestablish the sultan's suzerainty over the Khanate—a threat that remained real as late as 1777. It also could patrol the waters off Ochakov and the eastern coast as far south as Sucuk-Kale to support Russian forces holding the northern Caucasus.

But at the time of the Kuchuk-Kainarji Treaty the fleet had just thirty vessels, its frigates mounting just thirty-two to fifty-eight guns each, and its smaller "new model" two-masted ships only sixteen guns. This was too small a fleet to uphold cruiser operations across the entire Black Sea. The empress' decree of December 11, 1775, committed to find a new wharf near the mouth of the Dnepr for the construction of another twenty large ships of the line, some with sixty-four guns. But to build these bigger, deeper-draft vessels it was necessary to find a new harbor deeper than Taganrog or Kerch or any of the shallow harbors around the mouth of the Don.[65]

Initially Seniavin had selected Glubokaia pristan', an estuary of the Dnepr River, as the site for a new harbor and wharf. But Potemkin decided instead on a site to its north, near Fort Aleksandr-shanets. Here the new port of Kherson was founded in 1778 by Lt. General of Artillery I. A. Gannibal. The following summer construction began on the 66-gun *Slava Ekateriny*, but the shortage of lumber on the lower Dnepr delayed its completion until 1783 and the Kherson shipyard was able to finish and launch only one large warship a year on average before 1787. Kherson and the smaller wharfs on the lower Don did manage to produce fifty-two smaller frigates, pinks, and cutters over 1787–1788, however. Most of this construction that occurred after Ottoman agreement to the Treaty of Aynalikavak brought the war scare of 1777–1779 to an end.[66]

The business of expanding and administering the Black Sea Fleet remained concentrated in Potemkin's hands because of the region's distance from St. Petersburg, which made it necessary to establish a special Black Sea Admiralty Administration and award Potemkin the additional title of General-Admiral.

In 1782 the Turks tried to land troops at Taman' to exploit the rebellion in Crimea against Khan Shahin Girei, but by 1783 they had been driven below the Kuban and Crimea formally annexed to Russia. This presented the need to further expand the Russian Black Sea Fleet, so in May 1783 Counter-Admiral Thomas MacKenzie was instructed to build another new port and town near the Tatar village of Akhtiar on the southwest coast of Crimea. The bay off Akhtiar was large and deep enough to accommodate the biggest line ships and could be easily defended once batteries were established on the overlooking heights; the climate and terrain here also encouraged settlement on a larger scale. The port town at Akhtiar Bay was given the name Sevastopol' (Gk., "Venerable City") and was proclaimed the primary base of the Black Sea Fleet. Captain Fedor Ushakov, future commander of the port and the Black Sea squadron, built a fortress here and Potemkin planned roads connecting Sevastopol' to other parts of Crimea and a canal leading vessels to Kherson. By late 1784 the Sevastopol' squadron numbered a 66-gun line ship (*Slava Ekateriny*), two large frigates, nine frigates of forty-four guns, four frigates of 26–32 guns, two bombardiers, three schooners, two smaller schooners, two sailboats, two pinks, and one commercial vessel. This was large enough to maintain regular cruiser patrols along the route from Sevastopol' to Kafa and Ganzhibei and back.[67]

In 1780 Catherine II took the lead in organizing a League of Armed Neutrality, which aimed at establishing as international law the exemption from blockade of ports not already declared closed to warships of foreign powers, the exemption of nonmilitary goods from seizure as contraband—and Russia's right to use armed squadrons to protect her maritime commerce.[68]

The army under Potemkin

Between 1767 and 1786 the number of infantry increased by 75,000 and the cavalry increased by 30,000, so that by 1786 the total paper strength of the army was about 230,000 infantry (40,750 grenadiers, 128,046 musketeers, 29,940 jaegers, and 14,266 in field battalions) and 62,000 regular cavalry (5,530 cuirassiers, 21,014 carabiniers, 18,820 dragoons, and 16,572 light cavalry).[69] The increase in manpower after the Treaty of Kuchuk-Kainarji was achieved through territorial and population expansion— especially through the extension of recruiting to Ukraine and to the territories annexed from Poland-Lithuania. It was unnecessary in these years to raise the recruitment rate; there were no recruit levies in 1774 or 1775, and the levy rate over 1776–1786 remained stable at just one recruit from every 500 households. On the eve of the empress' second Turkish War, a slightly lower percentage (3.1 percent) of the Empire's population was in military service than had been the case in 1767 (3.3 percent). After the suppression of the Pugachev Revolt, Potemkin had even proposed reducing the term of service to eighteen years, although the Council of State did not implement this.[70]

Although Rumiantsev served as President of the VK from 1775 to 1784, the administration of the army was firmly concentrated in the hands of Potemkin. In 1774 and 1775 Potemkin was promoted to General-*anshef* and director of all light cavalry and irregular forces in the Empire; brought into the Council of State and made Vice-President of the VK; given the title of Count (and from Emperor Joseph II, Serene Prince of the Holy Roman Empire); awarded the orders of Aleksandr Nevskii, St. Andrew, and St. George Second Degree; and appointed Viceroy Governor-General of the New Russia, Azov, and Astrakhan governorates and commander-in-chief of all forces in those territories.[71] In 1784 he was appointed Field Marshal and President of the VK and the new viceroyalty of Tauris (Crimea) was added to his New Russian General-Governorate.

Potemkin had really been *de facto* head of the VK from 1774 and over the next decade he had assumed such great power from his appointments and from the special regard of the empress that the VK essentially ceased to function as a collegial body and assumed quasi-ministerial character. The Council of State also deferred to him in military affairs before the Second Turkish War. This enabled Potemkin to carry out without resistance his projects of enlarging the light cavalry and jaegers and reforming pay and service conditions to ease the lot of common soldiers. But it also led to some disorder because Potemkin was not by temperament inclined to give close attention to routine paperwork and his personal enthusiasms sometimes expressed themselves as favoritism distorting the promotion process. To compensate for these defects, a special Accounting Expedition and Inspectorate Expedition were formed within the VK in 1781 and 1785. The identification, promotion, and education of talented new commanders was also hampered by the weakness of the General Staff, which became essentially defunct after Bauer's departure in 1774.[72]

Under Potemkin, the army remained committed to the division principle because divisional organization had proven consonant with Rumiantsev's and Suvorov's doctrine of squares and attack columns. The experimentation with smaller "legions" and "cohorts" was ended, and in place of the small light "field commands" of the past war, field battalions for local defense were formed on the Ukrainian Line. The practice of shifting settled (*poselennye*) troops into the regular light cavalry continued, with the exception of some settled troops near Azov and Kerch who were reformed as battalions of Cossack infantry. The most important change in the organization of the infantry was the expanded role of the jaegers, which had shown their effectiveness in the last war. In 1777 separate jaeger battalions were established, and in 1785 some of these battalions were united in a Jaeger Corps.

Potemkin had supreme authority over the Empire's light cavalry, and he took advantage of this to increase their proportion relative to the heavy cuirassiers. Cuirassiers lost their breastplates and the only remaining distinction between cuirassiers and carabiniers was that the regiments of the latter had no regimental guns. More carabiniers were fielded by shifting Ukrainian Cossacks into the carabinier regiments. The sharpest departure from past practice was the increase in the number of dragoons (to ten regiments by 1783) and squadrons of dragoon-style "mounted jaegers" and mounted grenadiers. Cavalry regiments were no longer divided into companies; regular cavalry regiments now comprised six squadrons while dragoon regiments comprised ten squadrons.[73]

The VK did not issue any new infantry or cavalry ordinances, so officially the training ordinances of 1763 remained in effect. But in practice Rumiantsev's 1770 *Obriad sluzhby* and Suvorov's training principles were extended to all the southern frontier forces after 1776. This meant preference for the offensive, the adoption of the two-rank firing line, training for attack by bayonet, and practice in the forming of attack columns and squares (big divisional squares were de-emphasized and preference given to smaller regimental, battalion, and company squares). The most through training in such tactics was of course provided by Suvorov for his Kuban and Crimean Corps, which undertook regular maneuvers during 1774–1778. The most important new training precepts issued in this period were for jaeger firing and maneuvers, issued in 1786 and 1788 by Major-General Mikhail Kutuzov to his Jaeger Corps on the Bug River.[74]

Potemkin considered the infantry uniform of the last Turkish War uncomfortable and impractical. In 1783 he suggested some changes which became standard three years later: a shorter, looser coat, and trousers less impeding to movement, the elimination of gaiters and buckles, the elimination of powdered hair and pigtails (which had taken soldiers time to prepare he felt they could better spend catching up on sleep), and the replacement of the clumsy tricorne with a peaked felt casque with wool cross-roll, rather like the "Tarleton" helmet, to better cover the head and protect the neck from rain and sunburn.[75]

Before 1777 it was Russian strategy to avoid provocative actions along the Danube and focus on stabilizing Crimea and building up Russian naval power in the Black Sea. The single most important potential flashpoint for renewed war with the Turks was thought to be the Ottoman fortress at Ochakov, which threatened Kherson and Russian control over Crimea, so there was planning for the possibility of a campaign against Ochakov. After the overthrow of Shahin Girei and the breakdown of relations with the Porte, Russian war plans devoted more attention to besieging Ochakov so as to secure the lower Dnestr, and Potemkin even planned for naval attacks on Sinope and Constantinople by the Black Sea Fleet, but the focus remained on joint army–naval operations defending the Crimean coast. When war broke out again in late 1787, Russian forces in the south were deployed into two armies. A "Ekaterinoslav Army" numbered 132,000 troops in five corps: First Corps at Ekaterinoslav under the personal command of Potemkin, with 40,000 men; a Second Corps at Kherson and Kilburun, under Suvorov, with 18,500 men; a Third Corps in Crimea, under Kakhovskii, with 26,000 men; a Fourth Corps in the Caucasus, under Tekelli, with 30,000 men; and a Fifth Corps in the Kuban, under Rosen, with 12,000 men. The "Ukrainian Line Army," commanded by Rumiantsev, had a paper strength of 58,000 troops: First Corps under Elmpt, 32,000 men; Second Corps under Kamenskii, 15,000 men; and Third Corps under Volkonskii, 13,500 men.[76]

The issue of Russian "protection" of the Christian millets

The terms of the Kuchuk-Kainarji Treaty required that Russian forces evacuate Moldavia and Wallachia and that the principalities be placed again under the suzerainty of the sultan. Catherine II had abandoned her demand, made in 1771, that Russia be given occupation of Moldavia and Wallachia for twenty-five years as part of the Porte's indemnity; at Kuchuk-Kainarji she lifted the Russian military occupation despite the losses her armies had incurred against the Turkish garrisons and despite her own past manifestoes offering the Moldavians and Wallachians liberation and protection.

This is testimony to the exhaustion of the Russian army by 1774 and the urge to achieve a quick peace. It may also have reflected the difficulties the Russians had encountered in administering occupied Moldavia and Wallachia during the war, when the *diwan* councils were polarized between boyar factions making unfamiliar demands and the principalities were paralyzed by war devastation and pestilence.

Over the next decade Moldavia and Wallachia mattered much less to Catherine II than Russian relations with Crimean Khanate.[77] Then in the mid-1780s, she began exercising more aggressively her perceived right to "protect" the principalities against Ottoman oppression.

The first postwar Phanariot hospodar of Moldavia, Grigore III Ghica (r. 1774–1777) had been assassinated by agents of the Porte under mysterious circumstances, either because he was suspected of being too pliable toward the Russians, because he tried to block the Austrian annexation of Bukovina, or because his introduction of salary remuneration for officials threatened the corruption regime binding Moldavia to Ottoman elites. But Russian historiography has not been fair in stating that from the beginning the Porte tried to renege upon the pledges to the Moldavians and Wallachians imposed by Article XVI of the Kuchuk-Kainarji Treaty. On the contrary, the period from 1774 to 1787 was one of significant reform in the Danubian principalities, particularly in Wallachia, where the Phanariot Alexander Ypsilanti ruled as hospodar from 1774 to 1782. The hospodars were generally careful to avoid provoking civil unrest or Russian protest; they kept tax and tribute rates stable and payment schedules regular, and they tried to satisfy demands that confiscated lands be returned to the monasteries and boyars. Wallachia under Hospodar Alexander Ypsilanti (r. 1774–1782) saw the greater reform: Ypsilanti introduced salary remuneration for public officials, simplified tax laws, founded charitable institutions, and issued a comprehensive code of administrative and judicial law.[78] The hospodars in these years had to contend with divisions within the boyar nobility and head off controversies that might excite Russian or Austrian protest, but they had in their favor a significant economic revival as their principalities were reintegrated into the Ottoman and European commercial networks. This economic boom made it enable Istanbul to hold back from making exorbitant new fiscal demands upon the principalities.[79]

An indication of how willing Istanbul was to avoid provocation was the Aynalikavak Treaty of 1779, which tried to defuse the crisis in the Crimean Khanate and bound the Porte to recognize Shahin Girei as Khan. On the subject of the Danubian principalities this treaty reaffirmed Kuchuk-Kainarji: the sultan's tribute was to be imposed "with moderation and humility," to be collected very two years; the hospodars and their high officials were to be Orthodox Christians; and Russia was supposed to limit its right of representation "solely to conserve the conditions specified."[80]

Russo–Ottoman relations concerning the Danubian principalities began to deteriorate in 1781 when Russia finally established consuls in Iaşi and Bucharest in response to merchants' complaints about rights of passage across the border. The sultan's government, possibly encouraged by the French ambassador Saint-Priest, protested the appointment of S. L. Lashkarev as Consul. He was finally accredited and allowed to reside at Bucharest, and I. I. Severin was subsequently recognized as Russian Consul at Iaşi. Both consuls began working to win over the hospodars as political allies and build support among the boyars and churchmen for the idea of Russia as a more active protector. They were especially successful in winning the support of Moldavian hospodars Alexander Mavrocordatos Delibey (r. 1782–1785) and Alexander

Mavrocordatos Firaris (r. 1785–1786). In 1784 the Russian ambassador in Istanbul, Ia. I. Bulgakov, protested the sultan's plan to replace Delibey before the lapse of his term and announced that Delibey and his family would be given Russian refuge and citizenship. The next year Bulgakov protested the replacement of Mavrocordatos Firaris and Wallachian Hospodar Mihai Draco-Suțu. The sultan responded in 1787 with a memorandum to Catherine II demanding that she replace her vice-consul in Iași.[81]

The more aggressive stance taken by the Russian consuls in the 1780s may have been connected with Russia's intensified competition with Austria for spheres of influence in the Danubian principalities. Austrian consulates in Moldavia and Wallachia were established in 1783, and Prussian consulates were founded in 1785. In 1771 Thugut's proposed Austro–Ottoman alliance had aimed at getting the Turks to cede back Oltenia (Lesser Wallachia), held by the Austrians between 1714 and 1739; St. Petersburg had agreed to it in 1772, to cement the agreement to partition Poland; and the 1774 Kuchuk-Kainarji Treaty had acknowledged it. In September 1774 Emperor Joseph I annexed Bukovina as well, on the grounds that it had once been part of Podolia, which Austria had taken in its partition of Poland, and because it offered a corridor linking Transylvania with Galicia.[82] The Porte ceded Bukovina to Austria by the Convention of Pera in May 1775. This met with no protest from Catherine's government, from Nikita Panin or anyone else. But the recognition that Austria was pursuing further territorial advantage from the defeat of the Ottoman Empire gave the empress additional reason to develop a scheme to contain and channel that aggrandizement by providing Austria and Russia with mutual satisfaction in delineated spheres of influence produced by partitioning the Ottoman domains in the Balkans. In the event of resumed war with the Turks, Catherine reasoned, let it be conducted with the ultimate aim of a partition of the Ottoman Empire—a kind of payback for Austrian and Prussian insistence in 1772 that the partition of Poland be the price for their continued acquiescence to her last Turkish War. This was part of the logic behind her "Greek Project" emerging over 1779–1782.

The Greek Project has intrigued historians for a number of reasons. It illustrated the extent to which the enlightenment was able to mine classical literature and ancient history for inspiration for political action—rediscovering and romanticizing the heroic potential of the Greek nation, for example. Its vision of a Byzantine Empire restored to glory by Russian feats of arms was truly grandiose, and it raises the question of how Catherine II's Turkish Wars helped lay some of the foundations for the Greek and Serbian revolutions in the early nineteenth century.

Potemkin was a major source of inspiration for the Greek Project. Catherine II's second grandson, born to Grand Duke Paul and Mariia Fedorovna in 1779, had been christened Konstantin Pavlovich, and Potemkin, whose influence with the empress was then at its peak, had encouraged her to give Konstantin Pavlovich a Greek nurse, have him taught Greek, and prepare him for the destiny of ruling his own Eastern Empire as a new Constantine. "Prince Potemkin … is continually occupied with the raising of an Empire in the East," wrote the English ambassador James Harris, and he had "infected the Empress with these sentiments."[83] Potemkin was an ardent Hellenophile, had a thorough education in the classics and Greek theology, and had been a proponent of settling émigré Greeks within the Empire; he had appointed the Greek intellectual Eugenios Voulgaris as first archbishop in the new city of Kherson (Chersonesos). The 1780 *Notes on Political Affairs* laying out the elements of the Greek Project were less likely the work of secretary Aleksandr Bezborodko than Potemkin's dictation to Bezborodko.[84]

As laid out in the *Notes*, the Greek Project envisioned a successful war against the already weakened Porte, conducted by Russia and Austria in military alliance, and resulting in the partition of the Ottoman Empire. Russia would be awarded Crimea, the northern Caucasus, the northwestern Black Sea coast, including Ochakov, and some island bases in the Aegean. Austria would receive additional parts of Wallachia, Serbia, Bosnia, Herzegovina, and the Venetian provinces of Dalmatia and Istria. Two new independent states would be created: parts of Wallachia, Moldavia, and Bucak would form a new kingdom of Dacia, to be ruled by Prince Potemkin, while Greece, Macedonia, and Bulgaria would become a revived Greek Empire ruled from Constantinople by Catherine II's grandson Konstantin Pavlovich. Dacia and the Greek Empire would maintain the balance of power in southeastern Europe by serving as buffers between Russia and Austria; Konstantin Pavlovich would renounce all claims to the Russian throne. French acquiescence to such a partition would have to be obtained, of course; to win it Joseph II suggested compensating France with Egypt.

This was not an entirely original fantasy. There had been a long history of Russian rhetoric about the conquest of Constantinople, the liberation of the Balkan Christians, and the rollback of the Hagarites to their Asian deserts. Such rhetoric had been heard during Peter's Azov campaigns and his Prut expedition, in Ostermann's memoranda, in Münnich's 1736 report predicting a short victorious war ending in the Russian occupation of Constantinople, and more recently in Münnich's 1768 memorandum to Catherine II. Voltaire had been tireless in urging Catherine to crush Turkish "barbarism" and restore civilization to the Greeks: "Nature destined you to rule over Greece. In ten years' time...the Turkish Empire will be partitioned, and you will have Sophocles' *Oedipus* performed at Athens."[85] Catherine herself had employed such rhetoric in her 1770 instructions for Orlov on his Archipelago Expedition: "Having united various Greek peoples under your leadership, make of them something visible as quickly as possible...that would appear to the world as a new and complete people," conveying to the world the message that "the numerous Greek peoples, by God's will subjected to the heavy yoke of Hagarene iniquity...have joined together, constituting a new member of the Christian republic."[86]

Catherine II hinted at but did not fully reveal the details of her Greek Project during her 1780 summit with Joseph II; her priority at that time was securing an alliance with Austria, more possible now that the ever-suspicious Maria Theresa was dead and Joseph II bent once again upon annexing Bavaria. Joseph II wrote to Count von Cobenzl that he had learned, "Russia with us, and we with Russia, can achieve anything we like, but without each other we find it difficult to achieve anything important and worthwhile."[87] The prospect of winning more territorial gains in a war of alliance with Russia against the Porte appealed to him, as did the idea of further marginalizing Prussia. The terms of a Russo–Austrian alliance against the Porte were worked out in an exchange of letters over 1781 but kept secret for the next two years, and then the Greek Project in its full grandiosity, with its provisions for the partition of the Ottoman Empire, was revealed to the emperor in September 1782. It may be that Joseph's acceptance of the scheme finally emboldened Catherine II to the risky action of abandoning Shahin Girei and annexing Crimea in 1783.

This put the final nail in the coffin of Panin's Northern Accord. The empress had shed her partnership with Prussia (although it remained in her pact of Armed Neutrality) and subordinated Baltic interests to Potemkin's proposed Eastern System, a far more ambitious campaign of Russian power aggrandizement in the Black Sea, Caucasus, and eastern Mediterranean.[88]

But the Greek Project would not actually shape Russian strategy in the 1787–1791 Turkish War. Catherine II and Potemkin may have been earnest about it as a program, but it was never translated into a plan of military operations. There was no opportunity to do so; Russia had begun the war financially unprepared to carry it out; the empress admitted to S. R. Vorontsov, her ambassador to England, that Russian finances could not support a war on such a scale, so "the possibility of executing the grand plan … is quite remote."[89] Kaunitz doubted the Greek Project was achievable and preferred that the war come to an early end favorable to Austrian interests without destroying the Ottoman Empire. Political considerations also militated against the Project: by the summer of 1790 any hope of arranging French complicity in the partition of the Ottoman Empire had been dashed by the French Revolution; Austria had left the war and signed a peace treaty with the Turks at Sistova, following the death of Joseph II and the outbreak of revolt in the Low Countries; and the Polish Diet, encouraged by Prussia, had acclaimed a new Constitution and demanded the withdrawal of Russian forces from Poland. There was no possibility of carrying the war into Greece or bringing Russian forces up to Constantinople. Potemkin was not greatly disturbed by collapse of his Greek Project: it had served its purpose for a few years, to get Emperor Joseph II to align with Russia, and to isolate Prussia; and already in 1785 he had assured Comte de Ségur, the French ambassador, that the Project was just a chimera.[90]

Catherine II and Potemkin may have indulged wishful fantasies about the Greek Project up to their deaths—the empress insisted that the renewal of the Austro–Russian alliance in 1793 give lip service to it—but the Project was unlikely thereafter to be revived and made policy. Emperor Paul was very opposed to it, as were most Russian ministers.[91]

But it was true that from 1768 Russia had established closer links with the Greeks as well as Balkan Slavs and was helping to promote the emerging national liberation movement in Greece. The Orlovs' Archipelago expedition had put together an intelligence and political agitation network across the eastern Mediterranean, and by the 1780s Russia had consulates in several Ottoman cities that worked to strengthen links between the Orlov network and Greek prelates and notables.[92] Certain useful figures later played leading roles in the Greek Revolution had been identified and given Imperial patronage.[93] After 1774 there was a mass exodus of Greeks to the Russian Empire. Orlov resettled some of his Greek Aegean veterans at the Kerch garrison; in the 1780s and 1790s Potemkin, as Governor-General of New Russia and *de facto* Satrap of the South, resettled great numbers of Greeks in the new cities he built at Kherson, Ekaterinoslav, Nikolaev, and Odessa. By permitting Greek merchants to sail under the Russian flag, the Kuchuk-Kainarji Treaty had positioned Greek merchants and captains to become the principal carriers in Russia's grain export trade. The idea of Russian commitment to the liberation of the Greeks and the revival of Greek glory was celebrated in the works of such Greek émigré poets as Voulgaris and Antonii Palladoklis as well as the Russian poets Mikhail Kheraskov and Vasilii Petrov.[94]

Meanwhile, the ability of the sultan's central government to police the Balkans was hampered by the rise of the Valley Lords (*derebeys*), provincial *ayan* whose power had been greatly enhanced by the military responsibilities given them in the war of 1768–1774. By the 1780s and 1790s *derebey* warlords like Osman Pazvantoglu, Pasha of Vidin, and Ali Pasha of Janina were acting independently of central government control and expanding their own authority over large parts of Greece, Serbia, and Albania.

The problem of Poland

In 1772 the Russian ambassador to Warsaw, Otto Magnus von Stackelberg, had exerted great pressure on Poland's King Stanisław August to get the Partition ratified by the Polish Diet. Stackelberg continued to "manage" the Commonwealth for Catherine II until 1788. He was generally smoother and less bullying in his conduct toward King Stanisław than had been his predecessor, Repnin, and he was not adverse in allowing some limited reforms that would strengthen the king's authority vis-à-vis the *Familja*, the Hetmans, and the Diet—as long as such reforms kept the Commonwealth politically stable and tranquil. In 1775 he therefore pressed King Stanisław to establish a Permanent Council (*Rada Nieustająca*) to manage state affairs in the intervals between Diets and to bring greater continuity and cabinet coordination to the royal government. The Permanent Council had five departments, internal affairs, foreign affairs, finance, the army, and justice; half of its thirty-six members could be selected by the king, while the other half was "recommended" by Stackelberg and the Russian government. Stackelberg also permitted the king to establish a Commission for National Education, the Pope's 1773 bull abolishing the Jesuit Order having now created the opportunity for Stanisław to use the wealth and the colleges of the Jesuits to endow a national educational system. The special Diet commission Repnin that had created to adjudicate conflicts with Dissidents was dismantled and Stackelberg leaned on Protestant leaders to make some concessions reducing religious tensions (made easier by the fact that the majority of the Commonwealth's Protestants were now in the Prussian partition). In 1717 the size of the army had been constitutionally capped at 18,000 Polish and 6,000 Lithuanian troops; in 1776 that was raised to 30,000 men, despite the Commonwealth's reduced population, and over the next several years, Jan Komarzewski, the Director of the Military Office, modernized the army's equipment and training and ended the practice of buying officer commissions. Komarzewski liquidated the old *husarz* and *pancerz* trains in favor of regular cavalry brigades, introduced division organization, and made soldiers' pay more regular. The Crown and Field Hetmans were placed under tight control by the Military Office.[95] Some mitigation of the Crown's financial crisis was also promised when Stackelberg gave his approval to significantly raise the state budget to 29 million *złotys* in 1775.[96]

King Stanisław's distribution of honorific posts and Stackelberg's largesse with Russian subsidies packed the 1776 Diet enough to get these measures ratified. But there were ominous disturbances in several provincial dietines preceding the Diet, and after 1776 political factionalism became harder to manage as it had grown increasingly complicated. The Russian Party formed through Stackelberg's money was only up to a point the King's Party, and Stanisław was quite aware of this. The *Familja* was no longer headed by the Czartoryskis but by Stanisław Lubomirski, son-in-law of August Czartoryski, and the *Familja* had intermarried with Ignacy and Stanisław Potocki and Seweryn Rzewuski, formerly its enemies. Crown Grand Hetman Franciszek Ksawery Branicki also now allied with the *Familja* in reaction to Komarzewski's limitation of the authority of the hetmans. The *Familja* continued to assail Stackelberg for suppressing Polish liberties and the king for failing to defend those liberties, although as yet it advanced no plan as to how to undo the Partition or what to put in place of Poniatowski's monarchy. Austria sought political advantage through the *Familja*, counting on the fact that the Czartoryskis and Rzewuskis owned great estates in Galicia. To further complicate the situation Potemkin was also courting the support of the *Familja*. Potemkin had bought vast lands in Kiev Palatinate, north of Kiev and around Kremenchug and Uman', and by the early 1780s he had settled these estates with over 112,000 serfs and received royal certification as a Polish noble. In 1775 he had become the political patron of Grand Hetman Branicki, who had fallen out with King Stanisław. In 1781 Branicki became Potemkin's nephew-in-law. The two of them may have intrigued against the king by recruiting the Potockis and Rzewuskis into a project to raise Cossack forces and form a Confederation to defend Poland in the event of a new Turkish War. After Potemkin's death his niece Countess Alexandra Branicka stated that Potemkin had planned "to win over all the Cossacks, unite with the Polish Army, and proclaim himself king of Poland."[97] As with the Greek Project, Potemkin may only have been keeping his future political options open in the event of future crises, but his encouragement of the *Familja* worked at cross purposes with Catherine's efforts to sustain King Stanisław through the guidance of Stackelberg. The political situation was uneasy enough that Stackelberg urged the empress to continue to keep Russian troops in Poland until 1780. Meanwhile, King Stanisław was blocked by both the empress and Potemkin from building a strong party of his own. He could use appointments and art patronage to build a network of clients, but Stackelberg would not allow his followers to coalesce around any political program.

Another destabilizing factor was Prussia. In the first few years after the First Partition, Frederick II had focused on exploiting economically his West Prussian partition to the point of using his customs officials to strangle Poland's grain export down the Vistula to Danzig. Tariffs on Polish imports were more than doubled and in certain years imports of Polish grain were forbidden outright. This hurt the lesser *szlachta* the most, as the great magnates of the *Familja* had vast estates in the south and could still export to the Austrians or the Russians.[98]

Reports of the 1781 alliance between Austria and Russia enraged Frederick II. He feared that it would embolden Joseph II to challenge him for hegemony over the German states. He responded by organizing a League of Princes uniting Prussia, Hanover, Saxony, and several lesser Protestant states to block Austria's designs on Bavaria and present Prussia as the natural defender of German liberties. After his death on August 17, 1786, his successor King Frederick William II moved to develop ties with the opposition in Poland as a counterweight to Russian and Austrian influence. Such a Prussian Party might be used either to position Prussia to mediate in the event of another Russo-Turkish War or even to ally Prussia with England, Sweden, Turkey, and a "liberated" Poland to roll back Austrian power in the east. The new Prussian ambassador to Warsaw, Ludwig Büchholtz, agitated to raise dissatisfaction with the king and anger toward the Russians, and Ignacy Potocki and other leaders of the *Familja* welcomed Büchholtz's support and began to propagandize for Prussia as the new defender of Polish liberties. But to mobilize the lesser *szlachta* in the dietines and mount a disciplined opposition in the next Diet they had to remake themselves ideologically. Potocki met with Adam Czartoryski and other *Familja* magnates at Karlsbad in 1786 and developed plans to form "a new party, a Patriotic Congress, that would win a majority in the Seym, confederate, abolish the monarchy and establish a Quattuorvirate (Czartoryski, Potocki, Karol Radziwiłł, and Seweryn Rzewuski) which would rule the country."[99]

Sultan Abdul Hamid I's declaration of war on Russia on August 24, 1787, broke the political stalemate in the Commonwealth and united the *Familja* with the lesser *szlachta* in a Patriotic Opposition in the Diet of 1788. The Diet defied expectations and refused to dissolve after its six-week term; instead it confederated under Marshal Stanisław Małachowski, forced the king and Stackelberg to withdraw a bill for a formal Russo-Polish alliance against the Turks, demanded that Russia withdraw its forces from Right Bank Ukraine, and got the Diet to order the expansion of the Commonwealth Army to 100,000 troops.[100]

The last days of the Crimean Khanate

Although Devlet Girei's campaign to raise a revolt against the Russians in Kuban had been approved by the sultan before the Treaty of Kuchuk-Kainarji, it continued to build in the months after the Turks had signed the treaty. The Cherkess and Abaza tribes inhabiting the mountains below the Kuban steppe had not been asked to ratify the khanate's "protectorate" over Kabarda and still considered themselves Ottoman subjects; the Yedichkul Nogai Horde in the Kuban preferred to support Devlet Girei over Khan Sahip Girei; and Sahip Girei himself was suspicious of the Russians and so disinclined to cooperate too far with them he even imprisoned the Russian resident, P. P. Veselitskii. Devlet Girei and his supporters were therefore able to land in Crimea and occupy Kafa, forcing Sahip Girei to flee to Ottoman Rumelia.[101]

Although Devlet Girei sent envoys to Istanbul to ask the sultan to annul the Treaty of Kuchuk-Kainarji and send a fleet and army to expel the Russians from Crimea, the Porte took no military measures other than to retain troops in Taman' as a counterweight to Russian forces in the Kuban, so the Russian government decided for the time being to recognize Devlet Girei as khan but keep in reserve a more favorable alternative: young Shahin Girei, who had played a major role in arranging the 1772 Karasubazar Agreement establishing Crimea's independence under Russian protection. It had been agreed in October 1774 that Russia would support Shahin Girei with 100,000 rubles to form his own separate government over the Nogais in the Kuban, and Shahin Girei saw in this the opportunity to someday lead a Nogai army to retake Crimea and enthrone himself as Crimean Khan. The empress' Council of State reasoned that the Turks lacked the military resources to intervene and overthrow Shahin Girei, and the numerical superiority of the Kuban Nogais would discourage Devlet Girei and the Crimean Tatar nobles from moving against him.[102]

The Turks had been required by the terms of the Kuchuk-Kainarji Treaty to turn over their garrison on the Taman' Peninsula to the Crimean Khanate. They had not yet done so, however, so Shahin Girei convinced St. Petersburg to give him another 50,000 rubles to organize the Nogais for an attack on the Turkish garrison. Concerns about how the Porte would respond deterred an actual attack, but the Russians began building up their forces along the Perekop Line, at Azov, and in the Kuban, and a few hundred Russian troops under Brigadier Brink were attached to Shahin Girei's Nogai army in the Kuban in 1775. With the help of Russian troops Shahin Girei secured a base at Kopyl'. Meanwhile, Russian diplomacy tried to reason with the Turks to withdraw their support from Devlet Girei on the grounds that the Nogais, subjects of the Crimean Khanate, had not participated in Devlet's election as khan.[103]

But Devlet Girei had been underestimated. His support among the Crimean *ulema* and some Nogai tribes remained firm, and in the winter he sent troops into the Kuban and defeated Shahin Girei's forces near Kopyl'. The Yedisan Horde now joined the Yedichkul Horde in supporting Devlet Girei, and Devlet Girei received from the sultan in April 1776 a more formal patent of investiture not only confirming him as khan but stating that the Treaty of Kuchuk-Kainarji had been nullified and the khanate was once again under Ottoman protection. However, the Porte was too preoccupied with preparations for a Persian campaign to send Devlet Girei any actual military support at this time other than to maintain a few hundred troops at Taman' and increase its garrison at Ochakov.

The empress' Council of State had become divided as to how to deal with the Crimean crisis: Nikita Panin urged diplomacy and avoidance of armed force, while Grand Chancellor Aleksandr Bezborodko called for stronger measures to take Crimea under control. Catherine II sided with Bezborodko, calculating that French preoccupation with the war in the North American colonies reduced the risk of conflict with the Porte drawing in France. The regiments on the Perekop Line were reinforced and a corps stationed in Kuban, support to Shahin Girei was strengthened, and Shahin Girei's project for an elite Besli Guard trained in the European manner was approved and provided with arms from Tula. On November 21 Russia resorted to armed force: a corps of about 15,000 troops under General Prozorovskii captured the fortress of Or-Kapi without resistance. This incursion was explained to the Crimean notables as necessary because the Turks had violated the Kuchuk-Kainarji Treaty by refusing to evacuate Taman'. Iakup Aga, a Russian informant in Bakhchisarai, kept Prozorovskii and Rumiantsev posted as to the defection of the Shirin and Mansur clans to Shahin Girei's cause. Notables from other clans, including the Girei house, began emigrating from Crimea in anticipation of the spread of civil war to the Crimean peninsula.[104]

In January 1777 Shahin Girei attempted to seize the Taman' garrison by force, hoping this would broaden his support among the Kuban Nogais. But his attack failed, costing him heavy losses in manpower and strategic credibility. Fortunately, a change in government at Istanbul—the replacement of Grand Vizier Mehmed Dervish Pasha by Darendeli Mehmed Pasha, a supporter of Ahmed Resmi Efendi and a proponent of peace with Russia—finally pressed Devlet Girei to abdicate, along with Prozorovskii's long-delayed march on Bakhchisarai. Devlet Girei departed for Istanbul in March 1777. Shahin Girei assumed power as khan the following month.[105]

Shahin Girei had much in common with the autocratic modernizers Sultan Selim III and the Egyptian Khedive Muhammad Ali Pasha: he sought to build a more centralized, autocratic regime and tame the notables and *ulema* through a modernization campaign inspired by the European Enlightenment. He packed the *diwan* and excluded from it the clerics and the heads of the more recalcitrant clans. He tightened control over the *ulema* through his *mufti* and *kadiasker*. He replaced the old system of local administration, managed by the beys of the more powerful clans, with a new system headed by forty-four *kaimakam*s, appointed deputies of the khan. He confiscated *vakif* properties to carry out a land reform endowing the Tatar peasantry, and he introduced income-graduated taxes to be paid directly by land tenants past their mirza and bey landlords. The landlords were expected to continue paying to the treasury their traditional tax of one-tenth of the produce from their estates. The lands of Tatar notables who had fled Crimea reverted to the khan's treasury. Shahin Girei asked St. Petersburg for masons and craftsmen who could build a new palace at Bakhchisarai in the European style—at great expense. He also moved to expand his Besli Guard into a regular standing New Model army of 20,000 men equipped, uniformed, and trained along European lines, to be formed by levying recruits at the rate of one man from every five households.[106]

Such measures did increase the khan's revenue to an annual average of 345,612 rubles, of which 138,561 rubles were spent on administration and 85,000 on the court.[107] But imposing these reforms required unquestioned political supremacy that Shahin Girei had not yet obtained for himself, and certain features of the reforms outraged the Tatar elite and masses. His new tax regime had to be run through tax-farming, and the khan had sold tax-farming rights at Kafa, Gozlev, and Or-Kapi to a Christian Greek merchant, Mavroeni.[108] The *ulema* were distressed to see tax rates equalized for Muslims, Christians, and Karaim Jews and to see their *vakif*s confiscated while the monastery lands were not. The khan's military recruiting proved all the more unpopular when Muslim recruits learned that they would be serving in the new Besli regiments alongside

Christian recruits. The Russian government's resettlement at Yenikale of 1,200 Greek veterans of Orlov's Aegean campaign under thirty years' tax immunity and other special privileges sparked conflict with their jealous Tatar neighbors.[109] Shahin Girei had made new friends among the Christian and Jewish millets in Crimea but had alienated many of the Muslim Tatars. At court he was surrounded by Christian advisors; when venturing out he traveled in a European carriage; and rumors spread among the Tatar clerics and the Ottoman grand vizier that he had become an apostate. The Ottoman *şeykhülislam* considered him a "swine and a dog."[110]

The disorder near Yenikale eventually spread to Bakhchisarai, where the khan's palace was plundered and his vizier killed. Members of the Besli Guard went over to the rebels. Report came that the former Khan Selim III Girei, supported by 7,000 Turkish soldiers from Ochakov, had landed near Gozlev. Prozorovskii was forced to use Russian troops to put down the rebellion and to surround Selim Girei and place him under arrest. But suppressing the rebellion cost more than 12,000 dead. General Antoine de Balmain unleashed the Greek colonists from Yenikale upon the Tatar villages along the coast; at Kafa they slaughtered over six hundred Tatar men, women, and children and torched the town. The Kuban Nogais, especially the Yedichkul Horde, turned against Shahin Girei, and his brothers Arslan and Batyr offered themselves to the Nogais as leaders. In April 1778 the Ottoman sultan declared Shahin Girei an apostate and decided to send a larger force to Crimea to defend the faith. Suvorov's corps managed to prevent it from landing; the Turkish expeditionary force lost seven ships and 7,000 troops in failed attempts to win a beachhead on the coast. Ahmet Resmi Efendi opposed the expedition, which he considered yet another instance in which the "Ottoman treasury has been squandered in vain."[111] Finally, the French envoy Saint-Priest and the Russian envoy Stakhiev convinced the sultan's diwan that the Porte lacked the military resources to risk a full-scale war with Russia. In January 1779 Ottoman envoys signed a convention at Aynalikavak acknowledging Shahin Girei as khan on condition that both Russia and the Porte withdraw all forces from Crimea within three months and Shahin Girei recognize the sultan as his guardian in religious affairs.[112]

Suvorov, commanding Russian forces in the Kuban, saw the formation of a Nogai opposition around Batyr Girei as a threat to Russian interests in Kabarda. In 1777–1778 he occupied the entire right bank of the Kuban River and began building a series of new fortresses (Kopyl', Mar'insk, Aleksandrovsk, and Novotroitsk) to link up with Mozdok and deter attack by Batyr's Nogai allies.[113]

The withdrawal of Russian troops from the Crimean peninsula was completed by June 1779. This left Shahin Girei more vulnerable to reprisals. But the Christian millet in Crimea also feared reprisal for their role in the massacres at Yenikale and Kafa; they communicated this to Rumiantsev through the Karaim Rabbi, and Rumiantsev instructed Prozorovskii to persuade the Crimean Christians to leave with the departing Russian army and resettle in Russia. By the fall over 31,000 Crimean Greeks and Armenians had emigrated to Azov Governorate.[114] This left Shahin Girei even more isolated and reduced his tax revenue. He asked Potemkin for 100,000 rubles in compensation.[115] Yet at this point Shahin Girei embarked upon his most dangerous project yet. He tried to strengthen his position by campaigning in the North Caucasus: against the Cherkess and Abaza, to place Kabarda under the control of the khanate; against the Nogais in the Kuban, to remove the challenge to his power from his brothers Arslan and Batyr; and in Taman', to intimidate the Turks into abandoning their fortress at Sucuk-Kale.

Naturally, Istanbul responded by sending agents to agitate among the Nogais, Cherkess, and Abaza. By 1780–1781 a new revolt against Shahin Girei swept across the Kuban region. It threatened to link up with the Kabardans dislocated by the construction of Suvorov's new fortified line. It provoked Crimean Muslims to send deputations to St. Petersburg to complain about oppression at the hands of Shahin Girei. Russian troops in the Kuban managed to contain but not extinguish the revolt there.[116]

On May 26, 1782, Rumiantsev received at Kremenchug a report from Major-General Iazykov in Crimea.[117] A party of Tatars from Taman' led by Halim Girei had landed in Crimea, linked up with Shahin Girei's Crimean opponents, and marched on Kafa, forcing Shahin Girei to flee to Yenikale. They had proclaimed Batyr Girei the new khan and were preparing to bring him over from the Kuban.[118]

Catherine II sent Russian troops back into Crimea to restore Shahin Girei. General de Balmain seized Or-Kapi and marched on Bakhchisarai, and even Potemkin landed at Kafa. The rebels were defeated, Halim Girei arrested, and Shahin Girei reinstalled, this time under a new minder, resident S. L. Lashkarev. But it had become clear to St. Petersburg that Shahin Girei could only be kept on the throne by military force, and the brutality with which he retaliated against his enemies showed that he would continue to provoke opposition and isolate himself.[119] Catherine instructed Stackelberg to tell Shahin Girei, "As Our generosity and kindness is not only meant for him, but for all the Crimean peoples, he must stop this shocking and cruel treatment and not give them just cause for a new revolt."[120] Through Iakup Aga Potemkin began negotiating with leaders of the Shirin clan to explore the deposition of Shahin Girei. By December 1782, Potemkin and the empress were ready to remove Shahin Girei, nullify Crimean independence, and annex Crimea to restore order and preserve their investments in the Kuban and the new naval base at Sevastopol'.

The annexation of Crimea

Even before the revolt against Shahin Girei Potemkin had urged Catherine II to annex Crimea to the Russian Empire. As an independent state no longer under Ottoman suzerainty the khanate still "creates a breach in our borders … Now, just imagine that the Crimea is yours and no longer a thorn in your side; suddenly our frontier situation becomes splendid: along the Bug the Turks adjoin us directly and therefore have to deal with us themselves and not use others as a cover. Here we can see every step they take. As for the Kuban side, in addition to a dense series of forts manned with garrisons the numerous Don Host is always in readiness. The security of the population of New Russia would then be beyond doubt; navigation on the Black Sea would be free … We should rid ourselves of the difficulties of maintaining the forts we now have in remote outposts in Crimea ... Believe me, you will acquire immortal fame such as no other sovereign of Russia ever had ... With the Crimea will come domination of the Black Sea; it will be in your power to blockade the Turks, to feed them or to starve them." He concluded by invoking the origin of Russian Orthodox Christianity in Prince Vladimir's baptism at Crimean Chersonesus and how the empress' annexation of Crimea would restore "the peace of a Christian rule" to Kherson of Taurida. In the fall of 1780 Potemkin had submitted to Grand Chancellor Bezborodko a memorandum recommending the annexation of Crimea.[121]

On April 8, 1783, Catherine II decreed the annexation of the Crimea, the Taman' peninsula, and the right bank of the Kuban River to the Russian Empire.[122] Her manifesto cited the inability of the khanate's inhabitants since independence to enjoy the fruits of their freedom. The task of garrisoning and maintaining order in the khanate had cost twenty million rubles and many lives, and independent Crimea had continued to spark disputes between Russia and the Porte; now the attempt by Ottoman troops to occupy Sucuk-Kale on the Taman' peninsula and declare its inhabitants Ottoman subjects "has nullified our former mutual obligations concerning the freedom and independence of the Tatar peoples ... and restores to us all those rights which we acquired by our victories in the last war." The inhabitants of Crimea were to "make every effort to liken themselves to our ancient subjects in loyalty, zeal and moral conduct." In return "we make a sacred and unshakeable promise pledged on behalf of ourselves and our successors upon the throne to maintain them on a basis of equality with our hereditary subjects and to preserve and defend their persons, property, temples, and ancestral faith ... and to allow each social condition among them all those rights and privileges enjoyed by the corresponding condition in Russia."

This might have provoked the government of Sultan Abdul Hamid I and Grand Vizier Halil Hamid Pasha to declare war, especially as it came atop other outrageous provocations: the implicit threat in Potemkin's Greek Project, the Russian protectorate just established over Kartli-Kakheti, Russian operations in the North Caucasus, and the efforts of Russian consuls to suborn the Moldavian and Wallachian hospodars. The expansion of Russian power in the Black Sea and eastern Mediterranean had alarmed the French and English governments. But they were preoccupied with the war in America and cautioned the sultan to exercise restraint, pointing out that an Ottoman declaration of war upon Russia might spur Joseph II to war in the western Balkans. Halil Hamid Pasha was also concerned that the Ottoman army and fleet were not yet strong enough to retake Crimea. On January 9, 1784, the Ottoman representatives at Aynalikavak signed a new convention acknowledging the Russian annexation of Crimea.[123] A sign of Potemkin's personal commitment in retaining and developing Crimea was that he had already dispatched his personal envoy to the Porte, Iakov Bulgakov, to monitor the war party within the sultan's diwan and offer further talks to head off conflict.[124]

The commander of Russian forces in Crimea, General de Balmain, had alienated many Crimean Tatars by the cruelty with which he had suppressed their recent revolt, so Potemkin replaced him with the much gentler Otto Heinrich von Igel'strom, who was also given supervision over *vali* Mehmed-Shah's Tatar administration of *kaimakam* deputies and *kadi* judges centered at Karasubazar. Igel'strom recommended that the Russification of Crimean administration proceed carefully and solicitously to defuse the three Tatar concerns most likely to provoke unrest: fears of interference with the practice of Islam; fears of the offense to Muslim privacy and family honor from the billeting of Russian troops; and fears that Muslim households might be subjected to recruit levies. In February 1784 the Crimean peninsula, the Crimean steppe above Perekop as far west as the Dnepr, and the Taman' peninsula were formed into a Tauride Region (*Tavricheskaii oblast'*) of seven districts under General Kakhovskii. It was in turn subordinated to Governor-General Potemkin's new Viceroyalty of New Russia and Tauris. A few months later, the Tatar *kaimakam* administration was dissolved and replaced by Russian *uezd* administration, although effort was made to place some Tatar notables in *uezd* civil courts hearing litigation between native Tatars.[125]

Three other measures attempted to make good on the empress' pledge to tolerate Islam and extend to the Crimean Tatars the rights enjoyed by Russian subjects.

During the final years of Khan Shahin Girei's rule the offices of *mufti* and *kadiasker* had come under the khan's direct control, filled by his appointments rather than by men appointed by the Ottoman sultan. This made it easier for Potemkin to assume authority over the Muslim religious establishment in Crimea; the Governor-General could now appoint the *mufti* and place him on salary from the Russian treasury, while the *mufti* retained supreme authority over mosques and schools and over the *kadi* religious judges, with the exception that the *kadi*s now had power of verdict only in religious disputes. Support for the mosques and the *ulema* came from the Russian treasury, and the Russian government issued passports for the *hajj*. The *ulema* and their *vakif* foundations were exempted from taxation and the Russian government provided funds for the building of mosques and schools and for the printing and distribution of Qurans. The oath of allegiance Tatar notables took to the empress was worded to accord with shar'ia principles. In this manner Potemkin tightened Russian control over Crimea while adhering to the empress' promise that the "unhindered practice of this faith, with all its lawful ceremonies, would remain inviolable."[126] Once again the Enlightenment principle of religious toleration was put in the service of Russian imperialism. Twenty years before it had been used in Poland.

It was also decided to organize "native" military units as a means of maintaining control over the Tatar population while simultaneously integrating them into the imperial system as military subalterns. In March 1784 Potemkin formed a five-squadron light cavalry regiment of Tatar volunteers.[127] He called it the Besli Regiment, after the new formation force Khan Shahin Girei had tried to organize as the core of a standing army. It seemed to offer a number of advantages: it was primarily a parade unit, for political display; it co-opted the beys and mirzas by restoring their role as troop mobilizers and appointing them to squadron commands; by enabling Tatar notables to hold rank in the Imperial Russian army it entitled them to receive the legal privileges of Russian nobles; and it drew Tatars into Russian military service voluntarily, without having to subject them to recruit levies. But the Tatars were slow to enlist in it, and the regiments disintegrated during the next war when it was sent off to Kiev for campaign duty.[128]

In Ukraine the cossack *starshyna* and *szlachta* had been politically coopted by extending to them the rights and privileges of the Russian nobility. Catherine and Potemkin saw no cultural obstacle in doing the same for the Muslim Tatar beys and mirzas, and they acted quickly on it, issuing a decree to this effect on February 22, 1784.[129] A list of 334 notables acknowledged as *dvoriane* was compiled within a few months. The issue of whether the rights of Russian imperial nobility included allowing Tatar nobles to hold Tatar peasants as serfs was left unresolved for the time being.[130] St. Petersburg considered Tatar peasants on Tatar lords' estates to have the juridical status of state peasants; Tatar landlords were able to turn their tenants into dependent sharecroppers but unable to deprive them of their right of removal and bind them to the land.

Managing the political integration of the Crimean Tatar population was made easier by the fact that it had been so sharply reduced by waves of emigration before and during the last war and during the reign of Shahin Girei. Estimates of the scale of Tatar emigration before the Turkish War of 1787–1791 varied widely, and Ottoman sources did not refer to the matter. But Vasilii Zuev, who visited Crimea in 1782, wrote that informants had told him that two-thirds of the Tatar population had emigrated or died in the 1768–1774 war and he estimated only about 50,000 Tatar males remained in the Crimean peninsula. Igel'strom tried to use the district records of the *kaimakams* to gauge population, and he counted 55,917 Tatar and Hebrew male souls (this did not include Greeks and Armenians).[131] Zuev thought that large numbers of Greeks and Armenians had already departed under Shahin Girei's permission so that their lands and vineyards could be redistributed to his supporters; he thought that this was why only a third of the houses in Kafa remained occupied.

In addition to land left vacant by the emigration of Tatar notables, Greeks, and Armenians, the overthrow of Shahin Girei had turned over to Potemkin's administration title to the estates of the khan, *kalga*, and the leaders of the five main clans. Therefore, there was a considerable state land fund available for distribution to Russian colonists: to high-ranking nobles (including those like Chancellor Bezborodko, whose support was necessary for Potemkin's projects in Crimea and New Russia); to some 1,600 Greeks (who had performed valuable naval service in the Aegean campaign and were now resettled at Balaklava, Sevastopol' and Kherson), and to merchants, *meshchane*, state peasants, and former Ukrainian and Zaporozhian Cossacks taking up parcels of treasury land under the rules of the 1764 colonization plan. In the first year Potemkin and Kakhovskii distributed over 24,000 *desiatiny* of treasury land. This fell off to 2,660 *desiatiny* in 1785 and 4,695 *desiatiny* in 1786, apparently because it took time to survey the land and vet applicants, but 1787 saw a surge to 116,555 *desiatiny*. Some of the land went to soldiers too old to perform military duty but not feeble enough for invalid homes; some went to soldiers' wives invited to resettle in Crimea to be with their husbands; some went to Old Believers from Elizavetgrad province and northeastern Ukraine; enrollment as treasury colonists with right of free movement was even permitted to fugitive serfs from Russia, Lithuania, and Ukraine. A few Tatar notables—the bey of the Shirin clan, certain *kaimakams*—also benefited from the land redistribution, and of course, Potemkin awarded himself with 86,000 *desiatiny* and gave estates to his envoy

Bulgakov, his secretary Popov, and the naval commanders Ushakov and Mordvinov. Most of the treasury lands issued to colonists were on the steppe north of Perekop, which was better suited for livestock grazing; a smaller number of colonists were settled in the peninsula's southern foothills and along the coast, where conditions were more favorable for cereal culture, viticulture, gardening, and tobacco cultivation. But as in New Russia, loans, temporary tax exemptions, and subsidy money were provided and settlers preserved the right of free movement. For the time being serfdom remained even scarcer in Crimea than in New Russia (as late as 1793, there were just 226 resettled serfs in Tauride Governorate).[132] The construction of Sevastopol' stimulated maritime commerce and prompted population growth in other coastal cities such as Bakhchisarai, Karasubazar, and Akhmecet (now renamed Simferopol'). However, Crimea's position in the Black Sea maritime trade had changed. In the days of Ottoman hegemony, Kafa had been of primary importance as a port and market, servicing Trabzon and Sinope on the southern Black Sea coast and Istanbul. But the Russian settlement of New Russia had begun to shift Crimean maritime trade to the ports and depots on Crimea's west coast, to Simferopol, Balaklava, and Sevastopol', to service the coast of New Russia to the west, along the outlets of the Dnepr and Dnestr. This new trade pattern would be firmly consolidated from 1794, when the small Ottoman fortress town of Haji-bey, captured by the Russian navy in 1789, was expanded under the new name of Odessa.[133]

In the violent final days of Shahin Girei's Khanate, it had been necessary for Balmain and Igel'strom to keep 37,000 Russian troops in Crimea. Suvorov's Crimean and Kuban Corps had returned to the Kuban, to Fort St. Anna, to restore order among the Nogais. But as the Black Sea Fleet provided new protection against invasion and the Porte had for the time being accepted the annexation of Crimea to Russia, it was thought possible to reduce Russian forces on the Crimean peninsula to 26,000 by spring 1784 and to 20,000 by November 1774. It would be easier to support this smaller number from the land taxes paid by treasury colonists and the state peasant *obrok* paid by tenants on abandoned Tatar estates, and Crimean salt could be exported to pay for whatever grain and flour needs these revenue sources could not cover.[134] Progress in treasury colonization allowed Potemkin to begin forming settlers into a reserve force of six new regular infantry regiments and one new regiment of "settled cuirassiers" to assist the army in the defense of New Russia and Tauride.[135]

The joining of Tauris Governorate to New Russia Governorate in the Ekaterinoslav Viceroyalty (*Ekaterinoslavskoe namestnichestvo*) further enhanced Potemkin's executive power in the south and accelerated colonization, especially in New Russia. Ekaterinoslav was under construction as the capital of the new viceroyalty, and from March 30, 1783, the Governor-General's administration was being formed in accordance with the 1775 Statute for the Administration of the Governorates.[136] The viceroyalty was divided into fifteen *uezd* districts; its total area, including Tauris Governorate, was 12.7 million *desiatiny*, and its total population in 1783 was 708,190 (375,583 males). Its largest cities were the older towns of Poltava (77,839), Aleksopol' (75,447), and Kremenchug (72,945), but by the following year some of the more recently founded towns had reached impressive size if one counts their district as well as urban populations: Kherson (23,886),

Mariupol' (38,904), and Ekaterinoslav (40,124). Not long before Fort Elizavetgrad had only been a garrison; now it had a *posad* including 2,108 *meshchane*, merchants, and guild members and a district population of 51,461.[137]

Most of the Viceroyalty's male inhabitants were peasants (351,507 souls, of whom 200,736 lived on treasury lands, 148,949 lived on private lands, and 1,822 on court lands). Of the 148,949 living on private lands, only 4,139 were legally serfs (just 2.7 percent of the rural population). By origin 144,270 were Ukrainians (former Ukrainian Cossacks, commoners fleeing the spread of serfdom in Ukraine, and former Zaporozhian Cossacks retaining right of free movement).[138] The next largest group was men of Russian origin, and then several thousand Greeks, Armenians, Gypsies, German Mennonites, Polish Jews, Georgians, and other nationalities, with the proportion of such foreigners increasing over the next two decades. Of the 200,736 male souls on treasury lands, 159,516 were classified as "military settlers" (*voinskie posel'iane*) paying land taxes for the support of the army and furnishing recruits for the territorial cavalry regiments. About 18,000 on the treasury lands in northern New Russia (Bakhmut, Donetsk, Mariupol', and along the Ukrainian Line) were Russian *odnodvortsy*; when the next war came in 1787 they were put back in service in Cossack cavalry regiments.[139] The land tax collected from colonists totaled 119,262 rubles in 1787.[140]

By 1793 the population of Ekaterinoslav Viceroyalty would reach 819,731.[141] "Until the invention of steamships and railroads in the nineteenth century opened up such comparatively distant and landlocked regions as the American Midwest, the Argentine Pampas, the Canadian prairies, and the Australian backlands to commercial farming, this Russian expansion remained unparalleled in the scale, scope, and rapidity with which it was carried through."[142]

If there was one factor capable of disrupting Potemkin's "civilizing" of Crimea rousing the Crimean Tatars to another revolt and provoking a new Ottoman military intervention, it was the continuing unrest in Kuban and the North Caucasus. It endured even without Girei power struggles to incite it, because it was partly a response to Russian expansion across the Caucasus, the advance of the Mozdok Line from the north and the founding in the south of Vladikavkaz (1784), in North Ossetia, to control the Dar'ial Pass into Georgia.

The Nogais in the Kuban region had been placed under the new Caucasus Viceroyalty and divided from the Crimean Tatars by a ban forbidding them entry into the Taman' peninsula and the territory Tauris Governorate. Chancellor Bezborodko considered the Kuban Nogais a "very dangerous people" because of their "inherent wildness" and recommended that they be resettled outside the Kuban steppe, beyond the reach of Ottoman agitators: those preferring to adhere to nomadism were to be moved to the Volga-Don steppe and Ural steppe, and those electing to sedentarize as farmers could be resettled along the Volga from Astrakhan through Saratov and Penza and as far north as the eastern part of Tambov Governorate. Potemkin accepted the idea and in June 1783 ordered Suvorov to escort the Yedichkul Horde as far as the lower Don. But very soon there were clashes between them and the Russians and the Jamboiluk Horde, and by August 1783, 5,000 Nogai rebels were attacking Russian posts along the Ei River and threatening Azov. Potemkin ordered Suvorov to deal with them as enemies rather than subjects of the Empire, and in October, Suvorov, with fifteen squadrons of dragoons and fifteen companies of infantry, joined with Ilovaiskii's Don Cossacks and attacked several *auls*, arresting their chiefs. A few Nogai princes renewed their fealty to Russia; some perished in battle; and others withdrew into the foothills of the Caucasus Mountains. General Tekelli found it necessary to carry out a second pacification campaign in 1787, and Potemkin addressed the Nogai "threat" in the east by forming a Black Sea Cossack Host.[143]

The civil wars against Khan Shahin Girei had convinced Potemkin to authorize construction of a line of Russian fortresses running from Mozdok all the way to the Kuban River and Azov. Cossacks were resettled along this Mozdok Line, and it became even more important strategically with the annexation of Crimea and Russian assumption from the Khanate of suzerainty over Kabarda and the Muslim mountain peoples of the North Caucasus. But the Mozdok Line had the opposite of a pacificatory effect on the Kabardans, as the Line ran through a vast tract of grazing land essential to the survival of Kabardan peasants and blocked certain *pshis* from collecting tribute from particular tribes. Kabardan attacks on the Line had already occurred in 1779 and 1780, and Russian anxieties about revolt in Kabarda had been raised again in the early 1780s during the Turks' attempt to reoccupy Sucuk-Kale and the Taman'.[144]

In 1785 a new threat arose in Chechnya and Daghestan. Ushurma, a Chechen shepherd from a small village on the Sundzha River, had returned from Daghestan as a Naqshbandi Sufi imam, al-Mansur, and had launched a Muslim spiritual revival among the Chechens. It led to the proclamation of a holy war (*gazavat*) against the Russians and Cossacks of the Mozdok Line, and the Russians escalated the conflict by plundering and burning al-Mansur's village, killing several hundred. Al-Mansur's campaign against the Russians continued until 1794. The fighting in Chechnya set what would become a familiar pattern: "The Russians send in large forces and raze the places where the Chechens live; the Chechens retreat to the dense forests and high mountains where the 'war leader' announces a holy war to expel the Russians from Chechen lands; all the Chechens rally around the 'war leader', and under his leadership they ambush and kill startling numbers of Russian soldiers in well-executed guerrilla attacks."[145] There was a real danger that al-Mansur would not confine his holy war to Chechnya; he traveled into Kuban in 1787 to try to spread his revolt, and he established contacts with some *ulema* in Crimea. He also sent envoys to the sultan asking for support.[146]

In January 1786 Grand Vizier Halil Hamid Pasha was deposed and executed. His successor, Koca Yusef Pasha, was inclined to prepare for war with Russia.

Triumphal march

Potemkin had considered the successful colonization of New Russia and Crimea essential to his career at court and his continued place in the empress' trust; if his project succeeded, "I shall soon be seen in another light and then if my conduct is not approved

I will retire to the country and never again appear at Court."[147] But he had also spoken of Crimea and New Russia as gifts to the empress and tokens of his love for her as Mother of the Nation.[148] His nephew A. N. Samoilov wrote that Potemkin "to the glory of his Empress strove to bring about in the South what Peter the Great had accomplished in the North." Potemkin sought to lay symbolic foundations for his Greek Project by renaming Crimea *Taurida*, Kafa *Feodosiia*, Yenikale *Pentikapium*, and Akhtiar *Sevastopol'*, "to root out and extirpate all memory of the barbarians ... [so that] new light shone in the ancient kingdom of Pontus under the leadership of the conqueror of Tauris, and the first unstoppable step was taken toward cleansing Europe of Mohammedans and conquest of Istanbul."[149] By calling on volunteers from so many nations to resettle in New Russia and Crimea he was demonstrating, wrote the poet V. P. Petrov, "Under whatever native sky/They were born/ Catherine is mother to all ... // Be known as adoptive parent/Of all tribes on earth/ Plants from alien lands/ Are transported to the north./ You transform these alien peoples/ Into Rosses."[150]

On Potemkin's invitation Catherine II set out after New Years' 1787 on a six-month, 6,000-kilometer tour through Ukraine and New Russia to the Crimea. She had made inspection tours of her domains before—the Baltic coast in 1764, the middle Volga in 1767, the annexed Lithuanian districts in 1780—but this journey was especially long and costly and she was accompanied by a large and illustrious retinue: several of the principal figures at her court; Stackelberg; the British ambassador Alleyne FitzHerbert; the Austrian ambassador Count Ludwig von Cobenzl; the French ambassador Charles-Philippe, Comte de Ségur; her Vice-Admiral Karl Heinrich von Nassau-Siegen; Charles-Joseph Lamoral, Prince de Ligne; the Saxon diplomat Georg von Helbig; and the Italian composer Giuseppe Sarti. At Chwastów Catherine had her final meeting with her former lover, King Stanisław August; and as her barges sailed down the Dnepr, Samuel Bentham rowed out on his latest invention, a 250-foot river vermicular, to greet them. Near Kherson Emperor Joseph II joined her party under the pseudonym Count von Falkenstein. In Crimea the party visited Perekop, Kherson, Bakhchisarai, Inkerman, Sevastopol', Balaklava, and Kafa. The new towns, orchards, vineyards, and botanical gardens they toured impressed her considerably. On May 16 she wrote, "I am very happy to have seen it all with my own eyes ... This land is an earthly paradise," and on May 20, at Bakhchisarai, she recorded, "Not only will Kherson and Taurus pay for themselves in time, but one may hope that if Petersburg yields one eight of the empire's revenue the aforementioned places will surpass those barren places with their fruits."[151]

But this was not only a ruler's inspection tour: Catherine II was as much on display to her European guests, and through them, to European opinion, as her new provinces were on display for her own approval. The journey was carefully created political theater, a kind of *durbar* to demonstrate not only Russia's power but Russian taming of Asia, Russia's civilizing mission, and her embrace and defense of Western European cultural values. Great expense was taken to entertain her entourage all along the way with fireworks displays, parades by Kalmyks and Besli Guards and "mounted Amazons," mock battles, and concerts. The Comte de Ségur compared it all to a page from *The Arabian Nights*. The Prince de Ligne remembered the tour as "our triumphant and novelistic march [with] at each moment new objects of surprise: fleets created suddenly, squadrons of Cossacks and Tatars hastening up from the depths of Asia, illuminated routes, mountains on fire, enchanted palaces, gardens created in one night, savage caverns, temples of Diana, delicious harems, nomadic tribes, camels and dromedaries wandering in the desert, hospodars of Wallachia, princes of the Caucasus, persecuted kings of Georgia, all offering their homage and addressing their prayers to the queen of the North."[152] The letters Ligne wrote from his Crimean estate at Parthenizza (awarded to him by Potemkin) had great effect on the shaping of European Orientalism in the early nineteenth century. Besides giving vent to the European vogue for Orientalist fantasy, the tour was an exercise in a "triangulating" Orientalism allowing Russia to begin shedding European stereotypes as an Asiatic "other."[153]

But there was an element of hubris to the tour as well. It came on the heels of a series of provocations to the Porte: Russian efforts to suborn the hospodars and to use the consulates to make mischief in Greece and the Balkans; the annexation of Crimea; the Russian grip upon Kuban and Kabarda; and the Russian protectorate established over King Irakli's Kartli-Kakheti. In August 1787, just weeks after Catherine II returned to St. Petersburg, Grand Vizier Koca Yusef Pasha began preparations for war on Russia.

CONCLUSIONS

The Russo-Turkish War of 1768–1774 resulted in one of the most dramatic shifts in the balance of power in eighteenth-century Eastern Europe. Russia's victory in that war greatly weakened Ottoman power in the Balkans and laid foundations for the Greek and Serbian Revolts in the early nineteenth century and another Russian occupation of Moldavia and Wallachia. It pushed Russian power deeper into the Caucasus. It led to the liquidation of the once-independent Cossack Hosts and completed the transformation of Ukraine into a governorate of the Russian Empire. It detached the Crimean Khanate from the Ottoman Empire and led to its annexation by Russia. It opened up New Russia (part of which is today's embattled eastern Ukraine) to an intense colonization campaign directed by the Russian government. It established Russia as a naval and maritime trade power in the eastern Mediterranean as well as the Black Sea. It initiated the partitioning of Poland-Lithuania out of existence, a process completed by the end of the century. The war also salvaged the political fortunes of the usurper Catherine the Great, reconciled a suspicious Russian nobility to her rule, and led her to one of her most significant political reforms, the reorganization and systematization of provincial government in 1775.

The war was a conflict between two very different political systems with different strengths and limitations in mobilizing and managing resources for war. Catherine II was intent upon further centralizing and standardizing Russian Imperial administration and she continued to base Russian military resource mobilization on the recruit system, the soul tax, and state peasant *obrok* while further expanding and standardizing the Governorate system of provincial administration. This centralizing approach offered advantages for military planning, especially in regard to budgeting and coordinating resources and subordinating frontier colonization to strategic needs. The Ottoman Empire was experiencing decentralization, with political power (including the power of military resource mobilization) shifting from the central government into the hands of provincial notables (*ayan*). The main advantage of this decentralizing approach was that it permitted some flexibility, allowing provincial garrison commanders to maintain border defenses even after the grand viziers in command of the field army had demonstrated their incompetence or lost their nerve. The Russian centralizing mode of resource mobilization was best suited for a decisive aggressive campaign, as shown in the 1770–1771 operations in Moldavia, the Aegean, and Crimea. The Ottoman decentralizing mode was best suited for a protracted defensive war of posts along the Danube aiming to ultimately exhaust the enemy; it did not finally succeed in that, but it did prolong the war past 1771.

The Enlightenment in Russia had promoted the spirit of technicalism and produced a military culture more open to innovation; in the Ottoman Empire military innovation still faced some resistance from *istidrâc* determinism and the investment of social status in traditional forms of military service. The shock of defeat in 1774 would begin to erode those sociocultural obstacles to Ottoman military innovation.

Catherine II has a place in the foreground of our narrative not just because her resourcefulness and intelligence make her a fascinating figure but because she did manage the Russian war effort more successfully than her predecessors Empress Anna and Empress Elizabeth Petrovna had overseen Russian conduct of the Turkish War of 1735–1739 and the Seven Years' War. Catherine was more adroit at balancing competing political factions. She kept her Council of State focused on processing information and planning. She pressed good service out of Zakhar Chernyshov War College and Viazemskii's Procuracy monitoring the Senate. She approved the adoption of new training ordinances more conducive to tactical innovation. She recognized and rewarded the talents of commanders like Rumiantsev, Suvorov, and Potemkin. In the partitioning of Poland-Lithuania she found a way—a drastic one, to be sure—to stop Joseph II and Frederick II from interfering to sabotage the Russian war effort in 1771–1772. After 1774 she and Potemkin took advantage of the terms of the Kuchuk-Kainarji Treaty to maximize Russian strategic gains in the Black Sea region.

The Russo-Turkish War of 1768–1774 was fought on five fronts: along the Danube, in Moldavia, Wallachia, Bucak, and Bulgaria; in Crimea and the Kuban steppe; in the Kabardas and Transcaucasia; in the Aegean and on the Peloponnesus; and in Poland, to defeat the Bar Confederation and prevent it from linking up with the Turks. Orenburg and the Volga region could be considered a kind of sixth front in the sense that the Pugachev Rebellion exploited the Russian army's preoccupation with the Turks and was for awhile suspected of having been incited by the Bar Confederates or the Turks as a diversion.

Each year's operations corresponded to a distinct "phase" of the struggle because Russian and Ottoman war plans required their armies suspend operations every autumn in order to recuperate in winter quarters.

The first year of combat, 1769, could be considered one of *indecisive operations*. Khan Kirim Girei's incursion into Elizavetgrad Province was ended prematurely by bad weather. General-*anshef* Golitsyn showed great reluctance to commit his army to a siege of Khotin lest he come under attack by the grand vizier's field army coming up from the Danube, and Golitsyn only made good on taking Khotin on his third try, just after it had been announced his command (and any credit for future success at Khotin) was about to pass to Rumiantsev. Logistical problems discouraged the grand vizier from taking his field army north to the relief of Khotin.

By contrast the year 1770 was marked by *decisive action* and produced several overwhelming Russian victories. Rumiantsev's First Army dealt crushing defeats to the Ottoman field army at Riabaia Mogila, Larga, Kagul, and Kartal, discouraging the grand viziers from ever again taking their field army in full strength across the Danube, and convincing the Crimean Tatars to scale back their support of the Ottoman army and fall back to Bucak to protect the western border of the Khanate. Panin, in command of the Second Army, conducted his siege of Bender in a way contrasting sharply with Golitsyn's performance at Khotin, doggedly continuing his siege despite distressingly heavy casualties. After Bender's fall the Ottoman fortresses at Ismail, Kiliia, Akkirman and Ibrail, left vulnerable by the grand vizier's refusal to cross the Danube, fell to the Second Army after putting up a fierce fight, provoking Stoffeln to take out retribution on the villages surrounding them. It was also in 1770 that the Russian Baltic Fleet entered the Aegean and won resounding victories over the Ottoman fleet at Chios and Çeşme. Russian operations in 1770 achieved such spectacular results that Vienna grew alarmed that Sultan Mustafa III was about to capitulate, leaving the Russians entrenched in Moldavia and Wallachia to the detriment of Austrian interests.

The year 1771 saw decisive action on the Black Sea front—Dolgorukov's quick and easy occupation of Crimea, made possible by the prior defection of the Nogai hordes— while operations on the Danubian front settled into a lower-intensity *war of posts* due to the spread of the plague and the logistical difficulties deterring Rumiantsev from taking his First Army across the Danube. The major opposition to the Russian First Army now came from the pashas commanding certain fortress garrisons along the Danube, Grand Vizier Silahdar Mehmed Pasha having refused to risk the Ottoman field army again on the northern side of the Danube. His decision not to concentrate as many troops at Babadagh left more manpower and other resources at the disposal of the fortress commandants, and the shift of power from the imperial center to the frontier notables had found reflection in a shift in military initiative from the grand vizier's field army to the border pashas and seraskirs. In Poland there was briefly the threat that French military assistance would unite and reinvigorate the Bar Confederation, but the Bar commanders failed to coordinate operations and were soundly defeated by Suvorov, who had devised a strategy of striking with small but well-trained flying detachments out from a central defense network hub at Lublin. The French reduced their support of the Confederate cause, and a sign of the increasing desperation of the Confederates was their attempt in November 1771 to kidnap King Stanisław. That backfired upon them, giving Frederick II, Joseph II, and Catherine II additional reason to proceed with the partitioning of the Polish–Lithuanian Commonwealth.

Military operations in 1772 were of less importance than diplomatic developments. In February 1772 Prussia, Austria, and Russia reached agreement to begin the partition of the Commonwealth. In March, Grand Vizier Muhsinzade Mehmed Pasha decided to participate in peace talks at Giurgiu and Bucharest. The election at Karasubazar of Khan Sahip Girei, his repudiation of the sultan's suzerainty, and his acknowledgment of a Russian protectorate over his "independent" Crimean Khanate were ratified by the Russian government and the beys of the Nogai hordes.

In 1773 the stalemate in the peace talks at Bucharest, the escalating Pugachev Rebellion in the east, and temporary economic dislocations caused by harvest failures and assignat inflation put new pressure upon Rumiantsev to end the war by finally sending the First Army across the Danube. But it took him most of the year to prepare for his main blow against the grand vizier's forces at Shumla. First the Ottoman garrisons along the Danube had to be captured or neutralized by small raiding forces using the new Danubian Flotilla and led by the more daring Russian commanders, Weissman, Potemkin, and Suvorov. The success of their raids, and the death of Sultan Mustafa III toward the end of the year, convinced his successor Sultan Abdul Hamid I to sign a peace treaty at Rumiantsev's headquarters at Kuchuk-Kainarji.

As early as 1770 Rumiantsev's new training ordinances for the First Army and the tactics Suvorov had refined in Poland revealed some interesting innovations in their strategic and tactical thinking. These innovations could not yet be said to represent a "new Russian military doctrine;" they would not be formally adopted until 1783, and then only for the army on the southern frontier. But military historians have devoted great attention to them because they foreshadowed in several ways the strategic and tactical thinking of the French Revolutionary and Napoleonic Wars: preference of the square over unrolled line deployment; less fixation upon firepower and more attention to shock, to be delivered by infantry bayonet and cavalry saber; march and attack by parallel columns; the castling of artillery batteries; more deliberate positioning of forces and magazines to form parallel lines of operations; and the discovery of the tactical utility of jaegers. These innovations are usually cited as the main argument for considering the 1768–1774 Turkish War an important juncture in European military history. It could even be argued they constitute an eighteenth-century European Military Revolution if one follows Jeremy Black in defining "revolutionary" impact in terms of European ability to regularly secure decisive victory over much larger Asiatic armies.[1] That ability was demonstrated at Larga, Kagul, Hârşova, Kozluji, and several other battles.

Naval power had played a significant supporting role in the Russian war effort. The Azov Flotilla contributed to the success of Dolgorukov's occupation of Crimea and subsequently deterred the Turks from landing forces to retake Crimea. A series of squadrons from the Baltic Fleet were sent around northern Europe and through the Gibraltar straits into the Mediterranean during 1770–1774; although unable to sustain a successful revolt on the Greek mainland, the Baltic Fleet's dramatic victories at Chios and Çeşme drove the Turkish fleet out of the Aegean and created panic in Istanbul even though its blockade of the Dardanelles was half-hearted. In retrospect the most impressive achievement of Russia's Archipelago Expedition was not the destruction of the Turkish fleet at Çeşme, which was partly a matter of good luck; it was the success of the Orlov brothers in assembling an intelligence, propaganda, and logistics network across the Mediterranean. This network served as a foundation for much greater Russian diplomatic engagement in the Mediterranean, inspired Potemkin's Greek Project, and helped prepare the ground for the Greek and Serbian revolutions in the early nineteenth century.

By Urlanis' estimate Russia's First and Second Russian Armies had lost about 45,000 dead and wounded, compared to 60,000 in the Seven Years' War.[2] But information is unavailable about Ottoman or Crimean Tatar casualties or about the toll of the war and epidemic upon the populations of Poland, the Danubian principalities, Greece and the Aegean, or the Caucasus.

By early 1774 both sides were exhausted enough to rush to peace at Kuchuk-Kainarji without long negotiation. The Porte was by then prepared to accept a serious strategic setback, the loss of Crimea; but to obtain peace the Russians were also prepared to moderate some of their demands: despite the losses in men and treasure they had incurred in fighting on the Danubian front, they agreed to evacuate Moldavia and Wallachia and the several Ottoman fortresses they had captured along the Danube in exchange for retaining Azov and Taganrog and securing their new gains in Crimea and the Kerch Straits.

Once the Kuchuk-Kainarji Treaty had been signed the Russians turned their attention to suppressing the Pugachev Rebellion; removing the last vestiges of independence of the Cossack Hosts; completing the absorption of Ukraine into the Empire; extending and reforming *guberniia* administration; and launching an ambitious program to colonize and develop New Russia. Kuchuk-Kainarji had committed the Russians to accepting an independent Crimean Khanate with sovereignty over Kuban and the Kabardas, but Shahin Girei's failure to legitimate his rule forced Russia to abandon that commitment and annex Crimea to the Russian Empire in 1783—which the Porte appeared to grudgingly accept.

The Greek Project Potemkin and Catherine II developed in the early 1780s has been the subject of much speculation because its eccentric grandiosity seemed to suggest they had become intoxicated by what they had gained in the Turkish War. As a plan for the creation of two new buffer states, the Kingdom of Dacia and the Greek Empire, the Greek Project never went beyond fantasy and the most it achieved politically was some further rapprochement with Joseph II that would have real consequences later by drawing Austria into the empress' second Turkish War as an ally. The real significance of the Greek Project was that it helped shape Potemkin's development plans for New Russia and Tauris and magnified their propaganda value during the empress' Grand Tour of her new southern dominions.

The two most potentially destabilizing problems Russian victory in the Turkish War of 1768–1774 had failed to resolve were the continuing unrest in Poland-Lithuania and the northern Caucasus. The challenges to Russian interests from both these regions had helped spark war in 1768; they would contribute to the outbreak of war again in 1787.

Peace in the northern Caucasus was essential to the continued colonization and development of Crimea, New Russia, and the lower Volga; it was essential for maintaining and expanding Russian power in the Georgian kingdoms in Transcaucasia; and it was essential for avoiding conflict with the Ottoman Empire and Persia. But Kuban and the Kabardas had never been truly pacified, either by Shahin Girei or the Russians, and by the 1780s Kuban and the Kabardas were becoming embroiled in a new conflict between the encroaching Russian garrison line and the mountain peoples of the Caucasus, the Chechen, Ingush, and Daghestanis. This new conflict was especially dangerous because the resistance of the mountain peoples was increasingly translated into *gazavat* holy war provoking an increasingly brutal and "extirpationist" Russian response that viewed as an obstacle to successful pacification the kind of Enlightened religious tolerance Catherine II had employed to carry out her annexation of Crimea.

The record supports Paul Bushkovich's judgment that the annexation of part of the territory of Poland-Lithuania was not an "an aim of the Russian government in Catherine's time or earlier." What did motivate Russian policy toward the Commonwealth was to maintain the Commonwealth as a buffer state with a government kept "weak and compliant" through political gridlock between the king and the aristocratic oligarchy. Bushkovitch sees the governments of Elizabeth Petrovna and Catherine II as needing the Commonwealth as a buffer all the more with the rise of Prussia under Frederick II.[3] The death of August III in 1763 "forced her hand," committing Catherine II to installing Stanisław Poniatowski on the Polish throne so she could pursue Nikita Panin's Northern Accord with Prussia. She had to resort to the First Partition of Poland in 1772 in response to Austrian machinations, encouraged by Prussia, which threatened her ability to carry her First Turkish War through to a victorious conclusion. She resorted to the Second and Third Partitions in part because of the increasing difficulty of playing King Stanisław off against an emerging "patriotic" party led by the *Familja* (and encouraged by Prussia), but also in part to try to preserve the balance of power with Austria and Prussia.

One has to agree further with Bushkovitch that the problem Poland-Lithuania posed was that it threatened to destabilize Russia's western frontier, where Russia needed a quiet and secure flank "to secure her primary expansionist aim, the conquest of the Black Sea coast. It was the Turkish front, so to speak, that was central for eighteenth-century Russia, once Peter's Baltic conquests were secure."[4] One might object this was not apparent during 1762–1767, when Russia's primary objectives appeared to be the taming of Poland-Lithuania in order to build Panin's Northern Accord; but in 1768 it became clear that the Northern Project could not be separated after all from the Ottoman problem, given that the Turks still viewed, as they had viewed over the previous decades, any increase in Russian military power in Poland as a threat to their security.

For a decade the Treaty of Kuchuk-Kainardji appeared to maintain peace between the Ottoman and Russian Empires. At the two Aynaklivak conventions the Porte appeared to reaffirm its terms and acknowledge the new balance of power it had imposed, even to the point of recognizing for the time being the Russian annexation of Crimea. But unresolved problems and new grievances were accumulating that would bring the Porte back to war in 1787: the suspicion that the Russians would eventually attack Ochakov to complete the rollback of Ottoman military and naval power from the northern coast of the Black Sea; the advance of Russian imperialism through the Caucasus, even through the Dar'ial Pass into the Georgian kingdoms; and the attempts by Russian consuls to subvert the Christian millets in the Balkans and the Danubian principalities. The empress' Grand Tour of New Russia and Tauris was an outrageous affront to the Porte, a propaganda campaign to humiliate the Ottoman Empire before all of Europe. Her rhetoric about a Greek Project was implicitly threatening to the Porte. The decision of Sultan Abdul Hamid I's government to declare a new war upon Russia was due to the Turks' unwillingness to tolerate these offenses any longer, their calculation that Ottoman military capacity had been rebuilt, and their identification of strategic opportunities in the explosion of *gazavat* holy war in the Caucasus and the emergence in Poland-Lithuania of a Patriot Party ready to use the Diet to challenge Russian *diktat*.

NOTES

Chapter 1

1   The coup was engineered by Count Grigorii Grigor'evich Orlov, a captain of artillery and Catherine's lover since 1761, and by Nikita Ivanovich Panin, recently Russian ambassador to Sweden. It was supported by Aleksei Orlov, General M. N. Volkonskii, Secretary G. N. Teplov, and Ukrainian Hetman Kyrilo Rozumovsky. It was executed with the help of forty officers of the elite Semenovskii and Preobrazhenskii Guards regiments. Catherine cooperated partly from fear that Peter III was about to repudiate her—she had given birth in April to a son sired by Grigorii Orlov—but also because she shared the conspirators' conviction that the continued rule of Peter III would be a disaster for Russia, for as soon as Peter III had succeeded to the throne upon the death of Empress Elizabeth Petrovna (Christmas Day 1761), he had unexpectedly thrown away the imminent Russian victory over Prussia and made peace with King Frederick II to plan a new war against Denmark to liberate Schleswig and unite it with his native home, the Duchy of Holstein-Gottorp. On July 5, 1762, Peter III died while in the custody of the Orlovs, apparently during a drunken quarrel. Two days later, Catherine II issued a manifesto declaring that Peter III had passed away from a hemorrhoidal colic. Isabel de Madariaga, *Russia in the Age of Catherine the Great* (New Haven, CT and London: Yale University Press, 1981), 32.

2   Evgenii V. Anisimov, *Five Empresses: Court Life in Eighteenth-Century Russia* (Westport, CT and London: Praeger, 2004), 287, 294.

3   *Polnoe sobranie zakonov Rossiiskoi imperii*, series 1, XV, no. 11. 444 (St. Petersburg: Vtoroe otdelenie sobstvennoi ego Imperatorskago Velichestva Kantseliarii, 1830), pp. 912–915.

4   David M. Griffiths, "The Rise and Fall of the Northern System: Court Politics and Foreign Policy in the First Half of Catherine II's Reign," *Canadian Slavic Studies* IV, 3 (1970), 549; Madariaga, *Russia in the Age of Catherine the Great*, 25, 188; Hans Uebersberger, *Russlands Orientpolitik in den letzen zwei jahrhunderten. Erster Band: Bis zum Frieden von Jassy* (Stuttgart: Deutsche Verlags-Anstalt, 1913), 263–265.

5   David Ransel, *The Politics of Catherinian Russia: The Panin Party* (New Haven, CT and Yale, 1975), 23–27, 106–115.

6   Ibid., 107–108.

7   Ibid., 116–117; Griffiths, "The Rise and Fall of the Northern System," 552.

8   "Opisanie sostoiannia del vo vremia Gosudaryni Imperatritsy Elizavety Petrovny," *Arkhiv kniazia Vorontsova*, XXV (Moscow: M. Katkov, 1882), 280.

9   "Zapiska o politicheskikh otnosheniiakh Rossii v pervyi god tsarstvovaniia Ekaterinoi Velikoi (Neizvestnago sochitel'ia)," *Arkhiv kniazia Vorontsova*, XXV, 324.

10 Before the First Partition in 1772 the Polish–Lithuanian Commonwealth covered over 733,000 square kilometers and contained about 11 million inhabitants. Orest Subtelny, *Ukraine: A History* (Toronto, Buffalo, London: University of Toronto Press, 1988), 176.

11 Norman Davies, *God's Playground: A History of Poland. Volume I* (New York: Columbia University Press, 1982), 507.

12 Ibid., 508.

13 A. V. Ignat'ev, N. Ponomarev, and G. A. Sanin, eds., *Istoriia vneshnoi politiki Rossii XVIII vek* (Moscow: Mezhdunarodnye otnosheniia, 1998), 175; John Le Donne, *The Russian Empire and the World: The Geopolitics of Expansion and Containment* (Oxford: Oxford University Press, 1997), 40; Hans Bagger, "The Role of the Baltic in Russian Foreign Policy, 1721–1773," in *Imperial Russian Foreign Policy*, ed. Hugh Ragsdale (Cambridge: Cambridge University Press, 1993), 58.

14 Franz Szabo, *The Seven Years' War in Europe, 1756–1763* (Harlow: Pearson Longman, 2008). 420.

15 On Biron's political career in Russia and the reasons for his exile to Siberia, see Anisimov, *Five Empresses*, 73–75, 96–98, 143–147.

16 Ignat'ev et al., eds., *Istoriia vneshnei politiki*, 174, 176.

17 Albert Sorel, *The Eastern Question in the Eighteenth Century* (London: Methuen, 1898), 14.

18 Hamish Scott, "Frederick II, the Ottoman Empire, and the Origins of the Russo-Prussian Alliance of April 1764," *European Studies Review* 7(1977): 155, 163; Joseph von Hammer-Purgstall, *Histoire de l'Empire Ottoman. Tome seizieme* (Paris: Bellizard, Barthes, Dufour et Lowell, 1839), 66–67.

19 Ignat'ev et al., eds., *Istoriia vneshnei politiki Rossii*, 176; R. R. Iusupov, "Pol'skii vopros v politike Rossii nakanune russko-turetskoi voiny 1768–1774 gg.," *Vestnik Moskovskogo universiteta* VIII, 3 (1980), 38.

20 Iusupov, "Pol'skii vopros," 38; N. D. Chechulin, *Vneshniaia politika Rossii v nachale tsarstvovaniia Ekateriny II, 1762–1774* (St. Petersburg: Tip. Glavnago upravleniia udelov, 1896), 223; S. M. Solov'ev, *Istoriia Rossii s drevneishikh vremen*, 15 vols. (Moscow, Leningrad: Izd. Sotsial'no-ekonomicheskoi literatury, 1962), XIII, kn. 25, p. 254.

21 Sorel, *The Eastern Question*, 20.

22 A. N. Petrov, *Voina Rossii s Turtsiei i pol'skimi konfederatami c 1769–1774 god.* 5 vols. (St. Petersburg: Tip. E. Veimar, 1866–1874), I, 2.

23 Petrov, *Voina* I, 2; Madariaga, *Russia in the Age of Catherine the Great*, 191.

24 Iusupov, "Pol'skii vopros," 39.

25 Ignat'ev et al., eds., *Istoriia vneshnei politiki Rossii*, 177; Daniel Stone, *The Polish-Lithuanian State, 1386–1795* (Seattle: University of Washington Press, 2001), 269.

26 This had been facilitated by the fact that the Convocation and Coronation sessions of the 1764 Diet had been held as General Confederations of the Commonwealth Estates, allowing voting to occur by simple majority, with the *liberum veto* suspended.

27 Marshal Münnich, in 1732: "The republican form of government makes it impossible for us to get any satisfaction from Poland by negotiations alone." Quoted in Jerzy Lukowski, "Towards Partition: Polish Magnates and Russian Intervention in Poland During the Early Reign of Stanislaw August Poniatowski," *The Historical Journal* 28, 3 (1985), 564.

28 Ignat'ev et al., eds., *Istoriia vneshnei politiki Rossii*, 178; N. I. Kostomarov, *Poslednye dni Rechi pospolity* (St. Petersburg: Tip. F. Sushchinskago, 1870), 101.

29 Quoted in Adam Zamoyski, *The Last King of Poland* (London: Weidenfeld and Nicholson, 1998), 146.

30 Petrov, *Voina* I, 16–17, 19–20, 26–27, 31, 33–37; Madariaga, *Russia in the Age of Catherine the Great*, 199–200.

31 Władysław Konopczyński, *Barska konfederacja*, 2 vols. (Warsaw: wyd. Kasymienia Mianowskiego-instytutu, 1938), 179.

32   Petrov, *Voina*, I, 37, 40–42.

33   Etienne-Francoise, Duc de Choiseul, Foreign Minister of France in 1758–1761 and 1766–1770.

34   Sorel, *The Eastern Question*, 24.

35   Ibid., 25; V. A. Ulianitskii, *Dardanelly, Bosfor, i Chernoe more v XVIII veke* (Moscow: tip A. Gatsuli, 1883), 172.

36   *PSZ* XVIII, no. 13.071, February 15, 1768.

37   Madariaga, *Russia in the Age of Catherine the Great*, 202; Ignat'ev et al., eds., *Istoriia vneshnei politiki*, 179.

38   Kazimierz Pułaski (1745–1779, son of Jozef Pułaski) would return to the struggle in 1769, commanding Bar units near Kamianets. He and his brother Francisek would prove the most talented military leaders of the Confederation. After the rebellion's collapse in 1773 he took refuge in Saxony and tried unsuccessfully to organize a Polish Legion for the Ottoman Army. In Paris in 1777 he encountered Benjamin Franklin, who recruited him to come to Massachusetts and advise the Continental Congress. He became a Brigadier General of cavalry in the army of the Continental Congress. He was fatally wounded at the siege of Savannah in 1779.

39   Petrov, *Voina* I, 42–45; Konopczyński, *Konfederacja barska* I, 39.

40   Zamoyski, *The Last King of Poland*, 169.

41   Ibid., 168–169.

42   Tomasz Ciesielski, "O hajdamaczyźnie w latach 1733–1763," in *W kręgu Hadiacza AD 1658. Od historii do literatury*, ed. Piotr Borek (Kraków: Collegium Columbinum, 2008), 181, 183–184, 190–191.

43   Paul Magocsi, *A History of Ukraine* (Seattle: University of Washington Press, 1996), 295–296.

44   Simon E. Dubnow, *History of the Jews in Russia and Poland* (Philadelphia: Jewish Publication Society of America, 1918), 87–91.

45   Petrov, *Voina*, I, 153–155; Subtelny, *Ukraine: A History*, 174, 191–193; Zenon Kohut, "Myths Old and New: The Haidamak Movement and the Koliivshchyna (1768) in Recent Historiography," *Harvard Ukrainian Studies* I, 3 (September 1977), 365–366, 368, 372–373, 375.

46   A. K. Baiov, *Istoriia russkogo voennogo iskusstva. Vypusk pervyi* (Moscow: FondIV, 2008, reprint of 1909 ed.) I, 566.

47   Ahmed Resmi Efendi, *Hulâsatu-l-I 'Tibâr: A Summary of Admonitions: A Chronicle of the 1768–1774 Russian-Ottoman War*, trans. Ethan Menchinger (Istanbul: Isis Press, 2011), 38.

48   Petrov, *Voina*, I, 57.

49   Madariaga, *Russia in the Age of Catherine the Great*, 204; Sorel, *Eastern Question*, 26.

50   Petrov blames Yakub-Aga, the khan's commandant at the nearby Tatar village of Galta, claiming that Yakub-Aga had encouraged the Confederates to pass through Balta so that he could have a border incident provoking war. Petrov, *Voina* I, 67–68.

51   Sorel, *The Eastern Question*, 26.

52   Ahmed Resmi Efendi regretted the dismissal of Muhsinzade Mehmed Pasha, "an experienced vezir who had assessed the army and provisions, and who had scrutinized the Russians for thirty years and was aware of their preparation in military tactics." Mehmed Emin he considered "demented by illness." Ahmed Resmi Efendi, *A Summary of Admonitions*, 37, 49.

Notes

53 Virginia Aksan, *An Ottoman Statesman in War and Peace: Ahmed Resmi Efendi, 1700–1783* (Leiden: E. J. Brill, 1995), 123; Hammer-Purgstall, *Histoire de l'Empire Ottoman*, XVI, 174–178, 182–185.

54 The Russian Imperial Senate acknowledged a state of war on November 18, 1768. *PSZ* XVIII, no. 13. 198; Uebersberger, *Russlands Orientpolitik*, 282–284.

Chapter 2

1 "Opisanie sostoiannia del vo vremia Gosudaryni Imperatritsy Elizavety Petrovny," 300.

2 Ibid., 300–301.

3 Ibid., 301–302.

4 Ibid., 303. But in May 1769, Count Kaunitz informed Panin that Vienna now considered the 1753 pact nullified.

5 Ibid., 307–308.

6 Ibid., 306–307.

7 Charles Louis de Secondat, Baron de Montesquieu, *Persian Letters* [1720] (Indianapolis: Hackett, 1999), Letter XIX, p. 36. Voltaire wrote to Catherine II, "Your Majesty may think me an impatient sick man, and that the Turks are even sicker."

8 Voltaire to Sir Prince Eugene, "Epitre VIII" (1716).

9 A. L. Kochubinskii, *Graf Andrei Ivanovich Osterman i razdel Turtsii. Iz istorii vostochnago voprosa* (Odessa: Tip. Shtaba Odesskago voennago okruga, 1899), 129–131.

10 Quoted in Solov'ev, X, kn. 20, 416–417.

11 By 1648, state expenditures were 550 million *akces* but revenues just 360 million *akces*; in 1692–1693, the state deficit was 262.2 million *akces*.

12 This scenario of a mounting self-complicating crisis of central power was described most clearly by Stanford Shaw in his *History of the Ottoman Empire and Modern Turkey. Volume I: Empire of the Gazis* (Cambridge: Cambridge University Press, 1976), 169–247.

13 Ibid., 175.

14 There were twelve grand viziers over the years 1683–1702. Karen Barkey, *Empire of Difference. The Ottomans in Comparative Perspective* (Cambridge: Cambridge University Press, 2008), 231; Iu. A. Petrosian, *Osmanskaia imperiia: Mogushchestvo i gibel'* (Moscow: Nauka, 1990), 131–132; V. J. Parry, Halil Inalcik, A. N. Kurat, and J. S. Bromley, *A History of the Ottoman Empire to 1730. Chapters from the Cambridge History of Islam and the New Cambridge Modern History* (Cambridge, London: Cambridge University Press, 1976), 181–184; Yuzkel Ozkaya, "The Consequences of the Weakening of the Centralized State Structure: Ayanlik System and the Great Dynasties,"in *The Great Ottoman Turkish Civilization. Volume III*, ed. Kemal Cicek and Halil Inalcik (Ankara: Yeni Turkiye, 2000), 565.

15 Immanuel Wallerstein and Faruk Tabak, "The Ottoman Empire, the Mediterranean, and the European World-Economy, c. 1560–1800," in *The Great Ottoman-Turkish Civilization. Volume II*, ed. Kemal Cicek and Halil Inalcik (Ankara: Yeni Turkiye, 2000), 125.

16 Murat Cizakca, "The Evolution of Ottoman Domestic Loans from the 15th to the Nineteenth Centuries," in *The Great Ottoman-Turkish Civilization. Volume II*, ed. Kemal Cicek and Halil Inalcik (Ankara: Yeni Turkiye, 2000), 129; Ariel Salzmann, "Privatizing

the Empire: Pashas and Gentry During the Ottoman 18th Century," in *The Great Ottoman-Turkish Civilization, Volume II*, ed. Kemal Cicek and Halil Inalcik (Ankara: Yeni Turkiye, 2000), 133; Barkey, *Empire of Difference*, 233.

17 Barkey, *Empire of Difference*, 235.

18 Ibid., 207–209; Rifa'at Ali Abou-el-Haj, *The 1703 Rebellion and the Structure of Ottoman Politics* (Leiden: Nederlands Historisch-Archeaologisch Instituut te Istanbul, 1984), 8–9; Bruce McGowan, "The Age of the Ayans," in *An Economic and Social History of the Ottoman Empire, Volume II, 1600-1914*, ed. Halil Inalcik and Donald Quataert (Cambridge: Cambridge University Press, 1994), 661–663.

19 Rifa'at Ali Abou-el-haj and Karen Barkey see the Edirne Mutiny (1703) which deposed Sultan Mustafa II as the product of multiple *kapi* factions coming together in uneasy temporary alliance to deal a fatal blow to the sultan's and *şeykhülislam*'s attempts to restore the traditional patrimonial system in which patronage power was monopolized within the sultan's household. Suraiya Faroqhi, *The Ottoman Empire and the World Around It* (London and New York: I. B. Tauris, 2004), 58; Abou-el-Haj, *The 1703 Rebellion*, 10, 91–92; Barkey, *Empire of Difference*, 209–213.

20 A. K. Baiov, *Russkaia armiia v tsarstvovanie imperatritsy Anny Ioannovny. Voina Rossii s Turtsieiu v 1736-1739* (St. Petersburg: N. la. Stoikovoi, 1906), I, 97.

21 These numbers, reported by Peter I's admiral Cornelius Cruys, are more believable than the 240,000 Ottoman troops claimed by the unknown authors of the *Poetical Tale of the Siege of Azov*. Brian Boeck, "The Siege of Azov in 1641: Military Realities and Literary Myth," in *Warfare in Eastern Europe, 1500-1800*, ed. Brian Davies (Leiden, Boston: EJ Brill, 2012), 176.

22 D. Fedosov, ed., *Diary of General Patrick Gordon of Auchleuchries 1635-1699. Volume III: 1677-1678* (Aberdeen: Arts and Humanities Research Council, 2012), 61.

23 Virginia Aksan, *Ottoman Wars, 1700-1870* (Harlan, London, and New York: Pearson Longman, 2007), 95; Ia. E. Vodarskii, *Zagadki Prutskogo pokhoda Petra I* (Moscow; Nauka, 2004), 46–47; Chantal Lemercier Quelquejay, "La Campagne dePierre le Grand sur le Prut," *Cahiers du monde russe et sovietique* 7, 2 (1966):223–224.

24 Rhoads Murphey, *Ottoman Warfare, 1500-1700* (London: UCL Press, 1999), 45.

25 Count Luigi Ferdinando Marsigli, *L'etat militaire de l'empire ottoman* (Amsterdam: Gosse, Neaulme, de Hondt, Moetjens, 1732); Baiov, *Russkaia armiia v tsarstvovanie imperatritsy Anny Ioannovny* I, 91–97.

26 Baiov, *Russkaia armiia v tsarstvovanie imperatritsy Anny*, I, 97.

27 R. Mikhneva, *Rossiia i Osmanskaia imperiia v mezhdunarodnykh otnosheniiakh v seredine XVIII veka* (Moscow: Nauka, 1985), 8.

28 McGowan, "Age of the Ayans," 711, 714–715.

29 Baron de Tott Francois, *Memoirs of Baron de Tott: Containing the State of the Turkish Empire and the Crimea, during the late war with Russia*. 2 vols. (London: G. G. J. and J. Robinson, 1785), II 166, 219, 222.

30 Tott, II, 144, 145, 148.

31 Murphey, *Ottoman Warfare*, 58–59, 70, 79, 82.

32 Ibid., 58–59, 70, 79, 82, 98.

33 Virginia Aksan considers the proliferation of fictional *esame* tickets to be "the most intractable problem of the janissary organization" and quotes Baron de Tott to the effect that only about 10 percent of the estimated 400,000 tickets in circulation were held by actual

serving soldiers. Virginia Aksan, "Whatever Happened to the Janissaries? Mobilization for the 1768-1774 Russo-Ottoman War," *War in History* V, 1 (1998), 27; McGowan, "Age of the Ayans," 714-716; Brian Davies, *Empire and Military Revolution in Eastern Europe: Russia's Turkish Wars in the Eighteenth Century* (London and New York: Continuum, 2011), 262-263.

34 M. R. Arunova and S. F. Oreshkova, eds. *Russkii posol v Shtambule. Petr Andreevich Tol'stoi i ego opisanie Osmanskoi imperii nachala XVIII v.* (Moscow: Nauka, 1985), 25-26, 45, 52, 58, 59, 61.

35 Tott, *Memoir*, I, 7.

36 V. A. Zolotarev, M. N. Menzhevich, and D. E. Skorodumov, *Vo slavu otechestva Rossiiskogo (razvite voennoi mysli i voennogo iskusstva v Rossii vo vtoroi polovine XVIII v.)* (Moscow: Mysl', 1984), 114-115; Brent Nosworthy, *The Anatomy of Victory: Battle Tactics, 1689-1763* (New York: Hippocrene Books, 1990), 36-37.

37 Tott, *Memoir*, II, 81, 85, 89, 92, 96-98.

38 Virginia Aksan, "Breaking the Spell of the Baron de Tott: Reframing the Question of Military Reform in the Ottoman Empire, 1760-1830," *The International History Review* XXIV, 2(2002): 265-268.

39 Ethan Menchinger, "A Reformist Philosophy of History: The Case of Ahmed Vasif Efendi," *Journal of Ottoman Studies*, XLIV (2014): 142, 147-148, 152, 154, 161.

40 Aksan, *Ottoman Wars, 1700-1870*, 38-39; Aksan, "Breaking the Spell of the Baron de Tott," 270, 272.

41 Hakan Yildiz, *Haydi Osmanli Sefere! Prut Seferi'nde Lojistik ve Organizasyon* (Istanbul: Türkiye Iş Bankasi Kültür Yayinlari, 2006), 120, 154, 187, 196.

42 Vodarskii, *Zagadki Prutskogo pokhoda*, 207; Davies, *Empire and Military Revolution*, 112-113.

43 Vasile Stati, *Istoriia Moldovy* (Kishinev: Centrala, 2003), 191.

44 Thus, Nicolae Mavrocordatos served as hospodar of Moldavia in 1733-1735, 1741-1743, 1745-1749, and 1769 and was hospodar of Wallachia in 1730, 1731-1733, 1735-1741, 1744-1748, 1756-1758, and 1761-1763.

45 V. N. Vinogradov, ed., *Vek Ekateriny II. Dela balkanskie* (Moscow: Nauka, 2000), 51.

46 H. W. Seton-Watson, *History of the Roumanians. From Roman Times to the Completion of Unity* (Hamden, CT: Archon, 1963, reprint of 1934 Cambridge University Press edition), 141.

47 Tott, *Memoir*, I, 307-308.

48 Ibid., 316-317.

49 Davies, *Empire and Military Revolution*, 240-241.

50 Andrei Otetea, ed., *The History of the Romanian People* (New York: Twayne Publishers, 1970), 259-262; Seton-Watson, *History*, 141-143.

51 A. I. Baranovich and B. B. Kaufengauz, eds., *Ocherki istorii SSSR. Period feodalizma. Rossiia vo vtoroi polovine XVIII v.* (Moscow: Akademiia Nauk SSSR, 1956), 712.

52 The other important Ottoman fortresses in Moldavia were at Sorocha, on the Dnestr southwest of Khotin, and Ibrail (Russ. Brailov) in the south on the Danube just west of Galați.

53 Under the Ottomans, Dobruja was part of the *eyalet* of Silistra, but today it comprises the Black Sea coast of Romania. Bucak corresponded to the southern half of what would be known after 1812 as the Russian Governorate of Bessarabia; it now lies in Ukraine.

54 McGowan, "The Age of the Ayans," 685.

55 Vinogradov, ed., *Vek Ekateriny II*, 61; L. S. Stavrianos, *The Balkans Since 1453* (New York and Chicago: Holt, Rinehart and Winston, 1958), 238, 239, 240.

56 Davies, *Empire and Military Revolution*, 110.

57 Elizabeth Roberts, *Realm of the Black Mountain: A History of Montenegro* (Ithaca, NY: Cornell University Press, 2007), 139, 140, 141. A volunteer force of Montenegrin Serbs under Major Ivan Albanez joined Peter's army on the Prut; they were later given permission to resettle at Sumy in Sloboda Ukraine.

58 Quoted in Roberts, *Realm of the Black Mountain*, 151; see also Vinogradov, 65.

59 Quoted in Roberts, *Realm of the Black Mountain*, 152.

60 Ibid., 153–158.

61 McGowan, "Age of the Ayans," 687; Vinogradov, ed., *Vek Ekateriny II*, 72–75, 78.

62 Stavrianos, *The Balkans*, 365–366.

63 Stavrianos, *The Balkans*, 271, 274–275. The largest Greek entrepot in Russia at this time was in Nezhin in Ukraine.

64 McGowan, "Age of the Ayans," 688–689.

65 Vinogradov, ed., *Vek Ekateriny II*, 83.

66 Petrov, *Voina Rossii s Turtsiei*, I, 95–96.

67 A. N. Petrov, *Vliianie turetskikh voin s poloviny proshlago stoletiia na razvitie russkago voennago iskusstva. Tom 1: Voina 1769–1774* (St. Petersburg: Voennaia tipografiia, 1894), 61, 62, 68.

68 Moldavian sources called Montecastro Cetataea Alba; Ukrainian sources called it Bilhorod. Kiliia was superseded by a new Ottoman fortress just to its west at Ismail.

69 A. D. Bachinskii and A. O. Dobroliubskii, "Budzhakskaia orda v XVI-XVII vv. (Istoriko-arkheologicheskii ocherk," in *Sotsial'no-ekonomicheskii i politicheskii istoriia Moldavii perioda feodalizma*, ed. P. V. Sovetov (Kishinev: Shtiintsa, 1988), 85–90; Johann Eric Tunmann, *Krymskoe khanstvo*, trans. N. L. Ernst and S. L. Beliavskaia (Simferopol': Tavriia, 1991), 56.

70 Alan Fisher, *The Crimean Tatars* (Stanford, CA: Hoover Press Publications, 1978), 24; Magocsi, *A History of Ukraine*, 174. Vorontsov estimated the Yedisan and Jamboiluk Tatars together to number only about 30,000. *Arkhiv kniazia Vorontsova*, XXV, 300; Tunmann, *Krymskoe khanstvo*, 45–46, 49–50.

71 Tott, *Memoirs*, I, 400.

72 One of the reasons reported for the Porte's decision to depose Khan Kirim Girei in 1764 was his "oppression" of the Yedichkul, Bucak, and Kuban Hordes. V. D. Smirnov, *Krymskoe khanstvo pod verkhoventsvom otomanskoi porty v XVIII v. Tom vtoroi* (Moscow: Rubezh XXI, 2005, reprint of 1889 edition), 83; Davies, *Empire and Military Revolution*, 16–17.

73 Tott, *Memoirs*, I, 322, 326–327.

74 B.-A. B. Kochekaev, *Nogaisko-russkie otnosheniia v XV-XVIII vv.* (Alma-Ata: Nauka, 1988), 158–160, 165.

75 *Arkhiv kniazia Vorontsova*, XXV, 308.

76 F. Brun, *Krym v polovine XVIII stoletiia* (Odessa: L. Nitche, 1867), 27.

77 Sandor Papp, "Die Inaugurationen der Krimhane durch die Hohe Porte (16.-18.) Jahrhundert," *The Crimean Khanate between East and West (15th-18th Century)*, ed. Denise Klein (Wiesbaden: Harrasowitz Verlag, 2012), 87–88; Tunmann, *Krymskoe khanstvo*, 28.

Notes

78   Sultan Selim I, r. 1512–1520.

79   Probably an exaggeration; for logistical reasons, 40,000 warriors would not have been able to return safely to Crimea with prisoners outnumbering them three to one. Brian Davies, *Warfare, State and Society on the Black Sea Steppe, 1500–1700* (London and New York: Routledge, 2007), 17, 24–25.

80   The khan's pretext had been to root out and punish Cossack raiders, but the sultan had also sanctioned his invasion to punish Polish magnates for their mischief in Moldavia. The next year the Diet elected as king Stefan Bathory, the candidate preferred by the sultan.

81   A. A. Novosel'skii, *Bor'ba Moskovskogo gosudartva s tatarami v pervoi polovine XVII veka* (Moscow, Leningrad: Akademiia Nauk SSSR, 1948), 435–436.

82   Davies, *Warfare, State and Society*, 25; Tunmann, *Krymskoe khanstvo*, 26.

83   Pavel Levashev, *Kartina ili opisanie vsekh nashestvii na Rossiiu tatar i turkov* (St. Petersburg: G. Zubov, 1792), 100–109.

84   Davies, *Warfare, State and Society*, 191.

85   Tott, *Memoirs*, I, 415–416. A French consul at Bakhchisarai in the late 1730s estimated the khan's annual revenue at 500,000 Brabant thalers—440,000 in Ottoman subsidy and 60,000 in customs duties and salt duties. The *kalga sultan*, who commanded the army and was usually the khan's nephew, received 150,000 thalers, the *nuraddin sultan* 36,000 thalers, and the *orbei sultan* (commandant of Perekop) received 50,000 thalers. Brun, *Krym v polovine XVIII stoletiia*, 27–28.

86   The Nogais found it harder than the Crimean Tatars to maintain their cohesion and momentum against the firepower of European armies. Nogai cavalry were also intimidated by the Russians' Kalmyk auxiliaries. Davies, *Warfare, State and Society*, 190–192; L. J. D. Collins, "The Military Organization and Tactics of the Crimean Tatars, 16th–17th Centuries," in *War, Technology and Society in the Middle East*, ed. V. J. Parry and M. E. Yapp (London: Oxford University Press, 1975), 257.

87   V. P. Zagorovskii, *Belgorodskaia cherta* (Voronezh: Voronezhskii universitet, 1969); V. P. Zagorovskii, *Iziumskaia cherta* (Voronezh: Voronezhskii gos. universitet, 1980), 149–153; Davies, *Empire and Military Revolution*, 171–172, 189.

88   Davies, *Empire and Military Revolution*, 17, 47.

89   Ibid., 189.

90   Ibid., 205–206.

91   Davies, *Empire and Military Revolution*, 17, 47, 241.

92   Mikhneva, *Rossiia i Osmanskaia imperiia v mezhdunarodnykh otnosheniiakh*, 92–93; Smirnov, *Krymskoe khanstvo*, II, 70–71.

93   Davies, *Empire and Military Revolution*, 189, 255–256.

94   The signatories were exempted from mutual defense obligations if the Ottoman attacks were upon Austria's Italian domains or Russia's Caucasus and Asian domains. Karl Roider, *Austria's Eastern Question, 1700–1790* (Princeton, NJ: Princeton University Press, 1982), 100–101; *Arkhiv kniazia Vorontsova*, 276, 280, 281.

95   *Arkhiv kniazia Vorontsova*, XXV, 308, 311.

96   *Arkhiv kniazia Vorontsova*, XXV, 309.

97   Kochekaev, *Nogaisko-russkie otnosheniia*, 164–168.

98   Major Aleksandr Fedorovich Nikiforov had served at Constantinople in 1742 on a commission to resolve the status of prisoners taken in the 1735–1739 Russo-Turkish

War; he subsequently served at Constantinople as deputy to emissaries Nepliuev and Veshniakov, and in 1748–1749, he was posted to the Zaporozhian Sich, again to manage prisoner exchanges. Gul'nara Abdulaeva, "Pervyi rossiiskii konsul v Krymskom khanstve," at www.avdet.org, number 26, 2/07/2013; Uebersberger, *Russlands Orientpolitik*, 269.

99 Alan Fisher, *The Russian Annexation of the Crimea, 1772–1783* (Cambridge: Cambridge University Press, 1970), 27; *Arkhiv kniaz'ia Vorontsova*, XXV, 310–311; Smirnov, *Krymskoe khanstvo*, II, 70–71, 87.

100 Khan Selim III Girei's official reason for expelling Nikiforov was the latter's attempt to recover a fugitive bondsman who had converted to Islam.

101 *Arkhiv kniaz'ia Vorontsova*, XXV, 312.

102 Ibid., 309.

103 Anapa, the site of the old Genoese fortress of Mapa, near the mouth of the Kuban just across the Kerch Straits from the Crimean peninsula.

104 Kochekaev, *Nogaisko-russkie otnosheniia*, 134–137.

105 Walter Richmond, *The Northwest Caucasus: Past, Present, and Future* (London and New York: Routledge, 2008), 40–43; Amjad Jaimoukha, *A Brief History of Kabarda*, 2, 20 (on-line).

106 Davies, *Empire and Military Revolution*, 144–147, 165–167; Richmond, *The Northwest Caucasus*, 43–44, 46–48; Ignat'ev et al., eds., *Istoriia vneshnei politiki*, 31; D. Iu. Arapov et al., eds., *Severnyi Kavkaz v sostave Rossiiskoi imperii* (Moscow: Novoe literaturnoe obozrenie, 2007), 41–42.

107 Kochetkov, *Nogaisko-russkie otnosheniia*, 140.

108 Boris Nolde, *La formation de l'empire russe* (Paris: Institut D'Etudes Slaves, 1952–1953), 341.

109 N. A. Sotavov, *Severnyi Kavkaz v russko-iranskikh i russko-turetskikh otnosheniiakh v XVIII v. Ot Konstantinopol'skogo dogovora do Kiuchuk-Kainardzhiiskogo mira, 1700–1774* (Moscow: Nauka,1991), 107–114; Richmond, *The Northwest Caucasus*, 48–49.

110 Sotavov, *Severnyi Kavkaz*, 131.

111 Ibid., 133; E. I. Druzhinina, *Kiuchuk-Kainardzhskii mir 1774 goda: ego podgotovka i zakliuchenie* (Moscow: Akademiia Nauk SSSR, 1955), 45–46.

112 *Arkhiv kniaz'ia Vorontsova*, XXV, 298–299.

113 Peter I had begun taking interest in the eastern Georgian kingdoms in 1688 when the exiled Kartli Prince Alexandre Bagration entered the tsar's service. Bagration became a close comrade of Tsar Peter and accompanied him on his Grand Tour of Europe in 1698.

114 W. E. D. Allen, *A History of the Georgian People* (New York: Barnes and Noble, 1971, 2nd ed.), 189; Donald Rayfield, *Edge of Empires: A History of Georgia* (London: Reaktion Books, 2012), 226.

115 Allen, *History of the Georgian People*, 196–204; Rayfield, *Edge of Empires*, 227–228, 231, 238, 240.

116 Ignat'ev et al., eds., *Istoriia vneshnei politiki Rossii*, 157.

117 Rayfield, *Edge of Empires*, 240–243.

118 Quoted in Druzhinina, *Kiuchuk-Kainardzhiiskii mir 1774*, 72; Sorel, *The Eastern Question*, 24–25.

119 Khan Devlet II Girei, Charles XII, Mazepa, Orlyk, and Stanisław Leszcynski appealed to Ahmed III for Ottoman military aid in driving the Russians from Ukraine and Poland and

reinstalling Leszczynski on the Polish throne (1709–1710); but the aid actually proffered by the sultan was limited to providing refuge at Bender and throwing *ultimata* at Tsar Peter. What the Porte was not prepared to accept was the continued presence of large Russian forces on Polish soil, close to Bucak and Moldavia, especially in light of reports that Moldavian Hospodar Dimitriu Cantemir and Wallachian Hospodar Constantin Brancoveanu were in secret correspondence with Peter I and probably negotiating to invite the Russian army into their principalities to liberate them. It was for these two reasons that Ahmed III declared war on Russia in November 1710 and defeated the Russian army in Moldavia in August 1711. The truce signed at Stanileşti left Peter I with his throne but required that Azov be returned to the Porte and Russian forces removed from Poland. Once these conditions were met (1713), Sultan Ahmed III ceased threatening Russia and deposed Khan Devlet II Girei to halt Crimean Tatar raids upon Russia. The sultan's government then tightened its control over Moldavia and Wallachia to introduce phanariot rule and increase its revenues. Ahmed III's next war (1714–1718) was not with Russia, but against Venice and Austria, which he saw as subverting Ottoman control of Morea and the Banat.

Chapter 3

1   This manifesto had been written by her secretary Grigorii Teplov and by Nikita Panin. Ransel, *Politics of Catherinian Russia*, 71.

2   Robert E. Jones, *The Emancipation of the Russian Nobility, 1762–1785* (Princeton, NJ: Princeton University Press, 1973), 172–173.

3   L. F. Pisar'kova, *Gosudarstvennoe upravlenie Rossii s kontsa XVII do kontsa XVIII veka* (Moscow: ROSSPEN, 2007), 348.

4   Arcadius Kahan, *The Plow, the Hammer, and the Knout: An Economic History of Eighteenth-Century Russia* (London, Chicago: University of Chicago Press, 1985), 8; Janet Hartley, *A Social History of the Russian Empire, 1650–1825* (London and New York: Longman, 1999), 9; Jones, *Emancipation of the Russian Nobility*, 179; Baranovich and Kafengauz, eds., *Ocherki istorii SSSR. Period feodalizma. Rossiia vo vtoroi polovine XVIII v.*, 45.

5   Quoted in Ransel, *Politics of Catherinian Russia*, 53.

6   Jones, *Emancipation of the Russian Nobility*, 46.

7   Ransel, *Politics of Catherinian Russia*, 79, 81, 91, 92.

8   Viazemskii was placed in direct charge of the new First Department of the Senate, which directed the College of State Revenue, the College of Census Revision, and those colleges most responsible for cameralist economic development. *PSZ XVI*, no. 11.989; Pisar'kova, *Gosudarstvennoe upravlenie*, 344; Jones, *Emancipation of the Russian Nobility*, 175; Ransel, *Politics of Catherinian Russia*, 121, 162.

9   Quoted in Ransel, *Politics of Catherinian Russia*, 163–164.

10   On the recruit levies instituted by Peter the Great, see Davies, *Empire and Military Revolution*, 65–66, and J. L. H. Keep, *Soldiers of the Tsar. Army and Society in Russia, 1462–1874* (Oxford: Clarendon Press, 1985), 105–108. See also Chapter 4 below.

11   During the Turkish War of 1736–1739 the levy rate averaged 4.4 recruits from every 100 male taxpaying "souls"; during the Seven Years' War it averaged 2.9 recruits from every 100 souls from 1756 until 1760, after which the Russian war effort had begun winding down.

12   Reduced to twenty-five years in 1793.

13 Walter Pintner, "The Burden of Defense in Imperial Russia, 1725–1914," *Russian Review* 43, 3 (1984), 246, 249.

14 Walter Pintner, "Russia as a Great Power, 1709–1856: Reflections on the Problem of Relative Backwardness, with Special Reference to the Russian Army and Russian Society," 29; L. G. Beskrovnyi, *Russkaia armiia i flot v XVIII v.* (Moscow: Ministerstvo oborony SSSR, 1958), 266, 295.

15 Beskrovnyi, *Russkaia armiia i flot v XVIII veke*, 294–295; Keep, *Soldiers of the Tsar*, 160; *PSZ* XVIII, nos. 13.181, 13.195, and 13.229.

16 Keep, *Soldiers of the Tsar*, 148, 151–154; Beskrovnyi, *Russkaia armiia i flot v XVIII veke*, 293–294.

17 Kahan, *The Plow, the Hammer, and the Knout*, 337; Andrei Kolomiets, *Finansovye reformy russkikh tsarei. Ot Ivana Groznogo do Aleksandra Osvoboditelia* (Moscow: Zhurnal Voprosy ekonomiki, 2001), 172–3.

18 Davies, *Empire and Military Revolution*, 162.

19 Davies, *Empire and Military Revolution*, 168; Kahan, *The Plow, the Hammer, and the Knout*, 333–334.

20 Isabel de Madariaga and Simon Dixon have estimated the reserve at closer to 8.5 million rubles. Kahan, *The Plow, the Hammer, and the Knout*, 334, 337; Kolomiets, *Finansovye reformy*, 185, 189; Jones, *Emancipation of the Russian Nobility*, 179–180; Simon Dixon, *The Modernisation of Russia, 1676–1825* (Cambridge: Cambridge University Press, 1999), 70–71; Madariaga, *Russia in the Age of Catherine the Great*, 482.

21 In the 1760s about 1.2 million quarters a year were consumed by the army and fleet. Kahan, *The Plow, the Hammer, and the Knout*, 59; Kolomiets, *Finansovye reformy*, 179.

22 Kolomiets, *Finansovye reformy*, 156–157, 183, 188; Madariaga, *Russia in the Age of Catherine the Great*, 481.

23 Pisar'kova, *Gosudarstvennoe upravlenie*, 47, 98.

24 The four most important officials under the *gubernator* were the *ober-komandant*, in charge of the military forces stationed in the governorate; the *ober-komissar*, in charge of cash tax collection; the *ober-proviantmeister*, in charge of grain tax collection; and the *landrikhter*, for the administration of justice.

25 Most of the old *gorodovye voevody* had been kept to 2- to 3-year terms, but the *gubernators* were appointed for indefinite terms. The governors of the two *guberniias* of greatest strategic importance at this time—Petersburg and Azov—were called *general-gubernatory*. Anisimov, quoted in Pisar'kova, *Gosudarstvennoe upravlenie*, 97.

26 Pisar'kova, *Gosudarstvennoe upravlenie*, 96, 100–101.

27 Madariaga, *Russia in the Age of Catherine the Great*, 53.

28 Pisar'kova, *Gosudarstvennoe upravlenie*, 249–257; Ibid., 54.

29 Pisar'kova, *Gosudarstvennoe upravlenie*, 368.

30 *PSZ* XVI, no. 12.137; Jones, *Emancipation of the Russian Nobility*, 176–178.

31 Pisar'kova, *Gosudarstvennoe upravlenie*, 344–348, 352; Jones, *Emancipation of the Russian Nobility*, 175.

32 In 1763 1.089 million rubles were spent, of which 49 percent went to central officials and 51 percent to officials in the governorates, provinces, and districts. In 1765 expenditure on the bureaucracy reached 1.54 million rubles. These figures do not include officials in the War College, the Admiralty, or the College of Foreign Affairs. Pisar'kova, *Gosudarstvennoe upravlenie*, 379.

Notes

33 Ibid., 379–387.

34 By contrast the Kingdom of Prussia had 14,000, although its territory was less than 1 percent of the land area of the Russian Empire. Jones, *Emancipation of the Russian Nobility*, 182–183.

35 *PSZ* XV, no. 11.444.

36 The Manifesto explained, "Manners have improved, knowledge has replaced illiteracy; devotion and zeal for military affairs has resulted in the appearance of many experienced and brave generals; civil and political concerns have attracted many intelligent people; noble thoughts have penetrated the hearts of all true Russian patriots who have revealed toward Us their unlimited love, devotion, zeal and fervor. Because of all these reasons, We judge it to be no longer necessary to compel the nobles into service as has been the practice hitherto." Quoted in Jones, *Emancipation of the Russian Nobility*, 29.

37 It was therefore stipulated that army officers (and civil officials in the upper eight ranks) could apply for retirement but would have to wait for release after war's end or when their department consented. Nobles' sons serving in the army as privates or non-commissioned officers could not apply for retirement until they had won officers' commissions or had put in twelve years' service in the ranks. Jones, *Emancipation of the Russian Nobility*, 31.

38 Under Catherine I and Peter II nobles had been given permission to take leaves from service for up to one year, without salary, in order to tend to their estates and families; this was of course in a time of peace. In 1736 Empress Anna decreed that families with more than one son could keep one son at home to manage family affairs provided he took a post in local civil administration. She also decreed that the term of compulsory state service was to be reduced to twenty-five years—although implementation of this was postponed until 1740, when her Turkish War was over. Jones, *Emancipation of the Russian Nobility*, 24, 26.

39 Pisar'kova, *Gosudarstvennoe upravlenie*, 371–375; Sievers quoted in Jones, *Emancipation of the Russian Nobility*, 184.

40 The black soil belt continued westward through Kiev and Zhytomyr into Ukraine, which was part of the Polish–Lithuanian Commonwealth until the formation of the Ukrainian Hetmanate in 1648–1654. The Ukrainian and Russian parts of the black soil belt together covered about 270 million acres. Today the Russian Central Black Soil Economic Region comprises the *oblasti* of Belgorod, Kursk, Voronezh, Lipetsk, and Tambov. At the time of the First Soul Tax Revision (1719–1722) the population of the Central Black Soil Region was about 3.1 million, of which 3 million were tax-bearing; the total population of the Russian Empire at the First Revision was about 15.5 million. By the Fifth Revision (1795) the population of the Central Black Soil Region had risen to 5.9 million, of which 5.73 million were tax-bearing; the Empire's total population in 1795 was 37.2 million (including Left Bank Ukraine but excluding Right Bank Ukraine, Courland, annexed Crimea, and the territories obtained through the Partitions of Poland). Ia. E. Vodarskii, *Naselenie Rossii za 400 let (XVI–XX vv.)* (Moscow: Prosveshchenie, 1973), 54, 91.

41 Iu. A. Mizis, *Zaselenie tambovskogo kraia v XVII–XVIII vekakh* (Tambov: Tambovskii Gosudarstvennyi Pedagogicheskii Institut, 1990), 97–98; Brian Davies, *State Power and Community in Early Modern Russia: The Case of Kozlov, 1635–1649* (London and New York: Palgrave MacMillan 2004), 30, 140, 146.

42 Davies, *Warfare, State and Society on the Black Sea Steppe*, 14.

43 On the construction and settlement of the Abatis Line and Belgorod Line, see Davies, *Warfare, State and Society on the Black Sea Steppe*, 40, 44–87.

44 It had been Kozlov's success in shutting down one of the major Tatar invasion roads that had inspired construction of the Belgorod Line in 1635.

45   Davies, *State Power and Community*, 245.

46   Brian Davies, "Service, Landholding, and Dependent Labour in Kozlov District, 1675," in *New Perspectives on Muscovite History. Selected Papers from the Fourth World Congress for Soviet and East European Studies, Harrogate, 1990*, ed. Lindsey Hughes (Houndmills: MacMillan Press/St. Martin's Press, 1993), 137, 144.

47   Ibid., 130.

48   Madariaga, *Russia in the Age of Catherine the Great*, 101.

49   Brian Boeck, *Imperial Boundaries. Cossack Communities and Empire-Building in the Age of Peter the Great* (Cambridge: Cambridge University Press, 2009), 132; Mizis, *Zaselenie tambovskogo kraia*, 84–85 n.

50   Davies, *Empire and Military Revolution*, 171–172; F. F. Laskovskii, *Materialy dlia istorii inzhenernago iskusstva, tom tretii* (Moscow: Imperatorskaia Akademiia Nauk, 1865), 68–73, 77–79; V. V. Penskoi, "Ukrainskii landmilitseiskii korpus v XVIII v.," *Voprosy istorii* 10 (2000): 148, 150.

51   Iu. R. Klokman, "Goroda Belgorodskoi cherty v gubernskoi reforme," in *Voprosy sotsial'no-ekonomicheskoi istorii i istochnikovedeniia perioda feodalizma v Rossii*, ed. N. V. Ustiugov (Moscow: AN SSSR, Institut istorii, 1961), 157–159.

52   In 1764 Kozlov's urban population consisted of 216 *posad* commune taxpayers, 1,442 *odnodvortsy*, 847 *meshchane* privileged taxpayers, 91 peasants, 8 clergymen, and 337 others. Mizis, *Zaselenie tambovskogo kraia*, 64, 90, 91, 94.

53   Mizis, *Zaselenie tambovskogo kraia*, 87–88.

54   Quoted in Hartley, *A Social History of the Russian Empire*, 102.

55   Madariaga, *Russia in the Age of Catherine the Great*, 150, 174, 181.

56   Ia. E. Vodarskii, *Dvorianskoe zemlevladenie v Rossii v XVII-pervoi polovine XIX v.* (Moscow: Nauka) 223.

57   Mizis, *Zaselenie tambovskogo kraia*, 92, 101, 102.

58   Alexander Etkind, *Internal Colonization: Russia's Imperial Experience* (Cambridge, UK: Polity Press, 2011), 123.

59   Robert E. Jones, "Opposition to War and Expansion in Late Eighteenth-Century Russia," *Jahrbücher für Geschichte Osteuropas* 82 (1984): 39–41; Robert E. Jones, "The Nobility and Russian Foreign Policy, 1560–1811," *Cahiers du monde Russe et sovietique* XXXIV, 1–2 (1993): 159, 162–163.

60   A. P. Pronshtein, "K istorii voznikoveniia kazach'ikh poselenii i obrazovaniia sosloviia kazakov na Donu," in *Novoe o proshlom nashei strany. Pamiati akademika M. N. Tikhomirova*, ed. Akademiia Nauk SSSR, Otdelenie istorii, Arkheograficheskaia komissiia (Moscow: Nauka, 1967), 167–168; N. Ianchevskii, *Kolonial'naia politika na Donu torgovogo kapitala Moskovskogo gosudarstva v XVI-XVII vv.* (Rostov: Severnyi kavkaz, 1930), 111, 118–122, 135, 170–171; Davies, *Warfare, State and Society on the Black Sea Steppe*, 29–31.

61   Brian J. Boeck, "The Siege of Azov in 1641: Military Realities and Literary Myth," in *Warfare in Eastern Europe, 1500–1800*, ed. Brian L. Davies (Leiden and Boston, MA: EJ Brill, 2012), 173–198.

62   Davies, *Warfare, State and Society on the Black Sea Steppe*, 96–97, 185–186.

63   E. V. Chistiakova and V. M. Solov'ev, *Stepan Razin i ego soratniki* (Moscow: Mysl', 1988), 32–35; Boeck, *Imperial Boundaries*, 77.

64   Boeck, *Imperial Boundaries*, 122–125, 134–146.

65 By 1700 there were 127 cossack settlements on the lower Don and Upper Reaches, with about 28,000 inhabitants. Vodarskii, *Naselenie Rossii v kontse XVII- nachale XVIII veka*, 193.

66 Boeck, *Imperial Boundaries*, 161–162; Davies, *Empire and Military Revolution*, 26–27.

67 Boeck, *Imperial Boundaries*, 168.

68 Davies, *Empire and Military Revolution*, 88–90; A. G. Makarov, *Bulavinskii bunt (1707–1708 g.) Etiud iz istorii otnoshenii Petra Velikogo k Donskim kazakam* (Moscow, St. Petersburg: Dm. Bulianin, 2004), 40, 43–44, 57–59, 66; Boeck, *Imperial Boundaries*, 182–183.

69 Don Cossack captain Ignat Nekrasov tried to revive the Bulavin movement later in 1708. He was defeated by Dolgorukii's troops at Panshin and fled into the Kuban steppe, from where he appealed to the Ottoman sultan for protection. The Turks allowed the surviving Nekrasovites to resettle near Anapa and the Taman' peninsula. Davies, *Empire and Military Revolution*, 90.

70 Boeck, *Imperial Boundaries*, 232–238.

71 Ibid., 224.

72 Some Nekrasovites were resettled near Trabzon on the Anatolian coast; others went to Rusçuk near the mouth of the Danube. Boeck, *Imperial Boundaries*, 241.

73 Madariaga, *Russia in the Age of Catherine the Great*, 70; Boeck, *Imperial Boundaries*, 190–199, 206–207.

74 Davies, *Empire and Military Revolution*, 130; Boeck, *Imperial Boundaries*, 200.

75 There were complaints that this expelled from the Cossack register some senior experienced men—some of them even officers—who had settled after 1696, so as a compromise St. Petersburg reset the eligibility deadline to 1710. Boeck, *Imperial Boundaries*, 218–222.

76 Boeck, *Imperial Boundaries*, 200, 202–204; S. G. Svatikov, *Rossiia i Don (1582–1917)* (Rostov-na-Donu: Donskaia Istoricheskaia Komissiia, 1924), 190.

77 Svatikov, *Rossiia i Don*, 190–194.

78 John T. Alexander, *Autocratic Politics in a National Crisis: The Imperial Russian Government and Pugachev's Revolt* (Bloomington, IN: Indiana University Press, 1969), 9–10.

79 Robert E. Jones, "Opening a Window on the South: Russia and the Black Sea, 1695–1792," in *A Window on Russia. Papers from the Fifth International Conference of the Study Group on Eighteenth-Century Russia, Gargnano, 1994*, ed. Mariadi Salvo and Lindsey Hughes (Rome: La Fenice Edizioni, 1996), 124–125.

80 Ulianitskii, *Dardanelly, Bosfor i Chernoe more*, 76.

81 At this time the Mediterranean-Levantine trade was threatened by corsairs and the French, while the trans-Caucasian trade was endangered by Ottoman-Persian warfare.

82 Ulianitskii, *Dardanelly, Bosfor i Chernoe more*, 71–76.

83 Jones, "Opening a Window," 125; Ulianitskii, *Dardanelly, Bosfor i Chernoe more*, 79–81.

84 Ulianitskii, *Dardanelly, Bosfor i Chernoe more*, 98–99.

85 The population of the Hetmanate in 1719 was 1.82 million; by 1795 it was 3.39 million. Vodarskii, *Naselenie Rossii za 400 let*, 92.

86 Solov'ev, *Istoriia Rossii* IX, kn. 18, 520–522; O. Hurzhii, *Get'man Ivan Skoropad'skyi* (Kiev: NAN Ukraina, 1998), 72.

87 V. F. Verstiuk, V. M. Gorobets, and O. P. Tolochko, *Ukrains'ki proekti v Rosiis'kyi imperii* (Kiev: Naukova dumka, 2004), 235; Magocsi, *History of Ukraine*, 169; E. V. Belova, "Russko-turetskie i migratsionnaia politika Rossii v pervoi polovine XVIII v." *Voprosy istorii* 5 (2008), 144; D. I. Doroshenko, *Narys istorii Ukraini*, 2 vols. (Kiev: Globus, 1991), II: 422.

88   In fact the abolition of Ukrainian customs barriers in 1754 deprived Hetman Rozumovsky of that traditional source of hetman's revenue, making it necessary for him to live off an annual 50,000-ruble subsidy from the Russian Imperial treasury. Verstiuk et al., *Ukrains'ki proekti*, 235; G. Ia. Sergienko et al., eds., *Istoriia Ukrainskoi SSR. Tom tretii. Osvoboditel'naia voina i vossoedinenie Ukrainy s Rossii. Nachalo razlozheniia feodalizma i zarozhdenie kapitalisticheskikh otnoshenii (vtoraia polovina XVII-XVIII v.* (Kiev: Naumkova Dumka, 1983), III, 442.

89   Sergienko et al., ed., *Istoriia Ukrainskoi SSR*, III, 442–443; Magocsi, *History of Ukraine*, 171.

90   M. N. Pokrovskii, *Izbrannye proizvodeniia. Kniga pervaia. Russkaia istoriia s drevneishikh vremen (toma I, II)* (Moscow: Mysl', 1966), 514.

91   Magocsi, *History of Ukraine*, 171; Zenon E. Kohut, *Russian Centralism and Ukrainian Autonomy. Imperial Absorption of the Hetmanate, 1760s–1830s* (Cambridge: Harvard Ukrainian Research Institute, 1988), 83, 87–90.

92   M. Vasylenko, "G. N. Teplov i ioho pasika pro neporiadki v Malorossii," *Zapysky Ukrainskoho naukhovoho tovarystva v Kyivi* 9 (1912): 29–52.

93   Madariaga, *Russia in the Age of Catherine the Great*, 72–73.

94   Viktor Petelin, *Fel'dmarshal Rumiantsev, 1725–1796* (Moscow: Tsentrpoligraf, 2006), 238.

95   The Ukrainian peasantry would finally lose the right to leave their landlords' estates in 1783. Verstiuk et al., *Ukrains'ki proekti*, 238–239; Magocsi, *History of Ukraine*, 173.

96   G. A. Maksimovich, *Deiatel'nost' Rumiantseva-Zadunaiskago po upravleniia Malorossiei. Tom pervyi* (Nezhin: Pechatnik, 1913), 90–92, 94, 104–105; Kohut, *Russian Centralism and Ukrainian Autonomy*, 109, 114. See also: N. V. Storozhenko, "Reformy v Malorossii pri grafe Rumiantseve," *Kievskaia starina* 3 (1891): 478–493; M. Sudienko, "Bumagi do upravleniia Malorossieiu grafa P. A. Rumiantseva-Zadunaiskago otnosiashchiasia," *ChOIDR* 1 (1861), pt. 5: 137–165; Fortunatov, *P. A. Rumiantsev*, 4 pts. (Moscow: Voennoe ministerstvo SSSR, 1953), II (1768–1775), no. 1, 3–6.

97   Fortunatov, *P. A. Rumiantsev*, II, no. 6, 12–13.

98   The anticipated yield of the ruble tax in 1768 was 251,000 rubles, but the amount actually collected was just 172,000 rubles. Maksimovich, *Deiatel'nost'*, 114; Kohut, *Russian Centralism and Ukrainian Autonomy*, 122–123; Magocsi, *History of Ukraine*, 172.

99   Petr Golovinskii, *Slobodskie kozach'i polki* (St. Petersburg: Tip. N. Tiblena, 1865), 55–66; Magocsi, *History of Ukraine*, 211–212, 265–267.

100   Golovinskii, *Slobodskie kozach'i polki*, 66–68.

101   Golovinskii gives the following population figures for 1732: 2,664 Cossacks in service in the five Sloboda regiments; 13,859 children and dependents of these Cossacks; 14,222 *podsosedniki*and their children; 25,495 *podpomoshchniki* and their children. Golovinskii, *Slobodskie kozach'i polki*, 88–89, 120–133, 143–155.

102   Peter the Great had founded the Ukrainian Land Militia in 1713 to support the field army by providing a cordon defense of the Ukrainian frontier in the rear. He had disbanded it in 1714 to meet the peace terms set by the Turks, but he revived it ten years later and in 1729 a military commission headed by Münnich doubled its size by forming ten new regiments of Land Militia cavalry on the grounds of its cost effectiveness. Because Land Militia cavalry were partly remunerated with plowlands and received their pay out of state peasant *obrok* rather than the soul tax, a regiment of them was 3.6 times cheaper than a dragoon regiment in the field army and 1.7 times cheaper than a regiment of garrison dragoons. Gennadii Shpitalov, *Ukrain'ska Landmilitsiia* (Kiev: Natsional'na Akademiia Nauk Ukraini,

2013), 39–44, 60–87; N. N. Petrukhintsev, *Tsarstvovanie Anny Ioannovny: formirovanie vnutripoliticheskogo kursa i sud'by armii i flota, 1730–1735* (St. Petersburg: Aleteiia, 2001), 121–123, 133–134, 154.

103 V. M. Kabuzan, *Zaselenie Novorossii (Ekaterinoslavskoi i Khersonskoi gubernii) v XVIII-pervoi polovine XIX veka* (Moscow: Nauka, 1976), 51.

104 D. I. Bagalei (Bahalii), *Istoriia Slobods'koi Ukraini* (Khar'kov, 1918), 103–104; Golovinskii, *Slobodskie kozach'i polka*, 162–170, 173.

105 Artem Kirpichenok, *Serbskie poseleniia na Ukraine v seredine XVIII veka* (St. Petersburg: Nestor, 2007), 50–51, 54, 59, 63–64.

106 Ibid., 76.

107 Kabuzan, *Zaselenie Novorossii*, 52, 84–85, 88–89; Kirpichenok, *Serbskie poseleniia*, 92, 95–96.

108 Kabuzan, *Zaselenie Novorossii*, 53.

109 The Serbian-Moldavian immigrants were offered thirty rubles a head to register in hussar/*pandura* formation in the regular army, permanently and without right of return; the Ukrainian, Polish, and Russian colonists were offered 12 rubles a head to register in military service. Kabuzan, *Zaselenie Novorossii*, 53, 101, 102.

110 Golovinskii, *Slobodskie kazach'i polki*, 202; Nikolai Gerbel', *Iziumskii slobodskii kazach'ii polk, 1651–1765* (St. Petersburg: Tip. Eduarda Pratsa, 1852), 113–115.

111 A. G. Sliusarskii, *Sotsial'no-ekonomicheskoe razvitie Slobozhanshchiny XVII-XVIII vv.* (Kharkov: Khar'kovskoe knizhnoe izd., 1964), 456–457.

112 The Kal'miuss River was its border with the Don Cossack Host; the Orel and Dnepr rivers formed its border with the Hetmanate. The Sich was initially based on Khortytsa Island in the Dnepr. By Mazepa's time it had moved to the mouth of the Chortomlyk River. Zaporozhia was divided into thirty-eight barracks settlements (*kureni*), each home to one or two Cossack companies; but there were no larger territorial regiments as in the Hetmanate or Sloboda Ukraine. By 1700 the Zaporozhian Cossack Host numbered about 10,000 men. Davies, *Empire and Military Revolution*, 46, 47.

113 Davies, *Empire and Military Revolution*, 48, 49, 88–90.

114 In fact the Ukrainian Cossacks standing with Mazepa at Poltava in 1709 were outnumbered by Hordienko's 7,600 Zaporozhians.

115 D. I. Iavornitskii, *Istoriia zaporoz'kikh kozakiv*, 3 vols. (Kiev: Naukova dumka, 1990), III, 325–326.

116 Iavornitskii, *Istoriia zaporoz'kikh kozakiv*, III, 401–412; N. D. Polons'ka-Vasylenko, "The Settlement of the Southern Ukraine (1750–1775)." *The Annals of the Ukrainian Academy of Arts and Sciences in the US*, IV, 14–15, V, 8–15.

117 Kabuzan, *Zaselenie Novorossii*, 79, 81–83.

118 Druzhinina, *Kiuchuk-Kainardzhiiskii mir*, 59; Kabuzan, *Zaselenie Novorossii*, 95, 98, 118–119; Madariaga, *Russia in the Age of Catherine the Great*, 68–69.

119 Polon'ska-Vasylenko, "Settlement of the Southern Ukraine," 319–320, 327.

120 Marc Raeff, ed., "Patterns of Russian Imperial Policy toward the Nationalities," in *Political Ideas and Institutions in Imperial Russia* (Boulder, CO, San Francisco, CA, Oxford: Westview Press, 1994), 126–136.

121 Marc Raeff, ed., "Uniformity, Diversity, and the Imperial Administration in the Reign of Catherine II," in *Political Ideas and Institutions in Imperial Russia* (Boulder, CO, San Francisco, CA, Oxford: Westview Press, 1994), 141–143, 146.

122 Ibid., 146, 151.

123 Willard Sunderland, *Taming the Wild Field: Colonization and Empire in the Russian Steppe* (Ithaca, NY and London: Cornell University Press, 2004), 73–74, 87. From 1764 Zaporozhians, Russians, and foreigners willing to resettle in New Russia were offered homestead tracts of twenty-six or thirty *desiatiny*, settlement subsidies of twelve rubles, and tax exemptions of 6–16 years; agents enlisting foreigners received special bonuses.

124 N. D. Chechulin, *Ocherki po istorii russkikh finansov v tsarstvovanie Ekateriny II* (St. Petersburg: Senatskaia tipografiia, 1906), 286.

Chapter 4

1 This included the field army regiments, the artillery, the garrison regiments, the Land Militia, and the Cossack and Kalmyk irregulars but excluded naval personnel. The recently introduced soul tax from forty provinces together with such indirect taxes as excise, customs, and the salt tax had been budgeted to covert the costs of the military establishment while still leaving a balance of 192,395 rubles. The yield of direct taxes (now primarily the soul tax) to indirect taxes was about 5:3. Expenditures on the army and fleet in 1725 counted for 73.2 percent of total state expenditure (9.14 million rubles). Keep, *Soldiers of the Tsar*, 138; P. Miliukov, *Gosudarstvennoe khoziaistvo Rossii v pervoi chetverti XVIII stoletiia i reforma Petra Velikago* (St. Petersburg: Tip. M. Stasiulevicha, 2nd ed., 1905), 497.

2 Petrukhintsev, *Tsarstvovanie Anny*, 107–108, 121–123, 133–134, 154, 306, 310–311.

3 Kersnovskii called the 1741–1743 war against Sweden a "listless affair" marked by just three battles, all easily won by the numerically and technically superior Russian land and naval forces under General Peter Lacy and Admiral James Keith. In 1748 Russia briefly entered the War of the Austrian Succession in alliance with Austria by sending an expeditionary force of 30,000 troops under Prince Vasilii Repnin to the Rhine. Repnin's army did not see combat but its discipline made a favorable impression on Maria Theresa and its arrival may have contributed to the pressures bringing Frederick II to sign the Treaty of Aix-la-Chapelle. A. A. Kersnovskii, *Istoriia russkoi armii. Tom pervi. Ot Narvy do Parizha, 1700–1814* (Moscow: Golos, 1992), 85–89; N. Shpilevskaia, *Opisanie voiny mezhdu Rossiei i Shvetsiei v 1741, 1742, and 1743 gg.* (St. Petersburg: Tip. Iakova Treia, 1859); A. Veidemeier, *Tsarstvovanie Elizavety Petrovny. Chast' vtoraia* (St. Petersburg: Tip. Khintsa, 1834), 112–113.

4 K. V. Tatarnikov, ed., *Stroevye ustavy, instruktsii, i nastavleniia russkoi armii XVIII veka. Sbornik materialov. Tom I* (Moscow: Russkaia panorama, 2010), 147–177; Baiov, *Istoriia russkogo voennogo iskusstva, Vypusk I*, 394.

5 By comparison France had 211,753 troops, Austria about 139,00, and Prussia about 142,000–145,000. D. F. Maslovskii, *Russkaia armiia v semiletniuiu voinu. Vypusk I* (Moscow: Tip. Okruzhnago shtaba, 1886), 8–9.

6 The infantry regiments Peter I had begun forming by recruit levy in 1704 had a standard strength of 1,364 men in eight companies of fusiliers and one company of grenadiers; this had been slightly larger than the standard Swedish line regiment of 1,200 men and considerably larger than the English regiment of 780–930 rank-and-file. In 1708 Peter shifted the grenadier companies into their own regiments. Davies, *Empire and Military Revolution*, 67.

7 Maslovskii, *Russkaia armiia v semiletniuiu voinu*, I, 19–27, 69–70; Baiov, *Istoriia russkogo voennogo iskusstva*, 394–396.

8   In the final years of Peter the Great the army had been unusually heavy in cavalry—about 40 percent, not counting the Cossack and Kalmyk irregulars—and the overwhelming majority of regular cavalry had been dragoons, who were cheaper to equip than heavy cavalry and were trained to fight dismounted with carbines as well as from horseback. With such a large dragoon formation the Petrine field army was better prepared for flying corps (*corps volantes*) operations and could still overwhelm the small cavalry contingent Charles XII had fielded at Poltava. It therefore became established wisdom among Soviet military historians that the dragoons were one of the great strengths of the Petrine military system and that Münnich's decision to enlarge the heavy cavalry and make cuirassiers a third of the field army cavalry was a betrayal of Russian national principles, a blind imitation of German military orthodoxy and another example of the destructive consequences of the Courlander camarilla wielding power under Empress Anna. However, the prerevolutionary historian Baiov acknowledged that the dragoons lacked shock power and the need for some heavier shock cavalry was legitimate. Peter himself had contemplated forming cuirassier regiments, but cuirassiers were expensive because they required larger and sturdier mounts that had to be imported from Germany at the cost of sixty to seventy rubles apiece. Beskrovnyi, *Russkaia armiia i flota v XVIII veke*, 61–62; Baov, *Istoriia russkogo voennogo iskusstva*, I, 325.

9   Maslovskii, *Russkaia armiia v semiletniuiu voinu*, I, 29–33; Baiov, *Istoriia russkogo voennogo iskusstva*, I, 397–398.

10   By keeping his attacking cavalry in echelons in close order with the riders nearly knee-to-knee, Frederick II counted on the full rush to deliver enough shock to break the enemy's line even before his horsemen began using their swords. In fact the shock from such close-order charge did not require heavy cavalrymen; it could be produced by lighter cavalry, even dragoons or hussars, provided their mounts were strong and they were superbly trained. Nosworthy, *Anatomy of Victory*, 168–171; William Balck, *Tactics. Volume II* (Fort Leavenworth, Kansas: US Cavalry Association, 1894), 34; J. L. H. Keep, "The Russian Army in the Seven Years' War," in *The Military and Society in Russia, 1450–1917*, ed. Eric Lohr and Marshall Poe (Leiden: E J Brill, 2002), 201.

11   Maslovskii, *Russkaia armiia v semiletniuiu voinu*, I, 55–62; Baiov, *Istoriia russkogo voennogo iskusstva*, I, 400–402.

12   Iu. R. Klokman, *Fel'dmarshal Rumiantsev v period russko-turetskoi voiny 1768–1774* (Moscow: Akademiia Nauk SSSR, 1951), 28.

13   O. Leonov and I. Ul'ianov, *Reguliarnaia pekhota, 1698–1801* (Moscow: AST, 1995), 70–71; Baiov, *Istoriia russkogo voennogo iskusstva*, I, 395; Maslovskii, *Russkaia armiia v semiletniuiu voinu*, I, 22.

14   Herbert Kaplan, *Russia and the Outbreak of the Seven Years' War* (Berkeley: University of California Press, 1968), 47; G. G. Frumenkov, "Rossiia i semiletniaia voina," *Voprosy istorii* 9 (1971): 109.

15   Apraksin was a courtier without much military experience and may have owed his appointment as commander-in-chief to the influence of Kyrilo Rozumovsky.

16   Kersnovskii, *Istoriia russkoi armii*, I, 97–99, 102, 106–107; Szabo, *The Seven Years' War in Europe*, 428–429.

17   Shuvalov devalued the currency three-fold by introducing copper coins cast from outmoded guns. Szabo, *The Seven Years' War in Europe*, 209; Christopher Duffy, *Russia's Military Way to the West. Origins and Nature of Russian Military Power, 1700–1800* (London: Routledge and Kegan Paul, 1981), 60.

18   Keep, "The Russian Army in the Seven Years' War," 204, 209, 213; Petrov, *Vliianie*, 36–37.

19   It did preserve some Petrine-era practice by allowing commanders to form a line of three ranks under special circumstances. Prussian ordinances had already found the three-rank line sufficient. D. F. Maslovskii, *Stroevaia i polevaia sluzhba russkikh voisk vremen Imperatora Petra Velikogo i Imperatritsy Elizavety* (Moscow: Tip. Okruzhnago shtaba, 1883; Moscow: Librokom, 2011, 2nd ed), 129–130, 134–135; Tatarnikov, ed., *Stroevye ustavy*, I, 201–279; Leonov and Ul'ianov, *Reguliarnaia pekhota*, 79.

20   Keep, "The Russian Army in the Seven Years' War," 200.

21   The ordinance employs the term *kolong*. The attack column had already received some attention through the works of Jean Charles, Chevalier de Folard (d. 1751).

22   Catherine II's troops could reportedly march at an average of 20 kilometers a day (factoring in a rest day every third day) and could make forced marches of 40 kilometers a day. Duffy, *Russia's Military Way to the West*, 120; Keep, "The Russian Army in the Seven Years' War," 202.

23   Tatarnikov, ed., *Stroevye ustavy*, I, 307–334.

24   Klokman, *Fel'dmarshal Rumiantsev*, 25–26; Petrov, *Vliianie*, 36; Maslovskii, *Stroevaia i polevaia sluzhba*, 154, 168–170.

25   Baiov, *Istoriia russkogo voennogo iskusstva*, I, 425–426.

26   Keep, "The Russian Army in the Seven Years' War," 201.

27   Kersnovskii, *Istoriia russkoi armii*, I, 112; Petrov, *Vliianie*, 36; Maslovskii, *Russkaia armiia v semiletniuiu voinu*, I, 61–62.

28   Szabo, *The Seven Years' War in Europe*, 162–169; Christopher Duffy, *Frederick the Great: A Military Life* (London and New York: Routledge, 1985), 171.

29   Frumenkov, "Rossiia i semiletniaia voina," 115. Duffy, *Frederick the Great: A Military Life*, 189.

30   Quoted in Pintner, "Russia as a Great Power, 1709–1856," 48–49.

31   Ibid., 46; Klokman, *Fel'dmarshal Rumiantsev*, 26. But they may be underestimating the desertion rate from the Russian army. Losses to desertion in the first year of Russian campaigning (1757) were about 7 percent of total losses, and J. L. H. Keep thinks the desertion rate rose over 1758–1761. Keep, "The Russian Army in the Seven Years' War," 199–200. One should also consider the possibility that the high sick rate could in some instances reflect reduced endurance, with some seeking refuge from battle in the hospital.

32   Austrian losses in the Seven Years' War were about 140,000; Prussian casualties were 200,000. Keep, "The Russian Army in the Seven Years' War," 199–200; B. Ts. Urlanis, *Istoriia voennykh poter'* (St. Petersbug: Poligon, 1994), 51, 59. Deaths from disease would likewise account for much of the Russian mortality bill during the Turkish War of 1768–1774.

33   Here I am speaking of "technicalism" in the sense used by Marshall Hodgson to describe the impact of the spread of technical specialization across early modern society, not exclusively but most pronouncedly in the West. Technicalism refers not merely to the development of new and more efficient technologies but to the construction of a new cultural attitude, a confidence that nature, including the performance abilities of individuals and groups, can be engineered scientifically for greater efficiency. The technicalist spirit in eighteenth-century European military thought expressed the idea "that the art of war was also susceptible to systematic formulation based on rules and principles of universal validity which had been revealed in the campaigns of the great military leaders of history." Marshall Hodgson, *The Venture of Islam, Volume III. Gunpowder Armies and Modern Times* (Chicago and London: University of Chicago Press, 1977), 186–201; Azar Gat, *The Origins of Military Thought from the Enlightenment to Clausewitz* (Oxford: Clarendon Press, 1989), 28–29.

34 Klokman, *Fel'dmarshal Rumiantsev*, 29–33; Szabo, *The Seven Years' War in Europe*, 369–371.

35 Peter III's "Prussian" alterations to uniforms and his March 27 Infantry Ordinance were eliminated; the fourth Guards Regiment he had established was abolished, replaced by a smaller Cavalier Guard; his project to recruit seven infantry regiments and six cavalry regiments in Holstein was ended; and his renaming of regiments after their commanders was reversed. M. P. Bogdanovich, *Russkaia armiia v veke Imperatritsy Ekateriny II* (St. Petersburg: Tipografiia Departamenta udelov, 1873), 4–7; Baiov, *Istoriia russkogo voennogo iskusstva, I*, 488; Tatarnikov, ed., *Stroevye ustavy*, I, 429–452.

36 This commission also comprised Petr Ivanovich Panin, VK President, and V. I. Suvorov, father of the future hero of the empress' Turkish wars. Münnich was also consulted about reforms even though he had remained loyal to Peter III during Catherine's coup. *PSZ* volume XVI, 1762, nos. 11.605 and 11.707; Klokman, *Fel'dmarshal Rumiantsev*, 34; Bogdanovich, *Russkaia armiia*, 5.

37 Klokman, *Fel'dmarshal Rumiantsev*, 34; John P. Le Donne, "Outlines of Military Administration, 1762-1796. Part I: Troop Strength and Deployment," *Jahrbucher fur Geschichte Osteuropas* 31 (1983): 321.

38 Le Donne, "Outlines," Part I, 321; Beskrovnyi, *Russkaia armiia i flot v XVIII veke*, 304, 317.

39 Leonov and Ul'ianov, *Reguliarnaia pekhota*, 133; Le Donne, "Outlines," Part I, 322; Baiov, *Istoriia russkogo voennogo iskusstva*, I, 491.

40 A. K. Petrov and A. K. Baiov disagree as to whether the fusils of the carabiniers had bayonets.

41 Bogdanovich, *Russkaia armiia, II*, 6; Beskrovnyi, *Russkaia armiia i flot v XVIII veke*, 317–318.

42 Keep, "Outlines," Part I, 325–326; D. F. Maslovskii, *Zapiski po istorii voennogo iskusstva v Rossii*, 2 pts. (St. Petersburg: V. Bezobrazov, 1891), I, 65–66.

43 Villebois would be succeeded by the less diligent Grigorii Orlov in 1765.

44 Initially grenadier and jaeger battalions had no regimental guns, but in the course of the Turkish War these battalions received two guns each.

45 These five regiments, each of ten companies, were organized for administration; for tactical purposes field guns were deployed as batteries, the size of which was determined by need.

46 Bogdanovich, *Russkaia armiia, II*, 6, 7; Beskrovnyi, *Russkaia armiia v XVIII veke*, 322; Klokman, *Fel'dmarshal Rumiantsev*, 37; Maslovskii, *Zapiski*, 72–75.

47 The divisions and corps established in 1763 were the St. Petersburg, Moscow, Finland, Estland, Lifland, Smolensk, Sevsk, and Ukraine divisions, the Siberian Corps, and two Orenburg corps. Klokman, *Fel'dmarshal Rumiantsev*, 37.

48 Le Donne, "Outlines," I, 328–329.

49 Edward Luttwak, *The Grand Strategy of the Roman Empire: From the First Century AD to the Third* (Baltimore, MD and London: Johns Hopkins University Press, 1976), 55–60.

50 Baiov, *Istoriia russkogo voennago iskusstva* I, 493.

51 This cannot be fixed more precisely because it was still common practice to appoint supernumerary officers, especially to the Guards regiments. John Le Donne, *Absolutism and Ruling Class. The Formation of the Russian Political Order, 1700–1825* (New York, Oxford: Oxford University Press, 1993), 42.

52 Duffy, Russia's *Military Way to the West*, 144.

53 John Le Donne, "Outlines of Russian Military Administration, 1762–1796. Part II: The High Command," *Jahrbucher fur Geschichte Osteuropas* 33 (1985): 189–191; Duffy, *Russia's Military Way to the West*, 148.

54 Duffy, *Russia's Military Way to the West*, 152.

55 Ibid., 146; Beskrovnyi, *Russkaia armiia i flot v XVIII veke*, 443.

56 Klokman, *Fel'dmarshal Rumiantsev*, 38, 39.

57 Duffy, *Russia's Military Way to the West*, 166; Beskrovnyi, *Russkaia armiia i flot v XVIII veke*, 342; Baiov, *Istoriia russkago voennago iskusstva*, I, 513–515.

58 The Council had the authority to devise the general war plan and operational plans; to examine matters of mobilization, staffing, provisioning, and pay, in both the field army and the fortress garrisons; to follow diplomatic developments bearing upon the war and organize peace negotiations; and to discuss extraordinary taxes, loans, and military budgeting. During 1773–1775 the Council would plan and review operations against the Pugachev Revolt, and in 1775 it would advise the empress on her project to reform Governorate administration. The Council's decisions were issued as manifestoes, decrees and rescripts under the empress' signature. The legal issues its work raised were addressed in the Senate; its instructions to the army were fleshed out by the War College (VK), which was taking on the features of a *Stavka* or General Staff. *Arkhiv Gosudarstvennago soveta. Tom I* (St. Petersburg: Vtoroe otdeleniia Sobstvennoi E. I. V. Kantseliarii, 1869), 1–4. *PSZ XVIII*, nos. 13.232 and 13.233, January 17, 1769.

59 John Le Donne, *Ruling Russia: Politics and Administration in the Age of Absolutism, 1762–1796* (Princeton: Princeton University Press, 1984), 30; Le Donne, *Absolutism and Ruling Class*, 84–85; William C. Fuller, Jr. *Strategy and Power in Russia, 1600–1914* (New York: Free Press, 1992), 141, 144.

60 Maslovskii, *Zapiski*, 56–57.

61 K. V. Tatarnikov, ed., *Stroevye ustavy, instruktsii i nastavleniia russkoi armii XVIII veka. Sbornik materialov, Tom II* (Moscow: Russkaia panorama, 2010), 5–51; Leonov and Ul'ianov, *Reguliarnaia pekhota*, 136; Nosworthy, *Anatomy of Victory*, 58. Klokman, *Fel'dmarshal Rumiantsev*, 37–38.

62 For a description of oblique fire see Maslovskii, *Stroevaia i polevaia sluzhba russkikh voisk*, 132.

63 Tatarnikov, ed., *Stroevye ustavy*, II, 41–42; Leonov and Ul'ianov, *Reguliarnaia pekhota*, 136; Nosworthy, *Anatomy of Victory*, 264–276, 382–383; Russell Weigley, *The Age of Battles: The Quest for Decisive Warfare from Breitenfeld to Waterloo* (Bloomington and Indianapolis: Indiana University Press, 1991), 268.

64 Tatarnikov, ed., *Stroevye ustavy*, II, 45–48; Petrov, *Vliianie*, 41, 42; Nosworthy, *Anatomy of Victory*, 380. A few Russian infantry regiments at this time still had pikes, at 216 per regiment.

65 Duffy, *Russia's Military Way to the West*, 170.

66 Tatarnikov, ed., *Stroevye Ustavy*, II, 90–156.

67 Kersnovskii, *Istoriia russkoi armii*, I, 121.

68 Maslovskii, *Zapiski*, 88–89.

69 Ibid., 92.

70 Baiov, *Istoriia russkago voennago iskusstva*, I, 522.

71 V. V. Penskoi, "Armiia Rossiiskogo imperii v XVIII v.: vybor modeli razvitiia," *Voprosy istorii* 7 (2000): 128–129.

Notes

72 Gat, *The Origins of Military Thought*, 38.

73 In 1737 Munnich wrote, "The Turks count upon their strong and numerous army and artillery, on the health, strength, and activity of their soldiers, and on the hardiness of their mounts; and in this they have the advantage over other European armies. We must count upon a disciplined army, on a well-formed order of battle, and on accurate and heavy musket and artillery fire." His chief adjutant, James William Fermor, authored a *Disposition of Battle Order and Maneuvers in General Battle with the Turks*. To counter the Turks' numerical advantage and their preference for bold attack Fermor prescribed a better-trained, better provisioned Russian army that could mobilize faster, march faster, carry the war into enemy territory, force the time and place of battle, and seize control of a military theater earlier on, forcing the enemy to negotiate for peace. This required that the Russian army learn to make night marches in silence and march in planned stages so that the baggage train could catch up with the forward battalions. In combat with the Turks it was crucial to maintain battle order and not present vulnerable intervals along the front, and it was especially important to heed Montecuccoli's advice and keep up a heavy rate of fire. The preferred firing system was by platoon, in sequence, with firing by rank within each platoon. Volley fire by rank across battalion or regiment was discouraged because it made too much smoke and noise, hampering directing officers from seeing the enemy move and making it harder for fusiliers to hear their officers' commands. In storming enemy fortifications attack should be made by column, with grenadiers in the front, the columns closing in near the attack point to support each other and to shift over to take and widen a breach. Although Fermor's *Disposition* did not instruct how to fold lines to form a square, in the course of the 1735–1739 Turkish War Münnich's forces came to make frequent use of squares, including multiple corps or regimental squares to catch the enemy in crossfire, and their deployment in squares paid off spectacularly well at the Battle of Stavuchany (1739). V. V. Penskoi, "Armiia Rossiiskoi imperiii," 126; Baiov, *Istoriia russkogo voennogo iskusstva*, I, 341–345; Baiov, *Russkaia armiia v tsarstvovanie*, 54–65.

74 Fortunatov, *P. A. Rumiantsev*, II, no. 43, 81–82.

75 A commander of hussars in the War of the Austrian Succession, Turpin de Crisse rejected the obsession with infantry firepower and proposed greater reliance on light units mixing infantry and cavalry and attacking with bayonet and saber. In 1769 Turpin de Crisse published commentaries on Montecuccoli's campaigns against the Turks in Hungary. Baiov, *Istoriia russkago voennago iskusstva*, I, 409; Armstrong Starkey, *War in the Age of the Enlightenment, 1700–1789* (Westport, CT and London: Praeger, 2003), 195.

76 Beskrovnyi, *Russkaia armiia i flot v XVIII veke*, 288–290, 385–424, 508–509; Baiov, *Istoriia russkogo voennogo iskusstva*, I, 653; Iu. R. Klokman, "P. A. Rumiantsev i A. V. Suvorov," in *Suvorovskii sbornik*, ed. A. V. Sukhomlin (Moscow: AN SSSR, 1951), 61–88; Iu. R. Klokman, "P. A. Rumiantsev kak voennyi teoretik," *Istoricheskie zapiski* 37 (1951): 81–103; A. N. Kochetkov, "Takticheskie vzgliady A. V. Suvorova," *Razvitie taktiki russkoi armii, XVIII- nachale XIX vv.*, ed. D. V. Pankov (Moscow: Ministerstvo oborony SSSR, 1957), 83–111; I. V. Semenova, *Chugun Kagul'skii, tyi sviashche: Iz istorii russkoi-turetskoi voiny 1768-1774* (Kishinev: Kartia Moldoveniaske, 1970), 18–22; Penskoi, "Armiia Rossiiskoi imperii," 129–130; V. A. Zolotarev, M. N. Menzhevich, and D. E. Skorodumov, *Vo slavu otechestva Rossiiskogo (razvitie voennoi mysli i voennogo iskusstva v Rossii vo vtoroi polovine XVIII v.* (Moscow: Mysl', 1984), 114–128; Fuller, *Strategy and Power in Russia*, 156–167. Bruce Menning, who has written extensively on the Russian army in the eighteenth century, acknowledges that there was indeed a tendency in the Elizabethan and Catherinian military establishments to posit "Prussianizing" versus "native Russian" military doctrine (although historians have exaggerated the dichotomy between them,

ignoring the extent to which each accommodated some elements of the experience of the other); that the strategic and tactical innovations Rumiantsev and Suvorov worked out during Catherine II's two Turkish Wars did represent a departure from Austrian and Prussian doctrine on line tactics; and that Rumiantsev's and Suvorov's ideas did in some ways anticipate French practice between 1792 and 1815. But he argues that Rumiantsev and Suvorov were building upon lessons from Münnich's as well as Peter I's campaigns and were consciously departing from Austro-Prussian convention not on general principle but because they recognized the need to revise strategy and tactics for the particular military environment of the southern steppe frontier. "The Russian Army of the Seven Years' War, wedded as it was to conventional European models, was ill-suited to engage in the kind of far-flung and far-reaching operations that would produce military decision in the south. The advent of decision required significant departures from the northern European ideal, which in the 1760s and the early 1770s was embodied in the army of Frederick II of Prussia. While native Russian genius remained an important factor governing the evolution of Russian military art, warfare on the steppe frontier encouraged that genius to seek and apply innovation in ways that were either ignored (as in the case of the North American precedent), unknown, or embryonic in the west until the era of the French Revolution." Bruce W. Menning, "Russian Military Innovation in the Second Half of the Eighteenth Century," *War and Society* 2 (1984), 36. See also Bruce W. Menning, "Russia and the West: The Problem of Eighteenth-century Military Models," in *Russia and the West in the Eighteenth Century*, ed. A. G. Cross (Newtonville, MA: Oriental Research Partners, 1983): 282–293.

77 In support of this conclusion they have cited a 1777 memorandum by Rumiantsev arguing that Russia should develop its own unique military organization corresponding to the particular "physical, moral, and political" character of the Russian nation. See Emelia'nov, "Razvitie taktiki," 59. Kersnovskii, *Istoriia russkoi armii*, I, 164–169; Beskrovnyi, *Russkaia armiiia i flot v XVIII veke*, 648–653; N. M. Korobkov, *Fel'dmarshal Rumiantsev. Sbornik dokumentov i materialov* (Moscow, Leningrad: OGIZ, 1947), 6.

78 We exclude here those ideas and practices appearing after 1774, even though Potemkin and Suvorov instituted their most important military reforms after the end of Catherine the Great's first Turkish War.

79 V. A. Zolotarev, ed., *Istoriia voennoi strategii Rossii* (Moscow: Kuchkovo pole, 2000), 65–66, 68.

80 Gat, *The Origins of Military Thought*, 35, 75–77, 80–81.

81 By 1769 Austrian military ordinances were prescribing the multiple-column march maneuver, but Austrian commanders still adhered to the traditional battle order of the unrolled line and they continued to use swine-feathers as a defense against Turkish cavalry. Christopher Duffy, *The Army of Maria Theresa. The Armed Forces of Imperial Austria, 1740–1780* (New York: Hippocrene Books, 1977), 78, 142–143.

82 "Divisional square" (*divizionnyi kare*) here refers to the larger hollow square comprising several regiments and battalions rather than to the firing divisions within battalions. It is not to be confused with the "squared division," a division of two brigades, each of two regiments.

83 Menning, "Russia and the West," 287–288.

84 Nosworthy, *Anatomy of Victory*, 258–259.

85 Marshal Saxe had recommended as early as the 1740s supporting infantry battalions with light infantry using aimed fire. Zolotarev et al., *Vo slavu otechestva*, 116; Fortunatov, *P. A. Rumiantsev*, II, 334 and 627; Nosworthy, *Anatomy of Victory*, 157.

Notes

86　Bruce W. Menning, "Train Hard, Fight Easy: The Legacy of A. V. Suvorov and his 'Art of Victory,'" *Air University Review* (November–December 1986), 5; Beskrovnyi, *Russkaia armiia i flot v XVIII veke*, 390, 405.

87　"Nauka pobezhdat'," in L. G. Beskrovnyi, ed., *Khrestomatiia po russkoi voennoi istorii* (Moscow: Ministerstvo vooruzhennykh sil SSSR, 1947), 273–278.

88　"Iz prikaza General-poruchika Suvorova po voiskam Krymskogo i Kubanskogo korpusov," Beskrovnyi, ed., *Khrestomatiia*, 255.

Chapter 5

1　Solov'ev, XIV, kn. 28, 280–282. *Arkhiv Gosudarstvennago Soveta, Tom I.* (St. Petersburg: Vtoroe otdelenie Sobstvennoi E. I. V. Kantseliarii, 1869), 1–8.

2　It should be noted that these were modest objectives compared to those announced by Münnich in launching Russia's last war with the Turks. He had held out to Empress Anna the prospect of conquering Crimea and Kabarda, liberating Moldavia and Wallachia and Greece, and occupying Istanbul by the fourth year of war. Davies, *Empire and Military Revolution*, 191.

3　Solov'ev, XIV, kn. 28, 284.

4　Petrov, *Vliianie* I, 84, 85.

5　Aleksandr Mikhailovich Golitsyn (1718–1783), first cousin of Vice-Chancellor A. M. Golitsyn. In the Seven Years' War, he had distinguished himself at Thorn and Frankfurt, for which he was promoted from Lt. General to General-*anshef* and awarded the order of St. Aleksandr Nevskii. An influential member of Empress Catherine's Court Council, he was a political ally of Zakhar Chernyshov. The German military historian F. von Stein considered Golitsyn "respected and honest, but devoid of strategic brilliance." Solov'ev, XIV, kn. 28, 284; Dm. Bantysh-Kamenskii, *Biografii rossiiskikh generalissimusov i general-fel'dmarshalov* (Moscow: Biblioteka, 1994, facs. reprint of 1840 edition), 170–171; Richard Ungermann, *Der Russisch-Turkische Krieg, 1768–1774* (Vienna and Leipzig, 1906), 29.

6　Petr Aleksandrovich Rumiantsev (1725–1796), son of one of the leading commanders of the previous Turkish War, and rumored the bastard son of Peter I. Veteran of the Seven Years' War, rewarded for victories at Tilsit, Frankfurt, and Kolberg with the order of St. Aleksandr Nevskii and the orders of St. Anna and Apostle Paul; Governor-General of Little Russia, 1764–1768; once married to (and now separated from) Ekaterina Mikhailovna Golitsyna, sister of General-*anshef* A. M. Golitsyn. Bantysh-Kamenskii, *Biografii rossiiskikh generalissimusov i general-fel'dmarshalov*, 174–177.

7　Solov'ev, XIV, kn. 28, 284.

8　Petrov, *Vliianie* I, 85–88.

9　Three thousand of these recruits were *odnodvortsy* now made liable for Land Militia service.

10　A. B. Shirokorad, *Russko-turetskie voiny 1676–1918 gg.* (Moscow: AST, 2000), 142; Solov'ev, XIV, kn. 28, 286–287.

11　Petrov, *Vliianie* I, 104–112.

12　Petrov, *Voina* I, 55.

13　Khan Kirim Girei had been restored to power in October 1768. Smirnov, *Krymskoe khanstvo*, II, 99.

14 This was the war plan according to Petrov, who cites as source the testimony of a "Nonie" I have not been able to identify. Petrov, *Voina* I, 57–58, 82, 108, 113; Louis Felix Guinement de Keralio, *Histoire de la derniere guerre entre les Russes et les Turcs* (Paris: DeSaint, 1777), 48–50; Ungermann, *Der Russisch-Turkische Krieg*, 15–19.

15 Aksan, *Ottoman Wars*, 142, 143, 145; Virginia Aksan, "The One-Eyed Fighting the Blind: Mobilization, Supply, and Command in the Russo-Turkish War of 1768–1774," *International History Review* 15, 2 (1993): 229.

16 Aksan, "The One-Eyed Fighting the Blind," 231–232; Virginia Aksan, "Feeding the Ottoman Troops on the Danube, 1768–1774," *War and Society* 13, 1 (1995): 6, 9; Aksan, *An Ottoman Statesman*, 125.

17 Petrov, *Voina* I, 129.

18 Tott, *Memoirs*, I, 420.

19 Petrov, *Voina* I, 129.

20 Tott, *Memoirs*, I, 441; Ibid., 129–130.

21 Tott, *Memoirs*, I, 450. The arnauts and the *sipahi*s included many Christians.

22 Tott, *Memoirs*, I, 457.

23 Prozorovskii had twelve squadrons of hussars, 300 jaegers, four companies of grenadiers, and a carabinier regiment. After crossing the Dnestr on January 19, he received in reinforcement two more carabinier regiments and a regiment of infantry from Kiev. Petrov, *Voina*, I, 131.

24 P. K. Fortunatov, ed., *P. A. Rumiantsev* 2 vols. (Moscow: Voennoe ministerstvo SSSR, 1953), II, no. 35, 66–67.

25 Tott, *Memoirs*, I, 462. This tactic of dividing columns in dendrite fashion into branches and multiple smaller branches was the classic raiding tactic for Tatar invasion armies. It allowed Tatar forces to fan out across a broad front, running across the countryside in small raiding parties of a hundred men or fewer, and then reassembling at a predetermined rally point with their captives and stolen livestock.

26 Tott, *Memoirs*, I, 464.

27 Tott, *Memoirs*, I, 469.

28 Petrov, *Voina* I, 132–133.

29 Tott, *Memoirs*, I, 472–473.

30 Ibid., 475.

31 Petrov, *Vliianie*, 137; Petrov, *Voina* I, 295–6.

32 Tott, *Memoirs*, I, 475, 490, 503, 506; Ahmed Resmi Efendi, *A Summary of Admonitions*, 46; Hammer-Purgstall, *Histoire de l'Empire Ottoman*, XVI, 214. Smirnov considered Kirim Girei's death to have marked the beginning of the political demise of the Crimean Khanate. Smirnov, *Krymskoe khanstvo*, II, 103.

33 Fortunatov, *P. A. Rumiantsev*, II, no. 33, 62–63, and no. 36, 67–69.

34 Ahmed Resmi Efendi, *A Summary of Admonitions*, 46.

35 Fortunatov, *P. A. Rumiantsev*, II, no. 24 and *prilozhenie*, 39–41; Petrov, *Voina* I, 124, 148, 157–158. At full strength, a line infantry regiment was supposed to number 1,552 men—in ten companies, or two battalions—and a regular cavalry regiment was supposed to have 750 men.

36 Petrov, *Voina* I, 150; Petrov, *Vliianie* I, 126–128.

Notes

37 Petrov, *Vliianie*, 128–129.

38 Petrov, *Voina* I, 157–158.

39 Mustafa Kesbi, cited in Mezin Bezikoglu, "The Deterioration of Ottoman Administration in the Light of the Ottoman-Russian War of 1768–1774," MA Thesis, Bilkent University, 2001, p. 57.

40 Petrov, *Voina* I, 161.

41 Abaza Mehmed Pasha had been sent to reinforce Khotin with 10,000 horse. Petrov, *Voina* I, 162–164; Aksan, *An Ottoman Statesman*, 144–145.

42 Petrov, *Vliianie*, 135; Shirokorad, *Russko-turetskie voiny*, 145–146.

43 Keralio, *Histoire de la derniere guerre entre les Russes et les Turcs* I, 85; Petrov, *Vliianie* I, 136–140.

44 The details of the war plan issued at the end of 1769 projected that the Second Army would number 43,728 troops: five regiments of regular cavalry, seven hussar regiments, four pikinier regiments, 9,000 cossacks, fourteen regiments of infantry, and forty guns. Klokman, *Fel'dmarshal Rumiantsev*, 61.

45 Klokman, *Fel'dmarshal Rumiantsev*, 68.

46 Ibid., 61; Fortunatov, *P. A. Rumiantsev*, II, no. 24, 37–43.

47 Klokman, *Fel'dmarshal Rumiantsev*, 57, 61; Fortunatov, *P. A. Rumiantsev*, II, no. 30, 54.

48 Klokman, *Fel'dmarshal Rumiantsev*, 65–67; Petrov, *Vliianie*, 188.

49 A. A. Lebedev, *U istokov Chernomorskogo flota Rossii* (St. Petersburg: Gangut, 2011), 86–87, 227–229.

50 Petrov, *Voina* I, 296–298; A. Andreev, *Kniaz' V. M. Dolgorukov-Krymskii* (Moscow: Mezhregional'nyi tsentr otraselevoi informatiki Gosatomnadzora Rossii, 1997), 92.

51 Fortunatov, *P. A. Rumiantsev*, II, 346.

52 Stoffeln's column comprised one infantry regiment, one dragoon regiment, a regiment of Donetsk pikiniers, the Myrhorod Ukrainian Cossack *polk*, a regiment of Don Cossacks, and several guns. (This was Karl von Stoffeln, not to be confused with Christopher von Stoffeln, who was with Golitsyn's First Army. Romanius may be either Johan or Avram Romanius, both of whom were Major-Generals in the Second Army.) Romanius' column comprised one hussar regiment, one pikinier regiment, one regiment and company of Cossacks, and four guns. Petrov, *Voina* I, 299, 303, 304.

53 Fortunatov, *P. A. Rumiantsev*, II, no. 57, 107.

54 Petrov, *Voina* I, 305–306.

55 Petrov claims the army's strength approached 200,000 men. Petrov, *Vliianie*, 148.

56 Aksan, *An Ottoman Statesman*, 141.

57 Aksan, "The One-eyed Fighting the Blind," 235; Ahmed Resmi Efendi, *A Summary of Admonitions*, 49; Hammer-Purgstall, *Histoire de l'Empire Ottoman*, 219.

58 Baiov, *Istoriia russkogo voennogo iskusstva*, I, 568.

59 *Petrov, Vliianie*, 146–147.

60 To convince the grand vizier to focus on a campaign against New Russia, Potocki had offered a Treaty of Eternal Peace between the Republic of Poland and the Porte. This treaty, subsequently signed by some Confederate representatives at Tilsit, ceded Kiev palatinate to the Porte and offered a mutual defense pact in which Poland pledged to support the Porte with a Republican army of 100,000 troops. Petrov, *Vliianie*, 146–147; Petrov, *Voina* I, 187, 190.

61 Petrov, *Vliianie*, 150–152.

62 Petrov, *Vliianie*, 154; Bezikoglu, "The Deterioration of Ottoman Administration," 61.

63 Petrov, *Vliianie*, 155, 158.

64 According to testimony from Turkish prisoners, Mehmed Pasha's attacking force numbered 70,000 men. They apparently carried off most of their dead and wounded. Russian losses in this battle were: fifty-four killed, eighty-eight wounded, and forty-seven missing. Among those receiving commendations for valor were Stoffeln and Major-General Grigorii Potemkin, who was at this time attached to Golitsyn's army as a volunteer. Petrov, *Vliianie*, 156, 157; *Zhurnal voennykh deistviia armiei eia Imperatorskago Velichestva 1769–1771* (St. Petersburg: Gosudarstvennaia Voennaia Kollegiia, 1772), (unpaginated), frames 45–47; Simon Sebag Montefiore, *Potemkin: Catherine the Great's Imperial Partner* (New York: Vintage Books, 2000), 76, 80; Ungermann, *Der Russisch-Turkische Krieg*, 57–60.

65 Petrov, *Vliianie*, 158.

66 He had embezzled a large part of the 25 million piasters earmarked for purchasing stores in Moldavia, and 12,000 of his troops had deserted in disgust. Ahmed Resmi Efendi speculated that the grand vizier's illness must have demented him. Aksan, *An Ottoman Statesman*, 142–143; Petrov, *Voina* I, 228.

67 Petrov, *Vliianie*, 159.

68 Ibid., 160–165.

69 Petrov, *Voina* I, 220; *Zhurnal voennykh deistviia armiei*, frame 70.

70 Petrov, *Voina* I, 221.

71 Petrov, *Vliianie*, 167–169; Aksan, *An Ottoman Statesman*, 145–146.

72 Quoted in Sorel, *The Eastern Question*, 54.

73 Fortunatov, *P. A. Rumiantsev*, II, xii–xiii, no. 48, 90–91, 93, and no. 56, 105–106; Klokman, *Fel'dmarshal Rumiantsev*, 68–71; Solov'ev XIV, tom 28, 291.

74 Klokman, *Fel'dmarshal Rumiantsev*, 71; Petrov, *Vliianie*, 189–190.

75 Fortunatov, *P. A. Rumiantsev*, II, nos. 63 and 64, 119–121.

76 Shirokorad, *Russko-turetskie voiny*, 147.

77 Soloviev, XIV, tom 28, 291–292.

78 Ahmed Resmi Efendi, *A Summary of Admonitions*, 49.

79 Petrov, *Voina* I, 231.

80 Fortunatov, *P. A. Rumiantsev*, II, no. 64, 122–128; Ibid., 225, 227, 232.

81 These could be packed two to a mule.

82 Petrov, *Voina* I, 232–235, 238; Aksan, *An Ottoman Statesman*, 144.

83 The first abatis was held by jaegers, the middle and rear by regular infantry—in all about 2,600 men under the command of James Bruce and Aleksei Golitsyn. Count James Bruce (1732–1791) was the son of James David Bruce, Peter the Great's illustrious *General-fel'dtseikhmeistr*, and was married to Rumiantsev's sister. Petrov, *Voina* I, 236, 239.

84 Petrov, *Voina* I, 239.

85 Petrov, *Vliianie*, 172–174.

86 Ibid., 175–179.

87 Petrov, *Vliianie*, 180–181.

88   The historian A. N. Petrov considered the endurance of Bruce's regiments at the abatis lines praiseworthy, as well as the initiative taken by Saltykov and Glebov. But he subjected Golitsyn to some criticism for keeping his cavalry in camp until the final phase of the battle. Petrov discerned a lack of coordination between Ottoman infantry and cavalry. Virginia Aksan thinks the performance of the Ottoman cavalry suffered from too high a proportion of undisciplined *levendat* horsemen. Petrov, *Vliianie*, 181–183; Petrov, *Voina* I, 239–246; Aksan, *An Ottoman Statesman*, 151.

89   Aksan, *An Ottoman Statesman*, 147; Petrov, *Voina* I, 251–253, 260.

90   Petrov, *Voina* I, 258–262.

91   Petrov, *Vliianie*, 185.

92   Petrov, *Voina* I, 260–268.

93   L. E. Semenova, *Kniazhestva Valakhiia i Moldaviia konets XIV- nachalo XIX v.* (Moscow: Indrik, 2006), 317–318.

94   Petrov, *Voina* I, 271–276; Petrov, *Vliianie*, 185–186.

95   Semenova, *Kniazhestva Valakhiia i Moldaviia*, 318; Seton-Watson, *A History of the Roumanian People*, 145.

96   Petrov, *Voina* I, 265–267, 284; Seton-Watson, *History of the Roumanian People*, 145.

97   The advance post at Bereşti had been defended by one squadron of hussars and a hundred Cossacks, and they had just run out of ammunition at the moment Fabritsian arrived at the rescue. Petrov, *Voina* I, 285–290.

98   Karazin's detachment finally managed to slip out from Koman Monastery and return to Bucharest. Petrov, *Voina* I, 292–293.

99   Aksan, *Ottoman Wars*, 151.

100   Weimarn's Observation Corps consisted of three carabinier regiments, four infantry regiments, ten guns, and 2,000 Cossacks. Petrov, *Voina* I, 121.

101   Petrov, *Voina* I, 139, 142–148.

102   Petrov, *Voina* I, 151, 171, 175, 201, 217; Władysław Konopczyński, *Casimir Pulaski*, trans. Irena Mackarewicz (Chicago: Polish Roman Catholic Union of America, 1947), 18–20.

103   Petrov, *Voina* I, 153.

104   Aleksandr Vasilevich Suvorov (1729–1800), the most celebrated Russian commander of the eighteenth century, was the son of General-*anshef* and Senator V. I. Suvorov. He entered the Semenovskii Life Guards and Corps of Cadets in 1748. He served in the Seven Years' War, first as *oberproviantmeistr* and then as officer at Krossen, Kunersdorf, Berlin, and Breslau; he was appointed to Colonel in 1762.

105   Russian casualties at Orzechowo were five dead and sixteen wounded. A. E. Taras, *Anatomiia nenavisti. Russko-pol'skie konflikty v XVIII-XX vv* (Minsk: Kharvest, 2008), 84–85; V. I. Buganov and A. V. Buganov, *Polkovodtsy XVIII v* (Moscow: Patriot, 1992), 376–377; Petrov, *Voina* I, 248–249; Fridrikh fon-Smitt, *Suvorov i padenie Pol'shi. Kn. Pervaia* (St. Petersburg: I. Veimar, 1866), 30–31.

106   fon-Smitt, *Suvorov*, 32; Buganov, *Polkovodtsy*, 377–378; Klokman, *Fel'dmarshal Rumiantsev*, 40–41.

107   John Baddeley, *The Russian Conquest of the Caucasus* (New York: Longmans, 1908), 33–34; Richmond, *The Northwest Caucasus*, 52.

108   V. A. Potto, *Kavkazskaia voina v otdel'nykh ocherkakh, epizodakh, legendakh, i biografiiakh*, 5 vols. (St. Petersburg: Tip. E. Evdokimova, 1887–1889), I, 53–55.

109 N. A. Smirnov, *Politika Rossii na Kavkazev XVI-XIX vekakh* (Moscow: Izd. Sotsial'no-ekonomicheskoi literatury, 1958), 93–95; Sotavov, *Severnyi Kavkaz*, 157.

110 Sotavov, *Severnyi Kavkaz*, 157.

111 Ibid., 161.

112 Another 20,000 Kalmyks were serving as auxiliaries to Berg's corps in Rumiantsev's Second Army. Petrov, *Voina* I, 322–323.

113 Petrov, *Voina* I, 324; Potto, *Kavkazskaia voina*, I, 56.

114 Ratiev's losses in this operation were one Cossack and eight Kalmyks killed and twelve wounded. Petrov, *Voina*, I, 326; Potto, *Kavkazskaia voina*, I, 57–58; Smirnov, *Politika Rossii na Kavkaze*, 95.

115 Potto, *Kavkazskaia voina*, I, 59; *Zhurnal voennykh deistviia armiei*, frames 443, 444.

116 Petrov, *Voina* I, 329; Sotavov, *Severnyi Kavkaz*, 161, 162; Smirnov, *Politika Rossii na Kavkaze*, 100.

117 Potto, *Kavkazskaia voina*, I, 59–60; Michael Khodarkovsky, *Where Two Worlds Met: The Russian State and the Kalmyk Nomads, 1600-1771* (Ithaca, NY: Cornell University Press, 1992), 225–227; Beatrice Teissier, *Russian Frontiers: Eighteenth-Century British Travellers in the Caspian, Caucasus, and Central Asia* (Oxford: Signal Books, 2011), 89.

118 Count Gottlieb Heinrich Todtleben, a Saxon, had entered Russian service during the Seven Years' War and had acquired brief glory for occupying Berlin in 1760. In June 1761, he was exposed communicating secretly with Frederick II, offering full details about Russian and Austrian operational plans in return for the promise of a commission in the Prussian army after the war. Empress Elizabeth Petrovna had him convicted of treason and sentenced to death by quartering, but Peter III had his sentence commuted to Siberian exile. Catherine II recalled him from exile and promoted him to Major-General. Szabo, *The Seven Years' War*, 337.

119 Solov'ev, XIV, kn. 28, 295.

120 Petrov, *Voina* I, 331; Allen, *History of the Georgian Peoples*, 207–208; Rayfield, *Edge of Empires*, 243–244.

Chapter 6

1 At this time, new levies to rebuild the field army at Babadagh (including a call-up of boys over seven years of age to replace noncombat support personnel) were being ignored in the provinces. Petrov, *Vliianie*, 203.

2 Stoffeln had been appointed commander of the Moldavian Corps in October, 1769. The regiments and brigades of the Corps were under Major-Generals Podgorichani, Prozorovskii, and Zamiatnin, Colonel Vladimir Golitsyn, and Brigadier von Weissman. Potemkin had charge of a vanguard force. Fortunatov, *P.A. Rumiantsev*, II, no. 87.

3 V. G. Kipnis, "Razvitie taktiki Russkoi armii v Russkom-Turetskoi voine 1768–1774," in *Rossiia v XVIII veke. Voiny i vneshniaia politika, vnutrennaia politika, ekonomika, i kul'tura. Tezisy*, ed. T. G. Frumenkova (St. Petersburg: Minerva, 1996), 4–5; Petrov, *Voina* II, 41–44; Fortunatov, *P. A. Rumiantsev*, II, no. 109, 213–214.

4 Rumiantsev criticized Stoffeln for failing to take Ibrail, dividing his forces, and destroying resources that the Moldavia Corps could have used for a second assault on Ibrail. Petrov, *Voina* II, 50–53; Fortunatov, *P. A. Rumiantsev*, II, nos. 113a–115, 220–225.

5   Perhaps this order of battle had been encouraged by Potemkin's success with two-company squares at Focşani. Kipnis, "Razvitie taktiki russkoi armii," 5.

6   Petrov, *Voina* II, 55–61; Aksan, *Ottoman Wars*, 150–152.

7   Shirokorad, *Russko-turetsskoie voiny*, 152.

8   It could also have spread from the army supply depots in Poland (plague was reported at Bar and Vinnitsa) or through merchants and refugees from the Danube.

9   Fortunatov, P. A. Rumiantsev, II, nos. 85, 95, 130, 138; Alexander Melikishvili, "Genesis of the Anti-plague System: The Tsarist Period," *Critical Reviews in Microbiology* 32 (2006): 24–25; Petrov, *Vliianie*, 201–202; John T. Alexander, *Bubonic Plague in Early Modern Russia. Public Health and Urban Disaster* (Oxford: Oxford University Press, 2003), 101–110.

10   L. E. Gorelova, "Chuma v Moskve (771–1773 gg.)," at www.gumer.info/bibliotek__Buks. History/Article/Gorel__ChumaMosk.php.

11   The First Army in winter quarters comprised nineteen cavalry regiments, thirty-two infantry regiments, 6,000 Don Cossacks, 3,000 Ukrainians, 120 field guns, and ten unicorns. This included the Moldavian Corps. Second in command was General-*anshef* Olits. The Lt. Generals were Christopher von Stoffeln, Petr Plemiannikov, Christopher von Essen, James Bruce, Ivan Saltykov, Nikolai Saltykov, Nikolai Repnin, and Ivan von Elmpt. The Major-Generals were Vasilii Khrapovitskii, Aleksei Stupishin, Fedor Glebov, Aleksandr Kheraskov, Ivan Podgorichani, Ivan Izmailov, Aleksandr Prozorovskii, Semen Chernoevich, Aleksandr Zamiatnin, Mikhail Kamenskii, Sergei Trubetskoi, Aleksei Golitsyn, Grigorii Potemkin, and Brigadier Iurii Trubetskoi. Klokman, *Fel'dmarshal Rumiantsev*, 76–77; Fortunatov, *P. A. Rumiantsev*, II, nos. 73, 76, 77, 80, 106.

12   "Mysli generala grafa Rumiantsova o proshedshchei i budushchei kampanii," *Voennyi zhurnal* 11 (1853): 157, 160.

13   Although St. Petersburg did not officially approve this proposed division of labor between the First and Second armies, it gave Rumiantsev enough freedom of initiative to follow it.

14   "Mysli generala grafa Rumiantsova," 156.

15   Vinogradov, ed., *Vek Ekateriny II*, 134–136; Illie Ceausescu, "Military Aspects of the National Struggle of the Rumanian Principalities in the Eighteenth Century," in *East Central European Society and War in the Pre-Revolutionary Eighteenth Century*, ed. Gunther Rothenburg et al. (New York: Columbia Press, 1982), 377–379.

16   Klokman, *Fel'dmarshal Rumiantsev*, 86; Petrov, *Vliianie*, 201–202.

17   Klokman, *Fel'dmarshal Rumiantsev*, 78; Shirokorad, *Russko-turetskie voiny*, 143–144.

18   Fortunatov, *P. A. Rumiantsev*, II, no. 119–120, 231–254; "Obriad sluzhby," *Khrestomatiia po russkoi voennoi istorii*, ed. L. G. Beskrovnyi (Moscow: Ministerstvo vooruzhennykh sil SSSR, 1947), 215–221. It would be adopted by the rest of the Russian army in 1787, at the outset of the next Turkish War.

19   Petrov, *Vliianie*, 238.

20   Klokman, *Fel'dmarshal Rumiantsev*, 81–85.

21   The cavalry comprised 1,899 cuirassiers, 4,886 carabiniers, ninety-four hussars, and 408 Ukrainian Cossacks. The infantry comprised 7,044 grenadiers in regimental companies and separate battalions, 14,440 musketeers, and 839 jaegers. There were 13,620 troops at the field artillery, sixty-one in the Engineers' Command, and 132 pioneers—in all about 37,000 men, with 296 field guns and regimental guns, 16,000 horses, and 1,400 oxen. Petrov, *Vliianie*, 203.

22 The heavy baggage train was sent under cavalry escort down the opposite bank of the Prut, where the roads were more reliable, with instructions to rendezvous with the army at Cecora Bridge. Petrov Voina II, 83, 88, 92; Petrov, *Vliianie*, 205.

23 Petrov, *Vliianie*, 204. Repnin had been placed in command of the Moldavian Corps upon Stoffeln's death from plague.

24 Bauer had five grenadier battalions, a battalion of jaegers, four battalions musketeers, twelve squadrons of cavalry. His fourteen field guns were under the charge of Major-General Melissino. Friedrich Wilhelm Bauer (1734–1783) was Swedish-born, served in the Prussian army in the Seven Years' War, and had just entered Russian service in 1769. For his distinguished service at Larga and Kagul, he won the Order of St. Anna and the Order of St. George (2nd Degree). He became head of the General Staff in 1772. A hydraulic as well as military engineer, he helped build the canals and sewers of St. Petersburg and Tsarskoe Selo; he also authored *Memoires Historiques et geographiques sur le Valachie* (1778). Petrov, *Voina* II, 98; Petrov, *Vliianie*, 207.

25 Klokman, *Fel'dmarshal Rumiantsev*, 92; Petrov, *Vliianie*, 207–208.

26 Klokman, *Fel'dmarshal Rumiantsev*, 92; Petrov, *Vliianie*, 208.

27 *Zhurnal voennykh deistvii armiei*, frames 231–233; Klokman, *Fel'dmarshal Rumiantsev*, 94, 96; Petrov, *Vliianie*, 209–211.

28 Petrov, *Vliianie*, 213; Semenova, *Chugun Kagulskii*, 51, 54–55; *Zhurnal voennykh deistvii armiei*, frame 245.

29 *Zhurnal voennykh deistvii armiei*, frames 247, 252–253.

30 Petrov, *Vliianie*, 217–219; Klokman, *Fel'dmarshal Rumiantsev*, 98–100; Semenova, *Chugun Kagulskii*, 58–59.

31 Rumiantsev was subsequently awarded the Cross of St. George, Second Degree. Among the many junior officers promoted for the Larga action was Captain Mikhail Illarionovich Golenischev-Kutuzov, who was made an *ober-kvartermeitser*. In 1812, Kutuzov would be General Field Marshal and would bloody Napoleon's *Grande Armee* at Borodino. *Zhurnal voennykh desitvii armiei*, frames 259–260.

32 Petrov, *Vliianie*, 223–224; Beskrovnyi, *Russkaia armiia i flot v XVIII veke*, 479; Zolotarev et al., *Vo slavu otechestva Rossiiskogo*, 117.

33 Petrov, *Voina* II, 125–127, 136; Petrov, *Vliianie*, 224; Kapitonov, ed., *Fel'dmarshal Rumiantsev. Dokumenty, pis'ma, vospominaniia*, no. 44, 114–116.

34 In his letter to the empress, Rumiantsev stated that only 17,000 of these troops were combat effectives; other sources say 23,000 of them were combat effectives. Petrov, *Vliianie*, 236.

35 This was probably not part of the Roman emperor Trajan's wall in Dacia, but the remnant of a later defense line built by Athanaric in the third century.

36 Kapitonov, ed., *Fel'dmarshal Rumiantsev. Dokumenty*, no. 44, 122; Klokman, *Fel'dmarshal Rumiantsev*, 105.

37 Rumiantsev's critics attribute this to his decision not to protect his squares with swine-feathers. Beskrovnyi, *Russkaia armii i flot v XVIII veke*, 482.

38 Kapitonov, ed., *Fel'dmarshal Rumiantsev. Dokumenty*, no. 44, 119; Petrov, *Vliianie*, 230, 232.

39 Some of the Turks fleeing toward the Danube were attacked and robbed by a unit of Albanian arnauts sent to reinforce them. Kapitonov, ed., *Fel'dmarshal Rumiantsev. Dokumenty*, no. 44, 119–120; Petrov, *Vliianie*, 234.

40 Kapitonov, ed., *Fel'dmarshal Rumiantsev. Dokumenty*, no. 44, 121.

Notes

41 Petrov, *Voina* II, 135.

42 Ahmed Resmi Efendi, quoted in Aksan, *An Ottoman Statesman*, 153; Petrov, *Voina* II, 141, 144–145.

43 At the outset of the campaign in spring 1770, the Second Army had 49,000 men (22,000 infantry, 7,000 cavalry, and 20,000 irregulars, with 197 guns and 100 pontoons). Parts of this force were detached to defend the Ochakov region and the Ukrainian rear, so the force that Panin initially concentrated to besiege Bender consisted of just 32,814 men: 18,567 infantry, 5,145 cavalry, 5,528 irregulars, and 3,574 gunners and engineers. Fortunatov, *P. A. Rumiantsev*, II, no. 106, 205–206; P. A. Geisman and A. N. Dubovskii, *Graf Petr Ivanovich Panin (1721–1789)* (St. Petersburg: Tip. N. V. Vasileva, 1897), 32, 39.

44 Bender was defended by 354 guns and mortars and 11,794 Ottoman troops under *Seraskir* Mehmed Pasha. By early July he had died, perhaps poisoned, and the command of Bender passed to *Seraskir* Mehmed Emin Pasha. *Zhurnal voennykh deistvii armiei*, frame 417; Shirokorad, *Russo-turetskie voiny*, 165.

45 Of these 45,750 men, 34,191 were under arms; the rest were noncombatant *nestroevye* and support personnel. There were 29,408 horses and 7,953 oxen. The artillery comprised thirty-two siege guns, eight mortars, sixty field guns, seventy-nine regimental guns, and thirty-four Coehoorn mortars. Shirokorad, *Russko-turetskie voiny*, 165; Petrov, *Voina* II, 289.

46 Petrov, *Vliianie*, 245–246.

47 Petrov, *Voina*, II, 299.

48 Petrov, *Vliianie*, 246–247.

49 Petrov, *Voina* II, 324–327; Shirokorad, *Russko-turetskie voiny*, 167.

50 *Zhurnal voennykh deistvii armiei*, frames 414–417; Petrov, *Vliianie*, 248; Petrov, *Voina*, II, 333–334; Geisman and Dubovskii, *Graf Petr Ivanovich Panin*, 44–55. In Panin's defense, Geisman and Dubovskii point out that it was the first time he was in command of his own army; that he had little backing from Rumiantsev or from Chernyshov in the VK; that if he used too few troops on the storm assault, he had used his entrenching work, artillery, and mines effectively; and that he had been suffering from gout during the siege.

51 Petrov, *Voina*, II, 335. For purpose of comparison note that the US soldiers killed on all the Normandy beaches on D-Day 1944 numbered 2,499, according to the US National D-Day Memorial Foundation.

52 Panin detached 3,000 troops to garrison what was left of Bender and sent Kamenskii with another 3,000 toward Akkirman to assist the First Army. One of those deserting rather than returning to winter quarters was a Don Cossack cornet named Emel'ian Pugachev. Geisman and Dubovskii, *Graf Petr Ivanovich Panin*, 54–57.

53 Petrov, *Voina* II, 146–148; Korobkov, *Fel'dmarshal Rumiantsev*, no. 73, 189–191.

54 Petrov, *Voina* II, 151–154.

55 This outpost proved its worth on September 15 when its guns drove back twenty Turkish transports approaching the Dnestr estuary.

56 Five battalions of infantry, two regiments of cavalry, and ten guns, under the command of Kamenskii.

57 The Akkirman garrison was allowed to evacuate to Tulcea. Russian losses at Akkirman were twenty-three dead and 109 wounded. Petrov, *Voina* II, 164–167.

58 Petrov, *Vliianie*, 241–243; Petrov, *Voina*, II, 171–183; Fortunatov, *P. A. Rumiantsev*, II, nos. 183, 184, 188.

59 Petrov, *Voina*, II, 197.

60 Bucharest was defended by 6,000 Turks. They abandoned the town after some skirmishing with the Russians in the woods outside the city. Petrov, *Vliianie*, 243; Fortunatov, *P. A. Rumiantsev*, II, no. 192; Petrov, *Voina*, II, 197.

61 Major-General Baron Otto-Adolph Weissman von Weissenstein (1726–1773), a brigadier during the Seven Years' War, fought at Gross Jägersdorf and Zorndorf; commanded Russian troops fighting the Bar Confederates in Poland; served under both Golitsyn and Rumiantsev; and became acclaimed as "the Achilles of the Army" for his raids across the Danube.

62 Fortunatov, *P. A. Rumia*ntsev, II, nos. 186, 189, 193.

63 Petrov, *Voina* II, 207; Smirnov, *Krymskoe khanstvo*, II, 110, 114.

64 I. M. Smilianskii, M. B. Velizhev, and E. B. Smilianskaia, *Rossiia i Sredizemnomor'e. Arkhipelagskaia ekspeditsiia Ekateriny Velikoi* (Moscow: Indrik, 2011), 72–73.

65 Smilianskii et al., *Rossiia i Sredizemnomor'e*, 33–38; Madariaga, *Russia in the Age of Catherine the Great*, 193–195.

66 Smilianskii et al., *Rossiia i Sredizemnomor'e*, 38–43, 56–62.

67 Ibid., 64–69.

68 Smilianskii et al., *Rossiia i Sredizemnomor'e*, 75–77; Lebedev, *U istokov*, 374–375.

69 Smilianskii et al., *Rossiia i Sredizemnmor'e*, 53, 78–81, 86.

70 Grigorii Andreevich Spiridov (1713–1790) had entered Russian naval service at age ten and had commanded a succession of ships in the Baltic Fleet after 1741; he had participated in Rumiantsev's landing at Kolberg and had received appointment as Rear Admiral in 1762. His resignation from the navy in 1774 was reportedly prompted by resentment that Orlov had claimed all the glory for his victories in the Aegean.

71 Samuel Greig (1736–1788), a Scot, entered British Royal Navy service sometime before 1758. He had fought at Quiberon Bay and Havana but only made Lieutenant; his transfer into Russian service soon got him promoted to Captain, however.

72 Copper sheathing was already in use on some British ships but would not be adopted by Russian fleets until the 1780s. Lebedev, *U istokov*, 375–377.

73 Ibid., 378–379.

74 The empress blamed *Sviatoslav*'s captain Barsh ("such a coward as I had never before seen"). *Sviatoslav* had to be reassigned to Elphinstone's Second Squadron; it was replaced in the First Squadron by the *Rostislav*. Lebedev, *U istokov*, 384.

75 Lebedev, *U istokov*, 384–385.

76 John Elphinstone (1722–1785) was transferred to Russian naval service through the efforts of the British ambassador Charles Cathcart. After the foundering of the *Sviatoslav* in late 1770, Elphinstone was blamed and dismissed from Russian service. He returned to England after his wife died of plague in St. Petersburg. Elphinstone's papers on the Aegean expedition are preserved at Princeton University Library.

77 Lebedev, *U istokov*, 386, 388–391.

78 Quoted in Sorel, *The Eastern Question*, 81.

79 E. V. Tarle, "Chesmenskii boi i pervaiai russkaia eksepeditsiia v Arkhipelag, 1769–1774," in *Sochineniia v dvenadtsatii tomakh. Tom X*, ed. A. S. Erusalimksii (Moscow: Akademiia Nauk SSSR, 1959), 35; Lebedev, *U istokov*, 395; Smilianskii et al., *Rossiia i Srednezemnomor'e*, 114, 116, 121.

80 Vinogradov, ed., *Vek Ekateriny II*, 153.

81   Quoted in Smilianskii et al., *Rossiia i Sredizemnomor'e*, 125.

82   The siege of Methodi by Russian landing troops under Lt.-General Iurii Dolgorukov was ended on May 6 after taking heavy losses. N. V. Novikova, ed., *Boevaia letopis' russkogo flota* (Moscow: Voennoe izdatel'stvo Ministerstva vooruzhennykh sil SSSR, 1948), 92–93.

83   After visiting Morea in 1776, the Comte de Choiseul expressed the opinion that the Morea Revolt could have succeeded if Orlov had not ended his support of it in March 1770. The rebels who suffered the heaviest retaliation were those following Daskalogiannis on Crete; they would be slaughtered and Daskalogiannis caught and skinned alive. Smilianskii et al., *Rossiia i Sredizemnomor'e*, 118–119, 127–128.

84   Spiridov had been sent to rendezvous with Elphinstone because the latter's transports were then in great need for the defense of Navarino, which was now under siege by the Turks. Tarle considered Ibraim Hassan "a completely insignificant figure, ignorant of naval affairs and a great coward." Tarle, "Chesmenskii boi," 40.

85   Lebedev, *U istokov*, 397; Novikova, *Boevaia letopis'*, 94.

86   Lebedev, *U istokov*, 398–401; Tarle, "Chesmenskii boi," 39–40.

87   Lebedev, *U istokov*, 401–403.

88   This choice may have been partly predicated on the construction of the Turkish line ships, which were massive, with excessively high poops and superstructures, and nearly as wide as they were long, making them difficult to maneuver. John Tredrea and Eduard Sozaev, *Russian Warships in the Age of Sail, 1696–1860: Design, Construction, Careers and Fates* (Barnsley, Yorkshire: Seaforth, 2010), 84–85.

89   Tredrea and Sozaev, *Russian Warships*, 85; Lebedev, *U istokov*, 403–408.

90   Lebedev, *U istokov*, 409; Novikova, *Boevaia letopis'*, 95; Tarle, "Chesmenskii boi," 45–48.

91   Lebedev, *U istokov*, 419. Turkish losses are not recorded.

92   A ship moving at three knots could cover 350 meters in about five minutes, in which time the opposing enemy could get off only two to three volleys. When within a cable length, the attackers could turn alongside and batter the enemy line, or "cross the T" by slipping through the intervals of the enemy line. Lebedev, *U istokov*, 410–416.

93   If Baron de Tott is to be believed, Gagarin and Il'in had been able to bring their branders through because some Turkish captains had momentarily mistaken them as defectors trying to take refuge with the Ottoman fleet and had tried to take the branders in tow as prizes. Tarle, "Chesmenskii boi," 52.

94   This may have sparked an anti-Greek pogrom at Izmir. Tarle, "Chesmenskii boi," 55; Lebedev, *U istokov*, 421–422.

95   Lebedev, *U istokov*, 423; Tredrea and Sozaev, *Russian Warships*, 85. The Russian victory has also been attributed to *Grom*'s use of unicorn-fired incendiary carcasse rounds.

96   Shirokorad, *Russko-turetskie voiny*, 218.

97   At the start of the Aegean expedition, the treasury had issued it 500,000 rubles for expenses; by late 1770, expenditures had risen to 1.19 million rubles. Lebedev, *U istokov*, 428; Shirokorad, *Russko-turetskie voiny*, 222.

98   Lebedev, *U istokov*, 430–433.

99   Ulianitskii, *Dardanelly, Bosfor, i Chernoe more*, 345.

100   The total strength of the Austrian army in 1771 was 151,700 men, down from 177,947 in 1762, and 3/8 of the army still consisted of foreign-born enlistees. Michael Hochedlinger,

Austria's Wars of Emergence, 1683-1797 (London and New York: Longman, 2003), 294-294, 300; T. C. W. Blanning, *Joseph II* (London and New York: Longman, 1994), 127.

101 Roider, *Austria's Eastern Question*, 113, 116-117; Ulianitskii, *Dardanelly, Bosfor, i Chernoe more*, 341-344, 349-352.

102 Druzhinina, *Kuchuk-Kainardzhskii mir*, 126-135. When these new terms were added, Catherine abandoned her demand for the cession of an Aegean island.

103 Madariaga, *Russia in the Age of Catherine the Great*, 220.

104 Jerzy Lukowski, *The Partitions of Poland: 1772, 1793, 1795* (London and New York: Longman, 1999), 58.

105 Ulianitskii, *Dardanelly, Bosfor, i Chernoe more*, 376-381; Roider, *Austria's Eastern Question*, 119-123.

106 The idea was actually Frederick's; there is no record of it in Lynar's papers.

107 Roider, *Austria's Eastern Question*, 134-136; Madariaga, *Russia in the Age of Catherine the Great*, 217-219; Hochedlinger, *Austria's Wars of Emergence*, 352-354; Lukowski, *The Partitions of Poland*, 56-62.

108 Ulianitskii, *Dardanelly, Bosfor, i Chernoe more*, 346.

109 Frederick II wrote to Voltaire, "I know that it is pretty generally believed in Europe that the partition which has been made in Poland is a result of political maneuvers which are attributed to me. Nothing, however, is further from the truth. After different treatments had been vainly proposed, recourse had to be had to this partition as the only means of avoiding a general war ... I played the part of an extinguisher; I put out the fire." Quoted in Sorel, *The Eastern Question*, 222.

110 Ulianitskii, *Dardanelly, Bosfor, i Chernoe more*, 383-391; Sorel, *The Eastern Question*, 177-178.

Chapter 7

1 All of this was supposed to be paid for by debasing the coinage. Petrov, *Voina* III, 59-62; Fortunatov, *P. A. Rumiantsev*, II, no. 199, 416.

2 Klokman, *Fel'dmarshal Rumiantsev*, 113.

3 A smaller division of 1,650 infantry and 1,500 cavalry protected the magazines back in Poland. Petrov, *Voina*, III, 62-63; Fortunatov, *P. A. Rumiantsev*, II, no. 195, 408-412.

4 These six-month portions for 1771 totaled 139,191 quarters of flour, 8,698 quarters of groats, and 139,232 quarters of oats. Petrov, *Voina* III, 67.

5 Petrov, *Voina*, III, 63-69; Fortunatov, *P. A. Rumiantsev*, II, no. 195, 405-406.

6 Petrov, *Voina*, III, 70-71.

7 Fortunatov, *P. A. Rumiantsev*, II, no. 348, 687-689.

8 Maslovskii, *Zapiski*, II, 260-262.

9 Petrov, *Voina*, 18-23; Fortunatov, *P. A. Rumiantsev*, II, no. 208, 428-430; Lebedev, *U istokov*, 464-465.

10 Fortunatov, *P. A. Rumiantsev*, II, nos. 197, 198, 206, 413, 414, 426; Petrov, *Voina*, III, 8-14.

11 Petrov, *Vliianie*, 254; Petrov, *Voina*, III, 79; Fortunatov, *P. A. Rumiantsev*, II no. 211, 433.

12 Petrov, *Voina*, III, 81-87; Klokman, *Fel'dmarshal Rumiantsev*, 118; Fortunatov, *P. A. Rumiantsev*, II, nos. 220-221, 449-453.

Notes

13 Rumiantsev congratulated Repnin on this victory but also criticized him for letting slip the opportunity to deal the enemy a total route when Ahmed Pasha's troops retreated through a narrow ravine. "Had you, with your overwhelming superiority, turned your army toward the pursuit of the shattered enemy, not only would he have suffered a total route but he would have been in such terror as to abandon Giurgiu to us." Fortunatov, *P. A. Rumiantsev*, II, no. 224, 458–459; Solov'ev, XIV, kn. 28, 449.

14 Seventeen officers killed or fatally wounded, fifty-eight officers heavily wounded, twenty-seven officers lightly wounded; 497 soldiers killed, 1,393 heavily wounded, and 321 lightly wounded. Catherine wrote to Rumiantsev, "I very much regret this turn of events, but what are we to do? Where there was water once there can be water again .... I hope that we can accept this failure cheerfully. I trust you will not delay in putting this misfortune to rights as soon as the opportunity arises." Petrov, *Voina*, III, 120–127; Solov'ev, XIV, kn. 28, 449.

15 Petrov, *Vliianie*, 262, 268.

16 Petrov, *Voina*, III, 150–153; Petrov, *Vliianie*, 272–273; Fortunatov, *P. A. Rumiantsev*, II, no. 245, 484–485.

17 *Zhurnal voennykh deistviia armei*, frames 512–517.

18 The Austrians now had 30,000 troops nearby at Zemlin in the event Thugut's secret alliance talks with the Porte produced an agreement to restore Oltenia to Austria.

19 Petrov, *Voina*, III, 52–53, 79–80; Petrov, *Vliianie*, 258, 260; Fortunatov, no. 215, 440–441.

20 His detachment on the October attacks on Tulcea, Isaccea, and Babadagh comprised seven battalions of grenadiers and musketeers, one battalion of jaegers, five squadrons of hussars, and 300 Don Cossacks.

21 Ahmed Resmi Efendi, *A Summary of Admonitions*, 60; Fortunatov, *P. A. Rumiantsev*, II, no. 226, 461, no. 247, 487–488; *Zhurnal voennykh deistvii*, frames 480, 518–526; Petrov, *Voina*, III, 96–109, 155–169.

22 "While Muhsinzade Mehmed was ostensibly reappointed as grand vizier because of his recent success in quelling a rebellion in Morea, Mustafa III was perfectly aware of his initial opposition to the Ottoman entrance into the war, perhaps a tacit recognition by the central government of the now pressing need to pursue peace." Aksan, *An Ottoman Statesman*, 156; Hammer-Purgstall, *Histoire de l'Empire Ottoman*, XVI, 305.

23 Fortunatov, *P. A. Rumiantsev*, II, no. 243, 482.

24 In January 1771 the First Army lost 461 to disease; the death toll from disease rose to 538 by June and to over 3,000 by September. Shirokorad, *Russko-turetskie voiny*, 176.

25 Petrov, *Vliianie*, 277–284.

26 F. F. Lashkov, "Shagin-Girei, poslednii krymskii khan," *Russkaia starina* (September 1886):39; Alan W. Fisher, *The Russian Annexation of the Crimea, 1772–1783* (Cambridge: Cambridge University Press, 1970), 33–35; Solov'ev XIV, kn. 28, 451.

27 Andreev, *Kniaz' Vasilii Mikhailovich Dolgorukov-Krymskii*, 97.

28 Prince Vasilii Mikhailovich Dolgorukov (1722–1782). The Dolgorukiis had been disgraced in 1730 over their intrigue against Peter II, so when the 13-year-old Prince Vasilii enrolled in the dragoons in 1735 it had been under the name Vasilii Mikhailov. He served on Münnich's 1736 Crimean campaign and was promoted to lieutenant for distinguishing himself at the walls of Perekop. He fought in the 1741–1743 Russo-Swedish War. Empress Elizabeth Petrovna lifted the ban on the Dolgorukiis, enabling Vasilii to rise by six ranks in

just six years. He participated in several of the major operations of the Seven Years' War and was wounded several times. On the day of her coronation (September 22, 1762) Empress Catherine II promoted him to General-*anshef*. He was then just forty years old. Five years later he received the Order of St. Andrei. Shirokorad, *Russko-turetskie voiny*, 176–177; Andreev, *Kniaz' Vasilii Mikhailovich Dolgorukov-Krymskii*, 88.

29 Solov'ev, XIV, kn. 28, 451; Andreev, *Kniaz' Vasilii Mikhailovich Dolgorukov-Krymskii*, 91.

30 Smirnov, *Krymskoe khanstvo*, II, 116–117.

31 Andreev, *Kniaz' Vasilii Mikhailovich Dolgorukov-Krymskii*, 98.

32 Davies, *Empire and Military Revolution*, 194–200, 205, 211–215, 232–233.

33 Maslovskii, *Zapiski*, II, 242.

34 Shahin Girei had been born in Edirne and raised in Thessalonika and Venice, where he had received a European education. He was just twenty-five years old in 1771. Lashkov, "Shagin-Girei," 38.

35 Lashkov, "Shagin-Girei," 41.

36 Under Dolgorukov: 11,650 regular infantry, 2,600 regular cavalry, 2,000 hussars, 1,600 pikiniers, 2,400 Don Cossacks, and 3,700 Ukrainian Cossacks. In contrast to previous Russian armies sent into Crimea, Dolgorukov's division had a much higher proportion of regular infantry and cavalry—reflecting the fact that its mission was to seize and garrison coastal towns rather than hunt down Crimean irregular cavalry throughout the interior of Crimea. The Dnepr Line, built in 1770–1771, ran for about 130 kilometers along the Verda and Moskovska rivers to Konskie vody; unlike the older Ukrainian Line, it was an unbroken line of magazines and great redoubts manned by regular troops. Maslovskii, *Zapiski*, II, 246–249.

37 Petrov, *Voina* III, 175–177; *Zhurnal voennykh deistvii armiei*, frames 541–542.

38 Maslovskii, *Zapiski*, II, 244.

39 *Zhurnal voennykh deistvii armiei*, frame 555.

40 Enemy losses at the Battle of Perekop were estimated at 1,200 killed; Russian losses were twenty-five killed, 135 wounded, six missing. Petrov, *Voina* III, 180–181; Andreev, *Kniaz' Vasilii Mikhailovich Dolgorukov-Krymskii*, 101; *Zhurnal voennykh deistvii armiei*, frame 555; Maslovskii, *Zapiski*, II, 253–255.

41 Lebedev, *U istokov*, 249–250, 252, 253.

42 The sultan would later have him executed for this. Smirnov, *Krymskoe khanstvo*, II, 121, 124.

43 Lebedev, *U istokov*, 254; Petrov, *Voina*, III, 186–187.

44 Petrov, *Voina* III, 187–188; *Zhurnal voennykh deistvii armiei*, frames 566–567; Maslovskii, *Zapiski*, volume II, 257.

45 N. N. Petrukhintsev, "Voina s prostranstvom," *Rodina* 5,6 (1998): 64; Davies, *Empire and Military Revolution*, 199–200.

46 The sultan deposed Khan Selim III and appointed Maksud Girei in his place. Selim died in exile a few months later. Grand Vizier Silahdar Mehmed Pasha was also deposed and replaced by Muhsinzade Pasha. Petrov, *Voina* III, 191.

47 *Zhurnal voennykh deistviia armiei*, frames 566, 567, 573; Fisher, *Russian Annexation of the Crimea*, 43–44; Solov'ev XIV, kn. 28, 455.

48 One 32-gun frigate, eleven shallow draught frigates, three "sail boats," five transports, four flat-bottomed prams for cargo and troop transfers, and thirty-two smaller vessels. At this

time the Ottoman fleet in the Black Sea, headquartered at Istanbul, had nine line ships and a host of xebecs and smaller vessels. Lebedev, *U istokov*, 277–278, 282.

49 Lebedev, *U istokov*, 289, 296, 303–308.

50 Ibid., 326–335.

51 Tredrea and Sozaev, *Russian Warships*, 86; Lebedev, *U Istokov*, 428–431; Novikova, *Boevaia letopis'*, 97–98.

52 Novikova, *Boevaia letopis'*, 98; Shirokorad, *Russko-turetskie voiny*, 223.

53 Lebedev, *U istokov*, 455–460.

54 Lebedev, *U istokov*, 432–434; Tredrea and Kozaev, *Russian Warships*, 86.

55 Novikova, *Boevaia letopis'*, 99, 101.

56 Smilianskii et al., *Rossiia i Sredizemnomor'e*, 136–140.

57 Ibid., 147–152.

58 Ibid., 152–161.

59 Hammer-Purgstall, *Histoire de l'Empire Ottoman*, XVI, 350–355.

60 Paul du Quenoy, "Arabs under Tsarist Rule: The Russian Occupation of Beirut, 1773–1774," *Russian History* 41 (2014): 130–137; Smilianskii et al., *Rossiia i Sredizemnomor'e*, 393–405.

61 Donald W. Mitchell, *A History of Russian and Soviet Sea Power* (New York: MacMillan, 1974), 66.

62 Tredrea and Sozaev, *Russian Warships*, 86.

63 Konopczyński, *Casimir Pulaski*, 28.

64 Philip Longworth, *The Art of Victory. The Life and Achievements of Field Marshal Suvorov* (New York, Chicago, San Francisco: Holt, Rinehart and Winston, 1965), 56.

65 Zamoyski, *The Last King of Poland*, 172.

66 Dumouriez (1739–1823) had seen action at Rossbach in 1757 and in the French expeditionary army garrisoning Corsica in the 1760s. It was his memoranda on Corsica that brought him to the attention of Choiseul but also of the king, who made him an agent of his secret service. Dumouriez would later play an important role in the political and military events of the French Revolution. He began as a Jacobin, was promoted to Major-General in 1791, and switched his loyalty to the Girondists in 1792. He participated in the 1792 campaigns against the Austrians and Prussians. In 1793 he tried to save Louis XVI from execution and attempted to lead his troops in a march on Paris to overthrow the National Convention. He then defected to the Austrians and from 1804 resided in England.

67 fon-Smitt, *Suvorov i padenie Pol'shi*, 42–43; Longworth, *Art of Victory*, 50–51.

68 Sorel, *The Eastern Question*, 156–157; Ulianitskii, *Dardanelly, Bosfor i Chernoe more*, 200.

69 fon-Smitt, *Suvorov i padenie Pol'shi*, 44.

70 Ibid., 48–50; Longworth, *Art of Victory*, 58–59; Buganov, *Polkovodtsy*, 381–382.

71 Suvorov's losses at Stolowicze were eight dead and six wounded. For his victory Suvorov received the orders of St. Aleksandr Nevskii and St. George, Third Degree. Ogiński was amnestied and allowed to return to Lithuania in 1775. fon-Smitt, *Suvorov i padenie Pol'shi*, 51–53; Longworth, *Art of Victory*, 62–64.

72 Baron Charles Joseph Hyacinthe du Houx de Viosmenil (1734–1827). Viosmenil later fought in alliance with George Washington against Lord Cornwallis at Yorktown in 1781.

73 Sorel, *The Eastern Question*, 157.

74 Zamoyski, *The Last King of Poland*, 179–180.

75 Great-grandfather of the composer Igor Stravinsky.

76 Zamoyski, *The Last King of Poland*, 190.

77 Taras, *Anatomiia nenavist'*, 92–94; Longworth, *Art of Victory*, 69–71; Ion Smitt, *Suvorov i padenie Pol'shi*, 61–63. During 1780–1783 Choisy would command French troops in Lauzun's Legion, fighting in Rhode Island, Maryland and Virginia in alliance with the Continental Congress.

78 Taras, *Anatomiia nenavist'*, 95; Konopczyński, *Casimir Pulaski*, 34.

79 Lukowski, *The Partitions of Poland*, 82; Taras, *Anatomiia nenavisti*, 98.

80 Zamoyski, *The Last King of Poland*, 201.

81 Quoted in Davies, *God's Playground*, I, 521–523.

82 Davies, *God's Playground*, I, 521; Hochedlinger, *Austria's Wars of Emergence*, 355; Lukowski, *The Partitions of Poland*, 93, 100.

83 Zamoyski, *The Last King of Poland*, 203–206, 212, 217.

84 Sorel, *The Eastern Question*, 225–226.

85 Ibid., 226.

86 Korobkov, *Fel'dmarshal Rumiantsev*, nos. 91 and 92, 217–219.

87 Aksan, *An Ottoman Statesman*, 156–158; Madariaga, *Russia in the Age of Catherine the Great*, 226; Solov'ev, XIV, kn. 28, 546.

88 Druzhinina, *Kuchuk-Kainardzhskii mir*, 172–176.

89 Sorel, *Eastern Question*, 228; Madariaga, *Russia in the Age of Catherine the Great*, 227; Druzhinina, *Kuchuk-Kainardhzskii mir*, 180. Upon his return to St. Petersburg Orlov was not allowed to see the empress and was held in custody at Gatchina. This was to protect Vasil'chikov and because Catherine had qualms about receiving Orlov fresh from pestilential Moldavia. She subsequently paid Orlov off with an enormous pension, 10,000 serfs, and the title of Prince.

90 Shirokorad, *Russko-turetskie voiny*, 184; Soloviev, XXVIII, 549.

91 Aksan, *An Ottoman Statesman*, 162; Druzhinina, *Kuchuk-Kainardzhskii mir*, 189–237 offers the most detailed summary of the course of negotiations at Bucharest.

92 Solov'ev, XIV, kn. 28, 550.

93 Beskrovnyi, *Russkaia armiia i flot v XVIII v.*, 295–296; Alexander, *Autocratic Politics*, 19–20; Madariaga, *Russia in the Age of Catherine the Great*, 233.

94 Chechulin, *Ocherki po istorii russkikh finansov v tsarstvovanie Ekateriny II*, 272, 283.

95 Ibid., 272, 326. The subsidy from Prussia amounted to 400,000 rubles a year. Russia acquired her first foreign loan in 1769, a 5 percent loan of 3.7 million rubles over ten years, from the De Smet bankers in Amsterdam; Mavrucci subsequently arranged a second loan of 1.17 million rubles from Genoese bankers in 1771–1772.

96 Ibid., 322, 324; Alexander, *Autocratic Politics*, 16–17; Marc Raeff, "Pugachev's Rebellion," in *Preconditions of Revolution in Early Modern Europe*, ed. Robert Forster and Jack P. Greene (Baltimore: Johns Hopkins University Press, 1971), 165–166.

97 Alexander, *Bubonic Plague in Early Modern Russia*, 116–118, 162–167, 177–195.

98 N. F. Dubrovin, *Pugachev i ego soobshchniki* (St. Petersburg: Tip. Skorokhodova, 1884), vol I, 112–118.

Notes

99 In English a good short overview of the subject is Raeff's "Pugachev's Rebellion,"161–202. Alexander, *Autocratic Politics* remains unsurpassed in examining the impact of the revolt on state policy, the army, the court, and the provincial nobility. A summary of the basic narrative of the rebellion useful for popular readers is Paul Avrich, *Russian Rebels, 1600–1800* (New York: W. W. Norton, 1976), 180–255. Alexander Pushkin, *A History of Pugachev*, trans. Earl Sampson (Ann Arbor, MI: Ardis, 1983) makes available the narrative Pushkin produced from documents and interviews with survivors as foundation for his great novella *The Captain's Daughter* (1836).

100 Koiti Toekava, *Orenburg i Orenburgskoe kazachestvo vo vremia vosstanii Pugacheva 1773–1774 gg.* (Moscow: Arkheograficheskii tsentr, 1996), 91–92; Dubrovin, *Pugachev*, I, 250–251.

101 Toekava, *Orenburg i Orenburgskoe*, 97; Dubrovin, *Pugachev*, I, 27, 33.

102 After visiting the Orlov estates near Samara the empress wrote, "Everything that you can imagine is here in plenty and I do not know what else they could need: everything is available and everything is cheap." Quoted in Roger Bartlett, *Human Capital: The Settlement of Foreigners in Russia, 1762–1804* (Cambridge: Cambridge University Press, 1979), 94–95.

103 Tarakanova posed as a daughter of Empress Elizabeth Petrovna and was supported by Karol Radziwiłł and the Polish Confederates. After the signing of the Kuchuk-Kainarji Treaty she was enticed aboard Aleksei Orlov's flagship and sent back to St. Petersburg, where she died in the dungeon of the Petropavlovsk Fortress. Dubrovin, *Pugachev*, III, 352, 354; Madariaga, *Russia in the Age of Catherine the Great*, 619, n. 36.

104 Dubrovin, *Pugachev*, III, 355; Alexander, *Autocratic Politics*, 74–75, 197–198.

105 Dubrovin, *Pugachev*, II, 63, 67, 95, 167, 179.

106 A week after the signing of the peace treaty with the Turks Catherine reluctantly appointed Panin supreme commander over operations against the rebels in Orenburg, Kazan' and Nizhegorod governorates and assigned him nearly 20,000 troops. He had pressed her relentlessly for this appointment in order to restore his reputation, besmirched by Zakhar Chernyshov and the Orlovs. The empress cautioned him against unnecessary bloodshed in suppressing the rebellion and set up two counterweights to his authority by keeping Pavel Potemkin in charge of the secret investigative commissions at Moscow and Kazan' and by recalling Suvorov from medical leave to serve as Panin's second in command. Suvorov did not arrive at the Tsaritsyn front until August 25, the day Lt-Colonel Mikhelson finally crushed Pugachev's army at Chernyi Iar. Alexander, *Autocratic Politics*, 168; Dubrovin, *Pugachev*, III, 133, 144–147; Geisman and Dubovskii, *Graf Petr Ivanovich Panin*, 74–76.

107 Hamish Scott, *The Emergence of the Eastern Powers, 1756–1775* (Cambridge and New York: Cambridge University Press, 2001), 226, 236; Madariaga, *Russia in the Age of Catherine the Great*, 259.

108 Solov'ev, XV, kn. 29, 11–12; Klokman, *Fel'dmarshal Rumiantsev*, 126–127, 130; P. M. Sakovich, *Deistviia Suvorov v Turtsii v 1773 goda* (St. Petersburg, 1853), 18–19; Fortunatov, *P. A. Rumiantsev*, II, no. 296, 580–584; no. 301, pp. 595–598. At this time Lt.-General Saltykov's Second Corps was in winter quarters across southern Wallachia, protecting a sector about 300 kilometers wide, from Craiova and Oltenia in the west to the mouth of the Călmățui River in the east. Including garrison troops and Tekelli's Oltenian Command, Saltykov had a total of just 17,000 troops under arms: 6,500 infantry, 3,510 regular cavalry, 2,500 Don Cossacks, and 500 Wallachian arnauts. Major-General Grigorii Potemkin's Reserve Corps was headquartered at Likorești, across the Danube from Silistra, defending a cordon about 200 kilometers across, from Negoești to Ibrail. Including garrison troops

and troops stationed in redoubts, Potemkin had about 10,000 troops: 4,200 infantry and jaegers, 2,000 regular cavalry, and 2,000 Don and Zaporozhian Cossacks. Major-General Otto-Adolf Weissman's Corps of about 4,000 troops was stationed in Bucak near Ibrail, securing the eastern Danube and links to Dolgorukov's Second Army. Rumiantsev's Corps of 14,839 men (10,564 of them infantry) was camped far behind the Danube line, in Moldavia, with headquarters at Iaşi. The First Army had in all 66,685 field and garrison troops, but about 8,000 of them were on the sick lists.

109   In spring 1773 the Ottoman garrison at Rusçuk had 10,000 troops and many heavy guns; the enemy garrison at Silistra had 8,000–12,000 men and 75 guns. Petrov, *Vliianie*, 285–286.

110   Klokman, *Fel'dmarshal Rumiantsev*, 127–128.

111   Maslovskii, *Zapiski*, 265–266.

112   Of these diversionary raids in April the most successful were undertaken by Colonel Klichko, out of Weissman's corps. With just 1,000 infantry and 1,400 Don Cossacks he raided Tulcea and Babadagh and captured Karasu and Karaurman. Klokman, *Fel'dmarshal Rumiantsev*, 130–132; Petrov, *Vliianie*, 287–288.

113   Sakovich, *Deistviia Suvorova v Turtsii*, 34–52; Klokman, *Fel'dmarshal Rumiantsev*, 132; V. S. Lopatin, *Potemkin i Suvorov* (Moscow: Nauka, 1992), 12–15; Petrov, *Vliianie*, 288–290.

114   Some anecdotes relate that Rumiantsev had not authorized Suvorov's attack on Turtukai and had moved to have him court martialled. This was not true, but Suvorov did take ill with fever and had to take leave to Bucharest. Klokman, *Fel'dmarshal Rumiantsev*, 132; Maslovskii, *Zapiski*, II, 275–228; Lopatin, *Potemkin i Suvorov*, 15.

115   Klokman, *Fel'dmarshal Rumiantsev*, 133; Maslovskii, *Zapiski*, II, 282–283.

116   Klokman, *Fel'dmarshal Rumiantsev*, 134; Fortunatov, *P. A. Rumiantsev*, II, nos. 319–321, 623–625; Maslovskii, *Zapiski*, II, 284–287.

117   The center, under Rumiantsev, comprised five musketeer regiments, one grenadier regiment, one grenadier battalion, three carabiniers regiments, three cuirassier regiment, and a regiment of Don Cossacks. Stupishin's left flank had four musketeer regiments, one grenadier regiment, one grenadier battalion, two jaeger battalions, two carabinier regiments, one hussar regiment, and two regiments of Don Cossacks. Potemkin commanded four musketeer regiments, one grenadier battalion, one jaeger battalion, one cuirassier regiment, one hussar regiment, two hussar squadrons, one pikinier squadron, and two regiments of Don Cossacks. In each of these three armatures the infantry would form narrow rectangles after crossing the river, with grenadiers along each face and smaller battalion squares of jaegers on the flanks. Cavalry would proceed in two-line echelons between the great infantry squares; the artillery would be distributed so that each square had ten guns in front and four howitzers on the flanks; the remaining six guns would be placed in reserve. Klokman views this as similar to the order of battle Rumiantsev had used successfully in 1770, but with some tactical innovations. This time Rumiantsev placed special emphasis on using his forward guns to open gaps in the enemy line, then turning to maintain heavy fire in enfilade while the Russian infantry attacked these gaps. The infantry was expected to keep up its pace and maintain formation while attacking, even when rolling over enemy fortifications, and regardless of how heavy was the enemy's cannon-fire. This also meant they could not afford to slow to take prisoners. The main role of the Russian cavalry was to preoccupy the Turkish cavalry, attacking them only upon special order, and then by moving through the intervals of the infantry regiments with jaegers protecting their flanks. This time Rumiantsev's cavalry was under orders not to fire from horseback but to rely instead on cold steel; if they needed firing to protect them against enemy counterattack, it would come from the jaegers. To guard the river

crossing and the baggage train—which would remain for awhile on the Russian side of the Danube—Rumiantsev stationed one regiment of infantry and one regiment of Don Cossacks with four unicorns in the rear. About 8,900 troops would be left to protect the rear and the flanks: another two regiments of infantry and one of cavalry stationed in the right flank rear, to secure the road toward Silistra, while the roads on the left flank would be guarded by one infantry regiment out of the Ismail garrison. Klokman, *Fel'dmarshal Rumiantsev*, 136–137; Maslovskii, *Zapiski*, II, 288–291; Fortunatov, *P. A. Rumiantsev*, II, no. 323, 627–628.

118   Montefiore, *Potemkin*, 92; Klokman, *Fel'dmarshal Rumiantsev*, 137–138; Petrov, *Vliianie*, 291, 293.

119   Petrov, *Vliianie*, 293, 295; Klokman, *Fel'dmarshal Rumiantsev*, 139–141.

120   Turtukai did not have to be burned as it still lay in ruins.

121   Fortunatov, *P. A. Rumiantsev*, II, no. 325, 630–631 and no. 330, 637; Maslovskii, *Zapiski*, II, 295–298; Sakovich, *Deistviia Suvorova v Turtsii*, 74–87.

122   Solov'ev, XV, kn. 29, 14–15; Klokman, *Fel'dmarshal Rumiantsev*, 142–143.

123   Solov'ev, XV, kn. 29, 15–18.

124   Aksan, *Ottoman Wars, 1700–1870*, 156.

125   Solov'ev, XV, kn. 29, 18.

126   Petrov, *Vliianie*, 298–300.

127   Ibid., 300–301.

128   Ibid., 300–302; Longworth, *The Art of Victory*, 87–89; Fortunatov, *P. A. Rumiantsev*, II, no. 341, 668–669.

129   Klokman, *Fel'dmarshal Rumiantsev*, 146–147; Petrov, *Vliianie*, 303–304; Fortunatov, *P. A. Rumiantsev*, II, no. 343, 675–677.

130   Solov'ev, XV, kn. 29, 83.

131   Petrov, *Vliianie*, 304–308; Klokman, *Fel'dmarshal Rumiantsev*, 148; Fortunatov, *P. A. Rumiantsev*, II, no. 347, 682–684.

132   Klokman, *Fel'dmarshal Rumiantsev*, 153–154; Fortunatov, *P. A. Rumiantsev*, II, no. 348, 687–689, and no. 350a, 697–700.

133   Suvorov was to command the Second Division until his replacement, Repnin, arrived; then he was to take command of the Reserve. As for the other military theaters, Dolgorukov's Second Army in Crimea comprised three carabinier regiments, two dragoon regiments, four hussar regiments, two pikinier regiments, ten infantry regiments; the "Moscow Legion"; two light field commands, 360 jaegers, 3,000 Don Cossacks, 3,000 Ukrainian Cossacks, an unspecified number of Zaporozhians, and fifty-six field guns. Also under Dolgorukov's command were forty companies of retired infantry along the Ukrainian Line, five squadrons of Sloboda Hussars, and some Don Cossacks along new Dnepr Line. Major-General Romanius' corps in Poland comprised one cuirassier regiment, one carabinier regiment, one infantry regiment, two light field commands, 2,000 Don Cossacks, and ten field guns. Lt.-General Medem's corps in Kuban had been reduced to one light field command, two squadrons of hussars, four guns, 1,000 Don Cossacks, 490 Iaik Cossacks, and 150 Terek Cossacks. General-*anshef* Bibikov had been sent to Orenburg to suppress the Pugachev rebels; his corps comprised two carabinier regiments, eight hussar squadrons, three infantry and grenadier regiments, four light field commands, 500 Don Cossacks, 1,000 Ukrainian Cossacks, and twenty-two field guns. Petrov, *Vliianie*, 309–310; Petrov, *Voina*, V, 122–126. Fortunatov, *P. A. Rumiantsev*, II, no. 352, 702–707.

134 Quoted in Montefiore, *Potemkin*, 92–93.

135 Lopatin, *Potemkin i Suvorov*, 24.

136 Klokman, *Fel'dmarshal Rumiantsev*, 156 158; Petrov, *Vliianie*, 312.

137 The rivalry between Kamenskii and Suvorov was partly personal and partly over disputed seniority. Both were Lt.-Generals, but Kamenskii, age 36, had received his commission a year before Suvorov, who was 45 years old. Fortunatov, *P. A. Rumiantsev*, II, no. 375, 752–753, no. 376, 753–756; Klokman, *Fel'dmarshal Rumiantsev*, 159; Petrov, *Vliianie*, 315; Longworth, *Art of Victory*, 91–97.

138 Klokman, *Fel'dmarshal Rumiantsev*, 161; Petrov, *Vliianie*, 317–318.

139 Fortunatov, *P. A. Rumiantsev*, II, no. 373, 746–747; no. 379, 757–758; no. 380, 758–759; nos. 383 and 384, 762–764.

Chapter 8

1 Druzhinina, *Kiuchuk-Kainardzhiiskii mir*, 254–256.

2 Quoted in Petrov, *Voina*, V, 185.

3 It was probably not coincidental that he chose July 10 as a deadline, given that it fell upon the anniversary of Peter I's unfortunate capitulation on the Prut in 1711.

4 Druzhinina, *Kiuchuk-Kainardzhiiskii mir*, 261–272.

5 Vinogradov, ed., *Vek Ekateriny II*, 119.

6 "Treaty of Kuchuk-Kainardji," Art. XXIV, Art. XVIII, Art. XX, Suppl. Article I, English translation at www.fofweb.com/History

7 Ibid., Art. III.

8 Ulianitskii, *Dardanelly, Bosfor, i Chernoe mor'e*, 469.

9 "Treaty of Kuchuk-Kainardji," Art. XI.

10 Ibid., Art. XVI.

11 Ibid., Art. XXIII.

12 Ibid., Art. XXI.

13 Ibid., Art. VII.

14 Sorel, *The Eastern Question*, 250.

15 Roderic Davison, "Russian Skill and Turkish Imbecility: The Treaty of Kuchuk Kainardji Reconsidered," *Slavic Review* XXXV, 3 (1976): 465, 467, 470–475.

16 *PSZ* XX, no. 14.274.

17 "The Treaty of Kuchuk-Kainardji," Suppl. Art. II.

18 Geisman and Dubovskii, *Graf Petr Ivanovich Panin*, 80–82.

19 Quoted in Alexander, *Autocratic Politics*, 185.

20 Ibid., 211.

21 Ibid., 288–289, 311.

22 Alexander, *Autocratic Politics*, 221–222.

23 Alexander, *Autocratic Politics*, 227–232, 235, 239–240; Madariaga, *Russia in the Age of Catherine the Great*, 279–280.

24 *PSZ* XX, no. 14.392.

25 Ibid., 230–231.

26 In 1774, there had been 12,712 officials employed in local and provincial administration; by 1796, there were about 27,000, about one-third of whom were salaried. The cost of local and provincial administration therefore rose from 1.7 million rubles to 10.9 million rubles. Madariaga, *Russia in the Age of Catherine the Great*, 290.

27 J. Le Donne, "Catherine's Governors and Governors-General, 1763–1796," *Cahiers du monde russe et sovietique* 20, 1 (1979): 30–31.

28 Alexander, *Autocratic Politics*, 242–243.

29 Le Donne, *Ruling Russia*, 71, 74–75.

30 Madariaga, *Russia in the Age of Catherine the Great*, 296–303.

31 Montefiore, *Potemkin*, 393–394.

32 Vladimir Kuznetsov, *Donskoe kazachestvo v voinakh po zashchite otechestva (1618–1918 gg.)* (Simferopol': DAR, 1997), 60–64.

33 Madariaga, *Russia in the Age of Catherine the Great*, 239.

34 *PSZ* XX, no. 14.251; *PSZ* XX, no. 14.252; Aleksandr Rigel'man, *Istoriia ili povestvovanie o donskikh kozakakh* (Moscow: Universitetskaia tip., 1846), 142; Kuznetsov, *Donskoe kazachestvo v voinakh*, 65–67; Le Donne, *Ruling Russia*, 293.

35 Part of New Russia between the Chernyi Tashlik and the Samotkan' rivers; land along the southern edge of the Ukrainian Line; part of Kodak district on the Domotkan' River; from 1770, territory along the new Dnepr Line; and from 1773, parts of Elizavetgrad Province.

36 Polons'ka-Vasylenko, "The Settlement of the Southern Ukraine (1750–1775)," 293, 294, 298, 299–309, 310, 323, 327.

37 *Arkhiv gosudarstvennogo soveta*, I, 219–222.

38 *PSZ* XX, no. 13.354; Montefiore, *Potemkin*, 266–267; Madariaga, *Russia in the Age of Catherine the Great*, 360–361; Aleksandr Rigel'man, *Letopisnoe povestvovanie o Maloi Rossii i ee narode i kazakakh voobshche. Chast' vtoraia, kniga chetvertaia* (Moscow: Universitetskaia tip., 1847), 29–31.

39 Kabuzan, *Zaselenie Novorossii*, 118; Madariaga, *Russia in the Age of Catherine the Great*, 361.

40 John Le Donne, "The Territorial Reform of the Russian Empire, 1775–1796. [II. The Borderlands, 1777–1796]," *Cahiers du monde Russe et Sovietique* XXIV, 4 (1983), 414, 420.

41 Kohut, *Russian Centralism and Ukrainian Autonomy*, 179, 182, 187–190.

42 Ibid., 209–210, 214.

43 The one exception was that Rumiantsev could not interfere with judicial decisions.

44 Kohut, *Russian Centralism and Ukrainian Autonomy*, 216–217.

45 Le Donne, *Ruling Russia*, 309.

46 Kohut, *Russian Centralism and Ukrainian Autonomy*, 218.

47 Sudienko, "Bumagi do upravleniia Malorossieiu grafa P. A. Rumiantseva Zadunaiskago otnosiashchiesia," 153–161; Storozhenko, "Reformy v Malorossii pri gr. Rumiantseve," 482–493; Magocsi, *History of Ukraine*, 275–276; Kohut, *Russian Centralism and Ukrainian Autonomy*, 219–220.

48 *PSZ* XX, no. 15.724; Madariaga, *Russia in the Age of Catherine the Great*, 313.

49 Sergienko et al., eds., *Istoriia Ukrainskoi SSR*, 586.

50 The Organic Law—the Statute for the Administration of Governorates of November 7, 1775—had provided for each *guberniia* to have its own Governor-General. But this was never carried out for all *gubernii*. Le Donne, *Ruling Russia*, 68.

51 Le Donne, "The Territorial Reform," 420.

52 V. Kabuzan, *Russkie v mir. Dinamika chislennosti i rasseleniia (1719–1989)* (St. Petersburg: Blits, 1996), 57, 63.

53 Polons'ka-Vasylenko, "The Settlement of the Southern Ukraine," 183–187, 193.

54 Of these, about 65,000 were Ukrainians, 38,000 were Russians, and the rest were Hungarians, Serbs, Greeks, Macedonians, Poles, Moldavians, Wallachians, Georgians, and some Swedes. E. I. Druzhinina, *Severnoe Prichernomor'e v 1775–1800 gg.* (Moscow: Akademiia Nauk SSSR, 1959), 53–55.

55 *PSZ* XVI, no. 12.099.

56 But they could not proselytize among the Orthodox within the Empire; Muslims, for example, could only proselytize beyond the frontier.

57 Druzhinina, *Severnoe Prichernomor'e*, 63–64; James Duran, "Catherine II, Potemkin, and Colonization Policy in Southern Russia," *Russian Review* 28, 1 (1969), 28.

58 D. I. Bagalei, *Kolonizatsiia Novorossiiskago kraia i pervye shagi ego po puti kul'tury* (Kiev: Tip. Korchaka-Novitskogo, 1889), 72; Druzhinina, *Severnoe Prichernormor'e*, 163.

59 *PSZ* XX, no. 14.552.

60 Bagalei, *Kolonizatsiia Novorossiiskago kraia*, 73.

61 Druzhinina, *Severnoe Prichernomor'e*, 65, 69.

62 Ekaterinoslav was originally situated at the confluence of the Samara and Kil'chen rivers, but the site proved too marshy; after the annexation of Crimea, Potemkin re-established Ekaterinoslav on a much more ambitious scale on the Dnepr near Zaporozhia, intending it to the be the new capital of Ekaterinoslav Viceroyalty. Today, Ekaterinoslav is Dnipropetrovsk.

63 D. P. Miller, *Zaselenie Novorossiiskago kraia i Potemkin* (Khar'kov: Tip. Zil'berberg i synov'ia, 1901), 35–36; Druzhinina, *Severnoe Prichernomore*, 71–73, 79, 81.

64 At the end of the war, the Azov Flotilla comprised eleven "new model" ships, nine frigates, two bombardiers, twenty-two galiots, ten single-masted extended longboats, and fifty-six smaller vessels and was based at Azov, Taganrog, and Kerch. The Danube Flotilla had seven galleys, five galiots, and twenty smaller vessels. Beskrovnyi, *Russkaia armiia i flot v XVIII veke*, 335.

65 F. F. Veselago, *Kratkaia istoriia russkogo flota* (Moscow, Leningrad: Voenno-morskoe Izd. NKVMF SSSR, 1939), 106–107; Lebedev, *U istokov*, 499.

66 Veselago, *Kratkaia istoriia*, 108; Lebedev, *U istokov*, 501, 517.

67 Counting the Kherson and Nikolaev squadrons, the fleet in 1785 numbered twenty-two ships of the line, twelve frigates, seventeen cruisers, two bombardiers, eight brigantines, six transports, and a number of smaller ships. Veselago, *Kratkaia istoriia*, 109–110; Lebedev, *U istokov*, 537, 542, 648–649; Beskrovnyi, *Russkaia armiia i flot v XVIII veke*, 336.

68 Bogdanovich, *Russkaia armiia*, 18.

69 The number of Don Cossacks doubled to more than 10,000, but they now served in the regular cavalry. Maslovskii, *Zapiski*, II, 62, 69.

70 Beskrovnyi, *Russkaia armiia i flot v XVIII veke*, 299; Alexander, *Autocratic Politics*, 221.

71 Buganov and Buganov, *Polkovodtsy*, 344–345; Maslovskii, *Zapiski* II, 57–59.

72 Baiov, *Istoriia russkogo voennogo iskusstva*, I, 511; Duffy, *Russia's Military Way to the West*, 181–182.

73 Maslovskii, *Zapiski*, II, 59–62, 67–69, 83; Alexander Svechin, *Evoliutsiia voennogo iskusstva* (Moscow: Akademicheskii Proekt, 2002), 260–262; Bruce Menning, "The Imperial Russian Army, 1725–1796," in *The Military History of Tsarist Russia*, ed. Frederick Kagan and Robin Higham (New York, Houndmills: Palgrave, 2002), 67–68.

74 Leonov and Ulianov, *Reguliarnaia pekhota*, 138; Maslovskii, *Zapiski*, II, 85, 122–124; Tatarnikov, ed., *Stroevye ustavy*, II, 65–87.

75 Leonov and Ul'ianov, *Reguliarnaia pekhota*, 152.

76 Maslovskii, *Zapiski*, II, 303–306, 310–313.

77 Vinogradov, ed., *Vek Ekateriny II*, 190–191.

78 Seton-Watson, *History of the Roumanians*, 152; Otetea, ed., *History of the Romanian People*, 265.

79 For example, cattle ranching in Moldavia expanded from 400,000 head in 1774 to 800,000 head in 1786. Stati, *Istoriia Moldovy*, 193–194.

80 Seton-Watson, *History of the Roumanians*, 151; Semenova, *Kniazhestva Valakhiia i Moldaviia*, 325–326.

81 Semenova, *Kniazhestva Valakhiia i Moldaviia*, 328–329.

82 M. S. Anderson, *The Eastern Question, 1774–1923* (London and New York: MacMillan, St. Martin's, 1966), 5; Blanning, *Joseph II*, 130.

83 Andrei Zorin, *By Fables Alone: Literature and State Ideology in Late-Eighteenth—Early-Nineteenth Century Russia* (Boston, MA: Academic Studies Press, 2014), 25.

84 Montefiore, *Potemkin*, 218–221.

85 Zorin, *By Fables Alone*, 32.

86 Ibid., 44; for other examples, see Smilianskii, *Rossiia i Sredizemnomor'e*, 416–422.

87 Quoted in Blanning, *Joseph II*, 135.

88 By 1779, Panin's Northern Accord had already outlived its usefulness. England and Sweden remained outside the Accord, Prussia less useful within it, and the nations against which it had been directed—Austria and France—were now more attractive as strategic partners. Le Donne, *The Russian Empire and the World*, 107; Ransel, *The Politics of Catherinian Russia*, 251–252.

89 Hugh Ragsdale, "Evaluating the Traditions of Russian Aggression: Catherine II and the Greek Project," *Slavonic and East European Review* XLVI, 1 (1988): 111–112.

90 Montefiore, *Potemkin*, 243.

91 Ragsdale, "Evaluating the Traditions," 113.

92 Besides the General Consuls at Trieste, Morea, Salonika, Smyrna, Alexandria, and Said, there were consuls at the Dardanelles, Beirut, Damascus, Crete, Cyprus, Negroponte, Rhodes, Santorini, and Chios. Smilianskii, *Rossiia i Sredizemnomor'e*, 218.

93 For example, Ioannis Varvakis (1745–1825) had distinguished himself in the Russian fleet at Çeşme and became a client of Potemkin. After the war he got rich in Volga shipping and the caviar trade. In 1812 he settled in Taganrog and received the orders of St. Anna and St. Vladimir, and in his final years, he returned to Greece and played a major role in the Greek Revolution.

94 Zorin, *By Fables Alone*, 54–57.

95 This represented a political victory for the king, in that Komarzewski's Military Office was under royal control and worked to reduce the authority of the Military Department within Stackelberg's Permanent Council. But in the early 1780s the *Familja* moved to block further military reform, and they even had the Diet investigate Komarzewski on charges of conspiring to poison Adam Czartoryski.

96 But that sum could only have been reached by risking a dangerously steep increase in tax rates Zamoyski, *The Last King of Poland*, 215; Lukowski, *The Partitions of Poland*, 98–99.

97 Davies, *God's Playground*, I, 529; Montefiore, *Potemkin*, 237–238; Madariaga, *Russia in the Age of Catherine the Great*, 399; Lukowski, *The Partitions of Poland*, 115–117.

98 Lukowski, *The Partitions of Poland*, 110–111.

99 Zamoyski, *The Last King of Poland*, 301.

100 Stone, *The Polish-Lithuanian State*, 277.

101 Fisher, *The Russian Annexation of Crimea*, 60; Smirnov, *Krymskoe khanstvo*, II, 133–134, 138.

102 Ibid., 64–65.

103 Ibid., 68–69; Lashkov, *Shagin Girei*, 51, 53.

104 Fisher, *The Russian Annexation of Crimea*, 74–77; Lashkov, *Shagin Girei*, 54–55.

105 Fisher, *The Russian Annexation of Crimea*, 80; Lashkov, *Shagin Girei*, 55.

106 Fisher, *The Russian Annexation of Crimea*, 82–89; Lashkov, *Shagin Girei*, 56, 60–61.

107 Lashkov, *Shagin Girei*, 60.

108 This tax farm was later assigned to a Russian, Khokhlov, and then to a Jew, Beniamin-Aga.

109 Fisher, *The Russian Annexation of Crimea*, 87, 89, 91–92.

110 Smirnov, *Krymskoe khanstvo*, II, 153.

111 Quoted in Fisher, *The Russian Annexation of Crimea*, 106.

112 Fisher, *The Russian Annexation of Crimea*, 92–95, 99, 105–110; Lashkov, *Shagin Girei*, 63–64.

113 Smirnov, *Politika Rossii na Kavkaze*, 112.

114 The Greeks founded the new town of Mariupol', at the mouth of the Kal'miuss River, with their own Greek "Gothic" eparchy; the Armenians founded the new town of Nakhichevan' on the Don. A. A. Skal'kovskii, *Khronologicheskoe obozrenie istorii Novorossiiskogo kraia*, 2 vols. (Odessa: Gorodskaia tipografiia, 1836–1838), I, 138–139.

115 Fisher, *The Russian Annexation of Crimea*, 100–105.

116 Ibid., 114, 120–122.

117 N. F. Dubrovin, *Prisoedinenie Kryma k Rossii*. Tom IV (St. Petersburg: I. Glazunov, 1885–1889), no. 190.

118 Iazykov's report identified Arslan Girei rather than Batyr Girei as the rebel's choice for khan.

119 Lashkov, *Shagin Girei*, 67–68.

120 Quoted in Fisher, *The Russian Annexation of Crimea*, 133.

121 S. M. Solov'ev, *Istoriia padeniia Pol'shi* (Moscow: Grachev i komp., 1863), 156–157; Lashkov, *Shagin Girei*, 67.

122 *PSZ* XXI, no. 15.708.

123 Fisher, *The Russian Annexation of Crimea*, 137–138; Vinogradov, ed., *Vek Ekateriny II*, 189.

124 Lopatin, *Potemkin i Suvorov*, 92.

125 The Kuban was moved into the new Caucasus Governorate. Fisher, *The Russian Annexation of Crimea*, 142–143; Druzhinina, *Severnoe Prichernomore*, 94, 96.

126 Fisher, *The Russian Annexation of Crimea*, 149; *PSZ* XXI, no. 15.708; Edward Lazzerini, "The Crimea Under Russian Rule, 1783 to the Great Reforms," in *Russian Colonial Expansion to 1917*, ed. Michael Rywkin (London and New York: Mansell, 1988), 131–132.

127 *PSZ* XXII, no. 15.945.

128 Kelly O'Neill, "Bearing Arms for the Empire: Crimean Tatars as Soldiers and Subjects," Conference Paper, 2008, 11, 14; cited with the author's permission.

129 *PSZ* XXII, no. 15.936.

130 Druzhinina, *Severnoe Prichernomore*, 99; Fisher, *The Russian Annexation of Crimea*, 143.

131 Druzhinina, *Severnoe Prichernomore*, 105; Fisher, *The Russian Annexation of Crimea*, 145–146. Lazzerini, "Crimea Under Russian Rule," 126, considers the largest wave of Tatar emigration from Crimea the one following the Treaty of Iaşi in 1792, which "dashed Tatar hopes of recovering their independence."

132 Druzhinina, *Severnoe Prichernomore*, 108, 111, 119–120, 122, 130, 132, 141; Fisher, *The Russian Annexation of Crimea*, 147.

133 Named after the ancient Greek colony of Odessus. Charles King, *The Black Sea: A History* (Oxford: Oxford University Press, 2004), 162–163; Bartlett, *Human Capital*, 124–130.

134 Druzhinina, *Severnoe Prichernomore*, 135.

135 *PSZ* XXI, nos. 15.768 and 15.679; Druzhinina, *Severnoe Prichernomore*, 148.

136 *PSZ* XXI, no. 15.696.

137 Druzhinina, *Severnoe Prichernomore*, 149–151, 153.

138 Some of these Ukrainian settlers had been recruited in the Kiev and Podolia palatinates of Polish Ukraine by agents sent by Potemkin. Druzhinina, *Severnoe Prichernomore*, 156–157.

139 Ibid., 157–160.

140 Skal'kovskii, *Khronologicheskoe obozrenie*, I, 196.

141 Druzhinina, *Severnoe Prichernormore*, 200.

142 William H. McNeill, *Europe's Steppe Frontier, 1500–1800* (Chicago: University of Chicago Press, 1964), 200.

143 Kochekaev, *Nogaisko-russkie otnosheniia*, 232–248; Fisher, *The Russian Annexation of Crimea*, 144–145.

144 Richmond, *The Northwest Caucasus*, 52–53.

145 Robert Schaefer, *The Insurgency in Chechnya and the North Caucasus: From Gazavat to Jihad* (Santa Barbara, CA and Denver, CO: Praeger Security International, 2011), 56–57.

146 Druzhinina, *Severnoe Prichernomore*, 100–101. For a more detailed account of al-Mansur's war in Chechnya and Kabarda see N. F. Dubrovin, *Istoriia voiny i vladychestva russkikh na Kavkaze*, volume (St. Petersburg: Tip. Departamenta udelov, 1886), 86–136.

147 Quoted in Montefiore, *Potemkin*, 251.

148 "If gentle is thy rule, then Russia needs a Paradise." Quoted in Soloviev, *Padenie Pol'shi*, 157.

149 Potemkin's nephew A. N. Samoilov, quoted in Zorin, *By Fables Alone*, 97, 105; see also Sarah Dickinson, "Russia's First 'Orient': Characterizing the Crimea in 1787," *Kritika* III, 1 (2002): 12.

150   Quoted in Zorin, *By Fables Alone*, 114.

151   Quoted in Ibid., 113, 114.

152   Quoted in Larry Wolff, *Imagining Eastern Europe: The Map of Civilization on the Mind of the Enlightenment* (Stanford, CA: Stanford University Press, 1994), 139–140.

153   Dickinson, "Russia's First 'Orient,'" 4; Wolff, *Imagining Eastern Europe*, 140–141.

Conclusion

1   Jeremy Black, *European Warfare, 1660–1815* (New Haven, CT and London: Yale University Press, 1994), 135, 157, 166–167, 208; Davies, *Empire and Military Revolution*, 282–283.

2   Urlanis, *Istoriia voennykh poter'*, 55, 58.

3   Paul Bushkovitch, "Russia," in *The Imperial Moment*, ed. Kimberley Kagan (Cambridge: Harvard University Press, 2010), 126.

4   Ibid., 127.

BIBLIOGRAPHY

Abdulaeva, Gul'nara. *Bitvy iz istorii Krymskogo khanstva* (Simferopol': Krymchupedgiz, 2013).

Abou-el-Haj, Rifaat Ali. *The 1703 Rebellion and the Structure of Ottoman Politics* (Leiden: Nederlands Historisch-Archeaologisch Instituut te Istanbul, 1984).

Agoston, Gabor. "Empires and Warfare in East-Central Europe, 1550–1750: The Ottoman-Habsburg Rivalry and Military Transformation," in *European Warfare, 1350–1750*, ed. Frank Tallett and DJB Trim (Cambridge: Cambridge University Press, 2010), 110–134.

Agoston, Gabor. *Guns for the Sultan. Military Power and the Weapons Industry in the Ottoman Empire* (Cambridge: Cambridge University Press, 2005).

Ahmed Resmi Efendi. *Hulâsatu-l-I 'Tibâr: A Summary of Admonitions: A Chronicle of the 1768–1774 Russian-Ottoman War*, trans. Ethan Menchinger (Istanbul: Isis Press, 2011).

Aksan, Virginia. "Breaking the Spell of the Baron de Tott: Reframing the Question of Military Reform in the Ottoman Empire, 1760–1830," *The International History Review* XXIV, 2 (2002): 253–277.

Aksan, Virginia. "Feeding the Ottoman Troops on the Danube, 1768–1774," *War and Society* 13, 1 (1995): 1–14.

Aksan, Virginia. "Locating the Ottomans among Early Modern Empires," *Journal of Early Modern History* 3, 2 (1999): 103–134.

Aksan, Virginia. "The One-Eyed Fighting the Blind: Mobilization, Supply, and Command in the Russo-Turkish War of 1768–1774," *International History Review* 15, 2 (1993): 221–238.

Aksan, Virginia. "Ottoman Ethnographies of Warfare, 1500–1800," in *Empires and Indigenes: Intercutural Alliance, Imperial Expansion, and Warfare in the Early Modern World*, ed. Wayne Lee (New York: New York University Press, 2011), 141–163.

Aksan, Virginia. "Ottoman Military Power in the Eighteenth Century," in *Eastern European Warfare, 1500–1800*, ed. Brian Davies (Leiden: E. J. Brill, 2011).

Aksan, Virginia. "Ottoman Military Recruitment Strategies in the Late Eighteenth Century," in *Arming the State: Military Conscription in the Middle East and Central Asia, 1775–1925*, ed. Erik Zurcher (London and New York: I. B. Tauris, 1999), 21–39.

Aksan, Virginia. *An Ottoman Statesman in War and Peace: Ahmed Resmi Efendi, 1700–1783* (Leiden: E. J. Brill, 1995).

Aksan, Virginia. *Ottoman Wars, 1700–1870. An Empire Besieged* (Harlow, London, New York: Pearson Longman, 2007).

Aksan, Virginia. "Whatever Happened to the Janissaries? Mobilization for the 1768–1774 Russo-Ottoman War," *War in History* V, I (1988): 23–36.

Al'bovskii, Evgenii. *Istoriia Khar'kovskago slobodskago kazach'ago polka (1651–1765 gg.)* (Khar'kov: Tip. Gubernskago pravleniia, 1895).

Alexander, John T. *Autocratic Politics in a National Crisis: The Imperial Russian Government and Pugachev's Revolt, 1773–1775* (Bloomington, IN and London: Indiana Unversity Press, 1969).

Alexander, John T. *Bubonic Plague in Early Modern Russia. Public Health and Urban Disaster* (Oxford: Oxford University Press, 2002).

Allen, W. E. D. *A History of the Georgian People* (New York: Barnes and Noble, 1971, 2nd ed.).

Anderson, M. S. *The Eastern Question, 1774–1923* (London and New York: MacMillan, St. Martin's, 1966).

Andreev, A. *Kniaz' V. M. Dolgorukov-Krymskii* (Moscow: Mezhregional'nyi tsentr otraselevoi informatiki Gosatomnadzora Rossii, 1997).

Anisimov, Evgenii. *Five Empresses: Court Life in Eighteenth-Century Russia* (London and Westport, CT: Praeger, 2004).

Anisimov, Evgenii. *Gosudarstvennye preobrazovaniia i samoderzhavie Petra Velikogo* (St. Petersburg: Dmitrii Bulanin, 1997).

Anisimov, Evgenii. "The Imperial Heritage of Peter the Great in the Foreign Policy of his Early Successors," in *Imperial Russian Foreign Policy*, ed. Hugh Ragsdale and V. N. Ponomarev (Cambridge: Cambridge University Press, 1993), 21–35.

Anisimov, Evgenii. *Podatnaia reforma Petra I: vvedenie podushnoi podati v Rossii, 1719–1728* (Leningrad: Nauka, 1982).

Anisimov, Evgenii. *Rossiia bez Petra* (St. Petersburg: Lenizdat, 1994).

Arapov, D. Iu. et al., eds. *Severnyi Kavkaz v sostave Rossiiskoi imperii* (Moscow: Novoe literaturnoe obozrenie, 2007).

Arkhiv Gosudarstvennago Soveta. Tom I (St. Petersburg: Vtoroe otdelenie Sobstvennoi E. I. V. Kantseliarii, 1869).

Arunova, M. R. and Oreshkova, S. F., eds. *Russkii posol v Shtambule. Petr Andreevich Tol'stoi i ego opisanie Osmanskoi imperii nachala XVIII v.* (Moscow: Nauka, 1985).

Ascherson, N. *Black Sea* (New York: Hill and Wang, 1996).

Aurova, N. N. *Sistema voennogo obrazovaniia v Rossii; Kadetskie korpusa vo vtoroi polovine XVIII- pervoi polovine XIX veka* (Moscow: Institut Rossiiskoi istorii RAN, 2003).

Avrich, Paul. *Russian Rebels, 1600–1800* (New York: W. W. Norton, 1976).

Avtokratov, V. N. "Pervye komissariatskie organy russkoi reguliarnoi armii," *Istoricheskie zapiski* 68 (1961): 163–188.

Avtokratov, V. N. "Voennyi prikaz (K istorii komplektovaniia i formirovaniia voisk v Rossii v nachale XVIII v.," in *Poltava: K 250-letiiu poltavskogo srazheniia*, ed. L. G. Beskrovnyi and B. B. Kafengauz (Moscow: AN SSSR, 1959), 228–245.

Bachinskii, A. D. and A. O. Dobroliubskii. "Budzhakskaia orda v XVI-XVII vv. (Istoriko-arkheologicheskii ocherk)," in *Sotsial'no-ekonomicheskii i politicheskii istoriia Moldavii perioda feodalizma*, ed. P. V. Sovetov (Kishinev: Shtiintsa, 1988), 82–93.

Baddeley, John. *The Russian Conquest of the Caucasus* (New York: Longmans, 1908).

Bagalei (Bahalii), D. I. *Istoriia Slobods'koi Ukraini* (Khar'kov: Soiuz, 1918).

Bagalei (Bahalii), D. I. *Kolonizatsiia Novorossiiskago kraia i pervye shagi ego po puti kul'tury* (Kiev: Tip. Korchaka-Novitskogo, 1889).

Bagger, Hans. "The Role of the Baltic in Russian Foreign Policy, 1721–1773," in *Imperial Russian Foreign Policy*, ed. Hugh Ragsdale (Cambridge: Cambridge University Press, 1993), 37–74.

Baiov, A. K. *Istoriia russkogo voennogo iskusstva. Vypusk pervyi* (Moscow: FondIV, 2008, reprint of 1909 ed.).

Baiov, A. K. *Russkaia armiia v tsarstvovanie imperatritsy Anny Ioannovny. Voina Rossii s Turtsiei v 1736–1739.* 2 vols. (St. Petersburg: N. Ia. Stoikovoi, 1906).

Balisch, Alexander. "Infantry Battlefield Tactics in the Seventeenth and Eighteenth Centuries on the European and Turkish Theaters of War: The Austrian Response to Different Conditions," *Studies in History and Politics* 3 (1983–1984): 43–60.

Bantysh-Kamenskii, Dm. *Biografii rossiiskikh generalissimusov i general-fel'dmarshalov* (Moscow: Biblioteka, 1994, facs. reprint of 1840 edition).

Baranovich, A. I. and Kaufengauz, B. B., eds. *Ocherki istorii SSSR. Period feodalizma. Rossiia vo vtoroi polovine XVIII v.* (Moscow: Akademiia Nauk SSSR, 1956).

Bardach, Juliusz, Leśnodorski, Bogusław and Pietrzak, Michał, eds. *Historia ustroju i prawa polskiego* (Warsaw: PAN, 1994).

Bibliography

Barkey, Karen. *Empire of Difference. The Ottomans in Comparative Perspective* (Cambridge: Cambridge University Press, 2008).

Barrett, Thomas M. *At the Edge of Empire: The Terek Cossacks and the North Caucasus* (Boulder, CO: Westview Press, 1999).

Bartlett, Roger P. *Human Capital: The Settlement of Foreigners in Russia, 1762–1804* (Cambridge: Cambridge University Press, 1979).

Bauer, Friedrich Wilhelm von. *Memoires historiques et geographiques sur la Valachie* (Frankfort and Leipzig: Henry-Louis Broenner, 1778).

Baugh, Daniel. *The Global Seven Years' War, 1754–1763* (London and New York: Longman, 2011).

Bazhova, A. P. "Nachalo tsarstvovaniia Ekaterine II. Rossiia v sisteme mezdunarodnykh otnoshenii," in *Istoriia vneshnei politiki Rossii. XVIII vek*, ed. A. V. Ignat'ev, V. N. Ponomarev, and G. A. Sanin (Moscow: Mezhdunarodnye otnosheniia, 1998), 111–116.

Bazhova, A. P. "Rossiia i balkanskie zemli," in *Istoriia vneshnei politiki Rossii. XVIII vek*, ed. A. V. Ignat'ev, V. N. Ponomarev, and G. A. Sanin (Moscow: Mezhdunarodnye otnosheniia, 1998), 125–129.

Bazhova, A. P. "Voina 1768–1774 godov, Kiuchuk-Kainardzhiiskii mir," in *Istoriia vneshnei politiki Rossii. XVIII vek*, ed. A. V. Ignat'ev, V. N. Ponomarev and G. A. Sanin (Moscow: Mezhdunarodnye otnosheniia, 1998), 116–125.

Belova, E. V. "Russko-turetskie voiny i migratsionnaia politika Rossii v pervoi polovine XVIII v." *Voprosy istorii* 5 (2008): 141–145.

Beskrovnyi, L. G. *Russkaia armiia i flot v XVIII veke* (Moscow: Ministerstvo oborony SSSR, 1958).

Beskrovnyi, L. G., ed. *Aleksandr Vasil'evich Suvorov* (Moscow: Nauka, 1980).

Beskrovnyi, L. G., ed. *Khrestomatiia po russkoi voennoi istorii* (Moscow: Ministerstvo vooruzhennykh sil SSSR, 1947).

Bespalov, Aleksandr. *Bitvy severnoi voiny* (Moscow: Reitar, 2005).

Bezikoglu, Metin. "The Deterioration of Ottoman Administration in the Light of the Ottoman-Russian War of 1768–1774," MA Thesis, Bilkent University, 2001.

Black, Jeremy. *European Warfare, 1660–1815* (New Haven, CT and London: Yale University Press, 1994).

Black, Jeremy. *A Military Revolution? Military Change and European Society, 1550–1800* (Atlantic Highlands: Humanities Press International, 1991).

Blanning, T. C. W. *Joseph II* (London and New York: Longman, 1994).

Bobrovskii, P. O. *Voennoe pravo v Rossii pri Petre Velikom. Chast' vtoraia. Artikul' voinskii. Vypusk 2. Perekhod Rossii k reguliarnoi armii* (St. Petersburg: V. S. Balashev, 1886).

Boeck, Brian J. *Imperial Boundaries. Cossack Communities and Empire-Building in the Age of Peter the Great* (Cambridge: Cambridge University Press, 2009).

Boeck, Brian J. "When Peter I Was Forced to Settle for Less: Coerced Labor and Resistance in a Failed Russian Colony (1695–1711)," *Journal of Modern History* 80 (September 2008): 485–514.

Bogdanovich, M. I. *Russkaia armiia v vek Imperatritsy Ekateriny II* (St. Petersburg: Departament udelov, 1873).

Brewer, John. *The Sinews of Power: War, Money, and the English State, 1688–1783* (Cambridge, MA: Harvard University Press, 1990).

Brun, F. *Krym v polovine XVIII stoletiia* (Odessa: Tip. L. Nitcha, 1867).

Buganov, V. I. and Buganov, A. V. *Polkovodtsy XVIII v* (Moscow: Patriot, 1992).

Bushkovitch, Paul. "The Romanov Transformation, 1613–1725," in *The Military History of Tsarist Russia*, ed. Frederick Kagan and Robin Higham (New York and Houndmills: Palgrave, 2002), 31–45.

Bushkovitch, Paul. "Russia," in *The Imperial Moment*, ed. Kimberly Kagan (Cambridge: Harvard University Press, 2010), 109–140.

Buturlin, D. P. *Kartina voin Rossi s Turtsieiu v tsarstvovaniia Imperatritsy Ekateriny II i Imperatora Aleksandra I* (St. Petersburg: Tip. Imperatorskago Vospitat. Doma, 1829).

Căzănişteanu, Constantin. "The Consequences for the Rumanian Principalities of the Ottoman Wars with Austria and Russia," in *East Central European Society and War in the Pre-Revolutionary Eighteenth Century*, ed. Gunther Rothenberg, Bela Kiraly, and Peter Sugar (New York: Columbia University Press, 1982), 401–414.

Ceauşescu, Ilie. "Military Aspects of the National Struggle of the Rumanian Principalities in the Eighteenth Century," in *East Central European Society and War in the Pre-Revolutionary Eighteenth Century*, ed. Gunther Rothenberg, Bela Kiraly, and Peter Sugar (New York: Columbia University Press, 1982), 371–386.

Chandler, David. *The Art of Warfare in the Age of Marlborough* (New York: Sarpedon, 1994).

Chechulin, N. D. *Ocherki po istorii russkikh finansov v tsarstvovanie Ekateriny II* (St. Petersburg: Senatskaia tipografiia, 1906).

Chechulin, N. D. *Vneshniaia politika Rossii v nachale tsarstvovaniia Ekateriny II, 1762–1774* (St. Petersburg: Tip. Glavnago upravleniia udelov, 1896).

Chernushkin, A. V. *Russkaia armiia XVIII-XIX vekov. 1700-1801: Pekhota—kavaleriia—artilleriia. 1801-1825: Gvardeiskaia i armeiskaia pekhota* (Moscow: Astrel-AST, 2004).

Chistiakova, E. V. and Solov'ev, V. M. *Stepan Razin i ego soratniki* (Moscow: Mysl', 1988).

Ciesielski, Tomasz. *Armiia koronna w czasach Augusta III* (Opol'e: Instytut Historii Uniwersytetu Opolskiego, 2009).

Ciesielski, Tomasz. "O hajdamaczyźnie w latach 1733–1763," in *W kręgu Hadziacza AD 1658. Od historii do literatury*, ed. P. Borek (Kraków: Collegium Colombinum, 2008), 181–198.

Cizakca, Murat. "The Evolution of Ottoman Domestic Loans from the 15th to the Nineteenth Centuries," in *The Great Ottoman-Turkish Civilization. Volume 2*, ed. Kemal Cicek and Halil Inalcik (Ankara: Yeni Turkiye, 2000), 128–131.

Collins, L. J. D. "The Military Organization and Tactics of the Crimean Tatars, 16th–17th Centuries," in *War, Technology and Society in the Middle East*, ed. V. J. Parry and M. E. Yapp (London: Oxford University Press, 1975), 257–276.

Constantiniu, Florin. "Tradition and Innovation in the Eighteenth-Century Military Structures of the Rumanian Lands," in *East Central European War and Society in the Pre-Revolutionary Eighteenth Century*, ed. Gunther Rothenberg, Bela Kiraly, and Peter Sugar (New York: Columbia University Press, 1982), 387–399.

Cracraft, James. *The Petrine Revolution in Russian Culture* (Cambridge and London: Harvard University Press, 2004).

Cross, Anthony Glenn. *By the Banks of the Neva: Chapters from the Lives and Careers of the British in Eighteenth-Century Russia* (Cambridge: Cambridge University Press, 1997).

Davies, Brian L. *Empire and Military Revolution in Eastern Europe: Russia's Turkish Wars in the Eighteenth Century* (London and New York: Continuum, 2011).

Davies, Brian L. "Military Engineers and the Rise of Imperial Russia," in *Military Engineers and the Making of the Early-Modern State*, ed. Bruce Lenman (Dundee: Dundee University Press, 2013), 201–215.

Davies, Brian L. "The Razin Rebellion at Tambov and Kozlov, 1670–1671," *Russian History/Histoire Russe* 34, 1–4 (2007): 262–276.

Davies, Brian L. "Service, Landholding, and Dependent Labour in Kozlov District, 1675," in *New Perspectives on Muscovite History. Selected Papers from the Fourth World Congress for Soviet and East European Studies, Harrogate, 1990*, ed. Lindsey Hughes (Houndmills: MacMillan Press/St. Martin's Press, 1993), 129–155.

Davies, Brian L. *State Power and Community in Early Modern Russia: The Case of Kozlov, 1635-1649* (London and New York: Palgrave MacMillan, 2004).

Davies, Brian L. *Warfare, State and Society on the Black Sea Steppe, 1500-1700* (London and New York: Routledge, 2007).

Bibliography

Davies, Norman. *God's Playground: A History of Poland. Volume I* (New York: Columbia University Press, 1982).

Davison, Roderic H. " 'Russian Skill and Turkish Imbecility': The Treaty of Kuchuk Kainardji Reconsidered," *Slavic Review* XXXV, 3 (1976): 463–483.

Dickinson, Sarah. "Russia's First 'Orient': Characterizing the Crimea in 1787," *Kritika* III, 1 (2002): 3–25.

Dolgorukov, P. "O Vasilii Mikhailoviche Dogorukove-Krymskom," in *Istoriia Kryma. Kratkoe opisanie proshlogo Krymskogo poluostrova*, ed. A. R. Andreev (Moscow: Mezhregional'nyi tsentr otraslevoi informatika Gosatomnadzora Rossii, 1997), 249–250.

Donnelly, Alton. *The Russian Conquest of Bashkiria, 1552–1740* (New Haven, CT: Yale, 1968).

Dorn, Walter. *Competition for Empire, 1740–1763* (New York: Harper and Brothers, 1940).

Doroshenko, D. I. *Narys istorii Ukraini*. 2 vols. (Kiev: Globus, 1991).

Druzhinina, E. I. *Kiuchuk-Kainardzhskii mir 1774 goda: ego podgotovka i zakliuchenie* (Moscow: Akademiia Nauk SSSR, 1955).

Druzhinina, E. I. *Severnoe Prichernomor'e v 1775–1800 gg.* (Moscow: Akademiia Nauk SSSR, 1959).

Dubnow, Simon. *History of the Jews in Russia and Poland* (Philadelphia, PA: Jewish Publication Society of America, 1918).

Dubrovin, N. F. *Istoriia voiny i vladychestva russkikh na Kavkaze*. 6 vols. (St. Petersburg: Tip. Departamenta udelov, 1871–1888).

Dubrovin, N. F. *Prisoedinenie Kryma k Rossii*. 4 vols. (St. Petersburg: Imperatorskaia akademiia nauk, 1885–1889).

Dubrovin, N. F. *Pugachev i ego soobshchniki* (St. Petersburg: Tip. Skorokhodova, 1884).

Duffy, Christopher. *The Army of Maria Theresa. The Armed Forces of Imperial Austria, 1740–1780* (New York: Hippocrene Books, 1977).

Duffy, Christopher. *Frederick the Great: A Military Life* (London and New York: Routledge, 1985).

Duffy, Christopher. *The Military Experience in the Age of Reason* (London and New York: Routledge, 1987).

Duffy, Christopher. *Russia's Military Road to the West. Origins and Nature of Russian Military Power, 1700–1800* (London: Routledge and Kegan Paul, 1981).

Duffy, Christopher. "The Seven Years' War as a Limited War," in *East Central European Society and War in the Pre-Revolutionary Eighteenth Century*, ed. Gunther Rothenberg, Bela Kiraly, and Peter Sugar (New York: Columbia University Press, 1982), 67–74.

Duran, James. "Catherine II, Potemkin, and Colonization Policy in Southern Russia," *Russian Review* 28, 1 (1969): 23–36.

Duran, James. "The Reform of Financial Administration in Russia during the Reign of Catherine II," *Canadian Slavic Studies*, IV, 3 (1970): 485–596.

Elfimov, S. V. and Makovskaia, L. K., eds. *Arkhiv general-fel'ddtseikhmeistera Iakova Vilimovicha Briusa* (St. Petersburg: Shchelkovaia, 2004).

Emel'ianov, A. P. "Razvitie taktiki russkoi armii vo vtoroi polovine XVIII v.," in *Razvitie taktiki russkoi armii, XVIII- nachalo XX vv.*, ed. D. V. Pankov (Moscow: Ministerstvo oborony SSSR, 1957), 58–82.

Epifanov, P. P. and Komarov, A. A. "Voennoe delo. Armiia i flot," in *Ocherki russkoi kul'tury XVIII veka. Chast' vtoraia*, ed. B. A. Aleksandrov et al. (Moscow: Moskovskii universitet, 1987), 186–257.

Etkind, Alexander. *Internal Colonization. Russia's Imperial Experience* (Cambridge: Polity, 2011).

Faroqhi, Suraiya. *The Ottoman Empire and the World Around It* (London and New York: I. B. Tauris, 2004).

Fedosov, D., ed. *Diary of General Patrick Gordon of Auchleuchries 1635–1699. Volume III: 1677–1678* (Aberdeen: Arts and Humanities Research Council, 2012).

Fedyukin, Igor. "An Infinite Variety of Inclinations and Appetites': *Genie* and Governance in Post-Petrine Russa," *Kritika*, 4 (2010): 741–762.

Ferguson, Alan. "Russian Landmilitia and Austrian Miltargrenze (A Comparative Study)," *Sudostforschungen* 13 (1954): 139–158.

Fichtner, Paula Sutter. *Terror and Toleration: The Habsburg Empire Confronts Islam, 1526–1850* (London and Chicago: Reaktion Books, 2008).

Finkel, Caroline. *Osman's Dream. The History of the Ottoman Empire* (New York: Basic Books, 2005).

Fisher, Alan W. *The Crimean Tatars* (Stanford, CA: Hoover Press Publications, 1978).

Fisher, Alan W. *The Russian Annexation of the Crimea, 1772–1783* (Cambridge: Cambridge University Press, 1970).

Fortunatov, P. K., ed. *P. A. Rumiantsev*. 2 vols. (Moscow: Voennoe izd. Ministerstva oborony SSSR, 1953).

Frost, Robert I. *The Northern Wars: War, State and Society in Northeastern Europe, 1558–1721* (London: Longman, 2000).

Frumenkov, G. G. "Rossiia i semiletniaia voina," *Voprosy istorii* 9 (1971): 107–119.

Fuller, William C., Jr. *Strategy and Power in Russia, 1600–1914* (New York: Free Press, 1992).

Gat, Azar. *The Origins of Military Thought from the Enlightenment to Clausewitz* (Oxford: Clarendon Press, 1989).

Geisman, P. A. and Dubovskii, N. *Graf Petr Ivanovich Panin (1721–1789)* (St. Petersburg: Tip. N. V. Vasileva, 1897).

Gerbel', Nikolai. *Iziumskii slobodskoi kazachii polk, 1651–1765* (St. Petersburg: Tip. E. Pratsa, 1852).

Gerovskii, Iu. (Gierowski, Jozef Andrzej) "Otnoshenia Pol'shi k Turtsii i Krymu v period personal'noi unii s Saksoniei," in *Rossiia, Pol'sha i Prichernomor'e v XV- nachale XVIII v.*, ed. B. A. Rybakov (Moscow: Nauka, 1979), 344–366.

Gerovskii, Iu. (Gierowski, Jozef Andrzej) "The International Position of Poland in the Seventeenth and Eighteenth Centuries," in *A Republic of Nobles: Studies in Polish History to 1864*, ed. J. K. Fedorowicz (Cambridge: Cambridge University Press, 1982), 218–237.

Gerovskii, Iu. (Gierowski, Jozef Andrzej) "The Polish-Lithuanian Armies in the Confederations and Insurrections of the Eighteenth Century," in *East Central European Society and War in the Pre-Revolutionary Eigheenth Century*, ed. Gunther Rothernberg, Bela Kiraly, and Peter Sugar (New York: Columbia University Press, 1982), 215–238.

Gierowski, Jozef Andrzej and Kaminski, Andrzej. "The Eclipse of Poland," in *The New Cambridge Modern History. Volume VI: The Rise of Great Britain and Russia, 1688–1725*, ed. John Selwyn Bromley (Cambridge: Cambridge University Press, 1970), 681–715.

Gil'denshtedt, Iogann Anton. *Puteshestvie po Kavkazy v 1770–1773* (St. Petersburg: Peterburgskoe Vostokovenedie, 2002).

Golovinskii, Petr. *Slobodskie kozach'i polki* (St. Petersburg: Tip. I. Tiblen i komp., 1864).

Grant, Jonathan. "Rethinking the 'Ottoman Decline': Military Technology Diffusion in the Ottoman Empire, Fifteenth to Eighteenth Centuries," *Journal of World History* X, 1 (1999): 179–201.

Griffiths, David M. "Catherine II Discovers the Crimea," *Jahrbücher für Geschichte Osteuropas* LVI, 3 (2008): 339–348.

Griffiths, David M. "The Rise and Fall of the Northern System: Court Politics and Foreign Policy in the First Half of Catherine II's Reign," *Canadian Slavic Studies* IV, 3 (1970): 547–569.

Gusev, I. *Artilleriia Petra I* (Moscow: AST, 2002).

Gusev, I. *Chesmenskoe morskoe srazhenie* (Moscow: AST, 2002).

von Hammer-Purgstall, J. P. *Histoire de l'Empire Ottoman. Tome seizieme* (Paris: Bellizard, Barthes, Dufour et Lowell, 1839).

Bibliography

Hartley, Janet. "Russia as a Fiscal-Military State, 1689–1825," in *The Fiscal Military State in Eighteenth-century Europe*, ed. Christopher Storrs (Farnham and Surrey: Ashgate, 2009), 125–146.

Hartley, Janet. *A Social History of the Russian Empire, 1650–1825* (London and New York: Longman, 1999).

Hickok, Michael. *Ottoman Military Administration in Eighteenth-Century Bosnia* (Leiden and New York: E. J. Brill, 1997).

Hochedlinger, Michael. *Austria's Wars of Emergence, 1683–1797* (London and New York: Longman, 2003).

Hochedlinger, Michael. "The Habsburg Monarchy: From 'Military-Fiscal State' to 'Militarization,'" in *The Fiscal-Military State in Eighteenth-Century Europe*, ed. Christopher Storrs (Farnham, Surrey: Ashgate, 2009), 55–94.

Hodgson, Marshall. *The Venture of Islam. Volume 3. Gunpowder Armies and Modern Times* (Chicago and London: University of Chicago Press, 1977).

Hurzhii, O. (Gurzhii, A.) *Evoliutsiia feodal'nykh otnoshenii na levo-berezhnoi Ukraine v pervoi polovine XVIII veka* (Kiev: Naukova Dumka, 1986).

Hurzhii, O. (Gurzhii, A.) *Get'man Ivan Skoropad'skyi* (Kiev: NAN Ukraina, 1998).

Hurzhii, O. and Chukhlib, T. V. *Get'mans'ka Ukraina. Tom 8* (Kiev: Al'ternativy, 1999).

Iakovenko, I. P. *Nyneshnee sostoianie turetskikh kniahzhestv Moldavii i Valakhii i Rossiiskoi Bessarabskoi oblasti* (St. Petersburg: Tip. A. Smirdina, 1828).

Iavornitskii, D. I. *Istoriia zaporoz'skikh kazakiv.* 3 vols. (Kiev: Naukova dumka, 1990).

Ignatev, A. V., Ponomarev, N. and Sanin, G. A., eds. *Istoriia vneshnoi politiki Rossii XVIII vek* (Moscow: Mezhdunarodnye otnosheniia, 1998).

Il'enko, A. K., ed. "Istoricheskii ocherk. Komplektovanie vooruzhennykh sil v Rossii do 1802 g.," in *Stoletie voennago ministerstva 1802–1902. Glavnyi shtab.* Tom 4, ch. 1, no. 1, otd. 1, ed. D. A. Skalon' (St. Petersburg, 1902), 139–143.

Iusupov, R. R.. "Pol'skii vopros v politike Rossii nakanune russko-turestkoi voiny 1768–1774 gg.," *Vestnik Moskovskogo universiteta. Seriia 8: Istoriia* 3 (1980): 35–45.

Ivanics, Maria. "Enslavement, Slave Labour and the Treatment of Captives in the Crimean Khanate," in *Ransom Slavery Along the Ottoman Borders*, ed. Geza David and Pal Fodor (Leiden and Boston, MA: E. J. Brill, 2007), 193–220.

Ivanov, P. I. *Obozrenie sostav I ustroistva reguliarnoi russkoi kavalerii ot Petra Velikago do nashikh dnei* (St. Petersburg: Tip. Departament udelov, 1873).

Itzkowitz, Norman. "Eighteenth-Century Ottoman Realities," *Studia Islamica* 16 (1962): 73–94.

Jaimoukha, Amjad. *A Brief History of Kabarda* (on-line), Jaimoukha.synthasite.com

Jelavich, Chales and Jelavich, Barbara. *The Establishment of the Balkan National States, 1804–1920* (Seattle, WA: University of Washington Press, 1977).

Jones, Robert E. *The Emancipation of the Russian Nobility, 1762–1785* (Princeton, NJ: Princeton University Press, 1973).

Jones, Robert E. "Opening a Window on the South: Russia and the Black Sea, 1695–1792," in *A Window on Russia. Papers from the Fifth International Conference of the Study Group on Eighteenth-Century Russia, Gargnano, 1994*, ed. Maria di Salvo and Lindsey Hughes (Rome: La Fenice Edizioni, 1996), 123–129.

Kabuzan, V. M. *Russkie v mire. Dinamika chislennosti i rasseleniia (1719–1989)* (St. Petersburg: Blits, 1996).

Kabuzan, V. M. *Zaselenie Novorossii (Ekaterinoslavskoi i Khersonskoi gubernii) v XVIII-pervoi polovine XIX veka* (Moscow: Nauka, 1976).

Kahan, Arcadius. *The Plow, the Hammer, and The Knout: An Economic History of Eighteenth-Century Russia* (London and Chicago: University of Chicago Press, 1985).

Kalinina, E. *Istoriia goroda Voronezha* (Voronezh: Voronezhskoe oblastnoe knigoizdatel'stvo, 1941).

Kapitonov, A. P., ed. *Fel'dmarshal Rumiantsev: dokumenty, pis'ma, vospominaniia* (Moscow: Vostochnaia Literature, 2001).

Kaplan, Herbert. *The First Partition of Poland* (New York: Columba University Press, 1962).

Kaplan, Herbert. *Russia and the Outbreak of the Seven Years' War* (Berkeley, CA: University of California Press, 1968).

Karman, Gabor. *The European Tributary States of the Ottoman Empire in the Sixteenth and Seventeenth Centuries* (Leiden: E. J. Brill, 2013).

Keep, J. L. H. "Feeding the Troops: Russian Army Supply Policies during the Seven Years' War," *Canadian Slavonic Papers* 29, 1 (1987): 24–44.

Keep, J. L. H. "The Russian Army in the Seven Years' War," in *The Military and Society in Russia, 1450–1917*, ed. Eric Lohr and Marshall Poe (Leiden: E. J. Brill, 2002), 197–220.

Keep, J. L. H. *Soldiers of the Tsar. Army and Society in Russia, 1462–1874* (Oxford: Clarendon Press, 1985).

Keralio, Louis Felix Guinement de. *Histoire de la derniere Guerre entre les Russes et les Turcs* (Paris: DeSaint, 1777).

Kersnovskii, A. A. *Istoriia russkoi armii. Tom pervi. Ot Narvy do Parizha, 1700–1814* (Moscow: Golos, 1992).

Khodarkovsky, Michael. *Where Two Worlds Met: The Russian State and the Kalmyk Nomads, 1600–1771* (Ithaca, NY: Cornell University Press, 1992).

King, Charles. *The Black Sea: A History* (Oxford: Oxford University Press, 2004).

Kipnis, B. G. "Razvitie taktiki Russkoi armii v Russko-turetskoi voine 1768–1774 g," in *Rossiia v XVIII veke. Voiny i vneshnaia politika, vnutrennaia politika, ekonomika, i kul'tura. Tezisy*, ed. T. G. Frumenkova (St. Petersburg: Minerva, 1996), 4–5.

Kirpichenok, Artem. *Serbskie poseleniia na Ukraine v seredine XVIII veka* (St. Petersburg: Nestor, 2007).

Kleeman, Niklous Ernst. *Reisen Von Wien Ber Belgrad Bis Kilianova … in Die Crimm … in Den Jahren 1768, 1769 and 1770* (Charleston, SC: Nabu Press, 2012 reprint).

Kliuchevskii, V. O. *Sochinenii v deviati tomax. Tom IV. Kurs russkoi istorii, chast' IV* (Moscow: Mysl', 1989).

Klokman, Iu. R. *Fel'dmarshal Rumiantsev v period russko-turetskoi voiny 1768–1774* (Moscow: Akademiia Nauk SSSR, 1951).

Klokman, Iu. "Goroda Belgorodskoi cherty i gubernskoi reform 1775 g.," in *Voprosy sotsial'no-ekonomicheskoi istorii i istochnikovedeniia. Sbornik statei*, ed. N. V. Ustiugov (Moscow: AKademiia Nauk SSSR, 1961), 157–162.

Klokman, Iu. "P.A. Rumiantsev i A. V. Suvorov," in *Suvorovskii sbornik*, ed. A. V. Sukhomlin (Moscow: Akademiia Nauk SSSR, 1951), 61–88.

Klokman, Iu. "P. A. Rumiantsev kak voennyi teoretik," *Istoricheskie zapiski* 37 (1951): 81–103.

Klokman, Iu. *Sotsial'no-ekonomicheskaia istoriia russkogo goroda. Vtoraia polovina XVIII veka* (Moscow: Nauka, 1967).

Kochekaev, B.-A. B. *Nogaisko-russkie otnosheniia v XV-XVIII vv.* (Alma-Ata: Nauka, 1988).

Kochetkov, A. N. "Takticheskie vzgliady A. V. Suvorova," in *Razvitie taktiki russkoi armii, XVIII-nachale XX vv.*, ed. D. V. Pankov (Moscow: Ministerstvo Oborony SSSR, Voennoe Izd., 1957), 83–111.

Kochubinskii, A. L. *Graf Andrei Ivanovich Osterman i razdel Turtsii. Iz istorii vostochnago voprosa* (Odessa: Tip. Shtaba Odesskago voennago okruga, 1899).

Kohut, Zenon. "Myths Old and New: The Haidamak Movement and the Koliivshchyna (1768) in Recent Historiography," *Harvard Ukrainoan Studies* I, 3 (1977): 359–378.

Kohut, Zenon. *Russian Centralism and Ukrainian Autonomy. Imperial Absorption of the Hetmanate, 1760s–1830s* (Cambridge: Harvard Ukrainian Research Institute, 1988).

Kołodziejczyk, Dariusz. *The Crimean Khanate and Poland-Lithuania: International Diplomacy on the European Periphery* (Leiden: E. J. Brill, 2011).

Bibliography

Kolomiets, Andrei. *Finansovye reformy russkikh tsarei. Ot Ivana Groznogo do Aleksandra Osvoboditelia* (Moscow: Zhurnal Voprosy ekonomiki, 2001).

Konopczyński, Władysław. *Casimir Pulaski*, trans. Irena Mackarewicz (Chicago: Polish Roman Catholic Union of America, 1947).

Konopczyński, Władysław. "The Early Saxon Period, 1697–1733," in *The Cambridge History of Poland*, ed. W. F. Reddaway et al. (Cambridge: Cambridge University Press, 1951), 1–24.

Konopczyński, Władysław. *Konfederacja barska.* 2 vols. (Warsaw: wyd. Kasymienia Mianowskiego-instytutu, 1938).

Konopczyński, Władysław. *Polska a Turcja, 1683–1792* (Warsaw: Nakładem Instytutu Wschódniego w Warszawie, 1936).

Korobkin, N. M., ed. *Fel'dmarshal Rumiantsev. Sbornik dokumentov i materialov* (Moscow, Leningrad: OGIZ, 1947).

Korzon, Tadeusz. *Dzieje wojen i wojskowości w Polsce. Tom III. Dokończenie epoki przedrozbiorowej. Epoka Porozbiorowa* (Lwów, Warsaw, and Krakow: Wydawnictwo zakładu narodowej im. Ossolińskich, 1923).

Kostomarov, N. I. "Fel'dmarshal Minikh i ego znachenie v Russkoi istorii," in *Russkaia istoriia v zhizneopisaniiakh eia glaneishikh deiatelei. Tom vtoroi. XVIII-oe stoletie. Vypusk sed'moi* (St. Petersburg: M. M. Stasiulevich, 1888), 1–107.

Kostomarov, N. I. *Poslednye dni Rechi pospolity* (St. Petersburg: Tip. F. Sushchinskago, 1870).

Krotov, P. A. "Opyt gosudarstvennoi reform Petra Velikogo i sovremennaia Rossiia," *Trudy Istoricheskogo fakul'teta Sankt-Peterburgskogo universiteta* 15 (2013): 58–71.

Krotov, P. A. "Sozdanie lineinogo flota na Baltike pri Petre I," *Istoricheskie zapiski* 116 (1988): 313–331.

Kumacheva, M. "Polkovodets A. V. Suvorov v otsenke russkogo obshchestva," in *Russia and the West in the Eighteenth Century*, ed. A. G. Cross (Newtonville, MA: Oriental Research Partners, 1983), 271–281.

Kutishchev, A. V. *Armiia Petra Velikogo: Evropeiskii analog ili otechestvennaia samobytnost'* (Moscow: Sputnik, 2006).

Kuznetsov, Vladimir. *Donskoe kazachestvo v voinakh po zashchite otechestva (1618–1918 gg.)* (Simeropol': DAR, 1997)

Lang, David M. "Count Todtleben's Expedition to Georgia, 1769–1771, According to a French Eyewitness," *Bulletin of the School of Oriental and African Studies, University of London* 13, 4 (1951): 878–907.

Lappo-Danilevskii, A. S. *Ocherk vnutrennoi politiki Imperatritsy Ekateriny II* (St. Petersburg: Tip. M. M. Stasiulevicha, 1898).

Lashkov, F. F. *Shagin-Girei, poslednii krymskii khan* (Simferopol', 1886).

Laskovskii, F. F. *Materialy dlia istorii inzhenernago iskusstva v Rossii.* 3 vols. (Moscow: Imperatorskaia Akademiia Nauk, 1858, 1861, 1865).

Lazzerini, Edward. "The Crimea under Russian Rule: 1783 to the Great Reforms," in *Russian Colonial Expansion to 1917*, ed. Michael Rywkin (London and New York: Mansell, 1988), 123–138.

Lebedev, A. A. *U istokov Chernomorskogo flota Rossii* (St. Petersburg: Gangut, 2011).

Le Donne, John. *Absolutism and Ruling Class. The Formation of the Russian Political Order, 1700–1825* (New York and Oxford: Oxford University Press, 1993).

Le Donne, John. "Catherine's Governors and Governors-General, 1763–1796," *Cahiers du monde russe et sovietique* 20, 1 (1979): 15–42.

Le Donne, John. "Outlines of Russian Military Administration, 1762–1796. Part I: Troop Strength and Deployment," *Jahrbücher für Geschichte Osteuropas* 31 (1983): 320–347.

Le Donne, John. "Outlines of Russian Military Administration, 1762–1796. Part II: The High Command," *Jahrbücher für Geschichte Osteuropas* 33 (1985): 325–347.

Le Donne, John. "Outlines of Russian Military Administration, 1762–1796. Part III: The Commissary Budget of 1780," *Jahrbücher für Geschichte Osteuropas* 34 (1986): 188–216.

Le Donne, John. *Ruling Russia: Politics and Administration in the Age of Absolutism, 1762–1796* (Princeton, NJ: Princeton University Press, 1984).

Le Donne, John. *The Russian Empire and the World: The Geopolitics of Expansion and Containment* (Oxford: Oxford University Press, 1997).

Leonov, O. and Ul'ianov, I. *Reguliarnaia pekhota, 1698–1801* (Moscow: AST, 1995).

Levashev, Pavel. *Kartina ili opisanie vsekh nashestvii na Rossiiu tatar i turkov* (St. Petersburg: G. Zubov, 1792).

Levy, Avigdor. "Formalization of Cossack Service under Ottoman Rule," in *East Central European Society and War in the Pre-Revolutionary Eighteenth Century*, ed. Gunther Rothenberg, Bela Kiraly, and Peter Sugar (Boulder, CO: Social Science Monographs, 1982), 491–506.

Levy, Avigdor. "Military Reform and the Problem of Centralization in the Ottoman Empire in the Eighteenth Century," *Middle Eastern Studies* 18, 3 (1982): 227–249.

Lewis, Bernard. "Some Reflections on the Decline of the Ottoman Empire," *Studia Islamica* 9 (1958): 111–127.

Lewitter, L. R. "The Partitions of Poland," in *The New Cambridge Modern History. Volume VIII. The American and French Revolutions*, ed. A. Goodwin (Cambridge: Cambridge University Press, 1965), 333–359.

Lewitter, L. R. "Poland Under the Saxon Kings," in *The New Cambridge Modern History. Volume VII. The Old Regime, 1713–1763*, ed. J. O. Lindsay (Cambridge: Cambridge University Press, 1966), 365–390.

Litavrin, G. G. *Osmanskaia imperiia i strany tsentral'noi, vostochnoi, i iugovostochnoi Evropy v XVII v.* (Moscow: Pamiatniki istoricheskoi mysli, 2001).

Liubavskii, M. K. *Istoricheskaia geografiia Rossii v sviazi kolonizatsii* (Moscow: Moskovskii universitet, 1996).

Liubavskii, M. K. *Obzor istorii russkoi kolonizatsii* (Moscow: Moskovskii gosudarstvennyi universitet, reprint 1996).

Liudi Ekaterinskago vremeni: Spravochnaia kniga (St. Petersburg: Tip. V. S. Balasheva, 1882).

Longworth, Philip. *The Art of Victory. The Life and Achievements of Field Marshal Suvorov* (New York, Chicago, and San Francisco, CA: Holt, Rinehart and Winston, 1965).

Lopatin, V. S. *Potemkin i Suvorov* (Moscow: Nauka, 1992).

Lukowski, Jerzy. *The Partitions of Poland: 1772, 1793, 1795* (London and New York: Longman, 1999).

Lukowski, Jerzy. "Towards Partition: Polish Magnates and Russian Intervention in Poland During the Early Reign of Stanisław August Poniatowski," *The Historical Journal* 28, 3 (1985): 557–574.

Luttwak, Edward. *The Grand Strategy of the Roman Empire: From the First Century AD to the Third* (Baltimore, MD and London: Johns Hopkins University Press, 1976).

De Madariaga, Isabel. *Russia in the Age of Catherine the Great* (New Haven, CT: Yale University Press, 1981).

Magocsi, Paul Robert. *A History of Ukraine* (Seattle, WA: University of Washington Press, 1996).

Magocsi, Paul Robert. *This Blessed Land: Crimea and the Crimean Tatars* (Toronto: University of Toronto, 2014).

Makarov, A. G. *Bulavinskii bunt (1707–1708 g.) Etiu is istorii otnoshenii Petra Velikogo k Donskim kazakam* (Moscow, St. Petersburg: Dmitrii Bulianian, 2004).

Maksimovich, G. A. *Deiatel'nost' Rumiantseva-Zadunaiskago po upravleniia Malorossiei. Tom pervyi* (Nezhin: Pechatnik, 1913).

Bibliography

von Manstein, C. H. *Contemporary Memoirs of Russia from the Year 1727 to 1744* (London, 1770; New York: Da Capo Press, 1968 reprint).

Markova, Evgeniia. *Ocherki Kryma. Kartiny krymskoi zhizni, prirody i istorii* (St. Petersburg and Moscow: M. D. Vol'f, 2nd ed., 1884).

Marsigli, Count Luigi Ferdinando. *L'etat militaire de l'empire ottoman* (Amsterdam: Gosse, Neaulme, de Hondt, Moetjens, 1732).

Maslovskii, D. F. "Materialy k istorii voennago iskusstva v Rossii," *Chteniia obshchestva istorii i drevnostei rossiiskikh* 153, 2 (1890): i–xvi, 1–294.

Maslovskii, D. F. *Russkaia armiia v semiletniuiu voinu* (Moscow: Tip. Okruzhnago shtaba, 1886).

Maslovskii, D. F. *Stroevaia i polevaia sluzhba russkikh voisk vremen Imperatora Petra Velikogo i Imperatritsy Elizavety* (Moscow: Tip. Okruzhnago shtaba, 1883; Moscow: Librokom, 2011, 2nd ed.).

Maslovskii, D. F. *Zapiski po istorii voennogo iskusstva v Rossii* 2 pts. (St. Petersburg: V. Bezobrazov, 1891).

Mavrodin, V. V. *Rozhdenie novoi Rossii* (Leningrad: Leningradskiii universitet, 1988).

McGowan, Bruce. "The Age of the Ayans, 1699–1812," in *An Economic and Social History of the Ottoman Empire, Volume 2: 1600–1914*, ed. Halil Inalcik and Donald Quataert (Cambridge: Cambridge University Press, 1994), 637–758.

McKay, Derek and Scott, Hamish. *The Rise of the Great Powers, 1648–1815* (London and New York: Longman, 1983).

McNeill, William H. *Europe's Steppe Frontier, 1500–1800* (Chicago: University of Chicago Press, 1964).

Mears, John A. "The Influence of the Turkish Wars in Hungary on the Military Theories of Count Raimondo Montecuccoli," in *Asia in the West: Encounters and Exchanges from the Age of Explorations*, ed. Cyriac Pullapilly (Notre Dame: Cross Roads Books, 1986), 129–145.

Melikishvili, Alexander. "Genesis of the Anti-Plague System: The Tsarist Period," *Critical Reviews in Microbiology* XXXII (2006): 19–31.

Menchinger, Ethan. "A Reformist Philosophy of History: The Case of Ahmed Vasif Efendi," *Journal of Ottoman Studies*, XLIV (2014): 141–168.

Menning, Bruce W. "The Army and Frontier in Russia," in *Transformation in Russian and Soviet Military History*, ed. Carl Reddell (Washington, DC: USAF Academy, Office of Air Force History, 1990), 25–38.

Menning, Bruce W. "The Imperial Russian Army, 1725–1796," in *The Military History of Tsarist Russia*, ed. Fredrick Kagan and Robin Higham (New York and Houndmills: Palgrave, 2002), 47–75.

Menning, Bruce W. "Russian Military Innovation in the Second Half of the Eighteenth Century," *War and Society* 2 (1984): 23–41.

Menning, Bruce W. "Russia and the West; The Problem of Eighteenth-Century Military Models," in *Russia and the West in the Eighteenth Century*, ed. Anthony Cross (Newtonville, MA: Oriental Research Partners, 1983), 282–293.

Menning, Bruce W. "Train Hard, Fight Easy: The Legacy of A. V. Suvorov and his 'Art of Victory,'" *Air University Review* (November–December 1986): 1–11.

Meshcheriakov, G. P., ed. *A. V. Suvorov* (Moscow: Voennoe ministerstvo SSSR, 1949–1953).

Miakotin, V. *Ocherki sotsial'noi istorii Ukrainy v XVII-XVIII v.* 3 vols. (Prague: Vataga i plamia, 1926).

Mikhneva, R. *Rossiia i Osmanskaia imperiia v mezhdunarodnykh otnosheniiakh v seredine XVIII veka* (Moscow: Nauka, 1985).

Miliukov, Pavel. *Gosudarstvennoe khoziaistvo Rossii v pervoi chetverti XVIII stoletiia i refoma Petra Velikago* (St. Petersburg: Tip. M. Stasiulevicha, 2nd ed., 1905).

Miller, D. P. *Zaselenie Novorossiiskogo kraia i Potemkin* (Khar'kov: Tip. Zil'berberg i synov'ia, 1901).

Mironov, Boris N. *The Social History of Imperial Russia, 1700–1917. Volume 2*, trans. Ben Eklof (Boulder, CO: Westview Press, 2000).

Mitchell, Donald W. *A History of Russian and Soviet Sea Power* (New York: MacMillan, 1974).

Mitev, Plamen, ed. *Empires and Peninsulas: Southeastern Europe between Karlowitz and the Peace of Adrianople, 1699–1829* (Munster: LIT Verlag, 2010).

Mizis, Iu. *Zaselenie tambovskogo kraia v XVII-XVIII vekakh* (Tambov: Tambovskii gosudarstvennyi pedagogicheskii intsitut, 1990).

Montefiore, Simon Sebag. *Potemkin: Catherine the Great's Imperial Partner* (New York: Vintage Books, 2000).

Morawski, Wojciech and Szawłowska, Sylwia. *Wojny rosyjsko-tureckie od XVII do XX wieku* (Warsaw: Trio Wydawnictwo, 2006).

Murphey, Rhoad. "Ottoman Military Organization in South-Eastern Europe, c. 1420–1720," in *European Warfare, 1350–1750*, ed. Frank Tallett and D. J. B. Trim (Cambridge: Cambridge University Press, 2010), 135–158.

Murphey, Rhoads. *Ottoman Warfare, 1500–1700* (London: UCL Press, 1999).

Muzagovskii, E. A. *Istoriia chernomorskogo flota 1696–1912* (St. Petersburg: Tip. A. S. Suvorina, 1914).

Neale, Adam. *Travels through some parts of Germany, Poland, Moldavia and Turkey* (London: Longman, Hurst, Rees, Orme and Brown, 1818).

Nedosekin, V. I. "Istochniki rosta krupnogo zemlevladeniia na iuge Rossii v XVIII stoletii," *Izvestiia Voronezhskogo gosudarstvennogo pedagogicheskogo instituta* 63 (1967): 252–323.

Nelipovich, S. G. "Pozitsiia B. Kh. Fon Miunnikha v diskussi 1725 o sokrashchenii armii i voennogo biudzheta Rossii," *Voenno-istoricheskii zhurnal* 8 (1990): 3–7.

Nelipovich, S. G. *Soiuz dvuglavykh orlov: Russko-avstriiskii voennyi al'ians vtoroi chetverti XVIII v.* (Moscow: Kvadriga, 2010).

Nolde, Boris. *La formation de l'empire russe* (Paris: Institut D'Etudes Slaves, 1952–53).

Nosworthy, Brent. *The Anatomy of Victory: Battle Tactics, 1689–1763* (New York: Hippocrene Books, 1990).

Novikova, N. Ia., ed. *Boevaia letopis' russkogo flota* (Moscow: Ministerstvo vooruzhennykh sil SSSR, 1948).

Novosel'skii, A. A. *Bor'ba Moskovskogo gosudartva s tatarami v pervoi polovine XVII veka* (Moscow and Lenigrad: Akademiia Nauk SSSR, 1948).

Okhliabinin, Sergei. *Povsednevnaia zhizn' russkoi armii vo vremena suvorovskikh voin* (Moscow: Molodaia gvardiiia, 2004).

"Opisanie sostoiannaia del vo vremia Gosudaryni Imperatritsy Elizavety Petrovny," *Arkhiv kniaz'ia Vorontsova* XXV (1882): 272–312.

Otetea, Andrei, ed. *The History of the Romanian People* (New York: Twayne Publishers, 1970).

Ozkaya, Yuzkel. "The Consequences of the Weakening of the Centralized State Structure: Ayanlik System and the Great Dynasties," in *The Great Ottoman Turkish Civilization. Volume 3*, ed. Kemal Cicek and Halil Inalcik (Ankara: Yeni Turkiye, 2000), 554–570.

Pallas, Peter Simon. *Puteshestvie po raznym provintsiiam Rossiiskoi imperii. Chast' pervaia* (St. Petersburg: Imperatorskaia Akademiia Nauk, 1773).

Pallas, Peter Simon. *Travels Through the Southern Provinces of the Russian Empire in the Years 1793 and 1794* (Pickadilly: John Stockdale, 1812; Arno Press, 1970 reprint).

Panova, V. I. "Voronezhskoe Pribitiuzh'e v XVII vek," in *Voronezhskii krai na iuzhnykh rubezhakh Rossii XVII-XVIII vv.*, ed. V. P. Zagorovskii (Voronezh: Voronezhskii gos. universitet, 1981), 68–76.

Panzac, Daniel. "The Manning of the Ottoman Navy in the Heyday of Sail (1660–1850)," in *Arming the State: Military Conscription in the Middle East and Central Asia, 1775–1925*, ed. Erik J. Zürcher (London and New York: I. B. Tauris, 1999), 41–57.

Bibliography

Papp, Sandor. "Die Inaugurationen der Krimhane durch die Hohe Porte (16.–18. Jahrhundert," in *The Crimean Khanate between East and West (15th–18th Century)*, ed. Denise Klein (Wiesbaden: Harrasowitz Verlag, 2012), 75–90.

Parry, V.J., Inalcik, Halil, Kurat, A. N., and Bromley, J. S. *A History of the Ottoman Empire to 1730. Chapters from the Cambridge History of Islam and the New Cambridge Modern History* (Cambridge and London: Cambridge University Press, 1976).

Pelevin, Viktor. *Fel'dmarshal Ruminatsev, 1725–1796* (Moscow: Tsentrpoligraf, 2006).

Penskoi, V. V. "Armiia Rossiiskoi imperii v XVIII v.: vybor modeli razvitiia," *Voprosy istorii* 7 (2001): 119–136.

Penskoi, V. V. "Ukrainskii landmilitseiskii korpus v XVIII veke," *Voprosy istorii* 10 (2000): 147–153.

Petrosian, Iu. A. *Osmanskaia imperiia: Mogushchestvo i gibel'* (Moscow: Nauka, 1990).

Petrov, A. N. "Largo-Kagul'skii operatsiia 1770 g.," *Voennyi sbornik* 214 (1893): 195–214.

Petrov, A. N. *Vliianie turetskikh voin s poloviny proshlago stoletiia na razvitie russkago voennago iskusstva. Tom 1: Voina 1769–1774* (St. Petersburg: Voennaia tipografiia, 1894).

Petrov, A. N. *Voina Rossii s Turtsiei i pol'skimi konfederatami c. 1769–1774 god.* 5 vols. (St. Petersburg: Tip. E. Veimar, 1866–1874).

Petrukhintsev, N. N. *Tsarstvovanie Anny Ioannovny: formirovanie vnutripoliticheskogo kursa i sud'by armii i flota* (St. Petersbury: Aleteiia, 2001).

Pintner, Walter. "The Burden of Defense in Imperial Russia, 1725–1914," *Russian Review* 43, 3 (1984): 231–259.

Pintner, Walter. "Russia as a Great Power, 1709–1856," Kennan Institute for Advanced Russian Studies, Occasional Paper Series, No. 33 (1978).

Pintner, Walter. "Russia's Military Style, Russian Society, and Russian Power in the Eighteenth Century," in *Russia and the West in the Eighteenth Century*, ed. Anthony Cross (Newtonville, MA: Oriental Research Partners, 1983), 262–270.

Pintner, Walter. "Russian Military Thought: The Western Model and the Shadow of Suvorov," in *Makers of Modern Strategy: From Machiavelli to the Nuclear Age*, ed. Peter Paret, Gordon Craig, and Felix Gilbert (Princeton, NJ: Princeton University Press, 1986), 354–375.

Pisar'kova, L. F. *Gosudarstvennoe upravlenie Rossii s kontsa XVII do kontsa XVIII veka* (Moscow: ROSSPEN, 2007).

Pollock, Sean. "Russia and the Ottoman Empire: Transregional and Comparative Approaches," *Central Asia Studies Review* 7, 1 (2008): 30–33.

Polnoe sobranie zakonov Rossiiskoi imperii (PSZ), 1st series, 45 vols. (St. Petersburg: Vtoroe otdelenie sobstvennoi ego Imperatorskago Velichestva Kantseliarii, 1830).

Polons'ka-Vasylenko, N. D. "The Settlement of the Southern Ukraine (1750–1775)," *The Annals of the Ukrainian Academy of Arts and Sciences in the US*, IV–V, 14–15 (1955).

Porfir'ev, E. I. *Petr I. Osnovopolozhnik voennogo iskusstva russkoi reguliarnoi armii i flota* (Moscow: Voennoe ministerstvo SSSR, 1952).

Porfir'ev, E. I. "Taktika russkoi reguliarnoi armii v pervoi chetverti XVIII v.," in *Razvitie taktiki russkoi armii, XVIII- nachalo XX vv.*, ed. D. V. Pankov (Moscow: Ministerstvo oborony SSSR, Voennoe izdatel'stvo, 1957), 31–57.

Potto, V. A. *Kavkazskaia voina v otdel'nykh ocherkakh, epizodakh, legendakh, i biografiiakh.* 5 vols. (St. Petersburg: Tip. E. Evdokimova, 1887–1889).

Quelquejay, Chantal Lemercie. "La Campagne de Pierre le Grand sur le Prut," *Cahiers du monde russe et sovietique* 7, 2 (1966): 221–233.

Rabinovich, M. D. "Formirovanie reguliarnoi russkoi armii nakanune severnoi voiny," in *Voprosy voennoi istorii Rossii. XVIII i pervaia polovina XIX vekov*, ed. V. I. Shunkov (Moscow: Nauka, 1969), 221–232.

Rabinovich, M. D. "Sud'by sluzhilykh liudei 'starykh sluzhb' v periode formirovaniia reguliarnoi russkoi armii v nachale XVIII veke," Candidate's dissertation, MGIAI, 1953).

Raeff, Marc, ed. "Patterns of Russian Imperial Policy toward the Nationalities," *Political Ideas and Institutions in Imperial Russia* (Boulder, CO, San Francisco, CA and Oxford: Westview Press, 1994), 126–140.

Raeff, Marc. "Pugachev's Rebellion," in *Preconditions of Revolution in Early Modern Europe*, ed. Robert Forster and Jack P. Greene (Baltimore, MD: Johns Hopkins University Press, 1971), 161–202.

Raeff, Marc., ed. "Uniformity, Diversity, and the Imperial Administration in the Reign of Catherine II," *Political Ideas and Institutions in Imperial Russia* (Boulder, CO, San Francisco, CA and Oxford: Westview Press, 1994), 141–155.

Ragsdale, Hugh. "Evaluating the Traditions of Russian Aggression: Catherine II and the Greek Project," *Slavic and East European Review* 66 (1988): 91–117.

Ransel, David. *The Politics of Catherinian Russia. The Panin Party* (New Haven, CT: Yale University Press, 1975).

Rauchensteiner, Manfred. "The Development of War Theories in Austria at the End of the Eighteenth Century," in *East Central European Society and War in the Pre-Revolutionary Eighteenth Century*, ed. Gunther Rothenberg, Bela Kiraly, and Peter Sugar (New York: Columbia University Press, 1982), 75–82.

Rayfield, Donald. *Edge of Empires: A History of Georgia* (London: Reaktion Books, 2012).

Richmond, Walter. *The Northwest Caucasus: Past, Present, and Future* (London and New York: Routledge, 2008).

Rieber, Alfred. *The Struggle for the Eurasian Borderlands* (Cambridge: Cambridge University Press, 2014).

Rigel'man, Aleksandr Ivanovich. *Istoriia ili povestvovanie o donskikh kozakakh* (Moscow: Universitetskaia tip., 1846).

Rigel'man, Aleksandr. *Letopisnoe povestvovanie o Maloi Rossii i ee narode i kazakakh voobshche* (Moscow: Universitetskaia tip., 1847).

Roberts, Elizabeth. *Realm of the Black Mountain: A History of Montenegro* (Ithaca, NY: Cornell University Press, 2007).

Roider, Karl. *Austria's Eastern Question, 1700–1790* (Princeton, NJ: Princeton University Press, 1982).

Roider, Karl. *The Reluctant Ally: Austria's Policy in the Austro-Turkish War, 1737–1739* (Baton Rouge, LA: Louisiana State University Press, 1972).

Rostworowski, Emanuel. "War and Society in the Noble Republic of Poland-Lithuania in the Eighteenth Century," in *East Central European Society and War in the Pre-Revolutionary Eighteenth Century*, ed. Gunther Rothenberg, Bela Kiraly, and Peter Sugar (New York: Columbia University, 1982), 165–182.

Rumiantsev, P. A. "Mysli generala grafa Rumiantseva o proshedshii I budushchii kampanii," *Voennyi zhurnal* 11 (1853): 154–160.

Rycaut, Paul. *History of the Present State of the Ottoman Empire* (London: John Starkey and Henry Brome, 1675).

Sakovich, P. M. *Deistviia Suvorova v Turtsii v 1773 godu* (St. Petersburg: Tip. K. Krai, 1853).

Sakovich, P. M. *Suvorov i padenie Pol'shi. Chast' pervaia* (St. Petersburg: Tip. E. Veimar, 1866).

Salzmann, Arie. "Privatizing the Empire: Pashas and Gentry During the Ottoman 18th Century," in *The Great Ottoman-Turkish Civilization, Volume 2*, ed. Kemal Cicek, Ercument Kuran, Nyat Goyunc, and Ilber Ortayli (Ankara: Yeni Turkiye, 2000), 132–139.

Sanin, G. A. "Razdely Rechi Pospolitoi," in *Istoriia vneshnei politiki Rossii. XVIII vek*, ed. A. V. Ignat'ev, V. N. Ponomarev, and G. A. Sanin (Moscow: Mezhdunarodnye otnosheniia, 1998), 168–197.

Bibliography

de Saxe, Herman Maurice. *Reveries on the Art of War*, trans. Thomas Philips (Mineola, NY: Dover, 2007).

Schaefer, Robert. *The Insurgency in Chechnya and the North Caucasus: From Gazavat to Jihad* (Santa Barbara, CA and Denver, CO: Praeger Security International, 2011).

Schimmelpenninck van der Oye, David. *Russian Orientalism: Asia in the Russian Mind from Peter the Great to the Emigration* (New Haven, CT and London: Yale University Press, 2010).

Schumpeter, Joseph, ed. "The Crisis of the Tax State," *Imperialism and the Social Classes* (New York: Kelley, 1951), 141–219.

Scott, Hamish. *The Emergence of the Eastern Powers, 1756–1775* (Cambridge: Cambridge University Press, 2001).

Scott, Hamish. "The Fiscal-Military State and International Rivalry during the Long Eighteenth Century," in *The Fiscal-Military State in Eighteenth-Century Europe: Essays in Honour of P. G. M. Dickson*, ed. Christopher Storrs (Farnham and Surrey: Ashgate Books, 2009), 23–54.

Scott, Hamish. "Frederick II, the Ottoman Empire, and the Origins of the Russo-Prussian Alliance of 1764," *European Studies Review* 7 (1977): 153–175.

Semenov, I. V. *Chugun Kagul'skii, Ty Sviashchen: Iz istorii russko-turetskoi voiny 1768–1774* (Kishinev: Kartia Moldoveniaske, 1970).

Semenova, L. E. *Kniazhestva Valakhiia i Moldaviia konets XIV-nachalo XIX v.* (Moscow: Indrik, 2006).

Sergienko, G. Ia. et al., eds. *Istoriia Ukrainskoi SSR. Tom tretii. Osvoboditel'naia voina i vossoedinenie Ukrainy s Rossii. Nachalo razlozheniia feodalizma i zarozhdenie kapitalisticheskikh otnoshenii (vtoraia polovina XVII-XVIII v.* (Kiev: Naumkova Dumka, 1983).

Seton-Watson, H. W. *History of the Roumanians. From Roman Times to the Completion of Unity* (n.p., Hamden, CT: Archon, 1963, reprint of 1934 Cambridge University Press edition).

Shaw, Stanford. *History of the Ottoman Empire and Modern Turkey. Volume 1: Empire of the Gazis* (Cambridge: Cambridge University Press, 1976).

Shirokorad, A. B. *Russko-turetskie voiny 1676–1918 gg.* (Moscow: AST, 2000).

Shkalon, D. A., ed. *Stoletie voennago ministerstva 1802–1902. Glavnyi shtab. Tom IV, ch. pervaia. Istoricheskii ocherk. Komplektovanie vooruzhennykh sil v Rossii do 1802 g.* (St. Petersburg: Voennoe ministerstvo, 1902).

Shpilevskaia, N. *Opisanie voiny mezhdu Rossiei i Shvetsiei v 1741, 1742, and 1743 gg.* (St. Petersburg: Tip. Iakova Treia, 1859).

Shpital'ov, Gennadii. *Ukrains'ka Landmilitsiia* (Kiev: Natsional'na Akademiia Nauk Ukraini, 2013).

Sivkov, K. V. "Finansovaia politika Ekaterina II," in *Tri veka. Rossiia ot smuty do nashego vremeni. Tom IV*, ed. V. Kallash (Moscow: GIS, 1992), 488–500.

Skal'kovskii, A. A. *Khronologicheskoe obozrenie istorii Novorossiiskogo kraia*. 2 vols. (Odessa: Gorodskaia tipografiia, 1836–1838).

Sliusarskii, A. G. *Sotsial'no-ekonomicheskoe razvitie Slobozhanshchiny XVII-XVIII vv.* (Khar'kov: Khar'kovskoe knizhnoe izd., 1964).

Smilianskii, I. M., Velizhev, M. B., and Smilianskaia, E. B. *Rossiia i Sredizemnomor'e. Arkhipelagskaia ekspeditsiia Ekateriny Velikoi* (Moscow: Indrik, 2011).

Smirnov, N. A. *Politika Rossii na Kavkaze v XVI-XIX vekakh* (Moscow: Izd. Sotsial'no-ekonomicheskoi literatury, 1958).

Smirnov, V. D. *Krymskoe khanstvo pod verkhoventsvom otomanskoi porty v XVIII v. do prisoedineniia ego k Rossii. Tom vtoroi* (Moscow: Rubezhi XXI, 2005, reprint of 1889 ed.).

fon Smitt, Fridrikh. *Suvorov i padenie Pol'shy. Chast pervaia* (St. Petersburg: I. Veimar, 1866).

Solov'ev, N. "Kratkii istoricheskii ocherk raskhodov na armiiu i denezhnago dovol'stviia voisk v Rossii v pervoi polovine XVIII stoletiia," *Voennyi sbornik* 214, 12 (1893): 215–257.

Solov'ev, S. M. *Istoriia padeniia Pol'shi* (Moscow: Grachev i komp., 1863).

Solov'ev, S. M. *Istoriia Rossii s drevneishikh vremen.* 15 vols. (Moscow, Leningrad: Izd. Sotsial'no-ekonomicheskoi literatury, 1962).

Sorel, Albert. *The Eastern Question in the Eighteenth Century* (London: Methuen and Co., 1898).

Sotavov, N. A. *Severnyi Kavkaz v russko-iranskikh i russko-turetskikh otnosheni-iakh v XVIII v. Ot Konstantinopol'skogo dogovora do Kiuchuk-Kainardzhiiskogo mira, 1700–1774* (Moscow: Nauka, 1991).

Starkey, Armstrong. *War in the Age of Enlightenment, 1700–1789* (Westport, CT: Praeger, 2003).

Stati, Vasile. *Istoriia Moldovy* (Kishinev: Centrala, 2003).

Stavrianos, L. S. *The Balkans Since 1453* (New York and Chicago: Holt, Rinehart and Winston, 1958).

Stevens, Carol Belkin. "Evaluating Peter's Army: The Impact of Internal Organization," in *The Military and Society in Russia, 1450–1917*, ed. Eric Lohr and Marshall Poe (Leiden and Boston, MA: E. J. Brill, 2002), 147–174.

Stevens, Carol Belkin. "Modernizing the Military: Peter the Great and Military Reform," in *Modernizing Muscovy. Reform and Social Change in Seventeenth-Century Muscovy*, ed. Jarmo Kotilaine and Marshall Poe (London and New York: Routledge Courzon, 2004), 247–262.

Stevens, Carol Belkin. *Russia's Wars of Emergence, 1460–1730* (London and New York: Longman, 2007).

Stone, Daniel. *The Polish-Lithuanian State, 1386–1795* (Seattle, WA: University of Washington Press, 2001).

Storozhenko, N. "Reformy v Malorossii pri gr. Rumiantseve," *Kievskaia starina* 3 (1891): 478–493.

Stoye, J. W. "The Austrian Habsburgs," in *The Cambridge Modern History of Europe*, vol. VI, ed. J. S. Bromley (Cambridge: Cambridge University Press, 1970), 572–607.

Stoye, J. W. *Marsigli's Europe, 1680–1730* (New Haven, CT: Yale University Press, 1994).

Strumilin, S. G. "K voprosu ob ekonomike petrovskoi epokhi," in *Poltava. K 250-letiiu poltavskogo srazheniia*, ed. L. G. Beskrovnyi and B. B. Kafengauz (Moscow: AN SSSR, 1959), 179–189.

Subtelny, Orest. *Ukraine: A History* (Toronto, Buffalo, and London: University of Toronto Press, 1988).

Sudienko, M. "Bumagi, do upravleniia Malorossieiu grafa P. A. Rumiantseva Zadunaiskago otnosiashchiesia," *ChOIDR* 1 (1861): 137–165.

Sugar, Peter. *Southeastern Europe under Ottoman Control, 1354–1804* (Seattle, WA and London: University of Washington, 1977).

Sugar, Peter. "Unity and Diversity in the Lands of Southeastern Europe in the Eighteenth Century," in *East Central Euopean War and Society in the Pre-Revolutionary Eighteenth Century*, ed. Gunther Rothenberg, Bela Kiraly, and Peter Sugar (New York: Columbia University Press, 1982), 255–270.

Sumarokov, Pavel. *Puteshestvie po vsemu Krymu i Bessarabii v 1799 godu* (Moscow: Universitetskaia tipografiia, 1800).

Sunderland, Willard. *Taming the Wild Field: Colonization and Empire on the Russian Steppe* (Ithaca, NY and London: Cornell University Press, 2004).

Svatikov, S. G. *Rossiia i Don (1582–1917)* (Rostov-na-Donu: Donskaia Istoricheskaia Komissiia, 1924).

Svechin, Aleksandr. *Evoliutsiia voennogo iskusstva* (Moscow: Akademicheskii Proekt, 2002).

Sykes, Sir Percy. *Persia* (Oxford: Clarendon Press, 1922).

Syromiatnikov, B. I. *"Reguliarnoe" gosudarstvo Petra Pervogo i ego ideologiia"* (Moscow: AN SSSR, 1943).

Bibliography

Szabo, Franz. *Kaunitz and Enlightened Absolutism, 1753–1780* (Cambridge: Cambridge University Press, 1994).

Szabo, Franz. *The Seven Years' War in Europe, 1756–1763* (Harlow: Pearson Longman, 2008).

Szczygielski, W. *Konfederacja Barska w Wielkopolsce, 1868–1770* (Warsaw: Pax, 1970).

Taras, A. E. *Anatomiia nenavisti. Russko-pol'skie konflikty v XVIII-XX vv.* (Minsk: Kharvest, 2008).

Tarle, Evgenii V. "Chesmenskii boi i pervaiai russkaia eksepeditsiia v Arkhipelag, 1769–1774," in *Sochineniia v dvenadtsatii tomakh. Tom X*, ed. A. S. Erusalimksii (Moscow: Akademiia Nauk SSSR, 1959).

Tatarnikov, K. V., ed. *Stroevye ustavy, instruktsii i nastavleniia russkoi armii XVIII veka. Sbornik materialov*, 2 vols. (Moscow: Russkaia panorama, 2010).

Teissier, Beatrice. *Russian Frontiers. Eighteenth-Century British Travellers in the Caspian, Caucasus, and Central Asia* (Oxford: Signal Books Limited, 2011).

Tkach, V. I. "Organizatsiia tsentral'nykh organov russko-moldavskoi administratsii v period russko-turetskoi voiny 1768–1774 gg.," in *Sotsial'no-ekonomicheskaia I politicheskia istorii Moldavii perioda feodalizma*, ed. P. V. Sovetov (Kishinev: Shtiintsa. 1988), 127–134.

Tkachev, N. K. "Iz istorii odnodvortsev v XVIII v," in *Ezhegodnik po agrarnoi istorii vostochnoi Evropy za 1968 g.*, ed. A. M. Anfimov (Leningrad: Nauka, 1972), 133–141.

Toekava, Koiti. *Orenburg i Orenburgskoe kazachestvo vo vremia vosstanii Pugacheva 1773–1774 gg.* (Moscow: Arkheograficheskii tsentr, 1996).

de Tott, Francois Baron. *Memoirs of Baron de Tott: Containing the State of the Turkish Empire and the Crimea, during the late war with Russia*, 2 vols. (London: G. G. J. and J. Robinson, 1785).

Tredrea, John and Sozaev, Eduard. *Russian Warships in the Age of Sail, 1696–1860* (Barnsley, Yorkshire: Seaforth, 2010).

Trepavlov, V. V. *Istoriia nogaiskoi ordy* (Moscow: Vostochnaia literature, RAN, 2001).

Troitskii, S. M. *Finansovaia politika russkogo absoliutizma v XVIII veke* (Moscow: Nauka, 1966).

Tunmann, Johann Eric. *Krymskoe khanstvo*, trans. N. L. Ernst and S. L. Beliavskaia (Simferopol': Tavriia, 1991).

Uebersberger, Hans. *Russlands Orientpolitik in den letzen zwei jahrhunderten. Erster Band: Bis zum Frieden von Jassy* (Stuttgart: Deutsche Verlags-Anstalt, 1913).

Ulianitskii, V. A. *Dardanelly, Bosfor, i Chernoe mor'e v XVIII veke* (Moscow: Tip. A. Gatsuli, 1883).

Ulianitskii, V. A. *Russkie konsul'stva za granitsei v XVIII veke*. 2 vols. (Moscow: Lissner i Geshel', 1899).

Ungermann, Richard. *Der Russisch-Turkische krieg, 1768–1774* (Vienna and Leipzig: Wihelm Braumüller, 1906).

Urlanis, B. Ts. *Narodonaselenie: Issledovaniia, publitsistika: Sbornik statei*, ed. B. Ts. Urlanis (Moscow: Statistika, 1976).

Urlanis, B. Ts. *Istoriia voennykh poter'* (St. Petersburg: Poligon, 1994).

Ustiugov, N. V. et al., eds. *Ocherki istorii kal'mytskoi ASSR. Do-oktiabr'skii period* (Moscow: Nauka, 1967).

Uyar, Mesut and Erickson, Edward J. *A Military History of the Ottomans. From Osman to Ataturk* (Santa Barbara, CA: Praeger/ ABC Clio, 2009).

Vasylensko, Mikola. "G. N. Teplov i ioho pasika pro neporiadki v Malorossii," *Zapysky Ukrainskoho naukhovoho tovarystva v Kyivi* 9 (1912): 29–52.

Veidemeier, A. *Tsarstvovanie Elisabety Petrovny*. 2 vols. (St. Petersburg: Tip. Khintsa, 1834).

Verstiuk, V. F., Gorobets, V. M., and Tolochko, O. P. *Ukrains'ki proekti v Rosiis'kyi imperii* (Kiev: Naukova dumka, 2004).

Veselago, F. F. *Kratkaia istoriia russkogo flota* (Moscow, Leningrad: Voenno-morskoe Izd. NKVMF SSSR, 1939).

Vinogradov, V. N., ed. *Vek Ekateriny II. Dela balkanskie* (Moscow: Nauka, 2000).

Vodarskii, Ia. E. *Naselenie Rossii v kontse XVII- nachale XVIII veka* (Moscow: Nauka, 1977).

Vodarskii, Ia. E. *Zagadki Prutskogo pokhoda Petra I* (Moscow: Nauka, 2004).

Volkonskii, M. A. and Mukhanov, V. M., eds. *Kavkazskii vector Rossiiskoi politiki. Sbornik dokumentov. Tom I. XVI-XVIII vv.* (Moscow: MVD Rossii, 2011).

Volkov, S. V. *Russkii ofitserskii korpus* (Moscow: Voenizdat, 1993).

Vozgrin, V. E. *Istoricheskie sud'by krymskikh tatar* (Moscow: Mysl', 1992).

Wallerstein, Immanuel and Tabak, Faru. "The Ottoman Empire, the Mediterranean, and the European World-Economy, c. 1560–1800," in *The Great Ottoman-Turkish Civilization. Volume 2*, ed. Kemal Cicek and Halil Inalcik (Ankara: Yeni Turkiye, 2000), 120–127.

Weigley, Russell. *The Age of Battles: The Quest for Decisive Warfare from Breitenfeld to Waterloo* (Bloomington, IN and Indianapolis, IN: Indiana University Press, 1991).

Wilson, Peter H. *German Armies: War and German Politics, 1648–1806* (London and New York: Routledge, 1998).

Wolff, Larry. *Inventing Eastern Europe: The Map of Civilization on the Mind of the Enlightenment* (Stanford, CA: Stanford University Press, 1994).

Yildiz, Hakan. *Haydi Osmanli Sefere! Prut Seferi'nde Organizasyon ve Lojistik* (Istanbul: Turkiye Bankasi, 2006).

Zagorovskii, V. P. *Belgorodskaia cherta* (Voronezh: Voronezhskii universitet, 1969).

Zagorovskii, V. P. *Iziumskaia cherta* (Voronezh: Voronezhskii gos. universitet, 1980).

Zagorovskii, V. P. "Voznikovenie i razvitie gorodov v voronezhskom krae v XVII-XVIII vekakh," in *Istoriia zaseleniia i khoziaistvennogo osvoeniia voronezhskogo kraia v epokhu feodalizma*, ed. V. P. Zagorovskii (Voronezh: Voronezhskii universitet, 1987), 62–93.

Zagorovskii, V. P. "Obshchii ocherk istorii zaseleniia i khoziaistvennogo osvoeniia iuzhnykh okrain Rossii v epokhu zrelogo feodalizma," in *Istoriia zaseleniia i khoziaistvennogo osvoeniia Voronezhskogo kraia v epokhu feodalizma*, ed. V. P. Zagorovskii and A. N. Akinshin (Voronezh: Voronezhskii universitet, 1987), 3–23.

Zamoyski, Adam. *The Last King of Poland* (London: Weidenfeld and Nicholson, 1998).

"Zapiska o politicheskikh otnosheniiakh Rossii v pervyi god tsarstvovaniia Ekaterinoi Velikoi," *Arkhiv kniaz'ia Vorontsova* XXV (1882): 313–339.

Zhurnal voennykh deistvii armii eia Imperatorskago Velichestva, 1769–1771 (St. Petersburg: Gosudarstvennaia Voennaia Kollegiia, 1772).

Zolotarev, V. A. *Donskie kazaki i gosudarstvennaia sluzhba* (Rostov-na-Donu: Rostizdat, 2001).

Zolotarev, V. A., ed. *Istoriia voennoi strategii Rossii* (Moscow: Kuchkovo Pole, 2000).

Zolotarev, V. A., Menzhevich, M. N. and Skorodumov, D. E. *Vo slavu otechestva Rossiiskogo (razvite voennoi mysli i voennogo iskusstva v Rossii vo vtoroi polovine XVIII v.)* (Moscow: Mysl', 1984).

Zorin, Andrei. *By Fables Alone: Literature and State Ideology in Late Eighteenth- Early Nineteenth-Century Russia* (Brighton, MA: Academic Studies Press, 2014).

INDEX

Note: Locators followed by the letter "n" refer to notes.

Index

Index

Index

Kapudan-Pasha 157
Kara Mustafa, Ottoman Grand Vizier 21
Karasubazar 39, 41, 173, 176, 177, 188, 231, 236,
    238, 245
Karazin, Nazar Aleksandrovich 130
Karlowitz, Treaty of 4, 17, 33, 40, 47, 66, 80
Kartal 27, 119, 144–6, 149, 244
Kartli 44–6, 134, 161, 235, 242, 257 n.113
Kaunitz, Wenzel Anton 160–3, 183, 186, 227, 252 n.4
Kazan' 54, 57, 65, 82, 192, 209, 288 n.106
Kazykirmen 40
Keith, James Francis 265 n.3
Kerch Straits 44, 173–7, 188, 205, 206, 208, 222,
    227, 247, 257 n.103, 293 n.64
Khar'kov 39, 40, 74, 79
Khotin 12, 29, 30, 32, 107–35, 137–42, 160, 169,
    201, 206, 244, 245, 254 n.52, 274 n.41
Kiev 10, 11, 37, 42, 54, 70, 71, 74, 76, 77, 79, 87,
    107, 109, 113, 114, 138, 139, 182,
    214–16, 229, 236, 260 n.40, 274 n.60,
    296 n.138
Kilburun 32, 36, 188, 201, 205, 206, 217, 223
Kiliia 36–8, 138, 144, 148–50, 165, 201, 206, 245,
    255 n.68
Kishinev 12, 138, 147
klephts 35
Koca Yusef Pasha, Ottoman Grand Vizier 240,
    242
Kochubei, Semen 72, 73
Kolberg 92, 93, 139, 272 n.6, 281 n.70
Koliivshchyna 11
Kolomak Articles 71
Konskie Vody 174, 285 n.36
Köprülüs, Ottoman Grand Vizier 17, 20
Kopyl' 133, 231, 233
Koroni 155
Korsun' 11
Kozlov 59–63, 76, 260 n.44, 261, n.52
Kozluji 203, 246
Krasiński, Adam 9, 10, 131
Krasiński, Michał 9, 10, 110, 130, 132, 181
Krechetnikov, Mikhail Nikitich 11, 126, 166, 167,
    170
Kremenchug 69, 74, 113, 114, 147, 216, 229, 234,
    238
Kruz, Aleksander Ivanovich 158
Kuban 17, 37–45, 59, 64, 66, 67, 107, 110, 132, 133,
    172, 177, 187, 190, 201, 206, 213, 220–3,
    230–5, 238–40, 242, 244, 247, 255 n.72,
    257 n.103, 262 n.69, 290 n.133, 296
    n.125
Kuchuk-Kainarji 195, 196, 204
Kuchuk-Kainarji, Treaty of 134, 177, 180, 192,
    205–8, 217, 220–5, 228, 230–2, 244, 246,
    247, 288 n.103

Kunersdorf 88–91, 104, 192, 276 n.104
Kurbeşti 136
Kursk 63, 81, 109, 260 n.40
Kutaisi 45, 134, 207
Kutuzov. See Golenishchev-Kutuzov

Lacy, Peter 85, 119, 173, 175, 265 n.3
Lamoral, Charles-Joseph, Prince de Ligne 241
Lanckorona 181–3, 185
Land Army Commission 85
Larga 26, 104, 142–4, 147, 149, 160, 165, 172, 197,
    198, 244, 246, 279 n.24, 279 n.31
League of Armed Neutrality 221, 227
Le Donne, John 211
Legislative Commission of 1767 73, 74
Lemnos 32, 159, 178, 179
Leont'ev, Mikhail Ivanovich 42
Lesghians 46, 134
Leszczyński, Stanisław 4, 71, 258 n.119
Lifland (Livonia) 7, 13, 89, 186, 190, 268 n.47
Lublin 131, 132, 138, 181–3, 245
Lubny 74
Lubomirski, Stanisław 131, 229
L'viv 115, 131, 138, 185

Mačin 36, 165, 169, 171, 172
Magnaterja 1, 3–8, 10, 11, 50, 186, 230, 256 n.80
Mahmud I, Ottoman Sultan 16, 41, 42, 44, 45, 47
Mahmud Ghilzai 44, 45
Maksimen 150, 166
Malorossiia. See Ukraine
Malta 36, 151, 152, 154
Mamluks 171, 180
Manifesto of the Emancipation of the Nobility 58,
    97, 191, 211, 260 n.36
Maniots 35, 102, 154, 155
Maria Theresa, Archduchess of Austria, Holy
    Roman Empress 184, 226, 265 n.3
Mariupol' 218, 219, 239, 295 n.114
Marsigli, Liugi 21
Martineşti 200
Mavrocordatos, Alexander 224
Mavrocordatos, Konstantin 129
Mavromichalis, Georgios 152, 154
Mazepa, Ivan Stepanovych 67, 71, 80, 257 n.119,
    264 n.112, 264 n.114
Medem, Ivan Fedorovich (Georg Johann Friedrich,
    Baron von Medem) 108, 132, 133, 290
    n.133
Mediterranean Company 151
Mediterranean Sea viii, 29, 35, 36, 107–9, 151, 152,
    178 passim
Medzhibozh 115, 116, 121, 122, 128, 129, 139
Mehmed Emin Pasha 120–2, 135, 169, 275 n.64,
    280 n.44

Index

Orthodox Church 1, 6, 8, 11, 15, 30, 33–5, 43, 45,
    53, 66, 77, 82, 129, 134, 182, 208, 224,
    235, 293 n.56
Orzechowo 131, 181, 276 n.105
Osman III, Ottoman Sultan 16
Osman Pasha 195
Ostermann, Andrei Ivanovich 39, 47, 226
Ostrogozhsk 61, 75, 76, 79
Ottoman Empire
    borderlands 28–46 *passim*
    diplomacy and grand strategy viii, 2–4, 6, 9,
        11–13, 15–19, 29, 30, 32, 34, 35, 38–42,
        44–7, 67, 69, 70, 83, 92, 110–12, 187,
        188, 191, 206, 207, 208, 213, 220, 224–7,
        231, 233, 235, 243, 248, 258 n.119,
        274 n.60
    diwan and central government 12, 17, 26, 32,
        35, 40, 120, 145, 188, 233, 235
    finances (*see* State finances and taxation,
        Ottoman)
    grand vizier 12, 13, 16, 17, 19, 20, 21, 28, 29
        passim
    land tenure (*see ciftlik*; *malikane* tax-farming;
        timar revenue grant)
    millets 30, 40, 165, 208, 223–8, 233, 248
    "new notables" (*ayan*) 19, 21, 23–5, 59, 111,
        198, 228, 243, 245
    provincial government 19–23, 25, 59, 111, 198,
        228, 243
    "reconfiguration" of the state 19, 20, 23, 243, 245
    religion and ideology 27, 28
    timar revenue grants 18, 19, 21–3
    See also army, Ottoman; Moldavia; State
        finances and taxation, Ottoman;
        Wallachia
Ozerov, Semen Petrovich 145, 166

Pac, Michał 131
Palatino, Ivan 151, 154
Palladoklis, Antoni 228
Palzig 90
Panin, Nikita Ivanovich 2–7, 15, 50, 72, 107, 118,
    150, 152, 171, 179, 186–8, 192, 195, 205,
    225, 231, 248, 258 n.1
Panin, Petr Ivanovich 26, 42, 92, 93, 97, 98, 102,
    108, 118, 124, 137–9, 142, 144–8, 150,
    172, 173, 191, 192, 202, 208, 209, 217,
    268 n.36, 280 n.43, 288 n.106
Papazoli, Georgios 35, 36, 151, 154
Paris 153, 181, 183, 251 n.38, 286 n.66
Paros 156, 159, 178, 180
Patriot Party 214, 230, 248
Patronage 12, 20, 25, 68, 211, 227, 229, 253 n.19
Pazvantoglu, Osman 228
Peloponnesus 35, 151–5, 244

Pereiaslav 70, 71
Perekop 37, 61, 66, 118, 119, 147, 173–6, 231, 236,
    238, 241, 256 n.85, 284 n.28, 285 n.40
Persia 15, 16, 41, 44–6, 67, 69, 76, 134, 231, 247
Peter I, Emperor of Russia 49–51, 80, 82, 83, 85,
    90, 92, 93, 102, 167, 241, 253 n.21, 253
    n.119, 258 n.10, 265 n.6, 268 n.8, 271
    n.76, 272 n.6, 278 n.83, 291 n.3
Peter III, Emperor of Russia 1, 2, 5, 34, 49–51, 53,
    58, 92–4, 97, 109, 152, 191, 249 n.1, 268
    n.36, 277 n.118
Petrov, Andrei Nikolaevich 171, 276 n.88
Petryk 80
Peysonnel, Louis Charles de 27
Phanariots 30–2, 35, 224, 258 n.119
Plemiannikov, Petr Grigor'evich 125, 141–5, 278 n.11
Podgorichani, Ivan Mikhailovich 125, 135, 136,
    142, 149, 166, 277 n.2, 278 n.11
Podolia 10–13, 32, 36, 39, 110, 182, 225, 296 n.138
Pokutia 137
Polish-Lithuanian Commonwealth viii, 3, 4, 6, 8,
    38 *passim*
    Diet, Senate and dietines 3, 4, 6–8, 10, 15, 72,
        186, 187, 209, 227–30, 248, 250 n.26,
        295 n.95
    First Partition of viii, 7, 52, 63, 162, 163, 184,
        185, 248
    Hetmans and armed forces 4, 7–10, 131, 182,
        183. 184, 228–30
    Kingdom of Poland, monarchy 162, 184–7, 192,
        205, 216, 228, 229, 243–5, 248, 249 n.10,
        283 n.109
    Lithuania, Grand Duchy of 4, 6, 7–9, 39, 52, 89,
        131, 182–6, 228, 237, 241
    political factionalism 4, 6, 7, 185, 229
    Second and Third Partitions of 248
    See also August III Wettin; Bar, Confederation
        of; Familja; Magnaterja; Repnin,
        Nikolai Vasil'evich; Stackelberg; Otto
        Magnus von; Stanislaw II August
        Poniatowski
Poltava 4, 40, 71, 74, 76–8, 94, 113, 173, 216, 238,
    264 n.114, 266 n.8
Potemkin, Grigorii Aleksandrovich 101, 102, 125,
    126, 135, 136, 142–4, 149, 166, 168–70,
    191–200, 202, 210–13, 216–23, 225–7,
    229, 233–42, 244, 246, 247, 271 n.78,
    275 n.64, 277 n.2, 278 n.5, 278 n.11, 288
    n.108, 289 n.117, 293 n.62, 294 n.93,
    296 n.138
Potemkin, Pavel Sergeevich 209, 288 n.106
Potocki, Ignacy 230
Potocki, Joachim 4, 9–12, 110–12, 115, 120, 123,
    130, 131, 168, 181, 274 n.60
Potocki, Stanisław 229

Index

Rzewuski, Seweryn 229, 230
Rzewuski, Wacław 8, 9, 229
Rzhevskii, Stepan Matveevich 126, 127, 136, 147, 149, 166, 212

Safavids 44, 45
Sahip Girei 173, 177, 188, 230, 245
St. Petersburg 2, 4, 6, 34, 46, 54–7, 63, 67, 68, 71, 72, 78, 81, 89, 92, 95, 98, 109, 110, 117 *passim*
Salgir River 176, 177
Salonika 294
Saltykov, Ivan Petrovich 8, 116, 125–7, 141–5, 168, 193–6, 198–203, 278 n.11, 288 n.108
Saltykov, Nikolai Ivanovich 125, 278 n.11
Saltykov, Petr Semenovich 89–92, 97–9, 190
Samara 108, 174, 293 n.62
Sambor River 169
Sandomierz 135, 181, 182, 185
Sapieha, Jozef 131
Sapieha, Michał 183
Sărat 120, 138, 166, 171
Saratov 154, 239
Sari Mehmed Pasha 196, 197
Sarti, Giuseppe 241
Savran River 113, 114
Saxony 4, 5, 7, 130, 131, 161, 181, 230, 248, 251 n.38
Secret Howitzers 87, 94
Segur, Charles-Philippe, Comte de 227, 241
Selamet II Girei, Crimean Khan 41
Selim II Girei, Crimean Khan 41
Selim III Girei, Crimean Khan 42, 150, 173, 174,176, 233, 257 n.100
Seniavin, Aleksei Naumovich 118, 174, 175, 177, 220
Serbia 32–5, 41, 77, 78, 83, 225–8, 243, 246, 264 n.109
Sevastopol' 220, 221, 234, 237, 238, 241
Seven Years' War 2, 9, 17, 47, 49–52, 73, 85–95, 97, 99, 101–3 *passim*
Sevsk 95, 268 n.47
Shahin Girei, Crimean Khan 173, 176, 177, 220, 223, 224, 227, 231–8, 240, 247
Shakhovskoi, Iakov Petrovich 57, 58, 77
Shamkhal 54, 55
Shcherbatov, Grigorii Alekseevich 146, 174, 175
Shcherbinin, Evgenii 172, 173, 177
Shirin Girei 45
Shumla 21, 171, 193–6, 198–206, 245
Shuvalov, Aleksandr Ivanovich 88
Shuvalov, Petr Ivanovich 54, 72, 77, 85–92, 94, 101, 102
Silahdar Hamza Pasha, Ottoman Grand Vizier 13, 110

Silahdar Mehmed Pasha, Ottoman Grand Vizier 150, 165, 171, 198, 245, 285 n.46
Silistra 21, 32, 36, 129, 165, 172, 193–205, 254 n.53, 288 n.108, 289 n.109
Sistova 174, 227
Sivash Straits 119, 174, 175
Skoropads'kyi, Ivan 71
Slavonic Serbia 41, 70, 81, 94, 212, 216
Sloboda Ukraine 39, 56, 61, 65, 66, 70, 74–82, 94, 95, 172, 212, 216, 255 n.57, 263 n.101, 264 n.12, 290 n.133
Slobozia 168, 198, 201
Slutsk 8, 9
Solomon I, King of Imereti 46, 134
Sorocha 29, 115, 138, 254 n.52
Spiridov, Grigorii Andreevich 108, 152–9, 178–80, 281 n.70
Stackelberg, Otto Magnus von 186, 228–30, 234, 241, 295 n.95
Stanileşti 28, 258 n.119
Stanislavov 117, 121, 122, 138
Stanisław August II Poniatowski, King of Poland 1, 6–10, 15, 89, 110, 131, 161, 162, 183–7, 228–30, 241, 245, 248, 295 n.95
Starodub 59, 74
Staro-Konstantinov 108, 114, 137
State finances and taxation, Ottoman
   accounting and assessment, role of *kadis* and *ayan* in 25
   arrears and debt 18, 25, 207
   avariz extraordinary tax 25
   decentralization and competition for revenue 23–5, 29, 31, 32, 243
   malikane tax-farming 18–20, 23, 25, 30, 34
   reform efforts 19, 29
   tax exemptions 28, 33
State finances and taxation, Russian
   arrears and debt 52–4, 74, 189
   assignats 54, 109, 136, 166, 189, 190, 245
   austerity measures 52, 53
   budgeting 7, 49, 57, 72, 189, 243, 259 n.32, 265 n.1, 269 n.58
   debasement and devaluation 53, 89
   excise, customs, and indirect taxes 53, 54, 189, 209, 265 n.1
   fiscal exploitation of Ukraine 53, 71–4, 76, 77, 216, 263 n.98
   military expenditure 49, 52, 53, 58, 87, 265 n.1, 282 n.87
   obrok rent from state peasants 53, 61, 85, 189, 190, 218, 238, 243, 263 n.102
   soul tax (*podushnaia podat'*) 51–7, 59, 61, 63, 64, 68, 76, 79, 83, 85, 210, 243, 258 n.11, 260 n.40, 265 n.1

326

Index